History of
MODERN
EUROPE

History of
MODERN
EUROPE
1789–1850s

M**ONMAYEE** B**ASU**

Orient BlackSwan

HISTORY OF MODERN EUROPE, 1789–1850s

ORIENT BLACKSWAN PRIVATE LIMITED

Registered Office
3-6-752 Himayatnagar, Hyderabad 500 029, Telangana, India
e-mail: centraloffice@orientblackswan.com

Other Offices
Bengaluru, Chennai, Guwahati, Hyderabad, Kolkata,
Mumbai, New Delhi, Noida, Patna

© Orient Blackswan Private Limited 2025
First published 2025

ISBN 978-93-6973-051-3

Typeset in
Adobe Garamond Pro 11/13
by Le Studio Graphique, Gurgaon 122 007

Printed in India at
B B Press, Tronica City, Ghaziabad, U.P. 201103

Published by
Orient Blackswan Private Limited
3-6-752 Himayatnagar, Hyderabad 500 029, Telangana, India
e-mail: info@orientblackswan.com

All figures and maps used in this book are in the public domain and sourced from Wikimedia Commons, unless specified otherwise.

Dedicated to the boundless grace and blessings of

My Sweet Mother
and
My Beloved Baba

Contents

Figures and Maps

FIGURES

MAPS

Preface

Much has already been written on the history of Modern Europe. Innumerable books are available, and any fresh attempt to write on it, even if on a select period, must involve some risk of repetition. Yet, during my long years of teaching this paper, I have found my students grappling with the problem of finding a book that would not only furnish them with necessary and relevant facts and details but would provide them with analyses, debates and interpretations of scholars on each topic as well. In other words, a comprehensive book with facts as well as historiographical evaluation was what they were looking for. Then I decided to write one for them myself. Therein lies the secret of the origin of this book. While teaching this paper to my students year after year, I collected a considerable pile of valuable information from the works of several scholars—historians, sociologists, economists, political scientists—that are extremely crucial to a study of this paper. They not only helped broaden my own vision of the subject, but at the same time, enriched my process of teaching, and undoubtedly made it a lot more interesting. Here in this book, I have endeavoured to compile and consolidate the material I have accumulated during my long teaching career for the benefit of my students. If my students in particular, and the world of students in general, find it useful, I would think my efforts to be successful.

While writing this book, I incurred considerable debt to many individuals and institutions. First of all, I thank my students who inspired me to undertake this project and were a great source of encouragement. The library of Hansraj College where I teach, the Central Library, Arts Faculty, University of Delhi, and the erstwhile Nehru Memorial Library (NML) at Teen Murti Bhavan were of immense help; I am deeply indebted to them.

In my research work of all kinds, the staff members of NML particularly, have been of invaluable assistance. I am indebted to my friends and my colleagues at Hansraj for boosting my morale with their constant support. I am specially indebted to my friend and colleague, Neeru Ailawadi for her indispensable help with valuable suggestions, books and reading material. No words would be adequate to record my deep sense of gratitude to Dr Monica Juneja, formerly professor at University of Delhi, and now Global Art History Professor at Heidelberg University, for kindling my interest in the study of Modern Europe.

Lastly, my special thanks to my parents for making me what I am today. I would also like to acknowledge my deep loving gratitude for my family—my husband Prabeer Basu for his support and forbearance during my preoccupation with this work, and my sons Amitabh and Pathikrit as well as daughters-in-law Deepthi and Riju, for their sustained help and encouragement.

Monmayee Basu
February 2025

History of Modern Europe
An Overview

The period between 1789 to 1939 was one of significant transition in the history of Europe. This period marked a blossoming of unique thoughts and ideas, and heralded some fresh concepts leading to events that the world had never seen before, for example, revolutions! The ancient and medieval world had seen wars—violent, brutal wars. Life in Hobbes' state of nature was 'nasty, brutish and short'. But 'revolution' was a completely unknown phenomenon. There had been occasional revolts, uprisings, but a revolution bringing about a complete upheaval and fundamental transformation in the existing state of affairs was unheard of. And this metamorphosis happened not only in the political and social spheres but in the economic sphere as well. This led, as **E.J. Hobsbawm** observed, to the coinage of new terms like 'industry', 'factory', 'middle class', 'working class', and so on. Several new concepts or 'isms' also sprung up—*absolutism, conservatism, liberalism, radicalism, nationalism, capitalism, industrialism, socialism, imperialism, colonialism, militarism, fascism, romanticism, realism, impressionism, positivism*—and so on and so forth. These were unknown in the vocabulary of the period before 1789. The aforesaid period, therefore, struck a new chord in the flow of history in Europe. So, it is known as the **modern** period of European state of affairs. It is sandwiched between the medieval and the contemporary eras.

It is worthy to note that all the major events (or phases) of this period can precisely be classified on the basis of the ideologies or 'isms' mentioned above. The period between 1789 and 1848 is characterised by the recurrent outbreak of a number of revolutions in various places, starting with the revolution in France. Hobsbawm calls this the **Age of Revolution**, which saw the tug of war between conservatism on the one hand, and liberalism and radicalism on the other. This time also coincides with the Industrial Revolution that brought about a train of social and economic occurrences. The Age of Revolution was therefore, comprehensive and encompassed political, social as well as economic elements. This period saw the interplay of the forces of **liberalism, radicalism, nationalism** and **industrialism**. The Age of Revolution started with the French Revolution and was followed by several other revolutions during the 1820s, in 1830 and also in 1848. These were organised by the liberals, radicals, and nationalists (their goals and methods, which often overlapped and occasionally differed) have been discussed at length in the relevant chapters.

It was also the time for the growth of industrialism and socialism. Starting with England, one after another European country developed a social and economic system in which manufacturing industries prevailed. Factories developed all over Europe throughout the 19th century. An extensive working class emerged. The inhuman conditions of the workers led social and political thinkers to develop doctrines to ameliorate their conditions. These divergent theories collectively came to be called 'socialism'. Thoughts of socialism pervaded throughout the 19th century and beyond.

The **Napoleonic era** of **1799–1815** is an interregnum between the revolutions. It can be called a prelude to the conservative consolidation that followed with the Congress of Vienna, and unleashed an intense and bitter strife between efforts to restore conservatism and a bid to demolish it with the weapons of liberalism and radicalism.

Nationalism transcended the boundaries of 1848. Territories that were not regarded as national units so far demanded their identity as composite 'nations'. The unification of Italy, and that of Germany were completed by 1871. In the Balkans, the European states under the Ottoman Turkish Sultan started revolting to declare independence and establish their own entities, on the basis of racial and ethnic identities. Their struggle became prominent in the third quarter of the 19th century, although Greece had attained her independence by 1829.

The period between 1870 and the First World War (1914–1918) is specifically known as the **Age of Imperialism**. Among the major powers of Europe, imperialism followed from industrialism to fulfil the needs of raw materials, cheap labour, fresh markets, and engage in military expansion for increased combative prowess over each other. **Militarism,** therefore, now took centre stage in European diplomacy. By the turn of the century, Europe came to be divided into two armed camps—the **Triple Alliance** (Germany, Austria-Hungary and Italy) and the **Triple Entente** (Great Britain, France and Russia). A series of crises complicated and strained relations between the countries forming these two groups beyond redemption, which resulted in the outbreak of World War I.

The post-War socio-economic crises along with political turbulence paved the ground for the emergence of a new ideology in certain countries. It came to be called **fascism**. Although its form varied from country to country depending upon the specific circumstances prevailing in them, fascism had certain common features which were prevalent in the countries of its origin. A few countries became virulently fascist while others remained liberal, notwithstanding the fact that within the liberal countries too, fascist groups and parties prevailed. **Parti Populaire Français** and the **British Union of Fascists** are cases in point. The post-War era also saw the gradual end of Empire as well as colonialism. However, those are beyond the time frame of the modern period of European history. Developments since World War II are studied under the contemporary era.

As far as possible, I have tried to classify the chapters of this book on the basis of these isms. Let us now embark together on this journey of unravelling the 'History of Modern Europe', which is embedded with such isms.

Chapter 1

The French Revolution

Conservatism, Liberalism and Radicalism

The period starting with the French Revolution (1789) and extending upto the revolutions of 1848 and beyond was characterised by the interplay of liberalism, radicalism and conservatism. **Conservatism**, generally speaking, referred to a preference for tradition and authority. The period prior to the French Revolution reflected a penchant for traditional institutions and old values. A love for continuation and stability is the characteristic feature of conservatism. **Liberalism** and radicalism developed from the Age of Enlightenment. They indicated a critical approach to the existing state of affairs, and sought to rectify prevalent vices. The American writer Ambrose Bierce considered the conservative as, 'a statesman who is enamoured of existing evils, as distinguished from the Liberal, who wishes to replace them with others'. **Radicalism** goes a step farther than liberalism. The radicals aspire for everything that the liberals want, but they are not contented like the liberals with only rectifications and amendments, and wish to metamorphose the weary conservative system into something entirely new. For example, the liberals are happy with the change of a tyrannical absolutist monarchy into a constitutional one; while the radicals wish to abolish the monarchical system altogether, and replace it with a new republican experiment.

The topics of the French Revolution, Napoleon Bonaparte and the Age of Revolution come under the interplay of these three isms.

The Fall of the Bastille

A violent crowd, hundreds in number, stormed the fort of Bastille, the symbol of despotism and arbitrary imprisonment, on 14 July 1789. This unprecedented mob fury was sparked off by the dismissal of Jacques Necker, the only non-noble minister, by King Louis XVI on 11th July. Immediately, there was an outburst of public wrath as Necker was a minister with popular sympathies. Necker was replaced by Baron de Breteuil, a nominee of the queen. In the midst of a financial crisis, the King had been forced by the aristocracy to convene the Estates-General (a National Assembly comparable to the English Parliament where all the social classes of France were represented but which had not been allowed to meet after 1614) after 175 years; it met on 5 May 1789. Necker's dismissal was sharply resented because he had put forth the proposal at the Estates-General that matters of common interest should be discussed jointly.

On 12 July 1789, the day after Necker's dismissal, a rebellion broke out in Paris. Soldiers (*Garde Française*) in charge of protecting the royal palace joined the rebels. Throughout 13th and 14th of July, the Parisian rebels engaged in search of arms and ammunition, with the purpose of preparing to break out in open revolt against an intransigent monarch and his insensitive corrupt ministers. A group of notables including Camille Desmoulins (a journalist, politician and a prominent revolutionary) joined the common people and formed a citizens' militia. This militia, known as the **National Guard**—formed the day before the Bastille was stormed on 14 July 1789—was created in order to protect the country against external attack and to promote internal stability. It was, however, dominated by the affluent bourgeoisie, and excluded the lumpen proletariat. According to influential French lawyer and politician **Antoine Barnave**, the National Guard comprised the 'bonne bourgeoisie' or the 'respectable' middle classes.[1]

Throughout 13th July and the intervening night of 13–14 July, a frantic search for weapons went on. Gunsmiths' shops were looted. The **Monastery of St. Lazare** (where food, guns and supplies were presumed to be stored) was attacked and other than arms, cartloads of corn and flour were carried away to be sent to the local market. At the dawn of 14th July, **Hôtel des Invalides** (a complex of buildings in Paris, which was also presumed to be a storehouse of essential commodities and ammunition) was captured by the crowd and 32,000 muskets were seized. Then they thought of storming the fort of Bastille with the same objective of collecting arms. It was believed that considerable powder and ammunition were stored in Bastille. The cry of 'On to Bastille' tore through the air. Victor Besenval, the Commander of the Paris garrison, withdrew to **Champs de Mars** (a large open area in Paris that has witnessed many historical events. We will refer to it again and again through our discussion on the French Revolution).

FIG. 1.1: *Storming of the Bastille* (1789) by Jean-Pierre Houël

Marquis de Launay, the military governor in charge of the fort, politely received a deputation of besiegers at about 10 AM of 14th July and promised not to open fire unless attacked. However, the crowd waiting outside lost patience as considerable time had passed and the deputation did not reappear; they attempted to storm into the courtyard. Launay became apprehensive of a frontal attack and ordered the opening of fire. As Rudé says, "in the affray that followed the besiegers lost ninety-eight dead and seventy-three wounded."[2] Launay was dragged by the besiegers to the Hotel de Ville and brutally slaughtered. Six other of his associates met with the same fate including Prevot des Merchandands or chief municipal magistrate, Flesselles.

The question now is—Who were the besiegers and who were the vanguards of the Bastille? What was their composition? The legend goes that they were mostly "vagabonds, criminals or mercenary, rabble hired in the wine-shops of the St. Antoine quartier."[3] However, Rudé points out that the lists drawn up by the National Assembly (the Assembly formed by the bourgeoisie after the Estates-General met on 5th May) show that the attackers numbered nearly 600, and were mostly members of the citizen's militia belonging to the St. Antoine quartier and neighbouring areas.[4]

The fall of the Bastille is one of the most significant events in the history not only of France and the French Revolution, but of modern Europe and the entire world. Some scholars think that it signalled the beginning of the French Revolution. The fall of this embodiment of despotism symbolised liberty; that is why the French celebrate this day as their day of independence. However, according to another opinion, it was the meeting of the Estates-General on 5 May 1789 that heralded the starting point of the revolution—a significant landmark, especially because it was being convened after 175 years.

Whatever may have been the immediate triggering factor, thus began the revolution in France that, in the words of **A.J.P. Taylor**, "originated revolutions in the modern sense and it was not until it that people knew what revolutions were like. Its events echoed down the corridors of history."[5] The crisis of Bastille and the summoning of the Estates-General did not happen all of a sudden. **William Doyle** says, "The Revolution that was to sweep away the political institution of old France, and shake her society to its foundations, did not begin on 14th July 1789. By that time the old order was already in ruins beyond redemption."[6] This was the result of a chain of events that in fact can be traced farther back. It is, therefore, important to analyse what led to these series of momentous events.

Background to the Fall of Bastille:
Causes of the French Revolution

ECONOMIC FACTORS: FINANCES UNDER THE MONARCHY

On 20 August 1786, **Calonne**, the then Controller-General of the royal treasury came up to **King Louis XVI** to inform him that finances of the

State were in acute crisis. While the income from revenue amounted to 475 million livres, the expenditure stood at 587 million livres—a deficit of 112 million.[7]

What were the reasons for this enormous shortfall? The reasons could be traced back to prolonged days of poor harvest. After Calonne's time, from the summer of 1788, the price of bread spiralled rapidly. A 4lb loaf of bread, normally costing 8 to 9 sous (20 sous added up to 1 livre) had reached 9.5 sous on 17th August, 10 sous on the 20th and 11 sous on 7th September.[8] Crisis became acute in the winter of 1788–1789. As a result of a hailstorm in July 1788, harvest was already bad and with the unexpected severe winter that followed, there was a dearth of work and thousands of people flocked to Paris for jobs. According to Sebastien Hardy, almost 80,000 were unemployed.[9]

But had there not been similar failure of harvests earlier also? For example, 1775 was a year characterised particularly by bad crops, hunger and consequently popular unrest. Rudé records grain riots or 'flour war' in 1775.[10] Then why did not a revolution break out then? Clearly, apart from the factors mentioned by Rudé like lack of involvement of the majority of peasants or quick suppression of the revolt by **Turgot**, the then Controller-General, there were several other reasons why a revolution broke out in 1789 and not in 1775.

The recurring deficits of 18th-century France, however, may be attributed predominantly to the cost of the country's wars. In the Seven Years' War, besides maintaining her own forces, France had heavily financed those of her new ally Austria. France's participation in the war of American Independence had even more disastrous consequences. Turgot's warning to young Louis XVI in August 1774 when the latter came to power was that the first gunshots would drive the State into bankruptcy. Louis XVI inherited a huge public debt from the old monarchical system. Over three quarters of the annual State expenditure was being incurred on defence and the service of public debt. The essence of the financial crisis on the eve of the revolution was, therefore, the impossibility of reducing these heavy items of national expenditure. Defence expenses were unavoidable; otherwise, security of the nation would be in peril. This meant that economic retrenchment could be attempted in the field of civil expenditure alone. The civil estimates for 1788 represented only 23 per cent of the total expenditure.[11] Louis XVI was unable to curtail expenditure on luxury in the Royal Court. As it is, the cost of maintaining the royal establishment and the grants to prisoners and courtiers constituted under 6 per cent of the total outgoings. New methods of agriculture were suggested which could have enhanced the yield from the land. One of these methods was the **enclosure system**, which entailed cultivating the common land that was used for cattle grazing by the people. Due to loss of these collective rights, the enclosure system was fiercely resisted. The archaic system of communication required to be seriously overhauled. This could have been of great benefit to the ordinary people, especially in times of crisis like famines, delivering food efficiently even to the distant corners of the empire. Scientific methods of cultivation were equally discouraged by the peasantry as that involved investment of capital which they did not have. Large-scale cultivation in France was, therefore, an exception.

Corruption was rampant in administration. Misappropriation and wasteful expenditure were common. Further, inter-state duties and customs posed a major impediment to the growth and the smooth flow of trade and commerce. Internal customs raised barriers in the movement of goods between different parts of France. Prices varied, causing untold sufferings to the common people.

In 1787 and 1788, therefore, France was certainly facing an economic crisis of unprecedented magnitude. Even so, historians are divided regarding the importance of economic factors in the outbreak of the revolution. **William Doyle** quotes elaborately from **Ernest Labrousse** who showed that the revolution was not the product of prolonged economic crisis, but rather a short-term malaise.[12] According to Labrousse, the years between 1730 and 1770 were of flourishing trade and substantial agricultural yields. It was a shorter period—the two decades of 1770s and 1780s—which faced incriminating climatic conditions leading to catastrophic harvests. This agricultural debacle naturally had its ramifications on the industrial sector. The poor harvest pushed food prices so high that almost the entire income of common people were spent on food, with little left for other expenses. Demand for other goods, therefore, drastically fell, causing a slump in industries and manufactories. A cyclic economic depression followed. The result was widespread popular revolt. But it was not the effect of "a long-endured misery" but rather an agony felt sharply "by the sudden contrast with relatively recent prosperity."[13] **J.F. Bosher** thought the revolution to be an outcome of a backward underdeveloped economy where the agricultural sector was of supreme importance. And France's sufferings were primarily due to the fact that in France there had not been, unlike England, an agricultural revolution.[14] Echoing Bosher's argument, **Michel Morineau** said that in France there was neither an agricultural revolution nor a demographic revolution. Although, on the face of it, the population, according to Morineau's figures, had risen from 19 million in 1700 to 25 million in the 1790s, it had merely compensated for the human losses France had suffered as a result of recurrent wars.[15] **Emmanuel Le Roy Ladurie** raised the question as to how could a steadily growing population in France in the 18th century be managed and fed if there was no agricultural revolution.[16] While Morineau defends his argument by saying that earlier, though the country was under-populated, its agricultural production too was under-utilised, and that with the rise in population, the food produced also began to be utilised optimally. Therefore, in order to feed the growing population, additional agricultural production was not necessary.[17]

Some other historians, on the other hand, do not agree with the view that economic conditions were deplorable when the revolution broke out. **J.C. Toutain**, for example, argued, that the 18th century was marked by a remarkable agricultural growth.[18] A similar opinion had been expressed in 1933 by **Alexis de Tocqueville**, who had argued that the French Revolution was not a result of grinding poverty and declining wealth, but occurred rather when economic conditions were improving. Tocqueville thought that growing social and political awareness among the middle classes and growing literacy among the peasantry hastened the revolution. He believed that *extreme misery does not necessarily bring about a revolution*. Rather a stage of steady progress and improvement is far more capable of sparking a revolt, because it is at this time that the "slightest acts of arbitrary power" become intolerable.[19] Roger Price observed that economic issues became significant in the 1840s when with the advent of the railways, agriculture transcended the boundaries of regionalism and the lack of economic reforms became glaring.

SOCIAL ISSUES

Society in 18th-century France had a pyramidical structure. Extreme social and economic inequality was at the root of all evils.

Monarchy

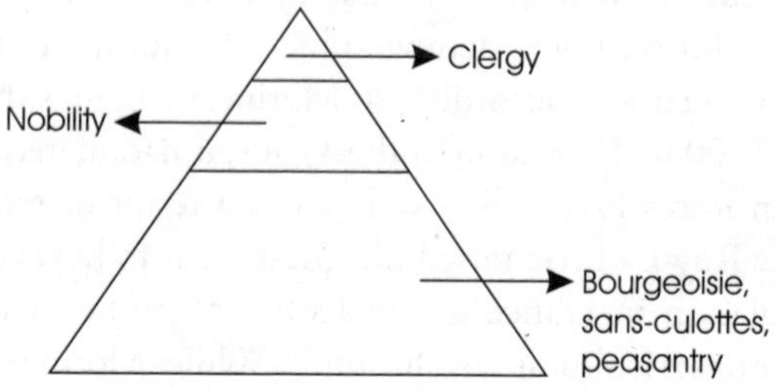

FIG. 1.2: The Three Estates

At the apex of the societal pyramid stood the monarchy that enjoyed what Jean Bodin called *summa potestas*, a Latin phrase which means the "**sum and totality of power**". In other words, the King was the embodiment of supreme power, authority and jurisdiction. His words were the law. Royal power was hereditary and transmitted down through generations, and not confined to any one king. A royal dynasty thereby continued to rule through ages. The King, infallible as he was, received his power from the Divine and was answerable to Him alone. However, despite being infallible and ruling by divine right, the King was still bound by certain fundamental principles. According to **Francois Furet**, these were: (*i*) primogeniture; (*ii*) property rights of the subjects; (*iii*) the integrity of the royal domain.[20] These principles being "inalienable and untouchable", were precluded from monarchical powers. Furet wrote,

> Above the law, yet subject to law, the King of France was no tyrant: The French monarchy, a State based on law, must not be confused with despotism, which is the unfettered power of a master. Nevertheless, despotism was monarchy's temptation, as Montesquieu explained, to degenerate; it needed only to ignore the established body of laws.[21]

Responsibility of King Louis XVI

The monarchy of Louis XVI was to a large extent responsible for the revolution given that there were many actions that the King could have taken that might well have averted its outbreak. The government of France was arbitrary and anachronistic. The evils emanating from the disorder and misrule added to the discontent of the masses. The monarchy was thoroughly incompetent and despotic. The prevailing social anomalies, financial embarrassments, administrative complexities and mass distress of France required a strong and efficient sovereign to steer the country's administrative machinery. Regrettably, however, the French monarchy was hopelessly incompetent to deal with the variety of problems it was called upon to tackle. It has often been suggested that had the monarchy been efficient and sagacious, the revolution would never have occurred. On the contrary, the weak personality and a few erroneous acts of Louis XVI served to infuriate the people and hastened the revolution. Undoubtedly, Louis XVI was a man of noble intentions, endowed with every private virtue, honesty, piety, amiability and good sense, but he could not govern. As **Norman Hampson** says, "French society was also becoming increasingly humane and tolerant; it was during the reign of Louis XVI that torture was abolished and the Protestants obtained limited religious toleration."[22] Yet, this was a regime which fell with such little regret. Instead of directing events, Louis XVI drifted with the tide. He was often under the influence of his imperious queen, Marie Antoinette. A spendthrift and an Austrian by birth, she came to personify an unpopular foreign alliance against France. She was strongly condemned by the people, and appeared to be the siren who was drawing the ship of the State on to the rocks.

The only way the monarchy could put a brake on the rapid collision of the ship of the State against the iceberg of ruin was by carrying out well thought-out reforms of the system under which the King ruled; and it was the system, not the person of the monarch, which the French people disliked. The best chance of forestalling revolution by reform was lost when the young King, in search of popularity, summoned the *Parlement*, the supreme and highest court of appeal under the *ancien régime* (or the old social, political order of France before 1789), overriding René Nicolas Charles Augustin de Maupeou, the Chancellor in 1774. Historically, the Parlement grew out of the King's Court, where early kings of the Capetian Dynasty (987–1328) would summon their principal vassals to discuss political issues. The opinions of the Parlement, a powerful and influential body, frequently clashed with those of the Church, the monarchy and the common people. According to some historians like **Marcel Marion**, it was the Parlement rather than the monarchy which obstructed reforms,[23] while others like **Jean Egret** are full of praise for the Parlement and criticise Maupeou, who, according to Egret, did not allow the former to function[24] (This debate will be taken up under the discussion on political issues).

FIG. 1.3: *Louis XVI of France* (1777) by Joseph Duplessis

The point to be noted is that due to the differences of opinion between the King and the Parlement, the desired and urgent reforms could not be pushed through. Hence, the people of France could not be pacified.

Since the dismissal of Maupeou, the Chancellor, in 1790, Louis XVI displayed a strange inability to take the right decisions and exercise correct judgement almost at every crucial moment. In 1788, he summoned to his council the Genevan banker, **Jaques Necker**. Necker was the Director-General of France between 1777 to 1781. In 1788, he was still a great favourite of the people, as he wanted to distribute capitation tax more equitably. However, in 1788 he fell into deep unpopularity as soon as he began to set up provincial assemblies which were to curb the authority of the Parlements.

The last chance of reform was lost when, after a close scrutiny of the *cahiers* (*cahiers de doléances*) or list of grievances drawn up by the people on the eve of the revolution, the King failed to chalk out a path of reforms in order to appease the rebellious mood of the people. **Georges Lefebvre** argued that while Louis XVI remained unclear about the best course of action and was probably most concerned with avoiding bloodshed; Necker suggested doubling the representation of the Third Estate in the Estates-General to mollify the people. But the King dismissed Necker. This enraged the people as they believed there would be a royalist *coup d'etat* after the Estates-General had met where the royal army would arrest some and disperse the remaining deputies of the National Assembly formed by the Third Estate. Ignoring their appeal for the removal of the royal army, the King instead dismissed Necker, the popular Chancellor. This resulted, as discussed above, in the outbreak of a violent insurrection and the fall of the Bastille. Immediately, however, the King in his characteristic oscillations between severity and surrender, reappointed Necker and promised the dispersal of extra troops.

Louis XVI was known to be a good man because of his lack of cruelty and his freedom from personal vices, but a bad king because of his indecisiveness and inconsistency, which often were looked upon as conscious chicanery. Even so, the people remained intensely loyal to the King who was a father figure to them. Yet, the tides of opinion were that in all probability only a royal genius could have worked out a solution and rescued the State from inevitable disaster. The monarch was required to assume the role of a just ruler who rose above parties and special interest groups, and to transcend his special affection for the nobility and a privileged Church. Louis XVI, in his very nature of oscillation between obstinacy and showering favours at just the wrong times, failed to comprehend the exigencies of the situation.

The Clergy

As shown in the pyramidical structure above in Figure 1.2, French society was divided into three estates—the **clergy** (First Estate), the **nobility** (Second Estate), and the **bourgeoisie and the common people** (Third Estate). According to data furnished by Lefebvre, out of a total population of 23,000,000, the priests numbered about 100,000, and 400,000 were nobles; the rest comprised the people of the Third Estate.[25] The same statistics have been provided by Hampson.[26]

The Church was an autonomous institution which owned about one-tenth of the entire land of France. Moreover, it collected the **tithe** (tax paid by the common people to the Church) and exercised enormous influence over the monarchy. Being exempt from any kind of taxes, it paid the Crown a portion of its revenue. This was essentially voluntary and instead of the King making any kind of financial demand on the Church, it was the Church which exerted pressure on the monarchy in lieu of the economic support it lent. The clergy was an organised institution, with its own administration, courts, and an independent assembly which met every five years to decide its affairs. The Church became powerful since 1685 when the Edict of Nantes established the predominance of the Roman Catholic religion in France. The clergy exercised its control over education, registration of marriages, births and deaths, and extended its supremacy over almost every sphere of society and social life. The King too had to rely on the Church for his coronation and for the legal inheritance of his children or successors. These powers and privileges enjoyed by the clergy became an important source of disaffection for the people.

Both Lefebvre and Abbe Sieyes were of the opinion that the clergy was not a social class or an estate in that sense. Sieyes was a French Roman Catholic clergyman and constitutional theorist, whose concept of popular sovereignty guided the National Assembly in the initial years. While Lefebvre calls the clergy an order, Sieyes considers it to be a profession.[27] And like all orders or professions, it was strictly hierarchal in structure, and could be broadly be classified into two groups—nobles and commoners. The clash of their interests created a schism in the body of the Church. As a result, a substantial portion of the clergy joined hands with the revolutionaries.

The clergy was clearly divided between the **upper clergy** and the **lower clergy**. The upper clergy consisted of bishops, abbots and chapters— the upper echelons of the ecclesiastical order who were in charge of the administration and management of the episcopal offices, controlled the finances and presided over the quinquennial assemblies. Norman Hampson wrote, "the organisation of the Church mirrored that of lay society in the sense that there was a fairly sharp distinction between ruling hierarchy and an impoverished rank and file, a distinction based essentially on noble birth."[28] **Voltaire**'s sharp condemnation of such inequity and discrimination within the Church organisation also dealt a severe blow to traditional Christianity and the existing ecclesiastical system, thus contributing further to the split within the clergy. The lower clergy was also inspired by the French theologician **Edmund Richer** (1560–1631), who professed ecclesiastical democracy and denounced the emergence of any inequity or difference within the episcopal body. Richer upheld theories of **Gallicanism**, which placed the authority of the Church councils above that of the Pope and thereby demolished any barrier of power.

The privileges and special powers of the higher clergy became a serious bone of contention for the lower clergy on the eve of the French Revolution. The clergy or First Estate joined hands with the nobility or Second Estate when the King, advised by Calonne, in view of the impeding financial bankruptcy, decided to tax these two upper estates, which had till then been immune from any kind of taxation. It was at this juncture that the final schism within the clergy took place. While the higher clergy allied themselves with the Second Estate, the thoroughly dislllusioned lower clergy joined the Third Estate. The division within the clerical structure was complete, and this helped to accentuate and fortify the forces of the revolution.

The Nobility

The privileges and prerogatives enjoyed by the nobility, like those of the clergy, became an eyesore for the large body of common people in France. There were three most important privileges. *First* and foremost, their freedom from the liability of paying taxes to the State. This liability was imposed on the common people, particularly the peasantry. It was an unnatural system: the richer classes did not pay while the poorer classes had to meet the expenses of costly wars, an extravagant administration and a spendthrift court. Of the total revenues of France, about 96 per cent had to be paid by the Third Estate: the remaining 4 per cent came from the rich clergy and nobility. Additionally, the nobility, most of whom were big estate owners, also received taxes from their peasants in the form of feudal dues.

Second, the nobility enjoyed the privilege of monopoly of appointment to high official posts. All important posts in the government and army belonged to the aristocracy. Privilege divorced from responsibility provoked jealousy and hatred in the non-privileged class.

Third, as feudal landowners they enjoyed exclusive privileges like the right to hunt or to own a mill, an oven or a wine press. These were sharply resented by the common people, who were compelled not only to use facilities owned by the lord, but also pay for their use. A life of pleasure and oppression of the poor had become an integral part of the aristocratic lifestyle.

The aristocracy, like the clergy, was divided into two main groups— the *noblesse d'épée* or **Nobles of the Sword** (by birth) and *noblesse de robe*, or **Nobles of the Robe**, that is, those who had been promoted by the King, for various reasons, to the rank of nobility. During the days of acute financial crisis, a portion of the bourgeoisie or middle class who were engaged in trade and commerce and had thereby accumulated immense fortune, bailed out the monarchy by donating substantial amounts of money to the royal treasury. In return for such valuable services, the King in his turn, rewarded some of them by endowing upon them the rank of nobility. These promoted nobles came to be known as the noblesse de robe.

Quite naturally a relationship of intense jealousy and competition raged between these two groups of aristocracy. The nobles by birth looked down upon those who were promoted to nobility with deep contempt and fiercely strove to limit their number. A constant strife, therefore, ensued between the two classes of aristocracy, each denouncing the other. There was effort from the upper bourgeoisie to forge ahead and open wider the door to nobility, while the other side endeavoured to violently push them down and slam the door on them forever.

The conflict between the two persisted for other reasons as well. Since the **Civil Wars of the Fronde**,* the hereditary nobles had fallen out of favour with the monarchy for their anti-establishment role. Consequently, they were precluded from the membership of the Parlements, the great legal courts of France. The Parlements, therefore, began to be filled up by the promoted nobles or nobles of the robe, which only caused the rivalry and the schism between them to deepen further.

There was another serious issue of conflict and jealousy between them. This was the exclusion of the noblesse de robe or promoted nobility from services in the army. Armed services were specially reserved for the hereditary nobles by *Loi Segur* or Army Law of 1781, which restricted promotions in the army to the rank of captain and above only to those whose families

---

*The word refers particularly to two revolts against the absolutism of the Crown in France between 1648 and 1652. The first Fronde began in 1648 by the Parlement of Paris, joined by the Parisian population, as a protest against war taxation. Disaffected nobles joined in and intrigued with France's enemy Spain. Peace was restored in March 1649. The second Fronde began in 1651. Widespread revolt broke out against the chief minister-ship of Jules Mazarin during the minority of Louis XVI. The revolt was led by Louis II or the Great Conde which represented a junior branch of the French Royal House of Bourbon. A large number of disaffected nobles joined Conde, but all of them soon lost popularity. Mazarin who had fled from France during the civil war, returned and quickly recovered Paris for the King. The Fronde ended in Paris in October 1652.

had been nobles for at least four generations. This automatically excluded everybody who was a first-generation aristocrat or second generation at best. This discrimination helped further widen the cleavage between the two groups of nobles.

Historians, however, have different opinions regarding these social distinctions in France under the ancien regime. According to historians like **Franklin Ford**, the division within the body of the aristocracy was illusory. In fact, on the eve of the revolution, according to Ford, both groups of nobility sank all their differences and presented a united front against the monarchy on the one hand and the commoners on the other.[29] **John McManners** went a step ahead and suggested that not only did the nobles unite, but that there was also a union of the bourgeoisie and the nobility based on wealth. However, **Norman Ravitch** saw a sharp and bitter conflict between the Nobles of the Sword and Nobles of the Robe, which, he believed, was a distinct feature of French society prior to the revolution.[30] **Marxist historians**, on the other hand, led by **Georges Lefebvre** and followed by **Albert Soboul** and others held that the French Revolution was the *culmination of a protracted economic transformation resulting in the rise of capitalism in France*, as a result of which a significant social remoulding took place that slowly shifted power from the aristocracy, the feudal class to the capitalists, that is the bourgeoisie. Lefebvre in his study of 18th-century Orleans society, *Études Orléanaises*, also claimed that entry to the Orleans nobility was open and accessible to the wealthy bourgeoisie, and that some old nobles were also pursuing commercial ventures.[31] **George V. Taylor** and **Alfred Cobban**, however, critiqued the Marxist reading of the revolution and argued that the wealth of all social classes in France before the revolution was 'proprietary' in nature, primarily because industrialism had not yet dawned in France, although it had started in England. Capitalism in France before the revolution was, therefore, mostly land-based and hardly resembled industrial capitalism of the 19th century. And in this sense, the landed bourgeoisie and the nobility, the majority of whom were big-estate owners, formed a single proprietary elite.[32] **Pierre Goubert** agreed with them, emphasising the links that bound the nobility and the upper bourgeoisie together into a single plutocratic elite.[33] He refused to accept the French Revolution as the triumph of the capitalist bourgeoisie over a feudal aristocracy. Similarly, **Robert Forster** and **Herbert Luthy** substantiated Cobban's arguments.[34] The same view was expressed by the *Annales* historian and hard revisionist,

Francois Furet who, like G.V. Taylor and Cobban, concluded that the nobles and the bourgeoisie shared the same class on the basis of their proprietary wealth.[35] The question, therefore, arises that why then were the nobles and bourgeoisie at loggerheads with each other on the eve of the revolution.

George V. Taylor has tried to explain it in political terms. The bourgeoisie, whose economic contribution to solve the financial crisis of the State was tremendous, aspired for political power in return. This clashed with the interests of the nobles, who enjoyed the political limelight as they occupied all the prominent official posts in the State. The result was the **Segur Ordinance of 1781** which reserved important posts in the army for those who had been nobles for four generations. The purpose was to eliminate the bourgeoisie as well as the newly elevated nobles from such posts. The increasing ennoblement of the bourgeoisie was also another bone of contention because it meant there were more claimants on the limited resources and privileges earlier enjoyed only by the hereditary nobles. Matters reached a height with the summoning of the Estates-General in May 1789. The Estates-General was divided into three estates and differences appeared regarding the procedure of voting as soon as the Estates-General met. The first two estates—the clergy and the nobility—directly confronted the Third Estate led by the bourgeoisie over the methods of casting votes. Thus started a bitter conflict that raged throughout the revolutionary period.

Colin Lucas calls these differences 'stress zones'. But the existence of such differences did not imply that the landed rich were not part of the same class. Lucas, while agreeing with Taylor and others that the bourgeoisie and the nobles all belonged to a single propertied elite, believes that constant tensions and frictions occurred within them. However, a separate union of these 'stress zones' did not take place because, as Lucas has interpreted, the decision of the Parlement of the Paris in September 1788 was that the Estates-General would be summoned according to the forms of 1614. And this was accepted by all the classes. It was in 1614 that the Estates-General had last met. And in the meeting of 1614, the interests of the bourgeoisie and nobility were in such opposition that the bourgeoisie decided to head a separate campaign of their own with the aim of capturing control of the Estates.[36]

Lefebvre also agreed with this interpretation of Lucas. But this has been contradicted by **Elizabeth Einstein**. She referred to the **Committee of Thirty** formed on 6 July 1789 to draft a constitution in order to voice protest against the Parlements and the ancient regime. The Committee of Thirty had many noble as well as bourgeois members who worked hand in hand in their protest against the government. Rudé also agrees with Einstein and says that the Committee was "composed of lawyers, liberal aristocrats and clerics."[37] It is not very clear, therefore, why the lower bourgeoisie and petty nobles did not form a common unit whereas the upper nobles and the upper landed bourgeoisie formed one class of propertied elite. It was the upper mercantile bourgeoisie or the rich commercial class whom Lefebvre called the capitalist bourgeoisie,[38] which became the 'revolutionary bourgeoisie'. This meant, as William Doyle reiterates, "that France was now to be ruled not by men of birth but by men of property, not by nobles, but by 'notables'".[39]

The Third Estate

The Bourgeoisie

As mentioned earlier, out of a population of 23 million, Lefebvre noted, about 1 million was clergy, 4 million constituted the nobility, and the rest the Third Estate. Abbe Sieyes, a priest and a Vicar General born in Frejus in France in a modest bourgeois family, was renowned as a great intellectual thinker. He popularised the Third Estate by his three famous utterances in his well-known 1789 pamphlet *Qu'est-ce que le Tiers Etat*, in which he asked: What is the Third Estate? And he answered—the Nation. He then asked: What has it become uptill now? He answered—Nothing. He further asked: What does it want to become? And he replied: Everything. The bourgeoisie was an important component of the Third Estate. As shown in the pyramid in Fig. 1.2, the Third Estate was broadly divided into two main classes—the bourgeoisie, and the common people. Common people included the peasantry, the **sans-culottes** and the **proletariat**. Each had its own share of grievances, which we shall discuss here one by one. The accumulated grievances piled up to create an explosive situation, and a spark alone was needed to set it ablaze. The acute economic crisis and the intense misery of the common people provided that spark, and revolution broke out.

Albert Soboul, the eminent French historian, thought that it was the French Revolution that brought into focus the ideas and principles of the bourgeoisie not only in France but in the entire world. He said,

'The French Revolution, along with the English revolutions of the 17th century, constitutes the crowning achievement of a long economic and social evolution that made the bourgeoisie the master of the world.'[40]

Georges Rudé too has assigned primary responsibility for the outbreak of the revolution on the bourgeoisie. He raised a pertinent question: Why was there a revolution in France in 1789, and nowhere else in Europe? The same conditions prevailed in almost all the countries in Europe as they did in France in the 18th century—despotic monarchy, disgruntled nobility, restless bourgeoisie, sharp financial crisis, impoverished peasantry. These conditions, in some combination or the other, existed in all European countries. Still the revolution broke out only in France. That is because, Rudé thinks, two factors were typical of France alone. These were: *first*, the role of Paris in the life of the French people, not only as the capital city but as a thriving centre of administration, law, culture and education; and *second*, a highly talented and 'challenging' bourgeoisie with 'a widely circulated corpus of radical political ideas', along with the common people, made the revolution happen.[41] The role of the bourgeoisie in the coming of the revolution is therefore undeniable. This *spirited and dynamic bourgeoisie* was the *strongest feature of French society in the 18th century* and contributed vigorously towards the opening of a new era in French social history of which the French Revolution was the culmination.

The bourgeoisie was divided into a number of categories. The first and foremost was the **landed bourgeoisie**. They, like the nobility, were owners of sprawling lands and landed estates. Their wealth and ownership of property eroded the fine distinctions between them and the nobility and clubbed them together to form one single plutocratic elite. However, there was another group who owned land, but not large enough to distinguish them from the huge mass of peasantry. Lefebvre called them the '**rural bourgeoisie**'. Both these groups of landed bourgeoisie had a substantial number of peasants working on their lands, the number varying according to the size of the landholdings.

Then there was the **commercial or capitalist bourgeoisie** who were mostly engaged in overseas mercantile activities and were owners of seaports. As part of French colonial ambitions, they were involved in competition and conflict with the British over Canada and India. Besides, there were the merchant manufacturers who owned industrial houses and manufacturing units in France. These men along with big bankers like Samuel Bernard played a significant role in financing the government in times of deep crisis, especially wars. In return they expected, and often received, special favours like promotion to the rank of nobility. There was constant friction between the capitalist bourgeoisie and the State. Moreover, the internal tolls and customs were onerous and lacked uniformity. This impeded the smooth flow of trade and commerce. The merchants resented it fiercely and this further embittered the relationship between them and the monarchy.

Another significant part of the bourgeoisie class was what was called the *fermiers generaux* or **financier bourgeoisie**. They, on behalf of the monarchy, collected indirect taxes on income from the royal domain. They paid large sums out of it to the royal exchequer and also kept substantial amounts to invest in their private industrial ventures, for example, the factories of Dupin de Francueil at Chateauroux. By virtue of their commercial activities, they were not only an integral part of the government but invariably exercised enormous influence on the King as well as the entire administrative machinery. Their existence being intricately integrated with the monarchy and the ancien regime, the fermiers generaux naturally were interested in their sustenance. However, things went wrong in times of crisis when their share in the collection dwindled as the Controller-General withdrew as much as he wished in favour of the monarchy. This made the position of the financier bourgeoisie rather uncertain, thereby creating a cleavage in their abiding loyalty to the royal authority.

The relationship between these different categories of bourgeoisie was one of suspicion and jealousy. As Antoine Barnave has pointed out, "a new distribution of wealth produces a new distribution of power. In the same way possession of lands raised the aristocracy, industrial property raised the power of the people" (here by 'people', Barnave meant the bourgeoisie).[42] So, they scrambled for power and fiercely competed against each other for the few coveted positions, each trying to win the King's favour. The struggle accentuated their rivalry and deep undercurrents of antagonism developed.

Another category within the bourgeoisie was **the professionals**—the lawyers, the doctors, the journalists, the teachers, etc. Early in the ancien regime, many of these men were accommodated in the fabric of the bureaucracy and innumerable law-courts.[43] With the passage of time and rise in population, opportunities shrank and consequently competition intensified. On the eve of the French Revolution, prominent professional bourgeois men included, for example, **Jean-Paul Marat**, a scientist and newspaper-owner who held extreme views in support of the political and economic rights of the common people; **Georges Danton**, another leader of the extremists; **Maximilien Robespierre**, the most influential supporter of democracy. Born in a middle-class family, the latter's political ideas were deeply influenced by the philosopher Jean-Jacques Rousseau. Both Danton and Robespierre were lawyers. An important **Girondist** (a group of middle-class republicans hailing from a place called Gironde) revolutionary was **Jacques-Pierre Brissot** who was a small-estate owner. Although the professional bourgeoisie were progressively advancing in education and political consciousness, they had no part to play in politics and administration. They deeply resented the fact that despite their education they were debarred from most of the important posts in the administrative and legal sphere, which were reserved for the clergy and the nobility alone.

Lastly, there was the category of the **petty bourgeoisie**. They included small entrepreneurs, modest landowners, humble traders, petty shop-owners, small publishers along with the petty government servants, who were known for their venality and utter lack of integrity. They were envious of all upper classes, including the landed and commercial bourgeoisie for the greater prosperity and higher social status they enjoyed.

The Peasantry

The peasantry formed the bulk of the Third Estate, comprising about, as Norman Hampson estimates, 20 million out of a total population of 26 million, while according to Lefebvre the total figure was approximately 23 million. The peasantry in 18th-century France encompassed the mass of humanity integrally associated with soil and cultivation in some way or the other and who derived their income by working on the land. They were central to the agricultural system, which the eminent physiocrat **Francois Quesnay** distinguished into *grande culture* and *petite culture*.[44] The grande culture referred to regions where large-scale cereal cultivation was the characteristic feature. The land was parcelled out into large units cultivated by tenant-farmers working on the lands of absentee landlords. Share-cropping was non-existent. The areas under petite culture were, however, cultivated by share-croppers. Grain cultivation was not popular as the soil was not suited for it, and although cereals were produced in order to meet the requirements of the local population, crops like rye or maize were preferred to wheat or rice.[45]

French peasantry was broadly divided into the ***gros fermiers*** or ***coqs de village*** (the rich, large tenant-farmers, or independent landowners), and the ***laboureurs*** (or the rural bourgeoisie). They stood, as **P.M. Jones** points out, 'at the apex of the peasantry'. The gros fermiers were the big estate-owners who staunchly supported the **physiocrats**, a group of eminent economists advocating the enclosure and use of common lands for scientific and capitalist agriculture. As grain prices skyrocketed on the eve of the revolution due to harvest failure, landowners rushed to grab more and more land to make enormous profits from enhanced grain production. This was called **enclosure**.

P. M. Jones identifies two types of 'engrossment' or enclosure. In 18th-century France and England, patches of common or fallow land and pastures were meant for collective use. Generally, villagers used them for grazing cattle. These common lands were held in the **open-field system** prevalent in much of Europe from the Middle Ages. This meant that each village had large fields which were parcelled out in strips to be cultivated by individual families. Under enclosure, however, this collective ownership was replaced by individual ownership. Rich landowners used their control of state processes to appropriate public land for their private benefit. In most cases it was a story of arm-twisting, force and superior power. According to Jones, 'two forms of engrossment caused particular dismay: proprietors stealthily enlarged their estates by absorbing adjacent holdings, either by purchase or fore-closure; or they acquired scattered farms one by one.'[46] In short, the rich became richer and the poor poorer. As a result, deep grievances and profound antagonism emerged within the lower echelons of the peasantry.

The laboureurs were yeomen farmers or rich peasant proprietors engaged in scientific farming. They formed the most important segment of the upper category of peasants because, although relatively few, they were still more in number than the gros fermiers. However, according to Jones, laboureurs could also 'refer to peasant proprietors of less exalted status' than the gros fermiers.[47] Lefebvre grouped the enriched gros fermier and laboureurs into one broad category which he called the 'rural bourgeoisie', while the poorer peasants were grouped into the large body of the 'rural proletariat'. Then there were the ***menagers***. Sometimes they referred to prosperous peasants with independent land and, therefore, were synonymous with laboureurs,[48] but on the other hand, Lefebvre calls them poor peasants with little land and who were a part of the 'rural proletariat'.[49]

The lower echelon of the peasantry comprised several layers. The petty peasant proprietors or *haricotiers* also worked as day wage-earners or part-time artisans as their land was not enough to make both ends meet. In some parts of France, haricotiers were known as *sossons* and elsewhere, as *bordiers*. A large number of peasants were *metayers* or share-croppers who owned insufficient land, and therefore worked on the land of their landlords on a contract of sharing the total produce on a fifty-fifty basis. They had no capital and were supplied with animals and tools by their landlords. There were tenant-farmers as well who like share-croppers had very little land of their own, and hired plots of land to cultivate from landowners in exchange for a rent. In times of bad or failed harvest, however, often the share-croppers and tenant-farmers were forced to take up jobs in factories or the domestic industry as wage-earners to supplement their income.

The conditions of landless peasants and serfs were the most precarious. The landless peasants worked on others' land as day labourers, or took up odd jobs elsewhere. **Florence Gauthier** called them the 'rural proletariat'. However, Derouet has noted that 50 per cent of such households owned their dwellings; between 60 per cent and 70 per cent owned a small garden; 27 per cent owned a cow and 7 per cent owned some sheep.[50] Tied to the lands of nobles, landed bourgeoisie, rich peasants and the Church were serfs, who, however, were as entitled as others to royal justice.

The peasantry was subjected to an onerous system of **taxation**. First of all, they had to pay *tithe* to the Church; *taille, vingtieme* (or, twentieth in French; an income tax amounting to one-twentieth part of the income), *capitation* and *gabelle* to the State. *Taille* referred to the principal tax levied on personal income paid by all commoners; *capitation* was a tax levied on individual income though, however, it fell entirely on the Third Estate. The clergy and the nobility were exempt from it. And *gabelle* was a salt tax. A huge range of feudal rents were paid to the landlord as well. These included *corvee* which meant forced labour, especially rendered on roads; *cens* or rent in cash; *champart* or rent in kind, and the *lods et ventes* or tax charged for transfer of land. They were also supposed to pay for the use of the landlord's property like wine press, mill, or bakery.[51] It was extremely difficult for the peasantry to pay such a large number of taxes. Moreover, in times of bad harvest, when the price of grain soared, the landlords prospered while the poor peasants reeled under the heavy weight of expenses and frequently starved. Along with the prices of food, rents of land also skyrocketed. While enclosures reduced the lands available for common use like cattle grazing, high rents curtailed the scope of renewing the lease of lands for common peasants. The system of taxation was highly exploitative, excessive and unfair. As the woes and struggles of the poor landless farmers to pay the bloated rents and feed their families became more acute, their helplessness, bitterness and anger at being unable to live a life of minimum dignity gave rise to deep schisms that further divided the lower peasantry from the upper peasantry.

The entire French population can thus be divided into two broad categories: the privileged and the non-privileged. The clergy, the nobility, the upper landed bourgeoisie along with the 'rural bourgeoisie' enjoyed enormous privileges arising out of their possession of land. These were referred to as seigneurial privileges. P.M. Jones defines *seigneurie* as 'a system of land tenure, as a jurisdiction of rights and as a unit of judicial administration'.[52] **Seigneurie** was, therefore, essentially related to land, that is, to the First and the Second Estate (the clergy and the nobility), but also to the substantial landlords of the Third Estate. As Jones observes, "all nobles were seigneurs, even if all seigneurs were not nobles."[53]

Seigneurialism impinged upon all aspects of rural life. The resentment of the peasants hovered round two specific issues—*first*, the extraction of taxes, surplus harvest and services and *second*, the apathy and total lack of interest of the seigneurs to improve the pitiable conditions of peasants. Many seigneurs were interested in pursuing agricultural capitalism by producing food-grains and non-food-grains like oil-seeds, cotton, etc. in bulk for trade and commerce. To increase production, they promoted the adoption of better technology and modernised farming. This was what the physiocrats also advocated. There was, therefore, a so-called entente between the big estate-owners and the physiocrats. That is why in the context of Burgundy, **Pierre de Saint Jacob** saw the emergence of *seigneurie* in the latter part of the 18th century as 'physiocratic'.[54] The mass of the peasantry, on the other hand, staunchly opposed scientific agriculture as their fear was that it would drastically curb society's need for and dependence on their services.

Many peasants in 18th-century France resented *the free movement of grain across the country and the abolition of tolls and customs on grain*. This was due to several factors. The free movement of grain, particularly when coupled with the abolition of tolls and customs, meant that grain could be shipped from regions with abundant harvests, often at lower prices to regions experiencing shortages, where they would be sold at much higher rates. This could *disrupt local markets* in areas where grain was already very cheap, which would then be replaced by goods from other places, the prices of which would be exorbitant. High costs of inland transport would control the prices which would definitely benefit the free traders and landowners but conversely crush the peasants.

Further, peasants also feared *exploitation by merchants and landlords*, who hoarded grain to profit from price fluctuations. Free movement of grain meant those who already held more power exercised even greater control over the grain supply, thus leading to higher prices and reduced availability of grain in times of dire need. In the period leading up to the revolution, *rumours of a 'famine plot' by the aristocracy* to starve the population were rife. The free movement of grain, combined with all these factors, fuelled fears among peasants who saw it as a direct threat to their livelihood, and a symbol of the broader inequalities and injustices of the existing social order.

Georges **Lefebvre** and Emmanuel **Le Roy Ladurie** have argued that it was this capitalist interest of the seigneurs which infuriated the peasantry and ruined their relationship.[55] According to Le Roy Ladurie, the prior servile attitude of the peasants changed significantly after 1750.[56] He further thinks that the **seigneurial demesne** (i.e., land directly controlled and utilised by the seigneur, including his manor house and farm, as opposed to the land given to and worked upon by his tenants) were harbingers of modern capitalist agriculture and had the French Revolution not intervened, it might have brought about, as in England, an agricultural revolution in France.[57] **G.V. Taylor**, however, does not think that this peasant-seigneur relationship was in any way responsible for the revolution. By analysing the *cahiers* (list of grievances drawn up by different social classes), Taylor found that only a small proportion of the rural population protested vehemently against seigneurialism. "Of the 428 parish cahiers which he examined, only 21 per cent demanded an end to monopoly rights (banalities [or feudal dues that compelled peasants to use their lord's mills, ovens and wine presses for processing their crops, baking bread and making wine and pay for their use, even if they had their own facilities]); 11 per cent demanded the abolition of seigneurial courts; and a mere 4 per cent called for the destruction of the feudal regime completely."[58] **William Doyle** concludes that political issues rather than social or economic tension were the primary factors behind the outbreak of the revolution.[59] **P.M. Jones** conducts a detailed scrutiny of the cahiers and concludes that Taylor's analysis was piecemeal, not comprehensive, and argues that the peasants did indeed protest seriously against seigneurialism. **John Markoff** has also conducted a detailed research in order to establish a connection between peasant grievances and peasant insurrection in France in 1789. According to Markoff, the cahiers formed an important source of the desires, aspirations as well as grievances of the peasants. By examining 748 cahiers at random, about the peasant actions undertaken collectively, it was found that generally four kinds of actions took place—attacks on landlords, attacks on government personnel or institutions, desperate actions for securing food and for basic subsistence, and actions generated by imaginary fear.[60] The grievances of the peasants, therefore, could be summed up as follows:

(*i*) the heavy burden of taxation;

(*ii*) the enclosure system which encroached upon their collective rights on common pastures;

(*iii*) seigneurialism and its associated evils;

(*iv*) the modernisation and commercialisation of agriculture with the adoption of scientific methods;

(*v*) the rising price of bread due to both capitalism and bad harvests.

According to **James Scott**, the central concern common to different peasant mobilisations was the threat to subsistence. Many peasants were risk-averse and preferred negotiations with their lords to militant outbursts. **Jeffery Paige** argued that the peasantry also had political ambitions; however, George V. Taylor emphasised local interests and local issues to be the primary cause of most peasant unrest. **Ernest Labrousse** suggested that rising rural literacy showed the way towards awareness and some kind of enlightenment.[61] Markoff argued that peasants, in general, showed little interest in foreign affairs and colonial issues, were mostly interested in commerce, transportation, agricultural matters and that they mainly complained against taxes, specifically taille and capitation. Markoff also pointed out that grievances of the poorer peasants differed from those of the richer ones. While the former were concerned with community rights to common lands and forests, the latter with tolls and customs for improving their market interests. Markoff looked upon the cahiers as "a political act, a joint statement of a community."[62]

The Sans-culottes

An important social group—central to the revolution—was the *sans-culottes*. Who were these sans-culottes? Literally it meant 'without breeches'. Sans-culottes were ordinary patriots who did not wear fine clothes, and collectively referred to the lower classes and common people who wore long trousers instead of the knee breeches worn by the rich and the aristocrats. More specifically, it included all the urban poor and ordinary townspeople comprising petty traders, small shop-owners, skilled craftsmen, journeymen, among others, that is, a medley of people from different social origins. They were the most significant and radical militant component of the revolution who impacted the direction that it took, and represented 'the great mass of little men' who existed between the two poles of the bourgeoisie and the proletariat.

The main enemy of the sans-culottes were the aristocrats and the rich bourgeoisie. The sans-culottes believed in the concept of social equality, which the aristocrats did not. The pride and vanity of the aristocrats prevented them from being a part of the revolution; they felt they were socially and culturally superior to the mass of the common people, whom they looked down upon and deeply despised. The sans-culottes, too, could never accept them as one of themselves. Albert Soboul held: "For such men are incapable of bringing themselves to the heights of our Revolution; their hearts are always full of pride and we shall never forget their former grandeur and their domination over us." Soboul gives a number of examples of the rich and privileged being taken to task by the sans-culottes for the disdain shown by the former towards the latter. A clock merchant Etienne Gide was arrested by the Committee of the Revolutionnaire Section (of which the sans-culottes were members) in 1793 for being haughty and insolent.[63] On 12th October in the same year, a solicitor, that is a bourgeois man, was arrested for extending support to the aristocrats in the general assemblies.[64] A music merchant Bayeux was similarly apprehended by the revolutionary committee of the Marches Section because he had expressed his 'abomination' on seeing the meeting being presided over by a badly dressed cobbler.[65]

The bitterness of the sans-culottes against this haughty and supercilious behaviour of the upper classes originated from their intolerance of the sharp class distinctions that marred the French society of the time and the way the sans-culottes were looked upon and condemned by the former. Louis-Claude Cezeron of the Committee of the Poissonniere Section, for example, stated in a meeting of the general assembly on 31 May 1793 "that the poor depended on the rich and that the sans-culottes were never anything more than the lowest order possible."[66] This violated their sense of dignity and strong belief in social egalitarianism. The sans-culottes, therefore, saw as their enemies not only the aristocrats but anybody who transgressed their ideas of equality and refused to give them due respect.

The question then is: Can this enmity be simply treated as a war between the haves and the have-nots? No. The social and economic status of the sans-culottes cannot be easily fixed, for, as stated earlier, the term denoted a mixed population. It would be wrong to consider them as poorer elements belonging to the bottom of the society, devoid of any culture or refinement, and sometimes even associated with, as **Edmund Burke** held, a certain criminality and uncouth behaviour which prompted him to refer to them as the "swinish multitude". This definition of Burke was later supported by Abbe Barruel and Hippolyte Taine as well. However, as **Geoffrey Ellis** has rightly pointed out, there were many prosperous traders, artisans and craftsmen among the sans-culottes who were very much men of property. Rudé called them the **urban menu people** (common people) like small shopkeepers and craftsmen, servants and day labourers. The sans-culottes, therefore, could be better identified not by their economic status but rather by their common political beliefs, ideology and shared virtues like intense patriotism, love for equality and liberty, self-dignity and pride. "No man could be a good revolutionary without virtue", says **Richard Cobb**,[67] and indeed the sans-culottes were mostly militant revolutionaries. Their activities in and contributions to the revolution will be discussed later.

The Workers

The class at the lowest ebb of French society in the ancien regime were the workers, although they do not figure prominently in most historical writings, mainly because of the smallness of their number as there were few units of manufacture and industries at that time. The term 'proletariat', popularised by Karl Marx later, meant urban factory workers. According to **Albert Soboul**, prominent Marxist historian, they belonged more to the 19th century after the coming of the Industrial Revolution, than to the 18th. **Daniel Guerin**, another well-known Marxist historian, however, held that within the bourgeois revolution a working class with its own interests was already emerging, and tried "to bring to light the embryo of anti-bourgeois revolution concealed within the womb of the bourgeois revolution." Guerin claimed that later historians like Soboul and Cobb used his ideas without acknowledging him.[68] For his attempt to use the past to fit the present, Guerin was accused of anachronism. In his *Class Struggle in the First French Republic*, published in 1946, Guerin argued that the beginnings of a conflict of class interest had cropped up between the 'embryonic proletariat', the manual workers (*bras nus*), represented by the **Enragés** (a distinct group of firebrands who represented the demands of the lower class and the radical sans-culottes), and the bourgeoisie, represented by the **Jacobins**. Guerin says that the Jacobins on the one hand aimed at uniting the popular classes against the nobility; and on the other, endeavoured to create a solidarity of the wealthy people against the 'have-nots'. That is why they were so antagonistic against the Enragés led by Jacques Roux.

Such was the structure of society in France on the eve of the French Revolution. This, according to **Roland Mousnier**,[69] was a **society of orders or estates** rather than a **society of classes**. This has also been elaborated by **Pamela Pilbeam**.[70] Both scholars distinguished between the two and observed that a society of orders was one where social distinctions were decided by social values or positions and ranks in society. Prior to the 18th century, as already discussed, there were three orders or estates in France. The first order was the clergy and the second the nobility. This was determined entirely on the basis of the extraordinary pre-eminence they enjoyed in the State, particularly in the eyes of the King. Their status was exclusively decided by their birth. The third order included the rest of society. The topmost layer of the Third Estate was the bourgeoisie, many of whom were rich and prosperous by virtue of their possession of land and profitable commercial enterprises but lacked the privileges enjoyed by the nobility because of their lineage. Classes, on the other hand, in Marxian interpretation, were determined by the relationship of people to economic activity, i.e., production of material goods. The role of different people in the system of production assigned their position in society. Classes emerged in the 19th century largely in the wake of the Industrial Revolution and its concept of mass production. Then society became divided, in Marx's analysis, into distinct classes like labour and capital, the bourgeoisie and the proletariat.

The French Revolution, Mousnier says,[71] played a significant role in this transformation from social orders to classes. It stripped the two upper orders not only of much of their privileges but of their property as well. Particularly noteworthy in this connection, Pilbeam says, was the issue of the **Report of 4 August 1789**. By this Report, feudalism and all relics of feudalism were condemned and abolished. Even tithes were swept away, inspite of a protest from Sieyes, and the nobility and the clergy all had to recognise it. In the judicial sphere, the Parlements (law courts under the ancient regime, primarily controlled by the nobility) were abolished and new legal courts consisting of elected judges and elected justices of peace were substituted. This was the first step towards erosion of the dominance and preeminence of the privileged classes. The society had begun to be reorganised, which continued through several legal provisions and constitutional changes that characterised the entire period of the French Revolution, particularly during the time of Jacobin rule. These changes in law and constitution will be discussed gradually.

Political Issues

Although the burden of taxation fell heavily upon the people, they had neither political rights nor personal freedom. As we have discussed already, in the eyes of the law there was no limit to royal power. The kings of France thought that they were entitled to rule by Divine Right and that they had no responsibility to the people; if they had any responsibility at all, it was to God alone. Thus, there was no connection between public opinion and the absolute monarch who was supposed to be protected by God. The King's orders imposed taxes and created laws; there was no question of people's participation in such matters. On all administrative issues, the King's orders were final. The ministers simply carried out the King's directives. They had no freedom or discretion to act according to their own views. As we have seen, France did have a National Assembly known as the Estates-General, which was comparable to the English Parliament, but it was not allowed to meet after 1614. There were no representatives of the people anywhere in any institution of the government. The system of government was, therefore, totally arbitrary. No individual or institution in France was legally entitled to oppose the royal will. The system of judicial administration was full of defects. Even innocent people could be kept in prison indefinitely without trial. Political rights which the people of England had won in the 17th century were totally absent in France in the 18th century.

In an autocratic system of government, efficiency of administration depends primarily on the personality and capability of the King. In the 18th century, the kings of France lacked in these qualities. Louis XV was pleasure-loving and indifferent to the duties of his high office. Louis XVI was personally generous and soft-hearted but in political matters, he was inexperienced and weak. Neither of these two kings had the capacity to control the ministers, the officials and the nobility. Although nominally invested with unlimited power, they were incapable of giving the country a strong and efficient government.

There were some important councils for different important functions of the government like the **Council of State**, the **Council of Dispatches** and the **Privy Council**. The highest decisions of the State were taken in the Council of State which was presided over by the King and a handful of members called the Ministers of State. The Council of Dispatches was attended by a number of Heads of Departments or Secretaries or Ministers, who were invited for the purpose of deciding internal policies. It was generally headed by the Keeper of Seals or the Head of the Judiciary. They also sat in the Privy Council which was a kind of administrative tribunal attended by 30 Councillors of State. They were assisted by a large number of Masters of Request. All these councils were scenes of intense jealousy, acrimony, cut-throat competition and conflict. In the Council of State presided by the King, the few ministers who were called were constantly engaged in proving their own superiority over others and therefore, endeavoured to show others in a poor light before the King. The atmosphere in other councils was also marred by discord and friction. The Masters of Request aimed at becoming *Intendants* or Provincial Governors, and fiercely competed against each other. Under circumstances such as these, good governance could only be assured by a competent king like Louis XIV. But Louis XV had left everything in the hands of his Minister Cardinal Fleury. Confusion and chaos reigned supreme under Louis XVI, as discussed above in detail.

The role of the Parlement (legal court) in France on the eve of the revolution was very significant. Laws and edicts issued by the King were not valid until they were sanctioned by the Parlement. Since the days of the Fronde, the Parlements were dominated by the noblesse de robe, who were against the passing of any royal edict that conflicted with their interests. This political acrimony paved the path for the **aristocratic revolution** that consisted of the **first phase of the revolution**. The Parlements, therefore, played a distinct role in generating the political climate of the revolution.

According to **George V. Taylor**, political issues are central to an understanding of the French Revolution. Political factors were ingrained in the age-old conflict between the monarchy and the nobility, as the reforms that the monarchy endeavoured to institute clashed with the vested interests of the nobility. This comprised the core of the aristocratic revolution that ended in the victory of the nobility over the monarchy. In this, the Parlements played an important role. Historians' opinions regarding the nature of the Parlements are divided. They are fiercely criticised by royalist supporters like Marcel Marion, Pierre Gaxotte and Francois Pietri. Lefebvre and Alfred Cobban also attacked the Parlements as engines of power that deliberately blocked reforms advocated by the King in order to preserve the privileges of the first two estates. Jean Egret and J.H. Shenan, on the contrary, regarded the Parlements as institutions that tried to protect the rights of citizens against the whims and fancies of the monarchy.

The Role of Intellectuals

France took a leading part in the intellectual revolution which Europe experienced in the Age of Enlightenment. It is imperative here to say a few words about **Enlightenment in Europe**.

In the 17th and 18th centuries, Europe passed through an age of unprecedented progress in philosophy and science. Historians have called it the **age of intellectual revolution**. During the Middle Ages, European genius flourished on the basis of Christian doctrines and ideals. Theology and Law were discussed in terms of Christian teachings; science was neglected because it was supposed to be anti-Christian. The **Renaissance** and the **Reformation** brought about a complete change in the approach to problems of knowledge and European life began to increasingly centre round reason and science. Not only did it lead to new discoveries in philosophy and science, it taught man to advance along new tracks in the political, social and economic fields. In the history of Europe, this is known as the Age of Enlightenment. It was enriched by contributions from many scientists, philosophers, litterateurs, artists, historians and economists.

In the Age of Enlightenment, natural science assumed new forms and adopted new methods. Social science began to be studied on the basis of scientific principles, new philosophical ideas began to influence religion, a new humanitarianism coloured social ideals, and in the field of art, old traditions were harmonised with the new romanticism. Naturally, these far-reaching changes also influenced political and social organisations. The spirit of enquiry and critical approach to problems of life which were reflected in the Renaissance in the 15th century were brought forward in new forms in the 18th century. The natural result was the triumph of rationalism. In all aspects of life—religion, society, law, economics, government—rationalism became predominant; it became a common practice to judge all human institutions and customs by the test of reason.

More than discoveries in natural science, scientists of this period devoted themselves mainly to fresh experiments based on the ideas of older scientists like Copernicus and Galileo. During this period science spread itself over a wider field and was no longer confined to laboratories. Kings and administrators became patrons of science and scientists. New scientific academies were established. Among them, the Royal Society of England established in 1662 deserves special mention. In France, the Academy of Science secured the patronage of King Louis XIV. Similar progress took place in the field of social science—history, political science, philosophy. The primary question which preoccupied political thinkers of the 17th and 18th centuries was: Which is the best form of government to reconcile social progress with the individual's happiness and freedom? It was discussed by two English philosophers, **Thomas Hobbes** and **John Locke**. The Dutch philosopher **Spinoza** and the German philosophers **Immanuel Kant** and **Johann Gottlieb Fichte** also deliberated upon this. Two other prominent names in the field of political science were those of two Frenchmen—**Montesquieu** and **Jean-Jacques Rousseau**. The Age of Enlightenment also saw the earliest studies of economics. A French physician named **François Quesnay** and his collaborators known as the physiocrats introduced the study of economics in France. British economist **Adam Smith** published *The Wealth of Nations* in 1776.

A number of prominent political thinkers and philosophers were born in France during the Age of Enlightenment. They largely moulded the ideas and ways of thinking of men and society and contributed tremendously to creating the ideological background of the French Revolution. The greatest literary figure in Europe in the 18th century was the French writer **Voltaire** (1694–1778). He was equally at home writing poems, dramas, historical works and literary essays, and his reputation travelled to all parts of Europe. Although a Frenchman, he enjoyed the patronage of Frederick II of Prussia and Catherine II of Russia. His writings were not appreciated merely for their literary excellence. Voltaire was also the leader of religious scepticism in the Age of Enlightenment. He was a vocal and fearless critic of traditional Christianity and the organisation of the Church and clergy. Many popular ideas and institutions were exposed to derisive attack as a result of the spread of Voltaire's ideas.

Towards the close of the 17th century the greatest English political philosopher and theorist was **John Locke** (1632–1704). His teachings emphasised the natural rights of men. He wrote, "to understand political power, and derive it from its original, we must consider, what state all men are naturally in, and that is, a state of perfect freedom to order their actions, and dispose of their possessions and persons, as they think fit, within the bounds of the law of nature, without asking leave, or depending on the will of any other man." When a monarch contravenes these rights, people have the right to revolt. Locke, therefore, proposed that governments could be overthrown by citizens under certain circumstances—a unique and a revolutionary theory in an age of absolute despotism.

A group of French scholars known as the **Encyclopaedists** (of whom **Baron d'Holbach** was the most well-known) confirmed the theories of Voltaire. Two of them, **Denis Diderot** and **Jean le Rond d'Alembert**, both Frenchmen, published their famous *Encyclopédie* in 17 volumes. It was a collection of writings of many scholars, scientists, philosophers and historians. The writers were loyal to one principle: **rationalism**. Some of them went farther than Voltaire in their criticism of Christianity, and propagated **atheism**. The wide *Encyclopédie* of the Encyclopaedia indicated the acceptance of the theories and remonstrances of Voltaire and the Encyclopaedists. The profound influence of their views brought about significant changes in the sphere of religion. Freedom of thought in religious matters fostered religious toleration. The cruel persecution of non-conformists which characterised the 16th and 17th centuries came to an end in the 18th century.

Contemporary French philosophers did not fail to note that the British Constitution circumscribed the powers of the King. Among them, **Montesquieu** (1689–1755) deserves special mention. His great work, *The Spirit of Laws*, which was largely influenced by the English Constitution, is one of the classics of political science. He was an admirer of the British Constitution and recommended that it should be followed in France. Montesquieu was enamoured by the English practice of what he called the 'separation of powers'—the independence of the three organs of the government, the executive, the legislature and the judiciary. However, it should be borne in mind that Montesquieu was wrong in thinking that the three branches of government in England were independent.

The *philosophe* who left the most indelible impression on French society and the revolutionaries was **Jean-Jacques Rousseau**. He has acquired immortality as a pioneer in political thought. His most important work is the *Contrat Sociale* (The Social Contract) published in 1762. His main thesis is that the *rights of the ruler are derived from the consent of the ruled*. From this emerged the concept of popular sovereignty. In other words, he believed that sovereignty actually rested in the people. The State owed its origin to a contract between the people and the ruler. This was indeed a supreme revolutionary principle in an age when the rulers of Europe claimed to rule by Divine Right. "Man is born free, but is everywhere in chains," said Rousseau. All men in all nations are born free, but they are enslaved by the chains of society. They are also enslaved by the chains of poverty, ignorance and superstition. When man is able to break free from these man-made fetters, and enter a world of equality, the world would become a far better place to live in. The implications of his theory were significant. The French Revolution bears traces of Rousseau's thought throughout.

There was another group that had significant contemporary influence on the workings of the revolution. They interpreted economics from a new rationalist point of view, and were deeply inspired by the writings of the Scottish economist Adam Smith, especially by his book, *The Wealth of Nations*. As mentioned earlier, they were known as the **physiocrats** and their chief representatives were **Mirabeau** and **Quesnay**. Some of the key ideas they propagated were:

(*i*) agriculture is the primary and only true source of wealth;

(*ii*) the economy comprised three classes: **productive** (farmers), **proprietary** (landowners), and **sterile** (industrial workers);

(*iii*) State control over trade and commerce was not desirable;

(*iv*) there should be *laissez-faire*, free trade and limited government intervention in the economy;

(*v*) all taxation should be reduced to a single land tax.

The physiocrats had an undeniable impact on the entire course of the French Revolution. Jean-Baptiste Say was another French economist, famous for articulating what became known as **Say's Law**: "Supply creates its own demand." Say was influenced by the physiocrats, but developed his own economic thought, influenced by Adam Smith.

Whether these philosophers were directly responsible for the revolution or not is a highly debatable question. According to Mallet du Pan, without the *philosophes*, revolution would never have taken place.

So they were undoubtedly 'a cause', if not 'the cause' of the revolution. **Roland Mousnier**, on the contrary, observed that these men, despite their fiery writings were not responsible for the revolution, for they were little read, and much less understood. The philosophers, according to him, only gave voice to the grievances of the people.

Karl Marx, too, was of the opinion that for the causes of the revolution, we must probe into the social and economic background of the writings which were mere symptoms of the grievances. In 1859, in his preface to *A Contribution to the Critique of Political Economy* Marx wrote, "Just as one does not judge an individual by what he thinks about himself, so one cannot judge such a period by its own consciousness."

Indeed, the connection between the philosophers' ideas and the outbreak of the revolution of 1789 is somewhat remote and indirect. The causes of the revolution, as Morse Stephens points out, were chiefly economical and political.

Among scholars who highlighted the importance of the Enlightenment in the outbreak of the French Revolution, Norman Hampson[72] and Lefebvre were prominent. They believed that intellectual convictions played a crucial role in shaping the minds of the people. Both emphasised upon the social perspective of the revolution. In Lefebvre's view,[73] the revolution was the handiwork of the bourgeoisie, and the capitalist bourgeoisie. In other words, the French Revolution was a bourgeois capitalist revolution. And the bourgeoisie was fascinated and inspired by the ideas of the philosophes. Alfred Cobban,[74] the English revisionist historian who revised the interpretation of Marxist historians like Lefebvre, vehemently opposed the idea that intellectual ideas in any way influenced the outbreak of the revolution. He and his pupil Joan McDonald[75] argued that philosophical discourse, including Rousseau's *Contrat Sociale* were considered seriously in France only after 1789. Therefore, they could in no way have formed the background of the revolution. Cobban's view was largely accepted by English historians with the exception of Norman Hampson.

In fact, a host of historians deny the importance of intellectual factors in the outbreak of the French Revolution and consider political issues to be of direct and paramount significance. They believe, as David Thomson has summarised in his book *Europe since Napoleon* (Chapter 1, p. 1), that the connection between the philosophers' ideas and the outbreak of the revolution was remote and indirect. The philosophes were not revolutionaries in any way. Nor did they intend to propagate revolution.

Daniel Mornet,[76] for example, said emphatically that the *philosophes neither planned revolution nor were directly responsible for it*. However, their ideas percolated down into society through the few people who read them. Historian **Alexis de Tocqueville**[77] who studied the cahiers, or the people's list of grievances, was struck by how many of them craved reforms and radical change in the existing system. He saw in the cahiers signs of political awakening, especially of the Third Estate, which showed awareness of its rights and injustices. The act of writing their grievances itself gave ordinary people a sense of participation and legitimacy in politics. In this sense, the influence of the Enlightenment on the people is undeniable. However, **Guy Chaussinand-Noagret**[78] observed that the cahiers of the nobility bore indelible imprints of the ideas of the philosophes. Like many other scholars whom we have discussed, Chaussinand-Noagret also believed that due to their grievances against the monarchy, the nobility joined hands with the landed bourgeoisie to form a single propertied elitist group called the '**notables**'. Enlightenment, therefore was the guiding light not only of the bourgeoisie, but of the aristocracy as well. Similar opinions have been expressed by Denis Richet.[79] George V. Taylor,[80] however, rejected the ideas of Enlightenment playing any significant role in the outbreak of the revolution, and believed that it was entirely the outcome of a continuing political crisis.

Nevertheless, even if the philosophes did not directly contribute to the making of the revolution, they certainly fostered a critical attitude of inquiry into the prevailing state of affairs. They contributed to the development of a new way of looking at things and, in that sense, were responsible for shaping the minds of the populace in general.

Phases of the French Revolution

THE ARISTOCRATIC REVOLUTION

The French Revolution can broadly be divided into two distinct phases: (*i*) the aristocratic revolution; and (*ii*) the revolution of the Third Estate. The first phase, known as the ***Revolte Nobiliaire***, began with Calonne's declaration on 20 August 1786 that the State was on the verge of a financial collapse. Since the closing of the American War of Independence in 1783—which was a tremendous drain on the country's resources—till

1786, Calonne had managed the finances by borrowing. In 1786, when the exasperated lenders finally began to refuse further loans, Calonne was left with no other option but to inform the King of the enormous crisis that was driving the State machinery towards a rapid and inevitable head-on crash. The situation demanded a thorough and drastic overhaul of the entire financial system through careful and meticulous fiscal reform.

One way of raising funds was to enhance taxes. However, this option was exhausted as the people were already too heavily taxed. Another option was to curb the court expenses which in popular perception were too wasteful and extravagant. But this also, as we have already seen, amounted only to 6 per cent of the entire expenditure. Calonne suggested, therefore, that the only other way left was to tax everybody, which meant that the social classes earlier immune from taxation—the clergy and the nobility—would now be obliged to pay. Calonne even prepared a revamped list of taxes which included: (*i*) a salt tax to be imposed uniformly throughout the country; (*ii*) all owners of land, irrespective of class, were to be charged a land tax; (*iii*) in order to boost the economy by ensuring smooth flow of trade and commerce, all internal tariffs were removed and grain trade was made completely free; and (*iv*) manorial properties belonging to the Church could now be sold in order to liquidate the debt incurred by the Church and to help the State. Calonne's apprehension was that the debt incurred by the Church would be used as a plea to avert taxes. The task of assessing the taxes was placed upon provincial assemblies to be elected by land owners of the three orders taken as a whole. As Lefebvre has pointed out,[81] the sacrifice asked of the privileged classes were modest in the sense that they remained as before exempt from taille or direct income tax or from maintaining the roads. The peasants could now make monetary payments in lieu of *corvee* (forced labour on land).

There was an immediate outburst of vehement protest within the first two orders. There was a serious breach of trust and violation of the age-old property rights, they claimed. Under circumstances such as these Calonne needed firm support from the monarchy, which was not forthcoming. The King was too weak and through his demeanour and actions had made himself a laughing stock among the people.[82] Calonne then devised another method. He carefully selected from among the nobles a few who, he thought, would support the King and approve of the reforms orchestrated by Calonne. This committee was known as the **Assembly of Notables**. Soon after, unfortunately, Calonne fell ill and the Assembly could not meet until 22 February 1787. Regrettably, when it finally met, things did not work out as Calonne had expected them to do. The 'notables' neither supported the King nor the reforms. On the contrary, they fiercely objected against the curtailment of manorial rights. In their view, it violated property rights. Moreover, they argued that the land tax which was imposed could not be universal and perpetual. Further, the Estates-General alone and not the monarchy had the right to impose taxes on the first two estates which were otherwise immune from any kind of taxation. They forcefully demanded the calling of the Estates-General. The King dismissed Calonne on 8 April 1787 and replaced him with **Lomenie de Brienne, Archbishop of Toulouse**.

Brienne, a sharp critic of Calonne earlier, now started treading his predecessor's path by not only revamping the land tax but also imposing a steep stamp tax. The notables continued to protest strongly and clung to their demand of summoning the Estates-General. Brienne then took recourse to borrowing, but he required the consent of the Parlement. The consent was not forthcoming. Brienne then promised to call the Estates-General in 1792 while, in the meantime, a fund of 120,000,000 livres could be raised. The King himself then placed before the Parlement a demand for registration of loan, but the Parlement did not relent. The Duke of Orleans opposed the King's plea by saying, "Sir, it is illegal". The King asserted, "It is legal because I wish it."[83]

The dispute continued. The Parlement on 3 May 1788 declared itself to be the custodian of the laws of the State and also pronounced the Estates-General to alone have the right to impose taxes. The unlimited powers of the King were thus challenged and a separation of powers was proposed. The monarchy retaliated by arresting the two most vociferous members of the Parlement—Duval **d'Epremesnil** and Goislart **de Montsabert**. The monarchy also established a Plenary Court, composed mostly of princes and close supporters of the King. Its task was to register royal edicts. The Parliament was suspended. Sharp protests, and even riots in some places, followed. Eventually on 5th July Brienne yielded before the demands of the Parliament and agreed to summon the Estates-General. The date for its meeting was fixed on 1 May 1789. On 8th August, Brienne dismissed the Plenary Court and on 24th tendered his resignation. The King summoned **Jaques Necker** to be his Comptroller-General. With the calling of the Estates-General, the capitulation of the monarchy to the wishes of the Estates-General was complete. The aristocratic revolution ended in triumph for the aristocrats.

THE BOURGEOIS REVOLUTION

The bourgeoisie denoted the middle class that included the **professionals** as well as the **capitalist class** which owned the means of production. As soon as the aristocratic revolution in France was over, it was the turn of the Third Estate (the bourgeoisie along with the common people), to step in to carry the banner of revolution ahead. As we have seen earlier, within the bourgeoisie, there were distinct groups, who for various reasons, found themselves in a state of profound discontent on the eve of the French Revolution. As they took upon themselves the cudgel of the revolution, they were joined by the common people, especially the sans-culottes, and thereafter the revolution progressed on the basis of a specific bourgeois-popular alliance. Historians like Elizabeth **Eisenstein** call this combination a common 'patriot' front and denied any particular bourgeois element in it. In fact, according to them, the French liberal aristocrats too played a significant role in it.[84] However, the distinct and widespread role of the bourgeoisie became manifest with the gradual unfolding of the revolution. Although the parts played by the bourgeoisie and the common people often merged and overlapped as the revolution proceeded, they can be identified and, for the purpose of easier understanding, dealt with separately.

The Tennis Court Oath

On **24 January 1789**, guidelines were issued for the election of deputies and drawing up of the *cahiers de doleances,* or list of grievances, of the three estates. In Paris, the suffrage was limited to the annual payment of six livres in capitation. Elsewhere, all males over the age of 25, whose names were there in the taxation list, whatever be the amount, were eligible to vote. In general, the deputies were to be elected by their own Estates meeting in separate assemblies.[85] As far as the cahiers were concerned, those of the bourgeoisie demanded equality of political and civil rights of the three estates—freedom of speech, publication and assembly, freedom from arbitrary arrest, eradication of all special privileges.

Serious differences arose regarding the method of voting. The clergy or the First Estate had approximately 308 votes; the nobility or the Second Estate had 285 votes while the Third Estate had 621. If the three estates voted separately (that is one vote for each estate) the clergy and the nobility, who were naturally opposed to all reforms, could combine their votes and defeat the reform programme of the Third Estate. But if the three estates **voted jointly**, the Third Estate would prevail and the reforms would have a fair chance of success. So differences regarding the procedure of voting appeared as soon as the Estates-General met on 5 May 1789. The King and the first two estates were in favour of voting by estates, but the Third Estate demanded joint voting. On 10th June, it invited the other estates to meet at a common deliberative assembly. If they refused, it decided to proceed without them. On 17th June, the representatives of the Third Estate assumed the title of National Assembly. The King adjourned the Estates-General by force and closed the doors of the chamber where they met. The members of the National Assembly met at a tennis court adjoining the Assembly chamber and took an oath that they would continue their work till the completion of the Constitution. This oath is known as the **Tennis Court Oath**. Necker advised the King to discuss matters of common interest together while particular interests could be attended to separately. He also pressed the King to summon a *séance royale* or a royal session. It ultimately met on 23rd June where it was decided that: (*i*) all matters of common interest would be decided at a common assembly; and (*ii*) reform of the institutions of the ancien

FIG. 1.4: *The Tennis Court Oath* (1791) by Jacques-Louis David

regime was the reform most urgently required. On 11th July Necker was removed from office and replaced by **Baron de Breteuil**. This heralded the beginning of events that would lead to the **storming of the Fort of Bastille** on **14 July 1789**.

Municipal Revolts Spread

July to August of 1789 also witnessed the revolutionising of the municipal administration in most of the cities and towns of France. Political upheavals occurring there rendered a return to the monarchical absolutism of the old regime impossible. Twenty of the 30 largest towns in France experienced municipal revolutions. The nature and intensity of these revolts varied from place to place. In some towns like Strasbourg, local patriots created entirely new municipal councils or committees, while in others like **Dijon** and **Pamiers**, newly formed authorities shared power with old regime officials. But here also mostly the old officials were in a minority. In a few cases as in **Marseilles**, the upheaval preceded the fall of Bastille and occurred in February 1789, but in most cities, it was in response to the news from Paris. In some towns, as in **Normandy** the municipal revolution was hardly successful in the sense that former local authorities continued to exercise power. In places like **Lyons** and **Troyes**, the municipal revolt was initially successful, but was soon to be toppled by a counter-offensive from the forces of the ancient regime. And finally, as in **Toulouse**, there was no municipal revolution at all because the local councils enjoyed the confidence of the people. Not all of the municipal revolutions were violent, but the threat of violence was always present. In addition to the creation of new political bodies, local revolutionaries also generally created bourgeois militias to preserve order, the forerunners of the National Guard. These combined phenomena made it clear to the King and his advisers that revolutionary upheaval was not confined to Paris, nor could it be undone solely in the capital.

The Constituent Assembly and the Constitution

Meanwhile, the National Assembly engaged itself in framing a new constitution and in introducing administrative reforms. It now renamed itself the **Constituent Assembly (9 July 1789)**. The capture of Bastille strengthened the base of the Constituent Assembly and removed the danger of its dissolution; the municipal revolts paved the path for the improvement of local government; the good harvest of 1789 put an end to the food crisis. In these new and favourable conditions, the work of constructive reform could proceed unhampered. By a **Report on 4 August 1789** feudal customs and all relics of feudalism were condemned and declared to be abolished. Even tithes were swept away and the clergy had to recognise it.

But it was not possible to restore peace and prosperity to France by the abolition of the relics of feudalism alone. The deputies of the Constituent Assembly were quick to destroy but slow to construct. For two months they wasted time instead of hastening to draw up a new Constitution for France. There were some differences first over the wordings of *Declaration of the Rights of Man and Citizen* (27 August 1789), which they resolved to compile in imitation of the founders of the American Republic. It declared that men are equal in the rights of liberty, equality and property, and that law is the expression of the general will. The Declaration has become memorable and influential in political thought and nationalist movements everywhere.

By the French Constitution, which the Constituent Assembly was engaged in preparing, important decisions of political principles had already been taken. The King was deprived of the right to prorogue or dissolve the future Legislative Assembly and of the powers to initiate legislation. His effective powers of delay were restricted to the exercise of a suspensive veto, valid for the space of two legislatures. The title of Louis XVI was changed from '**King of France**' to '**King of the French**' indicating that henceforth he *held office by virtue of the French constitutional law and the will of the people and not, that is to say, by divine right.*

The Assembly then proceeded to usurp national sovereignty for the exclusive benefit of the bourgeoisie by restricting the electoral franchise. In July 1789, a distinction was made between '**active**' and '**passive**' **citizenship**, the former conferring 'political rights' (such as the exercise of the **franchise or voting rights**) and the latter '**civil rights**' only. Effect was given to these principles by a decree of 22 December 1789. To be an active citizen, a man had to contribute to the direct taxation of the country an amount equivalent in value to three days wages in his locality. Further, to be eligible for office, a candidate had to pay taxes of the value of a silver mark, which inevitably restricted all offices to the bourgeoisie.

One striking feature of the **Constitution** was that it was drawn up and **applied piecemeal**, not as an organic whole. One of the most important and lasting principles was decreed on 12 November 1789, when it was resolved that all the old local divisions of France should be abolished, and that the country should be divided into 80 departments. Further, each department was divided into districts, and each district into cantons. On the basis of the new divisions, a new local government was established. Each department and district was to be administered by elected authorities, elaborately chosen by a system of double election.

Next to the local government, the judicial system was reorganised. The parlements were abolished, and local courts, consisting of elected judges and elected Justices of Peace were substituted. A uniform system of law was projected and juries were sanctioned in criminal but not in civil cases. In these sweeping reforms one flaw was perceptible: from one extreme, that is, having no elected officials, the other extreme was adopted of having all officials elected.

The mania of election affected the reform of the ecclesiastical institution, and directly brought about the schism which so largely contributed to the misfortunes of France. On 2 November 1789, it had been resolved that the property of the Church in France should be confiscated or resumed. On 13 February 1790, all monasteries and religious houses were suppressed. It was resolved to reduce the number of bishoprics to one for each department, and that all the beneficed clergy— from cures to bishop—was to be elected.* The Constituent Assembly drove matters to a crisis by ordering that every beneficed ecclesiastic should take an oath to observe the new Civil Constitution of the clergy. It was generally refused by the bishops and it was resolved by the Assembly on **27 November 1790**, that all who refused the oath within one week should be held to be dismissed from their offices. The King sanctioned this decree on 26 December 1790, and the **Great Schism in France** began. Many clerics disagreed with its strict subordination of the Church to the State

---

Beneficed clergy* are those who hold a **benefice, a church office that grants them certain responsibilities and the right to use property and receive income.

A **cure** (short for cure of souls) refers to the spiritual responsibility for a specific parish.

The phrase "beneficed clergy—from cures to bishop" means the entire spectrum of clergy appointed to church offices that came with income and responsibilities, ranging from local parish priests (with the 'cure of souls') to bishops overseeing entire dioceses.

and with the limitation of the Pope's jurisdiction to spiritual affairs. Only seven bishops and about one half of the parish priests took the oath. The consequences were far-reaching. The **Church** in France was split between the **non-jurors (refractory priests)** and the **jurors (constitutional priests)**. The opposition between the constitutional and non-juring or refractory clergy brought into existence rival factions, whose antagonisms were to prove irreconcilable. The schism ended under Napoleon's rule with the **Concordat of 1801**.

In financial matters, the record of the Constituent Assembly was less impressive. It failed to solve the basic problem of the annual deficit and did not succeed in establishing a modern budgetary system. Bankruptcy was only avoided by the nationalisation of the ecclesiastical establishments and this expedient, unwisely handled, failed to pacify the peasants and, in time, embroiled the country in galloping inflation. For the moment, however, there could be little doubt that their institution had saved the country from immediate bankruptcy.

The measures of the Constituent Assembly in abolishing the old provincial divisions and law courts, and substituting them with new and more modern arrangements were in the nature of great reforms, though marred by the mania of election. But the arrangements for the central administration were utterly absurd. The King under the new constitution, was left powerless. The ministers were invested with supreme executive authority, but more regulations were made to ensure their responsibility and limit their actual power than to define their functions. Under such regulations, the King and his ministers in the executive were put in a position of inferiority, which no self-respecting man could be expected to accept, to the inevitable derangement of the whole administrative machinery. In addition to the Constitution, the Constituent Assembly carried several measures of utmost importance to the State. All citizens, regardless of religion or class, were declared eligible for employment by the State. On 13 April 1790, a noble decree, declaring complete tolerance and acceptance of all forms of religion, was carried. The **Constitution of 1791** (as it was called because of its completion in that year) was, on the whole, a praiseworthy effort of untried legislators to give their country a representative Constitution. But it was by no means democratic. For, no man was to have a vote unless he was an 'active citizen'.

The Constitution, so prepared, was finally accepted and **proclaimed by the King on 28 September 1791** with the declaration that 'the revolution is over'. However, far from being over, the revolution was in fact, as Rudé observes, "entering a new and decisive phase." Well before the completion of the Constitution, some very important events were taking place in the course of the revolution. These had momentous effects on the bourgeoisie who became split over their aims and principles towards the revolution.

Momentous Events Before the Completion of the Constitution

The King's Attempt to Flee

The first of these events which had far-reaching consequences was the *attempt made by the King to flee from revolutionary France*. On the night of 21 June 1791, the King dressed as a man-servant, endeavoured to secretly cross the borders of France along with his family. The flight had been carefully planned down to the minutest detail by **Count Axel de Fersen**, a Swedish aristocrat and a friend of Queen Marie Antoinette. A special coach had been prepared for the purpose. Unfortunately, the King had not taken enough precaution to disguise himself, with the result that he was recognised by a postmaster's son at a place called Sainte-Menehould and his carriage was stopped at Varennes, a tocsin was sounded and barricades were erected. A large number of local villagers assembled and started escorting the royal family back to Paris. On the way, more and more local people joined the crowd. On the evening of 22nd June, the royal family, guarded by armed soldiers, entered Paris. The flight of the King signified a few basic facts. *First,* before the entire nation the King now emerged as the enemy of the revolution. *Second,* the national consciousness of the common people was strongly reinforced and the event acted as a cementing force in unifying them against the monarchy. *Third,* the bourgeoisie was divided on the issue of the nature of the revolutionary government. While the democratic elements wanted to overthrow the monarchy and establish a republic, the others, deeply apprehensive of the mob, wished to carry on with a constitutional monarchy. *Finally,* it spurred a series of events leading ultimately to the outbreak of the Revolutionary Wars.

The Jacobins and the Girondins

When the Constituent Assembly finished its work, it renamed itself the Legislative Assembly. It worked for one year only (October 1791 to

September 1792). The members of the **Legislative Assembly** were divided into several political parties, of which the **Jacobins** (opposed to the monarchy, and leftist in ideology) and the **Girondists/Girondins** deserve special mention. The latter dreaded all violent, or energetic measures and desired a peaceful republic. Like the Jacobins, they were inimical to the monarchy and were democrats as well as republicans. Yet they did not share the *ferocious fanaticism and ruthless opportunism* of their counterparts in the **Jacobin club**. Their main strength lay in the provinces, the name being derived from the department of Gironde, from where some of their leaders came. Among the leaders of the Girondist Party may be mentioned **Condorcet**, **Roland**, **Petion**, **Barbaroux**, **Vergniaud** and **Brissot**. After the name of their leader Brissot, they also called themselves **Brissotins**. The Girondins were opposed by the radical, extreme leftist Jacobin Club which was initially founded in 1789, and was composed of members like **Abbe Sieyes**, **Abbe Gregoire**, **Barnave**, **Petion**, **Alexandre de Lameth**, and of course, **Maximilien Robespierre**.

The Jacobins took the title *Societe des amis de la Constitution*, but changed it to *Societe des Jacobins, Amis de la Liberte et de l'Egalite*. It restricted its membership primarily to **educated and professional people**. They supported the monarchy for a long time, but were radicalised after the departure of the more conservative members in July 1791 to form the **Feuillant Club**. The Feuillants, led by Barnave, Lameth, Adrien Duport made up a substantial group in the Legislative Assembly and sat on the right of the Assembly, indicating their conservative attitude, and upheld the constitutional monarchy. The club disappeared when the insurrection of 10 August 1792 overthrew the monarchy. After the fall of the monarchy, Robespierre became the leading personality in the Jacobin Club and his followers came to be called the **Montagnard or the Mountain**. They were called the Mountain because they sat on an elevated seat in the National Assembly. Slowly, the party became identified with extreme radicalism, democratic egalitarianism, violence and terror. Universal manhood suffrage, popular education and freedom of the State from Church control were their key issues. The support of the sans-culotte was their main pillar of strength. Another political group also emerged from the Montagnard and founded the **Cordeliers Club** or *Societe des Amis des Droits de l'Homme et du Citoyen* in 1790 under the leadership of **Georges Danton** and **Camille Desmoulin**. It had its origins in the Cordeliers district, and the notable members, apart from Danton and Desmoulins, were Hebert,

Marat, Momoro, Chaumette, Carrier, etc. They were radical in outlook, were opposed to monarchy and had a highly populist programme. They were more populist than the Jacobins and individual rights and liberty were their primary concern. "Liberty, Equality and Fraternity" was their club's slogan. They stressed upon the problems of the working class and drew a large number of working people as their members. Danton played the leading role in the attack on Tuileries on 10 August 1792 and Hebert introduced an atheistic method of worship, that is the worship of Reason. In the Reign of Terror dominated by Robespierre the Cordeliers became an important target of attack.

The Champ de Mars Massacre

On 17 July 1791 the Constituent Assembly led by the Girondins, drew up a petition demanding the reinstatement of the King in less than one month of his attempt to flee from France. The fate of the King was a matter of heated discussion of the different political groups. The Girondins perhaps feared that the Constitution which was on the verge of completion would be invalidated if the King was deposed. And France might come under the grip of foreign powers if the King was removed. Therefore, they insisted that the King be reinstated. Several other political clubs, however, drew up angry petitions denouncing this decision. Such a petition, for example, was drawn up by the Cordelier Club which invited the people to the Champ de Mars (a huge field on the outskirts of the city) to support the petition. In response, a large crowd of about 6000 people assembled at Champ de Mars on 17 July 1791 to sign the petition. The **National Guard** (a militia separate from the regular army, created in each city in imitation of the National Guard in Paris) under the control of Lafayette tried to disperse them through warning shots. The mob retaliated by throwing stones. The **National Guard then opened direct fire** at the intransigent crowd as a result of which a number of demonstrators were left dead. A republican newspaper, *Les Revolutions de Paris*, reported: … "if the victims of Champ de Mars were not brigands, if these victims were peaceful citizens with their wives and children, and if that terrible scene is but the result of a formidable coalition, against the progress of Revolution, then liberty is truly in danger, and the declaration of martial law is a horrible crime, and the sure precursor of counterrevolution."[86]

The Declaration of Pillnitz

On 27 August 1791, a statement was issued at Pillnitz castle near Dresden by the **Hapsburg (or Habsburg) Emperor of Austria Leopold II**, brother of Queen Marie Antoinette, and the **Prussian King Frederick William II** which would serve as a warning to the French revolutionaries not to trample upon the prerogatives of Louis XVI and to ensure his smooth and unhampered resumption of power. This is known as the **Declaration of Pillnitz** which also clarified that Austria would go to war only if other major European countries declared war on France as well. It seems, as Rudé also points out, it was "more of a face-saver than a threat of war", an endeavour rather to soothe the sentiments of the émigrés who had taken refuge in his country and were insisting upon a foreign intervention in their country. However, the radical elements in France interpreted it as a provocation and used it as a means to galvanise the French people to embark upon a revolutionary war.

To War or Not to War

As mentioned earlier, on 28 September 1791 the hapless King accepted the Constitution and the Constituent Assembly renamed itself the Legislative Assembly. Initially the Girondists were in power and formed the government. They controlled the executive council and filled the ministry. The Girondins favoured a war with a view to placing the King in a dilemma. The chief enemies of the revolution, in their eyes, were the émigrés, the non-juring priest and the Austrian Emperor. Upon these, therefore, the Girondists concentrated their animosity. Nothing was, they thought, more likely to make the position of the King and the Queen impossible and open the path towards a republic than the passing of sharp decrees against the émigrés and the priests, followed by a foreign war against the brother of the Queen.

By vetoing the decrees against the émigrés and the priests, the King stood revealed as the enemy of the revolution and in league with the traitors. The foreign war would place Louis XVI in a hopeless position of sympathising with his enemies and fighting against his friends. **Narbonne**, the King's war minister, however, instantly declared that the King was ready for war for he hoped that, if the Austrian war was successful, the King would be sufficiently strengthened in popularity to regain his authority as the head of the executive; while if it failed, the nation in its extremity would turn to its legitimate sovereign and invest him with dictatorial power. The leaders of the Jacobin party understood this just as well as Narbonne and, therefore, opposed the war with all its might. *So, while Brissot and the other Girondist orators argued in favour of war, Marat, Danton and Robespierre opposed it.*

The Revolutionary War

Though the French army was disorganised and Austria and Prussia were leagued against them, the Girondists were confident of victory. At the shock of war, the people of Europe would rise against their tyrants. Everywhere thrones would fall. Principles of Liberty, Fraternity and Equality would conquer the world. A Girondist ministry with the able **Dumouriez** at the foreign office **swept the country into war on 20 April 1792**. Upon them rested the chief responsibility of waging a long and terrible battle which left France a permanently enfeebled member of the European society. Another consequence was inevitable. As the militant spirit of the French people was aroused, the idyllic professions of pacifism and cosmopolitan brotherhood which decorated so many revolutionary speeches passed swiftly to the background. Old diplomatic strategies resumed their pre-eminence. The **Revolutionary War**, thus begun, continued almost without interruption for **23 years** and came to an end only after the **fall of Napoleon in 1815**.

Although the Austrian and Prussian armies were initially victorious, the **French Revolutionary Army** scored an **important victory in the Battle of Valmy** (September 1792). Meanwhile, the Paris mob invaded the royal **Palace at Tuileries and imprisoned the King and the Queen** (10 August 1792). This historic event, which was followed by the fall of the monarchy and establishment of a republic was primarily the consequence of Brissot's propaganda against the King. There was also widespread rumour about the Queen's intrigues with her brother, the Austrian Emperor, and the latter's plan to invade France to rescue the French royal family. All these inflamed popular passions and there were widespread demonstrations in Paris on 20 June 1792.

Matters came to a head due to the **Duke of Brunswick's Manifesto** of 1 August 1792 issued by Charles William Ferdinand, Duke of Brunswick,

Commander of the Allied Army of Austria and Prussia. It threatened that if the French royal family was hurt, then French civilians would be harmed. The disturbances reached their peak on 10th August when a huge mob attacked the royal Palace at Tuileries, forced the King and the Queen to take refuge in the Legislative Assembly. Although the people were provoked by Brissot, the Girondists wavered in the last moment and the Jacobins led by Danton stepped in. They were supported by the armed *federes* (a 20,000 strong national guard created by the Assembly) dissolved the Department of Paris and instituted an insurrectionary commune. The aftermath was six week's chaos and confusion to be ended by the renaming of the Legislative Assembly as the new National Convention and the eventual end of the monarchy and the proclamation of a republic.

September Massacres

The overthrow of the monarchy was followed immediately by a wave of mob violence which took place in Paris in September. The angry mob massacred a large number of people under the suspicion that they were loyal to the King. This is known in the history of France as the **September Massacres** (1792). The killing began on 2 September 1792 when a group

Fig. 1.5: *September Massacre* (1793)

of prisoners who were being transferred to Abbaye prison was attacked by an armed band. Thereupon began an **orgy of violence** culminating in mass killing which the civil authorities were unable to stop. In all about 1200 prisoners were killed after being hastily tried by a clumsily constituted 'popular tribunal'. The September Massacres became **an important issue of conflict** between the Jacobins who tacitly supported the massacre and the Girondins who denounced the violence and held the extremist Jacobin leaders responsible for abetting the crime.

Expulsion of the Girondins

Meanwhile the Revolutionary Wars were in progress although the revolution had thoroughly disorganised the army, and the forces raised were insufficient for the invasion. Initially, therefore, the French Revolutionary Army was not successful; the Austrian and Prussian armies were victorious. However, the first victory was scored by the Revolutionary Army under the leadership of Dumouriez, the foreign minister, in the **Battle of Valmy (20 September 1792)**. Dumouriez then conquered Belgium by crushing an Austrian army in the **Battle of Jemappes on 6th November**. He later deserted to the Austrians in April 1793. His defection severely discredited his Girondin colleagues whose position was further undermined by popular uprisings on 27 and 31 May 1793. They were then expelled from the Convention by the Jacobins on 2 June 1793.

There were several reasons behind the expulsion of the Girondins. *First*, the Girondins supported *laissez faire* principles in economy, that is, the policy of least interference by the government in economic matters. The Jacobins also believed in the same policies, but "were closer to the people, more flexible in their attitudes, and more able and willing to bend gracefully to popular pressure and to adapt their views to meet the needs and exigencies of the moment."[87] Naturally, the Girondins were less popular compared to the Jacobins. Moreover, the prices of foodgrains were soaring. According to Eugene White, prices rose because of climatic conditions. In Andrew Dickson White's view, on the other hand, the rise in prices was due to the hopeless devaluation of the *assignats* (paper money issued by the National Assembly in France from 1790 to 1796).

According to Albert Soboul, bad harvests were not the reason behind high prices because harvest was good in 1792. The main reason was, as

Saint-Just had pointed out, the reluctance of the farmers to part with their produce because they did not want to sell their grains in exchange of assignats whose value was falling constantly.[88] This tendency of the farmers towards hoarding obstructed the free circulation of corn leading to high prices. And hoarding was precipitated by the declining value of the assignats. Since the government was bankrupt, it decided to issue assignats after the confiscation of Church properties. The government sought to solve its acute financial crisis by printing paper money representing the value of Church properties. Lack of proper precautions against their re-issue and mingling with general currency in circulation caused hyper-inflation. Therefore, instead of solving financial problems, the assignats became a catalyst for food riots. People were completely disillusioned. The unpopularity of the Girondist government intensified. They further aroused popular hostility by opposing economic controls like the Jacobin-sponsored Law of the General Maximum, which the common people hailed.

Second, the Girondins purged the Assembly of the revolutionary committees that had been formed. Although the Jacobins feebly protested against this measure, they agreed in the end. But the breach between the two widened.

Third, differences between the Jacobins and the Girondins were further accentuated on the issue of the quantum of punishment to be imposed on Louis XVI. While The Jacobin extremists settled on nothing less than death sentence, the Girondins wanted to save the King's life. However, almost the whole nation wished to see the King executed, especially in light of the recent revelation of irrefutable evidence of the King's correspondence with the Austrian Empire. The Girondins desperately proposed a referendum. But they lost, and the King Louis XVI was finally **guillotined on 21 January 1793**.

Fourth, the initial debacles of the Girondists in the international war and the defection of Dumouriez and Pache were the last nails in the coffin. On 31st May, an armed crowd, organised by Paris Sections, surrounded the Convention and demanded the arrest of the Girondists. In fact, such an insurrection had been attempted by the **Enragés** led by Jacques Roux, **Jean Varlet** and **Theophile Leclerc** on 10th March. The Convention at first resisted, but continued popular pressure succeeded in getting 29 Girondists arrested on 2 June 1793. Subsequently, leaders like Brissot, Vergniaud and others were executed one by one. The fall of the Girondists established the power of the Jacobins within the National Convention.

Worsening Conditions in 1793 and the Progressing War

During the greater part of 1793, the plight of France was worse than it was in 1792. An invasion of Holland had failed; Belgium and the Rhine conquests were lost. France was invaded by enemies with whom the idea of partition was rapidly replacing that of restoration of the Bourbons. Civil war was draining her strength and weakening her armies. The Jacobins took every advantage of France's desperate need and feebleness of the Girondins. They now had become converts to the war, for they saw that in a 'state of siege' their own aims could best be realised together with the welfare of the country. So, while they strove to strengthen the unity of France, to build up an effective defence against the enemy, they were working also to increase their own power. They embarked upon a vigorous campaign against the foreign enemy, against the internal rebel, against the non-juring priest and the émigrés noble.

Valmy was only the prelude to a series of revolutionary successes. The Sardinian possessions of Savoy and Nice were occupied. On the invitation of the Rhenish patriots, Custine, a prominent French general, made a dash into Germany and seized Spires, Worms and Mainz and held Frankfurt to ransom. The National Convention even declared that the French people would **fight throughout Europe against oppressive monarchs and feudal classes**. The French army was strengthened; the reforms of Carnot made it the most efficient instrument of fighting in Europe. In 1793, England, Holland and Spain joined Austria and Prussia against France. It was a powerful coalition, but it was broken up by successive victories. **Holland** became practically a **subordinate ally** of France (subordinate allies usually lost authority and became subjugated completely, although internally their administration was independent). Spain and Prussia made peace with France. Within three years (1793–1795), Revolutionary France established its military power and political influence. The Revolutionary Army pushed down in Lyons, Toulon was recaptured, the Austrians defeated at Wattignies and Fleurus, Belgium reconquered, Holland invaded; French soil everywhere was liberated from the invader.

The National Convention

The National Convention worked for three years (1792–1795) only but within this brief period it made its mark in the field of internal reforms.

Victories abroad enabled the revolutionaries to consolidate the reforms at home. The execution of the King strengthened the foundations of the Republic. They took in hand the conscription of new armies to supplement the volunteers of 1791 and 1792. They brought popularity by adopting economic programmes for common man. They taxed the rich, guaranteed the right to work, and regulated industry and trade in the interests of the people. They undertook the feeding of Paris **by fixing a maximum price for bread**. This was primarily the result of the demand of the sans-culottes who came out on the streets largely in view of the rise in the price of bread from the spring of 1793 after remaining stable in the preceding summer and autumn. Those abroad, especially cartoonists in England, mocked and satirised the dire shortage of affordable food in France.

In the meanwhile, in April 1793 the **Committee of Public Safety** was created by the National Convention and then was restructured in July. As a wartime measure, the Committee composed of nine, later twelve; members were given broad supervisory powers over military, judicial and legislative efforts. It was formed as an administrative body to supervise and expedite the work of the executive bodies of the Convention and of the government ministers appointed by the Convention. In fact, prior to the Committee of Public Safety, the **Committee of General Security** was established as a Committee of the National Convention on 10 March 1793. It was designed to protect the Revolutionary Republic from its internal enemies. On 10 March 1793, the **Revolutionary Tribunal** was created in the wake of the defeats suffered by the Revolutionary armies in Belgium. People wanted the establishment of a tribunal to judge the enemy agents in France. On 9th March Danton proposed: "Let us benefit from the mistakes of our predecessors"; "*Soyons terribles pour dispenser le peuple de l'être*" ("Let us be terrible so that the people will not have to be").[89] In May 1793, the Committee of Public Safety took the first step towards dealing with food shortages, inflation and wages pressures by introducing edicts fixing some prices. In September, it expanded the policy by passing the **Maximum Price Act**, also known as the **Law of the Maximum** or just "**the Maximum**." This radical attempt to counter hoarding and price gouging placed a maximum selling price on essential goods, chiefly food items. Merchants were required to display a full list of maximum prices outside their shops. The general public could inform the city authorities if mercantile prices exceeded the stated maximum; merchants were to be fined double the value of each overpriced item and the fine would then be paid to the informer. Wages as well as prices were also capped, at 50 per cent higher than their 1790 levels.

In principle, fixing prices and wages was indeed a noble idea intended to limit inflation and to make food cheaper and more accessible for ordinary citizens. Economically, it was a disastrous policy in the sense that price limitations were resisted bitterly by the peasant farmers and producers, who began hoarding their food crops rather than selling them at fixed prices. As a result, food supply became severely restricted. On the other hand, a black-market was formed and thrived among those who preferred to buy and sell at their own prices. In the Reign of Terror hoarders and black-marketeers were tried and guillotined alongside suspected counter-revolutionaries.

Further, the Committee of Public Safety attempted to re-establish discipline in the armies and to supply them with provisions and munitions of war.

Immense progress was made in the field of science. **Semaphore telegraph** or optical telegraph was a system invented by **Claude Chappe** in 1792 and was popular in the late 18th to early 19th century. Semaphore lines were a precursor of electrical telegraph. They were faster than post riders for bringing a message over long distances but far more expensive and less private than the electrical telephone lines that succeeded them. On 27 July 1792, an order was sent from Paris to the frontier in less than hour.

In the social field, important reforms were introduced. **Three laws** were brought about which radically transformed the lives of the peasants. By the law of 3 June 1793, the confiscated lands of the émigrés nobles and the Church were decided to be distributed among the landless and the poor. On 28th March, the laws against emigres had been codified. Those Frenchmen who had escaped from France since July 1789 and had not returned by 9 May 1792 were legally considered as having emigrated permanently and their property would become the property of the republic. They were considered to be banished forever and any breach of it would be punishable by death. These properties of the émigrés were to be distributed among the poor. On 10th June, the common lands were also to be divided in equal proportion among the residents of respective localities. On 17th June, all relics of feudalism were to be suppressed completely without any indemnity. All these provisions were embodied in the **Constitution of 1793** which now replaced the Constitution of 1791.

After the expulsion of the Girondins, the Jacobins were at the centre of power. The Jacobins and Girondins were both liberal and bourgeois, but the Jacobins desired a centralised, disciplined government under their full control with Paris as its capital. They joined hands with the sans-culottes to carry on the revolution. The number of members in the Committee of Public Safety went up to 12 from nine when Robespierre and his close associates Saint Just and Couthon joined it in July 1793 after Danton and his associates were purged from the Committee of Public Safety for trying to conclude peace with England. Robespierre and his group, that is the Montagnards, were now at the centre of power. They realised that an alliance with the sans-culottes would strengthen their base and could be the muscle power behind the movement. Robespierre and Saint-Just often used to say, "those living in misery and poverty are the real source of power on earth."[90] In that sense the Montagnards were the precursors of the Marxists of the 20th century. The difference was in numbers. The quantum of popular support the Russian Revolution could draw was far greater than what the Montagnards of the French Revolution could muster. Together with the sans-culottes they vowed to carry on the revolutionary war. As they came to power, they found the position of the National Convention to be quite fragile primarily because it was surrounded by

FIG. 1.6: Robespierre

revolts and protests from many fronts. One such important centre of protest was Lyon. The **Revolt of Lyon** against the National Convention was a counter-revolutionary movement involving the revolutionary government, breaking out in June 1793 and continuing till December of the same year. Lyon was a prosperous centre of silk weaving. The city of Lyon faced a serious economic crisis in 1789 resulting in the dismissal of a huge number of weavers. This was coupled with a tax riot that broke out in the same year. People were demanding a removal of the octroi which fell upon those least able to pay. The working-class activists set up *Societes Populaires des Amis de la Constitution.*

Consolidating the Committee of Public Saferty

These were the trying circumstances which persuaded Robespierre and his allies to take measures that would give them dictatorial control over the Committee of Public Safety for the purpose of pushing their ideas ahead. The influence of **Rousseau** and his concept of **General Will** (a unified popular will that aims at common good and general well-being of the common political body) on Robespierre also had an important part to play. However, the subsequent **Reign of Terror** which the Jacobins unleashed, was nowhere close to what Rousseau had preached. Robespierre expanded the power of the Committee of General Security and the Committee of Public Safety. The former was in charge of police and internal security. The latter was in charge of appointments, foreign policy, administration of local government, control of the *representants en mission* (representatives on mission)—civil agents of purest fanaticism— dispatched for the purpose of strict supervision of the generals on the field. The authority of the Paris Commune was also severely restricted and the Commune was subordinated to the power of the Committee of Public Safety. Initially, the representants en mission were invested with enormous power, but gradually the Committee of Public Safety centralised its authority and from **Frimaire II (December 1793)** onwards it extended closer supervision over the representants who were henceforth bound to report to the Committee every ten days.[91] Moreover, on **30 Germinal (19 April 1794)**, 21 representants including Carrier at Nantes and Tallien at Bordeaux, Barras and Freron from Toulon were summoned back to Paris. It was a blatant concentration of power in the hands of the Jacobin rulers.

Meanwhile, popular pressure for a fixed price of bread was mounting. Unruly crowds of people were assembling outside the bakers' shops demanding reasonable price of bread; with the support of the Paris Commune, they presented an address before the Convention: "You have decreed the principle that all essential consumer goods will be subject to price controls.... The people await your decision on this question with an impatience occasioned by genuine hardship."[92] The result was the passing of the **Law of the General Maximum** on 29 September 1793. By this both prices as well as wages were fixed, as discussed.

The Reign of Terror

As Soboul says, the **intense desire of meting out punishment was engrained in the revolutionary mentality**.[93] This propensity reached its climax when the sectional assemblies and committees purged all those who were moderate, passive or lukewarm in their attitude towards the revolution. The result was the passing of their death sentence by the Convention through the **Law of Suspects** passed on 17 September 1793. It expanded the definition of suspects to the widest possible limit; for example, it included within its orbit relatives of émigrés, unless they could prove specifically their love for the revolution. The Revolutionary Tribunal dealt with all cases of suspects and the dreadful, nightmarish period of coercion and terror followed. The Convention set up Military Commissions whose task was to identify people of suspect, especially the émigrés, the refractory priest, the royalists etc., and to initiate the propagation of their death sentence. Whoever was suspected to be opposed to the revolution was executed.

Anybody disagreeing with Robespierre's point of view could not survive. Danton was guillotined; so also was Hebert. This system of merciless killing instilled a chilling sense of fear running down the spine of the entire nation. It had commenced with the September Massacres and continued unabated. Within the span of a year (1793–1794) about 20,000 people were executed in France. Queen Marie Antoinette was guillotined on 16 October 1793. An orgy of violence and massacre was unleashed across France. This phase in the history of the French Revolution came to be known as the **Reign of Terror**. It was the will of the Montagnards or the Mountain. The Girondins could not prevent it; the Convention dared not. If the aim of the revolutionaries had been to put an end to everything of the ancien regime, they indeed achieved considerable success. The execution of the King swept away the last vestiges of the old order, and left the ground clear for a new France, entirely radical in outlook and opinion, to emerge from its ruins. With the execution of the King, the last tottering pillar of the ancien regime crumbled.

The King's Execution: A Symbolic Patricide

The King's execution, as Lynn Hunt discusses in her essay 'Band of Brothers', had a tremendous anti-patriarchal impact on the nation.[94] *First*, it was regarded as a symbolic patricide as the King was the 'father of the nation'. Some of the deputies of the Convention were in more sombre mood than others: "Today he has paid his debt; let us speak of it no longer, let us be human; all our resentment must expire with him." But many others like Marat celebrated the occasion: "Goodbye then to the splendour of thrones, goodbye to all human respect for constituted authorities themselves… when they assert any tendency to elevate themselves above the common level." In this way, observes Lynn Hunt, the more radical elements like Marat transferred the sacrality of the old monarchical government to the republic of the modern age.

Second, this symbolic patricide had a significant impact on the traditional position of fathers and dealt **a serious blow to the prevailing patriarchal society**. The attack on the fathers' rights found legal expression in the enumeration of new laws circumscribing fathers' unflinching authority within the family; on 7 March 1793 the father's right to disinherit some of their heirs, or preferring some children over others, through the making of wills was nullified, and the deputies declared the **equality of all inheritance in the direct line of succession**. On 2 November 1793, the Convention made the historic enactment of granting illegitimate children equal rights of inheritance upon proof of paternity. All these implied the establishment of the supremacy of the State over the family, and the subordination of the authoritarian father to the State.

Third, all forms of art and literature of the time reiterated one common element: the **father was absent everywhere and instead brothers were stepping in unitedly**. The brothers were joining hands to replace the father. David's *Oath of Horatii* provides an example. The effort of the French people to create the '**Band of Brothers**' was in contrast to the American example of heralding Washington as a father figure. The French rather elevated the dead heroes to the position of father—heroes like Lepeletier, or the regicide deputy who was assassinated by an ultra-royalist on the eve of the King's execution, Marat etc. The Band of Brothers was **a symbol of democratic equality** and **denial of tyranny and absolute power**.

The Execution of Robespierre

Soon, however, differences cropped up between the Committee of Public Safety and the Committee of General Security concerning the overlapping of duties. Matters came to a head when the Committee of Public Safety set up its own police department to take action against corrupt officials. This clashed with the jurisdiction of the Committee of General Security who was generally in charge of internal security and police duties. Their resentment was further accentuated with the passing of the law of the **22nd Prairial (10 June 1794)**, which speeded up the process of trial in the Revolutionary Tribunal and also deprived the accused of any benefit of a defense counsel. Robespierre's **cult of the Supreme Being** evoked lot of suspicions and misgivings, among especially the de-Christianisers who were apprehensive of a revival of Catholicism that had been suppressed with immense effort.

Moreover, dispute was brewing within the Committee of Public Safety itself. Serious differences emerged between Carnot and Saint-Just on the conduct of war. In fact, **Carnot, Lindet** and others who called themselves **moderates** opposed the **radicals** like **Robespierre**, **Couthon**, **Saint-Just**, especially with respect to their relation with the sans-culottes. The former wanted to deal with them more sternly than the latter. Many members of the Convention had never forgiven the Jacobins for the expulsion of the Girondins. Then there were the 'terrorists' like Billaud and Collot. They were the supporters of Hebert and were, therefore, opposed to Robespierre and allied with those represantant en mission like Barras and Freron at Toulon, Tallien at Bordeaux, Carrier at Nantes, etc., who had been recalled by Robespierre. Some of these had been expelled from the Jacobin Club and most of them feared the fate of the Dantonists. The spectacular victories against enemies—the suppression of agitation at Lyons, the recapture of Toulon, the defeat of the Austrians at Wattignies and Fleurus, the reconquest of Belgium, the invasion of Holland—convinced the moderate members of the Convention that the *terror had outlived its usefulness.* The tyranny of the Committee of Public Safety and the dictatorship of Robespierre, therefore, became intolerable. On 28 July 1794, Robespierre, along with 21 other victims, was guillotined. The long nightmare was over. The hateful epidemic of butchery came to a sudden end.

FIG. 1.7: *Execution of Robespierre (c. 1790)*

But if France ceased to be terrorist, she continued to be revolutionary. A new Constitution was framed in 1795 and according to its provisions the **Rule of the Five Directors**—known as **the Directory**—began in 1795. It was in office for four years (1795–1799). It could not do any useful work in internal administration. Their rule was marked by several popular uprisings and food riots, which the Directory suppressed with the help of **Napoleon Bonaparte**, a young commander of the armed forces. In the international field, the French army was winning important victories, but the credit went entirely to Napoleon for his leadership. His military reputation endeared him to the French people, who compared his successes with the failures of the Directors. In 1799, through a *coup d'etat* (forcible capture of power), Napoleon drove the incompetent Directors out of office and established himself as the ruler of France. We shall study about this in Chapter 2.

THE POPULAR REVOLUTION: WRITING HISTORY 'FROM BELOW'

The trend of history writing, till the turn of the 20th century, was to write 'from above', that is to emphasise upon the role or the ideology of the leaders like Mirabeau, Abbe Sieyes, Brissot, Danton, Hebert, Robespierre, Saint-Just, or the story of the National Assembly, the Royal Court or the Parlement in shaping the political, social and economic life of the nation. The thoughts, actions or the perception of the peasants and the urban *menu people* (i.e., urban common people organised into several guilds like tailoring, carpentry, cooking) were not considered to be of any serious consequence. It was the **socialist historian Jean Jaures** who for the first time, at the turn of the century, wrote a history of the French Revolution 'from below'. His *L'Histoire Socialiste de la Revolution Francaise*, first published in 1901–1904, stressed upon the problems, agony and desires of ordinary people. This new and unique endeavour was continued by the successors of Jaures—Mathiez, Lefebvre, Soboul and Rudé. In fact, according to Daniel Guerin, the anarcho-communist scholar, the maturity and the depth of the feelings of the mass made them the precursor of the socialist movements in the 19th and 20th centuries. Through the analysis of these scholars and historians, the viewpoints of the peasants, sans-culottes and the working class became entrenched in the history of France. Their role in the revolution is termed as the revolution of the people or the popular revolution.

The agitation of the common people was nothing unusual in the history of France. The grain riots of 1775 had a profound impact. But before that also, as Rudé says, the agitations of 1725, 1739–1740 and 1752 were indeed very significant. The introduction of free-trade principles in grain by Turgot, the Controller-General, and bad harvest in 1775 aggravated the situation. Price of food shot up. Open protest broke out in Bordeaux, Dijon, Rheims and soon spread to several other provinces. It is known in history as *la guerre des flarines* (the flour war). Rudé points out certain interesting characteristic features: (*i*) the movement was a massive attack on markets and was directed by small farmers and workers; (*ii*) mostly the prosperous farmers and merchants were targeted; and (*iii*) the *Parlement* of Paris gave its tacit support.

During the next twelve years, that is until 1787, there was a lull as far as popular outburst was concerned. The price of bread remained more or less steady and peace prevailed. There were occasional, sporadic cases of unrest here and there. From the end of 1787, the price of bread began to rise. There was a belief that the prosperous farmers were hoarding grains as a result of which prices were rising. Crisis deepened further in 1788 when harvest failed due to hailstorm and was coupled with a severe winter. Prices of food rose. Rudé quotes from Sebastien Hardy that almost 80,000 people were thrown out of work in Paris. Rise in prices of food implied that people were spending mostly on food items with very little money left in hand to buy other things. This brought about a slump in the manufacturing units. Rudé notes that there was sharp unemployment in places outside Paris. He writes that "from September 1788 to January 1789, there were 46,000 unemployed at Amiens, 10,000 at Rouen, 30,000 at Carcassone and 25,000 at Lyons, while at Lille and Troyes half the looms were idle."[95] One thing, however, is clear. The popular movement began as a protest against the rising price of bread and non-availability of food. Later it shifted also to the manufacturing centres where production fell and massive unemployment followed. The popular ire took several forms—pillaging granaries, attacking bakeries, assault on prosperous merchants, big farmers etc. In prominent industrial areas like Lyons sharp divergence of interests took the form of class dispute which divided the industrial population.

In April 1789, two similar and interesting incidents demonstrated the mood of the common people. These incidents have been extensively elaborated by Rudé.[96] Reveillon was a successful wall-paper manufacturer in the Faubourg St Antoine and his neighbour Henriot was a powder manufacturer. Reveillon was a good employer who paid none of his 350 workers less than 25 sous a day at a time when the average wage everywhere was 20 sous a day. On 23rd April, Reveillon commented in a public gathering that he regretted the time when 15 sous a day was the standard pay and how with the passage of time the burden on the industrialists have increased. On the same day Henriot also made some similar comments. Problems started on 27th April, that is Monday (workers' day off). Hundreds of workers assembled near Bastille and attacked Reveillon's factory which, however, they failed to take because of the presence of heavy troops that Reveillon had got stationed sensing trouble. The mob then turned towards Henriot's house which they ransacked and destroyed much of his personal property. Next morning also the agitation continued. There was no work the whole day and at six in the evening the crowd stormed the house of Reveillon. He had precious belongings and a huge library. These were badly damaged, ransacked and ravaged. Cries went up like,

"Long live the Third Estate! Long live the King! Long live Mr. Necker!" The words are significant. It shows that people still had lot of faith in the King. While the bourgeoisie in the Constituent Assembly were curbing the power and position of the King, the common people still rested their confidence in him, held him in high esteem and shouted slogans in his name. At the same time they upheld the Third Estate. So, although they were in a revolutionary mood, the King was even then their hero.

This attitude, however, was slowly waning. The change became clearly visible as time rolled by. The next noticeable participation of the people in the revolutionary upsurge was at the time of the attack on the Bastille fort. As the news of dismissal of Necker reached on 12 July 1789, mobs began rioting in Paris at the instigation of revolutionary leaders. On the evening of 13th July, mobs stormed the Paris arsenal and another armoury and acquired thousands of muskets. At dawn on 14th July, a great crowd armed with muskets, swords and various makeshift weapons began to gather around the Bastille. They rushed into the fortress, and Launay, the military governor of the Bastille, and his men took up a defensive position. Launay's men were able to hold the crowd back, but more and more Parisians were converging on the Bastille. Launay and 110 of his men were killed. The fall of Bastille symbolised the end of the *ancien regime* and provided the revolutionary passion an extraordinary momentum.

The popular revolution was not confined to Paris and the urban areas. It soon spread to the countryside. As Rudé observes, the popular revolution could be divided into two main parts—the peasant revolt and the revolt of the sans-culottes—which do overlap at certain points. In July-August 1789 a series of peasant revolts broke out which have been referred to by Lefebvre as the *Grande Peur* or Great Fear or Great Panic. The deep-seated causes for the grievances of the peasants and their revolts have been discussed earlier. The peasants were overburdened with onerous taxes as a result of which they continuously floundered in poverty. Poor harvests aggravated their sufferings. The harvests of 1787–1788 had been particularly poor, placing increased pressure on grain stocks. With the shortage of food grain, prices began to escalate and those who possessed stores of grain started hoarding. The small farmers suffered not only as producers but also as consumers, because the high prices adversely affected them also as purchasers. Moreover, the constant pouring in of migrant labourers and beggars or vagabonds into the countryside from cities and towns for food and work was a perennial source of tension for the peasantry. These newcomers not only competed for food and shelter, but they placed heavy demand on charitable institutions, mostly run by the Church. Such charity was not available to the locals, causing further wrath as well as acrimony.

All these grievances were coupled with the unnerving news from Paris of the Tennis Court Oath, the dismissal of Necker, the fall of Bastille, and the expansion of the royal troops. They also heard that after the attack on Bastille, the royalist troops that had been dispatched were disbanded and they were now on the prowl in the countryside, and after the crops of the poor peasants. There were also rumours that the nobles had hired brigands to march through the villages and destroy the peasant's new harvest and their homes. The peasants went crazy and attacked, ransacked and looted the chateaux (grand castles) of the seigneurs to whom they owed feudal dues. Their targets were the lists and records of the feudal dues and obligations of the peasants. These were seized and burnt. Sometimes the nobles themselves were held captive and, under threat, forced to renounce their rights over the peasants on the estate. The disturbances started on 20th July and continued till 6 August 1789. These events are referred to by Lefebvre as the Great Fear or *Le Grande Peur*.

The Great Fear fizzled out by 6th August, but left indelible effects. *First*, as Rudé points out, it forced the towns and newly created militias to reorganise themselves.[97] *Second*, the enmity in the relationship between the peasants and the seigneurs emerged as firm and crystallised. *Third* and most importantly, in response to the Great Fear, the Constituent Assembly issued the Report of 4 August 1789 by which all vestiges of feudalism, including the tithe, were swept away. Furthermore, the Great Fear was distinct from other peasant uprisings in its scope. No other revolt in rural France was so widespread and extensive. Expanding over almost half a dozen separate centres, nearly the whole of rural France was in uproar. The magnitude of the event only focuses upon the extent to which the passions of the common people were inflamed, how the toleration of the people crossed all limits of definition.

October 1789 constituted another crucial landmark of popular revolution. It was in response to the acute scarcity of bread which characterised the entire year of 1789. The short supply of bread was much to the chagrin of the French women. The harvest of 1788–1789 was poor and France was in debt. On 5th October, crowds of Parisian women met at City Hall to demand bread. When they got nothing, they grew into a mob of thousands and, armed with pikes, broomsticks, pitchforks and lances, marched 12 miles to Versailles to confront the royal family, chanting on the way, 'Let us fetch the baker, the baker's wife and the little baker's boy.' On listening to their ordeal, the King promised the women that he would send grain to Paris. The women insisted that the royal family should return to Paris along with them. The National Guard arrived to the aid of the women and the royal family was forced to accompany the crowd back to Paris. This was extremely significant because the King displayed that, after all, he yielded to popular pressure. The event effectively ended the King's independent authority and tilted the balance of power from the ancient privileged orders to the common people.

FIG. 1.8: *October Revolution, Versailles, 5 October 1789*

On 21 June 1791, the French royal family decided to escape to Austria, the homeland of the Queen Marie Antoinette. Unfortunately, they were recognised at Sainte-Menehould by a vigilant village post-master named Jean-Baptiste Drouet because of the King's carelessness to take proper precautions to disguise himself and the royal family was eventually arrested at Varannes, 50 km short of their ultimate destination Montmedy. Heavily guarded by the army and civilians, they were brought back to Paris. In escorting the King back, the people played an important role as more and more villagers joined the crowd as the news spread. In fact, they were in such a militant mood that they killed Count de Dampierre, a land-owner who came to greet the King when he heard that the latter was passing by his locality.

As Albert Soboul observes, "Varennes had two contradictory effects on the internal situation in France."[98] On the one hand, the Girondins or the moderate bourgeoisie who controlled the helm of affairs in France, felt that the institution of monarchy should be continued for some time more in order to keep the nation united under a legitimate King, to strengthen its own control over the people and also to keep foreign powers at bay by putting up a strong and normal front; while on the other hand, the radical bourgeois elements like the Cordelier Club thought that "at last we are free and without a King" and considered it to be the appropriate time to proclaim a Republic. Moreover, the patriotic passions of the people were inflamed intensely and their bitterness against the King crystallised further. A fear of foreign invasion gripped the minds of the people who now out of apprehension, points out Soboul, manned the borders spontaneously.[99]

Its impact abroad was also equally momentous. The Kings of Europe were aghast at the fate of the French monarch at the hands of his people and dreaded lest the same befell upon them. 'What a frightful example that presents to us all!' exclaimed the King of Prussia.[100] The result was the signing of the Declaration of Pillnitz on 27 August 1791 between the Emperor of Austria and the King of Prussia.

The revolutionary mood of the people was further evident when they met at Champ de Mars on 17 July 1791 in response to the invitation of the Cordelier Club to sign a radical petition they drew up denouncing the decision of the Constituent Assembly to reinstate the King in less than a month of his attempted flight to Varennes. More than 6000 people attended. Here also mob militancy was clearly noticeable as they decided to hang two suspected royalists. The signers also threw stones at the National Guard who fired and fell upon their attackers.

The crowd indeed played a very significant role in the fall of the monarchy following the storming of the Tuileries Palace. Around 10:00 AM on 10 August 1792 a mob of nearly 30,000 French citizens advanced towards the Tuileries with the objective of capturing the King. There was a background to this violent episode. On 20th June, groups of French people had met Louis XVI at Tuileries to convince him of how urgently the administration, society and economy of France needed a change for the better. The King had assured them that he would look into it. However, as the war with Austria and Prussia continued, the people became desperate. Believing that the King was in collusion with the foreign powers, they attacked Tuileries to arrest him. They killed a number of guards and staff at the palace and then moved to the Legislative Assembly where the royal family had taken refuge. The King was held captive by the Paris mob and this signified the end of the monarchy in France.

A series of counter-revolutionary popular insurrections broke out in the west of France between 1793–1796. The first and the most important clash broke out in the area known as the Vendee—a coastal region south of the Loire river in western France. In this economically backward and fervently religious region, the French revolution was of little significance. Disaffection was simmering since the passing of the Civil Constitution of the clergy, 1790, and developed into a general uprising in March 1793 soon after the issue of conscription orders by the National Convention in February. The Conscription of 30,000 on the whole of France for the sake of the war required Vendee to fulfil its quota and this infuriated the Vendeans. They started a guerrilla warfare which seriously threatened the revolution at a time when it had already suffered a severe debacle in the battle of Neerwinden (18 March 1793) before the Hapsburg Austrians allied with a small contingent of Dutch troops. The peasant leaders Jacques Cathelineau, Gaston Bourdic and Jean-Nicolas Stoffet were joined by royalist nobles like Charles Bonchamps and Maurice Gigost d'Elbee, among others. The Committee of Public Safety dealt with the rebels extremely sternly. General Turreau was despatched to crush the Vendean rebellion. The disaster of the Vendean army started from October onwards when it suffered a severe defeat on 17th October at the battle of Cholet. It was finally routed at the battle of Savenay in December. 20,000 to 50,000 civilians were massacred by Turreau from January to May 1794.[101]

The role of the sans-culottes was also of great consequence. We have already discussed who the sans-culottes were and what were their grievances. The sans-culottes were interested in an egalitarian democracy where all citizens would be equal, just wages, uniform distribution of food, fixed prices and control over fluctuation of prices, end to hoarding, end to free market which the Girondins, following the physiocrats, were advocating. They aspired for a voice for small farmers and petty traders in the nation. They formed a strong pillar of support in the revolutionary movement behind the Jacobins when the latter came to power in the National Convention. During the time of the Girondins, the sans-culottes took an active part in the attack on the Tuileries palace and played a violent role in the September Massacres. Some of them participated in the 48 sectional assemblies comprising the Paris Commune. The Grocer riots were organised by them in February 1792. There was a tremendous rise in the prices of essential daily use items like sugar, coffee, soap etc. The rising price of sugar was the matter of greatest concern. The sans-culottes in large numbers including women invaded the grocers' shops, ransacked and pillaged the goods and refused to pay more than what they paid the previous year. The women were particularly infuriated at the hoarders, who they felt should be severely punished. All of them were so agitated because sugar and coffee were an indispensable part of their daily habit. They generally took a large quantity of coffee every morning which sustained them till evening.[102] On 23rd February two deputations of women visited the National Convention. The Enragés leader Jacques Roux openly supported the regulation of prices. On 25th February, he upheld the riots in his speech at the Paris City Council. The result of all this agitation was the eventual passing of the Law of the General Maximum on 29 September 1793. The sans-culottes were responsible for aiding the Enragés leaders—Jacques Roux, Theophile Leclerc and Jean Valet—the extreme revolutionaries, in attempting to purge the Girondins on 10 March 1793. The move failed due to the lukewarm attitude of the Jacobins who were unwilling to let others, especially the Enragés, take the credit. In the final coup d'etat on the Girondins, in addition to the National Guard, a revolutionary militia was formed of 20,000 sans-culottes who would be compensated for their loss of work by payment at the rate of 40 sous a day.[103] The triumph of the Jacobins and the sans-culottes over the Girondins was complete.

Albert Soboul argues that Jaures denied in his *Histoire Socialiste* the significance of class in the *journees* of 31st May–2nd June. Indeed, Soboul agrees, both the Jacobins and the Girondins broadly belonged to the middle class, though with various shades of differences, which we have discussed earlier.[104] The most important factor about the *journees* was the role played by the sans-culottes on the political scene. The replacement of the Girondins by the sans-culottes gave these *journees* an unprecedented socio-political dimension and an entirely new turn to the revolutionary movement as a whole.

The fight of the sans-culottes against rising price of bread continued. The National Convention was under constant pressure from the sans-culottes to address to the problem of acute scarcity of food and escalating prices. On 4 May 1793 *loi du maximum* was initiated for setting the price limits and allowing the continuous supply of food supply to the people of France. Food shortages, however, continued and the Committee of Public Safety feared bitter outburst of popular reaction. In fact, on 5 September 1793 the sans-culottes invaded the National Convention demanding more forceful imposition of the law and sternest action against the offenders. The Law of the General Maximum was introduced, therefore, to conciliate the people on 29 September 1793. It was an extension of the Law of Suspects of 17 September 1793 whose purpose was to create a list of those who were to be arrested and examined before revolutionary tribunals. **Article 7** of the **General Maximum** declared, "The Municipal Police shall fine everyone who buys or sells merchandise for more than the Maximum… The buyer will not be subject of these penalties if he denounces the seller's violation, and each merchant must post in his shop a table of the maximum or the highest price of his merchandise."[105] Margaret H. Darrow, who has studied extensively the General Maximum in Montauban, observed how the government there used it to shift its responsibility to control prices to the retailers. And this is true of the whole of France. The National Convention, by introducing the law, transferred the entire blame of high prices on the bakers and the butchers and thereby turned the whole crisis into a traditional battle between the retailer and the consumer. Subsistence thereafter no longer remained a priority on the political agenda. In this way the General Maximum "defused and diffused the attack on commerce and the social and political revolution that lurked behind it."[106]

The Enragés, referred to earlier, advocated price controls on grain, suppression of counterrevolutionary activity, requisitioning of grain and government assistance to the poor. Allied closely with the sans-culottes, they demanded that hoarders be put to death, led food riots in Paris and participated actively in the popular agitation that led to the overthrow of the Girondins. Jacques Roux, who was elected to the Paris Commune (the municipality in Paris) in 1791, was blamed for inciting the soap riots in June 1793. Shortly thereafter, he was expelled by Robespierre from the Commune and the Cordeliers Club. It was then Jacques Rene Hebert who took over the programme of Jacques Roux and continued the popular agitation.

In order to conciliate the sans-culottes, Robespierre passed three laws in the social field—The laws of 3rd June, 10th June and 17th June, respectively as discussed earlier. The Constitution of 1793 was drawn up on 24th June which incorporated all these decrees and formally laid down the political outlines of a democratic regime.

Elimination of its adversaries was a characteristic feature of the revolutionaries from the very beginning. It was revealed since the days of the fall of Bastille. This streak of violence erupted again and again throughout the revolution. It reached its peak in the September Massacres of 1792. The news of the reverses of France in Belgium inflamed popular furore and there was outburst of street demonstrations on 9 and 10 March 1793. On 10th March, at the initiative of Danton, a tribunal was set up for trying extraordinary criminal offences. By a decree of 20 October 1793 it was given the name of the Revolutionary Tribunal. This slowly came to be exploited, particularly by Robespierre, for avenging personal vendetta, when he established his supremacy in the Committee of Public Safety. Thus, was unleashed what is known as the Reign of Terror or Robespierre's 'Republic of Virtue.' It reached its peak with the promulgation of the infamous Law of 22 Prairial (10 June 1794). It forbade the prisoners to employ defense counsel and made death the sole penalty. Thousands of people, including innumerable innocent victims, lost their lives within the span of a year. Marie Antoinette, Madame Roland, Olympe de Gouges, the Hebertists, the Dantonists and many Girondins were among the victims known to every household in France. As discussed earlier, the excesses of Robespierre were abhorred by the other members of the National Convention, especially at a time when the splendid victories against the foreign enemies as well as the abolition of monarchy and the complete suppression of the clergy and the aristocracy, made the Terror seem abundantly superfluous. This brought about the downfall of Robespierre. On 27 July 1794, he was held in the same containment chamber as Marie Antoinette and the next day met with the same fate.

As we have already mentioned, since the days of Jaures' *Histoire Socialiste de la Revolution Francaise*, published in four volumes in 1902–1904, the role of the common people has received a new dimension. Till then, as T. G. Parsons has correctly pointed out, the popular movement was regarded as being led by "debased, criminal and brutish" people.[107] This was underlined first by the contemporary historian Edmund Burke who, while agreeing that people indeed played a significant part in the revolution along with the literary, civilized men and 'philosophers', referred to them as the 'mob' or 'swinish multitude', who were given mostly to loot and fulfilment of their own selfish interests.[108] It was Jaures, and later following him, Albert Mathiez, Georges Lefebvre and Albert Soboul, who have written a history of the revolution 'from below'. T.G. Parsons has made a comprehensive study on the different works on the common mass and has given lot of emphasis on the history of the working class people. He particularly mentioned the works of Pierre Chauvet, *(Les ouvriers du livre en France de 1789 a la Constitution de la Federation du livre*, from where we get a picture of the lives of the workers in France based on several books; the work of M.M. L Trenard, (*La crise sociale Lyonnaise*) has dealt with the workers of the factories of Lyons; and the study of F. Evrard (*Les ouvriers du textile dans la region Rouennaise*, 1789–1802) which is a picture of the lives of the textile workers of Rouen.[109] The origins of the social composition of the army of the ancient regime has been examined in detail by M. Pierre Courvisier of Sorbonne university. According to him, the army in the ancient regime was mostly recruited from the poorer sections of the society and his work has been referred to by Richard Cobb as "possibly the most complete source of information concerning the petit people of French town and countryside."[110]

George Rudé, Albert Soboul and Richard Cobb have written extensively about the sans-culottes. The main concern of the sans-culottes was the acquisition of cheaper supply of bread. "This more than any other factor was the raw material out of which the popular revolution was formed."[111] Daniel Guerin borrowed from Michelet the term *bras nus* to refer to the common people. However, Guerin's effort to consider the conflict between the *bras nus* and the bourgeoisie to be the beginning of the proletarian revolution has been challenged by Parsons according to whom the very suggestion of the existence of a proletariat in a pre-industrial society like that of France in the eighteenth century is bizarre.[112] J. Zacker, R.B. Rose and W. Markov, on the other hand, discussed the significance of the role of the Enragés group. They looked upon the enrage movement as a serious challenge as well as an alternative to the predominance of Robespierre and his men.[113] Similarly, Richard Cobb regarded the *armee revolutionnaire* (Revolutionary Army) to be an alternative proposition to the 'Jacobin centralisation and war communism.'[114] As Parsons observed, "With sympathetic insight, this fine Oxford historian (Cobb) seeks to understand the men of the Revolution and they become living, suffering creatures, not merely categories or statistics."[115]

Women in the French Revolution

WOMEN IN THE AGE OF ABSOLUTISM

In order to comprehend the role of women in the French Revolution and its significance, it is essential to understand the position of women in general in Europe in the 18th century and earlier. It was undoubtedly a patriarchal world where male predominance reigned supreme. Even in this male world, women had a voice in the Middle Ages, that is to say, the intervening period between ancient and modern times (approximately from about 600 AD to about 1500 AD). Women had borne arms and played a significant role in governance. This position changed with the process of state formation and the advent of the modern age. **Joan Kelly**[116] analyses two important effects of state formation: (*i*) the erosion of power and status of women; and (*ii*) the formation of the pre-industrial, patriarchal household. From about the 14th century, the feudal lords could no longer withstand the continuous growth of trade and commerce and the might of the merchants or the middle class. In England, they were further weakened by the **War of the Roses** (a series of dynastic civil wars between the Houses of York and Lancaster) which were fought between two groups of feudal lords from 1455 to 1485. Henry VII established a strong monarchy. The **Hundred Years' War** between England and France from 1337 to 1453 helped French kings establish their authority. France became a modern state. The process of state formation had begun. England and France were, therefore, the two earliest nation-states. Finally, the **Treaty of Westphalia**, 1648, which ended the **Thirty Years' War** (1618–1648), played the most determining role in the emergence of the modern age and the formation of states. To sum up, the elements which brought about this change were: (*i*) the centralisation of power in the hands of the King; (*ii*) the rise of the mercantile class which ended the predominance of the feudal lords; (*iii*) the expansion, regulation and professionalisation of the Kings' armies, which helped him to suppress feudal lords and participate in wars against other countries. It established the principle that all states, regardless of their size and shape, were to be treated as equal in the eyes of international law. In this newly evolved political structure, patriarchy was firmly rooted. It started with the King who was *the highest patriarch*. Patriarchal households became the primary social and economic unit of the post feudal or pre-industrial societies. This was the beginning of the **Age of Absolutism** (when monarchs held absolute power).

The position of women in this formation of the modern absolutist State can be summarised as follows. They could no longer bear arms as earlier and take training in warfare as individual armies did not exist anymore. The army was now the King's army from which women were completely excluded. This led to a clear erosion of their importance in society. They remained confined to household activities.

WOMEN IN THE MODERN STATE

Coming to the discussion on French women, according to **Natalie Zemon Davis**, the emergence of the modern State had curious effects on women's freedom.[117] Broadly speaking, women could be divided into three categories—**aristocratic or noble women**, **bourgeois or middle-class women**, and **artisanal and working-class women**. Despite wage disparity, women of urban artisanal classes were involved in various professional activities along with their husbands. On the contrary, the decline of feudalism and rise of the merchants or the middle class, brought about a substantial decrease in the military, political, economic and juridical powers of the lives of the feudal lords or the aristocracy. Consequently, aristocratic women who, as has already been mentioned, played an important role in public affairs began to experience significant curb on their power and privileges. Between these two, were the bourgeois women who started forming a public space for themselves. Then there were the working-class women who, notwithstanding their commendable role in the family and society, had hardly ever received the attention which was their rightful due. However, what was the role of these women in the French Revolution? And what was the impact of this revolution on their status in society?

The Salon

As far as the aristocratic women were concerned, although there was an erosion of their former status, they managed to create a niche for themselves—*the salon*—which **Joan B. Landes** prefers to regard as "a rather unique institution of the early modern period".[118] It was cited as a "vast engine of power, an organ of public opinion".[119] The salons of early modern and revolutionary France played an integral role in the cultural and intellectual development of France. They emerged in Europe in early 16th century and generally continued till the end of the 18th century. Joan B. Landes, however, says that salons were established in France in the 17th century. **Steven Kale**, however, has stretched the period of salon until the revolution of 1848[120] because he thinks that the intellectual ideas, academic environment, political thoughts created by the salon did not end in 1789 but moved deeper into the folds of the 19th century. The salons were seen by contemporary writers as cultural centres, responsible for the dissemination of good manners and sociability. They were means of exchange of thoughts and ideas as well—social, political, economic, and intellectual—playing host to many members of the republic of letters. In contrast to other early modern institutions, women played an important and visible role within the salons. It is to be noted that the salons were generally held in the sprawling, luxurious living rooms of the aristocratic families, hosted by the lady of the house. An important aspect of the salons was that they included not only the noble-born but the ***haute bourgeoisie*** (the upper echelons of the bourgeoisie) as well. In that sense, the *salons transcended the barriers of sharp class distinctions*. In fact, the upper bourgeois ladies learnt some distinctive styles and fashions, dress and manners of the aristocrats and often competitions ensued. Even so, till the end it certainly remained a highly restrictive and elitist gathering with impressive activities like reading aloud novels, poems, essays; discussing matters of concern for all; important political, economic and social issues; organising plays, concerts, painting exhibitions and other cultural activities; published pamphlets and journals in which the members contributed.

The salons played a crucial role in shaping the minds and viewpoints of men as well as women during the period of the French Revolution. Nevertheless, the role of aristocratic women remained largely passive throughout the course of the revolution. After all, they shared in the privileges endowed upon the aristocracy and hence were not in a position to denounce the monarchy and the Old Regime. However, there were exceptions like Madame Roland. From her childhood, **Manon Philippon** (as **Madame Roland** was called by her friends), took immense interest in the writings of Voltaire, Montesquieu and particularly Rousseau. Under their influence she started questioning the ideas of an absolute monarchy. Her husband Jean-Marie Roland was a well-known politician and both of them extended their political support for the revolution through letters to the journal *Patriote Francaise*. Alongside her involvement in politics and her staunch support for the Girondins, Madame Roland, following Rousseau's model of femininity, took keen interest in domestic matters. Her salon in Paris became the rendezvous of Brissot, Petion, Robespirre and other popular revolutionaries. They discussed the rights of citizens and strategies to transform the absolute monarchy into a constitutional republic. The couple, however, stood against the excesses of the Reign of Terror and thereby earned the ire of the extremists. Eventually, Madame Roland was guillotined under the orders of Robespierre on 8 November 1793.

The extent and significance of the role of the salon has been heavily contested by some historians. Jürgen Habermas in his book *The Structural Transformation of the Public Sphere*[121] termed the salon a public sphere and emphasised its importance by elaborating the role it played in French society. He thought it to have emerged in contrast to court society. Joan B. Landes disagrees with him when she thinks it to be an extension of the institutionalised court.[122] However, she believes that the salon had certain distinct features of its own and therefore was unique in its own merit. The viewpoint of Landes has been carried on by Norbert Elias,[123] according to whom the behavioural pattern of the courtly people—*politesse, civilite* and *honnete*—were adopted by the salons as well. Steven Kale attempted to show how public and private spheres overlapped in the salon. Dena Goodman,[124] however, agrees with Habermas when she looks upon the salon as having structured the public sphere, press and other social institutions.

As far as the role of women in the salon—*salonnieres*, as they were called—is concerned, it is again contested by historians. S.G. Tallentyre and Julia Kavanagh[125] thought the salonnieres to be involved in jealousies, competition and petty intrigues. Jolanta T. Pekacz looked upon the salonnieres as amateurs, while men concentrated on the serious aspects of the Enlightenment. According to her, the salons played an important role in the "culture wars" that raged in the post-revolutionary period, in which the philosophes were criticised by many and were at the same time, eulogised by others. Prominent salonniere **Mme Geoffrin** euologised the philosophes, while **Mme du Deffand** criticised them. Mme Deffand was disparaged by contemporary men of letters. According to Jolanta, the most vociferous in his disapproval of Deffand was Morellet, who denounced her saying how could an ignorant woman analyse the most distinguished men of the time. And, although Mme Geoffrin was fondly remembered for her generosity, she was generally considered to be a woman "poorly educated and intellectually inferior".[126] In other words, the Enlightenment was considered by these scholars as exclusively 'masculine'. Joan B. Landes, however, viewed them as women of substance contributing significantly to the cultural and intellectual upliftment of the era. Carolyn Lougee,[127] too, emphasised the positive public role the salonnieres played in the French society. In Dena Goodman's view "the salonnieres were not social climbers, but intelligent, self-educated and educating women who adopted and implemented the values of the Enlightened Republic of Letters and used them to reshape the salon to their own social, intellectual and educational needs."[128]

However, the role of the salonnieres had also been a subject of serious discussion of contemporaries including prominent men like Francois de Salignac de la Mothe-Fenelon, Montesquieu and Jean-Jaques Rousseau. All of them extolled domesticity and condemned excessive liberty for women which might lead to corruption. Fenelon upheld the Aristotelian concept of family and felt that women's duties were at home where all her love and concern would be reserved for her family, who would be nourished by her affection and thus, each family would contribute towards strengthening the foundations of the society. Women participating in public life might go astray, weaken the base of the family and social disorder would follow.[129] Montesquieu in his *Persian Letters* has warned us of the adverse effects of both over suppression and too much freedom of women. He has also shown how women's high ambition, craving for fashion and desire to flaunt prosperity have ruined their families' economy and been a drain on the resources of the country.

> Paris, which is the most sensuous town in the world, is where pleasures are most subtly cultivated, but it is perhaps also the place where one leads the hardest life...A woman gets it into her head that she must wear a particular outfit on some occasion, and at once it becomes impossible for fifty craftsmen to get any sleep or have leisure to eat or drink; she gives her commands and is obeyed more promptly than our monarch, since self-interest is the greatest monarch on earth.[130]

In monarchy, where the pomp and splendour of the aristocracy is excessive, Montesquieu believes that women tend to be more corrupt, as compared to a republican democracy where social disparity is less.[131] Another deep critic of women's participation in public life was Jean-Jacque Rousseau who prescribed boundaries for women's lives in the private sphere. Through his novels and treatises he painted an ideal picture of womanhood—a caring wife, an affectionate mother, a loving sister, a dutiful daughter, fostering an ideology attempting to confine them in the private sphere of home and domesticity.

Rousseau's ideology of women was accepted as the general concept of feminine behaviour by the republican revolutionaries. As Lynn Hunt has observed, "The republican ideal of virtue was profoundly homosocial; it was based on a notion of fraternity between men in which women were relegated to the realm of domesticity."[132] This was precisely the reason why all women's clubs were eventually *outlawed*. It was a part of what Richard Cobb calls the "*revolutionary mentalite*". Bitter hostility against women who played prominent roles in public sphere during the French Revolution culminating in the guillotining of Madame Roland and Olympe de Gouge—women who were considered political enemies—was displayed.

The extreme example of this "*mentalite*" was the treatment accorded to the queen, **Marie Antoinette**. The vilification campaign raged against her snowballed into the publication of virulent pornographic literature—a series of as many 126 pamphlets—spilling all over the country. Unnatural sex, promiscuity, incest, poisoning of the heir to the throne were some of the charges brought against her. They were enough to generate enormous popular venom, which was further fanned by authors like Louise de Keralio in a political tract entitled *Les Crimes des reines de France* in which she analysed the history of the queens of France in general and that of Marie Antoinette in particular. She stressed upon her "private crimes", provided a list of her paramours, and called her "the soul of all the plots, the centre of all the intrigues, the foyer of all these horrors." Keralio called the queen a "political tarantula" and compared her with a tigress who had tasted blood and could never be satisfied with anything less.[133] In short, all the blame and disgrace revolved round the queen alone; she was maligned beyond redemption, while her male aides and paramours were spared. The question is not whether the queen was guilty of these crimes. What is important is that it revealed, as Lynn Hunt points out, "Jacobin attitudes towards gender and sexuality."[134] Sexuality is the easiest weapon used through ages to denigrate and exploit women. It is an expression of the popular mindset.

Among the well-known salonnieres were Madame de Graffigny, Madame d'Epinay, Madame de Lambert, Madame de Mercier, Madame de Beaumer Madame de Tencin, Madame Geoffrin, Madame du Deffand

and Mademoiselle de Lespinasse. **Mme Francoise de Graffigny** was a novelist and playwright who authored *Letters d'une Peruvienne* (Letters from a Peruvian Woman), *Cenie* and *La fille d'Aristide* (The Daughter of Aristide). She, however, hesitated to call herself an 'author' because she did not think it appropriate.[135] **Mme de Lambert** and **Mme de Tencin** taught conversational art and **Mlle de Lespinasse** encouraged the encyclopedists.[136] **Madame Genlis** and others wrote plays which were put up for theatrical performances organised by salonnieres. **Mme Stephanie Félicité de Genlis** was known for her didactic epistolary novel on the education and upbringing of children, *Adelaide and Theodore or Letters on Education*, a highly influential work widely read across Europe during the late 18th and early 19th centuries. Of her 120 published volumes, many key texts were translated into all major languages, as well as widely read in original French. They addressed various social and political issues of the times the purpose being generating awareness among the audience. Many salonnieres were members of the well-known monthly paper *Journal des dames*, launched three times between 1759 and 1778 after being withdrawn by censors. It dealt with long-ranging social issues and became widely popular with its readership, encompassing men and women from varying social classes. The first editor of the paper was **Madame de Beaumer** whom Joan Landes describes as "the most idiosyncratic and most radical in her feminist beliefs".[137] The paper encouraged contributions from all classes, especially the common people. The last editor of the paper was **Madame de Montanclos** who was known for her wisdom and praise for motherhood. She emphasised virtues like fidelity, chastity, love, honesty, which were the values practised by the Freemasons* of the time. This gives the idea, suggests Nina Rattner Galbert, who is known for her extensive research on the *Journal des dames*, that she might have belonged to the female Masonic lodges.

However, there were a few men who were strong advocates of women's freedom. One of them was the well-known French liberal aristocrat **Marquis de Condorcet**. He was a member of the Society of 1789, (a political club established on 12 May 1790 by Lafayette, the prominent aristocrat and military officer, along with Jean Sylvain Bailly, the then Mayor of Paris) and the Society of the Friends of the Blacks. He and his

---

*The Freemasons were a fraternal organisation in the middle ages who emphasised brotherly love, truth, charity, individual freedom. Since they claimed their origin to the stonemasons in the middle ages, they are called Freemasons.

wife had a salon which was known for hosting French philosophes as well as men of letters from outside France. Condorcet initiated the demand for women's political rights. He published in 1790 his famous essay 'On the Admission of Women to the Rights of Citizenship' in the *Journal of the Society of 1789*. In his view, it was extremely unjust to exclude women from the rights of citizenship because, firstly, many of them paid taxes, and secondly, they possessed equal power of reasoning and morality as men. "Either no individual of the human species has any true rights, or all have the same," he declared.[138] Moreover, if the grounds on which women are excluded (like lack of education, rationality and knowledge) are applied to the entire population, then only a small fraction of people would qualify for citizenship. Women were also considered unfit for any political activity because of their physical compulsions like motherhood. Condorcet, failed to comprehend why these could be problems more pressing than gout or bronchitis. Surprisingly, however, even such a resolute feminist expressed his apprehensions of women neglecting their domestic responsibilities once they attained emancipation and success in the public sphere. Perhaps, as Joan B. Landes concludes, Condorcet was "made nervous by overly ambitious public women".[139]

Another prominent writer of the times and a Prussian civil servant **Theodor Gottlieb Hippel** was a great champion of women's liberty and their rights for citizenship. He advocated women's active participation in matters of state administration. To enable them to successfully execute such responsibilities, Hippel suggested opening of institutions for specific training for interested women. He, therefore, strongly supported women's education. Until the age of 12, Hippel believed, both sexes should be trained in the same manner. Thereafter, they would be free to pursue duties that nature has designed for them. Thus, like Condorcet, this implies that Hippel too believed in specificities of the work 'nature' ordained for both sexes. In other words, even while advocating egalitarianism, determined defenders of liberty could not transcend barriers of 'differences' between the two.

The men who supported women's rights were mostly men of substance. **Pierre Guyomar** maintained that the only difference between men and women, in his eyes, were in the reproductive organs, and it was ludicrous to deprive women on grounds of such inconsequential physical differences. He wrote, "the Law of ... Justice, reason and humanity brings us back effortlessly to equality and liberty, the bases of a democratic republic."

Cordelier Labenette who started the newspaper *Journal des Droits de l'Homme* was a staunch supporter of women's rights as well.

The Bourgeois Public Sphere

Coming to bourgeois women, it is to be noted that many belonging to the haute bourgeoisie joined the salons. But with the rise of the bourgeoisie and growth of towns, there emerged a number of **public spaces** in several urban centres—like clubs, libraries, museums, operas, cafes—which were cultural hubs as well. A new world of public communication with its emphasis on print and publication came into being. Habermas called it **the bourgeois public sphere**.

There were distinct differences between bourgeois public spaces and **the salon**. *First*, the salon was essentially feminist in character in terms of the large participation of women. It was women of nobility who hosted the salons. In the bourgeois public sphere, on the other hand, woman's voices were not predominant. It was primarily a man's world where a few women also took part. Majority of the bourgeois women stayed aloof while a small section participated actively. Through them, bourgeois feminism flourished. They were active in drafting cahiers (list of grievances) which all the classes were asked to draw up on the eve of the meeting of the Estates-General. **Political rights** were a central concern of the **cahiers of the bourgeois women**. One of them stated that it was equally just to count their votes since women were obliged, like men, to pay royal taxes and fulfil business contracts. In another cahier, women of the 1789 National Assembly demanded the abolition of male privileges, including legal authority over wives, and the admission of women without restriction to all political functions. The legal tyranny of husbands was challenged in 1791 by a group of women in a petition to the National Assembly protesting against a law which permitted only husbands to complain against conjugal infidelity and also slammed on wives found guilty of such offence a sentence of two years, while adulterous husbands went scot-free.

Second, since the cities and towns were the chief centres of bourgeois activity, their public spaces were also developed in urban settings, where facilities like cafes, libraries, theatres, clubs and lecture halls were accessible to everyone. They were **public spheres in the true sense** of the term as they were less exclusive and less elitist than the salons where entry was restricted to a handful of people strictly on invitation. As Habermas observes, "citizens behave as a public body when they confer in an unrestricted fashion—that is, with the freedom of assembly and association and the freedom to express and publish their opinions—about matters of general interest."[140]

Third, the bourgeois sphere was far more economic than the salons and lacked lavish expenses which characterised the latter.

Fourth, the activities of the salons were varied while the bourgeoisie were mostly confined to literary and printed work from which majority of women automatically got excluded because of their limited education and writing skills. Participation of bourgeois women in revolutionary activities, therefore, remained restricted. However, there were a few bourgeois women who contributed substantially to the cause of womanhood in the era of the French Revolution. One such leading bourgeois feminist during the French Revolution was **Olympe de Gouges**.

Olympe de Gouges

Born Marie Gouze, the daughter of a butcher in Montauban, Olympe de Gouges later claimed that her real father was a local noble Jean-Jacques Lefranc, Marquis de Pompignan. Initially, she was a strong monarchist. She had practically no sympathy with the protesting women's procession to the King's palace in Versailles on 5 October 1789. She supported the Constitution of 1791. "It is madness to think of changing it (the constitution). Yet they do think of doing so. What a time!"[141] she said. However, she came to despise the monarchy after the King's flight to Varennes and became a devout revolutionary. Her most comprehensive contribution to the cause of bourgeois feminism during the revolution was the *Declaration of the Rights of Woman and of the [Female] Citizen* in 1791— a woman's reply to the male chauvinistic document *Declaration of the Rights of Man and of the Citizen*. The opening words were particularly remarkable: "This revolution will not be completed until all the women are conscious of their deplorable lot and of the rights they have lost in society."[142]

Even before she authored this document, as early as October 1789, de Gouges had urged the National Assembly to grant legal sexual equality, to throw open the doors of all occupations to women, ensure equality of education and political rights, suppression of the dowry system, fair measure of taxes, assistance to unwed mothers, secure shelter for prostitutes, and secure compensation for deceived, abandoned women from the man responsible. In the *Declaration of the Rights of Woman and of the [Female] Citizen* she insists on the natural, inalienable rights of women. The preamble stated,

> All women are born free and remain equal to men in rights…the aim of all political associations is the preservation of all inalienable rights of women and men…the nation is the union of women and men…Law is the expression of general will: all female and male citizens have the right to participate personally, or through their representatives, in its formation.[143]

A woman's right to speak was essential because, in the absence of scientific proof, her word and testimony was often the only way to establish who the father of her child was, De Gouges asserted. She criticised the *Declaration of the Rights of Man and of the Citizen* for discriminating among human beings on grounds of colour and sex. She pointed out the contradictions of the political revolutionaries who espoused liberalism, which theoretically presupposed equality for all. But when the Constitution was proclaimed by the Constituent Assembly, half the nation was excluded from citizenship— the slaves, the mulattos and the women.

Joan W. Scott in her essay on French feminists, vis-a-vis the rights of man,[144] particularly focuses on Olympe de Gouges because her works best reveal the *contradictions inherent in revolutionary liberal ideology*. Olympe de Gouges demanded equal rights for women based on the ideals of justice, natural rights and equality. While she may have invoked traditionally feminine qualities such as beauty, sacrifice, child-bearimg capacity, nurturing and sacrifice to bolster her argument, her central claim was rooted in Enlightenment ideals of reason and equality.

Thus, she regarded rights of citizenship as *universal*, but demanded it for women on reasons that were *particular*. Scott highlights how this strategy—asserting equality while referencing difference—revealed the paradox feminists faced in revolutionary discourse. Olympe de Gouges wanted removal of contradictions and redress of discrimination in the behaviour of revolutionaries; but her own claim, Scott argues, was also not free of contradiction.[145] This undermined the strength of her claims. Perhaps de Gouges believed nature to be the source of rights, and emphasised the fundamental similarities among all human beings. Scott analyses de Gouges' work at length with the purpose of exposing the inherent contradictions and hypocrisy within the discourse of revolutionary liberalism. Madame de Gouges' demands were never realised. In 1792, after the fall of the monarchy, citizenship was granted to all men over 21, and women were again excluded. One reason might have been that the physical distinctions alluded to by Gouges were seen by the revolutionaries as *natural*—and, therefore, politically irrelevant. This is evident from the remarks of people like Pierre-Gaspard Chaumette, a radical member of the Paris Commune:

> Since when is it permitted to give up one's sex? Since when is it decent to see women abandoning the pious cares of their households, the cribs of their children, to come to public places, to harangues in the galleries, at the bar of the senate? Is it to men that nature confided domestic cares? Has she given us breasts to feed our children?[146]

Olympe de Gouges opposed the Jacobin concentration of power and strongly upheld Montesquieu's separation of power. She put up an active campaign in favour of dissemination of authority and plastered posters on the walls of Paris urging the replacement of Jacobin authoritarian rule with a federalist system. This, as well as her close association with the Girondins were the foremost reasons—and not her advocacy for women's rights—for her being sent to the guillotine on 3 November 1793.

FIG. 1.9: *Olympe de Gouges* by Alexander Kucharsky

Etta Palm d'Aelders and Other Bourgeois Women Activists

Another eminent bourgeois contributor to feminism during the French Revolution was **Etta Palm d'Aelders**, a Dutch woman. She was the daughter of a Dutch merchant Aelders Von Nieuwenhuys, who owned a paper-mill and ran the local pawnshop in 1743. She moved to Paris in 1773 and became a courtesan for the rich aristocracy. She was recruited for French secret services by Comte de Maurepas. She set up a salon which was frequented by prominent revolutionaries like Jean Paul Marat, Francois Chabot and Claude Basire. She became involved in revolutionary politics and was especially active in feminist circles, like Societe fraternelle de l'un et l'autre sexe (Fraternal Society of Both Sexes), Societe Patriotique des Amite de la Verite and Societe Patriotique et de Bienfaisance des Amies de la Verite (Patriotic and Charitable Society of the Female Friends of Truth). A collection of her lectures on the position of women was published in July 1791. Her political views were embedded in the equal rights and citizenship and she strongly rejected conservative, traditional structures founded on privileges and hierarchy. She made her mark in the Societe des amite de la verite, also known as Cercle Social where she defended a male orator who was obstructed while speaking on the role of women in the revolution by other impatient male members. She said: "Gentlemen, can it be said that the holy revolution, that gives men their rights, has made the French unjust and dishonest towards the women! You have listened with patience to the other speakers, why interrupt the one who speaks in favour of women?"[147]

She proposed the formation of a woman's section within the Society and this was finally approved by the Cercle Social. In a speech before the Society on 18 March 1791, Etta Palm declared the woman's section to be the forum for demanding justice for women, demanded the passing of a comprehensive divorce bill for protection of women against bad marriages, and advocated opening a centre for education for children of poor and destitute mothers and free clinics for helpless women.[148] On 1 April 1792, she presented a petition to the Legislative Assembly which specified the aims of the bourgeois women. It demanded education for girls, legal majority for women at the age of 21, political freedom and equal rights for both sexes, the right to divorce, elimination of primogeniture and protection against wife-beating. However, even while eulogising women and demanding equal rights for them, Etta Palm, like Olympe de Gouges, emphasised specific female virtues, thereby conceding in a way the differences between the two sexes. She observed:

> Yes gentlemen, nature has created us to be your companions in your works and in your glory. If she gave you a better muscled arm, she made us your equals in moral force, and perhaps your superiors in vivacity of imagination, by the delicacy of the sentiments, by the resignation in misfortunes, by the fortitude in sorrows, the patience in sufferings, finally in generosity of soul and patriotic zeal.[149]

Here lay the ambiguity of her political ideology. Like Gouges, she resorted to differences to claim equality.

Another strong bourgeois activist in the French Revolution was **Theroigne de Mericourt** who appeared in public dressed in a white riding habit, plume on her head, pistol in her belt, which made her extremely striking. She did so, as she claimed, to assert equality with men and was also known for her vigorous speeches. A staunch supporter of the Girondins, she was stripped naked and flogged by the Jacobin women at the public garden of Tuilleries in May 1793 after which she slowly became insane and never recovered her rationality until she died on 9 June 1817.

Women, particularly bourgeois women, started taking parts in political clubs and associations very actively from 1790s onwards. They joined clubs like Societe fraternelle de l'un et l'autre sexes, Societe des Amite de la Verite, among others, and also began sending petitions to legislatures demanding political rights. **Societe des Amite de la Verite** which was a part of the Cercle Social (Social Club), was founded in October 1790 by Nicholas Bonneville and Claude Fauchet. In early 1791, it openly declared itself republican and became the rendevouz of prominent Girondist leaders like Louis-Sebastian Mercier, Jacque-Pierre Brissot, Jean-marie Roland, Marquis Condorcet. It stressed political and social issues through the publication of pamphlets, journals, newspapers, poetry, posters, etc. From the very beginning it devoted itself to women's issues also, like divorce, education and political rights. Etta Palm became a member of the Societe des Amis de la Verite and was in fact as Judith Vega points out, "the first woman who appeared on the tribune of the 'Cercle Social' in defence of feminist notions."[150] Etta palm proposed the formation of women's own club and this idea stirred the minds of numerous other women and activity in this direction began. The result was the formation of the **Society of Revolutionary Republican Women** in February 1793. Its founders were two noteworthy revolutionary bourgeois women—**Pauline Leon** and **Claire Lacombe**.

One of the foremost agenda of the Society was the demand for citizenship which women had been demanding for quite sometime. One woman went up to the National Convention and said:

> Citizen legislators, you have given men a constitution; now they enjoy all the rights of free beings, but women are very far from sharing these glories…We ask for primary assemblies and, as the constitution is based on the rights of Man, we now demand the full exercise of these rights for ourselves.[151]

Olympe de Gouges claimed the rights of citizenship in 1791 in her *Declaration of the Rights of Woman and of the [Female] Citizen*. The Society was inclined towards revolutionary radicalism and supported the activities of the Montagnards. They hailed the new **Montagnard Constitution** of June 1793. But slowly afterwards they started drifting towards the Enragés as they were greatly enamoured by their agenda, which included price control, repression of counter-revolutionary activities, and a progressive

Fig. 1.10: *La Liberté Guidant le Peuple* (1830) by Eugene Delacroix

income tax. Thereby they incurred the wrath of the Montagnards or the Jacobins. On the other hand, the market women who were not the members of the Society came to blows against the latter especially on economic issues like price control. These measures did not suit the interests of the market women at all because they meant less profit for their products in the markets. Violent clashes on the streets began between the two. This gave the Jacobins, who otherwise were also not pleased with the Society of Revolutionary Republican Women and felt threatened by their militancy, the plea to close it. Finally, on 30 October 1793 the National Convention decreed that henceforth **all women's clubs and societies would be banned**. The mentalite of the Jacobins towards revolutionary women and their clubs is further evident from the following words of Chaumette when he dissolved women's clubs in October 1793: "The sans-culotte had a right to expect from his wife the running of his home while he attended political meetings: hers was the care of the family: this was the full extent of her civic duties."[152]

Economic Demands of the Sans-culotte Women

The role of sans-culotte and working-class women was also no less remarkable. As Olwen Hufton observes, "their role was both unique and important and their attitudes demanding of consideration."[153] Their primary concerns, however, differed from those of their aristocratic and bourgeois counterparts. While the latter were preoccupied mostly with social and political issues, to the sans-culotte and working-class women, on the contrary, economic matters, especially procurement of food were of topmost priority. They hardly could afford the time and leisure of thinking about, let alone agitating, for demands of political equality and citizenship. Albert Soboul has summarised their problems in the following words: "In the case of women coming from the sans-culotterie, battling the difficulties of daily life, the struggle against high prices and food shortages obviously had a higher priority than political action: **daily bread ranked higher than the right to vote**."[154]

The cahiers de doleances presented by the working class and sans-culottes women before the Estates-General revealed their particular grievances. The working women complained about their low wages and abysmal working conditions. **Absence of wage protection** left them perpetually poor and forced them to prostitution to save their families from hunger. The flower-selling women complained of the abrogation of the old privileges they enjoyed as a group. Similarly, the fisher-women reiterated their faith and confidence in the King who, they believed, would protect their interests.

The working-class women played a key role in the family economy which depended on the contributions of each of its component members. The main occupation of unmarried young girls was to work as domestic help. The money earned by her was saved to serve as a part of her marriage expenses. The mothers generally worked in different manufacturing units for spinning wool and cotton, making of lace, shoes, gloves, ribbons, garments; as embroiderers, milliners and corset makers. The lowest order of the society, that is, the very poor and destitute women did all kinds of odd and casual jobs including carrying loads—wood, coal, water, other household goods from one place to another. The women earned money, prepared food at home, nursed the children and served as the main pillar supporting their families. Many of their lives were constant struggles to save their families from crossing the thin invisible barrier between poverty and destitution. In extreme cases, these women took recourse to prostitution to keep their children alive. Being a bread-earner, the mother in a working-class family enjoyed enormous power. Olwen Hufton refers to a contemporary feminist Madame de Coicy, who observed that because of her crucial role in the family economy **the working-class woman enjoyed within her home a position of equality which her aristocratic and bourgeois counterparts did not do**.[155] In fact, the bread riots at the time of the French Revolution were essentially feminine in character. "The bread riots of the French Revolution then, …were *par excellence* women's days. Where bread was concerned this was their province: a bread riot without women is an inherent contradiction," says Olwen Hufton.[156]

The women without property or *bras nus* (term coined by Michelet) were particularly distressed from 1789 onwards. There were various reasons behind this. *First*, the years 1787, 1788 and 1789 saw severe failure of harvests. According to Ernest Labrousse, the average expenditure of 50 per cent of the wage of a wage-earner on bread in 1762–1791, shot up to an appalling 88 per cent in the critical months of famine in 1789.[157] Hence, the acute scarcity of bread and the spiralling rise in prices. Rudé refers to an incident from Sebastian Hardy's journal in which a working housewife had commented "that it was monstrous to allow the poor to starve in this way."[158]

Second, their old means of livelihood got thoroughly disrupted by the events of the French Revolution. For example, due to the emigration of the nobles, disintegration of the Church and disruption of international trade, industries of fancy and luxury items like lace, ribbons, velvet, silk, brocade lost a huge clientele. Consequently, a significant number of these industries were closed down. The workforce of these industries, particularly that of lace, were predominantly women. A large number of working-class women thereby became unemployed. A similar fate befell the salt smugglers when the revolution abolished **gabelle or salt tax** in 1790. Almost 200,000 families who lived on salt smuggling were impoverished.

Third, the government at this critical hour failed to come up with adequate help. It is true, as Hufton points out, that the government did have a programme of poor relief. It abolished the system of almsgiving and replaced it with work for poor unemployed adult male…[159] Unfortunately, those who drew the programme hardly had any clue about the number of people they would have to assist. Soon it transpired that their resources were totally inadequate to deal with the situation. Earlier, some Church monasteries (for example, the Trappist monastery of Bonnecombe in Rodez district, as well as Bishop of Mende) used to distribute bread annually among the local destitute from the money collected through tithe from the small landholders. When tithe was abolished, this source of money dried up and distribution of bread also stopped. The bourgeois women of *clubs des femmes,* of course, did organise voluntary collection of alms and also arranged lotteries for charity among the poor. But these were never enough and what the unemployed poor needed most was some regular and stable means of livelihood and a steady price of bread. Neither of these, however, were forthcoming and popular discontent kept on mounting. In fact, the problem of unemployment multiplied since the signing of **free trade treaty with England in 1786** which had proved unfavourable to France and led to the fall of a number of industries. Bad harvest complicated things further and the result was a spiralling of prices. Rudé provides certain figures of price-rise. "The 4-lb loaf, having long remained at 8 to 9 sous, rose to 91/2 sous on 17th August, to 10 sous on 20th and to 11 sous on 7th September."[160] Subsequently, a **series of bread riots**, with heavy participation by women followed.

Riots on Bread, Milk and Soap

As we have discussed earlier, on 5 October 1789, a large crowd consisting mainly of women and children, marched on to Versailles to present a petition before the King and the Queen and brought them back to Paris. The day after the royal family returned to Paris, a huge crowd of women threw 150 barrels of rotten flour into the river. On 21st October, while rioting in the Hotel de Yule, the militant women got Francois, the baker hanged from a lamp-post. The riot continued the next day also during which the women demanded to search a house where they suspected grains to be hidden.[161]

Between November 1789 and September 1791, the prices of bread were stable and there were no bread riots. The prices started to rise again from October 1791 onwards. The value of paper money or assignats crashed. Working women again rose in arms. In mid-1792, the voice of working women was heard loudly and distinctly against the irregular supply of **milk**. They also were sharply demanding immediate lowering of prices. On 25 February 1793, they joined their menfolk to enter the shops and to force the shopkeepers to sell goods at prices fixed by themselves. On the following day, 26th February, a delegation of women went to the city hall to demand price fixation for all basic commodities.[162] Due to their persistent efforts, ultimately on 4 May 1793, the Convention took the first step to enact the **first Law of the Maximum** by which prices were fixed for all commodities. It was extended into the **Law of the General Maximum** on 29 September 1793.

Even after the first Law of Maximum, high prices and scarcity continued. This led to the **soap riots** of 26–28 June 1793. On the 26th, at the ports of Grenouillere, Saint-Nicolas, and so on, washerwomen unloaded soaps from boats and forced to get them sold at the rate of 20 sous a pound. On the 28th, a delegation of women demanded from the General Council of the Commune to fix the price of soap at 20 sous per pound. Simultaneously, a group of washerwomen protested at the National Convention against the soaring price of soap.

The soap riots continued intermittently till 15 April 1794. On that day, Soboul records, a group of militant women barged into the office of the Civil Committee of the Temple Section to protest against the irregular distribution of soap. Soboul writes, "The women complained about the 'very offensive' attitude toward them of the committee and the guard; the guardsmen declared that they had been 'ill-treated and scratched'; one young seamstress, twenty-two years old was arrested."[163]

In March 1794, the Convention imposed wage restraint. It sparked off widespread agitation by women and men throughout the country. A huge demonstration was organised at the City Hall of Paris on 9 Thermidor

(July). After the fall of Robespierre, price control on bread was removed with the result of prevailing inflation, rampant speculation, acute scarcity of bread bringing in its train extensive protests all-over. The worst hit were the poorer sections of the society—the working people, most of whom were turned into destitutes, a phenomenon their women ceaselessly and desperately endeavoured to resist all these years. Medical care was unavailable as the hospitals closed down due to lack of funds. Minor diseases, therefore, became major taking numerous lives especially that of children, infants and the old. Parents helplessly saw their children perish from hunger and malnutrition before their eyes. "The mothers of Caen in 1795 were allaying the cries of their new-born children with rags dipped in water..."[164] The last two bread riots of the revolution took place in April and May 1795. On 25 March 1795, a large of gathering of women marched on to the Convention demanding adequate bread. On 1st April, too, women invaded the Convention with the cries of "Bread! Bread!" However, it was not a well-organised movement, and as soon as the National Guard arrived, the crowd dispersed. A far larger and aggressive demonstration—of mostly women—attacked the Convention on 20th May with slogans pinned on their dresses like "Bread and Constitution of 1793," or "Bread or Death!" This rally was crushed forcefully. This was the end of the bread riots of the revolution after which the Convention excluded women from attending their meetings. Only wives of men carrying citizen's card were allowed to just sit and watch.

Women in the War of 1792

The commitment of women to the cause of the revolution is clearly evident in their attitude to the war when it broke out in 1792. They were passionately patriotic as well as emotional as far as the issue of war was concerned. They contributed without hesitation even their extremely essential items like household linen for bandages of soldiers; and also precious possessions like jewellery acquired in dowry—one of the main assets in a woman's life—including wedding rings, to raise funds for the nation's war efforts. Olwen Hufton writes,

> Women of Pontarlier, a frontier town, contributed their wedding rings—the most pawnable piece of property any woman had—to clothe volunteers; in Besancon, street walkers and women who had toiled all day turned up when they had put their children to bed to knit stockings for the soldiers at the front. In the summer of 1792 when war fever ran

> high, innumerable addresses were drawn up and sent to the Assembly
> wherein women stressed their patriotism and swore to feed their children
> the right sort of milk: the milk of *'bon principles, amour de la constitution,
> haine des tyrans'* (good principles, love of the Constitution, hatred of
> tyrants), or more specifically, hatred of the Austrians…[165]

They even were prepared to protect their houses in absence of their husbands who had gone for war, and armed themselves with pitchforks and kitchen knives. They expressed their intense venom and hatred against the non-juring priests, émigrés nobles or anybody who in their perception opposed the revolution. And examples of such militancy were not rare. Some women were committed completely to the Reign of Terror. **Widow Barbau**, for example, belonging to Section de l'Indivisibilite, was a virulent supporter of the Jacobins and would declare publicly that, "It would'nt matter if someone were my best friend, I would have him guillotined if he did not think like a true Jacobin…" because in her view, such insincere people were responsible for people dying of hunger as much as "the egotistical merchants, the former aristocrats" and the rich.[166] **Wife Baudray**, a sans-culotte and a cafe owner in the Lepeletier Section, said she wanted to eat "the hearts" of those who opposed the sans-culottes.

Working-class Women and their Political Rights

Although political aspirations were more or less an exclusive realm of the bourgeois women, some working-class women did take keen interest in their political rights. Rudé gives an example of a 23-year-old cook, **Constance Evrard**, who was arrested for joining the major republican demonstration on the Champ de Mars in July 1791 to sign the republican petition; she admitted not only of having visited the Cordeliers Club, but also of reading four newspapers regularly.[167] In fact quite a number of working-class women attended public gatherings, read revolutionary newspapers, participated in the meetings of the Convention. They participated most widely at the time of the ratification of the Constitution of 1793 and also the food crisis of the winter of 1794. In large numbers from all the sections women's delegations came to the Convention and swore their allegiance to the Constitution. The republican women of the Marches section declared,

> we accept the Declaration of the Rights of Men and the Constitutional
> Act that you have presented for the approval of the sovereign people. If

our husbands and our brothers have sworn to defend the Constitution by armed force, we ourselves swear to defend it either by raising our children in the principles of liberty and equality which form the base of this Constitution, and others by giving their hand only to true republicans who will have done something for the country.[168]

One *citoyenne* (female citizen) of the Baurepaire Section, however, vociferously demanded political equality. While men enjoyed rights of citizen, women were denied of it. "… they are not counted in the political system…and since the constitution rests on the rights of man, we demand today the full exercise of those rights."[169]

Urban and Rural Attitudes Towards the Church

In the sphere of religion, women—especially working class and peasant women—had a special role to play. The abolition of tithe (11 August 1789), the nationalisation of Church property (2 November 1789), the Civil Constitution of the clergy (12 July 1790), made the position of the Church extremely fragile. In the popular eye, the non-juring clergy had downright betrayed the revolution; the constitutional clergy had lost its former authority and glory. The Church, on the whole, along with the monarchy and the nobility were looked upon as enemies of the revolution. This popular belief turned into conviction when a **cult of reason** was established by radical revolutionaries like **Hebert**, **Momoro** and **Chaumette** as an alternative to Christianity. God was detached from religion, which now revolved round human reason. Adherence to the cult of reason was pervasive among the ranks of the sans-culottes and the working class. A large number of men and women, belonging to these classes expressed their loyalty to the revolution by closing the churches and resorting to iconoclasm and desecration of places of worship including image-breaking and dancing on the overturned tabernacles.[170] Things, however, changed when Robespierre opposed the atheism of the Hebertist faction, and restored the catholic Church. It had a deep impact on the minds of the women who now seriously regretted their own anti-clericalism and by 1796 were found to be working seriously towards reopening the churches. They knelt on their knees and begged for pardon. They wanted full restoration of the Roman Catholic religion of the ancien regime.

The peasant women, however, had an entirely different story to tell. *Their approach towards the French Roman Catholic Church was just contrary to their approach towards urban working women.* To them, as Olwen Hufton observes, the French revolution was an adversary, not a friend. The Church, the image of the deity, the traditional clergy and their sermons represented to these women the only form of worship. It was their firm belief that disasters could be averted only through the intercession of a priest who had the true knowledge of rites and rituals. They defied all attempts of the revolutionaries to replace this with any new method. "It had, after all, hallowed the great events of life—birth, marriage, and death—as well as vaunted the virtues of catholic motherhood.[171] Resolutely they declared, "*Les hommes font les lois; les femmes les traditions*" (Men make laws, women traditions). They did not bother whether a priest was non-juring or constitutional. Their loyalty was to individuals. There were occasions of mass boycott of the meetings of the new constitutional priests; there were allegations that in 1796, several hundreds of fanatical women threw an official to the ground and snatched the keys of the Church; there were cases where complete disrespect was shown to the alternative deities—Reason, Liberty, Robespierre's Supreme Being—during the dechristianisation process. Hufton calls them counterrevolutionary women. It was their effort that decided "the re-emergence of the Catholic Church on very particular terms, which included an express rejection of State attempts to control priesthood and the form of public worship."[172]

WOMEN IN REVOLUTIONARY ICONOGRAPHY AND THE FINAL RECKONING

In the final reckoning, however, women did win a few reforms for themselves. In **inheritance laws**, henceforth, sons and daughters were to be treated as equals. They got legal majority at 21. Women could now be witnesses in civil acts and their ability to administer their property was recognised. They also acquired the right to divorce. Mothers were given priority over the fathers to decide issues concerning their children. But women were completely denied political rights. They were refused citizenship, the right to vote, the right to be elected or the right to serve on jury. The system of women's education also could not be improved. They could not even sit in the Tibunaux de Famille which settled family disputes. The reforms they won were, however, short-lived. With the coming of the Napoleonic Code, not only were most of these swept away, but much stricter legislation was clammed upon them. As far as the working women were concerned,

> [H]ow could she assess the revolution except by examining her wrecked household; by reference to children aborted or born dead, by her own sterility, by the disappearance of her few sticks of furniture, by the crumbling of the years of effort to hold the frail family economy together and what could her conclusion be except that the price paid for putative liberty had been far too high?[173]

Why were the women's movements not a complete success? The main reason was the ambivalence of the women themselves. As already discussed, exigencies of their harsh daily lives did not allow majority of sans-culotte and peasant women much room to demand for more than the meeting of their day-to-day needs. Political status was of least priority to women of this category. Even those women who were militant among them, preferred to play at best a supportive role to that of men. The Republican women of the Marches Section made this very clear when they lent their support to the Constitution which their menfolk had sworn to defend. The women of Epinay, for example, said, "…it took stronger arms than ours to defeat the enemies of the Constitution; our weakness has prevented us from taking part in this Revolution."[174] The aristocratic women were entrenched in their own niche from which they never stepped out to press for women's rights. Even revolutionary women like Madame Roland or Madame de Stael never came forward to participate in public politics. The bourgeois women mostly, except a few, remained content in their private, secluded lives. Also, the revolutionary women found support among very few prominent men of the revolution. Marquis de Condorcet, Theodore Hippel and others were rare exceptions. The highly revered philosophes spoke against their political activities. As a result, while "revolutionary feminism began in a burst of enthusiasm, its unpopularity, its own mistakes, and the blissful incomprehension and dogmatism of its opponents combined to obliterate it."[175]

Nonetheless, once cannot deny that the part played by women, if not anything else, succeeded in planting them firmly at the centre of the revolutionary mind. Monica Juneja[176] shows how gender played a key role in conveying the message and implications of the revolution; how feminine images and icons were used to symbolise what after all the revolution stood for and the changes it brought about. The **revolutionary iconography** was thereby a gendered process. And this indeed was highly paradoxical. Because, astonishingly enough, women came to represent a revolution which had summarily rejected them as individuals with rational, legitimate claims. In other words, iconography and imagery of women have been extensively pressed forth as the instrument of expression of the mentalite of a revolution which had blatantly ignored the question of gender identity and individuality—a complete contradiction.

In the ancien regime, all symbols centred round the King, his body, palace, court, etc. The revolution, as a challenge to the monarchy had to develop its own symbols—symbol of free men in a democratic republic. The **Rococo style** was a predominant form of art since the mid-18th century. The 1730s represented the height of Rococo development in France. It emphasised on an intricate, ornate, decorative, colourful design, insisting on asymmetrical curves and natural patterns on light-hearted and erotic themes. The bourgeois public sphere while opposing the cultural practices of the absolutist era, sought to reject the Rococo style and develop technique and symbols of its own. New icons and art forms had to be invented to represent this new era. The symbols adopted by the revolution were simpler, straight-forward and transparent, stripped of the artificiality, ornamentation and duplicity of the symbolic language of the ancien regime. This was an influence of Rousseau who always emphasised on transparency.

Female allegory was adopted as the emblem of revolutionary art forms signifying radical political concepts. This was obviously a contradiction which possibly implied, argues Lynn Hunt, a clear-cut rejection of the age-old patriarchal model.[177] The figure of **Marianne**, the Goddess of Liberty, came to represent Liberty and Reason during the French Revolution. A Marianne is portrayed as the bust of a resolute woman wearing a Phrygian cap. The new seal of the State under the National Convention in 1792 depicted Liberty as a woman figure holding a spear with a **Phrygian cap** on its top. According to Maurice Agulthon, Catholicism made Marianne figures easily acceptable to the French public.[178] Monica Juneja alludes to a different reason, asserting that male forms always resented "anonymity and universality", while females, mostly residing beyond public structures "could lend themselves more easily to the representation of abstract notions."[179] Moreover, fundamental elements of the French Revolution like **Liberty**, **Equality**, **Fraternity**, **Justice**, **Law** could be best alluded through **feminine figuration**. She provides a long list of such figures—*La Liberte* (Liberty) *L'amour de la Liberte* (The love for Liberty), *La Liberte Triomphe et Detruit les Abus* (Liberty triumphs and destroys Abuses), *La Liberte ou la mort* (Liberty or Death), *Mere Republicaine allaitant son enfant* (Republican

Mother nursing her infant), *La nature* (Nature), *L'Egalite* (Equality), etc., are some of the prominent engravings in which the central themes are in female forms.[180] Almost the same view is echoed by Marina Warner, according to whom, Liberty was depicted as female because of woman's detachment from politics. As she writes, "a symbolised female presence both gives and takes value and meaning in relation to actual women, and contains the potential for affirmation not only of women themselves but of the general good they might represent."[181]

FIG. 1.11: Symbol of Égalité (Equality) in the French Revolution

Art and Culture in the French Revolution: Democratisation of Polity and Academies

The French Revolution brought about profound transformation in the life, society and body-politic of the people of France. The consequences of this revolution were epoch-making. They were evident in every field—politics, society, religion, law, literature, architecture, sculpture, painting, festivals, music. From these gigantic changes emerged a new era with a new culture. According to Emmet Kennedy, "The society and culture that replaced the Revolution were in some respects immeasurably richer, more efficient, more variegated, if more confused, than they had been."[182]

The Political Culture after the French Revolution

Historians have pondered seriously over the origins of this culture. Daniel Mornet, Keith Michael Baker and Roger Chartier have explained it in different but somewhat overlapping terms. These historians engaged themselves primarily in elaborate and lengthy discussion of the political culture of the French Revolution. Daniel Mornet's *Les Origins Intellectuelles de la Revolution Francaise* talks of a close connection between dissemination of ideas from about the middle of the 18th century and the outbreak of the French Revolution. The underlying thesis of **Mornet**'s book is that it was ideas that determined the French Revolution and its culture. He considered political issues to be important, but it was the Enlightenment which eventually drew them out and organised their consequences. In **Roger Chartier**'s view, this was nothing more than a mere teleological analysis which interpreted an event in relation to its outcome and an outcome in relation to the event. Therefore, if we say the Enlightenment caused a revolution, it would be equally apt to say that the revolution invented the Enlightenment. So, Chartier looks for something more than intellectual matters to explain the origins of the French Revolution. He not only explores the intellectual thoughts that have been put forth by the intelligentsia, but also takes into account "unmediated representations" that is, how people read, discussed and exchanged well-elaborated thoughts. These he called **cultural origins**. Chartier, therefore, went beyond **intellectual origins** of Mornet, examined, and included the impact of these thoughts on the minds of the people, on means of public exchange and communication, education process, modes of sociability etc. in his study. He referred to this form of exchange, discussion and representation as '**discourse**'. The term 'discourse' was borrowed by both Chartier and Keith Michael Baker from Foucault. Chartier added a political dimension to discourse and he searched not for culture per se, but **political culture**.[183] Although he considered Mornet's interpretation inadequate and added his own views to it, Chartier conceded, that a study of history, stripped of teleology would be an endless inventory of disconnected facts floating incoherently and aimlessly without any hypothesis to frame. So, whether we like it or not, we have to tread through the path chalked out by Mornet, trying to connect the cause and effect.

Chartier had endeavoured to replace intellectual origins with cultural origins which took into account political realities and political action. These political activities could follow two models. The first, also known as the **Cochin-Francois model** (contemplated by Augustin Cochin and Francois Furet), identified organisation of various associations like the Jacobin Club, the Cordelier Club, the Enragés, etc., who espoused egalitarianism and democracy. The second model, called the **Kant–Habermas model** (projected by Emmanuel Kant and Jürgen Habermas) introduced the concept of a public space like salons, cafes, clubs, etc., which sponsored free and open discussions and sometimes catapulted into formation of political parties. This public space presupposed an autonomous, free sovereign republic. Both the models, however, led to one common end— they created a new political culture.

The political culture of the French Revolution, as explained by Chartier, had certain characteristic features. It is important to note, he explained, that perfect harmony did not always prevail between the actions and the discourse governing them. Discordances often existed between them, and cultural origins stemmed from these discordances. In other words, the discourse, action as well as discordance—all taken together— shaped the political culture of the French Revolution. The **discordances** were as follows.

First, Chartier borrowed his concept of political public sphere from Habermas who distinguished between '**public authority**', that is, State power and '**public sphere**' denoting a space where individuals met for discussion and exchange of ideas removed from the influence of the State machinery. However, discordance lay in the fact that the 'public sphere' was not public in the true sense of the term, as it clearly excluded the common people from it because of their lack of ability to participate in critical debate.[184]

Second, Chartier also refers to Immanuel Kant for his ideas on the '**public**' and the '**people**'. Kant has projected the public space as a medium used by some scholarly private individuals to communicate their erudite thoughts to an unspecified group of listeners or readers whom he refers to as "a society of world citizens". The 'private', on the other hand, was a group or institution with limited, particular interests like the State or the Church. But like Habermas, Kant's assumption of a universal audience or "society of world citizens" remained extremely limited to a handful of people who could read, write, comprehend or publish. "The 'people', that is the majority of the population, were thus excluded from the 'public'."[185]

Third, it was postulated that in the public sphere, every citizen was welcome and every participant was equal. In that sense, the new political sphere transcended all distinctions between orders of the ancient regime and was truly democratic in character. But, for all practical purposes, only a tiny section of the population—the men of letters—could claim access to that sphere. They were the ones who constituted a kind of 'tribunal' and sat on judgement on different solemn issues of the day.

The discordances, along with discourse and action, constructed a new political culture, which was as Chartier observes, "recognised as a novelty by contemporaries in that it transferred the seat of authority from the will of the King alone, who decided without appeal and in secret, to the judgement of an entity embodied in no institution, which debated publicly and was more sovereign than the sovereign."[186]

Keith Michael **Baker** felt the necessity to reconstitute the political culture

> within which the creation of the revolutionary language of 1789 became possible…. this political culture began to emerge in the 1750s and 1760s and its essential elements were already clear by the beginning of Louis XVI's reign. In the course of these two decades, politics broke out of the absolutist mould. *Opinion* became *opinion publique*: not a social function but a political category, the *tribunal du public*, the court of final appeal for monarchical authority, as for its critics.[187]

He found the efforts to establish connection between 'ideas' and the French Revolution by scholars preceding him as inadequate. **Francois Furet**, for example, considered "revolutionary consciousness" as "offspring of *philosophie*". But, according to Baker, the influence of *philosophie* was highly manipulable, sensitive and was constantly changing though varying interpretations and therefore required much deeper analysis. Daniel Mornet had made a distinction between intellectual causes and political causes. Baker disapproved of such an outlook because in his perception, these two were inextricably intertwined and could hardly be separated. The intelligentsia wrote keeping the political realities in view and the political activist would like to fortify himself with the ideas of the philosophes. Not that Mornet did not realise it. Moreover, Baker felt, the exact intellectual ideas influencing specific political actions were not clearly elaborated in his study. Baker, therefore, endeavoured to overcome these shortcomings in terms of three basic forms of discourse. What he did was to disintegrate some virtues that were earlier vested in the King and to provide them with forms of discourse. He identified three principal discourses:

> (*i*) judicial discourse emphasising justice;
> (*ii*) political discourse emphasising will and
> (*iii*) administrative discourse emphasising reason.

Justice was the main instrument of opponents of royal despotism. Will symbolised Rousseau's General Will or will of the people. And reason meant growth of civilisation and progress of civil society.[188]

Baker observed, "The emergence, elaboration and interpretation of these three discourses, I think it can be argued, defined the political culture that emerged in France in the later part of the 18th century and provided the ideological framework that gave explosive meaning to the events that destroyed the Old Regime."[189]

Political culture of the French Revolution, therefore, has been defined in different ways by different scholars. What then do we mean by this political culture? All in all, political culture is the sum-total of all the transformation that the revolution has brought about in the realm of State, authority, politics and royal power. In short, it can be said that the revolution undoubtedly metamorphosed the age-old concepts of the ancien regime about kingship and governance and firmly established the transition from absolutism and royal will to republicanism based upon popular will or popular sovereignty. "The authority and mystical qualities formerly vested in the King as an image of God Himself were transferred to the collective people."[190] This was the crux of the new political culture. And new culture revealed new mentalite (mentality). This had its impact on every aspect of life in France. Everything changed—themes and style of architecture, sculpture, painting, music, drama, festivals—everything. All these now revolved round the new mentalite. We will see how.

The New Religious Culture

Along with State and politics, it was the field of religion which witnessed significant upheaval in its thought and structure. A new religious culture emerged. In the ancien regime, the Roman Catholic Church of France owning one-tenth of the land of the nation, enjoying tithe on all products of the soil, equipped with its own administration and its own system of law, represented by a periodical assembly, was an institution by itself. An onslaught on its authority was directed for the first time when the Constituent Assembly began a systematic clipping of its power through the various pieces of legislation formulated during the two years regime (1789–1791). The first blow was dealt on 11 August 1789 when tithes were abolished. On 2 November 1789, Church property were nationalised and was used as the backing for the assignats. On 13 February 1790, monastic vows were forbidden and, importantly, all ecclesiastic orders and congregations were dissolved. On 19 April 1790, all remaining Church property were transferred to the State. A major jolt came with the formulation of the Civil Constitution of the clergy on 12 July 1790. By it, the entire clergy was supposed to swear an oath of loyalty to the Constitution. This dealt a cleavage within the main body of the clergy which now became divided into the **constitutional clergy** and the **non-juring or refractory clergy**. Only seven bishops and about one-half of the parish priests took the oath. Under the provisions of the Civil Constitution of the clergy, enfranchised citizens would elect bishops and parish priests and the State would pay the clergy's wages. This severely dampened the position of the clergy. The internal structure of the Catholic Church in France was fundamentally altered, as also was the relationship between Church and State.

The final blow came with the establishment of the cult of reason—an atheistic belief system—intended as a replacement for Christianity during the revolution. Under this, no gods were to be worshipped at all. Reason alone was to be worshipped. Thus began the dechristianisation of France. The fundamental concepts were initiated by radical revolutionaries like Hebert, Momoro, Chaumette, Fouche. Destruction of churches, breaking of idols, etc. followed. The cult of reason, however, did not become very popular in France. A large section of the population, especially the peasants in the countryside, deeply resented the desecration of their Church which was so close to their hearts. Many in protest started joining counter-revolutionary forces.

The widespread rejection of the cult of reason as well as lack of divinity frightened Robespierre. He formerly discarded the cult and its proponents and introduced in its place his own concept of religion—the **cult of the**

Supreme Being. On 7 May 1794, it was announced before the National Convention to be the State religion of the new French Republic.

The new position of the Church radically altered the religious life of France. A new religious culture of anti-clericalism emerged. It divided the population of France down the middle. While one section of the people joined the revolutionaries in denouncing the Church and thereby vandalising Church properties and humiliating the clergy, another section, on the other hand, clearly expressed their bitterness against this anti-clerical attitude and rallied round the Church and their local priest as earlier. Such a situation and such dichotomy in the religious sphere, France had never experienced before. It was clear that nothing was eternal, nothing infallible, nothing sacrosanct. This was the impact the French Revolution left on the religious life of France.

Cultural Institutions after the Revolution

The effect of the revolution on traditional French cultural institutions was equally noteworthy. Some important cultural institutions of the ancien regime were academies, masonic lodges, salons and the press. From the 17th century to the early part of the 20th century, artistic production in France was controlled by the **academies**. They were the critiques as well as protectors of all cultural activities. Royal academies were created by the Bourbons between 1635 when Cardinal Richlieu founded the Academie Francaise, and 1776 when Societe Royal de Medecine was formed. The Academie de Peinture et de Sculpture was founded by Cardinal Mazarin 1648 and was soon followed by many other such academies like the Academie Royale des inscriptions et Medailles in 1663 (renamed the Academie Royale des inscriptions et belles-lettres) in 1716; the Academie Royale des Sciences in 1666; the Academie d'Opera in 1669 etc. The monarchy not only chartered and patented them but also appointed its personnel and organised its elections. In 1793, during the French Revolution the academies were suppressed, only to be revived under the Directory. The primary reason behind the repression of the academies was their predominance by the people of privilege, which provoked the ire of the people who were excluded. Talented scientists like Jean-Paul Marat, Franz Mesmer, Pascal, Journalists like Simon-Nicolas-Henri Linguet, painters like Saint-Germaine Drouais were left out. The whole system was deeply resented by Abbe Gregoire, Jacques-Louis David and others.

On 8 August 1793, Abbe Gregoire, the constitutional Bishop of Blois and a prominent revolutionary leader, brought before the Convention a proposal for a decree on the 'Abolition of the Academies'. It was seconded by David in the Convention on the same day. Abbe Gregoire declared that academies should go for the general good for the development of science and letters.

Masonic lodges were another institution which formed an integral part of the cultural life of France in the ancien regime. A Masonic lodge is the basic organisational unit of Freemasonry. *Freemasonry* is one of the world's oldest secular fraternal societies. It is a worldwide organisation based on the principle of the fatherhood of God and the brotherhood of man. It seeks to make good men better and thereby make the world a better place to live in. Masonic organisations throughout the world are engaged in many philanthropic and charitable projects. The first Masonic lodge in France was founded by some Englishmen in Paris "around the year 1725."[191] "Many members of the Convention were Masons, but so were many émigrés. The Masons of Dijon were mostly *parlementaires* and feudal seigneurs reluctant to see the death of a regime under which they had prospered."[192] In reality, there were Freemasons both in Republican as well as monarchical camps. Even so, they were forced to close their activities during the Reign of Terror between 1793 and 1794.

As we have discussed earlier, the **salons** played a significant role in French cultural life before the coming of the revolution. They formed the medium of cultural exchange among the social elite, intellectuals and literary figures—women as well as men—who visited them. The ladies of the house played a key role not only in entertaining the distinguished guests but also in participating and conducting discussions and in initiating ideas. Ideas of the Enlightenment largely shaped women's involvement in the salons. They did not encourage revolution in any overt way, but the ideas generated by their pamphlets, journals, etc., might have left an impact. Voltaire, Rousseau, d'Alembert, Diderot found eager listeners and supporters in the salons. Towards the middle of the 18th century, a shift in both subject matter and tone began to characterise the enlightened discourse of the elegant salons. In the words of Augustin Cochin: "mockery replaced gaiety, and politics pleasure; the game became a career, the festivity a ceremony, the clique the Republic of Letters."[193]

After 1789, these cultural hubs of the old regime were slowly relegated to the background, and they ultimately disappeared. During the Directory, a few were revived and some more during the Restoration. Finally, they were eclipsed by the **bourgeois cercles** where businessmen and entrepreneurs met to discuss economic and public affairs.

An important pillar of the cultural life of any nation is **the press** which like all absolute monarchs the French kings also sought to control. The concept of freedom of the press was unknown in France and was borrowed by the philosophes for the first time from England. Censorship—a regular phenomenon—was imposed through different agencies like the Parlement of Paris, the lieutenant general of Paris police force and some prominent men of letters. Journals, newspapers, periodicals, etc., were strictly regulated by the monarchy. This curbed their growth substantially. All these practices were radically changed under the revolution. Article 11 of the *Declaration of the Rights of Man and of the Citizen* 1789 of the Constituent Assembly proclaimed the freedom of the press: "The free circulation of thoughts and opinions is one of the most precious rights of man. Each citizen can therefore speak, write and print freely within the limits of the abuse of freedom prescribed by the law." This law remained in vogue till the National Convention on 30 March 1793 decreed that

> Anyone proved guilty of having written or printed texts proposing the re-establishment of the monarchy in France or the dissolution of the National Convention will appear before the Revolutionary Tribunal and be sentenced to death. Peddlers, sellers and distributors of prohibited prints will be sentenced to three months in prison if they give the names of the authors, and to two years in chains, if they refuse to do so.[194]

This new print culture of the revolutionary era, however, could not remain consistent. On 24 July 1789, the temporary Committee of the Commune of Paris declared that "all peddlers or distributors of defamatory prints…in which the name of the author or printer does not appear, will be sentenced to prison."[195] Numerous peddlers were arrested. There was, at the same time, an unprecedented outburst of intellectual activity. From one newspaper in 1788, the *Journal de Paris*, the number of newspapers proliferated to 184 in 1789 and 335 in 1790.[196] Everyday from early morning, fresh information flooded the streets of France. Camille Desmoulins observed, "newspapers rain down every morning."

This **print revolution** formed an essential feature of the culture of the French Revolution. As a result, number of printing press multiplied in order to keep pace with the rising demand. A mushroom growth of small and big printing shops took place. To cater to popular demand, for example, Marat gave his newspaper *L'Ami du Peuple,* to at least three printers.[197] At the same time, despite the solemn proclamation of 1789 on freedom of the press, clandestine or anti-revolutionary prints continued to be suppressed with zeal. In the first two years of the revolution, for instance, the Municipality of Paris, scared of popular revolt, began an organised onslaught against ultra-royalist or counter-revolutionary publications. Spearheaded by **La Fayette**, chief of the National Guards and **Bailly**, the Mayor of Paris, all forms of extremist publication were denounced. They attacked, through municipal decrees, the peddlers, booksellers and printers and even journalists. Some of the extreme left journals were Marat's *L'Ami du Peuple*, Hebert's sensational journals like *Le Pere Duchesne* and *La lantern Magique*. The most potent ultra royalist journal was *Actes des Apotres* edited by Rivarol. *Jean Bart ou je m'en fous* was a violent leaflet equally noteworthy.

Things, however, changed from the end of 1791 as a result of vehement protests of the Cordelier Club led by Danton against the attack on the press. In January 1792, Danton was appointed Assistant Deputy Public Prosecutor of the Commune and an atmosphere of total freedom of the press followed. It was, however, very short-lived and a radical change occurred after the storming of the Tuilleries on 10 august 1792. The fall of the monarchy was now complete. Strong anti-monarchical sentiments prevailed and the result was the **September Massacre**s. A special Tribunal was established on the 17th August to punish the people found guilty of crimes committed on the 10th. Severe blows were dealt at the royalist journalists. Du Rozoy, the editor of *Gazette de Paris*, was condemned to death on 29th August.[198] The entire printing world of France was subjected to relentless restrictions. *Freedom of the press was rigorously choked*. Carla Hesse observes, "Between 1792 and 1793, the number of journals published in Paris dropped by one-half, from 216 to 113."[199] The Reign of Terror resulted in the guillotining of a number of printers and booksellers suspected to be royalists like Gattey, Massot, Benard, Widow Lesclapart, Printer Girouard Momoro, and journalists like Brissot, Gorsas, Carra, Duplain, Jacques Roux, Hebert, Desmoulins etc. However, revolutionaries like Brissot, Momoro, Hebert, Jacques Roux, Desmoulins were guillotined not only because they were journalists but primarily because their political roles and ideological beliefs did not conform to those of Robespierre.

After the fall of Robespierre, restrictions on publication were withdrawn, though royalist or counter-revolutionary substances continued to be suppressed. But subsidies were sanctioned by the Convention for patriotic works for political and educational purposes. Republican newspapers like *Feuille Villageoise*, scientific treatises, school textbooks, almanacs, etc., were encouraged.[200] The regime under the Directory from 1795 re-established freedom of the press and helped the revival of the book trade.[201]

However, notwithstanding the provision of freedom of press promised by the Constituent Assembly in 1789, the stifling of the press and the violent excesses that went on in the subsequent years was clearly reminiscent of the controls imposed by the ancient regime. Assertion of control over the press was a common element between the old regime and the revolutionary era. The difference was that unlike the monarchy, the revolution carried out all its oppression in the name of popular sovereignty, in the name of replacement of a dwindling, tyrannical monarchy by a popular democratic republic. They sought a democracy through the most undemocratic means. Nevertheless, the vast quantity of printed material that was produced itself constituted a revolution. As Lise Andries said,

> The years 1789–1799 were a time of an extraordinary cultural revolution. The common people, the previously silent majority, won for the first time the right to speak and write. They expressed themselves passionately through pamphlets and journals, as well as a huge amount of petitions and memoirs, many of which were addressed to the National Assembly. Everything became politicized: readings, songs, theatre performances, festivals and celebrations. After the fall of the monarchy in 1792, revolutionary culture took a new step. Every aspect of daily life was meant to obliterate the symbols of the old regime. Names of babies, of streets and towns were changed. Bakers were even prohibited from cooking the traditional "gateau des rois" (cake for the King) on the 6th of January. New measures of space and time were also invented. The revolutionary calendar beginning in "Vendemiaire year I" was launched in September 1793. It is in such an exceptional context that the radicalization of the printing trade must be understood. Journals and pamphlets became both the means of personal commitment and the powerful instruments of mass political education.[202]

TRENDS IN ART AND ARCHITECTURE

The same trend is noticeable in different forms of art—architecture, sculpture, painting, music, theatre. In fact, a new style—**neo-classicism**—emerged to mark the distinctive features of revolutionary art, as distinguished from the **Rococo style** of the preceding era. Neo-classicism is a *revival of the styles and spirit of classic antiquity* inspired directly from the classical period, and was rather a reaction against the frivolity of the Rococo art, resulting in great over-simplification, perhaps to symbolise the sombre mood of the occasion, that is the revolution. In the place of decoration and ornamentation of the Rococo art, it ushered in gravity, balance, proportion and order. The themes of the two art styles were also different. While Rococo emphasised upon court grandeur, aristocratic romance, richness of design and insisted on intricate, colourful, to some extent cluttered motifs, neo-classicism excelled in simplicity and plain exterior, reflecting upon different events and personalities of the revolution. The subject matter of art also changed. From mostly traditional court scenes, portrayal of aristocratic life, imaging royal grandeur, building palatial structures, embellished gardens, the artists shifted to the depiction of life of common people, the sans-culottes, symbolising special events of the revolution like the fall of Bastille, construction or representation of republican icons etc.

In the field of painting, a prominent progenitor of neo-classicism was **Comte de Caylus** (or Count Caylus). He specialised in **encaustic painting** (painting with wax colours fixed by heat). Although he died in 1765, much before the outbreak of the French revolution, he and one of his close collaborators, **Comte Joseph-Marie Vien** left an indelible mark on French painting. As the director of the Academy of Painting and Sculpture, the latter revived the portrayal of historical events. He had a tremendous influence on his pupil **Jaques-Louis David**, a pre-eminent painter of revolutionary France. Being a friend of Maximilian Robespierre, it was David who dominated the art of the republic. His paintings on revolutionary themes, however, had begun long before his association with Robespierre. In 1784, he painted *Oath of the Horatii*, a piece based on Rousseau's *Social Contract*. David's *Oath of the Tennis Court* was based on the bitter conflict between the King and the Third Estate. David was an ardent supporter of the republican spirit and his love for the republic was clearly evident in his painting *The Lictors Bring to Brutus the Bodies of His Sons*. This unique piece of art along with his other works had a deep impact on the minds of the people of France. Perhaps, David's most renowned masterpiece was the *Death of Marat*, 1793, which had an intensely powerful impact on the revolution. It is "a moving testimony to what can be achieved when an artist's political convictions are directly manifested in his work."[203]

Fig. 1.12: *The Death of Marat* (1793) by Jacques-Louis David

Another well-known painter of the time was **Hubert Robert** noted for his landscape paintings. He was also known as *Robert des Ruines* for his picturesque depiction of ruins. His *Demolition of the Bastille* is famous for its vivid imaging and grace. He also designed gardens and painted for the royal palace. He was successively appointed Designer of the King's gardens, Keeper of the King's pictures.[204] He was briefly imprisoned during the French Revolution but continued to paint. As Diderot commented,

> The effect of these compositions, good or bad, is to leave us in a sweet melancholy. We fix our gaze on the debris of an *arc de triomphe*, a portico, a pyramid, a temple, a palace, and we return into ourselves. We anticipate the ravages of time, and our imagination disperses over the earth the very edifices we inhabit. For an instant, solitude and silence reign all around us; we alone remain of a whole nation which is no longer; and there is the first line of the poetics of ruins.[205]

The most famous revolutionary architect was the neo-classicist **Etienne-Louis Boullee**. His neo-classicism was a fusion of the **Doric order**, the oldest and simplest of the three main orders of classical Greek architecture, characterised by heavy fluted columns with plain, saucer-shaped capitals and no base, with the ancient Egyptian architecture characterised by massive structures with sloping walls with few openings and its elementary forms of cylinders, cubes, cones, spheres, etc. Boullee preferred geometrical forms and the circle, in his view, was most pleasing to the eye. Therefore, perhaps, his most famous structure—**Cenotaph for Issac Newton**—is circular in shape. He designed the Opera House, the National Library and also the National Assembly Hall. A supporter of the revolution, he, however, hated the Terror, and was condemned to be a royalist.

Other important architects of the revolutionary period were **Claude-Nicolas Ledoux** and **Jean-Jacques Lequeu**—both neo-classicists. It was Ledoux who built the **Wall of the Farmers-General** around Paris. Along with Boullee, they were the pioneers of a new architectural style which highlighted first, the neo-classical model as opposed to the Rococo techniques of the preceding era, and second, were an expression of love for the revolution in the buildings which embodied revolutionary concepts. As Emmet Kennedy puts it, "For all these men, the new simplicity in architecture was to serve the newly discovered simplicity of human nature. Architecture consciously mirrored in space what was cherished in people's hearts: liberty, equality, fraternity."[206]

In **sculpture**, the most prominent personality was **Jean-Antoine Houdon**. He is famous for his portrait busts and statues of philosophers, inventors and political figures of the Enlightenment. His works were on Denis Diderot, Benjamin Franklin, Jean-Jacques Rousseau, Voltaire, George Washington, Thomas Jefferson, Louis XVI, Napoleon Bonaparte Mirabeau, etc. He was more closely linked to the dilemmas of Louis XVI and the philosophical concepts of Voltaire, Rousseau, and the economic principles of Mirabeau, than to the radical bloodthirsty ideas of the Jacobins. "He had participated more in the wave that brought in the French Revolution than in the current that carried the old regime out."[207]

Further, the revolutionary period witnessed the creation by artists, known and anonymous, of several engravings, mostly coloured, which metamorphosed completely the theme and pattern of prevailing art forms. Some of these we have already discussed earlier. The change in *mentalite* or collective cultural attitude effected before and during the revolution was successfully captured in these unique pieces of art. A new language of art was to be found for the expression of the new mentalite in which men were to be cast into the mould of radical republicanism. The Rococo style was no longer tenable in the new world where art and politics were being melted together in the crucible of revolutionary transformation. The simpler convictions of neo-classicism came with far greater charm, appeal and adequacy. In the frantic search for new icons and images, feminine figurines seemed most acceptable. Monica Juneja calls it a strange paradox that female allegory was used to represent the political concepts of a revolution that categorically excluded women from all its agenda.[208] Historians have explained it in different ways. Monica Juneja gives a list of such pieces where female figures have been used to express the new philosophy. *L'amour de la Liberte*,[209] an anonymous engraving of 1792 depicts an angel holding the fasces. In Antoin Carre's coloured engraving of a drawing by Pierre Thomas Le Clerc—*La Liberte*, 1793[210]—presents liberty in the form of an attractive woman trampling upon a multi-headed hydra of despotism. In another anonymous coloured engraving—*Le Liberte*, 1790[211]—liberty is represented as a beautiful young woman standing with a pike at the top of which cap of liberty is perched, on her left hand, and her right hand resting casually on a tablet of the Declaration of Rights of Man and Citizen. *Mere republicaine allaitant son enfant*,1793,[212] an anonymous engraving, shows a young mother nursing her child who wears the republican cockade. The anonymous coloured engraving *La Nature*,[213] symbolises a mother nursing simultaneously a black and a white infant, indicating thereby the egalitarianism of a mother or the nation. In the famous engraving, *L'Egalite*, 1793,[214] by Jean-Louis Allais on the drawing of Alexandre-Evariste Fragonard, equality is presented in the form of a goddess, flanked by two other goddesses. In an oil canvas by Jean—Baptiste Regnault, *La Liberte ou la mort* in 1794 also liberty has been depicted as a young, pretty woman.

These are only a few of the engravings out of the long list elaborated in Monica Juneja's scholarly essay 'Imaging the Revolution'. They underline two very important elements. First, position of women seems glorified through these pieces of art where all the sublime concepts of the revolution were inextricably associated with and highlighted through female figurines. So, although the revolution denied them any political right, their importance was to some extent recognised in art forms of the time. This is in sharp contrast to some of the engravings of *ancient regime* where, on the contrary, the dual nature of women was revealed. An anonymous engraving of the 17th century—*Le Miroir de la Vie et de la Mort* (The Mirror of Life and Death)—suggests how woman tempts man through her physical beauty and sexuality and thereby drags him to the abyss of

FIG. 1.13: Symbols of Justice, Liberté (Liberty), Égalité (Equality) and Fraternité (Fraternity)

degradation. Another anonymous engraving of the 17th century,—*La vraye femme, ange al'Eglise et diable a la maison*—(True Woman, Angel in the Church, Devil at Home), is a unique one portraying the devil on the one side and the angel on the other, suggesting that they were the two sides of the same coin. This duality found expression in Diderot's essay *Sur les femmes* (On Women). However, canvases and engravings of the revolutionary period represented them in another light. Second, they were mostly based on one central theme, that is, the principles and events of the revolution.

In this connection, it should be mentioned that the greatest contribution of the revolution to art and culture was the creation of the famous and world's most visited museum, **Louvre** or **Musée du Louvre**, opened on 10 August 1793. Initially, it was a royal palace of the Bourbons. It served as an art gallery of paintings and sculptures and housed several artists like David, Vien, Boucher. It was merged with the Royal Palace of Tuileries by the Constituent Assembly by a decree of 26 May 1791: "The united Louvre and the Tuileries will be destined for the re-union of all the monuments of the sciences and arts." The invasion of Tuileries on 10 August 1792, the overthrow of the monarchy and confiscation of royal property resulted in the conversion of the palace into a museum. The day after the attack on Tuileries, that is 11th August, a commission was organised for the collection of all pieces of art belonging to the royal family, the Church and the émigrés. The opening of the museum was fixed on the first anniversary of the fall of Tuileries, 10 August 1793.

In the field of **music**, there were in the revolutionary period a few extraordinary musician-composers who have left an indelible mark on the music of their times and also for posterity. **Andre Gretry** composed music and operas for the revolution. His most famous opera comic *Richard de Coeur* the songs of which were extremely popular and widely sung. As Emmet Kennedy writes, "Gretry reflected on the connections between music, nationality and sensibilite."[215] Although a lover of sweet melody, he switched over to loud music and colourful attire for his opera dedicated to the republican spirit, *Guillaume Tall* written in 1791.

Luigi Cherubini was an Italian composer who spent most of his working life in France. Beethoven regarded Cherubini as the greatest of his contemporaries. During the revolutionary period he wrote three operas: *Ladoiska* in 1791, *Eliza* in 1794 and *Medee* in 1797, which received tremendous popular applause. Later, Cherubini was inclined to the composition of Church music and attained huge acclaim. In 1815 London's Royal Philharmonic Society commissioned to write a symphony, an overture and a composition for chorus and orchestra. He composed *Requiem in C minor* on the anniversary of the execution of King Louis XVI. It was a great success.

Etienne-Henry Mehul, another renowned composer of the age of the French Revolution composed operas devoted to the cause of the revolution, as well as duets like *Gardez-vous de la jalousie* which was a story of a shipwreck in the pre-romantic genre. Taken together, these musicians brought about an unprecedented musical revolution of the highest order. According to Rousseau and others, the music in the time of Louis XVI was plain and unnatural. It "lacked spontaneity and became controlled and measured." From the 1750s, a musical revolution started in France. It was undoubtedly the contribution of none other than Queen Marie Antoinette. She had invited and brought musicians like Gluck, Niccolo Piccinni, Antonio Sacchini, Luigi Cherubini to Paris and they truly contributed to the enrichment of the music of France. The influence of the Italian musicians was deep, and they soon came to loggerheads with the French musicians. But this quarrel since the 1750s led to the unfolding of a greater development of the 1790s rendering the culture evolving from the revolution much richer and much more splendid.

In the revolutionary period, a new kind of literature, in tune with the mentalite of the Reign of Terror, emerged and became extraordinarily popular. These came to be known as '**Black Novel**'. In the pre-revolutionary period too, a similar type of literature had become popular. Its author was **Francois-Thomas de Baculard d'Arnaud** who "believed in waking his readers with 'jolts of terror'" and was a friend of Voltaire. His novels like *Epreuves du Sentiment* (Ordeals of Sentiment) 1772, *Amants malheureux, Ou le Comte de Comminges* (Unhappy Lovers, or the Count of Comminges, an adaptation of Claudine Guérin de Tencin's 1735 novel *Mémoires du comte de Comminge*, considered one of the earliest French Gothic novels) and his *Epoux Malheureux* (Unhappy Spouses) were bestsellers and were printed several times. It was the age of *sensibilite* which was a curious combination of **sweetness**, **horror and terror** and the literature of the time fully reflected that. Best examples were novels like *Paul et Virginie* by Bernardin de Saint-Pierre, 1787, and *Coelina, ou l'Enfant du Mystere,* 1799 by Ducray-Duminil. In the early 18th century, *sensibilite* stood for the soft and good emotions of the heart—sympathy, benevolence, tearfulness, compassion. At the end of the century, however, sensibilite absorbed some opposite attributes of human character as well—melancholy, death, terror, horror, cruelty, murder. This can be assumed to be the effects of the whirlwind of terror and massacre that swept over France in the last decade of the century. Ducray-Duminil's *Alexis, ou La Maisonette dans le bois,* 1789 and *Coelina, ou l'Enfant du mystere.* Jean-Francois Arnould-Mussot's *Heroine Americaine,* 1786, is a portrayal of the opposite emotions of human nature—deceit and betrayal in the male and sincerity and compassion in the female. The novels obsessed with such *sensibilite* were undoubtedly products of the revolution. Apart from black novel or roman noir another form of literature associated with over-dramatisation, loud music and quasi-miraculous interventions, were melodramas, the themes of which were assassinations, loot, plunder, terror. In fact, it would be more appropriate to call *Heroine Americaine* a melodramatic pantomime. **Melodramas** continued to dominate the world of fiction even in early 19th century, long after the revolution. As Emmet Kennedy writes, "Psychological terror outlived political terror."[216]

Sensibilite was also expressed in theatres. **Drama**, in the era before the French Revolution, was generally known as the bourgeois drama. It was so called because they depicted the pleasures and pain of ordinary people. Two important writers of the time, Mercier and Diderot dealt with problems and experiences, happiness and sorrow of ordinary people in day to day life. Mercier's *Du Theatre, Ou Nouvel Essai Sur L'art* emphasises this. Some of his other famous works are *L'An 2440, Mon Bonnet de Nuit*. Bourgeois sensibilite was expressed passionately in Diderot's *Le Fils Naturel,* 1757, and *Le Pere de famille,* 1758.

The theatres were divided into two classes—the elitist theatre from which common men were excluded, and small theatres which the upper classes never visited. The elitist theatres had monopoly over certain plays which could not be performed in other theatres. All these privileges were eliminated by the revolution. The **Chapelier Law** or **Loi le Chapelier** was a piece of legislation passed by the Constituent Assembly in June 1791 banning special protection and proclaiming free enterprise. It established equal rights for all theatres and operas and any theatre could perform any play. Moreover, to mark the coming of the revolution, the names of many prominent theatres were changed. For example, Comedie-Francaise became *Theatre de la Nation*. Theatre Francais was given the name *Theatre Francais de la Liberte et de l'Egalite*, and later, *Theatre de la Republique*.

FESTIVALS—REVOLUTIONARY AND RELIGIOUS

The revolution left its mark comprehensively on another important aspect of culture, that is, festivals. The type and pattern of festivals changed completely. In the *ancien regime*, the festivals revolved round the King and God. *Voeux du Roi* and *Fete Dieu,* therefore, were the main festivals during this time. They were marked by solemn processions of people of the higher order. These ceremonies were highly hierarchical and reflected the sharp class distinctions of the society. Even the colour and the texture of the cloth of the dresses were prescribed according to social rank.[217] There were popular festivals as well in which people of all social orders participated. One such was the Carnival which came in the month of February every year. People then participated together, danced, ate and drank to their heart's content and wandered through the streets wearing masks of animals or of some people of the upper order. A festivity in the name of Saint John was merrily celebrated in summer when the whole countryside was lit up to mark the occasion and community feasts were held. In late summer another religious ceremony—Feast of the Assumption of the Virgin—was observed. Further, there were some popular seasonal festivals celebrating harvests in autumn. In winter, *fete des fous* or *calendes* were observed and most importantly, the celebration of Christmas filled the entire nation with joy and excitement.

The revolution brought about a momentous shift of focus as far as the festivities throughout the nation were concerned. According to Rousseau, "…far from attaching the hearts of citizens to the State, Christianity, detaches them from it and from all earthly things."[218] The revolutionaries, inspired by Rousseau, created a religion divorced from Christianity. First the Cult of Reason initiated by Hebert, Momoro etc., to be replaced later by the Cult of the Supreme Being projected by Robespierre, revolutionised significantly the culture of the French Revolution. They wanted, apart from many other things, to replace the old festivals with new ones that will pronounce and highlight the fundamental concepts and principles of the revolution. The first celebration they introduced was the *Fete Federation de la 1790*. It was a remarkable event to celebrate the fall of Bastille which was a symbol of despotic rule and arbitrary imprisonment. The event took place on the *Champ de Mars* far outside Paris. A mass was celebrated by Charles Maurice de Talleyrand, former Bishop of Aurun. He had become the Bishop in 1789, the same year when he attended the Estates-General, strongly supported the anti-clericalism of the revolutionaries, helped in the writing of the *Declaration of the Rights of Man and of the Citizen* and was a proponent of the *Civil Constitution of the clergy*. The King took the oath to abide by the Constitution (which, however, came a year later). The celebration ended with a huge popular feast.

A funeral ceremony was organised in July 1791 to remove Voltaire's mortal remains to the Church of Saint-Genevieve that had been converted into a pantheon (building containing memorials of illustrious dead). Bodies of those men adorned the pantheon whom the Republic held in highest esteem as true sons of the soil—Voltaire, Rousseau, Mirabeau, Lepeletier, Marat.

Festival of Unity or reunion was observed on 10 August 1793 to commemorate the attack on the royal palace of Tuileries on 10 August 1792 and the consequent end of the monarchy. It was marked by a huge procession attended by people from all social orders and ending at Champ de Mars, signifying loyalty to the Republic as well as elimination of all social inequalities and discrimination.

Fete de la Raison or Festival of Reason was organised by Hebert and Momoro on 10 November 1793 to epitomise the cult of reason, the new Republican religion. Its most redeeming feature was the conversion of the Churches across France into Temples of Reason. The Christian altar was dismantled and an altar to Liberty was installed. "To Philosophy" was carved in stone on the doors of the cathedrals. A beautiful woman represented Liberty in order to avoid idolatory. A procession of musicians, soldiers, young girls wearing tricoloured ribbons reached the Cathedral of notre-Dame which, along with other Churches, was declared the Temple of Reason. A hymn to Liberty, composed by Chenier was sung. Disdain, however, has been expressed by historians over the way they behaved. Emmet Kennedy, for instance, does not think the Festival of Reason of having left "any impression of rationality on the memories of contemporary observers."[219] According to Louis-Sebastian Mercier, people were aghast to see the living woman, an opera singer, to replace God. It was a sheer scandal. Mercier was a famous French dramatist and writer whose masterpiece *Le nouveau Paris*, written in 1799, gives a clear picture, "if one wants to get some idea", Robert Darnton writes, "of how Paris looked, sounded, smelled, and felt on the eve of the Revolution."[220] Kennedy believes that most possibly it was the raucousness of the Festival of Reason which had led to Robespierre's opposition to de-Christianisation.[221] Mona Ozouf, however, saw a lot of similarity between the Festival of Reason and the Festival of the Supreme Being seven months later.

After the introduction of the new State religion on 7 May 1794, Robespierre declared that 8th June would be the first day of national celebration of the Supreme Being. The festival was organised by the artist Jacques-Louis David and took place around a man-made mountain built from cardboard, plaster and wood, on the National Gardens (the Tuileries). At the top was a statue of Hercules, representing the indomitable French people, and holding a figure of Liberty in his hand. Robespierre assumed full leadership of the event, declaring the fundamental concepts and practical utility of his new religion and delivered the keynote speech.

Several other aspects of human life were also proposed by Robespierre to be celebrated, like, youth, marriage, agriculture, Liberty, the aged. However, these were never enforced during his lifetime and came into vogue through the Law of 3 Brumaire IV (25 October 1795), an entirely new calendar replaced the Gregorian anno domini system. Its years dated from year 1 of the Republic (1793). The 10 months were named to match agricultural patterns like Germinal (month of the seed), Floreal (month of the flower), Messidor (month of the harvest). Under the rational new metric system, even time itself went decimal. Each hour had now 100 minutes, clocks followed 10 hour cycles and French people worked 10 days a week.

The festivals were many and diverse; Mona Ozouf collectively calls them 'revolutionary festivals', that is, *la fete revolutionnaire*. Because, notwithstanding all their diversities, she sees in them certain common, basic elements. They all originated from the same need and underlined the same principles. Therefore, they were all one. Their ultimate purpose was to replace the old religion dominated by the Church and clergy by new religious practices. In this they followed the principle of imitation and purge. After discarding old forms of worship, the revolutionaries suddenly felt a *horror vacui* or "abhorrence of the vacuum," They filled it up by borrowing substantially from Catholicism, antiquity and freemasonry. From Catholicism they borrowed catechisms, altars, tabernacles, sermons. They retained prayers, songs; that is why they introduced patriotic anthems and civic sermons. The godfather, whosoever it is, wearing the republican cockade, would moisten the lips of the new-born, and in funerals deliver the oration and sprinkle honey around the coffin. Priests would be chosen not from among celibates but from among family men. At the same time they took from antiquity as well because it was looked upon as a golden era of the ancient world in which liberty and equality co-existed. Festivals of classical antiquity—Greek boat and foot races, disc throwing, dancing al fresco—were adopted extensively.[222] They purged also considerably. Whatever seemed to them superstitious, orthodox and retrograde were extirpated.

Mona Ozouf,[223] in her essay on revolutionary festivals, organised images of festivals into two models—the first promulgated by historians favourable to revolutionary festivals and the second consisting of those who were not exactly kind towards them. The first category, composed of scholars like Michelet, Durkheim etc. generally praised their serenity, invention of liberty, sharing of joy, energy and spontaneity. The second category, prominent among whom were scholars like Edgar Quinet, Lanfrey, Louis-Sebastien Mercier etc., criticised festivals for different reasons. For Quinet, lack of imagination made festivals boring. The infusion of Latin enthusiasm could have made the festivals interesting. But revolutionary festivals were essentially Roman by character. As the Romans could not free themselves from their old religious traditions, similarly the ceremonies of the French Revolution were trapped in the same stubborn bonds of formalism.[224] Another way of interpreting revolutionary festival was to link it with violence. Lanfrey who popularised this interpretation wrote, "A permanent orgy purported to be the Cult of Reason. No celebrants walking as on parade, but over-excited organisers, no strictly executed programme, but frenetic licentiousness." Louis–Sebastien Mercier considered the Cult of Reason as nothing but scandal. Jean Jaures, like Alphonse Aulard saw the Festival of the Supreme Being as an act of posthumous revenge on Hebertism.[225]

All the same, the revolutionary festivals aimed and succeeded in establishing equality and equanimity. The festivals of the old regime, as we have seen, were based upon class distinctions. Even the colour of the dresses signified social hierarchy. All discriminations were now extirpated. The revolutionaries—Hebert, Momoro, Chaumette, and then Robespierre,—organised festivals because they held them to be the only way to bring men together and to engrave firmly in them the changing concepts of the revolution. It was their dream. However, Edgar Quinet, called it not a dream but a utopia. Because, like Lanfrey, he also found in the festivals a streak of violence. People did not, as Michelet supposed, "set out for the sheer pleasure of doing so, to go beyond the familiar bounds…" They were going because they were ordered to do so. If they did not comply, they were not sure what would befall. Edgar Quinet wrote, "Unfortunately, our utopias are almost all born of servitude, and they have preserved its spirit.[226]

In the end, it can be argued that the French Revolution brought about far-reaching changes in the cultural life of France. The revolution and Terror brought forth devastation and ravages. These swept away the age-old cultural symbols of France. **Emmet Kennedy** rightly points out that nothing happened to the material structures. The streets, the bridges, the buildings, the palaces, the parks,—nothing changed. What really underwent a tremendous upheaval were the cultural institutions like the clergy, the academies, Masonic lodges, the salons, the theatres, music, literature, painting, sculpture, architecture, festivals. The revolution left an indelible impression on each of these icons of culture. In other words, a purely new culture was born that bore the new message, new principles, new hope the revolution proclaimed. All symbols of power—the monarchy, the Church, the aristocracy—were obliterated. The revolution replaced a class-ridden, oppressive, discriminating, feudal society by a "freer, more egalitarian, more tolerant society, one in which the individual and the State, rather than the order or the corporation, were the ultimate points of reference."[227]

A Historiography of the French Revolution

EARLY COMMENTATORS

The French Revolution is perhaps one chapter of modern history which has been subjected to most heated debate among historians. Threadbare discussion on various aspects—especially the causes and the nature—has been a passion of scholars, across continents, over a span of more than 200 years. **Edmund Burke**, contemporary Irish historian, was the first to write a comprehensive critique on the subject. His *Reflections on the Revolution in France* of 1790 created a considerable stir among historians, especially his comments on the mass of common people of France. According to him, the French Revolution was *brought about by the most civilised people, but they were followed by the crudest possible elements*—the '**swinish multitude**'. Although, considered liberal because of his support for the Americans in the American War of Independence vis-a-vis the British, Burke was, for all practical purposes, a conservative. Burke was staunchly supported by **Abbe Augustin Barruel**, who, in fact, surpassed him in condemning the revolutionaries. However, while Burke bitterly criticised the masses, Barruel was particularly critical of the revolution leaders, who, according to him, had hatched a 'conspiracy' against the monarchy and the clergy. Being a Jesuit priest himself, Barruel could never reconcile to such a 'plot'. **Michael Billig** summarised the thoughts of Barruel in the following words: "The conspirators had succeeded in poisoning the minds of the masses so that they turned from their natural allegiances to the monarchy to espouse the alien and internationalist ideas of republicanism."[228] Another scholar who, like Burke and Barruel laid deep faith in the monarchical regime was **Joseph de Maistre**, born in Savoy in Italy in 1753. His *Considerations on France*, published in 1796, not only opposed the overthrow of the monarchy, but at the same time firmly believed that counter-revolution will surely succeed someday. Others like **Bonald**, **Chateaubriand**, **Lamennais** and **Mallet du Pan** also looked upon the revolution as something 'abominable' and condemned it vehemently.

Not all contemporaries of the French Revolution were, however, opposed to it. **Mary Wollstonecraft**, for example, lashed out at Burke,

> … Reverencing the rights of humanity, I shall dare to assert them; not intimidated by the horse laugh that you have raised, or waiting till time has wiped away the compassionate tears which you have elaborately laboured to excite… Liberty… is a fair idea that has never yet received a form in the various governments that have been established on our beauteous globe … I perceive, from the whole tenor of your reflections, that you have a moral antipathy to reason.[229]

She was a feminist and a member of the group known as the **English Jacobins**. She was, therefore, a confirmed radical and a great supporter of the French Revolution. Her *A Vindication of the Rights of Woman: With Strictures on Political and Moral Subjects,* written in 1792, was on the same lines as **Thomas Paine**'s *Rights of Man* in which Paine, the famous English-American political activist, totally disagreed with Burke.

> Among the incivilities by which nations or individuals provoke and irritate each other, Mr. Burke's pamphlet on the French Revolution is an extraordinary instance. Neither the People of France, nor the National Assembly, were troubling themselves about the affairs of England, or the English Parliament; and that Mr. Burke should commence an unprovoked attack upon them, both in parliament and in public, is a conduct that cannot be pardoned on the score of manners, nor justified on that of policy….When the tongue or the pen is let loose in a frenzy of passion, it is the man, and not the subject, that becomes exhausted.[230]

THE LIBERAL HISTORIANS OF THE RESTORATION PERIOD

The historians of the Restoration period in France—the period between 1815 to 1830—who praised and criticised the events of the revolution in equal measure were primarily Anne Louise Germaine de Stael-Holstein, commonly known as **Madame de Stael**, daughter of Jacques Necker, Controller-General of Louis XVI; **Louis Adolphe Thiers**, Prime Minister of France three times and then President of France from 1871 to 1873; and **Francois Auguste Marie Mignet**, the French journalist and historian. They were great exponents of liberty and looked upon the revolution as "a legitimate political protest against the shortcomings of the ancient regime."[231] So, they were called the liberal historians of the

French Revolution. In her *Considerations Sur Les Principaux Evenements de la Revolution Francaise* (Considerations on the Principal Events of the French Revolution), published posthumously in 1818, Madame de Stael enumerated the weaknesses of the clergy, the selfishness and greed of the aristocracy and their degradation as a military class as the principal reasons for the outbreak of the revolution. But at the same time, she denounced the excesses of the Reign of the Terror in the strongest terms. Her natural sympathies lay with the **Girondins, the true liberals. Thiers**, on the other hand, looked upon the Terror as the inevitable price to be paid for the transition from feudalism to liberalism. **Mignet**, too, abhorred the years of the Terror, and described Robespierre as possessing all the "qualifications for tyranny;" but, as a liberal he was happy about the changes the revolution brought forth. He said,

> For these abuses, the Revolution substituted a system more conformable with justice, and better suited to our times. It substituted law in the place of arbitrary will, equality in that of privilege; delivered men from the distinctions of classes, the land from the barriers of provinces, trade from the shackles of corporations and fellowships, agriculture from feudal subjection and the oppression of tithes, property from the impediment of entails, and brought everything to the condition of one State, one system of law, one people.[232]

One thing, nevertheless, is clear about these historians—they all were **writing 'from above'**, that is, they viewed the revolution as an accomplishment of the bourgeois leaders who, according to them, were destined to endow the nation with the most cherished offering of the day—Liberty. So, they extolled and condemned, upheld and denounced the actions of the Girondins and the Jacobins, of Brissot and Desmoulin, Marat, Danton and Robespierre.

THE IDEALISTIC AND ROMANTIC HISTORIANS

Eminent historians like Thomas Carlyle, Jules Michelet, Francois Guizot, Edgar Quinet, Alphonse de Lamartine and Louis Blanc have been referred to by Peter Davies[233] as idealist and romantic historians. They were mostly writing in the middle years of the 19th century and emphasised the glorious, idealistic and romantic aspects of the revolution.

Thomas Carlyle was a Scottish-born essayist and historian, who wrote a highly romanticised history of the French Revolution which came out in three volumes in 1837. The most redeeming feature of his work was that he wrote it in the style of a fiction and a thriller, rather than narrative history. In fact, this was the greatest attraction of the work and it soon became extremely popular. Another important aspect of the book was his concern for the poor. The ordinary common man figured throughout its pages. Carlyle's love for liberalism was evident in his history of the revolution. He was full of praise for liberals like Mirabeau and Danton, and bitterly hateful of Robespierre, the blood thirsty tyrant. The work took much more time than expected because of a freak accident. Carlyle had sent its complete first draft to his friend the philosopher John Stuart Mill for his perusal, but the manuscript was accidentally burnt to ashes by Mill's maid. As is said, Carlyle had not kept any notes and was forced to start again from scratch. It is worthy of note that his liberalism, however, turned into reaction later and from 1849 onwards, he was writing essays defending slavery.

Jules Michelet, a French nationalist historian, was well-known for his monumental *Histoire de France* and also *Le Peuple*. He had an attractive style of narrating the past using a personal and emotive voice, thereby lending the work dramatic power. He saw the revolution as a "spontaneous upsurge" of the mass of people of the entire nation against the age-old injustice and despotism of the ancient regime and the consequent suffering of the people at large.[234] An ardent Republican and a true Democrat, Michelet believed in equal rights—political, economic and social. He depicted the common people—both urban and rural—as active revolutionaries and not mere "passive instruments" manipulated by other parties.[235] He was angry with the Church because he felt that the Church had failed in discharging its duties towards the poor and the common people. It only pandered to the rich and left the poor in the lurch. His romantic and dramatised portrayal of the people was a source of inspiration of later historians, even socialists like Jean Jaures. Nonetheless, even Michelet, like other earlier historians, wrote not 'from below' but 'from above'. For he envisaged a Republican democracy where the power struggle was between the King and the Parlements, the aristocracy and the bourgeoisie, the different groups of bourgeoisie like the Girondins and the Jacobins.

Francois Pierre Guillaume Guizot was a dominant figure in French politics prior to 1848 and was the Prime Minister of France under King Louis Philippe from September 1847 to February 1848. He was a romantic-idealist historian and wrote memoirs of the history of France, memoirs of the history of England, volumes of essays on the history of France, history of the Revolution of England from Charles I to Charles II etc. In the 1830s and 1840s, Guizot, however, moved towards the right and became a proponent of tradition, heredity and aristocracy. Guizot believed in the perfectibility of the human race, but one which was more historical, moral and institutional than the utopian or radical perfectibility imagined by Enlightenment thinkers like Condorcet or Rousseau. He was sharply opposed to uniformity of suffrage and strongly recommended voting rights to be restricted through property qualifications, advising those who demanded the right to vote to first enrich themselves; *"enrichissez vous"* is what he told them. And that is how he earned the hatred of liberals and republicans and politically aware common citizens. His open espousal of the *la classe moyenne* or the middle class was all the more vexatious. It is they alone, he argued, who possessed "not only the necessary fortune (to devote themselves to political work) but also the intelligence and the independence without which that work cannot be accomplished."[236]

Edgar Quinet, a romantic and anti-Catholic nationalist, was a poet, historian and political philosopher whose contribution to the cause of liberalism is undisputed. He denounced the Reign of Terror because he felt that it promoted absolutism and suppressed liberty. Staunchly anti-Catholic, he considered the Church as an instrument of greed and exploitation. In this he shared the same platform as Michelet. He is regarded as highly idealistic because he looked upon the revolution as a spiritual experience, carried out with the object of fulfilling certain ideals.

Louis Blanc was a well-known French socialist, referred to by George Sand as "possessing great ambition lodged in a small body; a soft insinuating voice; and a will of iron."[237] His socialist views were utopian in the sense that he dreamt of an ideal democratic republic in which the government would take the initiative of organising national workshops, or communal plants, in the most important industries. In his thirteen-volume *Histoire de la Revolution Francaise*, he was full of admiration for Robespierre's concept of a State, and felt that even the Terror was 'justifiable' in view of the abominable situation prevailing in France. Blanc was considered to be a romantic, an idealist as well as a utopian socialist.

Alphonse de Lamartine was a poet and liberal statesman known for his major role in both French Romantic literature and the Revolution of 1848 in France. He proclaimed the Second Republic and helped abolish slavery and the death penalty for political crimes. A visionary idealist deeply committed to liberty, democracy and humanitarian values, he shared many of Louis Blanc's romantic ideas, the difference between them being the former's support and admiration of the moderates—the Girondins. Like Blanc, he used epic language and style to express his ideas.

ALEXIS DE TOCQUEVILLE

Peter Davies, in his book *The Debate on the French Revolution* has devoted an exclusive heading to Alexis de Tocqueville, one of the most eminent French political thinkers and historians, because, as Davies said, it was difficult to fit Tocqueville in any of the other categories in view of his ideas which undoubtedly were so very distinct. I also share the same notion as his and, therefore, after much pondering, decided to follow suit. Toqueville was an aristocrat on the one hand, but an ardent liberal on the other. He wrote, "I have a passionate love for liberty, law, and respect for rights. I am neither of the Revolutionary party nor of the Conservative... Liberty is my foremost passion."[238] However, he also supported two laws restricting the liberty of the clubs and the freedom of the press. Although he admired the commitment and sacrifices of the Parisian revolutionaries in the revolutions of 1848, he was generally opposed to the revolution, being an aristocrat himself. Though as a liberal, Tocqueville was critical of the aristocracy, who he believed were indolent and purposeless political saboteurs. He was also sceptical of democracy because he felt that within democracy, too, might emerge a despotic government keeping its citizens as "perpetual children" and presiding over them in the same way as a shepherd looks after a "flock of timid animals".[239] While Tocqueville condemned egotism and selfishness as vices, he saw *individualism as a positive force* as it inspired people to work and achieve progress. According to political scientist **Joshua Kaplan**, Tocqueville saw individualism as a "calm and considered feeling which deposes each citizen to isolate himself from the mass of his fellows and to the circle of family and friends ... with this little society formed to his taste, he gladly leaves the greater society to look for itself."[240] These self-opposing characteristics that make him so distinctive also make it difficult to assign any specific label to Tocqueville.

As far as the **Revolution of 1789** is concerned, Tocqueville was strongly opposed to Michelet's contention that the revolution broke out because the people could no longer tolerate the misery they were seeped in. On the contrary, he argued, France was becoming richer. Her national income was rising, her trade flourishing and her agriculture expanding. Then why did a revolution break out in France and not in countries of central and Eastern Europe—Austria, Prussia, Russia, Poland—where the conditions of the people were far worse? The reason is, pointed out Tocqueville, the growth of consciousness of the middle class and increasing literacy of the peasantry. They were becoming more and more intolerant of the vestiges of feudalism.[241]

Moreover, Tocqueville observed that it is wrong to imagine that the French Revolution swept away the entire ancien regime. Rather, it continued many of its institutions and ideas, thereby establishing a strong link with its past. In his book *The Old Regime and the French Revolution,* he commented,

> I have always suspected that they unconsciously retained most of the sentiments, habits, and ideas which the old regime had taught them, and by whose aid they achieved the revolution; and that, without intending it, they used its ruins as materials for the construction of their new society.[242]

THE THIRD REPUBLICAN HISTORIANS

This section discusses historians writing in the period of the French Third Republic, that is, the period between 1870 and 1940, which is circumscribed by the crushing defeat of Napoleon III in the Franco-Prussian War and the Third Republic's defeat by Nazi Germany, resulting in its replacement by the Vichy Government. The two most prominent historians of this time were Hippolyte Taine and Alphonse Aulard. **Hippolyte Taine** was, like **August Comte**, a sociological positivist. Positivism confines itself to the data of experience and excludes metaphysical speculations. Taine was a sharp critic of the Jacobins and of their Constitution of 1793, which, he felt, was never properly implemented. He supported the moderates.

Alphonse Aulard promoted democratic republicanism and had no sympathy for the monarchy. The history he wrote interpreted the revolution in political and ideological terms. Democracy, he observed, emphasised equality, while republicanism represented national sovereignty. According to him, the despotic abuses of the ancien regime were responsible for the outbreak of the French Revolution. Aulard was full of praise for the Constitution of 1791, but felt that it allowed too much power to the monarchy. He hailed the fall of the monarchy and saw the establishment of the Republic as the greatest contribution of the revolution. He adored Robespierre for his commitment to the Republic, but criticised him for his 'ego' and tyranny. Similarly, he hailed the moderates for their revolutionary zeal, but disapproved of their willingness to accommodate the monarchy. Aulard wrote,

> He (Robespierre) loved his country and humanity; he was ready to die for the people. But he adored and constantly revealed his own ego. His hatreds were as eternal and inexorable as those of Madame Roland. If this magnanimous woman prevented the Girondins from becoming reconciled with the Montagnards, this magnanimous man prevented the Montagnards from becoming reconciled with the Girondins.[243]

The Marxist Historians

The Marxist analysis was the most predominant interpretation of the French Revolution in the first half of the 19th century. Substantial changes in the economic and social fields were taking place in France and also in several parts of Europe in the 19th century. France began to industrialise from 1830s onwards, and became a leading industrial country in Europe by the middle of the century. This had a profound impact on the traditional structure of the French society—from 'orders' it moved on to 'classes'. This change slowly began to be reflected in the historical writings as well. Till the beginning of the 20th century, political questions—ultra-royalist trends, democratic-republican issues, constitutionalism—of the revolution were the primary concerns of the scholars and historians. They engaged in writing a history 'from above'.

Since the turn of the century, however, with the writings of Jean Jaures, a shift was discernible in historical scholarship. The changing society and economy, marked by class conflict, now drew their sole attention. They began to look upon the French Revolution **not merely as a political struggle from an absolute monarchy towards democratic republicanism** but as a movement that represented a **deeper shift from feudalism to capitalism**. These scholars constituted the Marxist or classical school of historiography of the French Revolution. According to them, the French Revolution moved on a platform of a broad alliance between the bourgeoisie and the popular classes who were pitted against the aristocracy, and ended in the triumph and benefit of the bourgeoisie. So essentially it was a class struggle accentuated by the growing economic crisis in the State. It was a **history 'from below'**—a history created not by the kings, Parlements and nobles, but by ordinary men. The Marxist school was represented by Jean Jaures, Georges Lefebvre, Albert Mathiez, Albert Soboul and George Rudé.

Georges Lefebvre in his monumental work, *Quatre-Vingt-Neuf* (published in 1939 and translated by Robert R. Palmer into English as *Coming of the French Revolution*, published in 1947), propounded the view that medieval society was dominated by a landed nobility, because in those days landed property was the main source of wealth. In course of time, however, overseas trade and commerce expanded and commercial fortunes surpassed landed wealth. The mercantile entrepreneurs of the capitalist class acquired predominance and aspired for political power which they had never tasted. In 1789, the commercial bourgeoisie overthrew the aristocracy and usurped long-cherished power. In typical Marxist style, the revolution was explained in terms of a contradiction between relations of the system of production and the productive forces. As Soboul pointed out, "the traditional social structure was undermined by the evolution of the economy which increased the wealth and power of the bourgeoisie."[244]

Although some of the mercantile bourgeoisie were being ennobled by the King as he was indebted to their support at a time when the country was facing a financial crisis, it was not enough to satisfy them. More and more yearned to be endowed with nobility and enjoy larger political privileges, but things were not happening according to their satisfaction. The nobility also strongly resented the coming up of the bourgeoisie to their own rank. This conflict of interest turned the bourgeoisie into a potent revolutionary force. It was, therefore, *a bourgeois capitalist revolution overturning an aristocratic, feudal society, "the steam mill replacing the hand mill."*[245] But it was successful owing to the support of the urban masses, especially the sans-culottes "who furnished the physical force necessary to overthrow the old regime."[246] According to Lefebvre, there were in fact not one but four revolutions: (*i*) the **aristocratic revolution**; (*ii*) the **bourgeois revolution**; (*iii*) the mobilisation of the urban masses or the **popular revolution**; (*iv*) the uprising of the peasants or the **peasant revolution**. All these forces combined together to seal the fate of the ancien regime. In this sense, in Lefebvre's view, the revolution was **a 'bloc' revolution**, that is, each phase emerged dialectically out of class conflicts, and, therefore, each phase represented the predominance of a particular 'bloc' with certain typical characteristics.

Lefebvre was supported by **Albert Goodwin, Albert Soboul** and **George Rudé**. Soboul focussed particularly on the *sans-culottes* movement which according to him, played the key role in supporting the bourgeoisie by providing the muscle power, especially after 1792, and ensured its success.

THE REVISIONIST SCHOOL

The Soft Revisionists

A group of historians emerged who endeavoured to challenge and revise the main tenets of Marxist historiography. They came to be known as the revisionist historians of the French Revolution. It started with **Alfred Cobban** who is regarded as the vanguard of revisionism, particularly 'soft revisionism.' In fact, the revisionists could be categorised into two groups— the **soft revisionists** and the **hard revisionists**. The soft revisionists, like the Marxists, emphasised the social and economic aspects of the French Revolution, but had strong reservations about certain specific issues of Marxist analysis. They saw the **revolution**, notwithstanding its anomalies, **as an instrument of progress**. The hard revisionists (to be discussed later) on the other hand, not only supported the soft revisionist argument, but asserted that the revolution could not be analysed only in social and economic terms and expressed serious concerns about its significant political facets, which they felt, had to be taken into careful consideration. According to them, the revolution was an illiberal concept because of its emphasis on the Terror, which rather put the clock back. They, therefore, consolidated and further expanded the soft revisionist viewpoint.

The soft revisionist point of view was initiated by Alfred Cobban, a newly appointed Professor of French History at the University of London, through his inaugural lecture entitled 'Myth of the French Revolution' in 1954. These were further elaborated and along with a series of lectures delivered in 1962, were published as *The Social Interpretation of the French Revolution* in 1964. Cobban challenged all the arguments of the Marxist or orthodox interpretation which is also known as the social interpretation.

First, Cobban contradicted the concept of the rise of capitalism and the theory that the French Revolution was brought about by the rising capitalist class. According to Cobban, French commerce and industry remained restricted and regional in terms of their markets till well into the 19th century. Industrialisation, therefore, did not penetrate into France until the third decade of the 19th century.

Second, he thought it to be a myth that feudalism was ended by the bourgeoisie in 1789. Feudalism actually did not exist in France in the 18th century in its medieval form and order. What existed were the **vestiges of feudalism** and these were overthrown not by the bourgeoisie, but by the **peasantry** through their uprising in July 1789. Lefebvre himself gave a vivid account of the peasant movement in his work. **Roland Mousnier** supported Cobban by saying that there were indeed fundamental political, social and economic differences between 18th century France and her 'feudal' past.[247] Pierre Goubert also denied vehemently "the triumph of an unidentifiable capitalist bourgeoisie over an unidentifiable feudal aristocracy".[248] Furet, through detailed research, showed that by 1789, several parts of France were long since freed from seigneurial payments.

Third, Cobban argued on the basis of a detailed study of the background of the bourgeoisie elected to the Estates-General that they were not capitalist in any way because only 13 per cent of them came from the commercial world, whereas 43 per cent were professionals like lawyers, petty office-holders and government servants or *officiers*. Some of them belonged to the landed class. Cobban observed, "The bourgeois of the theory are a class of capitalists, industrial entrepreneurs and financiers of big business; those of the French Revolution were landowners, *rentiers* and officials…. The revolution was theirs, and for them at least it was a wholly successful revolution."[249] **George V. Taylor** argued in an unpublished thesis that even the small number of capitalists that existed before and in 1789, were not interested in politics.[250] Capitalism, therefore, was not so dominant in French economy in 1789. *Fourth*, Cobban refuted the Marxist concept of 'bloc' revolution on the ground that the course and nature of the revolution could be changed any moment by a chance happening. The concept has also been rejected by hard revisionists like Francois Furet and Denis Richet.

Marxist historians have been subjected to further criticism by scholars for their inadequate and inconsistent definition of 'class' and class struggle in France on the eve of the revolution. **Jack Amariglio** and **Bruce**

Norton are such two scholars. *First*, they found Lefebvre's division of the French people into three social orders—the clergy, the nobles and the commoners—too simplistic. In fact, as Lefebvre himself, following Abbe Sieyes, had accepted that "strictly speaking, the clergy was a profession and not a social class."[251] There were, therefore, basically two social classes—nobles and commoners. However, in this analysis, Amariglio and Norton point out, Lefebvre had overlooked the subtle divisions within them, for example, the nobles by birth and the nobles by promotion. Similarly, "the bourgeoisie in effect included everyone in the Third Estate who was economically active and was neither peasant, nor a journeyman or worker."[252] The **bourgeoisie** was, therefore **a widely varied class**, the finer nuances of which Lefebvre overlooked. Moreover, Lefebvre called the French Revolution a bourgeois revolution and at the same time included the peasants and the workers within it. In other words, non-bourgeois elements, as Lefebvre himself admitted, played a crucial role in making the revolution a success. **Soboul**, too, was emphatic about the role of the sans-culottes, who were the real physical energy behind the bourgeois revolution, although, their objectives were remarkably anti-bourgeois, like price controls on food, reduction of road toll taxes, customs on grain, etc., and general "restoration of the old system of regulation which blocked the expansion of capitalism."[253] Francois Furet objected "to this notion partly on grounds that it is an over-simplification wrought from modern Marxism's tendency to squeeze complex and contradictory events into the straitjacket of a simplistic teleology…"[254] Furthermore, Lefebvre did not take into consideration the frequent overlapping of the nobility and the bourgeoisie. The views of Furet, George V. Taylor, Colin Lucas, and others have been discussed in detail earlier.

Second, and the most important argument of Amariglio and Norton is that the Marxist historians' explanation of class as a concept, that is their social interpretation, did not at all fit with Marx's concept of class exploitation, in which surplus labour production and deprivation of labour by the producer was the main concern and not whether the form of the property was landed or commercial. Their concept of class was, therefore, entirely different from that of Marx himself. "Our understanding of the notions of class deployed in the social interpretation identifies several problems, but problems which are in no way inherent in Marxian theory."[255]

The Marxists argued that one of the most important causes of the revolution was the shrinking of the number of posts in the nobility for the bourgeoisie. Their anguish and frustration pushed them into planning a revolution. This view has been challenged by a number of historians. **George J. Cavanaugh** in his article 'The Present State of French Revolutionary Historiography: Alfred Cobban and Beyond', has summarised the points of view of such scholars. **Francois Blucher** and **Jean Egret**, for example, refused to accept that there was any curb on the number of recruitments from bourgeoisie to nobility. According to Vivian Gruder, the administration rather became more open to ennoblement. Lefebvre himself in his study of the Orleans nobility contended that it was an open group. In the views of Furet and Denis Richet, the nobility was never a closed but rather an "open elite" and "a perpetually expanding elite".[256]

Hard Revisionists or Neo-Conservative Historians

The most prominent historians of this school were Jacob Talmon, Francois Furet, Denis Richet and Keith Michael Baker and this historiography was developed from 1950s onwards, especially since the publication in 1952 of Talmon's classic, *The Origins of Totalitarian Democracy*. They had reversed the main thrust of the earlier liberal perspective which, as mentioned above, saw the revolution as a great instrument of progress. Cobban, for example, considered the revolution as indispensable for putting an end to the incongruities of the ancient regime. The hard revisionists or the neo-conservative historians, on the contrary, saw the revolution as essentially illiberal and placed the Reign of Terror at the centre-stage of the whole revolutionary era. At the same time, they criticised the Marxist historians and others who highlighted the socio-economic aspects and overlooked the political and ideological manifestations which, according to them, were of supreme importance.

In 1952, **Jacob Talmon**, in a new approach to the history of the French Revolution, gave immense importance to the Reign of Terror during which, he argued, the French State became a totalitarian democracy. Robespierre ruled in the name of the people, though he reigned despotically and tyrannically—the same way in which totalitarian regimes in certain parts of Europe ruled in the 20th century. Like Furet, Talmon also regarded Rousseau as the main source of inspiration of this democracy, which turned oppressive at the hands of the Montagnards. *The*

French Revolution, although based upon enlightened concepts, therefore, was an essentially conservative revolution. It handed down liberalism, but soon metamorphosed into tyranny at the hands of the extreme revolutionaries. Talmon's theory continued to motivate a whole generation of later historians.

The vanguard of hard revisionism, **Francois Furet** emphasised the political aspects of the revolution and sidelined the predominance of the social and economic paradigm of the Marxist interpretation. Political issues like the conflict of the weak monarchical regime and the Parlements, the Estates-General and the National Assembly, the constitutional process, the clashes of political ideologies of the moderates and the extremists, the Terror, were the primary concerns of Furet. At the same time, he was enormously enthused by the ideas of Rousseau, which as Collingwood says, "became the heart and soul of the French Revolution".[257] That is how Furet endorsed and expanded the age-old idea that the Enlightenment was an important cause of the French Revolution. Rousseau's concept of popular sovereignty became the major guideline of the Jacobin Republic. To *rule despotically in the name of popular sovereignty* was adopted and absorbed not only by the Jacobin democracy but later on by Napoleon Bonaparte as well. The democratic ideology later mutated into the Terror. Furet, therefore, considered "the early years of the French Revolution as a prologue to the Terror, and he viewed the Napoleonic Empire as its epilogue."[258] Furet supported Cobban in opposing the Marxist view that the revolutionary bourgeoisie were capitalist in character. As Doyle wrote, "now at last Cobban received some praise in France for showing how few links the bourgeois revolutionaries of 1789 had with capitalism. Like Taylor, Furet concluded that nobles and bourgeois were economically members of the same class, and that the essence of their wealth was proprietary."[259]

We have discussed that the Marxist historians argued that the revolution was a 'bloc'—each phase arising out of the conflicts existing within a particular class. As **Cavanaugh** observed, this view, however, has been countered by the revisionist historians, both the soft revisionists and the hard revisionists. Cobban, for example, refuted 'bloc revolution' concept on the ground that the course and nature of such a revolution could be changed any moment by a chance happening. The 'bloc' concept has similarly been summarily rejected by the hard revisionists like Furet and Richet. They have given the examples of the Girondins and the Mountain (the Jacobins). Both belonged to middle bourgeoisie, and were "hardly distinguishable", but predominated in separate phases as we have seen above.[260]

Furet belonged to the Annales school of historians, established in 1920s by **Lucien Febvre** and **Marc Bloch** who promoted a new form of history emphasising the role of geographical factors like climate, oceans, demography, agriculture, commerce, technology, transportation, mentalite of different social groups, the ordinary common people in particular. They emphasised upon long-term social history. Later on, however, he shifted from the Annales school and long-term socio-economic factors, and rather insisted that all aspects of French history could not be explained by the French Revolution.

Keith Michael Baker, earlier an assistant professor of European History in the University of Chicago and later Professor in Stanford, was one of the staunch supporters of Furet. He, too, laid immense stress on the cause of the Enlightenment. His masterly essay *The Ideological Origins of the French revolution* is not only a tribute to intellectual history, but demonstrates the close link between the Enlightenment and the French Revolution. The foundations of the revolution were, according to him, three discourses which he derived from the Enlightenment of the philosophes, particularly Rousseau. His elaboration of the discourse of will uphold the desires of the majority or 'national will'. He wrote, "… liberty appears as the active expression of general political will; despotism occurs through the exercise of any will that is individual or particular, rather than collective or general."[261] Discourse of justice provides the basis for the construction of the constitution which restrained the arbitrary will of the monarchy and the authoritarianism of his ministers. Discourse of reason "was a discourse of modernity, a discourse that emphasised the growth of civilisation and the progress of civil society."[262] It added rationality to the discourse of will. The Enlightenment of Rousseau later turned into revolutionary Jacobinism. The roots of this transformation lay, according to Baker, not in the wars of 1792–1793, but rather in the decisions of the Constituent Assembly when it accepted Rousseau's general will as the basis of all its reforms. Violence emerged from the sense of political power which was endowed upon the nation. Collingwood, therefore, said that Baker, "like Furet, placed the Terror squarely at the centre of the revolutionary process."[263]

Denis Richet, like Furet, belonged to the hard revisionist or neo-conservative group and cherished a profound faith in the Enlightenment.

Colin Lucas and Michel Vovelle also contributed significantly to the hard-revisionist historiography.

Neo-Liberal or Post-Revisionist Interpretation

The neo-liberal historians challenged the revisionist point that the Terror was the central and most important feature of the French Revolution. Rather, according to them, the period of the Constituent Assembly was a constructive and reformative phase of the French Revolution. It is true that there were eruptions of violence during this period also—the attack on Bastille, the peasant uprisings of July–August 1789 or the Great Fear—but, these were necessary, argued the neo-liberal scholars, for the establishment of a modern, liberal State. And there lay the greatest success of the revolution. The revolutionaries successfully constructed a State based upon egalitarian principles that placed an example before the entire world. Although they contradicted the Marxist view that a rising bourgeoisie brought about the French Revolution, they did not undermine the contributions of the bourgeoisie in general. **William Sewell** and **Colin Jones** were prominent neo-liberal historians.

Feminist Historiography

Historians writing through the lens of women of France at the time of the revolution, focussing on their participation, their hopes and aspirations, fulfilment and dismay—came to be known as feminist historians. This group emerged mostly in the last two decades of the 20th century. Lynn Hunt, Olwen Hufton, Joan B. Landes, Monica Juneja, Simon Schama were some of them. **Lynn Hunt** discussed the impact of the execution of the hapless King Louis XVI on the whole nation; haunted by patricide, it not only demolished the old patriarchal edifice, with the King as the symbol of the father, on which the whole country rested, but saw the rise of a '**Band of Brothers**', who now became responsible for the future in the absence of a father. This was the **triumph of fraternity**. Women came to be associated with Marianne. In her essay on Marie Antoinette, Hunt illustrated how woman is often vilified through her sexuality. **Olwen Hufton** not only emphasised the problems, attitude, mentality as well as the role of the sans-culotte women, but also elaborated the reactions of the peasant women. Unlike the sans-culottes women who participated in many ways in the radical phase of the revolution, the peasant women opposed the revolution as they were thoroughly disconcerted at the desecration of the Church, which they held close to their hearts.

Joan B. Landes in her book, *Women and Public Space in the Age of the French Revolution*, demonstrated how women from different walks of life played distinct roles in the private and public spaces like the salons, cafes, clubs etc. She has dealt at length on the views and ideology of the aristocratic and bourgeoisie women alike. However, it was the Jacobins who endeavoured more than anyone else to confine women within the four walls of the domestic sphere. This attitude, according to Landes, was the result of the influence of Rousseau, who had rigidly excluded women from any participation in politics and relegated them to their homes taking care of their family and children. **Monica Juneja** has shown how female imagery and iconography had been used extensively to symbolise the principles and achievements of the revolution, without, however, any realisation of women's due rights and expectations. **Simon Schama**, too, devoted substantial space to the discussion of women's issues in his book *Citizens*. Collingwood observed,

> It has been seen that the Revisionists and the new feminist scholars shared two essential attitudes about the French revolution. First, both groups believed that the French Revolution marked a step backwards for women's rights. Second, both gave credence to the works of Jean Jacques Rousseau and it was his highly contentious ideas that gave rise to new notions of female domesticity. The post-Revisionists, like the Revisionists do not have an ultimate theory for the beginning of the French Revolution.[264]

HISTORIANS OF THE LATE 20TH CENTURY

From the earlier discussion it is evident that even in the second half of the 20th century—**William Doyle** and **T.C.W. Blanning** were in fact writing in the 1980s and even later—nearly 200 years after the revolution broke out, scholars continued to debate various aspects of its anatomy with equal interest and curiosity. They can all be clubbed together as a broad group entitled contemporary historians. The revisionist school—both the soft revisionists and hard revisionists—as well as others like the neo-liberals and feminist historians were all writing during this period, therefore, are all **contemporary historians**. Apart from them, there were a few other contemporary historians who deserve special mention. In the early 1970s, for example, a professor of California, Berkeley, **Gerald J. Cavanaugh**, while analysing the French historiography at length, concluded that **a shift in paradigm takes place when an ideology fails to explain**, in the words of Thomas Kuhn, **"anomalies" emerging out of extensive research**. Influenced by Kuhn, Cavanaugh argued that when the Marxist and neo-Marxist interpretations proved to be inadequate to answer the anomalies arising out of the conditions prevailing in France, an "outsider", that is Cobban appeared with his revisionist explanation. Unfortunately, Cavanaugh observed, Cobban's thesis was also not a foolproof one and was countered by the later hard revisionist and other explanations. But Cavanaugh in his essay also analysed the points of agreement between the soft and the hard revisionists, discussed above.[265]

Sasha Weitman observed, taking cues from ideas expressed by Tocqueville and Robert Forster, that the bureaucrats, comprising mainly the aristocrats, treated the peasants as 'citizens', because they had to collect taxes from them. The **acknowledgement of citizenship involved certain degrees of equality**. This was in sharp contrast to the behaviour meted out by the seigneurs who treated the peasants as vassals. This was indeed a new perspective put forth by Weitman, although conceived first by Tocqueville and Forster.[266]

As pointed out earlier, volumes of indisputable scholarship have come out, like Doyle's *The Oxford History of the French Revolution* published in 1989, and his *Origins of the French Revolution* which came out earlier in 1980.

Impact of the French Revolution: A Short Review

The story of the fundamental elements, the major aspects and events of the French Revolution have been beautifully summarised by Holland Rose in the following words: "The French Revolution was a conquest in the spheres of thought, society and politics, effected by a people over the old systems of authority, class privilege and absolute rule."[267] I think this is an apt definition of the great revolution. Within a decade, 1789–1799, the monarchical system in France was obliterated, the political influence and leadership of the aristocracy were suppressed, the Church was humiliated, privileges based on birth were replaced by privileges based on property and wealth. With the nobility gone, the only other propertied class, that is the bourgeoisie, now grabbed these privileges. The job market being thrown open to talent, most of the high positions in the State also went to the bourgeoisie. Undoubtedly, therefore, as Soboul had commented, the bourgeoisie were the principal beneficiaries of the revolution. The sans-culottes watched in astonishment how aristocratic domination was quickly replaced by bourgeois supremacy. The monarchy was turned into a republic based upon democratic principles. The ideas of the philosophes were now the driving force behind the new republican State and Rousseau's general will and popular sovereignty were its gospel.

An era of quick reforms was accelerated through the writing of the Constitution—unprecedented in the history of France. It was the first written Constitution in the continent of Europe. Reforms were particularly manifest in the distribution of land. By the Constitution of 1793, the land of the Church and the émigrés nobles were confiscated and parcelled into small plots of land and were distributed among the landless and the poor. This was perhaps the direct and combined result of Baker's discourses of justice, will and reason. Furthermore, a new culture, comprising sweeping changes in the fields of architecture, sculpture, music, painting, literature, and festivals emerged as the ethos, behind which again revolutionary republicanism was the most predominant spirit. The revolution signified the end of feudalism by the Report of 4 August 1789. The differences between the privileged and the non-privileged were sought to be ended. It marked the **beginning of the end of despotism**. The entire administrative structure was reorganised. The whole country was divided into 80 departments. The changes spearheaded by the French Revolution reached their pinnacle under the Industrial Revolution. Steven Kreis rightly remarked, "The individual, formerly a subject in the old order, was now a citizen, with specific rights as well as duties....While the French Revolution politicised the sans-culottes, the industrial revolution industrialised them. Both events had the ultimate effect of making the European working class."[268]

All the above changes took place with remarkable rapidity, but was the transformation sweeping enough to be called a revolution? Did it really improve the lot of every social group? Was there any dramatic change as far as the social questions of poverty, scarcity and the unequal distribution of wealth were concerned? In other words, the question is: ***How revolutionary was the French Revolution?*** Historians are divided in their opinion on this issue. Peter McPhee broadly categorised them into two groups—the **minimalist historians** and the **maximalist historians**. For a long time, the historians more or less were agreed on the view that the French Revolution had brought about far-reaching changes in almost every facet of life in France. Today, however, the scenario has changed as some historians believe that the transformation that the French Revolution ushered in was of a limited nature. The impact, they argued, was rather minimal. These 'minimalist' historians were the revisionist or the neo-conservative historians like Francois Furet.

The minimalist historians, however, agreed with the maximalist scholars that the political and ideological changes brought about by the revolution were profound and epochal. The establishment of a republic along democratic lines, and overthrowing an absolutist monarchy was an exemplary accomplishment. **The former subjects now became citizens**. A representative government on an electoral basis initiated a new political culture. According to Malcolm Crook, almost three million people were involved in the voting process across the country in the revolutionary period.[269] The revolution nurtured, the minimalists agreed, significant ideologies of egalitarianism, republicanism, constitutionalism, popular sovereignty and endeavoured, in its own way, to translate them into practice. Certainly, the practice of these ideologies was not associated with same congenial consequences for everybody. Nor were they remembered with the same fondness by the entire French people. The elections prescribed by the Constitution of 1791 stripped the old authorities—monarchy, nobility, clergy—of much of its past glory and preponderance; the land reforms agenda of the Constitution of 1793 deprived the nobility as well as the clergy (even those who joined the Third Estate) of their ancestral land. The policy of mass conscription resulted, as we have seen, in the civil war in Vendee that cost thousands of lives; Jacobinism transformed into the Reign of Terror that became a nightmare for thousands of innocent people and their families. Nonetheless, whatever be the consequences, the minimalists concurred that an important political and ideological transformation did happen.

Where the minimalists disagreed was regarding the **socio-economic impact of the revolution**, especially on the common people—the conditions of work and their availability, the position of the poor and the destitute, and the status of women in society. Work became scarce, especially because big landed estates had now been disintegrated and broken up into small plots to be distributed among the poorer farmers and the landless. So, the peasants working on the lands of big landlords were now jobless as their masters had emigrated. Many of them did get their share of small plots, but these were not enough to sustain the whole family. There was an acute need for work which was not forthcoming. As McPhee points out, "France remained essentially a rural society dominated by small farm units on which households used ancient methods and techniques to produce mainly for their own survival."[270] In urban areas too, there was paucity of work, until the Industrial Revolution came with its bustling factories and plentiful opportunities for employment. But that did not happen till the middle of the 19th century.

Work being scarce, the **number of unemployed was swelling** and the number of poor and destitute in the country reached unprecedented heights. Earlier the Church played a crucial role in poor relief and had various schemes of charity. Ever since its disintegration and the confiscation of Church properties, the support it gave to the poor ceased. After 1794, the situation became extremely precarious with the suppression of Catholicism at the hands of the Hebertists and then of Robespierre. The new government was unable to replace the Church in poor relief owing to absence of adequate funds and also its preoccupation with war. The misery of the destitute was further aggravated by the severe winter of 1795–1796 and failure of harvests. In the final reckoning, therefore, inequality prevailed and sharp social divisions continued. Despite the emigration of innumerable nobles, and brutal killing during the Terror of a large number of those who remained, bulk of the property property was retained by them. The Church still continued to be an important and powerful aspect of social life. The poor remained poor and the rich continued to be rich.

According to the minimalists, the revolution was a hindrance to the growth of a capitalist economy. The main reason was the victory of the landowning peasantry and the emergence of France as a country of small land units. The absence of big landlords interested in capitalistic trade, and protracted war which ruined overseas trade of France, proved severely detrimental to the growth of a capitalistic economy.

The maximalist historians, on the other hand, looked upon the revolution as an event of profound transformation. They were the Marxist historians who characteristically emphasised on its socio-economic consequences. For Soboul, it was "A classic bourgeois revolution, its uncompromising abolition of the feudal system and the seigneurial regime make it the starting point for capitalist society and the liberal representative system in the history of France."[271] In short, it was a highly successful revolutionary event that thoroughly transformed the cultural and institutional structures of France. Not only were a new culture and a new administration introduced, but several century-old impediments in the path of growth were swept away. Abolition of onerous tolls and customs, for example, ensured a smooth flow of trade and commerce within the country. A uniform system of weights and measures was another notable achievement. Before 1789, in the department of Lot-et-Garonne alone there were 65 ways of measuring length and 26 measures of weighing grain. Now all these anomalies were removed and one single way of measurement was introduced for the entire nation. Similarly, all local legal systems were replaced by a single uniform legal code. The **triumph of nationalism over regionalism** was complete. The uniform legal system of the revolution took the shape of *Code Napoleon* in 1804, which we shall discuss in the following chapter.

Notes

1. George F. E. Rudé, *The French Revolution* (London: Weidenfeld and Nicolson, 1988), 43.

2. Ibid., 55.

3. Ibid.

4. Ibid.

5. A. J. P. Taylor, *Revolutions and Revolutionaries* (London: Hamish Hamilton Ltd., 1980), 17.

6. William Doyle, *Origins of the French Revolution* (New York: Oxford University Press, 1980), 43.

7. Doyle, *Origins of the French Revolution*, 43.

8. Rudé, *The French Revolution*, 29.

9. Ibid., 31.

10. Ibid., 26.

11. Georges Lefebvre, *The Coming of the French Revolution*, trans. R. R. Palmer (Princeton: Princeton University Press, 2005).

12. Doyle, *Origins of the French Revolution*, 31.

13. Ibid., 32.

14. Ibid.

15. Ibid., 33.

16. Emmanuel Le Roy Ladurie, *The French Peasantry, 1450–1660*, trans. Alan Sheridan (Berkeley and Los Angeles: University of California Press, 1987), 338.

17. Doyle, *Origins of the French Revolution*, 33.

18. Ibid., 32–33.

19. Rudé, *The French Revolution*, 14–15.

20. François Furet, *The French Revolution, 1770–1814* (New Jersey: John Wiley and Sons, 1987), 4.

21. Ibid., 4.

22. Norman Hampson, *A Social History of the French Revolution* (London: Routledge, 1963), 13.

23. Doyle, *Origins of the French Revolution*, 36.

24. Ibid., 37.

25. Lefebvre, *The Coming of the French Revolution*, 7.

26. Hampson, *A Social History of the French Revolution*, 28.

27. Georges Lefebvre, *The French Revolution: From Its Origins to 1793*, trans. Elizabeth Moss Evanson, vol. 1 (New York: Columbia University Press, 1962), 41.

28. Hampson, *A Social History of the French Revolution*, 28.

29. Doyle, *Origins of the French Revolution*, 18.

30. Gerald J. Cavanaugh, 'The Present State of French Revolutionary Historiography: Alfred Cobban and Beyond,' *French Historical Studies* 7(4)(Autumn 1972): 593.

31. Ibid., 594.

32. Doyle, *Origins of the French Revolution*, 19.

33. Ibid.

34. Cavanaugh, 'The Present State of French Revolutionary Historiography,' 592–593.

35. Doyle, *Origins of the French Revolution*, 23.

36. Ibid.

37. Rudé, *The French Revolution*, 33.

38. Doyle, *Origins of the French Revolution*, 8.

39. Ibid., 24.

40. Albert Soboul, *Understanding the French Revolution* (New Delhi: People's Publishing House, 1989), 15.

41. Rudé, *The French Revolution*, Introduction.

42. Soboul, *Understanding the French Revolution*, 21–22.

43. Hampson, *A Social History of the French Revolution*.

44. P. M. Jones, *The Peasantry in the French Revolution* (Cambridge: Cambridge University Press, 1988), 15.

45. Ibid.

46. Ibid., 11.

47. Ibid., 10.

48. Ibid.

49. Ibid.

50. Ibid., 9.

51. Rudé, *The French Revolution*, 2.

52. Jones, *The Peasantry in the French Revolution*, 44.

53. Ibid., 42.

54. Ibid., 53.

55. Ibid.

56. Ibid., 50.

57. Ibid., 53.

58. Ibid., 58.

59. Doyle, *Origins of the French Revolution,*34–40.

60. John Markoff, 'Peasant Grievances and Peasant Insurrection: France in 1789,' *The Journal of Modern History* 62(3) (September 1990): 150–153.

61. Ibid., 155–156.

62. Ibid., 179.

63. Albert Soboul, *The Sans-culottes: The Popular Movement and Revolutionary Government, 1793–1794* (Princeton: Princeton University Press, 1980), 3–4.

64. Ibid.

65. Ibid.

66. Ibid., 4–5.

67. Richard Cobb, *The French and Their Revolution: Selected Writings* (New York: The New Press, 1988).

68. Geoffrey Ellis, 'The Marxist Interpretation of the French Revolution,' *The English Historical Review* 93, no. 367 (April 1978): 360.

69. Roland Mousnier, quoted in Doyle, *Origins of the French Revolution*, 18.

70. Pamela Pilbeam, 'From Orders to Classes: European Society in the Nineteenth Century,' in *The Oxford History of Modern Europe*, ed. T. C. W. Blanning (Oxford: Oxford University Press, 2000), 101–125.

71. Roland Mousnier, quoted in Doyle, *Origins of the French Revolution,*18.

72. Doyle, *Origins of the French Revolution*, 15, 27.

73. Ibid., 26.

74. Ibid., 27.

75. Ibid.

76. Ibid., 25–28.

77. Ibid., 27.

78. Ibid., 28–29.

79. Ibid., 29.

80. Ibid., 28.

81. Lefebvre, *Coming of the French Revolution*, 25.

82. Ibid., 25.

83. Ibid., 29.

84. Rudé, *The French Revolution*, 36.

85. Ibid., 37.

86. *Les Révolutions de Paris*, no. 106 (July 16–23, 1791): 65–66. Edited and translated into English by Margaret H. Darrow and Marielle Battistoni, courtesy of Dartsmouth College Library.

87. George Rudé, *Revolutionary Europe* (Great Britain: Fontana/Collins, 1964), 134.

88. Albert Soboul, *A Short History of the French Revolution, 1789–1799* (Berkeley: University of California Press, 1977), 293.

89. Ibid., 303.

90. Ibid., 256.

91. Ibid., 384.

92. Ibid., 337.

93. Ibid., 384.

94. Lynn Hunt, 'Band of Brothers,' in *The French Revolution: The Essential Readings*, ed. Roland Schechter (Oxford: Blackwell Publishers, 2000), 236–262.

95. Rudé, *The French Revolution*, 30.

96. Ibid., 50–52.

97. Ibid., 49.

98. Soboul, *A Short History*, 223.

99. Ibid., 224.

100. Ibid., 226.

101. 'Wars of Vendee' by Robert Anchel. *Encyclopedia Britannica*. Volume 27, 1911.

102. Charles Alexandre, 'Women's Participation in Riots over the Price of Sugar, February 1792,' in *Women in Revolutionary Paris, 1789–1795*, eds Darline Gay Levy, Harriet Branson Applewhite, and Mary Durham Johnson (Illinois: Illinois University Press, 1979), 115–118.

103. Rudé, *The French Revolution*, 85.

104. Soboul, *A Short History*, 223.

105. Ibid., 311.

106. Margaret H. Darrow, 'Economic Terror in the City: The General Maximum in Montauban,' *French Historical Studies* 17(2) (Autumn 1991): 498–502.

107. T.G. Parsons, 'The Popular Movement during the French Revolution: A Note on Recent Work,' *Labour History*, no. 7 (November 1964): 11–13.

108. Quoted in Rudé, *The French Revolution*, 12.

109. Parsons, 'The Popular Movement during the French Revolution,' 11.

110. Ibid.

111. Ibid.

112. Ibid.

113. Ibid.

114. Ibid.

115. Ibid.

116. Joan Kelly, *Women, History and Theory: The Essays of Joan Kelly* (Chicago: University of Chicago Press, 1984).

117. Natalie Zemon Davis, *Society and Culture in Early Modern Europe* (Stanford, CA: Stanford University Press, 1975).

118. Joan B. Landes, *Women and the Public Sphere in the Age of the French Revolution* (Ithaca: Cornell University Press, 1988), 23.

119. Ibid.

120. Steven Kale, *French Salons: High Society and Political Sociability from the Old Regime to the Revolution of 1848* (Baltimore: Johns Hopkins University Press, 2006), 9.

121. Jürgen Habermas, *The Structural Transformation of the Public Sphere: An Inquiry into a Category of Bourgeois Society*, trans. Thomas Burger with Frederick Lawrence (Cambridge, MA: MIT Press, 1989).

122. Landes, *Women and the Public Sphere in the Age of the French Revolution*.

123. Norbert Elias, *The Civilising Process: The History of Manners*, vol. 1 (Oxford: Blackwell Publishers Ltd., 1978), 39–40.

124. Dena Goodman, *The Republic of Letters: A Cultural History of the French Enlightenment* (Ithaca: Cornell University Press, 1994), 14.

125. S.G. Tallentyre, *Women of the Salons* (New York: G.P. Putnam's Sons, 1926); Julia Kavanagh, *Women in France during the Enlightenment Century* (New York: G.P. Putnam's Sons, 1893).

126. Jolanta T. Pekacz, 'Les Amies des Philosophes: The Making of Enlightenment Salons in Nineteenth Century France,' *Conservative Tradition in Pre-Revolutionary France*, no. 36 (Toronto: Carinal Press, University of Toronto Press), 2. See https://h-france.net/rude/vol1/peckacz5

127. Carolyn Lougee, 'Women, Salons, and Social Stratification in Seventeenth-Century France,' *Journal of Social History* 12(2) (December 1, 1978): 327–331.

128. Goodman, *The Republic of Letters*, 76.

129. Landes, *Women and the Public Sphere*, 28.

130. Montesquieu, *Persian Letters*, trans. C. J. Betts (Harmondsworth: Penguin, 1973), letter no. 106.

131. Ibid.

132. Lynn Hunt, 'The Many Bodies of Marie Antoinette,' in *The French Revolution: Recent Debates and New Controversies*, ed. Gary Kates (New York: Routledge, 1998), 297.

133. Ibid., 292.

134. Ibid., 279.

135. Landes, *Women and the Public Sphere*, 50.

136. Ibid., 53.

137. Ibid., 59.

138. Ibid., 114.

139. Ibid., 117.

140. Ibid., 12.

141. Tony Cliff, *Class Struggle and Women's Liberation* (London, 1984), Marxists' Internet Archive, see https://www.marxists.org/archive/cliff/works/1984/women/00-intro.htm.

142. Ibid.

143. Ibid.

144. Joan Wallach Scott, 'French Feminists and the Rights of Man,' in *The French Revolution: The Essential Readings*, ed. Roland Schechter, 222. Oxford: Blackwell Publishers, 2000.

145. Ibid.

146. Ibid., 216.

147. Judith Vega, 'Feminist Republicans and Etta Palm d'Aelders on Justice, Virtue and Men,' *History of European Ideas* 10, no. 3: 391.

148. Landes, *Women and the Public Sphere*, 119.

149. Vega, 'Feminist Republicans and Etta Palm d'Aelders on Justice, Virtue and Men,' 341.

150. Ibid.

151. Soboul, *Understanding the French Revolution*, 161.

152. Olwen Hufton, 'Women in Revolution 1789–1796,' in *French Society and Revolution*, ed. Douglas Johnson (Cambridge: Cambridge University Press, 1976), 160.

153. Ibid., 148.

154. Soboul, *Understanding the French Revolution*, 158.

155. Hufton, 'Women in Revolution 1789–1796,' 150.

156. Ibid., 153.

157. Cliff, *Class Struggle and Women's Liberation*.

158. Rudé, *The French Revolution*, 30.

159. Hufton, 'Women in Revolution 1789–1796,' 155.

160. Rudé, *The French Revolution*, 29.

161. Cliff, *Class Struggle and Women's Liberation*.

162. Ibid.

163. Soboul, *Understanding the French Revolution*, 164–165.

164. Hufton, 'Women in Revolution 1789–1796,' 162.

165. Ibid., 158.

166. Darline Levy, Harriet Branson Applewhite, and Mary Durham Johnson, eds., *Women in Revolutionary Paris, 1789–1795* (Urbana: University of Illinois Press, 1979), 292–293.

167. George Rudé, *The Crowd in the French Revolution* (Oxford: Oxford University Press, 1967), 86–87.

168. Soboul, *Understanding the French Revolution*, 161.

169. Ibid., 161.

170. Cliff, *Class Struggle and Women's Liberation*.

171. Olwen Hufton, 'In Search of Counter-Revolutionary Women,' in *The French Revolution: Recent Debates and New Controversies*, ed. Gary Kates (New York: Routledge, 1998), 310.

172. Ibid., 305.

173. Hufton, 'Women in Revolution 1789–1796,' 166.

174. Jane Abray, 'Feminism in the French Revolution,' *The American Historical Review* 80(1) (February 1975): 59.

175. Ibid., 62.

176. Monica Juneja, 'Imaging the Revolution: Gender and Iconography in French Political Prints,' *Studies in History* 12(1) (January–June 1996).

177. Ibid., 12.

178. Ibid.

179. Ibid., 13.

180. Ibid., 18–38.

181. Marina Warner, *Monuments and Maidens: The Allegory of the Female Form* (Berkeley: University of California Press, 1985).

182. Emmet Kennedy, *A Cultural History of the French Revolution* (New Haven: Yale University Press, 1989), xxvii.

183. Chartier, 'Cultural Origins of the French Revolution,' 75–105.

184. Ibid., 89.

185. Roland Schechter, ed., *The French Revolution: The Essential Readings* (Oxford: Blackwell Publishers, 2000), Editor's Note.

186. Chartier, 'Cultural Origins of the French Revolution,' 98.

187. Keith Michael Baker, 'Ideological Origins of the French Revolution,' in *The French Revolution: The Essential Readings*, ed. Roland Schechter (Oxford: Blackwell Publishers, 2000), 71.

188. Ibid., 72–73.

189. Ibid., 73.

190. Kennedy, *A Cultural History of the French Revolution*, xxiii.

191. 'Mémoire historique sur la maçonnerie,' supplement to the *Encyclopédie* (Paris, 1773).

192. Kennedy, *A Cultural History of the French Revolution*, 19.

193. Roger F. Devlin, *From Salon to the Guillotine*, trans. Nancy Derr Polin (Rockford, IL: Chronicles Press, 2007), 38.

194. Lise Andries, 'Radicalism and the Book in Paris During the French Revolution,' CNRS Paris, undated, available at https://www.princeton.edu/csb/conferences/march_2006/…/andries.doc (accessed September 2013).

195. Ibid.

196. Ibid.

197. Ibid.

198. Ibid.

199. Ibid.

200. Ibid.

201. Ibid.

202. Ibid.

203. Albert Boime, *Social History of Modern Art: Art in the Age of Revolution 1750–1800*, Vol. 1 (Chicago: University of Chicago Press, 1987), 454.

204. *Encyclopedia Britannica* on Hubert, Robert.

205. Kennedy, *A Cultural History of the French Revolution*, 128.

206. Ibid., 96.

207. Ibid., 102.

208. Juneja, 'Imaging the Revolution, Gender and Iconography in French Political Prints,' 12.

209. Ibid., 18.

210. Ibid.

211. Ibid., 20.

212. Ibid., 37.

213. Ibid.

214. Ibid., 38.

215. Kennedy, *A Cultural History of the French Revolution*, 120.

216. Ibid., 136.

217. Ibid., 48.

218. Ibid., 330.

219. Ibid., 344.

220. Robert Darnton, *The Forbidden Bestsellers of Pre-Revolutionary France* (New York: W. W. Norton, 1996), 118.

221. Kennedy, *A Cultural History of the French Revolution*, 344.

222. Mona Ozouf, 'Revolutionary Festival: A Transfer of Sacrality,' in Roland Schechter, ed., *The French Revolution* (Manchester: Manchester University Press), 306–8; also see Mona Ozouf, *Festivals and the French Revolution*, trans. Alan Sheridan (Cambridge, MA: Harvard University Press, 1988).

223. Ibid., 309–11.

224. Ibid.

225. Quoted in ibid.

226. Quoted in ibid.

227. Kennedy, *A Cultural History of the French Revolution*, xxviii.

228. M. Billig, 'The Extreme Right: Continuities in Anti-Semitic Conspiracy Theory in Post-War Europe', quoted in Peter Davies, *The Debate on the French Revolution* (Manchester: Manchester University Press), 24.

229. Quoted in Davies, *The Debate on the French Revolution*, 18.

230. Quoted in ibid., 18–19.

231. Rudé, *The French Revolution*, 12–13.

232. F. Mignet, *Histoire de la Révolution Française* (The History of the French Revolution) (London 1913), Vol. 1 originally written and published in 1824.

233. Davies, *The Debate on the French Revolution*, 51.

234. Quoted in Rudé, *The French Revolution*, 13.

235. Quoted in ibid.

236. Quoted in Gordon Craig, *Europe Since 1815* (New York: Holt, Rinehart and Winston, 1966), 83.

237. Ibid., 88.

238. Alexis de Tocqueville, *Democracy in America*, Vol. 1, Part 1, Chap. 3 (Chicago: University of Chicago Press), 3.

239. Joshua Kaplan, *Political Theory: The Classic Texts and Their Continuing Relevance* (The Modern Scholar Series, 2005).

240. Ibid.

241. Rudé, *The French Revolution*, 14–15.

242. Quoted in Davies, *The Debate on the French Revolution*, 82.

243. James Harvey Robinson, 'Aulard's Political Theory of the French Revolution,' *Political Science Quarterly* 26 (March 1911): 139.

244. Albert Soboul, *Précis d'Histoire de la Révolution Française*, 2nd ed. (Paris: 1963).

245. Gerald J. Cavanaugh, 'The Present State of French Revolutionary Historiography: Alfred Cobban and Beyond,' *French Historical Studies* 7(4) (Autumn 1972): 588.

246. Albert Soboul, *Les Sans-culottes Parisiens en l'an II* (Paris, 1962), 10.

247. Roland Mousnier, 'Recherches sur les soulèvements populaires en France avant la Fronde,' *Revue d'Histoire Moderne et Contemporaine* (1958), quoted in Cavanaugh, *French Historical Studies*, 592.

248. Pierre Goubert, *L'Ancien Regime*, 234, quoted in Cavanaugh, *French Historical Studies*, 592.

249. Alfred Cobban, *The Social Interpretation of the French Revolution*, 2nd ed. (New York: Oxford University Press), 13.

250. William Doyle, *The Origins of the French Revolution*, 2nd ed. (Oxford: Oxford University Press), 13.

251. Lefebvre, *The Coming of the French Revolution*, 8.

252. Jack Amariglio and Bruce Norton, 'Marxist Historians and the Question of Class in the French Revolution,' *History and Theory* 30(1) (February 1991): 43.

253. Lefebvre, *The Coming of the French Revolution*, 181.

254. Amariglio and Norton, 'Marxist Historians and the Question of Class in the French Revolution,' 45.

255. Ibid., 47.

256. Cavanaugh, *French Historical Studies*, 594–95.

257. R. G. Collingwood, *Historiography of French Revolution*, in posthumously published *The Idea of History* (1946; rev. ed., 1993).

258. Ibid.

259. Doyle, *The Origins of the French Revolution*, 19–20.

260. Cavanaugh, *French Historical Studies*, 590, 595.

261. Keith Michael Baker, 'Sieyès and the Creation of the French Revolutionary Discourse,' 1989. Discover Archive. http://hdl.handle.net/1803/7172 (accessed May 2025).

262. Ibid.

263. Collingwood, *The Idea of History*.

264. Ibid.

265. Cavanaugh, *French Historical Studies*, 596–97.

266. Ibid., 599–601.

267. Holland J. Rose, *The Revolutionary and Napoleonic Era, 1789–1815* (Cambridge: Cambridge University Press, 1935), Chapter 1, 1.

268. Steven Kries, 'The French Revolution: The Radical Stage, 1792–94,' Lecture 13 of *Lectures on European Intellectual History*.

269. Malcolm Crook, *Elections in the French Revolution: An Apprenticeship in Democracy, 1789–99* (Cambridge: Cambridge University Press, 1996), 124–28; also quoted in Peter McPhee, *The French Revolution, 1789–99* (New York: Oxford University Press, 2002), 179–80.

270. McPhee, *The French Revolution*, 1789–99, 182.

271. Soboul, *The French Revolution*.

Chapter 2

Napoleon Bonaparte

Napoleon: The Early Years

Napoleon was born in a middle class family in the small town of Ajaccio in the island of Corsica on 15 August 1769. The island was under Genoese rule from 1453 till 1729 when a rebellion against Genoa culminated in the establishment of a **Corsican Republic** under the nationalist leader **Pasquale Paoli**. In 1768, the Genoese sold off their rights to France by the **Treaty of Versailles**; Paoli was defeated by the French and went into exile in England. Carlo Bonaparte, the father of Napoleon, although a close aide of Paoli, reconciled himself with French rule and was assigned an important post. A year later **Napoleon** was born and that is how his fate became linked up with the destiny of France, although he was ethnically Corsican-Italian.

In his early youth Napoleon dreamt of securing the leadership of the Corsican nationalist movement against French rule. His heroes were Paoli and Rousseau. The French government brought him to a wider field of action. He secured his military education in France and joined the Revolutionary Army. He received education in three schools of France, at Autun and at the military schools of Brienne and Paris. Napoleon developed a soft corner for France when the Constituent Assembly allowed Paoli to return to Corsica in November 1789. Napoleon returned to Corsica to join Paoli's group, but Paoli did not look upon him favourably as Napoleon's father had deserted his cause and joined hands with the French. Disappointed, Napoleon returned to France and was appointed the **first lieutanant** in the **4th regiment of artillery** in Valence. In April 1793. Paoli condemned the entire Bonaparte family to 'perpetual execration and infamy', whereupon they were left with no other option but to settle down in France.

Napoleon was attracted towards Jacobin radical ideas, joined the Jacobin Club. During the Revolutionary Wars, he was able to save the port of Toulon against the British attack in 1793. The officer in charge of Toulon was wounded and Napoleon was given command—a very significant responsibility for a young officer like him. He brilliantly took up the challenge, held the Fort of Eguilette and made the inner harbour inaccessible to the enemies. Immediately after this success he was promoted to the post of lieutenant-colonel in September 1793. His contributions were highly appreciated by **Augustin Robespierre** who wrote commendatory reports about Napoleon to his brother Maximilien Robespierre, who was at that time the virtual head of the government. In February, Napoleon was promoted to the post of **brigadier-general**.

However, he shot to further prominence and fame under the rule of the Directory. We have mentioned in Chapter 1 that by removing the Directory through a coup, Napoleon attained political power in 1799. Before that, both at home and abroad, again and again Napoleon had saved the Directory from falling into disgrace. There were repeated popular revolts against the **misrule of the Directory**. The crisis reached its height in 1795 when the streets of Paris witnessed a series of popular revolts and bread riots. The cry of 'Bread and Constitution of 1793' tore through the air of Paris. In May 1795, the revolts were suppressed by General Pichegru, and in October, Napoleon under the leadership of **General Paul Barras** thwarted the attempts of the rebels instigated by some Jacobin leaders. Soon the Directory came to depend upon Napoleon's military skill for several of the problems with which it was beset from the beginning. Napoleon was promoted to major-general and soon afterwards succeeded Barras as **the Commander of the Army** of the interior.

The **most intimidating enemy of France**, apart from **Britain**, were **Sardinia** and **Austria**. Holland, Spain, Portugal, Prussia, Naples, Parma and the Pope had been befriended by the National Convention. Austria sullenly resented the annexation of Austrian Netherlands (Belgium) by Napoleon on behalf of the Convention. He compelled Austria to conclude the **Treaty of Campo Formio** on 17 October 1797 after inflicting several defeats on the Hapsburg army. This marked Napoleon's brilliant victory in the Italian expedition. This treaty brought a portion of North Italy and the Netherlands under French rule. This success led to the disintegration of the **First Coalition of European powers** against France. Thenceforth, England alone continued the war against France.

It was now necessary to reduce the power of England to protect the interests of revolutionary France. With a view to cutting off the route between England and India, Napoleon **invaded Egypt in 1798**. After initial success, he found serious resistance in Syria. The famous English **Admiral Nelson** defeated him in the **Battle of Nile** in August 1798. Napoleon then returned to France. Although unsuccessful in Egypt, his bold expedition to that distant land added to his prestige and influence in his own country. In 1799 the **Second Coalition** was formed by **England, Austria and Russia** to weaken revolutionary France. The French army was expelled from Italy. When Napoleon returned to France from Egypt, he found the French people in a state of despondency, if not despair. The Directors had completely forfeited the confidence of the people. Napoleon took full advantage of the situation. In **November 1799, he deposed the Directors** in a coup with the help of his loyal regiments and seized political power for himself.

Napoleon's Coup

The politics of France was in the hands of a number of **factions**. One was led by **Paul Barras** and his colleagues; the one led by Jacobin military general **Jean-Baptiste Jourdan** was another; a third one was led by **Abbe Sieyes** who had entered the Directory in May 1799. He shared his aims of overthrowing the Directory and seizing power with men like Daunou, Roederer and Talleyrand. All the factions wanted a brilliant military man like Napoleon on their side. Napoleon himself, however, chose to join the faction led by Sieyes, but secretly nurtured ambitions to use them as a stepping stone to concentrate power in his own hands.

The Directory had a bi-cameral legislature known as the '**Corps Legislatif**'. The lower house was known as the '**Council of Five Hundred**' (*Conseil de Cinq-Cents*); the upper house known as the '**Council of Ancients**' (*Conseil de Anciens*). On **19th Brumaire** (10th November), both the councils were persuaded to meet at Saint Cloud ostensively to save the councils from an impending '**Jacobin plot**'. This was done under the auspices of **Lucien, Napoleon's brother**, who had recently been elected the President of the Council of Five Hundred. The opposition in the

Council of Ancients started complaining of not receiving proper summons on the previous day, while the Council of Five Hundred expressed its determination to take an oath to preserve the Constitution. A serious strife broke out and confusion reigned supreme. Napoleon began a speech but it was so incoherent that the real intention of Sieyes and his followers as well as Napoleon was suspected by the members of the legislature, and a storm of abuse and pandemonium broke out. Napoleon fled the scene.

The irony of fate is that he had to face fierce opposition from the Jacobins whom he had once so admired, and it was by crushing the Jacobins that he had to come to power. Lucien Bonaparte, and **Joachim Murat**, a Marshal of France and Napoleon's brother-in-law (husband of Napoleon's sister Caroline), somehow brought the situation under control. Napoleon organised the grenadiers of the Conciliar Guard and despatched them under Murat to enter the hall. Most of the deputies of the Council of Five Hundred fled, and the *Ancients were forced to decree the end of the Directory and the creation of the Consulate*, composed of three Consuls—Napoleon, Sieyes and Ducos. Napoleon was the **First Consul** in whose hands power were concentrated. Napoleon therefore succeeded in sidelining Sieyes and capturing supreme power. A new Constitution was framed vesting the governing power in three Consuls. The two other Consuls were to be in subordination to the First. Alfred Cobban wrote, "The result was whereas the age of divine right monarchy had ended in 1789, the age of dictatorship began in 1799. Sieyes, who had written the birth certificate of the revolution, also signed its death warrant."[1] *Within ten years of the commencement of the revolution, constitutional government in France was replaced by military dictatorship.* From the ashes of the revolution, Napoleon sprang to attain supreme power. In that sense, he was the son of the revolution. At the same time, he destroyed it by establishing a dictatorship.

The first duty of the First Consul after capture of power was to resist the Second Coalition which had been formed by Russia, Austria and England. He made peace with Russia. Austria was defeated in the **Battles of Marengo** and **Hohenlinden** in 1800, and was compelled to sign the **Treaty of Luneville** in **1801**. Once more French ascendancy was established in Italy. But Napoleon was unable to deal with England on the sea. Nelson expelled the French army from Egypt (1800) and destroyed the anti-British naval squadron at Copenhagen in 1801. This was followed by a truce between England and France known as the **Treaty of Amiens 1801**.

Reforms in Internal Administration

The peace with England gave Napoleon the requisite respite to devote his entire attention towards laying the secure foundations of a stable and sound administrative structure. The period between 1800 to 1803 were the years when Napoleon carried out significant reforms within the state. As an administrator, Napoleon introduced several reforms which contributed to the prosperity of France and the happiness of her people. He was not content with occupying the throne with the help of the sword. *He aimed at consolidating his political power by good government.* Even after his downfall, his reforms endured in France and helped her to develop as a progressive modern state. In Napoleon, we find a *unique combination of military genius and administrative capacity*, which characterised the great Roman hero Julius Caesar in ancient times.

In the field of administration, the primary goal of Napoleon was to get things done. Therefore, he assembled people from different corners of the nation regardless of their past—their proficiency being the main criterion. **Martin Gaudin** and **Portalis** of the *ancien regime*, regicide administrator of the Committee of Public Safety, **Jean Bon Saint-Andre**, ex-revolutionaries like **Merlin de Douai, Treilhard, Thibaudeau** are some prominent examples. However, it is to be noted that although he entrusted these people with various works of reorganisation, he held the ultimate strings in his own hands. As David Thomson observed, "He was the architect, they the technicians."[2] Napoleon himself used to say, "There were good workmen among them; the trouble was that they all wanted to be architects."[3] **Centralisation**, therefore, remained the supreme characteristic feature of his internal reorganisation. He retained the centralisation started by Richelieu (the Chief Minister of Louis XIII from 1624 to 1642), and himself nominated the Prefects and Mayors in charge of the districts and cities.

The overhauling of the finances, codification of laws, agreement with the Church, reforms in education were some of the lasting reorganisations that took place. The system of reorganising public debt was already been done by Joseph Cambon in 1793. Napoleon established a central bank, known as the **Bank of France** in 1800 with a view not only to streamline government loans and the deposits of the tax-collectors, but also to organise systematic issuing of bank notes. The collection of taxes which was earlier in the hands of autonomous local authorities, was now centralised under the supervision of Gaudin. Trade and commerce were regulated, especially active measures were initiated to extend French commerce in North America. For the purpose of development of overseas trade, French ports were improved and reconstructed.

THE NAPOLEONIC CODE

Under the ancien regime, there was no common law. In fact, as we have seen, the King's words were law. There was no proper codification even during the revolution. The National Convention had started the work in 1792, but the work of the final code began under the Consulate in 1800. The entire legal system was a medley of feudal customs, royal edicts and age-old practices. Napoleon reformed the current laws and arranged them in the form of a Code (1804) which later came to be known as the **Code Napoleon (1807)**. It was done through the **Council of State** which held about 84 sessions out of which Napoleon himself presided over 36. Property rights particularly needed an urgent overhauling. The north and south of France were divided as far as the property laws were concerned. The **teutonic customary law prevailed in the north**, while the **south was guided by the Roman Law—the Code of Justinian (*Corpus Juris Civilis*)**. But the property system underwent severe upheavals during the revolutionary period. The Constitution of 1793 had parcelled out the lands of émigré nobles and the Church into several units and distributed them among the poor and the needy. All these had now to be regularised and sanctified. *The Napoleonic Code came to be based upon the Roman Law.* This made it more acceptable to other European countries which were significantly influenced by Code Napoleon.

But the Code remained both *progressive as well as regressive*. It was an amalgamation of **five codes**—the Civil Code, the Code of Civil Procedure, the Commercial Code, the Code of Criminal Procedure, and the Penal Code. Of these, the **Civil Code** was by far the most important. In family matters, especially, the conservative, patriarchal aspects of the Roman Law were conspicuously prominent. The authority of the father over the children, the control of the husband over the wife were enlarged and enforced. The grounds of divorce were made stricter. Adulterous wives could be severely punished, even imprisoned. Upto one-fourth of the whole property could be bequeathed away from the family. The recognition of illegitimate children was discouraged. As David Thomson argued, these stringent measures were intended to mitigate the moral lapses that prevailed under the Directory. The most pernicious feature of the Civil Code was the element of patriarchy involved in it. The provisions clearly were *highly discriminatory against women*.

Nevertheless, the Code underlined several progressive liberal principles as well. The revolutionary legacy of distribution of land of the Church and émigré nobility among the poor was upheld by Code Napoleon. *The Code recognised liberal principles such as civil equality, religious tolerance, abolition of feudalism and emancipation of the serfs.* All civil rights including **voting rights**, acquired by the people as a result of the revolution were confirmed and consolidated by the Code. The influence of Napoleon's legislation crossed the boundaries of France and entered neighbouring countries like Germany and Italy. Even today, the laws of a large part of Europe are based directly or indirectly on the legal reforms of Napoleon.

Religion under Napoleon

During the revolution, tumultuous changes took place in religion. The power and privileges enjoyed by the clergy in the ancien regime were substantially curtailed by the **Civil Constitution of the Clergy**. A deep split emerged within the body of the clergy in the form of a constitutional and refractory clergy. Under Jacobin rule, the churches were desecrated and dechristianisation followed. The State was separated from the Catholic Church. This was deeply resented by a section of the population. With the aim of putting an end to the religious strife, Napoleon brought about a reconciliation with the Catholic Church through an agreement or **Concordat in July 1801** with **Pope VII**. By this, Roman Catholicism was regarded as the 'religion of the majority of the French men'. The State took the responsibility of the payment of salary to the clerics in return for the acceptance by the Pope of the practice of nomination of the Bishops by the State. *In April 1802, Napoleon introduced a general law of public worship applicable to all religions* and embodied the Concordat in it. This is why many devout Catholics as well as virulent anti-clericals alike disliked his Concordat. And he did all this to set his government in order. He realised that establishment of peace and stability at home was an urgent necessity. Otherwise his dreams of founding a world empire would remain unfulfilled forever. It was political motivation, therefore, and not religious, that lay behind his idea of the Concordat. He said, "I once had faith. But when I came to know something, as soon as I began to reason, which occurred early in life, at the age of thirteen, I found my faith attacked and that it staggered."[4] He candidly admitted that popular welfare was his main objective behind the Concordat. "It is said that I am a Papist. I am nothing. In Egypt I was a Mussulman; here I shall be a Catholic, for the good of the people. I do not believe in religions. The idea of a God!"[5]

EDUCATION UNDER NAPOLEON

Napoleon created a new aristocracy of merit by introducing the **Legion of Honour** in 1802. It was particularly reserved for military men but was sometimes also bestowed upon civilians under very special circumstances.

Napoleon introduced reforms in the field of education as well. He established the **University of France** in 1808. Careers were thrown open to talent. Many schools and colleges—*ecoles* and *lycees*—were established throughout the country under State control. The **Bibliotheque Nationale** (the National Library) was further expanded and developed. A new building was constructed for the **Archives Nationale** (the National Archives). Napoleon was a patron of art. Artistic objects were collected from different countries and displayed in the famous Paris museum called the Louvre. *Paris became the first city in Europe in beauty, art, refinement and culture.* The progress of **science** was encouraged. The earlier generation of mathematicians like Lagrange, Laplace, Monge, scientists like Lamarck, Ampere, the founder of electro-magnetism, Arago, the astronomer, the psychologists Destutt de Tracy and Cabanis contributed immensely to scientific advancement in Napolean's regime. Laplace (famous for his discovery of the Integral Transform, commonly known as Laplace Transform) had a special role to play in Napoleon's life. It was he who ranked Napoleon 42 in the final examination of the military school (**Ecole Militaire**) in Paris in 1784 by dint of Napoleon's extraordinary proficiency in mathematics. This achievement helped Napoleon to be directly commissioned as a lieutenant, jumping the posts of probationer and pupil. The technological education initiated by Carnot with his foundation of the Polytechnic School (**Ecole Polytechnique**) in 1794, was continued with vigour. Especially at the time of the continental blockade, French manufacturing received a boost because imports from Britain and her colonies were prohibited. The popular colonial imports like indigo, coffee and sugar were attempted to be substituted with woad (the production of which was promoted in south-west France), chicory and beetroot respectively. A prize of a million francs was announced by Napoleon for innovating a machine for manufacturing a substitute of cotton from flax. *The foundations of the French industrial revolution were laid during the Napoleonic regime.*

Napoleon introduced several reforms in public works with a view to improve the quality of life of his people. He built broad and long roads, and canals for the benefit of internal communication, transport and commerce. *Napoleon purged the French State of the chaos and confusion of the revolution and placed it on the secure platform of a durable administrative system.* "His immediate successors might repudiate his work, they could not undo it, and the Napoleonic state was long to outlive its author and the ends to which he had directed it."[6]

Napoleon: Son of the Revolution or Destroyer of its Spirit?

The Napoleonic rule embodied a unique synthesis of revolutionary traditions and their anti-theses. Napoleon rose, as already observed, by virtue of his superb military skill in several crises during the Revolutionary Wars—the recovery of Toulon from British hands and its retention; the preservation of the esteem of the Directory in both domestic as well as foreign affairs. In this sense, he was certainly child of the revolution. He also continued several works that had started under the different phases of the revolution. The reorganisation of France into divisions, districts and cantons, the posts of Mayors and Prefects were continued by Napoleon. Napoleon's technological contributions were primarily based upon the work of Carnot. The metric system introduced in 1794, and the unification of the systems of handling of public debt by Cambon in 1793 were also retained. The uniformity in assessment and collection of taxes introduced by the Directory in 1797, the codification of laws attempted in 1792 and 1796 were all carried to completion by Napoleon. As we have seen, so many bureaucrats and experts were appointed regardless of their past. It would not be wrong to say, therefore, that Napoleon erected the edifice of his rule on the foundation furnished by the revolution. In 1793, the National Convention had proposed a system of nationwide survey of property ownership, but it had not materialised. Napoleon now implemented this plan with the intent of controlling tax evasion. The metal currency introduced by the Directory in 1797 was now revived and re-established by Napoleon. The Directory used to encourage industrial development by organising fairs and exhibitions—a practice continued by Napoleon and later by his nephew Napoleon III during the period of the Second Empire. The revolution had envisioned a proper system of education; the National Convention had designed the structure of education and had divided it into primary, secondary and higher levels. But these had been left unaccomplished due to paucity of time. Napoleon carried this reform to its completion and not only established ecoles and lycees, but also founded the Imperial University in 1808.

In various ways, therefore, Napoleon carried on the traditions of the revolution. At the same time, his **deviations** were also no less remarkable. *First* of all, in the place of the Jacobin republic, Napoleon established a dictatorship. Napoleon used his popular image in the minds of the people to capture and concentrate power in his own hands. The French people, disillusioned by the incompetence and corruption of the Directory and blinded by his dazzling military success, offered him the mandate of establishing an empire, which soon turned into a military dictatorship. In place of the direct democratic methods of elections insisted upon by the Constituent Assembly in 1789, and upheld throughout the revolutionary era, Napoleon introduced the system of **plebiscite** and won massive popular consent for his singular leadership. In 1804, when he established his Empire, a national plebiscite was held asking whether Napoleon should become emperor, in which over 3.57 million people voted in favour of him, while only 2,569 voted against.[7] He repudiated the party system introduced by the revolution and initiated a one-man dictatorship—a system emulated by 20th-century dictators. But there was a difference. Mussolini and Hitler came to power through a party system in a democratic election process, whereas Napoleon wiped out all parties, especially the most prominent Jacobins, and emerged the sole dictator of France with overwhelming popular support that he had won by dint of his outstanding military glory. In that sense, he revived the despotism of the ancien regime—a system that the revolution had brought down with such great tenacity, toil and bloodshed. The revolution diffused power, Napoleon centralised it; the revolution was based upon the principles of *liberte, egalite, fraternite*, Napoleon overlooked and repudiated them. Although in his early life, he was fascinated by the ideals of Rousseau and the Jacobins, later on he crushed the Jacobins and used Rousseau's popular sovereignty only as a garb to carry on despotism.

Napoleon revived the nobility and re-endowed it with privileges, thereby nullifying the revolution's spirit of attack on aristocratic privileges. He revived the hereditary French nobles in descending order—princes, dukes, counts, barons and knights—and distributed hereditary fiefs among them in 1806.[8] He introduced the **Code of Criminal Procedure in 1808**, which virtually revived the retrograde **Letters de Cachet of the ancien regime**. It was a letter signed by the King and countersigned by the Secretary of State and was primarily used to imprison somebody. It was so widely misused in the 17th and 18th centuries that a plea for its abolition figured prominently in the cahiers de doleances (as we know, the list of grievances presented before the Estates-General in 1789). Napoleon restored the Chambers of Commerce of the old regime that the revolution had suspended in 1791. Napoleon revived the pyramidical social structure—a hierarchy of classes which occupied centre-stage of the ancien regime—that the revolution had so earnestly endeavoured to end. In all these ways, *Napoleon destroyed the revolution*. As M. Latey wrote, "the absolute monarchs who re-established themselves after his fall learned from Napoleon's techniques and in doing so helped to lay the groundwork of modern totalitarian rule."[9]

It is beyond doubt that Napoleon was a child of the revolution. We have seen how the circumstances of the revolution moulded and shaped his life and made him who he was. However, it would be wrong to say that he destroyed the revolution completely. It is true, as we have seen above, that he repudiated several basic principles of the French Revolution, but it is equally true that on many occasions he resurrected the spirit of the ancien regime. That is why many scholars think that he was a destroyer of the revolution. But in fact, *Napoleon evolved a new order of his own*. It was an unmatched combination of the legacies of the revolution as well as its past. It was this fusion of the old and the new that made it so distinctive. He developed a system of his own and while doing so, he borrowed whatever appealed to him and his sensibility, from distant or near past—whether the ancien regime or the revolution—and moulded them into a new order, **the Napoleonic order**. It was neither rejection nor destruction of any one regime or movement, but the creation of a new order by a synthesis of the different principles that Napoleon's vision and disposition found suitable.

Here we may ask: what exactly was Napoleon's perception of a ruler and a regime? Undoubtedly, Napoleon had a dictatorial streak, which was reflected in his personality as well as his actions. That came from his repeated military successes and the immense popular appeal that he enjoyed. This was why the precepts of the 18th-century absolute monarchs left an indelible impression upon his mind. Like **Cardinal Richelieu**, chief minister to Louis XIII (who aimed to end Spanish-Hapsburg hegemony in Europe and establish royal absolutism in France during the Thirty Years' War), Napoleon made centralisation the main theme of his administrative system. Napoleon's Commercial Code (1808), mentioned above, reflected the spirit of the Commercial Ordinance (1673) and Marine Ordinance (1681) of **Jean-Baptiste Colbert**,[10] the chief minister of Louis XIV from 1661 to 1683. Since Napoleon staunchly believed in central control, therefore like all absolute monarchs he repudiated the laissez faire principles and advocated mercantilism. No commercial enterprise or trade transaction could take place in his regime without his approval. But he was an enlightened despot all the same.

An Enlightened Despot?

The question now is who were the enlightened despots? In the 17th and 18th centuries, Europe passed through an age of unprecedented progress in literature and arts, philosophy and science. Historians have called it the age of **intellectual revolution**. It taught men to advance along new tracks in the political, social and economic fields. On the other hand, it was an era of absolute rule. But even the absolute rulers of Europe could not keep themselves free from the influence of the Enlightenment. Although they could not dream of allowing their subjects to participate in government as in that age, the tradition of absolute rule was universal, they recognised their responsibility for ensuring the welfare of the people. With this end in view, many of these rulers introduced comprehensive programmes of social reform, spread of education, religious toleration and economic development. *Such absolute monarchs who upheld this sense of responsibility for the people's welfare were known as the enlightened despots.*

The most prominent among them in the 18th century were **Frederick II or Frederick the Great of Prussia**, **Joseph II of Austria** and **Catharine II of Russia**. Joseph II of Austria famously said, "I have made Philosophy the legislator of my empire." So did Napoleon in the early 19th century. *The philosophy of rationalism was the guiding spirit of enlightened despotism.*

Like the enlightened despots, Napoleon believed in total control of the State and the people by the ruler. He wanted to purge all critics, and therefore, ensured his supreme power over the two other Consuls, personally selected members of the Council of State and his ministers, the Prefects and the Sub-Prefects. At the same time he felt responsible for the all-round development of his people, their peace and prosperity. Many systemic and transformative changes of the revolutionary period were, therefore, continued by him. "**I am the revolution**" is what he used to say. It is to be remembered that in his formative years, Napoleon was a great admirer of Rousseau and the Jacobins. Rousseau's theory of **popular sovereignty** which inspired the Jacobin leader Robespierre, also had a deep impact on the mind of young Napoleon. Although later he rejected the ideology of Rousseau and firmly suppressed the Jacobins because *he felt that it was his task "to close the romance of the revolution"*, he could never transcend completely its magnetic spell. And, therefore, although he strongly denounced the republic, established an empire, anointed and crowned himself the king, thereby sidelining even the Pope, he could not completely ignore his people. He knew in his heart that it was their support that brought him where he was. Therefore he ruled in an enlightened way in the name of the people.

He continued the revolutionary legacy of abolishing feudalism by distributing lands of the Church and of the émigré nobles among the people. In this matter, he went ahead of Frederick the Great and Catherine the Great. Napoleon threw careers open to talent, expanded government-funded education by opening several schools as well as the University of France in 1808. The other enlightened despot who had abolished feudalism was Joseph II. Like Joseph II, Napoleon ensured religious toleration. Merging enlightened despotism with revolutionary traditions, he was a successor of the revolutionary Jacobins who established a dictatorial rule in the name of the republic and popular sovereignty, as well as a precursor of the 20th-century dictators who established totalitarian rule through a cult of the personality and under the garb of popular rights. Francois Furet, therefore, considered the ties between Napoleon and the revolution inextricable. It was from the revolution that Napoleon drew his sustenance and vitality. This "**proletarian King**" ruled in the name of the French nation as well as in the name of its people. Furet thus looked upon the French Empire under Napoleon as the "dictatorship of public opinion."[11] As Soboul rightly observed,

> Napoleon taught the monarchs how to govern despotically in the guise of popular sovereignty and a Constitution, how to turn the rationalization of the Revolution to the profit of despotism. He showed the aristocracy that equality of rights, henceforth an untouchable principle, was not incompatible with the social authority of the *notables*...[12]

The First French Empire

Napoleon became the **First Consul for Life** in 1802 by a new plebiscite, in which he got the support of an overwhelming majority of 3.5 million as against the 8000 of his opponents. After such a resounding victory, the determination of his bitter opponents to resist him was fortified further. **Georges Cadoudal**, a royalist counter-revolutionary and one of the organisers of the counter-revolutionary uprisings of Vendee in 1793 and Chouannerie in 1794 was one such opponent. He attempted the assassination of Napoleon on 24 December 1800 while he was on his way to an opera, but the attempt failed. Cadoudal fled to England but plotted a second attempt with the connivance of **Jean Victor Marie Moreau**, French general and the hero of Hohenlinden. Moreau, a former ally of Napoleon, was aggrieved as he was overshadowed and denied due credit for the victory of Hohenlinden by Napoleon. Another opponent was **Charles Pichegru**, the General of the Revolutionary Wars who failed to topple the Directory. All three wished to end the military regime of Napoleon. Widely known as the **Pichegru Conspiracy** or the **Cadoudal Affair**, this attempt also failed and the conspirators were executed. Pichegru was thrown into Temple Prison where he strangled himself. Napoleon's major opponents the Jacobins had already been suppressed at the time Napoleon came to power by overthrowing the Directory in a *coup d'etat*. The Senate passed its approval and in the plebiscite which followed, Napoleon again, as we have seen, enjoyed a landslide victory in 1804—3.57 million votes as against 2569.

On 2 December 1804, he crowned himself the **Emperor of the French** at Notre Dame. And the era of **France's First Empire** began.

The Napoleonic Coronation was a memorable event in the history of the world for several reasons. *First*, it was an extraordinarily grand event marked by unmatched pomp and splendour. The ceremony was a fusion of the traditions of the Bourbon coronations with those of the coronation of Charlemagne. The ceremony started in the morning when a dozen processions symbolising important institutions of the State—the Army and Navy, the legislative assemblies, the judiciary, the Legion of Honour, the Chambers of Commerce—emerged from different points and converged at **Notre Dame Cathedral**. The papal procession in resplendent carriages, the imperial cavalcade led by Marshal Murat, the Governor of Paris, followed by the beautifully ornamented royal coach carrying the Emperor and the Empress Josephine gliding down the Champ Elysees were unforgettable scenes. *Second*, Napoleon **repudiated the traditional custom of receiving the Crown from the Pope**, took the Crown himself and placed it on his own head. Next he put the Crown of the Empress on Josephine's head as well. It was an unusual sight. Napoleon did it because he did not want to accept the supremacy of the Pope and the Vatican in the anointment of

FIG. 2.1: *The Coronation of Napoleon* (1807) by Jacques-Louis David; Depicting Empress Josephine Kneeling before Emperor Napoleon at their Coronation in the Notre Dame

Kings and Emperors. His aim was to demonstrate before the world that he would not bow before anybody, including the Pope. The **Pope Pius VII**, being practical and sagacious, accepted it in return for extensive papal territories and other benefits. *Third*, the Coronation marked a significant landmark in the political history of France. For the first time, France was declared an empire and like all empires embarked upon a decisive imperial policy which we will discuss later in this chapter. It embodied the zenith of Napoleon's power and glory.

The **First Empire (1804–1814)** was marked by several important changes. The most significant one came in the character of the Emperor himself, and it radically influenced his actions and decisions. Napoleon, as we have seen, had always been overbearing and sought to concentrate power in his own hands. But with growth of power, this characteristic trait took a turn towards obsessive authoritarian conceit. His intolerance knew no bounds. He listened to no advice. This was a feature that marked the character of Hitler as well 135 years later. This dangerous trait is a clear foreboding of imminent disaster that both the dictators subsequently encountered. Napoleon's wise, well-intentioned and independent advisers—Roederer, Chaptal, Talleyrand, Fouche—were all removed and replaced by unworthy mediocre men who were at the same time crafty and self-seeking. Chaptal observed, "he wanted valets, not counsellors".[13]

In this connection, Felix Markham, however, points out that, "It would be a mistake to think of Napoleon simply as an inhuman intellect and a cold-blooded tyrant. To some extent this aspect of his personality was a mask…"[14] He mentions how Napoleon refused to dismiss a drunken coachman in his service, simply because he had been with him at Marengo, and the tears that he shed at the death of Lannes and Duroc who were his old companions-in-arms and died in wars. He was indulgent with his family; he was a very loving brother as is evident from the way he bestowed royal thrones on his brothers Joseph, Lucien and Louis.

Nevertheless, Napoleon passed many arbitrary orders that betrayed his authoritarian traits. The Tribunate was made defunct, the powers of the Legislature were curbed. Heavy censorship was imposed upon the press. There were almost 74 newspapers in circulation under the Directory, and these were reduced to only four. The notorious *Letters de Cachet* of the ancien regime that had been abolished by the Constituent Assembly during the French Revolution were revived by Napoleon in 1810. They gave considerable arbitrary powers in the hands of the ruler. The Ministry of Police which had been suppressed in 1802 was again revived under

Joseph Fouché in 1804. The noblesse as a class ended in 1790 but was recreated by Napoleon.

But at the same time, several benevolent measures were undertaken like the establishment of the University of France (1808), as well as the University of Berlin in Germany (1810) after his victory over Prussia for facilitating the imparting of higher education to a large number of students. The best technical school in Europe, Ecole Polytechnique, founded by Gaspard Monge in 1794, was further developed and militarised in 1804. Napoleon put the Empire on a stable economic platform by imposing indirect taxes on liquor and tobacco, which brought revenue that not only sustained much of his war expenses, but also kept at bay the bread riots, which had become a regular feature of the Directory.

The Continental System

The most important feature of the Empire was Napoleon's imperialistic ventures. Napoleon began to conquer one by one as many countries as possible. In the beginning of 1814 he said, "I am not afraid to admit that I have waged war too much. I wanted to assure for France the mastery of the world." The boundaries of France were drastically altered. A brief account of them is given below.

By the time he became the Emperor of the French in 1804, he was the master of a large and apparently invincible army. The people of France stood by him inspite of his repudiation of the revolutionary heritage of democracy. Fully aware of his own strength, he became anxious to establish his political ascendancy over Europe. As the First Consul he tried to follow the policy of peace, but as Emperor his reign of ten years was devoted primarily to wars.

War with **England**, temporarily suspended in 1801 by the Treaty of Amiens was renewed in 1808. Napoleon began his preparations for the invasion of England. England was determined to defend herself with strength derived from an expanding commerce and an exceedingly powerful navy. The British Prime minister William Pitt the Younger organised the **Third Coalition in 1805**. England, Austria, Russia and Sweden combined their forces to bring about the fall of Napoleon.

In order to resist the anticipated attack from the east, Napoleon gave up his plan for invading England. He first defeated Austria in the **Battle**

of Ulm in 1805 and advanced towards Vienna. After occupying Vienna, he inflicted a severe defeat on the combined armies of Austria and Russia in the **Battle of Austerlitz in 1805**. Austria now concluded peace with France by the **Treaty of Pressburg in 1805**. Napoleon secured the Italian province of Venice. In 1806, Prussia declared war against France, but her army was almost destroyed in the **Battle of Jena**. Napoleon entered Berlin in triumph. A large chunk of Prussia fell into his hands. In **1807** he defeated Russia in the **Battle of Friedland**. The Czar of Russia, Alexander I entered into friendly relations with him and signed the **Treaty of Tilsit in 1807**. The **Third Coalition** broke up. Meanwhile, Nelson had destroyed the French navy in the **Battle of Trafalgar in 1805** and established complete British ascendancy over the sea. He was mortally wounded, but his achievement ensured the supremacy of the British navy for more than a century.

After the Treaty of Tilsit, Napoleon attained the zenith of power and glory. He was not only the ruler of France; he was the ruler of North Italy as well. The Pope was his ally and his elder brother Joseph ruled over Naples in South Italy. Another brother of Napoleon, Louis, was the King of Holland. The Kings of Spain and Denmark were his subordinate allies; the Czar of Russia a friend. Prussia and Austria were weakened by successive defeats. Practically the whole of Germany was in his hands. Formerly there were more than 300 principalities in Germany; Napoleon reduced them to less than 100 principalities and named it the **Confederation of the Rhine**. It extended from the Elbe to the Alps. It became a French vassal state as the last Holy Roman Emperor Francis II was humbled in 1805 after his defeat at the hands of Napoleon in the Battle of Austerlitz. Napoleon announced in **1806** that the Holy Roman Empire no longer existed. The **end of the Holy Roman Empire** that survived over a thousand years was complete. *Only England remained unconquered.* Although Napoleon was invincible on land, he had in England a far stronger rival on the sea. The French navy was no match for the English navy. It was due to French weaknesses on the sea that Napoleon could not send his army across the English Channel. Unable to defeat England in any direct battle, *Napoleon devised an economic warfare in order to subdue England.* In his eyes England was "a nation of shop-keepers". Trade and commerce was the backbone of her economy. Napoleon was convinced that a decisive assault on English commerce was sure to bring her to his knees. Napoleon, therefore, decided to destroy England's economic power by destroying her commerce.

ECONOMIC BLOCKADE AGAINST ENGLAND

Between the years 1806 and 1810, Napoleon issued from Berlin and Milan certain decrees **prohibiting European countries under his control from trading with England**. France and the countries politically associated with her would not allow any British ship to enter any of their ports. This system of **economic blockade against England** is known as the **Continental System**. England of course did not accept it quietly. England's reply was direct. She issued Orders-in-Council on 11 November 1807 by which her navy cut off the trade of France and her satellite nations with Great Britain and instructed the Royal Navy to blockade French and allied ports. The neutral nations were the worst sufferers. They were completely sandwiched between the two warring nations. On the one hand, Napoleon declared that the neutral countries which endeavoured to carry on independent trade with England would be treated as enemy ships and would be seized. On the other hand, England required the neutral traders to secure a licence before entering English waters. Otherwise, the consequences would be dire. It created enormous confusion. The trade and commerce of a neutral country like the USA, for example, suffered immeasurable losses. American ships were searched and even bonafide American citizens were captured under the notion that they were alleged deserters from the British navy, and **forcibly impressed**, that is, they were compelled into service by force or physical coercion. A huge furore followed. The worst incident took place in 1807 when an American warship, the *Chesapeake*, was attacked on the sea by the British frigate *Leopard*, following which four members of the crew were impressed into the British navy. Three out of these men were Americans. An unprecedented outrage of emotions burst out in the USA against British policy. The national humiliation coupled with economic distress inflamed public sentiment and finally snowballed into the **War of 1812 between Britain and the United States**.

The consequences on England were severe. Her trade and commerce slowed down; her textile industries languished because of cutting off of the supply of cotton from the USA. This provoked a new movement in England known as the **Luddite Movement**. This movement represented the machine-breaking riots that rocked the wool and cotton industries. The Luddites were named after Ned Ludd, a mythical figure who lived in the Sherwood Forest and supposedly led the movement. They were also called the '**Luddite Riots**'. The machine-breaking spree began in Nottingham in

1811 and quickly spread throughout the country, especially to Yorkshire and Lancashire in 1812 and also to Leicestershire and Derbyshire. They also attacked factory-owners and magistrates. It continued till the middle of the 19th century. The South American colonies of Spain also constituted another important source of raw materials for British factories. But Spain was Napoleon's subordinate ally and was, therefore, forced to accept the Continental System. So the smooth flow of raw materials from the Spanish colonies was greatly affected. Because of Napoleonic domination over Italy and Germany, Britain's trade with them was ruined completely. Britain was slowly embroiled in a war with the United States in 1812, which proved to be a further drain on her men and resources.

But as a result of the commercial war, Napoleon was injured much more than England. His primary aim was to subdue England by destroying her commerce, but he also had another interest. *Napoleon had never been accepted among the royal dynasties of Europe because of his humble origins.* He was refused the hand of the daughter of the Czar of Russia. After the annulment of his marriage with Josephine, in 1810 he married Marie-Louise, the daughter of the Austrian Emperor Francis, who condescended to 'sacrifice' his regal vanity and oblige Napoleon after his repeated defeats at his hands. Napoleon married Marie-Louise in order to secure a legitimate heir (he had no children with Josephine), forge a political alliance with Austria, and enhance his imperial legitimacy in Europe. Napoleon felt deeply humiliated at being frequently referred to as 'the Corsican', 'the usurper'. He, therefore, craved to start his own dynasty, placed his siblings on the thrones of dynastic sovereigns in different countries after removing the legitimate rulers—Holland, Spain, Naples, Westphalia—and founded his '**Grand Empire**'. For this he has been bitterly criticised for having destroyed the revolution. People had hailed him, his critics contended, for being a popular ruler and one among themselves, but he betrayed their faith by creating an Empire and emulating age-old imperial traditions. Failing to elicit recognition at par, Napoleon wanted to avenge his humiliation by conquering them through his military might. Therefore, war was carried on relentlessly. Napoleon observed, "**Conquest has made me what I am, and conquest can alone maintain me.**"[15]

France was ruined economically, politically, psychologically and materially. She lost enormously in terms of men and resources. Her army was depleted. The economic growth of France was disrupted. As trade with Britain was disrupted, the French aristocracy and the middle class—who were accustomed to relishing their coffee and tea from Britain and her colonies or sugar from South America—had to make do with poorer substitutes like chicory for coffee, beetroot for sugar and woad for indigo. The exasperation of the French nobility and the middle class was rising. Smuggling was rampant as it was not possible for Napoleon to keep watch over the long European coastline to cut off illegal British imports. The French navy was not strong enough for this task. On the other hand, England was so strong on the sea that she could blockade European ports and at the same time destroy the overseas trade of France and her satellite nations. Napoleon slowly realised that it was not possible to make his orders effective in all countries allied with France. In England, the **Industrial Revolution** had increased production through the factory system, but industrial production was almost at a standstill in the continental countries devastated by war. Naturally *there was a growing demand for British goods in all these countries. The Continental System created a serious economic crisis in Western Europe by prohibiting importation of British goods*. There was large-scale suffering of the people and they held Napoleon responsible for this state of affairs.

Here, however, one point has to be conceded. There was a silver lining around the dark clouds that were gathering. As I have mentioned above, the foundations of the **French industrial revolution** were laid by this economic warfare. The base of rigorous technical training was established. Inspite of the economic blockade, however, the free exchange of technological know-how prevailed. British technicians were invited to impart specialised technological education to the French workers. French entrepreneurs visited English factories to observe the operation of machines there. Prominent French chemists like **Berthollet** contributed immensely in the fields of dyeing, bleaching, tanning. Berthollet was the first to demonstrate the bleaching action of chlorine gas, and was first to develop a solution of sodium hypochlorite as a modern bleaching agent. The number of looms increased enormously. This generated employment and the number of workers went up by leaps and bounds. The number of workers which was almost 76,000 in 1788 went up to 131,000 approximately in Paris in 1812. The industrial and technological scenario of France was fast evolving.

Political Conflicts with Spain and Portugal

Napoleon was not unaware of the political effects of the intense discontent in the allied and neutral countries. In many respects, he was a realist.

Political necessity compelled him to modify at moderate scale. But the political problem was not solved by such measures. The policy of ruining England commercially, involved Napoleon in a series of political conflicts.

First, his friendly relations with the **papacy** were severed. He occupied the papal territories in February 1808. During his Wagram campaign against Austria in 1809, he annexed Rome to the French Empire. The **Pope** was **imprisoned in Savona**. This made him extremely unpopular with the Catholics. It had severe repercussions all over Europe, and further worsened his relationship with Spain and Austria. Their struggle against Napoleon was intensified.

Second, the Continental System brought Napoleon into bitter conflicts with Spain and Portugal. In order to enforce his Continental System by prohibiting the import of British goods, Napoleon needed to control the entire coastline of the Iberian Peninsula. At first the combined armies of France and Spain invaded Portugal in 1807. The Portuguese royal family fled to Brazil which was a part of the Portuguese Empire. Next **Napoleon turned against Spain**, his earlier ally. The scathing antipathy between Spanish King Charles IV and his son and heir Ferdinand, along with the decadence and confusion that prevailed gave Napoleon the impression that the path to the annexation of Spain was effortless and smooth. Unfortunately, he had greatly *underestimated the resilience of the Spanish people*. He forced Charles IV to abdicate and placed his brother Joseph on the Spanish throne. The Napoleonic Code was introduced in all countries that he subjugated. The patriotic people of *Spain broke out in open revolt*. The peasantry joined hands with the nobles to resist the foreign invader. Immediately the British leaped to assist the Spanish. Thus started the long-drawn **Peninsular War** that dragged on from 1811–1812, and thereby drained the life-blood of Napoleon's Grand Army.

Napoleon later bitterly regretted that the '**Spanish ulcer**' ruined him. Napoleon had so long fought against the mercenary troops of autocratic monarchies. In the Peninsular War, he confronted, for the first time, national armies fighting for preservation of national independence. Napoleon believed that the greatest impediment in Spain was the intervention of Great Britain, and thought if the latter could be checked, victory was certain. He failed to assess the resolution of the Spanish people who adopted **guerrilla tactics** of warfare to fight the foreign rule tooth and nail. It was a dispersed kind of a fighting in an unknown terrain with which his soldiers and commanders were not familiar. The people in general were extremely hostile. Joseph Bonaparte sadly exclaimed "I haven't a single supporter here". A major portion of Napoleon's army remained engaged in the peninsula when they were desperately needed elsewhere. Although initially Napoleon won against the Spanish in **July 1808** at the the **Battle of Medina del Rio Seco**, he was quickly defeated by the Spanish at the **Battle of Baylen** within a few days. In 1809 Napoleon engaged Massena to lead the French army in Spain. Regrettably, however, Massena was decisively defeated by the British General Arthur Wellesley, the Duke of Wellington at the **Battles of Salamanca and Vittoria** who thereupon entered Madrid in 1812 and compelled Joseph to retreat. Napoleon's costly Spanish expedition ended in a disaster.

War with Austria, Italy and Germany

Meanwhile, the spirit of intense nationalism transcended the boundaries of Spain and entered the lands of Austria, Italy and Germany. **Austria** reorganised her army and renewed war against France in 1809. But Napoleon secured a victory in the **Battle of Wagram** and compelled Austria to conclude a treaty on humiliating terms. Austria lost a part of her territories; she also promised to cut off her trade with England and to reduce the size of her army. But the victory was earned by Napoleon at the cost of huge losses in men and money. Despite the friendship with the Czar no help came from him in the war against Austria. In 1810, Napoleon married Marie-Louise, the daughter of the Emperor of Austria. But neither treaty relations nor family ties could remove the **spirit of hostility towards Napoleon**, which had so long guided Austrian policy.

Napoleon established the northern kingdom of **Italy** and the southern kingdom of **Naples** in 1805 and 1806 respectively. Between 1807 and 1810 the annexation and subjugation of Italy was completed. Napoleon's policy brought about a stern attitude of resentment in Italy. The humiliation of the Vatican and the Pope, the imposition of high taxes, introduction of Code Napoleon, and conscription of Italians into the Grand Army aroused intense nationalistic spirit among the Italian people. This was the starting point of the **Risorgimento** (a movement that would help arouse the national consciousness of the Italian people) which later flowered into the movements for unification in middle of the 19th century. Moreover, the economic effects of the blockade were too pressing for Italy. The important ports of the Italian peninsula like Ancona, Civitavecchia, Genoa, Naples, Venice were crucial as far as Italy's trade with Britain was concerned. England shipped colonial goods to Italy in exchange for precious Italian raw silk, wine and olive oil. Napoleon aimed to dominate the entire Italian coastline in order to cut off this particularly crucial centre of British commerce. When the Pope refused to close the port of Civitavecchia (near Rome), Napoleon occupied Rome and other papal states and finally imprisoned the Pope. This ignited the national movement in Italy.

The main centre of the rise of nationalism was in **Germany**. The 300 German principalities of the **Holy Roman Empire** were reduced by Napoleon to the **Confederation of Rhine** and he became its Protector. As we have already seen, in the 17th and 18th centuries Europe was going through the Age of Enlightenment. The spirit of enquiry and critical approach to problems of life which were reflected in the Renaissance in the 15th century were brought forward in new forms in the 18th century. The natural result was the triumph of rationalism. In all aspects of life—religion, society, law, economics, government—reason became predominant; it became a common practice to judge all institutions and customs by the **test of reason**.

Many great philosophers during this age contributed to the political thought of the time. Of them, the German philosophers Kant and Fichte are most prominent. The predominance of Romanticism was another characteristic feature of this era. **Lessing** and **Herder** were the pioneers in replacing the classical style by romantic expression. What they began was carried to its logical culmination by **Goethe** and **Schiller**. The thoughts of these great thinkers contributed immensely to the shaping of the German nationalist movement against French domination. **Immanuel Kant** argued that republicanism is especially conducive to peace. The people, he argued, would consent to war if only the economic burden was commensurate with the truly dire threat that the denial of war represented. Going to war only because of the will of the monarch was an abhorrent idea to Kant. Napoleon's craze for war, sometimes even despite all dissuasions by his own commanders, was not liked by Kant. **Johann Gottlieb Fichte** was, like Kant, against absolutism. His approval of revolutionary France was loud and clear. Initially he wrote, "I am more than certain that if the French do not acquire dominance and make changes in Germany …in a few years no one in Germany who is to have practised freedom of thought will have a haven."[16] In 1804, however, his ideas towards France changed drastically. When Fichte saw Napoleon's armies advancing through Europe with the aim of conquering German territories with the purpose of subjugating them to foreign rule, Fichte fiercely opposed Napoleon. **Johann Wolfgang Von Goethe** was, on the other hand, totally conservative in politics. At the time of the French revolution, for example, he was exceedingly skeptical of the capabilities of the masses to govern. So he was not the least enthusiastic about the French Revolution. Similarly he remained aloof at the time of the **War of Liberation** (1813–1815) waged by the German states against Napoleon. He wrote when persuaded by his countrymen to write patriotic poems and songs, "How could I write songs of hatred when I felt no hate?" Goethe remained an admirer of Napoleon to the end. The discomfiture at Jena further awakened the spirit of resistance and the dream of unification. The shock of misfortune infused new life into Prussia. Two capable ministers, **Stein** and **Hardenberg**, reorganised and improved her military and administrative institutions. Educational reforms were introduced. The University of Berlin was established in 1809. Prussia was ready to rise against Napoleon.

The friendly relations reached at Tilsit (1807) between Napoleon and the Russian Emperor Alexander I were strained by the Continental System. The Czar could not accept Napoleon's directive to cut off Russia's trade with England. Differences gradually led to hostility; *in June 1812 Napoleon invaded Russia* with his Grand Army—an act that was in the words of Rudé, "of unspeakable folly". The Russian General Kutuzov blocked the further advance of the French beyond the town of Borodino, 110 km west of Moscow, in September 1812. A bitter battle ensued; Napoleon won a narrow victory and occupied Moscow unopposed a week later, but the Russians were yet to surrender and the war dragged on. The approaching severe winter of Russia, the exhaustion of his men, the scarcity of supplies and the determined resistance of the Russians irrespective of their army also being badly mauled, compelled Napoleon to retreat soon to France. His army was hugely depleted. This weakened him tremendously from the military point of view. According to David Thomson, no expedition against Russia in the extreme east could be undertaken without first coming to terms with England in the west. Support from either of these "two great flanking powers" was essential for a monarch who aspired to be the Emperor of Europe. Napoleon made the same mistake that was repeated by Hitler 130 years later. As Thomson observed, "Each precipitated an east-west alliance and was then crushed, as in a nutcracker, by a devastating war on two fronts."[17]

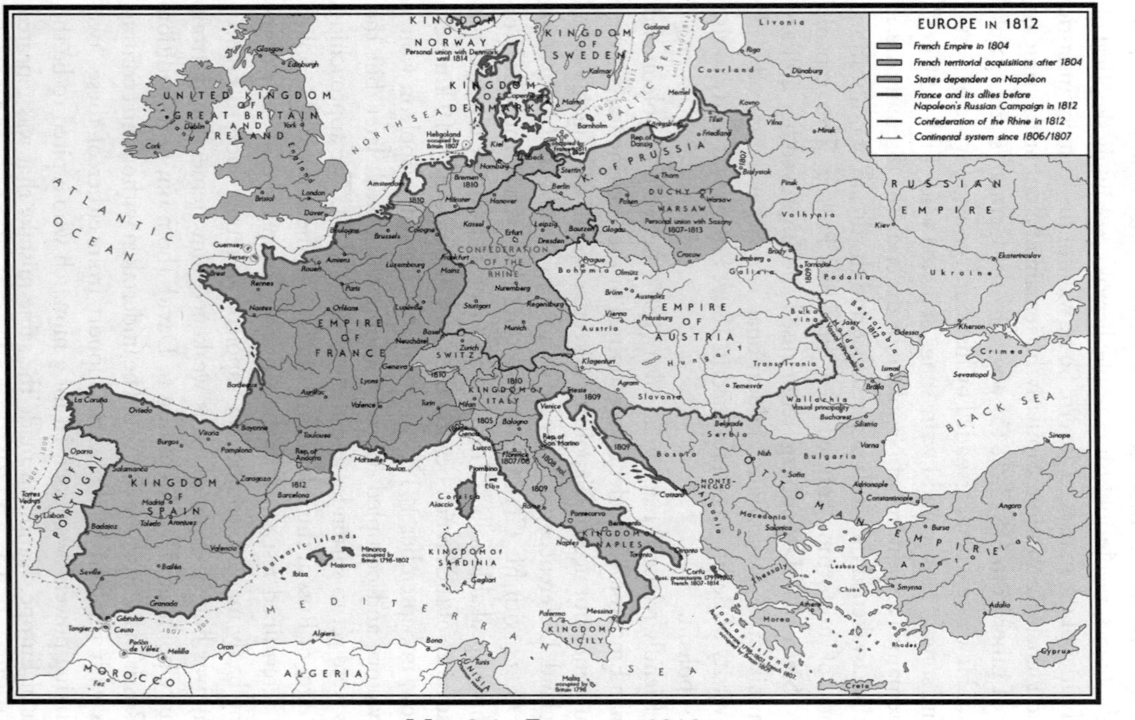

MAP 2.1: Europe in 1812

Source: Available at https://en.m.wikipedia.org/wiki/File:Europe_1812_map_en.png (accessed July 2025)
Note: Created by Alexander Altenhof, licensed under CC BY-SA 3.0, https://creativecommons.org/licenses/by-sa/3.0/deed.en

On the face of it, Napoleon embarked upon the precarious Russian adventure primarily to teach Czar Alexander I a lesson for not agreeing to enforce the Continental System in his lands. But for all practical purposes, the real reason was the clash of interests of France and Russia, in the Near East and the Mediterranean. The size of Napoleon's army was double that of Russia, but the extreme fluctuations of Russian weather, the shortage of supplies and the onset of diseases in a long-drawn war made victory completely elusive for the French. The tired, worn-out, disease-stricken Grand Army began to deplete very fast. Retreat remained the only option. In the words of Thomson, "it was his most dramatic and costly defeat."[18]

Napoleon: The Fall

Taking advantage of Napoleon's discomfiture **Prussia joined Russia against Napoleon in 1813**. This is known in German history as the **War of Liberation**. The success of popular resistance to French domination in Spain had inspired the Germans. In the **Battle of Leipzig**, also known as the **Battle of Nations**, the combined forces of **Prussia, Russia and Austria defeated Napoleon in 1813**.

The Battle of Leipzig not only liberated Germany from the yoke of Napoleon but also brought about the collapse of the Napoleonic Empire. Subordinate rulers gave up their allegiance to Napoleon. In 1814 the combined armies of Russia, Prussia and Austria invaded France. England also joined the coalition. In spite of his best efforts, Napoleon was unable to resist this invasion; Paris fell into enemy hands. Napoleon had to conclude a treaty by which he had to give up his claim on the throne of France. The successful invaders recognised him as the ruler of the small island of Elba in the Mediterranean Sea in April 1814. *The victorious powers restored the Bourbon dynasty to the French throne; Louis XVIII, brother of the executed King Louis XVI, became the King of France.*

Napoleon could not reconcile himself to the position of the ruler of a small island. In February 1815 he suddenly left Elba and returned to France. The people rallied round him with enthusiasm; so did the soldiers. Strengthened by such support, he entered Paris. Louis XVIII fled to Belgium. But the victorious powers were not prepared to accept Napoleon's restoration in France. The combined armies of **England and Prussia** defeated him in the **Battle of Waterloo** in **June 1815**. The British army was led by the Duke of Wellington. The Prussian Commander was Blucher. Napoleon had to give up his claim on the throne for the second time. He surrendered to the English in July 1815. This entire period from his return from Elba to his fall in Waterloo, is known as **Napoleon's 100 days**. During the remaining years of his life, 1815–1821, he lived as a prisoner of the English on the remote island of St. Helena in the Atlantic Ocean.

FIG. 2.2: Battle of Waterloo, 1815

What were the factors that precipitated Napoleon's downfall? While in St. Helena, Napoleon once observed, as written in *Le Memorial de Sainte Helene* by Emmanuel-Auguste Dieudonne Las Cases (a compilation of conversations with the Emperor published in 1823), that his fall was due to Spain, Pope and Russia. In the **Peninsular War** and in the Russian expedition, his military power suffered a serious setback and his military reputation lost its former glamour. The War of Liberation in Germany was the logical result of this change in Napoleon's position. The quarrel with the Papacy deprived him to a large extent of the sympathy of the Catholics who constituted the majority of the population of France. Indeed, it is doubtful whether he would have fallen prematurely from power if he had not drained his strength and energy in Spain, Portugal and Russia.

Truly speaking, however, the most serious of the causes of Napoleon's downfall was the **hostility with England**. Although he concluded several treaties with his older rivals, he never concluded any treaty with England. The Treaty of Amiens was merely a truce. It is the antipathy to England which led him to introduce the Continental System which in its turn led to the Peninsular War. The disputes with the Papacy and Russia were also primarily due to Napoleon's efforts to restrict England's foreign trade. But he was unable to match the invincible naval power of England. On the other hand, by trying to weaken England economically, he involved France in the Peninsular War and in the disastrous expedition to Russia. The intensity of his hatred towards England may have prevented him from acknowledging England's persistent hostility and naval supremacy among the causes of his downfall.

Nationalism became a dominant force in European politics as a result of the French Revolution. But there was no recognition of nationalism in the Napoleonic Empire. In embarking on his policy of imperialism, Napoleon never took the question of nationalism or national self-determination into consideration. That is why he removed the legitimate rulers of different countries and placed his own brothers there instead. In the name of imposing his own administrative system in these countries, he introduced Code Napoleon in all nations that accepted his subordination. But the peoples of other countries could not accept French political domination. The Napoleonic Empire could not garner the loyalty of all its subjects. Its foundation remained insecure. Felix Markham wrote,

> It is true that at Saint Helena, when he could see the trend of events, he fabricated the Napoleonic legend and tried to present his career as a struggle on behalf of the peoples and nationalities against the reactionary dynasties. But this was an after-thought and a travesty of the facts. The Napoleonic Empire was the negation of nationality...[19]

His empire was built up by military power and till the end, military power remained its sole basis. When that military power suffered serious setbacks in Spain and Portugal, in Russia and in Germany, the fall of the Empire became inevitable. All these countries fought tooth and nail to resist being swept away by the French army and to preserve their own right of national self-determination.

Napoleon's policy often betrayed lack of consistency. First, it was impossible for even the greatest of military might to keep a persistently uniform vigil over the entire European coastline. His police force often betrayed the cause, resorted to corruption and allowed smuggling. This obviously weakened the force of the Continental System. On rare occasions Napoleon himself relaxed his System. In 1811 when Britain was going through a chronic shortage of grain, he allowed grain supplies from France and also permitted limited imports from Britain on licence. He explained his motive clearly. France was also suffering and he intended to give his own farmers and traders some respite. He observed, "Undoubtedly we must harm our foes, but above all, we must live."

Even so, Napoleon failed to pacify the French traders and merchants who constituted the middle class or the bourgeoisie. They were the main beneficiaries of the French revolution, and, in their deep aversion to aristocracy, had helped to bring Napoleon—a common man—to power. But they turned against him completely when his Continental System damaged their trade and robbed them of their gains.

Certain traits of Napoleon's own character stood in the way of his success. As he grew in age and in power, there came a marked deterioration in his character, policy and methods. He listened to no advice; he was always guided by his own will. But it was not possible for even the mightiest of persons to carry alone the burden of a vast empire. This was the error that Hitler also repeated 130 years later. Blinded by his initial success, and then enraged by his reverses, Hitler refused to give a patient hearing to his sane advisers and well-wishers and thereby precipitated his own doom.

The composition and character of Napoleon's army were also changed. The enthusiasm of the Revolutionary Army had evaporated. Soldiers had to be recruited through conscription. Moreover, soldiers coming from different countries had entered Napoleon's Grand Army. It was no longer the national army of France. These were serious weaknesses of Napoleon's military empire.

Although gifted with brilliant genius in war and in peace, Napoleon failed on crucial occasions to follow realistic politics in international affairs. His unlimited self confidence and ambition dragged him to the wrong tracks. He did not realise the simple truth that France was not powerful enough to continue fighting indefinitely against practically the whole of Europe. France was bled white by his continuous wars. Engaged in war from the initial stage of the revolution, France was tired and eager for peace. After the failure of the Russian expedition, Napoleon's war policy no longer secured such support from the French people as it had enjoyed during the period of his uninterrupted victories. In a period of revolutions, no enduring empire can be sustained only by military conquests.

Napoleon and the Historians

History, as Peter Geyl says, is an argument without end.[20] Different scholars hold different views on the same issue. The same is the case with Napoleon. On the one hand, a Napoleonic legend was created about his rule which, the mass of the Frenchmen felt, brought unprecedented *gloire* to the history of their nation. They were blinded by the dazzling splendour of his relentless conquests. The legend—**Bonapartism**—as it is called, filled the hearts of the French with awe and inspiration. The successive regimes seemed too plain in their eyes. They were completely disappointed when Louis Philippe, the King of the French from 1830 to 1848, and his Prime Minister Guizot followed a cautious foreign policy and wanted to conquer Algeria only. They lamented the bygone Napoleonic days of glorious and daring foreign conquests. Some others like **Stendhal**, for example, hailed him as the 'son of the revolution'. "The true founders of present-day France" he wrote, "are Danton, Sieyes, Mirabeau and Napoleon."[21] Napoleon was thanked for ending feudalism, ensuring equality and subjugating the countries who had opposed the revolution. On the other hand, there were others like **Chateaubriand** who intensely hated Napoleon and referred to the fallen emperor in 1814 as

> the destroyer, the despiser of men, the foreigner, the Corsican, especially scornful of Frenchmen, careless of French blood, devourer of generations of young men, suppresser of all free opinion, demanding of writers a toll of flattering unction as the price of permission to publish—in a word, the tyrant.[22]

The polemic on Napoleon could broadly be divided into three categories—those who criticised him fiercely like Chateaubriand, those who were his admirers, and those who attempted at striking a balance between his virtues as well as vices. There were others apart from Chateaubriand who harboured unmitigated contempt for Napoleon. Pierre Lanfrey, Edgar Quinet, Hippolyte Taine, Jules Michelet, Jules Barni were among his strong critics who attempted to systematically shatter the legend that grew up around him. I have already discussed above the interpretations of Michelet and Taine on the French Revolution. Here we will see what they have to say about Napoleon. While **Lanfrey** accused him of brute force and his contempt for the people, as well as his opportunistic tendencies of concentrating power and issuing arbitrary orders, but then not owning up responsibility, and blaming the subordinates for the disastrous consequences; **Edgar Quinet** bitterly accused Napoleon of destroying the spirit of the revolution which embodied a mammoth resistance to absolutism, and to a worn out Church and its exploitation in the name of religion. Revolutionary France was reduced by Napoleon into a regime that was as authoritarian as the monarchy and revived the old relationship between the Church and the State. In Michelet's perspective, Napoleon was the ruthless self-seeker, betrayer of the revolution and of the people. In his earlier book on the revolution in 1851, he saw Napoleon as the champion of the revolution. But Michelet changed his opinion drastically in his three volumes on Napoleon published between 1872 and 1875, in which he regarded Napoleon as a '**corrupted soul**', although he continued to look upon the revolution as the carrier of the message of liberty and equality. Even when France fell in 1815, Napoleon was thinking of securing the succession of his son and the security of his possessions. **Hippolyte Taine**, also known as the **Third Republican historian** because he wrote during the period of the Third Republic, believed that Napoleon was nothing more than an 'evil demon' let loose upon Europe; like Chateaubriand, he considered Napoleon to be a foreigner—an Italian—who although reminisced his love for the Frenchmen, in reality only misused their emotions to fulfil his own dream and ambitions.

> The truth is that he loves it as a horseman loves his horse; all the grooming and smartening up, all the stroking and encouragement, is not for the benefit of the horse, but to prepare it as a useful animal for his service, so that it may fulfil his purposes, even to exhaustion, so that he may force it on over ever wider ditches and ever higher obstacles...[23]

Jules Barni, the prominent French philosopher and politician, was also extremely critical of Napoleon. He interpreted all the activities of Napoleon as a reversion to the methods and policies of the ancien regime and, therefore, clearly as a destroyer of the revolution. Moreover, his typical traits of contempt of humanity, insensitivity, his inordinate ego, were not in any way French characteristic features. He was **a foreigner** and remained so. The account of **Madame de Remusat**, another sharp polemic of Napoleonic regime, explained the causes why people adored him so; because they desperately looked for a deliverer, and thought Napoleon to be the one.

> I can understand how it was that men worn out by the turmoil of the revolution, and afraid of that liberty which had long been associated with death, looked for repose under the dominion of an able ruler on

whom fortune was seemingly resolved to smile. I can conceive that they regarded this elevation as a decree of destiny and fondly believed that in the irrevocable they should find peace…This belief, or rather the error, was… widespread…and he even succeeded in persuading foreign sovereigns that he constituted a barrier against republican influences, which, but for him, might spread widely… Had the new emperor granted a liberal constitution, the peace of nations and kings might really have been forever secured.[24]

All hopes, however, were dashed to the ground. The dismay can best be expressed in the words of Byron in the second stanza of 'Ode to Napoleon Buonaparte',

> Ill-minded man! Why scourge thy kind
> Who bow'd so low the knee?
> By gazing on thyself grown blind,
> Thou taught'st the rest to see.
> With might unquestioned—power to save—
> Thine only gift hath been the grave,
> To those that worshipp'd thee;
> Nor till thy fall could mortals guess
> Ambition's less than littleness![25]

At the same time, Napoleon had a host of admirers. Apart from Stendhal, there are many others like Henry Houssaye, Arthur-Levy, Frederic Masson, Madelin, who were clearly pro-Napoleon in outlook. **Houssaye** regarded Napoleon as a 'man of the people'. In the eyes of the people, he believed, France and Napoleon were inseparable. That is why people flocked around him *en masse* on his return in 1815 from Elba. **Arthur-Levy** was one of the most committed admirers of Napoleon. In his eyes, Napoleon was kindness and humanitarianism incarnate—over-indulgent in family, compassionate and just as a ruler. According to **Peter Geyl**, however, Arthur-Levy goes "too far" in his benevolent attitude in the estimate on Napoleon. He overlooks and undermines several incidents of Napoleon's cruelty and intolerance. Geyl has elaborated some of these in his own book to show that Levy was too liberal in endowing lavish praises on his dear Emperor. Napoleon's greatest admirer by far was **Frederic Masson**. Geyl wrote about him, "None was more wholehearted in his admiration, none more passionate, more one-sided, more partisan, and also none more sincere, more honest, none was more convinced that he (Napoleon) served truth, or more courageous in its service…"[26] Masson eulogised Napoleon in his book *Napoleon Chez Lui* after taking into account every aspect of Napoleon's life—public and personal—on the basis of hard facts. "The hero must appear entire, his every aspect illuminated by an implacable light."[27]

The majority of historians have made an effort to reach a balance between his greatness as well as his errors. In **Francois Auguste Mignet's** view, Napoleon was nothing less than a despot who marginalised the impact of the revolution. "Brought up in camps, a late arrival in the revolution, he understood only its material side… He believed neither in the moral cravings which had stirred up the revolution, nor in the cravings which had swayed it, and which sooner or later were bound to emerge again and bring about his downfall."[28] He entered into the Concordat with the Pope with the sole intention of dominating the Church and the people.

Here it is difficult to agree with Mignet. He erroneously assumed that Napoleon failed to grasp the spirit and the yearnings of the revolution. It was not so. He was inspired by the revolutionary fervour, the ideas of Rousseau and the Jacobins, and was slowly transformed from an ardent Corsican to a Frenchman. Many of these ideas he continued, and although he later turned away from Rousseau, the latter's philosophy of popular sovereignty he carried throughout his life. Though Napoleon established a military dictatorship, he **ruled in the name of the people** and sought to bring in egalitarianism in many respects. And so he is regarded as the **last enlightened despot of Europe**. This Mignet has conceded despite his strong criticism. He wrote, "As regards France, he was a counter-revolutionary because of his despotism, but as a conqueror of Europe he became a renovator. Several nations which slumbered before he came, will live with the life he brought them."[29] **Louis Adolphe Thiers** was undoubtedly an admirer of Napoleon, so much so that his account of Napoleon has been dubbed propagandist writing.[30] But it is an unfair comment as Thiers did not falter to criticise serious defects of Napoleon's character. He pointed out how jealous he occasionally was; how unreasonable and ruthless Napoleon was while giving orders to his subordinates. But these flaws of the Great Emperor he points out, Geyl observed, more with sorrow than in anger.[31] This reveals the softness he harboured for the Great conqueror. Thiers regarded Napoleon to be a great consolidator of the revolution at home and its great promoter abroad. At the same time Napoleon was a devoted and intense Frenchman. Unlike the Napoleon of Chateaubriand or of Taine or of Barni, Thiers' Napoleon was not a Corsican careless of

French blood and emotions, but rather a furtherer of France's fundamental interests, a true son of the soil.

Baron Bignon, the French diplomat who served under the Revolutionary Army and also under Napoleon, did not hesitate to praise and criticise him alike. He despised his despotism, condemned him for the excesses of his conquests, but at the same time held him high for the material benefits that his conquests brought to France, the improved education system that he tried to impart to his countrymen. No debate or interpretative account on either the French Revolution or Napoleon can be complete without a reference to Madame de Stael. **Madame de Stael** who turned against Napoleon after being dismayed at his arrogance and contempt for women, and criticised him virulently in public for destroying the republican ideology and thereby the essence of the French Revolution, for being a foreigner who knew nothing but tyranny and conquest, was once a great admirer of Napoleon herself. She was highly impressed by his splendid military genius which was first reflected in his deliverance of Toulon from British hands, his triumph against Italy, his march upon Egypt, and she sincerely congratulated him for bringing glory to France. Therefore, among the **ambivalent scholars** on Napoleon, Madame de Stael holds a distinctive place. In this connection, an interesting anecdote is worth mentioning. The great composer **Beethoven** was also an ardent admirer of Napoleon and compared him to the great consuls of ancient Rome. He dedicated in early 1804 a revolutionary symphony *Eroica Variations* (Op.35) to Napoleon and his heroic deeds. He named it in Italian—*Sinfonia, Intitolata Napoleon* (Symphony entitled Napoleon). However, soon after this he came to know that Napoleon had declared himself the Emperor of France. Beethoven flew into rage and shouted, "So he is no more than a common mortal…Now he will think himself superior to all men, (and) become a tyrant." He at once picked up his pen and scratched out the title with such force that the paper tore. Since then the symphony was simply known as *Sinfonia Eroica* (Heroic Symphony).[32]

George Rudé too, like many scholars, found the two completely opposing aspects of Napoleon's character highly enigmatic. On the one hand, he was a proponent of Jacobin philosophy, read Rousseau avidly, wanted to overthrow the old aristocracy, and many European liberals flocked around him, especially where his administrative system was successfully adopted, like by Westphalia, ruled by Napoleon's brother Jerome; *Napoleon successfully continued the peasant ownership of lands of émigrés nobility and* *the Church—the greatest achievement of the French Revolution.* In this sense, he was a revolutionary. On the other hand, as Rudé observed, this portrait of Napoleon did not seem to match with the personality who aspired to found a strong empire, who revived the old nobility, who prided himself on being the son-in-law of the Emperor of Austria, and claimed to be related to the Bourbons. So in Rudé's estimation, "Napoleon was indeed a military despot, but he did not destroy the work of the revolution; in a sense, in a wider European context, he rounded off its work."[33] In **Furet**'s opinion, he ruled in the name of the people and established a "dictatorship of public opinion".[34] For Furet, "Napoleon combined the qualities in his personality that were already despotic and uncontrollable. He himself had a clear understanding of the conditions that had brought him to power and of the civilian nature of his dictatorship."[35] Furet further elaborated,

> Nevertheless, he remained first and foremost the heir of the revolution, since the administrative state that he created in opposition to local powers was established upon the universality of law. Though in later years he resorted increasingly to arbitrary actions and established a nobility that owed its titles to the state, the source of his power over the nation was from the fact that he was the chosen embodiment of popular sovereignty, was its instrument for making and enforcing laws that were to be the same for all.[36]

Soboul too called it a despotic rule in the garb of popular sovereignty.[37]

We can end with the question posed by Max Sewell in his essay 'Feet of Clay: An Examination of Napoleon Bonaparte', that almost all the vices for which Napoleon was condemned again and again (Lord Acton's adage *'power corrupts and absolute power corrupts absolutely'* became synonymous with Napoleon Bonaparte) were present in almost all the contemporary monarchs of Europe—megalomania, immorality, involvement in continuous wars, accumulation of power in one's own hands, among others. *Why is then Napoleon singled out and so vehemently disparaged?*

The answer perhaps lies in the fact that Napoleon's brilliance was too dazzling; it made him not only stand out, but earned him the epithet '**Great**' and also led to his deification. He was placed on such an exalted pedestal that expectations from him became larger than life; people forgot that he was after all a human being with common human failings. In fact, the depravity of many of his contemporary monarchs had been much greater. But what is clear is that he fought too many wars, many unnecessary ones that cost millions of young innocent lives. Too much blood had been shed to satisfy one man's gigantic ego. The Frenchmen of his time and posterity never forgave him for that. He was hailed because the war-weary men of France looked upon him as their deliverer, their last hope. When that hope was dashed to the ground, Napoleon was heavily denounced. Even so, one must remember that the denunciation, too, was mostly among the intellectuals and scholars. The common man continued to adore him as was manifest from the passion with which they flocked around him when he suddenly came back from Elba. Deification and condemnation of Napoleon, both, therefore, were blown out of proportion.

Notes

1. Alfred Cobban, *History of Modern France*, Vol. II, 1799–1871 (England: Penguin Books, 1961), 13.

2. David Thomson, *Europe Since Napoleon* (London: Penguin Books, 1966), 37.

3. Felix Markham, *Napoleon and the Awakening of Europe* (England: Penguin Books, 1975), 63.

4. Hippolyte Taine, 'Napoleon's Views of Religion,' *The North American Review* 152(414) (May 1891): 567.

5. Taine, 'Napoleon's Views of Religion,' 567.

6. Cobban, *History of Modern France*, 38.

7. Stephen J. Lee, *Aspects of European History, 1789–1980* (London and New York: Routledge, 1982), 21.

8. Ibid., 24.

9. Ibid., 25.

10. Ibid., 2.

11. François Furet, 'Napoleon Bonaparte,' in *Recent Debates and New Controversies*, ed. Gary Kates (New York: Routledge, 1998), chapter 11.

12. Albert Soboul, *Understanding the French Revolution* (New York: International Publishers, 1988), 14.

13. Markham, *Napoleon and the Awakening of Europe*, 101.

14. Ibid., 102.

15. Ibid., 99.

16. Eugene Anderson, *Nationalism and Cultural Crisis in Prussia: 1806–1815* (New York: Octagon Press, 1966), 34.

17. Thomson, *Europe Since Napoleon*, 52.

18. Ibid., 53.

19. Markham, *Napoleon and the Awakening of Europe*, 122.

20. Peter Geyl, *Napoleon: For and Against* (New Haven and London: Yale University Press, 1964), 15–16.

21. Ibid., 32.

22. Ibid., 18.

23. Hippolyte Taine, quoted in Geyl, *Napoleon*, 139–140.

24. *Memoirs of Madame de Rémusat*, early 19th century, Document 4. Available at https://www.gutenberg.org/ebooks/33894 (accessed July 2025).

25. Lord Byron, 'Ode to Napoleon Buonaparte' (1814).

26. Geyl, *Napoleon: For and Against*, 177.

27. Ibid., 179.

28. Ibid., 35.

29. Ibid., 36.

30. Ibid., 54.

31. Ibid., 55.

32. Alexander Lee, 'Beethoven and Napoleon,' *History Today* 68(3) (March 2018).

33. George Rudé, *Revolutionary Europe, 1783–1815* (Great Britain: Fontana, 1975), 1st pub. 1964.

34. François Furet, 'Napoleon Bonaparte,' in *Recent Debates and New Controversies*, 346.

35. Ibid., 349.

36. Ibid., 349.

37. Soboul, *Understanding the French Revolution*.

CHAPTER 3

The Age of Revolutions (1815–1848)

The aftermath of the French Revolution and the Napoleonic regime was deep and pervasive. The ideas of Enlightenment that they generated transcended the borders of France and swept up a frenzy in the people of other parts of the European continent. The result was that revolutions, inspired by the enlightened ideas of the French Revolution, began to break out in various parts of Europe. Sporadic outbreaks occurred in the 1820s and snowballed into an extensive revolution covering a number of countries in 1830. Revolutions on a still larger scale—extending over almost the whole of Europe, with the exception of England in the west and Russia in the east—exploded in 1848. The first half of the 19th century also saw another spectacular revolution, albeit of a different kind—the **industrial revolution**. Eric Hobsbawm calls these two kinds of revolution—one political and the other economic—the **dual revolution** and places their centres in **France** and **England**, the political revolution for liberty and popular sovereignty in France and the industrial revolution in Britain. As he says, "The transformation of 1789–1848 is essentially the twin upheaval which took place in those two countries, and was propagated thence across the entire world."[1] Both the revolutions had one common element—the triumph of the bourgeoisie. In France, the revolution saw the definite victory of the bourgeoisie and establishment of the bourgeois liberal state. In Britain, it saw the victory of the capitalist industry and the capitalist bourgeoisie. This revolutionary period was significant also for the emergence of a number of new concepts, signified by certain terms which acquired prominence during this period. Hobsbawm says, "They are such words as 'industry', 'industrialist', 'factory', 'middle class', 'working class', 'capitalism' and 'socialism'. They include 'aristocracy', as well as 'railway', 'liberal' and 'conservative' as political terms, 'nationality', 'scientist' and 'engineer', 'proletariat' and (economic) 'crisis'."[2] These words indicate the profundity of the changes unfolding in Europe in the late 18th and early 19th century. All in all, this entire period of 1789–1848 therefore, can be aptly called the '**Age of Revolutions**'.

Background of the Revolutions of 1830 and 1848

In order to understand these revolutions, a probe is necessary into the circumstances leading to them, the series of events which formed their backdrop, the ideas that inspired them. That takes us to a brief discussion of what happened in the phase between 1815 to 1848, that is, between the fall of Napoleon and the eruption of the revolutions, first in 1830, and then far more widely in 1848. Without an assessment of this phase, any analysis of the revolutions is incomplete and inadequate.

THE CONGRESS OF VIENNA

After the fall of Napoleon at the hands of the European Coalition at Waterloo in 1815, the victorious powers concluded peace with France by the **First Treaty of Paris (30 May 1814)**. The Bourbon dynasty was restored under **Louis XVIII** (he ruled France from 1814–1824 with an interruption of a brief period during Napoleon's Hundred Days. He was also known as *Le Desire* (The Desired). He was the younger brother of Louis XVI. Louis XVII, the son of Louis XVI had died in 1795 at the age of 10). France was allowed to retain its boundaries of 1 January 1792, and was permitted to reclaim much of its colonies. The **Second Treaty of Paris** was concluded with France on **20 November 1815**, after Napoleon's defeat in Waterloo. Between the two treaties, many important developments had taken place—Napoleon's escape from Elba, his warm welcome by the French people, his re-occupation of the French throne, and consequently, war between France and the allies—all of which eroded the benevolent nature of the earlier treaty and exacted indemnities from France, redefined the French boundary from that of 1792 (as had been decided by the Treaty of 1814), to that of 1 January 1790, thus **stripping France of Saar and Savoy**. France had to pay a huge indemnity of 700,000,000 francs and accept an allied army of occupation on its soil for three to five years. Meanwhile, a **Congress of the victorious powers sat at Vienna** in order to determine the political changes which would be necessary to reconstruct Europe after the revolutionary and Napoleonic wars. The work of the Congress was disrupted temporarily with Napoleon's return from Elba and was again resumed after Napoleon's final defeat in the Battle of Waterloo. The Congress was attended by the **Russian Czar Alexander I, the Austrian Hapsburg Emperor Francis, the Prussian King Frederick William III**, and the **Kings of Denmark and Bavaria**. England sent her **Foreign Secretary, Lord Castlereagh**. Although France was a defeated power, she was admitted into the Congress and was asked to send her plenipotentiary. France sent her **Prime Minister, Charles Maurice de Talleyrand-Perigord**, commonly known as Talleyrand. Austria, the native country of Marie Antoinette, was the host nation and **Prince Metternich**, the Chancellor or Prime Minister of Austria, was the most predominant personality at the Congress of Vienna. He had great influence on the deliberations at the Congress of Vienna and also in the development of international relations till the revolutions of 1848. He was the Chancellor for about forty years, from 1809 to 1848. The entire period is known as **the era of Metternich**.

The primary objectives for which the Congress of Vienna was convened are as follows. *First*, to establish a new balance of power in Europe in order to prevent imperialistic activities of a European country towards any other nation, and to maintain lasting peace in the European continent. They wished to redraw the political map of Europe by obliterating the changes brought about by the imperialistic conquests of Napoleon Bonaparte. *Second*, the Congress also aimed at preventing any further revolutionary outbreak in Europe, such as the French Revolution, because, in their eyes, revolution was the root of all turmoil that engulfed Europe for so many years in the past in the form of the revolutionary and Napoleonic wars. *Third*, an important goal of the big powers who met at Vienna was to maintain the status quo in the continent.

After long discussions, the conclusions formulated at the Congress of Vienna were incorporated in an international treaty (**9 June 1815**)— the **'Final Act' of the Congress of Vienna**. These conclusions were based on three general principles, which in fact, can be subordinated under the headings of 'legitimacy', 'security', and 'compensation'. *First*, those ruling dynasties which had been displaced as a result of Napoleonic Wars were to be restored to their former rulers. In other words, the changes brought about by Napoleon in the map of Europe were now to be altered and everything was to be taken back to its original position. This was known as the **principle of legitimacy**. This was required to be applied in the cases of France, Spain, Piedmont and Holland. In all these kingdoms the old ruling dynasties—the Bourbon dynasties in France, Spain and Naples, the Orange dynasty in Holland and the Savoy dynasty in Piedmont—were once again placed on their respective legitimate thrones. But the principle had two exceptions: Holland was united with Belgium and Sweden with Norway. In these two cases the old arrangements were not restored.

Second, the countries which had taken up arms against Napoleon, or had been victimised by his militarism, were **territorially compensated**. This was known as the **principle of compensation or reward**. England got some colonial territories formerly under France and Spain in addition to Ceylon and South Africa from Holland. Territorial possessions in Europe did not interest England for her future lay in commercial and colonial expansion. Her gains at Vienna made England the greatest colonial power in the world. Holland, in exchange received Austrian Netherlands or Belgium. Austria, too, had to be compensated for handing over Austrian Netherlands and received, therefore, Lombardy and Venetia in North Italy. Moreover, Austrian princes were placed on the thrones of the central Italian principalities—Parma, Modena, Tuscany. Finland (a part of Sweden), was given to Russia; in return, Sweden got Norway. Prussia was given large territories in Germany—Pomerania, Westphalia and major portions of Saxony and the Rhineland. The strengthening of Holland and Prussia was intended to enable them to keep a close watch on France on her eastern and western borders. France was no longer to be allowed to disturb the peace of Europe. In Germany, a German Confederation was created comprising 39 German states ruled by independent German princes. Formerly there were more than 300 principalities in Germany; Napoleon reduced this number to 100 and established the Confederation of the Rhine. At the Congress of Vienna, the Confederation of the Rhine was further reduced to 39 states and was renamed the German Confederation. Austria was made the president of the confederation. Prussia also was a member. The territorial settlement of the Congress of Vienna is particularly significant because of its impact on the future history of Europe. In fact, political developments in the continent till about the 1870s revolved round the territorial arrangements accomplished at the Congress of Vienna.

Third, in applying the twin principles of legitimacy and compensation or reward, the leaders of the Congress were extremely careful in maintaining the **balance of power**. No power should be allowed to become so powerful as to dominate others and thereby endanger the existence of others. The Congress would not tolerate any country becoming stronger than what it was before the Revolution. In short, the status quo was to be maintained at any cost.

The Congress of Vienna was one of the most important diplomatic gatherings in the history of modern Europe, especially in view of the variety of issues it settled. One of the gravest charges brought against the members of the Congress of Vienna was that vested interests and self-aggrandisement of the big powers were the key to the welter of bargains and agreements. **Friedrich von Gentz**, the close confidant and adviser of Metternich and the Secretary to the Congress of Vienna, was a staunch critic of the Congress and his memoirs are a testament to his deep disillusionment with its workings. He wrote,

> The fine phrases, 'the reconstruction of the social order, the regeneration of the political system of Europe, an enduring peace based on a just redistribution of forces', etc., were intended only to tranquillise the people and give to the solemn reunion an air of dignity and grandeur; the real object of the Congress was to divide among the conquerors the spoils of the conquered.[3]

The real charge that was brought against the monarchs at Vienna was that they ignored the challenge of the French Revolution. *They failed to recognise the indelible influence of the ideals of equality and democracy brewing in the new Age of Revolution.* The personal rights and political privileges of the common man were completely denied. Metternich was intensely apprehensive of the prospect of a revolutionary outbreak. He looked upon **revolution as the source of all evils**, a terrible germ that would quickly spread from one country to another and assume the form of an epidemic. His partners in the leadership of the Vienna Congress also entertained the same idea. Therefore, all demands of the people for any kind of political rights or any voice in public domain were curbed instantly. For years the monarchs of Europe had condemned Napoleon for respecting neither the rights of princes, nor those of peoples. They now offered him a glowing tribute by simply following in his footsteps.

The leaders at the Congress of Vienna were equally disdainful of the **right of national self-determination**. A strongly nationalist idea had emanated from the French Revolution that people belonging to the same country and speaking the same language should remain under the rule of a single state. This was the principle of national self-determination. It was in utter defiance of this principle that two different countries—**Holland and Belgium**—speaking different languages were united. The union of Sweden with Norway ignored the difference in language and in historical tradition. Poland had already lost its national existence; different parts of the country remained under the rule of Russia, Austria and Prussia. Italy was virtually divided between the Hapsburgs and the Bourbons. Considerations of strategy, power and absolutist tendencies of big royal families took priority over national interests. From the beginning to the end, the Congress remained almost exclusively a congregation of the great powers, the smaller states being summoned only to participate in the deliberations of matters non-trivial, which pertained to them individually. A plenary session of all powers was never held.

In recent years, **Adam Zamoyski**, on the one hand agreed that "The **reconstruction of Europe at the Congress of Vienna** is probably the most seminal episode in modern history. Not only did the Congress redraw the map entirely, it determined which nations were to have a political existence over the next hundred years and which were not...It entirely transformed the conduct of international affairs," and "...brought into being a Europe of expanding prosperity and technological advance," but on the other, believed that all these came at a high price. He argued:

> The Vienna Settlement...enshrined a particularly stultified form of monarchical government institutionalised social hierarchies as rigid as any that had existed under the ancient regime; and preserved archaic disabilities (including serfdom in Russia). By excluding whole classes and nations from a share in its benefits, this system nurtured envy and resentment, which flourished into socialism and aggressive nationalism. And when, after the Concert of Europe had fought itself to extinction in the Great War, those forces were at last unleashed, they visited on Europe events more horrific than the worst fears Metternich or any of his colleagues could have entertained.[4]

In general, however, since the middle of the 20th century, historians have started taking a favourable view of the Vienna Congress and its activities. **Henry Kissinger**, for example, praised it because he believed that it brought forth a new 'legitimacy' that lasted for a hundred years. He observed that the achievement of the Vienna Settlement was that it not only restored balance of power, but restored it in such a way that all the great powers accepted it as legitimate. It is undeniable that no major state emerged from the settlement with such disappointment as Germany did after 1919. The conflict between Russia, Prussia and Austria was resolved in such a way that each nation emerged from the settlement with at least the minimum satisfaction of its requirements. But this is true only as far as the major states were concerned. It was not acceptable to the small powers, as a result of which there were upheavals in 1820s, 1830 and 1848 for overthrowing the order. And it was not that the leaders at Vienna were not aware of it. Yet, keeping in view the difficulties of the international situation of the times and considerations of the future, that was best solution they were able to work out. The protagonists of the Congress, therefore, should not be dismissed, as **Harold Nicolson** points out,

> as mere hucksters in the diplomatic market bartering the happiness of millions with a scented smile....It would be an error to imagine that the statesmen of 1814 were more cynical or selfish, more ignorant or unintelligent, than their successors of 1919 or 1946. Their common aim was to secure the stability, and therefore the peace, of Europe; and, before indulging in irritation or contempt, it is salutary to reflect that they did in fact prevent a general European conflagration for a whole century of time.[5]

Generally speaking, therefore, the Congress of Vienna has been hailed by scholars specifically for two reasons. Firstly, that it **preserved peace in Europe** for about forty years till 1853—notwithstanding the minor breaches of peace—in the intervening period. And second, it succeeded, it is claimed, in setting up **a balanced state system in Europe**. The general paradigm of 18th century was the 'balance of power'. **Edward vose Gulick** coined a new term—**alliance balance**—to define the most potent form of alignment system operating under the balance of power paradigm.[6] This meant manoeuvring the existing political system in such a way that no power was allowed to become strong enough to upset the balance. Here protection of individual self-interest was the primary driving force. This was transformed to a new coalition system—**'coalition equilibrium'**—where old enemies joined the common cause sinking their own interests to defeat hegemony and preponderance.[7] Community well-being and not self-interest was the foremost focus. In this paradigm shift, the Congress of Vienna played a crucial role. In fact, Austria took the lead in this—both by forming a coalition against Napoleon and also in convening the Congress of Vienna. Gulick wrote,

> The settlement as a whole, unfair in many respects, incomplete in numerous details, destined to be thus endlessly revised, was yet remarkably

consistent with the idea of re-establishing in Europe a balanced state system. If the Vienna Congress failed to satisfy the aspirations of Poland, if it ignored the population of Belgium, if it restored disunion to Italy and gave no permanent settlement to Germany, yet it showed both moderation and political wisdom and it provided a real foundation on which later Europe was to build.

Richard Langhorne analysed how the situation even at the end of the Second World War in 1945 was similar to that in 1815. The Congress of Vienna remained relevant even 130 years later.[8]

L.C.B. Seaman put forth a balanced critique of the historical significance of the Congress of Vienna. He has praised and criticised the Congress in equal measure. According to him, even if Belgium had been made independent in 1815, there was little chance for her survival because of her "perilous proximity to France." It was the high-handed attitude of the House of Orange that made things unbearable for the Belgians. Similarly, neither Austria nor Prussia—the two main powers in the German Confederation—were interested in unifying Germany, because that would have been tantamount to curtailing their own predominance. At least, argued Seaman, Germany in 1815 was much less divided than it had been in 1789. Austria was entrenched in Italy because otherwise Italy would have lapsed into French occupation. And same were the cases of Poland and Norway. Neither of them, felt the leaders at the Congress, were strong enough to sustain their independence. What they endeavoured, therefore, was to retain their autonomy as much as possible. Both Poland as well as Norway had their own governments, parliament and constitution. Seaman, therefore, believed that the men of 1815 at least could be spared of the "charge of cynical indifference." However, Seaman did not think that the Vienna Settlement *per se* had prevented the outbreak of a major European war for almost forty years, until 1853. Because, it was not treaties and settlements, but the determination of the big powers that prevented a war. "There might have been war in 1875, 1878, 1885, 1887, 1898, 1906, 1908, 1911 or 1912. That it was avoided on each of these occasions has nothing to do with the Congress of Vienna."[9] It is possible to say instead that none of its provisions contained the seeds of a future war between the great powers. It was after the **exit of Metternich** from the diplomatic scene and when **Louis Napoleon established the Second French Empire in 1851** that wars began to break out in 1850s and 1860s. That was because **Napoleon III** (the title Louis Napoleon assumed when he became the Emperor) had scant respect for any such international arrangement. The first assault on the system erected at Vienna was hurled when in 1831, Belgium declared independence from Holland; and it was by 1871 when the unifications of Italy and Germany had been accomplished that much of the settlement so assiduously built in 1815 withered away.

THE METTERNICH SYSTEM

During the first half of the 19th century, the most predominant political leader in Europe was **Prince Klemens Von Metternich**. He was the Foreign Minister of Austria for forty years, from 1809 to 1848, and also later the Chancellor from 1821 to 1848. The entire period is known as the era of Metternich. It came to be so called because it was Metternich's policies and diplomacy that played the key role in European politics during this time.

FIG. 3.1: Klemens von Metternich

Metternich was born into an aristocratic family on 15 May 1773 in Coblenz, Germany. He was taught by private tutors till the age of fifteen after which he went to study Philosophy at the University of Strasbourg.

There his education was disrupted by the French Revolution. He personally saw the chaos and disorder spreading over that city, and soon after he left for Mainz to study law in 1790. In Mainz, too, he heard disturbing tales of woe of the émigrés of France. These events were highly instrumental in sowing in his young mind the seeds of deep-seated revulsion against the concept of revolution and turning him into a hard-core reactionary. His marriage to Eleonore Kaunitz, the granddaughter of former Austrian Chancellor Wenzel Kaunitz in 1795 introduced him to the Viennese society. Metternich served as an envoy to the Congress of Rastadt (1797–1799) and then as Hapsburg's ambassador to Saxony (1801, Prussia (1803), and Napoleonic France (1806). A significant political event in 1809 brought about a momentous change in his professional career. In July of that year, Austria suffered a crushing defeat at the hands of Napoleon in the **Battle of Wagram**. Metternich was offered the post of Foreign Minister in place of Stadion who was discredited as a result of the defeat.

To increase Austria's power and influence and to utilise them in resisting the progress of revolutionary ideas in Europe, to promote her status quo interests and to maintain European stability were the primary objectives of Metternich's policy. He never deviated from these in the course of his long political career. The policies he undertook to achieve his goals may collectively be termed as his 'System'.

After the **Battle of Wagram**, the main thrust of his policy was to restore Austria's prestige by devastating Napoleon. In this he carefully cultivated Russia's friendship. His primary concern in this direction was also to prevent Russia from being drawn into any kind of understanding with Napoleon. However, he endeavoured to pretend before Napoleon to be his ally and even encouraged him to marry the Austrian archduchess Marie Louise in March 1810.

In the autumn of 1811, Napoleon was determined to defeat Russia decisively. The invasion began on 24 June 1812 when Napoleon's Grande Armee crossed the Niemen to attack Russia. What he expected from Austria was her neutrality. **Metternich faked neutrality**, and even promised military help. **Prussia**, which according to the terms of the Treaty of Tilsit, 1812, sent troops to support Napoleon's Russian invasion, later signed the **Convention of Tauroggen** with Russia on 30 December 1812. This was signed by the Prussian General York without the knowledge of the King. York was suspended but was absolved when the **Treaty of Kalisz** was finally settled between Prussia and Russia against Napoleon on 28 February 1813. Napoleon met Metternich and pleaded for his military help at Dresden on

26 June 1813, but Metternich now refused to oblige. Rather, he offered mediation for peace. In reply Napoleon flung his hat into the corner of the room, exclaiming,

> If I am to accept your policy I am required to evacuate Europe, half of which I still hold, lead back my legions across the Rhine, the Alps and the Pyrenees and, sign a treaty which amounts to a vast capitulation, deliver myself like an idiot to my enemies.[10]

Even so, Metternich did not budge. Rather, on 12 August 1813, Metternich formally joined hands with Russia and Prussia in their combined war against Napoleon and also supplied the largest number of troops. In the **Battle of Leipzig**, also known as the **Battle of Nations** (16–19 October 1813), the combined forces of Russia, Prussia and Austria defeated Napoleon. In 1814, the combined forces of Russia, Prussia, Austria and England invaded France. Napoleon was defeated and had to withdraw as the ruler of the small island of Elba in the Mediterranean Sea (April 1814), as we have seen in the previous chapter.

Apart from avenging the humiliation inflicted upon Austria by demolishing the Napoleonic Empire and restoring Austria's esteem in the eyes of the world, an important aspect of Metternich's policy was to reconstruct Europe after the ravages of the French Revolution and Napoleon, to establish peace and stability by resisting the progress of the revolutionary ideas in Europe. The experience of his early life had created in him a deep-rooted suspicion of everything connected with revolution. He looked upon revolution as the root of all social maladies. In his view, revolution was the disease which must be cured, the volcano which must be extinguished, the gangrene which must be burned out with hot iron, the hydra with jaws open to swallow up the whole social order. Everywhere, therefore, revolution was to be crushed at any cost. Austria under Metternich was vigilant all the while to smother the spirit of revolution wherever it tried to push up its 'ugly head'. The new political aspirations which had been awakened in the mind of the common man in the Age of Revolutions had no value for him.

In order to enhance Austria's preponderance in Europe, Metternich's first task was to solve her severe internal problems. The Austrian territories over which Metternich presided were riddled with immensely complicated problems—racially, politically and administratively. As Lipson commented, "… it is deficient alike in unity and coherence. This is due primarily to the fact that Austria was not a nation but a 'monarchical machine'."[11] The old territories of Austria fell into four distinct historical groups:—(*i*) the hereditary kingdom of Austria was a conglomeration of 11 nationalities which had been formed under the rule of the Hapsburg dynasty through forceful military subjugation; (*ii*) the kingdom of Bohemia; (*iii*) the Polish kingdom of Galicia; (*iv*) the Crown of St. Stephen. The French Revolution had aggravated the crisis by fanning the sentiments of freedom and nationalism of the diverse nationalities. Metternich sought to solve the perennial problem by devising his 'System'. His aim was not to bring the motley territories of Austria into greater unity, but rather to exploit their disunity on the basis of the time-honoured Hapsburg principle of 'divide and rule'.

Metternich was able to secure full recognition of his policy in the reconstruction of Europe at the Congress of Vienna. Austria, as we have seen, had given up Netherlands (Belgium) receiving in exchange the provinces of Lombardy and Venetia in North Italy and also some central Italian duchies. Practically, the **whole of North and Central Italy** came under **Austrian control**. Austria also secured the Presidency of the German Confederation. Thus, the ground was prepared for the application of Metternich's anti-revolutionary policy in Italy and Germany. In other countries as well the autocratic system of government of the *ancien regime* and the social system based on inequality were sought to be restored. Apparently, the whole of Europe submitted to the Metternich System.

In Germany, the Metternich System was dominant for many years, from 1815 to 1848. As the **president of the German Confederation**, **Austria** actually controlled the internal administration of all German States. No German prince could disobey or ignore the directives issued by Metternich. Throughout Germany he supported the reactionaries and prosecuted the revolutionaries. However, intense nationalist and patriotic feelings were simmering in several urban areas in Germany, particularly in **universities**. The students who participated in the War of Liberation went back and spread the message of unity and liberation. They formed societies called '**Burschenchaften**' which took a national form and by 1816 were organised in sixteen universities. These activities evoked in full measure the anger of Metternich who, through a conference of ministers from the major German states, got the **Carlsbad Decrees** issued in 1819. These Decrees attacked particularly the Burschenchaften, dissolving them and setting up inspectors for each university. They also enforced a more rigid censorship of the press. A central investigating commission was set up at Mainz with powers to curb ruthlessly any suspicious organisation. Ostensibly, the purpose was to suppress liberal and nationalistic tendencies within the states.

In Italy, Metternich endeavoured to exert his influence through the Austrian princes placed as rulers in the central Italian duchies of Parma, Modena, Tuscany, the omnipresent police force and a potent espionage system. The Italians were fiercely resentful and found Napoleon's rule over Italy less atrocious. Under Napoleon they enjoyed greater national solidarity, a thriving middle class and "**career open to talents**". The Metternich System was most resented in Lombardy and Venetia, especially the practice of appointing Germans and Slavs in all the important administrative posts. Equally vexatious was the absence of any autonomy in the real sense of the term. Metternich's venture to form a confederation in Italy similar to that in Germany was strongly resisted by the Pope and Kingdom of Piedmont-Sardinia. In fact, as David Thomson rightly says, "Italy was the Achilles' heel in the system of Metternich and it was to impose some of the earliest and most severe strains on its ingenuity."[12]

In spite of his efforts, however, Europe could not be kept free from revolutionary outbreaks. In Italy and in Spain, revolts broke out in the 1820s, but the Concert was able to suppress them. He failed in his plan of suppressing the rebellion in the Spanish Empire in South America. In 1830, the July Revolution brought about the fall of the Bourbon monarchy in France; Belgium was separated from Holland. Metternich could not resist these two serious violations of the Treaty of Vienna. In 1848 the revolutionary tide swept him away. Now the revolution was no longer confined to Germany and Italy; it assumed serious proportions in territories under the direct rule of the Hapsburgs: Austria, Hungary, Bohemia. Severe disturbances in Vienna compelled Metternich to seek shelter in England. *Ironically, his long political career came to an end as a result of revolutions, which he had sought so earnestly to suppress for decades.*

Metternich was one of the most famous statesmen Austria produced in the 19th century. He used to speak of himself as being born "to prop up the decaying structure" of European society. He felt the world "resting on his shoulders". He grasped that harmony was the utmost craving of the men of 1815. *For forty years, Metternich dominated the diplomatic and political scene in Europe, but in the end he failed; because while he could imprison revolutionists, he could not imprison ideals.* The inherent weakness of Metternich's System was that it only delayed but could not avert the day of final reckoning. Not that Metternich was not aware of this; he himself regretted that he came "too late" to save the ancien regime from its inevitable doom. He failed to identify the unforeseen strength of the new political current flowing underneath his own regime. He saw only one side of the revolution—the destructive side. The constructive side he never understood. A comprehension of that was essential for a statesman who felt the world resting on his shoulders.

In fact, there were two factors which in the long run undermined his system—**economic growth** and the **dissemination of intellectual ideas**. The Metternich System was built on the foundations of the ancien regime. The structure of the society and economy was that of the old order. When that edifice began to change with the advent of the industrial revolution, his system became outdated. *The French Revolution gave the middle-class political power; the industrial revolution brought them economic power.* While Metternich strove to put the clock back by crushing their political rise, the emergence of their economic supremacy blinded and overwhelmed him. The props supporting the Restoration were knocked away by the moral forces that sprang from the industrial revolution. Moreover, the eruption of new ideological concepts—a direct legacy of the American and French Revolutions—further tightened the noose around the Metternich System and his ancien regime which he so desperately sought to preserve.

Besides, the method of cultivation in Metternich's own Empire was obsolete and archaic. As a result, production was not improving, while, on the other hand, the population was growing enormously. The government of Vienna took no effective measures to remove economic disabilities, and the crisis reached its height in the 1840s.

A more underlying factor explains the weakness of his system. He had overstretched the resources of Austria in trying to maintain Vienna's paramountcy in Europe. Moreover, Metternich tried to manipulate the international situation in such a way that it would remain favourable for Austria. He wanted to control the political destinies of Europe—a task beyond the economic and military potential of Austria. Breakdown of the Concert, which was a part of Metternich's System shows how difficult the task of international manipulation was.

Nevertheless, his achievements should not be underestimated. One achievement will stand forever to his credit. Throughout his long tenure of power, he strove to **preserve the peace of Europe**, and he did secure for a world drenched with the blood of the Napoleonic wars the repose it sorely needed. It was hardly possible at that time to establish peace on the basis of nationalism and democracy. From this point of view, Metternich's policy was not irrational. He had a philosophy of **conservative peace**—an achievement which undoubtedly commands recognition. He prevented the success of revolutionary movements in Germany and Italy for more than thirty years. Moreover, it was no mean achievement to maintain Austrian ascendancy in European politics from 1815 to 1848. No other statesman of Europe succeeded in dominating European politics for so long a period of time. The heterogeneous empire of the Hapsburgs could not be preserved except on the basis of repudiation of revolutionary ideas. The empire would have crumbled if Metternich had not followed an anti-revolutionary policy.

THE CONCERT OF EUROPE

With a view to facilitating joint efforts to prevent further revolutionary outbreaks, **Austria, Russia, Prussia and England** entered into a treaty at the end of the Congress of Vienna. This is known as the **Quadruple Alliance (1815)**. The principal objective of these four powers was to stabilise the political situation in Europe in terms of the Treaty of Vienna. The alliance is also known as the **Concert of Europe**. France joined the Concert sometime later. About the same time the Russian Czar Alexander I, the Prussian King Frederick William III, and the Austrian Emperor Francis I, signed a treaty on 26 September 1815, by which they united in a 'Holy Alliance'. *Although a political act, the treaty in its wording is a statement purely religious in character.* The three monarchs pledged together to conceive the Christian principles—justice, love and peace—as the basis of their future administration. The rulers expressed their fraternal love towards each other and vowed to abstain from war with one another. They also exhorted their subjects to practise in their daily lives the principles of the Saviour in order to ensure the uninterrupted bliss and peace that arose from good conscience. The **Holy Alliance** was not taken seriously by most of the people, even by its members like Metternich, who saw it as nothing more than an insignificant and ephemeral association. However, the Holy Alliance has been regarded by scholars and historians as the **symbol of conservatism and repression** for the purpose of crushing people's revolutionary demands. The guiding spirit of both these organisations was Metternich. In spite of Metternich's best efforts and the constant vigil of the allied powers, the course of revolutions could not be arrested.

In **1820, Naples revolted** against its autocratic Bourbon King. Next year a revolt broke out in Piedmont. In both cases the local rulers succeeded in suppressing the revolts with military assistance from Austria. In 1820, revolution broke out in Spain. The Spanish king Ferdinand VII had fled to Brazil during Napoleon's conquest of Europe. He returned to Spain after Napoleon was exiled. Ferdinand was forced by the revolutionaries to grant a constitution, but at the same time he started negotiations with the Congress of Vienna to seek military help to crush the revolutionary outbreak. A French army, 100,000 strong was sent and the revolution was suppressed. Ferdinand continued as a ruthless autocrat.

The most powerful supporter of Metternich's anti-revolutionary policy was the Russian Czar Alexander I. The British Foreign Secretary Castlereagh gave him only half-hearted support. In 1822 following Castlereagh's death by suicide, Canning took over as the Foreign Secretary. He was in favour of a truly liberal policy. Metternich, therefore, lost the support of England. But he got the support of others in all the meetings of the Congress held between 1818 and 1822 at four different places—Aix-la-Chapelle, Troppau, Laibach and Verona.

Meanwhile, **revolution** had begun in the **Spanish Empire in South America**. After the restoration of the autocratic Bourbon monarchy in Spain in 1823, Metternich became anxious for the preservation of Spanish rule in South America. Here he encountered joint opposition from Canning in England and President Monroe of the United States. The latter two statesmen were, for their own interests, eager to see the Spanish colonies free and to establish independent economic relations with them. In 1815 after the Bourbon restoration on the Spanish throne, the Spanish King Ferdinand VII wanted to re-establish his control over the rebellious South American colonies and sought to invoke the assistance of the Holy Alliance for the purpose. The Concert of Europe led by Metternich entrusted France with the task of suppressing the revolt in Spanish America. This immensely enhanced the apprehensions of both Britain and the United States. **George Canning**, the British Foreign Minister, began negotiations in August 1823 with **Richard Rush**, the American minister in London in order to explore the possibilities of issuing a joint declaration along with the United States condemning the French intervention. Soon, however,

Canning gave up the idea of joint declaration and settled the matter through direct negotiation with France. On 9 October 1823, Canning and Jules de Polignac, the French minister in London, signed a document known as the **Polignac Memorandum** by which both the countries (France and Great Britain) agreed that neither nation had any desire to acquire territory in that region, or to gain exclusive commercial treaties. United States, on the other hand, decided to make an independent declaration that came to be known as the **Monroe Doctrine**. The failure of the Quadruple Alliance to help the Spanish King in suppressing the revolt in South America, virtually led to its dissolution.

On the whole, the Quadruple Alliance failed to achieve its purpose. This was largely due to **growing non-cooperation on the part of Great Britain**. She was not willing like others to interfere, militarily or otherwise, in the internal affairs of other countries. She, at best supported the policy of 'intervening to prevent intervention'. As David Thomson said, "The Concert of Europe, viewed by the conservative powers as a dam against revolution, was thought of by Britain as a sluice gate, allowing for a measured flow of national and liberal progress. This conflict of purposes was to last for half a century."[13]

The Revolutions of 1830

REVOLUTION IN FRANCE

The revolutions in Italy and Spain, which were suppressed by the local rulers with the assistance of the Concert of Europe, were confined to those countries and did not provoke outbreaks in any other country. But *the revolution which broke out in France in 1830 became a really international revolution*. From France it spread to some other parts of Europe as well.

After the fall of Napoleon in 1814 when he was forced to abdicate and was sent to Elba, **Louis XVIII of the Bourbon dynasty** ascended the throne of France with the help of the victorious powers. This heralded the beginning of what is known in history as the **Bourbon Restoration**. The First Restoration occurred when Napoleon fell from power and Louis XVIII became king. Louis's reign was interrupted by Napoleon's sudden return from Elba on 1 March 1815. Louis XVIII fled to Ghent in Belgium on 13th March. Napoleon was hailed by the common people of France who could not forget the glorious days—the unprecedented ascendancy of power France witnessed during his reign. But, as expected, this was not accepted by the big powers of Europe and again they formed a coalition on 25th March and eventually engaged in a serious battle against Napoleon, leading up to the Battle of Waterloo on 20 June 1815. On 22nd June, Napoleon abdicated for the second time. He was despatched as a prisoner to the British island of St. Helena in the far-off Atlantic. On 8th July, Louis XVIII was brought back to Paris. This is known as the **Second Bourbon Restoration** which lasted till 1830.

The Restoration was, however, not a full reinstatement with all its former attributes. In 1814, the Republic of the Jacobins (also known as **France's First Republic**), was replaced by a monarchy all the same. Even so, it was not the monarchy of the ancien regime in its form and content. The old absolutist monarchy now took the shape of a **constitutional monarchy**. The King would **rule by a Charter** which preserved many liberties proclaimed by the French Revolution. It established a **bicameral legislature** consisting of a Chamber of Peers, composed of members appointed by the King for life, and a Chamber of Deputies the members of which were elected for five years. Voting rights were conferred on those who were at least 30 years of age and paid taxes amounting to 300 francs per year. And only those people who were at least 40 years of age and paid 1000 francs annually as direct taxes, could be elected as Deputies. According to Gordon Craig, "…this meant that only about 100,000 men could vote and only 12,000 stand for election out of a population of 28 million."[14] The Charter guaranteed civil liberties, proclaimed religious toleration and acknowledged **Roman Catholicism as the state religion**.

During the reign of Louis XVIII, a serious rivalry developed in France between the liberal and reactionary political groups. Broadly speaking, four political groups could be identified in France in the period between 1814 and 1830. These were—the **ultra-royalists**, the **doctrinaires**, the **liberals** and the **radicals**. The ultra-royalists were the émigrés nobles and the clerics who returned after the French Revolution and were extremely bitter with not only the revolutionaries but also those who served the revolution and Napoleon, desecrated the Church and grabbed their properties while they were away. Both the doctrinaires and the liberals accepted the Charter and the constitutional monarchy; but, while the doctrinaires were blissfully happy about the reforms as they were and did not feel any need of tampering with them, the liberals, on the other hand, considered the reforms to be inadequate and were in favour of greater extension of the electorate and of endowing the Chamber of Deputies with more power by making the King's ministers answerable to them. The radicals vehemently advocated the overthrow of the constitutional monarchy and demanded the re-establishment of the republic.

Louis XVIII was able to comprehend the palpable forces of his times. He grasped the dangers of putting the clock back to the days of the ancien regime. He, therefore, decided to follow a balanced, moderate course between the two extreme groups. Although personally in favour of a compromise, he failed to control the reactionaries. There was a small, extremist group of nobility who earnestly coveted the old days to be back and sullenly resented the changes of the period of Restoration. He, therefore, dissolved the Chamber of Deputies with ultra-royalist majority (La Chambre Introuvable) or 'the Impossible Chamber', elected in 1815. This was followed by a relatively liberal interlude presided over by a chamber with liberal and doctrinaire majority supported by moderate ministers like Decazes and Richlieu. However, the assassination in February 1820 of the Duke of Berry, the son of Charles X (the latter was then Count of Artois and later became the King of France, changed the entire scenario. It infused into the minds of many that the earlier policy of liberalism was too lenient. Electoral procedures were revised in such a way that in the elections of 1820, the number of liberals in the Chamber was substantially reduced. When Villele, a leader of the ultra-royalist faction, succeeded Decazes as Prime Minister, reactionary cynicism reached its height. A period of repression was introduced, all liberal conspiracies were stamped out and stringent press laws were passed to muzzle opposition. In the elections of 1820, the number of liberals in the Chamber was reduced to 15.

On Louis's death in 1824, his brother **Charles X** (the Count of Artois) succeeded him. Charles X himself was also deeply conservative and, naturally became extremely unpopular with the people. He had once declared that he would rather be a wood-cutter, than be King of England,[15] who happened to be a constitutional monarch. That showed his love for absolutism and his contempt for constitutionalism. He replaced the moderate policies of Louis XVIII by reactionary policies leading to his own downfall. The blunders that he committed together sealed the fate of the Bourbon dynasty. In the period between his accession to power and the elections of 1827, Villele's reactionary policies found their full expression. Sacrilege was made a crime punishable by death by the **Anti-**

Sacrilege Act of 1825; new inheritance laws were attempted to be passed which would modify the principle of equal inheritance by restoring some measure of primogeniture; and above all, it was decided to indemnify the émigrés nobles for the loss of their lands at the time of the revolution by handing over to them the money set free by the conversion of state bonds from 5 per cent to 3 per cent. This money was accumulated through careful financial management and amounted to about a billion francs. These arbitrary measures led to **violent protests** and the elections of 1827 resulted in the victory of the liberals in large numbers.

The new Chamber was strongly opposed to Villele who resigned to make way for the moderate **Ministry of Martignac**. The latter was originally an ultra-royalist who later tilted towards the doctrinaires. He was responsible for getting some moderate ordinances passed through Charles X—the Press Ordinance to remove censorship; the ordinance of 16 June 1828 by which the Jesuits were to be expelled from France. The Jesuits were members of the Society of Jesus which was restored throughout the universal Roman Catholic Church on 7 August 1814, following the declaration by the Charter that Roman Catholicism would henceforth be the state religion. Since then, they were in control of educational establishments supervised by the Church hierarchy and thereby escaped state authority. Martignac was now exposed to attack both from the extreme left and the extreme right and on 29 April 1829, a coalition of these groups defeated him in the Chamber. On 8 August 1829 Charles X appointed Jules de Polignac as his foreign minister. He became the Prime Minister on 17th November.

Polignac was one of the most conspicuous ultra-royalists during the Restoration era. He was a former émigré and an over-zealous clergyman. His primary objective was, he claimed, "to reorganise society, to restore to the clergy its former preponderance in the state, to create a powerful aristocracy, and to surround it with privileges."[16] In the elections of 1830 the liberals won in much larger numbers than they did in 1827. Charles X dissolved the Chamber and ordered fresh elections. The new elections again returned a majority overwhelmingly liberal. An adamant Polignac goaded the king to issue a set of four ordinances on 25th July. These ordinances restricted the rights of the press, dissolved the Chamber of Deputies, deprived the voting powers of the three posts of the electors and new elections were ordered. Strong protests immediately broke out in newspapers and journals, the most prominent among them being

Le National, the editor of which was Adolphe Thiers. Resentment spread among different sections of the population—the workers, the teachers, the students, the journalists and other professionals. People were out on the streets and barricades went up. Revolution had begun. It came to be known as the **July Revolution**. Charles X was compelled to abdicate and leave for exile in Scotland. Never were any of his descendants destined to sit again on the throne of France. His successor was Louis Philippe, a member of the Orleans dynasty—a branch of the Bourbon dynasty. He was brought to the throne by the liberals with the general approval of the public. The accession of a popular King marked the elimination of Divine Right succession. The principle that the King should be the nominee of the people established itself through revolution. **Louis Philippe**, therefore,

Fig. 3.2: King Louis Phillippe

also came to be called the '**Citizen King**'. In France, the middle class established its political ascendancy. Alexis de Tocqueville wrote,

> The particular spirit of the middle class became the general spirit of the government; it ruled the latter's foreign policy as well as affairs at home; an active, industrious spirit, often dishonourable, generally orderly, occasionally restless through vanity or egoism, but timid by temperament, moderate in all things except in its love of ease and comfort, and, last but not the least, mediocre.[17]

However, political issues were not the only factor. As David Pinkney observed, an acute economic depression shook the entire French economy and impacted all sections of the society—artisans, middle class, workers, peasants—who blamed the government squarely for their misery. The great cholera epidemic broke out. All these led to a political explosion.[18]

Revolutions in Other Countries

The effects of the July Revolution were felt in other countries as well. In **Belgium**, for instance, a similar outbreak took place in October of the same year. As one of the effects of the Settlement of Vienna, the former Austrian Netherlands had been incorporated into the Dutch Kingdom. But the Belgians were separated from the Dutch by religion, language as well as by the different nature of their economic activity. The Belgians were Roman Catholics; the Dutch, on the other hand, were staunch Calvinists. While the Dutch were agricultural and commercial and advocated free trade; the Belgians developed their nascent industry and thereby needed tariff protection. The administrative policies of the Government of Holland were unfavourable to the dignity and interests of Belgium and conveyed the impression to the Belgian people that they were conquered vassals. The initial demands of the **Brussels rising** were moderate, but were rendered irreconcilable due to the intransigence of the King William I. Austria and Prussia turned a deaf ear to Holland's appeal for assistance. The Czar was more responsive, but was far away and much preoccupied with domestic difficulties. Even so, he expressed his desire to send an army of 60,000 to crush the Belgian revolt. France was alarmed by foreign intervention so close to its borders and Britain, appreciating France's concern, communicated their joint desire to hold an international conference on the issue. Subsequently, the **London Conference on 4 November 1830** ensured Belgian independence.

In Spain and Portugal, liberal constitutions were granted as a result of the July Revolution. In **Spain** the constitutional government of Ferdinand VII was challenged by the militant populist revolt that endured in the north till 1840. In **Portugal**, where a situation of civil war was already prevailing, a contest for the throne was going on between the two sons of King Joao VI since his death in 1826. The younger son Prince Miguel had already usurped the throne, ended the Constitutional Charter of 1822 and established absolute rule. He was being challenged by his brother Pedro I, the Emperor of Brazil and the legitimate successor to the throne of Portugal. In these circumstances, the outbreak of the revolutions in Europe encouraged the liberal factions in Portugal to oppose the absolute monarchy of Prince Miguel. Thereafter ensued what is known in history as the **Liberal Wars**—a war between progressive constitutionalists and authoritarian absolutists in Portugal over royal succession that lasted from 1828 to 1834. In 1834, finally the liberal forces won when on 24th May a peace was signed at Evoramonte by which Miguel formally renounced all claims to the throne of Portugal. Pedro restored the Constitutional Charter but died of tuberculosis on 24 September 1834.

In **Switzerland**, following the July Revolution in 1830, the assemblies in the cantons (26 cantons were the member states of the federal state of Switzerland) were called for framing new cantonal constitutions. They all emphasised two basic points. First, the constitutions were to be peacefully adjusted by systematising the way the seats were allocated. Second, the constitutions were to be amended if necessary. In **Britain**, the Great Reform Act was passed in 1832 in order to soothe the sentiments of the common people with the purpose of averting a revolution. By this Act the popular demand for universal adult suffrage was diverted by enfranchising one-fifth of adult men.

In **Poland**, however, the liberal aspirations of the Polish people were harshly repressed. Encouraged by the success of the Belgian revolt, the Polish nationalists put forth their radical demands for self-government before the Russian Czar. Russian Poland already enjoyed liberal institutions like a constitution that granted a bicameral parliament, religious toleration and civil liberties. All official positions were filled up by the Poles and Polish was the official language. But the Polish people preferred independence to any other privilege and in November 1830 a revolt was started in Warsaw by the aristocrats and intellectuals of Poland. Czar Nicholas I sent an army of a hundred and twenty thousand troops in February. The Russian Poles were flanked by the Austrians and Prussians whose outlook was similar to that of the Russians. The only hope was western intervention but that was not forthcoming. Poland was so far off from England and France that they remained indifferent to the happenings there. Left to themselves, the Polish insurgents had little chance of success. Ruthless suppression was meted out to the Polish uprising, eighty thousand Poles were imprisoned or exiled to Siberia and the country was subjected to severe attempts of Russification— her separate army dissolved, the parliament and universities closed.

Meanwhile, throughout the **lands of Central Europe**, revolutions were slowly spreading, particularly in **Italy**. In the central section of the peninsula, Papal Romagna, Bologna and the duchies (territories ruled by a duke or duchess), there were insurrections (organised by the **Carbonari** or the liberal secret societies) that Metternich helped to put down. In Parma, as John Merriman narrates, the rebels had locked out Duchess Marie Louise out of the city by locking the gates behind her and ultimately she was rescued by an Austrian army, which in March 1831 restored her to the throne.[19] In 1831, **Young Italy** (a new secret society) was founded by **Giuseppe Mazzini** to carry out a renewed attack in the backdrop of the repeated failures of the old type Carbonari. However, the Italian insurrections were eventually suppressed by Metternich and the country brought under complete Austrian control.

In **Germany**, the response to the revolutions in France and Belgium remained mostly confined to speeches and resolutions. In **Westphalia**, however, rent, tax and military records were burned. In some German states—such as Brunswick, Saxony, Hanover, Hesse-Kassel—demands were made for more liberal constitutional reforms. But they were sternly denied and Metternich obtained re-assertion and strengthening of the Carlsbad Decrees.

On general terms, the overall **outcome of the revolutions of 1830** could be summed up as follows. In Western Europe, there was progress— success in France and Belgium; while in eastern and central Europe, there were more reaction and restoration of the old order. Western Europe, therefore, grew more liberal, and eastern and central Europe more reactionary. So, Europe became divided into two parts—liberal and conservative. Such was the pattern of European settlement that emerged from the revolutions of 1830.

This new pattern was to a large extent conditioned by the actions of different foreign powers. The governments of Austria, Prussia and Russia wanted to check the Belgian Revolution and preserve the position of 1815. The governments of Britain and France wanted to prevent intervention and took initiative in summoning a conference of five powers—Britain, France, Austria, Russia and Prussia—in London to protect peace in Europe. The conference recognised the principle of Belgian independence and in January 1831, it issued a protocol proclaiming that "Belgium forms a perpetually neutral standing." In eastern Europe, in Poland for example, on the contrary, there was considerable lack of western support and as such the three eastern and central monarchies were free to crush liberal risings to restore the order of 1815. On the other hand, Austria and Russia, who had important Polish territories were solidly on the side of Russia, lest revolutions affected the people there too.

In central Europe, too, particularly in Italy, the chief hope of the revolutionaries was that Louis Philippe would send them help. This help was not forthcoming and Austria, unimpeded, sent her troops into Italy to restore the rulers to their thrones. In Germany by 1835, reaction was again triumphant. In Austria, where Metternich's system for preserving order was at its strongest, the ripples of revolution were hardly felt at all.

On the face of it, therefore, the wave of revolutions that rocked Europe in 1830 mostly ended in failure. It was **successful in the west**, while the hopes of the east and the centre remained unfulfilled. On a deeper probe, however, a different scenario emerged. Prominent changes were visible in every aspect of life—society, politics, economy, culture. France and Switzerland saw the triumph of liberalism; Belgium tasted the realisation of her nationalist aspirations. Britain gained wider franchise. Repression crystallised further the resolve of Italy and Germany to unify on national lines. In the west, the victory of the middle class over the aristocracy surfaced in unambiguous terms. As Hobsbawm says, "The ruling class of the next fifty years was to be the *grande bourgeoisie* of bankers, big industrialists and sometimes top civil servants, accepted by an aristocracy which effaced itself or agreed to promote primarily bourgeois policies…"[20] The situation was complicated further by signs of labour unrest, grievances of the artisans and petty traders. These were the people who were found building the barricades or joining the secret societies. A **new revolutionary culture** evolved—a culture of barricades and secret societies, distinct from that of the Great Revolution. Several secret societies sprang up—**Burschenchaften**

(Young Italy, Young Poland, Young Germany, Young Switzerland) under the aegis of Young Europe—which played a formidable role in shaping the minds of the people, especially the youth. All these factors brought about crucial transformation in the mindset of the entire continent. Revolutions were now inextricably linked with 'internationalism'. They were not confined to one country or one nation, but spread from one place to another and assumed different characters in different regions. The Concert of Europe was losing its grip. Europe was getting ready for a final reckoning which came in the form of the revolutions of 1848. The tide of mass rising swept all over the continent. The year 1830, therefore, not only prepared the stage but was also the **dress rehearsal** for a remarkable show in the future. Only the wise in 1830 could discern the potential signs of the beginning of the ruin of all efforts of the Congress and Metternich to prop up the ancien regime. The fire-bell had started ringing. Things did not remain the same after 1830.

The Revolutions of 1848

The changes that had come over the European canvas since the days of the French Revolution, and then the revolutions of 1830, reached their **climax in 1848**. The palpable and volatile forces of the age were progressing in stages. The events of 1789 originated in France and remained confined there as far as the movements and activities were concerned. The ideas and thoughts, concepts and philosophy, however, were not contained. Like a contagious disease, they transcended the boundaries of France and sowed their seeds wherever they went. Metternich grasped the matter fully and tried desperately to control and arrest their course, but in vain. They erupted and "showed their ugly heads" again in 1830. Again they emerged first in France and then spread elsewhere as we have seen. Nevertheless, this time a limited number of countries was affected. In 1848, it returned in a much bigger surge and swept Europe off its feet. The entire continent—with the exception of Russian Empire in the east and Britain in the west, and a few others like Spain, Portugal and Holland was in ferment. As Metternich regretted,

> I am not a prophet and I don't know what will happen, but I am an old physician and can distinguish between temporary and fatal diseases. We

now face one of the latter. We'll hold on as long as we can, but I have doubts about the outcome.[21]

ORIGINS

As far as the origins of the revolutions of 1848 are concerned, we have to remember one important point; that they all **sprang from the French Revolution** and the **American Revolution**. The American Revolution of **1776** bore a profound impact on the French Revolution. And the French Revolution inspired the subsequent revolutions in Europe. L.C.B. Seaman alluded to two interesting facts.[22] According to him, these revolutions of 1776 and 1789 taught the European man two remarkable lessons. *First*, they proclaimed that **man had every right to challenge his ruler** and even rise in revolt if the ruler failed to protect the fundamental rights of his subjects. The American colonies freed themselves from the King of Britain through violence; the French rebelled, overthrew and executed their King and established a republic. Such a thing was unprecedented in the history of Europe. There had been wars between dynasties, between kings, between feudal lords; but for the first time, the people learnt that even they could successfully wage war against their kings in order to assert their rights and even enjoy the fruits of their victory like the Americans and the French. *Second*, people earlier believed that rebellion was a crime and the rebels were criminals. But political philosophers like John Locke who motivated the American War of Independence, and Rousseau who was the driving force behind the French Revolution, hailed **revolution as dispenser of good and destroyer of evil** and the revolutionaries as messengers of hope and instruments of change. From revolution emerged the sublime concepts of equality, liberty and fraternity as well as the doctrine of popular sovereignty. To understand the cause of a revolution one essential fact has to be grasped. "The ideas and the discontents are secondary. The prime cause is that the years 1776 and 1789, and the events immediately following them, moulded hard and firm into the traditions of political life the notion that through revolution man could find a short cut to a paradise on earth."[23]

Third, according to Jacques Droz, the revolutions of 1848 were brought about by the conjunction of a **political crisis** and an **acute economic calamity**.[24] Any one-sided analysis would be beset with problems. It is essential, therefore, to examine closely both these intertwined factors one by one. As for the economic dilemma, it was, as Jacques Droz observed, due to a combination of two types of crises—an **agricultural crisis** and a **credit crisis**. Historians were all agreed on this. What they were in disagreement with was regarding the relative importance of these two factors. Some of them felt that it was the agricultural problem which was more serious and the credit crisis was its aftermath; while, on the contrary, another set of scholars preferred to situate the credit crisis higher in order of importance. The former group of scholars argued that in the mid-1840s, a **severe food crisis** was caused by widespread potato failure, particularly in Ireland, Prussia, Flanders in Belgium and France. It was harshest in **Ireland** from where alone about one million deaths and up to two million refugees were reported. This was followed in the next year by a grain crisis—an unforeseen drought and excessive heat destroyed the crops, particularly rye and wheat, and hardly any stock was left from the previous year. The combination of poor potato and grain harvests in a single place made things miserable and turned the whole period into the "hungry forties." The price increases "led to panic, popular unrest and privation."[25] Of course, the extent of distress varied from place to place.

As Eric Vanhaute observes, the national averages are often meaningless and famines and food crises are predominantly regional crises.[26] J. Mokyr, A. Maharatna, and M. Lachiver, too, agree with him on this point.[27] Mortality in Ireland, for example, was much higher than that in the Scottish Highlands, the primary reasons being, according to Tom Devine: (*i*) lower dependence of Scottish peasant society on only one crop; (*ii*) scope for temporary migration to industrial areas in the vicinity; and (*iii*) the role of relief organised by landlords and the Free Church of Scotland.[28] Similarly, Vanhaute believed that Flanders did not starve because of a more differentiated peasant economy, stronger village structures, the strong position of local elites and the church and protective State action.[29] In Denmark, Henriksen said, the crisis was mild because of a relatively small role of potato in consumption and production.[30] Helge Berger and Mark Spoerer, writing in the spirit of Marx, have argued recently that 1848 was the product of 'economic misery and the fear thereof', claiming that most of Europe's agricultural output led to a 'decline in manufacturing activity after a certain lag'.[31] Scholars like Vanhaute, Richard Paping, Cormac o Grada also believed that the financial crisis that spanned the continent in the 1840s was linked to poor grain and potato harvests.[32] Soaring prices of food left very little money in the hands of the people as wages were not increasing. Their **purchasing power**, therefore, almost **decimated**. This had serious repercussions on the industrial sector. People had no money left in their hands to buy anything other than food. This dealt severe blows to the manufacturing units. Many factories closed down and unemployment was rampant. As it was, the domestic industry was already staggering under the impact of competition with the machine. The agricultural crisis ensured its speedy death.

However, there were other historians who considered a financial or **credit crisis** to be of utmost importance in bringing about the economic disaster of the forties. Huge investments were made in railways and industry. People preferred to invest more in industry and land and less in agriculture. Even landlords were no exceptions. The result of such **excessive investments** was a phenomenal increase in fixed capital and corresponding decrease in circulating capital or liquid assets. To acquire liquid cash, the companies and financial institutions issued masses of shares and debentures whose value quickly fell and a depression set in. The agricultural crisis was a natural consequence of this. From the industrial sector, crisis travelled to agriculture. It was the credit crisis, therefore, that led to the agricultural crisis and not the other way round. Nevertheless, in some countries it led to bankruptcies and factory closures. But others like Jesus Huerta de Soto, the Spanish economist, blamed the crisis on the bursting of a bubble in railway shares. According to Huerta de Soto,

> As of 1840 credit expansion resumed in the United Kingdom and spread throughout France and the United States. Thousands of miles of railroad track were built and the stock market entered upon a period of relentless growth which mostly favoured railway stock. Thus began a speculative movement which lasted until 1846, when economic crisis hit in Great Britain. It is interesting to note that on July 19, 1844, under the auspices of Robert Peel, England had adopted the Bank Charter Act, which represented the triumph of Ricardo's Currency School and prohibited the issuance of bills not backed 100% by gold. Nevertheless this provision was not established in relation to deposits and loans, the volume of which increased five-fold in only two years, which explains the spread of speculation and the severity of the crisis which erupted in 1846.[33]

In 1847, the *Journal des Economistes* (a French academic journal of political economy founded in 1841 by Gilbert Guillaumin) also propounded that the agricultural crisis did not cause the credit crisis, rather it was a product of the financial distress of the 1840s.

Jacques Droz points out something interesting. He observes that the prices had skyrocketed by 100 to 150 percent, without any increase in wages during the period between 1845 and 1847. Understandably then, public misery had reached its climax. But strangely enough, the revolutions did not break out at this time. They came at a time when the flood of anguish was 'ebbing away'. "It left behind it a whole population in distress, with their savings gone."[34] Had the causes of the revolutions been only economic, they would have occurred when the economic misfortune was at its height. Clearly, therefore, there were other reasons behind the outburst. Vivier rightly defines the period as one of '**mixed crisis**'—a crisis with many dimensions: a crisis of harvest failure, an industrial and credit crisis as well as a social and political crisis.[35] This, I think is a proper assessment of the revolutions of 1848. Apart from crucial economic implications, the origins of the revolutions had important political and social significance as well. According to Jacques Droz, the discontent of 1848 was "essentially political in character".[36]

THE PATTERNS OF THE REVOLUTIONS OF 1848

In fact, *the French Revolution bequeathed a very rich political heritage to the people of Europe*. Its legacy of a democratic republic and popular sovereignty, of egalitarianism and liberalism had a magical impact on the entire continent and inspired them to emulate the example. It happened in 1830 but was easily crushed in most places. But the aspirations kept simmering. And finally, they exploded in 1848. The long tug-of-war between reaction and liberalism reached its peak. This long war came to an end with these revolutions as they were the last of their kind in that century. The **right of national self-determination** was firmly established in the heart of each nation. Even so, the political objectives assumed different forms in different countries. David Thomson identified two such forms or patterns.[37]

Some revolutions were in the pattern of that in Palermo in Sicily, which had broken out on 12 January 1848. The people there were out on the streets in **open revolt against King Ferdinand II of Naples**. The revolutions of Italy, Germany, Austria and Hungary were of the former pattern—that is, *revolt against foreign rule* and the utterly conservative Vienna Settlement. Another set of revolutions were on the **model of France** where revolutions broke out on **12th February** against the limited electoral and parliamentary reforms of King Louis Philippe and his chief minister Guizot. In some other countries, the problems were different. In Switzerland and Britain, where the issue was not one of foreign rule, the primary objective was acquisition of greater social and democratic reforms, including widening of franchise. At any rate, one important fact should be borne in mind. The political atmosphere in Europe was heavy with the fear of revolution in the period between 1815 and 1848. That was another legacy of the French Revolution. The constant spectre of revolution led to repression. That is how the 'Metternich System' was born. The sullen resentment against repression catapulted into revolution at the earliest opportunity in 1830. Again, repression followed except in France and Belgium. The situation was further vitiated by the economic crisis of the 1840s. The result was the revolutions of 1848. A vicious cycle dominated the European political scene.

REVOLUTION IN FRANCE, 1848

In France, the provisions of the Charter imposed upon the King Louis Philippe indicated the liberal ideas of the majority. The principle of popular sovereignty was tacitly admitted. It was a declaration of the rights of the nation. A cloud of opposition was gathering around the policies of Guizot who became Louis Philippe's Prime Minister in September 1847. Guizot believed that any further reform would not only be unnecessary but dangerous. The liberals, republicans and the newly emerging socialists demanded wider or even universal suffrage, Guizot and his conservative supporters felt that the existing eligibility of the payment of 200 francs in direct taxes for casting ballots was enough. On the contrary, **England** made appreciable progress along liberal lines under the **Reform Act of 1832**. Professional men and politicians were particularly dissatisfied for many of them were excluded from the franchise. Guizot's conduct of foreign policy was also pacific and failed to catch the popular imagination. He wanted to conquer for France the colony of Algeria only, while the French wanted in addition to conquer the colonies of England as well. For the people of France, it was a regime which was "neither a true monarchy, nor a true republic, nor true empire, but a hybrid." In 1839, therefore, the poet **Lamartine** declared that *France was a nation that was bored.* Another current which proved to be fatal for Louis Philippe's bourgeois monarchy was Bonapartism. As the years rolled by, the painful and fallacious aspects of the Great Emperor's policies were forgotten and forgiven, and the wonderful epic of his victories were cherished. The French people wanted desperately those glorious days to be revived. They wanted the government to follow a flashy foreign policy through which France would escalate again at the top of the comity of nations. Regrettably, *Louis Philippe had hardly anything to offer to a romantic generation.*

REVOLUTION IN CENTRAL EUROPE, 1848

The story in Central Europe is somewhat different. Central Europe meant **Germany**, the **Austro-Hungarian Empire** which included Austria, Hungary, the Czech lands (comprising Bohemia, Moravia, Silesia), **parts of Poland** and also **Italy** since half of it was under Hapsburg rule, according to the provisions of the Vienna Settlement. There the primary problem was foreign rule. In Germany, for example, Austria was made the President of the German Confederation and thereby sternly controlled the intellectual and political life of the German people. All secret societies were suppressed by the Carlsbad Decrees, public meetings prohibited, newspapers and other publications censored.

The Austro-Hungarian Empire was a medley of various territories and racial groups—the **Serbs, the Croats, the Magyars, the Slavs, the Czechs, the Poles**. They all strove to be independent of Hapsburg rule. In Italy, Austria was firmly entrenched in half of the peninsula. The whole of Central Europe was under the grip of despotic and reactionary rule. In Italy and Germany, insurrections broke out in a number of places in 1830, but they failed. High-handed rule and absolutism were ruthlessly clamped upon them and they were brought under more rigorous vigil than earlier. The French example of 1848 again ignited in them the embers of desire for freedom and liberty. Certain basic political demands were common for all the countries. Meetings were held across Central Europe and people stipulated for democratic constitutions providing for parliaments where the common people would sit and make decisions. The creation of National Guards was insisted upon in the place of armies of the ancien regime. Further, trial by jury, abolition of secret police, espionage and censorship, freedom of press, publication, association were insisted upon. They were urged by predominantly two political ideologies—**liberalism and radicalism**. Adherents of both were present in all the countries. The liberals tried to work out a compromise with the ruling establishment insisting upon a greater participation in matters pertaining to the government as well as wider democratic reforms catering to freedom in public and individual life. The radicals, on the other hand, aimed at total eradication of all monarchical authority and wanted the establishment of a republic. The secret societies under **Mazzini** belonged to the latter category and worked relentlessly for a republic in Italy.

There were skirmishes and agitations, food riots and artisanal disturbances all-over Central Europe, but the kings and princes were hardly concerned, until they received news of the **fall of Metternich in March 1848**. On 13th March—ten days after Kossuth, the national leader of Hungary delivered a fiery speech against Metternich—the people of Austria broke out in open revolt against **Metternich, "the Policeman of Europe"**. When the revolutionaries surrounded his palace, Metternich quickly resigned and left for exile to England. In the words of C.D. Hazen,

> Metternich, who for thirty-nine years had stood at the head of the Austrian states, who was the very source and fount of reaction, imperturbable, pitiless, masterful, was now forced to resign, to flee in disguise from Austria to England, to witness his whole system crash completely beneath the onslaught of the very forces for which he had for a generation shown contempt.[38]

It was only then that the German princes started responding and granting liberal constitutions to their subjects in Baden, Saxony, Wurttemberg, Hesse-Darmstadt and Bavaria. On 17th March, **King Frederick William IV** in Prussia granted, in response to the petitions from the Rhenish province and Cologne, regions he had erstwhile cold-shouldered, a manifesto in which he promised a liberal constitution, systematic internal reforms, and promised to convoke the Prussian Diet. Next day when a huge crowd gathered outside his palace, presumably to thank him, a highly apprehensive detachment of the royal cavalry **guard opened fire on the crowd** when they refused to disperse and pandemonium started. Street fighting between the royal troops and the mob continued the whole day and in the end, the King capitulated and promised the liberal leaders that he would summon a national Prussian assembly. On **28 March 1849**, the constitution was finally adopted by the Frankfurt National Assembly which provided for universal suffrage, parliamentary government and a hereditary emperor.

The fall of Metternich sparked off a rebellion in **Hungary** as well. The unique characteristic feature of the Hungarian revolt was that it came not from the bourgeoisie but from the **gentry**. The gentry's spokesperson Lajos or **Louis Kossuth**, the renowned Hungarian journalist, lawyer and politician, had already, before Metternich's fall, delivered a powerful speech on 3 March 1848, demanding parliamentary government for Hungary. He was determined to retain leadership of the nobility in the Hungarian movement. At the same time, he sought to protect the interests of the nobility by insisting on compensation to the feudal landlords who were being deprived of forced labour and also tax immunity. Kossuth himself had suggested that a uniform system of taxation be introduced in the petition to be placed before the Austrian Emperor. In this petition an autonomous Hungarian government was the foremost demand. It also claimed Hungarian authority over all taxes collected in Hungary and control over the entire area of the Crown of St. Stephen (a group of territories connected to the Kingdom of Hungary within Austria-Hungary, and included the prominent Principality of Transylvania and the Kingdom of Croatia-Slovenia, both of which were being ruled by governors appointed by the Hapsburgs). On 17th March, the Hungarian demands were approved. **Lajos Batthyany** was appointed the head of the first responsible government. A National Guard was forced to be formed. Even a separate Hungarian coinage was re-established. Kossuth, a Magyar (ethnic Hungarian) noble himself, emphasised upon the superiority of the **Magyars** and wanted to exclude all other racial entities.

Meanwhile, the success of Kossuth and his supporters enthused the other nationalities living in Hungary—**Serbs, Croats, Slovaks and Rumanians**—and they expected to share in the benefits and privileges of the new government. When Kossuth turned down this expectation, and made Magyar the official language, a virulent **anti-Magyar movement** cropped up. The Austrian government immediately took the anti-Magyar elements on its side with the intention of suppressing Kossuth and others, and the movement intensified. The anti-Magyar hostilities of these separate racial identities assumed different forms in different regions according to their circumstances. The Czech nationalities organised a Slavic Congress in Prague in the first two weeks of June 1848. Slavic people from different parts of the Empire attended the Congress. The Hapsburgs, the Germans and Hungarians denounced the Congress as a conspiracy of the Pan-Slav people who aspired to unite under the Czar. However, as Jonathan Sperber observes, this was a misplaced fear, as people attending from outside the Empire were very few and one very prominent Russian who attended it, Michael Bakunin, was "hardly the Czar's agent".[39]

Galicia was the largest and most populous northern-most province of the Austrian Empire. Among the several nationalities residing in Galicia, **the Poles** were the greatest in number in the whole province, although, only in the western parts, the Ukrainians exceeded the Poles in number. The Poles were desirous of extending their power over the entire province and held a national committee in Cracow. **The Ukrainians**, on the other hand, with a view to counteract the Poles, created a Supreme Ukrainian National Council in Lamberg and proclaimed its supremacy in the eastern half. The Hapsburg governor of Galicia, Stadion, found the most expedient situation to play the policy of 'divide and rule' and started backing the Ukrainians against the Poles. His ulterior motive was to scuttle the ambitions of both and to preserve the predominance of the Hapsburg Empire in the area.

Similar mass meetings, or 'national assemblies' were organised by different nationalities in several parts of the Austrian Hapsburg Empire. For example, the Croats called a meeting in Zagreb on 25th March, the Slovaks in Liptovsky Svaty Mikulas on 10–11th May, Serbs in Karlovci on 13th May and the Rumanians in Blaj on 15–17th May.[40] The demands of the Croats were firstly to create an **independent Croatian government** and a Croatian constituent assembly with the Austrian Emperor as the constitutional monarch. The Croatians, like the Magyars, wanted control over the taxes and the Croatian regiments in the imperial army. The Hapsburg government responded by appointing **Josip Jelacic**, a loyal Hapsburg official, as the governor of Croatia. As we have already seen, the Hungarian Diet wished to incorporate Croatia-Slovenia from the very beginning and, therefore, put up a fierce resistance against the appointment of Jelacic. The Hungarians had accepted the Austrian Emperor as the 'King of Hungary'. Jelacic argued that he was the legitimate appointee of the same Emperor, that is Ferdinand von Hapsburg. So, there was no question of his withdrawal. A civil war was in the offing.

A similar war like situation emerged in **Transylvania**, which also like Croatia-Slovenia, the Hungarians aspired to include within the unitary Hungarian State that was going to be created. Majority of the population of Transylvania were Rumanian serfs, and they hailed the decision taken at the national mass meeting at Blaj that serfdom would be abolished. The serf-owners in Hungary, on the other hand, were Hungarian Magyar nobles who strongly resented the idea of abolition. An ironic situation arose. The Hungarians themselves had liberated the serfs in their own land, but refused to grant the same to the people of Transylvania. Fearing atrocities from the Hungarians, the **Rumanian national leaders** who were **radical intellectuals**, looked to the Austrian Emperor for help and sent a delegation, one of whose leaders was **Baron Laszlo Nopcsa**, a Magyar aristocrat but also a loyal servant of the Emperor. He came to terms with the Rumanians because, after all, they preferred imperial authority to that of the Hungarian nationalists, who in the eyes of Nopcsa were nothing but rebels and, therefore, deserved to be repudiated and frustrated. Nevertheless, the Rumanians, Sperber rightly points out, were to lose either way. If they lost to the Hungarians, they were doomed; if they won, they would be subjected to the Hapsburgs, from the yoke of whose rule they always yearned to be free.[41] Frustration of all nationalist hopes, in any case, awaited the Rumanians.

Nature of the Nationalist Awakenings

All these nationalist awakenings in the Austrian Empire had certain common elements among them. *First*, there was nothing particularly radical about them. They were liberals. They were all constitutional monarchists. They aspired for a **liberal constitution and certain autonomy** in their own government. *Second*, they were all **intensely nationalist** in character. Everywhere in Austria-Hungary, there were nationalist and popular insurrections on the pattern of Palermo. The objective was to shake off foreign rule and to attain **national self-determination**, that is the freedom of people of a given area to determine their own political status and to control their own affairs. *Third*, as Sperber observes, "Through all the chaos and confusion, the empire as an institution remained in existence."[42] The authority of the Emperor was never transgressed. *Fourth*, the pattern everywhere was almost the same—(*i*) summoning of a national mass meeting, (*ii*) proclamation of a constitution or an independent court, (*iii*) formation of a national assembly, (*iv*) demand for liberal concessions like freedom of press, association and publication, abolition of serfdom, etc. Finally, whatsoever be the initial fervour, the movements all ended in frustration. In fact, L.C.B. Seaman has aptly called 1848 a "year of frustration".

In Italy: The First Revolution of the Year

Italy, as we know, was completely under the heels of foreign domination. The northern states of Lombardy and Venetia and all the central Italian duchies were under Austrian princes. In the south, in Naples and Sicily, the Spanish Bourbon monarchy was firmly established.

Charles Albert or Carlo Alberto, a descendant of the **House of Savoy**, was educated in the liberal and Francophile atmosphere of Geneva, then under Napoleon Bonaparte's First Empire. These initial years of his life played a key role in shaping his liberal inclinations. He succeeded his cousin Charles Felix to the **throne of Piedmont-Sardinia in 1831**. Being a liberal, he was not unfavourable to the ideas of a constitutional monarchy and promulgated a constitutional law code on the model of Code Napoleon. He further introduced a series of reforms that abolished customs barriers within the kingdom, reformed the army and promoted agriculture. Although an old Carbonaro (member of Carbonari, a network of secret revolutionary societies founded in 19th-century Italy), he was opposed to the radical republicanism of Mazzini, and preferred to lead a revolution at the end of which the peninsula would be unified into a **liberal monarchy** under Piedmont-Sardinia. Therefore, when Mazzini endeavoured to invoke his support in his revolutionary movement through a letter, an extract of which is as follows, "The men of freedom await your answer in your deeds. Whatever that answer may be, rest assured that posterity will either hail your name as the greatest of men, or the last of Italian tyrants. Take your choice…", Charles Albert responded by extending Mazzini's banishment. Meanwhile, **Pope Pius IX** had expressed liberal sympathies and granted several political and economic reforms. He also promoted progressive policies like promotion of railways, gas-lighting, and starting an agricultural institute. These reforms aroused popular hopes and people now looked to the Pope for supporting democratic reforms and the Italian national movement.

The **first revolution of the year** took place in **Palermo in Sicily** on 12 January 1848 against the arbitrary rule of **Ferdinand II**. The revolutionaries were able to regain the **Constitution of 1812** which included the principles of democracy and representative parliament. Revolts then broke out in March 1848 in Lombardy and Venetia, particularly in Milan, and the Austrian forces under Radetzky, the Austrian Commander in Lombardy, retreated to the Quadrilateral (the armed fortresses of Peschiera, Mantua, Legnago and Verona between the Mincio, the Po and Adige Rivers). There was popular pressure on Charles Albert to launch an attack on Austria, which he did by sending an army to the Quadrilateral. He was helped militarily from several quarters in Italy including 10,000 strong troops from the Pope. Even so, his forces were no match before the Austrians and though initially he won the **Battle of Goito** in May 1848 and even captured the fortress of Peschiera, eventually he was defeated at the **Battle of Custozza** on 24 July 1848. Meanwhile, after the Battle of Goito, the Pope was threatened by the Austrian Catholic Church of schism from papal authority. The Pope withdrew his support from Charles Albert. So did Ferdinand II of Naples and Sicily, who also had sent a large contingent. This was, by far, the most important cause of the defeat of Charles Albert at Custozza. The people were totally crestfallen and a violent uprising followed as a result of which **Count Rossi**, the Prime Minister of Rome was **assassinated**. The Pope fled from Rome and took refuge in the fortress of Gaeta in the province of Latina in November 1848. **Mazzini** and **Garibaldi** established a **Roman Republic in Rome** that guaranteed freedom of the press, secular education, distributed church lands among the poor. However, **Napoleon III**, the French Emperor, sent forces at the request of Pius IX and eventually the Roman Republic was defeated. In July 1849 Pius IX returned to Rome and ruled till 1870.

THE TIDE OF REVOLUTIONS ENDURES

According to Jonathan Sperber, it would be wrong to assume that with the close of 1848, the year of revolutions came to an end. The tide of revolutions had not subsided. There were fresh eruptions in a number of places and even revolutionary regimes were set up. In **France**, in fact, a reverberation of **insurrections** occurred in **June 1848** itself. In France, a provisional government had been set up composed of committees constituted from the Assembly until a new republican constitution could be proclaimed. The new government had set up national workshops, which, however, were decided to be closed on 23rd June. Bachelors were to be conscripted into the army and married men were to be sent to the provinces to work. The workers' associations and political clubs of the left burst out in open protest. This revolt is famous as the **"June Days"** which was put down brutally by **General Cavaignac**, **"the butcher of June"**. Karl Marx called this episode a **prelude to the future proletarian revolution** that would establish the rule of the working class. In **Italy**, as we have seen, the Roman Republic was established. In March 1849, Charles Albert, backed by the democratic forces, resumed his war with Austria which ended in a severe defeat of his army at the hands of the Austrian army in the **Battle of Novara**. In despair, Charles Albert exiled himself to Portugal and died shortly thereafter. In **Germany**, the 'little Germans' (those who wanted to unite German states without Austria) succeeded and finally elected the King of Prussia as the head of the new national state at the end of March 1849. In **Hungary**, the exiled Polish insurgent Jozef Bem drove out the Austrians from Transylvania in January 1849; **Arthur Gregory**, the brilliant Magyar General, defeated the Austrians in north-eastern Hungary in April 1849.

THE SOCIO-ECONOMIC CAUSES OF THE REVOLUTIONS OF 1848

Intense political aspirations, therefore, formed the background of the revolutions of 1848. What characterised European politics on the eve of 1848 was the **absence of liberty**. Even in France, where people expected that the middle-class monarchy of Louis Philippe would bring forth universal suffrage, the conservative government of the King and Guizot opposed any form of electoral and parliamentary reforms. In **Central Europe**, the political strife was directed against the Metternich System and foreign rule. There the chief political motivation was fulfilment of the principle of **national self-determination**. So, the political ideologies which mainly inspired them were nationalism and liberalism. They were not radicals like the French, because overthrowing the regime was not their ultimate goal. Rather, within the framework of the Austrian Hapsburg monarchy, they aspired for limited autonomy and liberal constitutions. National unity after the expulsion of foreign elements was what the people of Italy and Germany truly desired. They were not opposed to the idea of being united under a liberal monarch who fulfilled their political aspirations.

The French, however, had moved one step ahead by 1848—they had become thoroughly disgusted with the successive monarchies and yearned for a republic. Thus, was born **France's Second Republic**. In France, as Lipson commented, "the Revolution constituted an epoch in history of political democracy because the extension of the suffrage transferred power from the middle classes to the community at large."[43] *By 1848, France had experienced three revolutions* and each of them had taken her a step forward. Lipson observed, "the first revolution was directed against arbitrary monarchy, the second against aristocratic privilege, and the third against middle-class government: in other words, legal equality was established in 1789, social equality in 1830, and political equality in 1848."[44] In France, 1848 was not only an experiment of radicalism, but also of socialism. Liberalism and radicalism have already been discussed in Chapter 1. **Socialism** referred to a body of doctrines which were "a combined product of the Enlightenment, of the liberal and egalitarian principles of the French Revolution and the impact of the Industrial Revolution."[45] Generally they meant a social system based on the common ownership of the means of production and distribution. Socialism was one of the forces which brought down the Metternich System, and was a driving force behind the revolution in France in 1848. '**Right to work**' was a very important agenda of the revolutionaries "and Louis Blanc's *Organisation du Travail* (published 1839) was the gospel of 1848, just as the *Contrat Sociale* of Rousseau was the gospel of 1789."[46] Politics in Europe in 1848 was an interplay of these different ideologies—liberalism, radicalism, nationalism and socialism. The discontent and grievances of the times were essentially political in character and burst out in ideological expressions, assuming different forms in different countries.

The revolutions of 1848 had important social factors as well and the roles played by different social classes varied from country to country, depending upon the political, social and economic circumstances prevailing in the countries concerned. In France, for example, the bourgeoisie had attained political power since the days of the revolution of 1789. The Church and the nobility—the two privileged classes—had been humiliated. Such a thing had not happened in other countries of Europe. Therefore, the role of the social classes in the revolutions could not be the same in all countries. Even so, a broad classification of the classes in general could be made. For instance, the clergy and the nobility, the middle class or the bourgeoisie, and the workers and peasants were the common classes existing in almost all countries of Europe. In order to assess their role in the revolution, it is appropriate to study each case separately.

The Role of the Three Classes in the Revolutions

While discussing the French Revolution we had seen that the concept of nobility was inextricably linked with ownership of land. In France, feudalism or seigneurialism had been abolished as a result of the French Revolution. This had its impact on other parts of western Europe like Spain, Switzerland and also some states of Italy and western Germany where feudalism was abolished and **free capitalist market in agriculture** was initiated. Land there could be freely sold, purchased, rented or mortgaged. This, however, was not the case in other parts of Europe. In the Hapsburg lands and eastern Europe, including Czarist Russia, the effects of the French Revolution were non-existent. Feudalism and aristocratic preponderance were deeply anchored there. The concept of nobility in the Magyar-speaking and Polish-speaking regions was more widespread. The nobility there was "a mass nobility". Anybody who owned land and was not a serf was a noble. The nobles everywhere clung to their seigneurial rights and joined the counter-revolutionary forces against the peasant insurgents. A major demand of the revolutionaries in the regions where feudalism prevailed was **abolition of serfdom**.

The woes of the working class—that is, the **urban factory workers**—have been well documented in innumerable books and literature. Their main problems were their meagre income and the long hours of work. With almost all the members of the family working, they could hardly make their ends meet. With little furniture and a lack of heating arrangement, the conditions of the housing clusters of the workers were abysmal. They badly lacked sanitation and hygiene. As Peter N. Stearns narrates, they had to walk barefoot for miles to reach their workplaces. Their diet was poor, their children ill-nourished; in the words of Jacques Droz, "most workers saw their children die with indifference and sometimes with joy."[47] Scrofula, rickets and tuberculosis were the most common diseases. The working conditions inside the factories were extremely harsh. For the most trivial mistakes, they were punished severely, sometimes including physical chastisement like beating or financial reprimand like cut in pay. Labour laws were either non-existent or inadequate. Their conditions often led to serious psychological pressure. In their homes in villages, they unburdened themselves in the local church where the priest would often be a source of solace. In the cities, on the contrary, the church was far off, the priest was unknown and unfamiliar and the surrounding environment alien, stern and unsympathetic. Nervous breakdowns under such circumstances were not uncommon.

Historians like William Langer, Pierre Quentin-Bauchart, E.J. Hobsbawm, George Rudé, Louise A. Tilly, Arnost Klíma and Peter Jones have held such hardships to be significant causes of **labour unrest** which gradually crystallised into revolutionary outbreak. According to Klíma, deep-seated frustration led workers to resort to desperate and destructive steps like breaking machinery and equipment. Such incidents occurred, Arnost Klíma noted, mostly in places like Miedling, Perchtoldsdorf, Schwechat in Austria and Solingen in Germany in March 1848. Their grievance was similar to that of the **Bohemian workers in 1844**, "We have no work and no bread; the machines are to blame for this and that's why we came to smash them."[48] Workers' unrest was rampant throughout 1848. Karl Marx saw the '**June Days**' as a **colossal class struggle**—a struggle in which the workers were pitted against all other social classes including the artisans and peasants. It was a precursor of the intense class struggle of the future in which the workers' victory would help the emergence of a communist regime.[49] Sperber, however, argued that it was basically **a battle of workers versus workers**, in the sense that the insurgent workers were facing a Mobile Guard or special militia created by the new republican government. But who were the people the special militia was composed of? They were again the unemployed Parisian workers—the same kind of people on the other side of the barricades. The new government, therefore, attempted to crush one group of workers with the help of another.[50]

Klíma refers to outbreaks in March in Vienna and Berlin, in Prague in June, in Vienna in October and in Germany in May 1849. Special mention may be made of the **Battle of Prater** (Vienna) in **August in 1848** when the announcement by Schwarzer, the minister of labour, that 20,000 workers were to be laid off, resulted in a bitter conflict between a group of workers and the National Guard during which 18 workers were killed and more than 280 wounded.[51] Reference may also be made to the **Revolt**

of Silesian weavers in June 1844. Crowds of weavers attacked homes, factories, warehouses and indulged in wanton destruction and pillage. The Prussian army sought to suppress the movement and restore order, in the course of which 11 people were killed and several injured. According to Peter Jones, it was the working class "consciousness" which "manifested itself in 1848." And this was engendered by industrialisation. In fact, Jones referred to the Marxian theory that as an *impact of industrialisation, each class evolved its own consciousness.* The bourgeoisie owned the means of production and developed a faith in liberalism and freedom of enterprise. The working class, on the other hand, developed a belief in revolutionary socialism. This **revolutionary mentality** constituted the special 'working class consciousness' and was responsible for their role in the revolutions.[52] "It was the working class who died on the barricades."[53]

Peter N. Stearns has, however, argued that despite their conditions being deplorable and their extreme resentment and discontent as a result, factory workers were nevertheless not a potent force in the revolutions of 1848, for several reasons. *First*, industrialisation had not yet penetrated densely in most parts of the continent. For example, although cotton and wool were spun in machines, weaving was still done manually in most places. Notwithstanding enormous changes in the field of metallurgy, "in France a full half of the metallurgical product was still issued from small, traditional charcoal burning forges."[54] *Second*, since the industrial factories were located in the peripheries of the towns, the workers were situated far from the real centres of revolutionary action. *Third*, Stearns analysed that the workers were better off than the traditional artisans in Prussia and in many cases, in France. In both countries, the labour force was far less easily available compared to Britain, and therefore, was better paid. On the whole, Stearns ruled out the popular thesis among historians that the workers' grievances formed a major factor behind the outbreak of the revolutions of 1848. Of course, there were, he agreed, occasional outbursts of workers' wrath, especially in times of acute scarcity—in 1847 for instance—but they were mostly localised and for very limited purposes.[55]

Nevertheless, some measure of self-contradiction can be noted in Stearns' study. On the one hand, he portrayed a dismal and appalling picture of the conditions of the European workers, while on the other, he claimed that the workers in general in many parts of the continent were economically in a superior position than the artisans. In fact, in Stearn's opinion, "the key urban protest came from the ranks of artisans."[56] **Jonathan Sperber** also agreed with Stearns when he assessed that of the 12,000 insurgents of the 'June days' the largest group were artisans—masters as well as journeymen.[57] One of the **main grievances** of the artisans was the **coming of industrialisation** and **the invention of machinery**. With the machines came bulk production, while the artisans specialised in production of delicate and fancy items produced manually and, obviously in limited quantities. The prices of such exclusive products were many times higher than the mechanised ones. And it was natural that the demand for cheaper factory goods would be much higher. The specialised craft started losing quite a bit of its market and this difficulty gave birth to machine-breaking or '**Luddism**'.

Industrialisation largely transformed the traditional and basic structure of an artisan workshop. The master craftsman employed a number of apprentices or journeymen under him for the purpose of assisting him, while the main interest of the journeymen was to learn the trade as early as possible and to become a master craftsman one day. The erosion of the value of their trade dealt a hard blow to the young and enterprising journeymen whose dreams were now shattered and many of them drifted to other professions like teaching, religious preaching, petty government service etc. The **personal relationship** of the **master** and **journeymen** was traditionally one of comradeship and affection. In fact, the journeymen mostly lived and ate with their masters and were for all practical purposes part of their masters' families.

All this changed with the rise in population, increasing demand of craft items and urban growth as a result of which big merchants, through their middlemen, placed orders on the artisans who then, in the temptation of larger profits employed more workers. This was in other words, the '**domestic system**' or the '**putting out system**' which was widespread in 17th-century western Europe in which merchants, through middlemen, 'put out' materials to rural producers who returned the finished products for payment. This 'putting out system' or outsourcing craft often drove a wedge between the masters and their journeymen. For the masters were now more interested in production than training. The traditional, affectionate master–journeymen relationship was destroyed beyond redemption. This resulted in deep frustration of the latter. It did not benefit the artisans either. In order to protect the market of their own products, the master craftsmen sometimes did not allow their journeymen to become masters. This was a way of preserving the balance between the volume of production and popular purchasing power. It was, however, highly detrimental to the journeymen. The big merchants created competition among the artisans, many of whom began to shift from the countryside to the towns and cities.

With the **disappearance of the traditional guild system** (the Le Chapelier Law of 1791 abolished the guilds in France; thereafter, they fell in most European countries before the outbreak of the revolutions of 1848), the artisans could in no way protect their skill. Some of them, however, found entry into modern industries; for example, blacksmiths were welcomed in metal crafts. Similarly, in the newly growing towns there was a demand for tailors, drapers, embroiderers, confectioners etc. But others were severely threatened by industrialisation and replacement of guilds by free trade laws. In fact, they were a terribly anxious class caught between the bourgeoisie and the working class or the proletariat. In terms of their financial position or education they could not identify with the main body of the bourgeoisie, but at the same time, by dint of their skill and aptitude, they refused to be a part of the proletariat either. They felt extremely forlorn and insecure. Loss of their traditional livelihood, they feared, might compel them to join the factories and thereby throw them into the ranks of the proletariat.

Jacques Droz calls them the petite bourgeoisie. They were a volatile class, under great stress and, according to Droz, gripped by an **acute fear of proletarianisation**.[58] Their problems and dilemma have been beautifully summarised by Engels in 1848 as follows:

> Its intermediary position between the capitalists in trade and industry, the bourgeoisie proper, and the working class or proletariat, determines its special character. It aspires to the position of the bourgeoisie, but the slightest financial set-back plunges its members into the proletariat... Constantly torn between the hope of raising itself to the richest class and the fear of being reduced to the level of the proletariat or even to complete destitution: divided between the hope of advancing its interests by obtaining a share in the control of public affairs and the fear of provoking by untimely opposition the wrath of a government which could dispose of its very existence ...[59]

Hobsbawm also considered the petty bourgeoisie of independent artisans, shopkeepers, small farmers, skilled workers etc. to be the radical corps of Western Europe and an "invariable component" of the popular movement of 1848.[60] Like Droz, Hobsbawm too thought that the **petty bourgeoisie** suffered from a serious dilemma. "As little men they sympathised with the poor against the rich, as men of small property with the rich against the poor." Notwithstanding this dilemma they participated, according to Hobsbawm, in the revolution along with the proletariat. "Of the 350 dead in the Milan insurrection of 1848 only a dozen or so were students, clerks or from landowning families. Seventy-four were women and children and the rest artisans or workmen."[61] On 18 March 1848, there was a massive demonstration in Berlin of factory workers, independent artisans, craftsmen like potters, metal-workers, shoemakers, tailors etc. They clashed with the troops and almost 300 demonstrators were killed. This **Berlin workers' movement**, which was reminiscent of the June Days, was a classic example of a **proletariat-artisan alliance**. In fact, as mentioned above, according to Sperber, even in June Days, the maximum number of demonstrators came from the artisan class. **Droz**, on the contrary, felt that the fundamental cause of the failure of the men in 1848 was that petty bourgeoisie could not make a common cause with the 'disinherited classes' and "take up the banner of social revolution".[62] This *failure to merge* was due to the fact that while political notions evolved and liberalism and radicalism emerged, the social structure hardly changed and still bore all the characteristics of the ancien regime.

The grievances of the **peasants** were of a different nature. One of the most significant problems faced by them was the problem of common land. Certain portions of village land in Europe were owned collectively. They were mostly used for grazing cattle etc. In the first half of the 19th century, the population explosion increased the pressure on land tremendously. The common lands, therefore, had now to be taken under cultivation. Loss of common land, which was looked upon as collective property, caused seething discontent among the peasantry. Due to the rise in population, the lands in private possession of the peasantry proved to be inadequate, compelling the peasants to look for work elsewhere in order to augment their income. Domestic manufacturing by local artisans was an important source of work. As already discussed, because of the 'putting out system' the masters also needed more hands for higher production. A symbiotic relationship was thereby created. Soon, however, this source of work was seriously threatened with the advent of industrialisation. Spinning, weaving, metal work were seriously affected. The relationship between the peasants and landlords was further embittered over the issue of '**forest theft**' which meant the use of forests by cutting trees and collecting other forest resources by peasants desperately trying to make ends meet. The *forests largely belonged to the nobles* who fiercely resented this theft, while the peasants strongly insisted that they had such rights.

Population growth meant large-scale deforestation for the purpose of construction and heating and this entailed danger to the environment. Scuffles over this matter were quite common. In fact, in Westphalia a minor civil war broke out on the question of 'forest theft'.[63] As Marx observed, the forest conflict was a sure sign of the strain on social and economic structures.[64] Several state laws, too, irked the peasantry. Reference may be made to the **French Forest Code of 1827** which strictly prohibited the practice of grazing animals in the forests. It was felt that "A troop of goats scattered within them does one hundred times more damage than the axe."[65] The Code blamed the communal and collective woodland uses for the degraded state of France's forests. Similarly, by the Austrian government decree of 1839 all common village forests were decided to be sold off. Furthermore, the peasants protested vehemently against feudalism and demanded the abolition of serfdom. They refused to render labour services to their landlords and continued to graze their animals on the latter's lands and forests where earlier collective rights were prevalent. The nobles also retaliated sternly, often resorting to whipping and ruthless beating. The result was widespread peasant unrest which, however, took different forms in different places depending on the prevailing circumstances.

In France, the situation was relatively calm because peasants there had already gained some important concessions as a result of the French Revolution. Things were particularly bitter in Southern Italy where the peasants were losing their small holdings to the government and were being reduced to day labourers. In the Hapsburg Empire, peasants struggled incessantly to throw over the feudal and manorial burdens. In Hungary, serfdom seemed more intolerable than ever before. In Prussia, serfs had been freed in 1807 but they had to hand over a large chunk of their lands to their old landlords and subsequently faced unmitigated economic hardship. Manorialism was abolished in western Germany, but the peasants were subjected to cash redemption payments as well as higher taxes to the former landlords. And in Eastern Germany, **manorialism** still prevailed and was a constant bone of contention between the nobles and the peasants. In February 1846, the Polish-speaking peasants in the western districts of Galicia joined the Austrian troops to crush a national uprising led by Polish nobles and to uproot a Polish national government in the tiny **Republic of Cracow**. This is *a curious example where peasant-noble* *conflict goaded the peasants to join hands with the Emperor to rise against even the revolutionary nobles.* Marx and Engels saw this uprising as "the first in Europe to plant the banner of social revolution" and was a precursor to the "springtime of peoples" in 1848. The peasants near Magdeburg demanded more pasture for their geese. In general, one demand was common. The peasants strongly **demanded the right to own land** themselves and persistently **resisted unpaid and forced labour** which was called *robota* in the Czechland and *robot* in Hungary and Germany. The ire of the peasants could be fathomed, for instance, from the views expressed by a Galician peasant Kapusciak on the robot problem in the third session of the Vienna Parliament in July 1848 in the following words,

> Yes, the nobleman has treated the peasant lovingly [said Kapusciak]. After having been made to work all week, he was entertained on the Sunday—chained and locked up in the cowshed, so that he should work still harder the next week. Yes, the nobleman is humane, for he encourages the tired robot-peasant with the whip, and if the peasant complains that his draft-animals are too weak to perform the prescribed labour, he is told: 'Then harness yourself and your wife'…. Three hundred steps from the manor-house, he has humbly to take off his hat… and if the poor peasant wants to mount the stairs, he is told to stay in the court-yard, for he stinks …. And for such ill-treatment are we now to pay compensation? I say: "No!! The whips which came down on our heads and tired bodies must suffice. Let these be the compensation of the masters.[66]

Even so, as most scholars perceived, the peasants did not merge with the mainstream of the revolution, but remained confined within their limited vested interests. David Thomson observed that in the final analysis the ultimate fate of the revolution depended on the reactions of the peasantry.[67] As Paul Ginsborg commented, "The European peasantry, by its indifference or open hostility to the revolutionaries, sounded their death knell."[68] Indeed, the peasantry was a large, potent force, a powerful source of energy, which, if rightly tapped, was capable of doing wonders. Though the initiative lay in the hands of the bourgeoisie, they failed to manipulate this vast engine of power, and their clumsy manoeuvring threw the peasantry into the arms of the counter-revolution, which eventually triumphed. Ginsborg further observed,

> One of the central problems that needs careful analysis and explanation by any historian of the revolutions of 1848 is that of failure throughout Europe of the predominantly urban middle class revolutionary

governments to secure the support of the peasant masses. With the notable exception of the alliance that Kossuth formed between Magyar peasants and gentry, which resulted in the heroic resistance of the Hungarians until late in 1849, there seems little evidence of the peasantry being won wholeheartedly to the revolution.[69]

In Hungary, for example, the **April Laws** could free only a part of the peasantry from feudal subjection; the rest of the peasantry broke out in open revolt which was sternly repressed by Count Batthyany's revolutionary government.

An important reason for the apathy of the peasants was possibly the abolition of feudal restrictions in general, especially in the Hapsburg land, in the year of revolution. In Prussia, feudalism was swept away by a royal decree in 1850 and all feudal dues were converted into money rents. *Large number of peasants (approximately 640,000) were able to purchase lands*. In Piedmont and Sicily in Italy, agriculture was modernised. Because of these developments, peasants lost interest in revolutionary activities. The monarchies took advantage of this to woo the peasantry and the revolutionary governments failed to win them over to their side. In Vienna, in the imperial parliament in July 1848, the Silesian deputy Hans Kuldich proposed the abolition of all relics of feudalism. A law to that effect was issued by the Emperor on 7th September. This led to the cementing of the alliance between the monarchy and the peasants. The peasants expected from the revolutionaries that, as it had happened in the time of the French Revolution, portions of the noble estates would be confiscated and distributed among the revolutionaries. Unfortunately, that was not forthcoming. And as Hobsbawm analysed,

> politically once the peasantry reached the threshold of activity, nothing was more certain than that something would have to be done to meet its demands, at any rate in countries where revolutionaries fought against foreign rule. For if they did not attract the peasants to their side, the reactionaries would.[70]

And that was what exactly happened. The revolutionaries at most addressed the question of robota, feudal rents, taxes etc. The distribution of noble lands never happened.[71] The revolution thereby lost the golden opportunity to use the peasantry as a useful ally. The immaturity and ignorance of the peasantry was equally responsible for this unfortunate situation. They failed to transcend their limited vested interests and join the revolutionary movement as a national cause. Therefore, either they remained wholly inert, or they supported the monarchs in their efforts to crush the revolutions." And over most of Eastern Europe the Slav peasants in imperial soldiers' uniforms were the effective suppressors of German and Magyar revolutionaries."[72]

L.C.B. Seaman, however, has expressed his misgivings over the efficacy of the concept of including the peasantry in the revolutionary movement. He felt that even if the peasantry had been invoked into action and were out on the streets along with the workers to make the early months of 1848 a "springtime of the people" in the true sense of the term, the result would have been anarchy and confusion; the revolution, instead of being a success, would have ended in failure. In Hungary, Kossuth's call to the masses had created **bitter divergences** within them. The same was the fate with the appeal to nationalism. As discussed above, in the Hapsburg land, for instance, there was no united national front against imperial domination, but rather hectic scrambling among different racial groups to attain national identities. It paved the path for counter-revolution and repression on the basis of the policy of divide and rule. It is true that in the Russian Revolution nearly sixty years later, Lenin's slogan of 'Peace, Land and Bread' mobilised the peasants successfully, but the situation in Russia was different in the sense that the Russian army then was inefficient and could hardly be of any help to the Czar, while in 1848 the ruling dynasties, after their initial stupor, mustered their strength and were solidly backed by the army to contain the revolution.[73]

The leadership of the revolutions was provided by the middle class or the bourgeoisie. It is true that the workers and craftsmen provided the muscle power to the barricades and died on the streets, but the *ideas and direction* came from the bourgeoisie. **Lamartine**, the French poet and statesman, had defined the events of 1848 as "the product of a moral idea, of reason, logic, sentiment, and of a desire… for a better order in government and society." These moral ideas, logic and sentiments came from the bourgeoisie who were the *people with education*. **Sir Lewis Namier**, therefore, called the revolutions of 1848 primarily the **revolution of the intellectuals**— la *revolution des clercs*.[74] **Peter Jones** classified the bourgeoisie into three major groups—the *grande* **bourgeoisie**, the **middle bourgeoisie** and the *petite* **bourgeoisie**. The first group was either the landowning class or the big merchants who had amassed enormous wealth by dint of their commercial activities. In other words, they were the propertied class or *proprietaires*. The middle bourgeoisie were the professional classes—

doctors, lawyers, teachers, writers, journalists and government officials. The third category was composed of the shop-keepers, small entrepreneurs, petty businessmen, small farmers etc. According to Sperber, in Hungarian and Polish regions, unlike as in western Europe, anybody who owned land and was not a serf was considered to be a noble. To reiterate, the nobility in that region was, therefore, 'mass nobility'.[75] In France and Germany, on the other hand, as Namier pointed out, the middle classes comprised probably half the nation.[76] According to Veit Valentin, in Prussia alone two-thirds of the population consisted of the bourgeoisie.[77] Generally speaking, the bourgeoisie were highly sceptical of the mob or ordinary mass of the people whom they looked upon as crude trouble-makers.

Since the days of early industrialisation in the continent and expansion of market economy, the middle class was flourishing. The Industrial Revolution created enormous opportunities for all the classes of the bourgeoisie—mercantile, professional as well as entrepreneurial. New factories opened up, new enterprises were started, fresh business opportunities cropped up. People started pouring in from the countryside in search of jobs since the population explosion had made livelihood very difficult there. Professionals also thrived, as more people meant more legal disputes for lawyers to handle, more ailing people for the doctors to treat. More schools and educational institutions for the expanding population opened up opportunities for the teachers. In short, **the middle class was rising**. But, at the same time, their grievances were also increasing. *First*, they lacked the right to vote. Since the essential qualification for franchise was a requisite amount of property, a large chunk of the bourgeoisie did not qualify—especially the new entrepreneurs, professionals and petite bourgeoisie. *Second*, their access to government service was also extremely limited. The top positions in the bureaucracy were mostly dominated by the aristocracy in most countries of Europe. In Prussia where the nobles were removed from the bureaucracy, entry into it was on the basis of payment of money—an obnoxious practice which excluded a large number of people. At any rate, *the businessmen and merchants were not much interested in politics*. Their foremost interest lay in mercantile matters. They were interested in the proceedings of legislative assemblies in order to **safeguard their economic agenda** like removal of tariff barriers, ensuring smooth means of communication, construction of good roads and bridges, etc.

It was the professional class which craved political power. They coveted important positions in the bureaucracy but there were several hurdles in their way like qualification of law, passing a difficult entrance examination etc. Moreover, the number of jobs in the bureaucracy invariably fell far short of the number of aspirants. The professionals, therefore, sullenly resented the fact that they did not enjoy positions in the government commensurate to their education. They were disquiet, angry, disillusioned. In **Italy** and **Germany**, the professionals and intellectuals were the revolutionary forces—**Gioberti**, a professor of theology at the University of Turin, and his **Neo-Guelfs**; **Mazzini**, a doctor's son and himself a lawyer who practised as a "poor man's lawyer" and his Carbonari, the patriotic student societies or Burstenchaften in Germany.

Even so, the professionals, observed Stearns, "were not explicitly revolutionary."[78] It is a fact that a number of revolutionary leaders were professionals like Auguste Blanqui, Mazzini etc. and definitely played a key role, but eventually they were not effective enough. According to him, the artisans, and not the professionals, were the most significant factor. According to Sir Lewis Namier, the revolution of the proletariat and the artisans had ended with the June Days. And the peasants had been won over by the ruling dynasties. So, it was the middle class upon whom fell the task of carrying forward the torch of revolution. He wrote,

> The proletariat was defeated in Paris, the peasants were bought off in the Habsburg Monarchy. The social forces behind the revolution of 1848, disjointed and insufficient from the very outset, were practically eliminated. What remained was the middle classes led by intellectuals, and their modern ideology with which they confronted the old established powers and interests. Foremost in that ideology was their demand for a share in the government of states to be remodelled in accordance with the national principle.[79]

The most important political conflict of 1848 was the basic conflict between dynastic, monarchical rule on the one side and popular sovereignty and national self-determination on other. To the men of 1848, the former was arbitrary and retrograde, while the latter was in tune with the liberal ideas of the time, engendered by the French Revolution. Namier elaborated in his book the nationalist movements in different countries, particularly Central Europe where the aspirations of the Poles, the Slovaks, the Slavs, the Czechs, the Magyars, the Bohemians, the Germans were steered and manoeuvred by the intellectuals—Kossuth and Dahlmann, Palacky and Smolka, Robert Blum and Helfert. Stearn argued that there were **two perceptions of bourgeois revolution** espoused by two different ideological groups of bourgeoisie—the radicals and the liberals. *The radicals, as well as socialists like Marx and Engels, believed in the capture of power by the bourgeoisie* who then would take upon itself the task of bringing about revolutionary changes in the society, whereas the *liberals generally extracted reforms from the aristocracy without trying to overthrow them from power.* According to Klíma, even when counter-revolution triumphed, European society could not be returned to its original feudal structure. The civil liberties established during the revolution—freedom of press, association, publication, religious practices, etc.—could not be withdrawn. In other words, the revolution left its indelible mark on the European mind that the counter-revolution, despite the military successes, failed to wipe out. Therein lay the triumph of the bourgeois revolution.[80] For **Karl Marx**, on the other hand, it was the bourgeoisie who let down the cause of the revolution. *Out of fear of the proletariat, the bourgeoisie began to support the ruling authority and thereby sealed the fate of the revolution.*[81]

Sperber rightly considered religious divergences a highly sensitive and significant issue in the atmosphere of revolutionary conflict. Antagonisms were common between the Catholics and Protestants, Catholics and Jews, among different congregations within the Catholics. In fact, **conflict between clericalism and anti-clericalism** was a common phenomenon in most of the major conflicts in the Age of Revolution, especially in the Catholic states of France, Italy, south Germany and the Austrian Empire. In Bavaria, for example, in the Corpus Christi procession, all soldiers and militia accompanying it had to kneel before the sacrament—a common ritual disapproved sullenly by the Protestant regiments from the northern regions of the state. Similarly, when the Protestant King of Prussia ordered all army conscripts to attend Protestant church services on Sundays, the religious sentiments of the Catholic soldiers were seriously offended.[82] Although it is true that *religion, at any rate, was not a central issue in the revolutions of 1848*, it was bound to play a part in moulding the attitudes of the people and sometimes even provoking them to violent action. Most common among such violent outbursts were the **anti-semitic riots** occurring frequently in France, Germany and Hungary. The ire of the peasants was often directed against their money-lenders who charged exorbitant rates of interest. These creditors or money-lenders mostly happened to be Jews who became victims of violent attacks. The Jews retaliated and such conflicts, if not promptly nipped in the bud by the administrative authorities, often catapulted into bitter riots. The master

Map 3.1: Europe 1848–1849; Depicting the Main Revolutionary Centres

Source: Available at https://commons.wikimedia.org/wiki/File:Europe_1848_map_en.png (accessed July 2025)

Note: Created by Alexander Altenhof, licensed under CC BY-SA 4.0, https://creativecommons.org/licenses/by-sa/4.0/

craftsmen of the guilds also occasionally felt threatened when Jews started working as unlicensed craftsmen or shopkeepers selling merchandise not produced in the guilds.[83] Clashes were not uncommon under such circumstances. Religious conflicts broke out in different places of the Hapsburg Empire in the spring of 1848. Sperber referred to some of these. In Vienna, the convent of the Redemptorists, and in Graz in Syria the convent of the Jesuits were attacked and destroyed by the crowds. In the eastern provinces, the priests were agitating for a more democratic organisation of the church and for the abolition of clerical celibacy.[84] Religious issues created a split among the Germans as regards the leadership of a unified Germany. The Catholics wanted to include Austria whom they considered the stronghold of Catholicism, while the Protestants looked to Prussia as the leading Protestant power and wanted to exclude Austria. Riots and skirmishes, differences and disputes along religious lines were inseparable characteristic features of the revolutions of 1848.

Stearns also regarded the initial fumbling and unpreparedness of the monarchs to be important factors in the rapid spread of the revolution. The kings failed to comprehend the signals and to take proper measures to nip the trouble in the bud. That encouraged the rebels and the revolution began to spread like wild fire from one country to another. Within an amazingly short span of time, the whole continent—with the exception of Britain in the east and Russia in the west—was ablaze.

Broadly speaking, Jones believed that the revolutions of 1848 were marked by two major socio-economic elements. *First*, the beginnings of industrialisation and the growth of towns, particularly in England; and *second*, the rise in population which had a tremendous effect on the resources of the nations in Europe and slowly created the circumstances leading eventually to the Age of Revolutions, of which 1848 was the climax.[85]

Why Did the Revolutions of 1848 Fail?

On the revolutions of 1848, T.S. Hamerow wrote,

> it must have been exciting to be alive in the spring of 1848, that 'springtime of nations', when God smiled with favour upon every parliamentary sub-committee and the liberal millennium was just round the corner. Barricades were mushrooming in the capitals of Europe from the Seine to the Danube; angry mobs were stoning royal

palaces; unpopular ministers were signing resignations and hurrying into exile; exiled revolutionaries were hurrying home to a hero's welcome. To liberals witnessing these events it appeared as if a new world were about to be born, as if a new reign of liberty and justice were beginning. The sense of participation in the creation of a better society seemed to intoxicate them.[86]

The exhilarating zeal, however, was very short-lived. Within a few months, the provisional revolutionary governments were abolished, the constitutions withdrawn, revolutionary leaders were leaving for exiles and the hereditary kings recapturing power. The tables had been turned. **Odilon Barrot**, the liberal monarchist under the July Monarchy in France and later the Prime Minister in 1848–1849, wrote, "Never have nobler passions moved the civilized world, never has a more universal impulse of souls and hearts pervaded Europe from end to end: and yet all this was to result in failure…."[87]

But why did they fail? **With the exception of France and Switzerland, why were the revolutions quelled everywhere?** There were several reasons behind it. To begin with, the *lack of unity among the revolutionaries*, especially the middle class who were, after all, the leaders of the revolution, was indeed a disturbing phenomenon. In the first place, the middle class or the bourgeoisie were not unanimous on the question of the *form of the revolutionary government* in the respective states. *The liberals favoured constitutional monarchy, while the radicals wanted the formation of a republic. The socialists aimed at a complete overhaul of the socio-economic structure* either with the help of the republican government or without them. The **Neo-Guelphs in Italy** sought to establish a federation under the political as well as spiritual leadership of the Pope. In other words, ideological divergences ripped them apart. Furthermore, the liberals were averse to violence and disorder, while the radicals believed that bellicose, undaunted resistance was the only course to demolish the retrograde, obsolete order and to replace it with a new, progressive one based upon equality and popular sovereignty. The **socialists**, too, welcomed revolution as they were convinced that revolution was the only scientific and logical means through which an unprecedented social, economic and political transformation could emerge.

The **Bonapartists** in France seized the opportunity of this conflict to establish an imperial regime under the name of the Second Empire. Also, as Marxist historians as well as Karl Marx himself argued, *the* *bourgeoisie let down the artisans and the working class* who were the muscle power of the middle class and *fought on the barricades*. The most crucial dispute between them was over the issue of industrialisation. While the middle class sincerely believed in freedom of pursuit of independent enterprises including industrialisation, the artisans perceived an invincible enemy in the industrialists who compelled them to wind up their small manufacturing units or workshops owing to competition with machine-made cheaper goods. The industrialists, the artisans felt, crushed them under the wheels of their machines. According to Marx, the revolutions failed predominantly due to the '**treachery of the bourgeoisie**'. And the 'treachery' lay in the fact that the bourgeoisie, in order to counter the proletariat, began to side with the ruling class and facilitated the success of the counter-revolution. According to Marx and Engels, what the bourgeoisie should have precisely done was to grab power and carry out the reforms themselves; the bourgeoisie, on the contrary, preferred to collaborate with the aristocracy, who comprised the parliament of the constitutional monarchy, in order to extract reforms through negotiation.[88] The proletariat felt cheated, humiliated, forsaken. After all, they were the ones who had died on the barricades, only to discover now that the benefits were all being reaped by the bourgeoisie. Moreover, as in the case of the artisans, the capitalists or industrialists were the main enemy of the working class. But the liberals, on the contrary, wanted the development of the nation through capitalism. The **liberal bourgeoisie**, therefore, utterly failed to forge a common agenda and to find a common enemy, with the lower classes.

The same was true about the failing of the **radical bourgeoisie**. They also could not join hands with the socialists because their primary goal was the establishment of a democratic republic and not a government that was the 'supreme regulator of production'. The radicals, sincere though they were, *failed to identify themselves with the masses*—either with the peasantry or the proletariat. They depended mostly on militant action for which they received the greatest response from the student community. Their struggle frittered away due lack of cohesive unity, wider mass base and organisational skill. This explains the failure of the **movements of Ledru-Rollin** (the French lawyer and radical political activist who was instrumental in bringing about universal male suffrage in France on 2 March 1848); **Mazzini, Kossuth, Petofi** (renowned Hungarian poet whose poem 'Talpra Magyar' became the revolutionary anthem, was an extreme radical and an inspired agitator who led the peasants' insurgency in Hungary in March 1848 and was also the aide-de-camp of General Bem who led the Hungarian army in subduing Transylvania in the winter of 1848) and **Struve** (the German revolutionary and radical political agitator who took an active part in the Baden insurrection of 1848–1849). They were brilliant leaders with strong convictions and intense devotion to the revolutionary cause, but they lacked in experience and the support of powerful armed forces. The revolutions of 1848 were, therefore, marked by a *lack of effective leadership*. The bourgeoisie, who provided the leadership, despite their best intentions failed to come to terms with reality and sink their differences for a common cause. As the revolutions progressed, the divisive expectations grew sharper rendering all chances of cohesion practically impossible.

Inaction of the peasantry was another weakness the revolutions suffered from. Although there were sporadic peasant uprisings here and there, they were not, as we have seen, fused into the mainstream of the revolutionary movement. David Thomson, therefore, saw the revolutions of 1848 to be principally the *work of the towns*. Participation of the countryside, which could open up boundless force and energy, could not be manipulated. The scope of the revolution remained extremely limited. As we have discussed above, Seaman was, however, highly sceptical about the advantages of the involvement of the peasantry in the revolutions of 1848.

A serious *lack of unity prevailed among the different racial identities* in central Europe. As we have seen, different racial groups existed with spirited craving for liberty and independence, but regrettably these could not be coalesced into a united national movement against the Austrian imperial government. There were the Czechs, the Slovaks, the Magyars, the Poles, the Ruthenians, the Croats. On the other hand, there were the Germans whose liberal and national aspirations were voiced through the **Vorparlament** that met in Frankfurt in March 1848, composed of intellectuals and professionals who were opposed to violence and aimed at a united, constitutional Germany. The first draft of its constitution was prepared by one of its leading spokesmen, **Friedrich Dahlmann**, historian and professor of the University of Gottingen from where he was expelled for his revolutionary ideas. The members of the Vorparlament were not unanimous regarding the geographical borders of Germany and were divided between the '**Great Germans**', who wanted to include the

Austrian empire consisting of all its minority races except Hungary; and the '**Little Germans**', who aspired to unite the Germans alone leaving out all the mixed races. The latter wished to offer the crown to the King of Prussia, while the former wanted to make the Austrian Emperor the Emperor of united Germany. The plan of the 'Great Germans', who were the majority, did not suit the minority races which cherished different aspirations. The **Czechs** preferred to acquire autonomy within the loose structure of the Hapsburgs. They turned down the German invitation to attend the deliberations of the Frankfurt Assembly and rather wished to demonstrate their separate identity by summoning a **Slav Congress at Prague**, presided over by Palacky. The German nationalists in Prague, likewise, boycotted the Slav Congress. Even, among the Slavs, there were acute differences along ethnic lines. The **Slovaks** were happy if they gained equal rights within the Hapsburg Empire. The **Serbs** and the **Croats**, yearned for complete independence from Hungary and for the formation of a united Slav land. The **Rumanians** were extremely resentful because the Hungarian leaders wanted to incorporate Transylvania into the Hungarian national State. That was because since 1003 till 1683, when Transylvania finally fell under Hapsburg domination, she was under the rule of the Kingdom of Hungary. The Rumanians, who formed the majority of the population of Transylvania, however, doggedly opposed this decision and organised in May 1848 **a national assembly in Blaj** which drew a massive crowd of 40,000. The result was a violent civil war in June.

Similar was the situation in **Croatia-Slovenia,** which also the Hungarian government aimed at assimilating within its fold. The **Poles** dreamt of an independent Polish state in the province of Galicia, only to find that the eastern part of the province was being claimed by the Ukrainians, whom the Polish nationalists called the **Russian Austrians or Ruthenians**. They blamed Count Stadion, the provincial governor of Galicia for encouraging the Ruthenians. These disagreements among the Slav nationalities presaged the formation of the Slav nations of Czechoslovakia, Yugoslavia and Poland in 1919. The Magyars, who did not belong to the Slav race, accepted the Austrian Emperor as the king of Hungary, but demanded complete autonomy including final say in matters of the Hungarian armed forces in the Crown of St. Stephen. Moreover, they asserted the predominance of the Magyars in all official works in Hungary and also declared Magyar to be the official language. Only Magyar-speaking people could stand for elections. All these seriously alienated other racial identities in Hungary. However, there was *one common element among all these racial conflicts*. Till this time, *none of them desired to overthrow the Austro-Hungarian Empire*, but aspired for an independent, constitutional entity within it. The Hapsburg monarchy, in its turn, successfully played the policy of 'divide and rule' by taking full advantage of these divisive tendencies. It supported the Rumanians and the Croats against the Hungarian nationals; and the Ukrainians or Ruthenians against the Polish nationalists. The victory of the counter-revolution and frustration of the revolutions were warranted thereby.

While the **revolutionaries lacked unity**—the bourgeoisie was a divided house, the racial groups lacked in unity, the revolutionaries of Italy were divided into three different groups with varying political programmes, the Germans into 'Great Germans' and 'Little Germans'—*the rulers of the different countries of Europe, on the other hand, were absolutely resolute about one common goal*. That was the suppression of the revolutionary fervour which stirred the people all over Europe in 1848. In stemming the tide of revolution, they extended immediate and fullest cooperation to one another. Seaman, therefore, argued that if a government possessed the will to resist, which almost every government does, no revolution in the 19th century could hope to dislodge it, unless it was helped by another country. That is why, he said, it ultimately took a world war, in which so many countries were involved, to **dismember the Hapsburg Empire** and to set up national states in its place.

> The aims of 1848 could not be achieved by the methods of 1848, for the reason that the methods of 1848 were those of revolution; and, in the circumstances that existed, revolution was bound to fail. It is a fair generalisation that governments are almost always overthrown by other governments, and only on the rarest occasions by revolution. It needed the military coalition to achieve by 1919 what the men of 1848 expected to achieve by barricades and manifestoes.[89]

This statement of Seaman seems to be an exaggeration. Because, if it were so, how could the revolution in France in 1789 and the revolution in Russia in 1917 be successful? In both these cases, did not popular revolutions succeed in overthrowing age-old dynastic regimes without any external help? Or is it so because none of them occurred in the 19th century? Then, did Seaman imply that there was something special about the 19th century, so that revolutions on their own could not be successful at that time? Seaman's theory is applicable as far as the American Revolution of

1776 or the Belgian Revolution of 1830 was concerned. They won the wars with foreign support. He was right when he observed that the Hapsburg Empire was dislodged by the combined might of so many powers in the First World War. But Seaman seems to have overlooked the two greatest revolutions of the millennium.

Nevertheless, the fact remains that the reactionary monarchies promptly came to each other's assistance in the event of the slightest threat of the outbreak of a revolution. Austria, for example, was profusely helped by the Russians in the suppression of the insurgents. Russia's loyalty to the institution of monarchy and the Holy Alliance was unflinching. At the same time, the Czar was mortally scared of revolutions, particularly that of the Russian Poles, spilling over into the Russian Empire. Therefore, Czar Nicholas II earnestly felt that the monarchs should help one another against the revolutionaries. He despatched a contingent to the Hapsburgs to help the Rumanians in Transylvania against the Hungarian nationals. He also helped Turkey to crush the national uprising in Moldavia and Wallachia led by Nicolae Balcescu, a prominent historian and journalist. On 9 May 1849, the Czar promised aid to Austria again, and on 17th June Ivan Paskevich led a strong Russian army in an invasion of Hungary. In August the Hungarian army was routed after which Kossuth buried the Crown of St. Stephen which he had carried along with him and left for exile to Turkey.

France, too, like Russia, came to the aid of the counter-revolution. At the request of the Pope, for instance, Louis Napoleon, as the leader of a great Catholic nation, despatched his army to crush the Republic of Rome established by Mazzini in 1849. The Republic was ended and Mazzini left Rome. With the help of the French army which remained stationed in Rome, the Pope re-established his autocratic rule in Rome. Similarly, British intervention in the case of the duchies of Schleswig and Holstein in March 1848 upheld the rights of the Danish King under whose rule the duchies were attached. However, the whole population of Holstein and the minority population of some parts of southern Schleswig were German. Holstein was a member also of the **Bund** or the German Confederation. The German national awakening following the Napoleonic Wars led to a strong popular movement in Holstein and southern Schleswig for unification with a new Prussian-dominated Germany. Prussian troops, on behalf of the Bund mobilised in their support. But at this stage Lord Palmerston, the then British foreign Secretary, intervened and urged for an armistice. Eventually, by the **Treaty of London, May 1852**, the two duchies were restored to the dominions of the King of Denmark. The keynote of Britain's foreign policy at this time was the maintenance of the status quo and preservation of the balance of power. In short, the common approach of the different ruling countries towards revolution and their active support to each other were certainly instrumental in dampening the efforts of the revolutionaries.

The question is often asked: Why were the revolutions of 1848 unsuccessful? And *why did the monarchs of 1848 who had conceded before the revolutionary forces revive within a short span of time, whereas the French Revolution of 1789 which preceded the revolutions of 1848, and the Russian Revolution of 1917 which succeeded them, were able to get rid of their oppressive, age-old ruling dynasties for good?* According to Marx, certain socio-economic developments were responsible for this. In 1789, the bourgeoisie could successfully mobilise the masses for attacking the absolutist regime; but in 1848 a working-class movement led by socialist leaders had already emerged and this made popular mobilisation by the liberal bourgeoisie difficult. But at the same time, the workers were still not organised or enthused enough to be mobilised into a proletarian revolution that Lenin carried out in 1917.[90] Sperber observed, "**1848 was the revolution that fell between two stools—the bourgeoisie of 1789 and the proletarian of 1917.**" [91]

Sperber argued that there were several common features between the revolutions of 1789 and those of 1848. Both had constitutional monarchists and radical republicans; in 1789 there were sans-culottes who were the same as the master craftsmen and journeymen of 1848; revolutionaries in both were ardent and intense in their purpose. Even so, the most difficult problem of the revolutionaries of 1848 was that they were **haunted by the lessons and memories of 1789** all the while. The *conservative rulers learnt from the fate of Louis XVI the danger of turning a deaf ear to the demands of the people*; the constitutional monarchists learnt how negotiation with absolutism paved the path for the radicals; the *radicals were warned of the excesses of extremism* that reminded them of the fates of Marat, Danton and Robespierre. And in 1848, a **new element** had emerged which was not there in 1789–1799—the **rise of socialism**. The socialists, however, used the slogans of the Jacobins—popular sovereignty and popular rule— to woo the workers and peasants alike, but were suppressed by armed intervention at the instance of the rulers.

Loyalty of the armed forces was an important factor in the success of the counter-revolutionary forces in 1848. **Loyal soldiers** led by **dedicated commanders—Cavaignac and Radetzky, Jelacic and Windischgratz—** contributed immensely in crushing the revolutions and restoring the dynastic rulers to their thrones. They were the true upholders of the principle of legitimacy.

David Thomson, while discussing the collapse of the revolutions of 1848, assigned importance to another factor whose contribution in frustrating the revolutions indeed cannot be overlooked. This was the **spread of cholera**. In fact, Thomson called it a major force of counter-revolution.[92] Deadly cholera played a crucial role in substantial decimation, at intervals, of the population of Europe and unparalleled devastation of human life. The epidemic which started in China in 1844 reached Russia by 1847 and then spread rapidly westwards to other parts of the European continent. Hundreds of people died everyday and the survivors were petrified in shock and terror. There was not a single household that did not lose a member—most of the times more than one. It left the entire continent so incapacitated and shattered—physically, psychologically and emotionally—that they hardly remained capable of any sustained work for a long time to come. Building barricades and plotting revolts were the last things they could imagine. The spirit of revolution died down on its own.

The Features and Pattern of the Revolutions of 1848

About European revolutions, Metternich had once observed, "When France sneezes, the rest of Europe catches cold." This is exactly what happened in 1848. That year saw the entire continent of Europe—with the exception of Britain and Russia flanking the two extremities of the continent—gripped in the flame of revolutions. They started in France and like wild fire rapidly engulfed almost the whole of Europe. They were spurred by different grievances emerging out of varying circumstances; accordingly, therefore, the revolutions assumed various forms, with diverse characteristic features, in different countries. Even so, they were all woven together into one singular body that collectively came to be called the 'revolutions of 1848'. 1848 became known as the year of revolutions and could possibly be compared with an intricately embroidered piece of cloth—a masterpiece presenting a variety of embroidered designs in a spate of colours, all part of a single fabric of magnificence and style. They sprang from the fountainhead of varying conditions, merged into and followed the same currents and fell in the same sea of confusion, only to fade away into the horizon of obscure autocracy.

What were the diversities in unity? One important fact in this connection was that, as we had discussed earlier, the revolutions could be distinguished into two distinct forms. The revolutions of Switzerland, Spain and Portugal were **on the pattern of France**—that is, **democratic movements** for greater constitutional and electoral rights. Moreover, as a result of growing industrialisation, socialist doctrines had made rapid headway there. Apart from **political reforms**, therefore, the demand was also of **socio-economic** nature involving higher wages and better working conditions for the innumerable factory workers, and better living conditions like proper housing, sanitation facilities, etc.; while in **central Europe** the main problem was the **agrarian problem**, since industrialisation had not penetrated there. The primary concern of the peasantry was to shake off the feudal burdens and jurisdictions. Apart from that, there were the artisans struggling desperately to eke out an existence and to preserve an identity and not be submerged into a nameless proletariat. Being predominantly an agricultural world, serfdom was an extremely serious issue in central and eastern Europe. There the form of protest was as per **the model of Palermo**, that is, **national insurrection against foreign rule** and demand for greater social and economic freedom, including **abolition of serfdom**.

A significant difference between the western and eastern parts of the continent, as far as the revolutions were concerned was that revolutions mostly broke out in central Europe and much less in the west. As David Thomson observed, "the revolutions were pre-eminently central European events." The extreme west, that is **Britain and Belgium**, as well as the extreme east, like **Poland and Russia** remained *outside the orbit of the revolutionary outbreaks in 1848*. The reasons were different for each country. Both Britain and Belgium already had constitutional governments as well as strong parliamentary systems. Belgium established a new government after its successful revolution in 1830. **Britain**, through its **Great Reform Act of 1832** and the **Importation Act of 1846** by which the vexatious Corn Laws were repealed, had won immense good will among the people. *Through reforms, therefore, it had taken the wind out of the sail of popular revolt.* In **Poland**, the situation was most appropriate for a revolution as the nation was under the domination of three foreign countries—Russia,

Austria and Prussia. **Russian Poland** had risen in revolt in 1830 but the revolt was crushed and Poland was subjected to harsh Russian domination and all her earlier autonomy was gone. In 1846 again plans were made by several Polish organisations for a general Polish uprising against the Russians, the Austrians as well as the Prussians. On 21st February, it was supposed to start in Poznan, the capital of the Prussian Great Duchy of Posen, led by Ludwik Meiroslawski, but the plans failed before the uprising due to the betrayal of a conspirator and the leaders were arrested by the Prussian authorities. In the **Austrian part of Poland**, the uprising started in Cracow on the night of 20th February, but lasted only nine days ending in Austrian victory. Thereafter, Poland was not in a position to revolt again. Even so, in the Austrian Empire in 1848 the Poles in Galicia, taking advantage of the revolutionary situation, wanted to establish their authority there. However, they could assert themselves only in the western half, as the eastern half was claimed, with Austrian help, by the Ukrainians. **In Prussia**, too, they did not revolt because, in the wake of liberal movements there, the Poles also expected a better deal.

As far as **Russia** was concerned the question naturally arises that why did a revolution not break out in that country? Conditions prevailing there were abominable. Thomson alluded to Frederick J. Turner's **'safety valve' theory** (about America's westward expansion) to explain the phenomenon.[93] He observed that just as America in the west provided an outlet for the expanding population to settle there and fulfil their dreams and aspirations and thereby acted as a safety valve against the outburst of any plausible social tension, the Russian eastward expansion into Asia similarly offset the explosion of a cauldron of grievances brewing within the Russian society into a major revolution in 1848. Moreover, as most historians have pointed out, Russia did not have a bourgeoisie to lead the country through a revolution. Weak, intermittent ripples of discontent were cruelly repressed by the autocratic Czarist regime.

Notwithstanding these basic differences, the revolutions of 1848 formed one unitary whole, exemplifying unity in diversity. Their aims and objectives, the pattern they followed, the consequences they produced, the impact they created had certain fundamental common characteristics. Origins and outcome followed a particular singular model. Yet within this larger collective design there were several interwoven patterns.

The revolutionary movements in general were **all protests against the settlements of 1815**—their primary agenda being to revise it, if possible, to demolish it. In Italy and Germany, the revolutions were a direct onslaught on the territorial and dynastic settlement of Vienna and on the hegemony of the Hapsburgs which the 'Metternich System' had clamped upon Europe. At Vienna, the national aspirations for unification of the Germans and the Italians were completely frustrated and while Italy was brought under foreign domination, the Germans were placed under direct Austrian hegemony. Prussia sullenly resented Austrian presidency of the German Confederation created at the Congress of Vienna and was determined to revise it at the earliest opportunity. The preponderance of Austria at the Congress of Vienna and the policy and resolve of Metternich to maintain her status quo interests crushed all hopes of Hungary and racial minorities within the Hapsburg Empire to attain their freedom. Breakdown of the Vienna Settlement and the Metternich System were their only hope.

Another significant common element of the revolutions of 1848 was that they were all consciously **French in design**, inspired and directed by the **principles of liberalism and democracy** of the French Revolution. It is true that in 1848 the revolutions first started in Palermo in Sicily one month before it started in France. All the same, revolutions in Europe, since the days of the French Revolution in 1789, were associated and inextricably linked with France alone. In Europe it was in France in whose soil the seeds of liberalism, republicanism, popular sovereignty were sown, and France considered it to be her duty to share her noble ideas with others. And, other countries were indeed immeasurably inspired by her. Historian Edgar Quinet wrote, "France can no longer halt but a thousand tongues promptly shout in her ear: Onwards! Onwards!"[94] Although, therefore, the revolutions started in Sicily, the original source of inspiration was France. "If Italy set the example, it was France that gave the signal for a more general activity."[95] And within a few days of the French government banning the banquet and the people of Paris rushing out into the streets throwing up barricades, the same example began to be followed by one country after another. A German Deputy at the Frankfurt Assembly observed, "**Our revolutions, like our fashions, we were wont to receive from Paris.**"

Economic distress and financial crisis was an important underlying factor of all the revolutions of 1848. As we have discussed, the **harvest failure of 1846–1847** adversely affected almost all the European countries. This could be termed the immediate economic cause of the revolutions of 1848. However, behind this immediate cause was hidden a larger economic background deriving from several factors that built up a revolutionary mood. This economic backdrop was a common feature for all the countries concerned. In some countries, mostly of central and eastern Europe, the problem emanated from the **demographic pressure** upon land caused by enormous population growth. In others like France the unprecedented development of **transport and industry** contributed immensely to the build-up of the revolutionary passion. In the former case, population growth over the years created extreme pressure on the land forcing peasants to migrate to towns in search of extra income. At this juncture, **abolition of robot** (in Hungary in March 1848 and in Galicia in 1847) enabled more and more peasants to sell off their small plots of land to their landlords and migrate to the cities for livelihood. It facilitated the landlords also to buy the lands of the migrant peasantry and thereby to expand their area of consolidated cultivation. With the increase in income as well as the compensation they earned through abolition of robot, they ventured into industrial enterprises in which the migrant peasants served as the labour force. In France, on the other hand, the rapid development of industry and transport metamorphosed the entire economic scene, ushering in new problems of labour and capital and the concomitant issues of socialism. The erosion of the artisans' traditional crafts as a result of industrialisation, the consequent migration of many to the cities in search of work and the constant threat of proletarianisation were the crisis the artisans faced in countries like France and to some extent Germany, where industrialisation was rapidly progressing.

The **major centres** of revolutions were the **towns and cities**. The character of the revolutions of 1848 was therefore, essentially urban. I have discussed earlier at length how and why the vast mass of the peasantry could not be an integral part of the French Revolution. The landlords also were not content with the sum of money they received as compensation from the abolition of serfs and robot. With the countryside inert, the main centres of activities, therefore, turned upon the urban areas. It was, therefore, **Paris, Rome, Berlin, Vienna, Budapest, Zagreb, Poznan, Cracow and Prague**, with their bustling population, which became the nerve-centres of upheaval and hectic activity. Here also, as David Thomson pointed out, "this universal pattern concealed a basic difference." Paris and Berlin were revolutionary because they were **industrial cities** and therefore drew huge crowds of **migrant labourers and artisans** from different parts of Europe.

They were restless and aggrieved and formed a potent revolutionary force. Rome, Vienna, Prague, Zagreb were in revolutionary mood because they were capital cities.[96] Naturally they became the main hubs of activity of their respective states. In these towns and cities, the distraught workers and artisans struggled desperately and incessantly to improve their wretched existence. They were manoeuvred by the bourgeoisie who were resolute to change the existing order. A series of upheavals, **urban by nature and bourgeoisie-proletariat in character**, broke out.

Within the **bourgeoisie**, there was a prominent, outstanding group of intellectuals—**university professors and students, journalists and poets**, who prepared the ground for what Lewis Namier called "**the Revolution of the Intellectuals**." This, again, was a common element that characterised all the revolutions of 1848. It was **Lamartine and Ledru Rollin, Kossuth and Petofi, Palacky, Dahlmann, Mazzini, Balcesco** who lent the revolutions their ideas, style and intellectual direction. They not only provided the principles and concepts like the philosophes of the French Revolution, but shaped the course and methods of the uprisings as well as inspired and encouraged the people. However, being intellectuals, they were *perhaps romantic idealists who were visionary but also less practical and experienced than hardened politicians.* They were incapable of fighting seasoned military commanders like Windischgratz, Radetzky and Haynau, and imperial servants like Jelacic or Nopcsa. That was the tragedy of the intellectual leaders of 1848. "*It is their leadership that gave the revolutions their fragility and brittleness; if also their brilliance and heroism.*"[97]

Apart from liberalism and socialism, the most powerful general force in European politics at this time was the **spirit of nationalism** that bound all the European nations together in one string. It, again, took different forms in different countries. The French people, for instance, were anxious to liberate their nation from the grip of a dreary and uninspiring government that failed to fulfil the dreams of the nation to see herself placed again at the pedestal of the comity of European nations as she was under Napoleon Bonaparte. It was **Bonaparte**'s intense nationalism that imbued the entire country with a **hysteria of nationalist passion**. In Switzerland, it took the form of a civil war to preserve the unity of the nation by thwarting the attempts of the **Sonderbund** to secede from the Federal Diet which was being supported by the rest of the nation. In Italy, the foremost concern of the revolutionaries was to free the land from foreign domination and then to unify it into a dynamic nation. In Germany, the liberal and radical intellectuals strove to transform the loose structure of the German Confederation into a unified, powerful nation. The various national and racial identities within the Hapsburg Empire of Austria were also restless to attain the right to national self-determination. They clearly expressed their demand to establish their own provisional government and their own constitution. Here a point should be noted. *While the efforts at national self-determination in Germany, Italy and Switzerland were to integrate the fragmented portions into a unified, national whole, in the Hapsburg land, on the contrary, different nationalities bound by force under Austrian hegemony, struggled desperately to disintegrate themselves from the Empire by asserting independence through patriotic national movements.* Nationalism, therefore, could triumph somewhere through integration, and somewhere through disintegration. At any rate, whatever be its form, upsurge of nationalism was undoubtedly, a vastly potent influence in Europe in 1848.

The revolutions of 1848 brought about a system of mass agitation which, again, was a common general feature. Much of it was borrowed from Britain where various devices of mass politics—addressing common people through rousing public speeches, organisation of signature campaigns, demonstrations at open, public places etc.—were resorted to. The Chartist movement and the movement organised by the **Anti-Corn Law League** applied these stratagem. In fact, the revolutions followed a particular pattern and procedure and a typical sequence of events. *First*, there would be an insurrection arising out of popular discontent; *second*, people would pour out into the streets and barricades would go up; and *third*, a provisional government would be proclaimed and a constitution would be drawn up. This was the common general procedure that was being followed. The trend was set by France. On 22 February 1848, with the **failure of the banquets** (the name came from the leaders who attempted to raise money by giving rousing speeches at subscribed dinners in major urban areas), street agitation began. Barricades were built throughout Paris. The example was followed in Munich, Vienna, Budapest, Venice, Cracow, Berlin. The results were no less impressive. Metternich, the embodiment of reaction, escaped from Vienna and took shelter in England. The other governments, unprepared as they were, panicked and quickly gave in. Liberal constitutions were granted. Provisional governments sprang up. In fact, 1848 was the **year of parliaments**. Innumerable parliaments crammed the continent. Here, however, one must note that while in France, the monarchy of Louis Philippe was overthrown and a republic was proclaimed, the same was not the case in Central Europe. There, neither were the Kings and the Emperor overthrown, nor were republics proclaimed. Only **autonomous governments** were announced. Even Hungary, while announcing its separation from Austria, recognised the Hapsburg Emperor Ferdinand as its King.

Sperber, however, observed that the 'political choreography' of rallies and marches of the mass demonstrations of the 20th century had *not* been established in 1848. Mass demonstrations in those days, mostly took the shape of **insurrection**. Sperber referred to two major mobilisations of Parisian workers led by the **Luxembourg Commission** and a few radical leaders on 16 April and 15 May 1848. These were attempts either to intimidate or to overthrow the provisional government and were dispersed by the National Guard. The banquet campaign of Paris which eventually snowballed into the street struggles of 1848 could as well be cited as an example.

Secret societies and illegal organisations were a distinctive feature of the revolutions of 1848. They emerged in response to the stringent measures applied by Metternich on associations of people. As formal associations and societies were banned, secret societies sprang up everywhere, notable among them being **Young Italy** set up by Mazzini in 1831 and later in 1834, **Young Europe** comprising **Young Italy, Young Poland, Young Germany**. In 1835–1836, **Young France** was formed. Most of them were modelled on the Carbonari. There was also the **German League of Outlaws**, composed mainly of expatriate German journeymen.

One of the characteristics of the 1848 revolutions was the **explosion of the printed word**. The fall of Metternich brought about considerable relaxation of the press. Despite lack of freedom of the press and association in the Metternich era, the students and professors of German universities published pamphlets and newspapers which discussed the need for basic liberal reforms. After the end of censorship, however, newspapers and journals proliferated in almost all the major cities of Europe. In Paris alone, Sperber noted, there were at least 171 different newspapers during the spring of 1848.[98] *Le Monde, Le Journal, Le Peuple, L'ami du people, L'evenement* were some of the most important newspapers published from France. In Prussia out of the **70 newspapers** published in 1848, half of them (almost 34) were started only during that year. Unlike official sources, newspapers gave expression to a vast range of emotive ideas, convictions, opinions and expressions during these popular uprisings of a very important episode of the history of Europe. In Austria, only 19 out of 79 newspapers had the right to discuss politics. In 1848 this number jumped to 388, and 306 of them discussed politics. Most of these were in German language. The newspapers in regional languages—Croatian, Slovak, Slovene, etc.—were very few. The Czech newspapers alone numbered almost 52 in 1848. Though subjected to harsh censorship, there was an explosion of **political caricature journals**. They were perceived as more dangerous than the printed word, because while many of the *militant lower classes were illiterate, they were able to see and easily understand the visual images and cartoons of the caricature journals.*

Formation of **clubs and associations** was another common element of the revolutions of 1848. Since the days of the French Revolution, we have seen that political discourse played a very significant role in shaping public opinion. Clubs and cafes, **salons and libraries** were the public spaces where *ideas and opinions were freely exchanged.* The same was the case in 1848. That year saw a rapid proliferation of clubs and associations, many of them being essentially political in character. Sperber noted the existence of about **200 clubs in Paris alone**. The French Romantic novelist George Sand recounted that one evening when she had accidentally locked herself out of her Paris apartment and desperately called three locksmiths one after another, she found that none could be contacted as each was attending a club meeting![99] Political clubs were also very popular in Rome, Vienna, Prague and other cities. In the German universities, the **patriotic student societies** (Burschenchaften) were very popular much before the revolutions broke out. In Germany, the largest political club was the **Central March Association**, founded in November 1848. It attracted almost half a million members, mostly liberal middle-class, scattered over a thousand affiliate branches in different towns and cities.[100] In major towns of Europe—Rome, Berlin, Vienna, Budapest, Prague— mass meetings were often called in order to discuss important current issues and were attended by thousands of people. **Schools, public parks, municipal halls** were used for such purposes. In Prussia, there were some conservative political clubs, the more prominent among them being— **Prussian Association** and the **League of Loyalty** to King and Fatherland. In Germany, as well as in Austria there were branches of a well-known Catholic club known as the **Pius Association**. In Italy, secret societies were the main form of revolutionary politics, their key structure being that of the Carbonari. The best example was Mazzini's Young Italy. However, by the end of the year 1848 there sprang up a number of democratic clubs in Tuscany and the Papal States. These later merged themselves together to form the consolidated 'Central Committee of Italian Political Clubs.' In Budapest, '**Society for Equality**' was a prominent left-wing political club which vouched support for Kossuth. The Slav nationalities had their own separate political associations, especially the Czechs, the Croats and the Ukrainians.[101]

Such associations also led to the formation of **workers' associations**, many of which were encouraged and even founded by socialist thinkers like Louis Blanc, Proudhon and Sewell. In fact, the platform was provided by the Government Commission for Labourers or the Luxembourg Commission, established by the provisional government of France on 28 February 1848 following the February Revolution in order to implement its proclamation of the 'right to work'. The Luxembourg Commission emerged as an arbitral body of different workers' unions and established a standardisation of settlement among trades. Workers' associations, therefore, played a distinctive role in crystallising workers' grievances into strong political opinion which galvanised them into a powerful volatile force of the revolutions of 1848.

A significant universal feature which underlined the international character of the revolutions of 1848 was the **trend of exile**. Hobsbawm wrote, "One accidental factor which reinforced the internationalism of 1830–48 was exile."[102] Most of the political militants or most of the deposed princes and monarchs took the road of exile. After the February Revolution, Louis Philippe, for instance, fearful of what had happened to Louis XVI, quickly left for England under disguise. Prince Metternich also escaped to England in March 1848 when revolution broke out in Vienna, his own citadel. Charles Albert, the King of Piedmont-Sardinia, departed to Portugal after his humiliating defeat at the hands of Radetzky in the battle of Novara in March 1849. Similarly, Kossuth left for Turkey after Hungary finally capitulated before the Russian army at Vilagos in August 1849. Mazzini, too, went to Switzerland when his republic of Rome fell in July 1849 before the French army called in by the Pope. The revolutions of 1848, as a whole, were marked by 'spontaneity and surprise' as also by 'easy triumph and speedy disaster'. With the exception of France, they all ended in failure.

The Legacy of the Revolutions of 1848

On the face of it, the revolutions of 1848 failed everywhere. By the middle of 1849, with the exception of France and Switzerland, almost all the monarchs who had conceded constitutions at the demand of the revolutionaries, were withdrawing them and were being restored as absolute rulers. The revolutions were being crushed ruthlessly. Even though the revolutions were short-lived, their impact was not. In fact, in the words of A.J.P. Taylor, "its events echoed down the corridors of history".[103] The revolutions had deep political impact in the sense that parliamentary democracy and constitutionalism pervaded in a large number of countries. In France, a republic with Louis Napoleon as the President was established. In Italy, parliamentary monarchy in Piedmont was sustained, though that was not the case everywhere. In Prussia, the Parliament, though subdued, exerted significant moderation on the government. A real Federal State based upon a republican form of government with a Federal Legislature was established in Switzerland.

The revolutions of 1848 crystallised the spirit of nationalism among different countries and their peoples. *The sentiments of nationalism had been enkindled since the days of the Congress of Vienna where the smaller nations were treated as mere pawns in the fulfilment of territorial ambitions of bigger powers.* The issue of the unity of Italy and Germany were completely ignored. The resentment of these countries found expression partly in the revolutions of 1830 and then fully and in a wider canvas in the revolutions of 1848. Though the spirit of nationalism was suppressed again in 1848, its flickering embers persisted and came to fruition in the unifications of Italy and Germany by 1871, resulted in strong ferment in the Balkans and Ireland, and formation of the independent nations of Czechoslovakia, Yugoslavia, Rumania, Bulgaria out of the erstwhile mighty empires of Austria-Hungary and Turkey after the First World War.

Another important consequence of the revolutions of 1848 was the **solidification of working-class consciousness** that had emerged with the advent of the Industrial Revolution. In the revolutions of 1848 majority of the people who died on the streets and the barricades were mostly workers and artisans. Moreover, it dawned on the working class that the means of production were concentrated in the hands of the middle class. This created a divide between the bourgeoisie who masterminded the revolutions and organised the working class. This paved the path for the preponderance of socialism as the workers began to join different socialist groups. Frederich Engels participated in the revolutions at Baden and Palatinate in Germany. In June, Engels and Marx became editors of *Neue Rhinische Zeitung* in support of the revolutions and their constitutional demands. The revolutions had significant impact upon the *Communist Manifesto* published in 1848. It was the manifesto of the Communist League which was formed by the merger of the League of the Just of Karl Schapper and the Communist Correspondence Committee of which Engels and Marx were the leaders. The League, however, withered away by 1852. The **International Workingmen's Association** or the **First International** was established in 1864.

As Charles Breunig pointed out, the **revolutions ended an era of romanticism and idealism**. The idealistic world envisioned by the revolutionaries was dashed to the ground, and was replaced by the harsh realities of life. In mid-19th century, therefore, ensued an era of 'realism'.[104] This was expressed in literature and the art of the times. They depicted the dispassionate and hard realities of everyday life. In other words, life never remained the same after 1848. The contours of the political map and the social, economic and cultural aspects of European life were changed forever by this last significant revolution of 19th-century Europe.

Notes

1. E. J. Hobsbawm, *The Age of Revolution* (Delhi: Rupa & Co., 1992), 13.
2. Ibid., 13–14.
3. Quoted in Paul R. Sweet, *Frederich von Gentz: Defender of the Old Order* (Madison: University of Wisconsin Press, 1941), 192.
4. Adam Zamoyski, *Rites of Peace: The Fall of Napoleon and the Congress of Vienna* (London: Harper Press, 2007), xiii, 569.
5. Harold Nicolson, *The Congress of Vienna: A Study in Allied Unity, 1812–1822* (London: Methuen & Co. Ltd., 1970), 153–54.
6. Edward Vose Gulick, *Europe's Classical Balance of Power* (Connecticut: Green Wood Press, 1955), 77.
7. Ibid., 77.
8. Richard Langhorne, 'Reflections on the Significance of the Congress of Vienna,' *Review of International Studies* 12(4) (October 1986): 319–24.
9. L.C.B. Seaman, *From Vienna to Versailles* (London: Methuen & Co. Ltd., 1955), 1–9.
10. Albert Sidney Britt, *The Wars of Napoleon* (New York: Avery Publishing Group, 1985), 127.

11. E. Lipson, *Europe in the 19th and 20th Centuries*, 1960 ed. (London: Adam and Charles Black), 125.

12. David Thomson, *Europe Since Napoleon* (London: Longmans, 1957), 112–113.

13. Ibid., 112–113.

14. Gordon A. Craig, *Europe Since 1815*, 2nd ed. (New York: Holt, Rinehart and Winston, 1966), 75.

15. Alfred Cobban, *A History of Modern France*, vol. 2 (London: Penguin Books Ltd., 1961), 73.

16. Craig, *Europe Since 1815*, 80.

17. Quoted in ibid., 82.

18. David H. Pinkney, 'A New Look at the French Revolution of 1830,' *Review of Politics* 23 (1961): 217–19.

19. John Merriman, *A History of Modern Europe: From the French Revolution to the Present*, vol. 2 (New York: W. W. Norton & Company, 1996), 625.

20. Hobsbawm, *The Age of Revolution*, 140.

21. Robin Winks and Joan Neuberger, *Europe and the Making of Modernity, 1815–1914* (New York: Oxford University Press, 2005), 154.

22. Seaman, *From Vienna to Versailles*, 32–33.

23. Ibid., 37.

24. Jacques Droz, *Europe Between Revolutions, 1815–1848* (Glasgow: Fontana Collins, 1981), 245.

25. Eric Vanhaute, Richard Paping, and Cormac Ó Gráda, 'The European Subsistence Crisis of 1845–1850: A Comparative Perspective' (paper presented at IEHC, Helsinki, 2006), 25, available at https://www.researchgate.net/publication/24140493 (accessed May 2025).

26. Ibid., 22.

27. Ibid., 22.

28. Ibid., 23.

29. Ibid., 23.

30. Ibid., 24.

31. Helge Berger and Mark Spoerer, 'Economic Crises and the European Revolutions of 1848,' *Journal of History* 61(2) (June 2001).

32. Ibid., 26.

33. Jesús Huerta de Soto, *Money, Bank Credit and Economic Cycles*, 2nd ed., trans. Melinda A. Stroup (Auburn: Ludwig von Mises Institute), available at https://mises.org/books/desoto.pdf (accessed May 2025).

34. Droz, *Europe Between Revolutions*, 247.

35. Vanhaute, Paping, and Ó Gráda, 'The European Subsistence Crisis of 1845–1850', 24.

36. Droz, *Europe Between Revolutions*, 248.

37. Thomson, *Europe Since Napoleon*.

38. C. D. Hazen, *The Long Nineteenth Century: A History of Europe from 1789 to 1918* (e-artnow, 2019), chap. 16.

39. Jonathan Sperber, *The European Revolutions, 1848–1851* (Cambridge: Cambridge University Press, 1994), 130.

40. Ibid., 135.

41. Ibid., 137.

42. Ibid., 131.

43. Lipson, *Europe in the 19th and 20th Centuries*, 26.

44. Ibid., 25.

45. Alan Bullock, Oliver Stallybrass, and Stephen Trombley, eds, *The Fontana Dictionary of Modern Thought*, 2nd ed. (London: Fontana Press, 1988), 791.

46. Lipson, *Europe in the 19th and 20th Centuries*, 27.

47. Droz, *Europe Between Revolutions*, 66.

48. Arnošt Klíma, 'The Bourgeois Revolution of 1848–9 in Central Europe', in Roy Porter and Mikulas Teich, eds, *Revolution in History* (Cambridge: Cambridge University Press, 1986),75.

49. Sperber, *The European Revolutions*, 200.

50. Ibid.

51. Klíma, 'The Bourgeois Revolution of 1848–9 in Central Europe', 93.

52. Peter Jones, *The 1848 Revolutions* (Longman Group, U.K., 1981), 9–10.

53. Ibid., 26–27.

54. Peter Stearns, *1848: The Revolutionary Tide in Europe* (W.W. Norton & Company, New York, 1974), 17.

55. Ibid., 19.

56. Ibid., 20.

57. Sperber, *The European Revolutions*, 200.

58. Droz, *Europe Between Revolutions*, 255.

59. Quoted in ibid., 255.

60. Hobsbawm, *The Age of Revolution*, 155.

61. Ibid.

62. Droz, *Europe Between Revolutions*, 256.

63. Sperber, *The European Revolutions*, 41.

64. Ibid.

65. Keiko Matteson, 'The Revival of Tradition in France's Forests,' *Solutions Journal* 3(6) (February 2013).

66. Quoted in Sir Lewis Namier, *1848: The Revolution of the Intellectuals* (London: British Academy, 1944), 21.

67. Thomson, *Europe Since Napoleon*, 207.

68. Paul Ginsborg, 'Peasants and Revolutionaries in Venice and Veneto, 1848,' *Historical Journal* 3 (1974): 503.

69. Ibid.

70. Hobsbawm, *The Age of Revolution*, 155.

71. Klíma, 'The Bourgeois Revolution of 1848–9 in Central Europe', 91.

72. Hobsbawm, *The Age of Revolution*, 156–57.

73. Seaman, *From Vienna to Versailles*, 51–52.

74. Namier, *1848: The Revolution of the Intellectuals*, 4.

75. Sperber, *The European Revolutions*, 21–22.

76. Namier, *1848: The Revolution of the Intellectuals*, 7.

77. Ibid.

78. Stearns, *1848: Revolution Tide in Europe*, 44.

79. Namier, *1848: The Revolution of the Intellectuals*, 23–24.

80. Klíma, 'The Bourgeois Revolution of 1848–9 in Central Europe', 97–98.

81. Ibid., 97.

82. Sperber, *The European Revolutions*, 52.

83. Ibid., 123.

84. Ibid., 124.

85. Jones, *The 1848 Revolutions*, 5.

86. T. S. Hamerow, 'History and the German Revolution,' *American Historical Review* 60(1) (October 1954): 27–44.

87. Quoted in Namier, *1848: The Revolution of the Intellectuals*, 4.

88. Klíma, 'The Bourgeois Revolution of 1848–9 in Central Europe', 97.

89. Seaman, *From Vienna to Versailles*, 49.

90. Sperber, *The European Revolutions*, 246.

91. Ibid.

92. Thomson, *Europe Since Napoleon*, 197.

93. Ibid., 205.

94. Quoted in Droz, *Europe Between Revolutions*, 249.

95. Thomson, *Europe Since Napoleon*, 204.

96. Ibid., 206.

97. Ibid., 207.

98. Sperber, *The European Revolutions*, 151.

99. Ibid., 158.

100. Ibid., 160.

101. Ibid., 164–65.

102. Hobsbawm, *The Age of Revolution*, 160.

103. A. J. P. Taylor, *Revolutions and Revolutionaries* (Oxford: Hamilton, 1980).

104. Charles Breunig, *The Age of Revolution and Reaction* (New York and London: W. W. Norton and Company, 1977), 278.

CHAPTER 4

The Industrial Revolution in Britain

Capitalism is an economic and political system in which the systems of production, distribution and exchange are owned by private individuals and not by the state. It espouses the notions of free enterprise, profit accumulation, wage labour and private property. In other words, **freedom** is the key word of capitalism. Another hallmark of capitalism is **competition**. Capitalism involves **industrialism** which is a system in which manufacturing industries play a predominant role. In industrialism agriculture, handicrafts, commerce play a secondary part. Under these two 'ism's, in Chapters 4 and 5 of this volume, we will discuss at length the growth of the **Industrial Revolution** in England in the late-18th century as well as its dissemination into the continent.

Accumulation of wealth (capital) was encouraged and the existing system of **free trade** was given a new name in order to distinguish the world of free trade from the **age of industries**. In other words, the advent of capitalism is inextricably linked with that of industrialism. Together they transformed the entire world. Theodore S. Hamerow wrote in *The Birth of a New Europe*,

> Between the conclusion of the Napoleonic Wars and the outbreak of the First World War, Europe underwent a transformation unparalleled in its history. In the course of a century the system of production in industry and agriculture was profoundly altered, the population increased at an unprecedented rate, rapid urbanization shaped a new human environment, the standard of living began to improve dramatically, the relationship between classes and occupations suddenly shifted, learning became accessible to the propertyless, the function of the state expanded from security to welfare, the masses entered political life, economic and social reforms grew and multiplied, the Great Powers rushed into

a last spree of imperialist expansion, and the methods of warfare were revolutionized by technological movements.[1]

The Industrial Revolution was the key to this transformation.

The First Industrial Revolution

The Industrial Revolution was another very eventful landmark of the Age of Revolutions. As the revolution in France in 1789 and the revolutions in Europe in 1830 and 1848 brought about far-reaching social and political changes, so the Industrial Revolution ushered in sweeping social and economic changes in the countries where it occurred. In general terms, the *Fontana Dictionary of Modern Thought* described Industrial Revolution as "the process of the rapid onset of continued economic change and advancement through the application of industrial process to traditional forms of manufacture, the divorce of an economy from a restricted source and agricultural base, and a sustained increase in general living standards and in urbanisation."[2] The term '**Industrial Revolution**' was first used in 1837 by the French economist **Adolphe Blanqui** in the context of the transformation in the social and economic life of England. The term became popular with the writings of the brilliant English economic historian **Arnold Toynbee**, posthumously published as *Lectures on Industrial Revolution in England* in 1884. Later in 1906, a French historian **Paul Mantoux** spoke about it as "one of the most important moments in modern history, the consequences of which have affected the whole civilized world and are still transforming it and shaping it under our eyes."[3]

THE INDUSTRIAL REVOLUTION IN BRITAIN

The Industrial Revolution first started in England. By the end of 19th century, the island of Great Britain, was not only the mistress of the seas but also the largest empire in the world. How did a small island acquire military, naval and economic power to such an extent was indeed a pertinent question. One of the factors that made her a mighty power, according to Professor Jeremy Black ("by 1815 Britain was the most powerful empire in the world"),[4] was the Industrial Revolution which undoubtedly gave Britain a massive economical and technological head-start over the rest of the world. A number of factors were responsible for this; however, there is an enormous difference of opinion among historians about the exact cause that triggered the transformation. The question also arises: Why was there an Industrial Revolution in Britain alone in the late 18th century and not in other parts of Europe? Why did the Industrial Revolution arrive so late in other continental countries? Indeed, what is surprising is the fact that a number of favourable conditions which existed in Britain prevailed in many other countries as well. Especially in Holland, Austrian Netherlands or Belgium, France, Northern Germany and parts of the Ottoman Empire, there were significant technological progress, substantial agricultural growth as well as population rise. Yet, there was no Industrial Revolution in these countries in the 18th century. The reason might be explained by the fact that the peculiar set of factors that sparked off the revolution in England was not present in the same combination in any other European country at that time. We will discuss this in greater detail later in the course of our discussion.

When Did the First Industrial Revolution Begin?

There is enough controversy among historians about the exact time when the revolution began. Arnold Toynbee placed the starting point at **1760**, while majority of historians thought the **1780s** to be the actual starting point.[5] Some historians like Professor J.U. Nef stressed the concept of continuity in history and considered the British industrial phenomenon to be the climax of a long-drawn process that could be traced back to the **middle of the 16th century**.[6] British industrialism was, therefore, not a sudden occurrence, but rather a slow process developing over centuries. Other economic historians like Paul Mantoux, T.S. Ashton, W. G. Hoffmann, however, thought that in terms of output and economic growth, 1780s was the actual time when the first Industrial Revolution began. In fact, in 1948 when Ashton's brilliant monograph appeared, he had placed the time-frame between 1760 and 1830 and had warned against the error of overlooking the element of continuity. However, in his later book in 1955 he stressed upon a more precise starting point: 1782. "After 1782," he said, "almost every statistical series of production shows a sharp upward turn."[7] **Walter Hoffmann** had divided the process of industrialisation through which a country passes into three distinct stages:

(*i*) In the first stage, the production is maximum in the consumer goods sector, that is, textiles or food processing industries.

(*ii*) In the second stage, the production in heavy industries like those of pig-iron or engineering commodities rapidly increases, although the output of consumer goods still remains higher.

(*iii*) In the third stage, the output of both consumer goods and heavy industries becomes approximately equal.

According to Hoffmann, and also Simon Kuznets, **'long waves' of economic activity** preceded Britain's Industrial Revolution and this lasted for almost 15 to 23 years. Hoffmann argued that the third stage had reached Britain in 1780 approximately.[8]

W. W. Rostow also divided the industrialisation process into three stages.

(*i*) The first phase consists of a period of hundred years or more when the groundwork for a major economic, technological, social and political change from a predominantly agrarian to an industrial economy is prepared.

(*ii*) The second stage alludes to a brief period of about thirty years during which the rate of investment shoots up to 10 per cent from 5 per cent and important technical advances take place.

(*iii*) The third stage involves a long period of sustained industrial expansion during which the rate of investment remains steady and massive technological innovations happen.[9]

Rostow defined the second stage as the **"take off" period**, which is the most significant milestone in the industrialisation process of any country. As far as Britain is concerned, Rostow placed it between 1783–1802. It is, however, clear that both Hoffmann and Rostow, while maintaining that there was a specific starting point of the Industrial Revolution, also claimed that it was invariably preceded by a preparatory stage which might be a century or more depending on circumstances varying from country to country. In the case of Britain, both agreed that it took off in the 1780s.

Nevertheless, later historians, mostly writing in the late 20th century, felt reluctant to fix a rigid starting point and insisted on a long background as well. As **Patrick O'Brien** aptly puts it, "Historians have long preferred to present British industrialisation in 'evolutionary' rather than 'revolutionary' terms. They are predisposed to replace aeronautical metaphors ('take-offs') with words drawn from a Darwinian vocabulary."[10] Several points of continuity have been emphasised. For example, **Coleman** showed how energy was generated from fossil fuels even in the 16th century. According to **Cipolla**, the economic revolution which produced settled agriculture in the Near East about 10,000 years earlier was certainly more striking than what happened in Britain.[11] O'Brien, too, acknowledged the element of previously acquired ideas from places beyond her boundaries as well as capital accumulated over a long period of time. He wrote,

> It is indeed an example of precocious structural change, in the sense that the release of capital and labour from agriculture (for all kinds of fortuitous geographical as well as institutional reasons) proceeded further and faster in Britain than in other parts of Europe for at least two centuries before 1750.[12]

O'Brien further observed that fulling (a process to cleanse and thicken cloth) was used as early as the 13th century. Men, women and children in many factories continued to work using primitive methods without the aid of steam power or machines.[13] A wide range of manufacturing techniques were the same as in the days before the Civil War.[14] *The Industrial Revolution in Victorian England borrowed a lot from the scientific movement that blossomed during the Renaissance.*[15] Historians like Clark and Beckett, Cain and Hopkins looked upon the Industrial Revolution as a stable, gradual and civilised process, rather than an event that marked any sudden acceleration or discontinuity with the past.[16] "In brief, current emphasis from both economists and historians is 'back to continuity'."[17]

Conditions Favouring the Industrial Revolution in Britain

Several factors combined together to bring about the First Industrial Revolution. One of the most important among them was the **phenomenal rise in the population of Britain**. Economists and historians prefer to call it a demographic revolution. There was first a moderate rise in British population from 6.5 million in 1700 to 7.5 million in 1750. In the second half of the century, however, the country witnessed a remarkable acceleration in the process of population growth, culminating in a rise at the rate of 10 per cent per decade from 1781 onwards, and finally reaching a peak explosion of 17 per cent in the decade ending in 1821.[18] This was extra ordinary, especially when compared with other countries. For example, in the period between 1680 and 1820, while the population in

England rose by 133 per cent, that of France and Holland rose by 39 per cent and 8 per cent respectively.[19] Between 1810 and 1820, average family size reached five or six children per family, the highest rate in any decade in modern British history.[20] The sources for the purpose of determination of the size and growth of population were undoubtedly extremely limited, primarily because there was no census of population in England and Wales until 1801. **Gregory King**, the prominent English genealogist, engraver and statistician, had started estimating since 1695, when he was appointed a commissioner in charge of a new tax on marriages, births and burials, the demographic characteristics of the population of England and Wales predominantly on the basis of hearth taxes. This, however, was not a foolproof calculation. An attempt to introduce a bill in the Parliament in 1753 for counting people on the basis of the receipts of poor relief failed. **John Rickman**, the first director of the Census, tried to make an estimate depending on the church registers which, regrettably, were neither complete nor legible.[21] Nevertheless, Rickman is credited with drafting the first bill which became the **1800 Census Act** and became a law in December of the same year. According to Sir Edward Anthony Wrigley, the British historical demographer, the use of marriage data might offer a more reliable and exact guide to population trends than the estimates provided by Rickman.[22]

This **exponential population explosion** could be explained in various ways. One of the reasons, as historian Phyllis Deane, argued, was the absence in the second half of the 18th century of the sudden disruption of the balance of birth rate and death rate by natural phenomena like famines or epidemics. The normal balance between birth rates and death rates were generally found to be in the ratio of 30 (death rate) to 40 (birth rate) per annum. This ensured a slow and steady natural rise in population. However, this balance got disrupted completely by sudden natural calamities which swept away a substantial portion of the population. However, by the 18th century, in several countries of Western Europe, including Britain, famines became rare and epidemics became less endemic. Naturally, the population rose unhampered.[23]

The traditional view was that the population growth in the 18th century was to a large extent due to a fall in the death rate. And scholars like Griffith were of the opinion that advances in medical science contributed significantly in reducing the death rate.[24] Professor John Habakkuk, British economic historian, however, did not accept this explanation. According to him, it was rather "the rise in birth-rate which climbed to 1790, and remained thereafter for several decades at a very high level" which was the main reason of the population growth.[25] Habakkuk related this rise in birth-rate to expansion of economic opportunities. He wrote, "There is contemporary warrant for the view that the acceleration of population growth in the later 18th century was to a very large extent the result of a high birth rate, and that this in turn was the result of the economic developments of the period."[26] These economic developments were the new industrial changes which stimulated a high demand for labour. Higher demand for labour meant higher wages which in turn led to an increase in population; because, according to Ricardo's theory, workers were hopelessly addicted to "the delights of domestic society." Moreover, they did not have the incentive to limit births and as a result every increase in pay was promptly met with a rise in population.[27]

Thomas McKeown and R. G. Brown considered a decline in mortality to be a plausible cause of the rise in population. But, unlike Griffith, they refused to accept the progress of medical efforts as an explanation for this decline, although they agree that there was indeed a notable improvement of developments in medicine during the 18th century. It included expansion of hospitals and dispensaries, surgery and midwifery services, advances in medicines and protective therapy (inoculation against small-pox etc.). But McKeown and Brown made extensive studies of these conditions and found that these mechanisms had flaws and could not be relied upon to contribute effectively to a rise in population. To give an example, in Creighton's opinion, inoculation hardly had any effect on smallpox in Britain. Similarly, "the chief indictment of hospital work at this period is not that it did no good, but that it positively did harm."[28] After a careful scrutiny, therefore, McKeown and Brown concluded that changes in environment—"improvement in housing, water supply or refuse-disposal"—led to a decline in mortality by improving hygiene and controlling infectious diseases. Standards of living also improved which provided nutrition and thereby controlled diseases such as tuberculosis. They wrote, "Improvements in the environment are, therefore, regarded as intrinsically the most acceptable explanation of the decline of mortality in the late eighteenth and nineteenth centuries….whether we accept the birth rate or the death rate as more important influence on the rise of population, the conclusion that conditions improved in the late eighteenth century must follow rejection of the effectiveness of medical effort."[29]

The **demographic revolution** was inextricably intertwined with an **agricultural revolution**. In fact, each was dependent on the other. A rise in population meant more mouths to feed. The solution lay in an immense increase in agricultural productivity. This could only be achieved through a thorough transformation of the methods of cultivation. The agricultural revolution in England in the 18th century had certain characteristic features. They were:

(*i*) A new system of crop rotation.

(*ii*) Introduction of the system of 'enclosure' or integration of common land, generally used for cattle-grazing by the villagers.

(*iii*) New improved techniques of cultivation were introduced; for example, Jethro Tull's method of drilling (the horse-drawn seed drill) introduced extensively in the early 1730s.

(*iv*) The introduction of new plants like legumes replenished the soil and provided the feed for grazing animals.

(*v*) Improvements in drainage system.

(*vi*) Because of increase in demand due to population explosion, farmers began to produce for a national network of markets, rather than only for home or regional consumption. The lives of farmers now became more dependent on conditions in national or international markets, rather than on weather.

The agricultural revolution aided the Industrial Revolution by feeding the growing industrial centres and also by creating a surplus capital for investment in further industrial enterprises.

Classical economic historians like Adam Smith and physiocrats like Say (Say's law of markets) emphasised the role of the **growth of demand in the market**. Production and supply were conditioned by that. **Adam Smith** argued that division of labour was limited by the extent of the market. A congenial market with rising demand was an essential precondition of a flourishing economic growth. Hammonds wrote, "mass production demands popular consumption," and that "the command of a wide market is essential to the organisation of large-scale industry."[30] Although historians like Redford, Lipson and Ashton gave a lot of importance to **overseas trade** (because manufactures constituted a significant portion of exports), the real foundation of industrial expansion, according to Witt Bowden, was the growing demand of the home market. Britain in the 18th century had both these advantages. On the one hand, her home market was steadily expanding thanks to the population explosion, while on the other, she had a thriving colonial market as well. As Hobsbawm observed, the domestic market could grow due to four important reasons:

> There could be growth of population, which creates more consumers; a transfer of people from non-monetary to monetary incomes, which creates more customers; an increase of income per head, which creates better customers; and a substitution of industrially produced goods for older forms of manufacture or imports.[31]

And all these pre-conditions existed in England. As far as the foreign or export market was concerned, the **American colonies** as well as those of **West Indies** and **India** became important centres of exchange. The colonial markets were, according to liberal historiography, free markets, that is those that were not subjected to social or governmental restrictions. Britain's extensive colonies in the 18th century in different parts of the world served not only as trading markets, but as **free labour markets** and **free capital markets** as well. In the colonies, where there were few legal barriers to the free exchange of goods, wealth became broadly distributed, and credit easily available. This liberal notion of 'free market', however, has been challenged by scholars like O'Brien, Innes, Haines, Kussmaul and others who pointed out the tyrannical atmosphere of exploitation and absolute slavery in which the workers worked and how they were deprived of freedom to decide their own lives.

At the heart of Britain's trade and industrial revolution was her **mastery over the seas**. Not only was she close to the seas, but her navy was invincible in the world. Professor Jeremy Black wrote in his book *Why the Industrial Revolution Happened in Britain*, "naval power and imperial possessions enabled Britain to dominate trans-oceanic trade and to profit accordingly." Fortunately, her coal mines were located near the sea so that the coal that was extracted could easily be transported through ships, and coal was one of the most potent ingredients of the Industrial Revolution. And it was England's good fortune that she was immensely rich in natural resources, especially **coal**.

The role of parliament in the process of industrialisation was also very significant. The **Glorious Revolution of 1688** was a bloodless revolution which established the supremacy of the parliament over the monarchy and set England on the path towards a constitutional government. Various contested issues of power were resolved in favour of the parliament. The **House of Commons** particularly assumed extensive powers—legislative as well as administrative—and initiated, amended and approved wide-ranging bills covering matters relating to defence, foreign policies, fiscal questions (for instance, taxes, etc.), and economic development (like enclosures, developments of ports, roads, canals or railways), and also other national or local issues. All new taxes had to be approved by the parliament. It was hardly astonishing, therefore, that the parliament would play a key role in the country's industrial revolution. *It ensured freedom of the entrepreneurs from onerous financial encumbrances, established political stability and created the right environment for the pursuit of scientific innovations.* The House of Lords and a large proportion of the House of Commons consisted of people from the **landowning classes**. By the statutes of 1689 and 1694 respectively, landowners had been bestowed with exclusive rights over all minerals under their land except gold and silver. They, therefore, were naturally interested in industrialisation which might be in need of their mineral possessions. Harold Perkins argued, "They abolished most of the restrictions on internal industry, ignored those on building, forgot the anti-closure acts, and exchanged corn trade controls for bounties on coal exports. During the 18th century they allowed the wage-fixing and apprenticeship clauses of the Statute of Artificers to fall gradually into disuse."[32] The policy and attitude of the British government in the 18th century, therefore, was one of least interference or *laissez-faire*. They rather believed in Adam Smith's '**invisible hand**' to take care of the market and manufacture. The liberals had welcomed and commended the measures of the Hanoverian state (the British government), particularly its decision to refrain from the regulation of prices and wages and enforcement of the rules of apprenticeship.

Historians like Deane, however, did not agree with this traditional interpretation of the triumph of laissez faire. It is true, he observed, that a large body of laws prevailed that was not implemented rigorously. The **Usury Laws, 1714**, which restricted interest rates at 5 per cent on loans, the **Bubble Act, 1720**, which restrained the formation of joint-stock companies except under special provisions approved by the parliament and the apprenticeship laws were some of the more prominent ones. According to Deane, these laws were ineffective not because the government was not keen on enforcing them, but because they were beyond the government's control "without an effective police force or a widespread political intelligence system."[33] The passive attitude of the government was not the result of a deliberate policy, but rather an expression of helplessness and lack of authority. In the 18th century, British society, therefore, was hung between laissez faire and rigid mercantilism. Laissez faire was complete in Britain between 1820 and 1860. At any rate, historians like O'Brien have rightly pointed out that the entire entrepreneurial atmosphere created by the Hanoverian kings and their parliament was favourable to the landowners, merchants, industrialists, transporters, etc., and rather detrimental to the workers and 'lower orders'. The workers lacked the freedom to choose their work or employer, to withdraw their labour in search of better opportunities or to engage in an argument with their employers. Such conditions left ample economic and judicial authority in the hands of the employers over their workers which "left the labour market in a state of suspension between feudal servitude and the free contractual system of 19th century political economy."[34]

A **strong system of taxation** supported the Industrial Revolution. As mentioned above, since the days of the Glorious Revolution, all new taxes required the prior approval of the parliament. As O'Brien pointed out, *taxes in real terms rose by a factor of sixteen* between the reign of James II and George IV. Majority of the taxes were indirect, primarily the customs and excise taxes on imports. Direct taxes on income and wealth were less as it was felt that such impositions might lead to considerable resentment and unrest. Another important tax was the land tax. All taxes were charged uniformly throughout the year so that they did not become excessively burdensome in a time of crisis, like war. Unlike other European countries, France for example, where the burden of taxation was borne primarily by the peasantry and the nobles enjoyed sublime immunity, taxation in England transcended all class distinctions and social privileges. No eligible tax-payer could evade tax in England; no landowner was above land-tax which was carefully assessed by provincial assessors and collectors. In England, the cost of the Court fell heavily upon the gentry who were the main tax-paying class.

Moreover, an advantage which England enjoyed in the 18th century was the **facility of a national bank**. Established in 1694, the **Bank of England** became a source of credit for entrepreneurs in need of funds to promote their manufacturing ventures by issuing bank notes on the strength of issuable deposits. It also became a model for the development of several credit institutions like joint-stock companies and the London Stock Exchange. The Bank of England as well as other private banks and financial institutions issued as many currency notes as their deposits permitted. Many of these financial institutions faced problems when they failed to meet the depositors' demands for cash, as a large portion of their assets were tied up in different investments. Between 1772 and 1825, many of these private financial institutions failed. These problems gave rise to two schools of thought: **the banking school** and **the currency school**. According to the currency school, paper money should behave in the same way as metal coins. Only then could the balance between the exchange and the issuance of bank notes be maintained. Contraction of loan at the time of abnormally high prices was one solution. The banking school, on the other hand, held the view that sudden contraction of credit led to crises. The banks should keep enough bullion reserves in order to face such emergencies. The result of such controversy was the passing of the **Bank Charter Act of 1844** according to which *banks were required to keep at least one-third of their liabilities as bullion reserve*. In any case, notwithstanding several unforeseen ups and downs, financial institutions and joint-stock companies undoubtedly played a vital role in raising capital for the new industrial ventures of 18th-century England. These institutions supplied funds particularly to big projects like railways, canals, road construction, water-supply systems, ship-building etc. According to Phyllis Deane, smaller projects or factories were often set up through borrowing loans from resourceful friends, relatives or acquaintances. For example, Robert Owen went into partnership with a mechanic who made looms after borrowing 100 pounds from his brother. James Watt entered into a partnership with Boulton with a small loan taken from his friend Dr. Black. Richard Arkwright, famous for his invention of the spinning frame or water frame which revolutionised the textile industry, borrowed money from a friend to help finance his invention.[35] The list is long but it gives a glimpse into *how capital was raised to bring about collectively a sea-change in the industrial sector* of Hanoverian England. Apart from friends and relatives, the Bank of England too assisted the moderate entrepreneurs significantly.

In recent years, scholars like Williamson, Black and Gilmore, and Temin and Voth, have suggested that "British government borrowing crowded out private investment, and stifled what otherwise would have been a more robust industrial revolution prior to 1830."[36] The Bubble Act and the Usury Laws had paved the path of government borrowing, which certainly harmed private finance. As against this, William McColloch has argued recently that not only there is little evidence to show that the

Bubble Act blocked the access of the nascent firms to borrow funds in any significant way, but also that the 'crowding out' model had practically no relevance in 18th-century Britain. The role of the Bank of England, which had considerably financed the industrial enterprises, was thereby undermined.[37] Moreover, **charters for joint-stock corporations** for funding infrastructural investments were granted from time to time.

In 1776, Adam Smith wrote in his book *An Inquiry into the Nature and Causes of the Wealth of Nations* that "Good roads, canals, and navigable rivers, by diminishing the expense of carriage, put the remote parts of the country more nearly upon a level with those in the neighbourhood of the town. They are upon that account the greatest of all improvements."[38] The Industrial Revolution improved Britain's transport infrastructure with a turnpike road network, a canal and waterway network and a railway network. These facilitated the smooth and easy transportation of raw materials and finished products from one place to another—the source to the factory and from factory to the market.

Britain in the 18th century was flooded by **a cascade of scientific innovations** which made the first Industrial Revolution possible. The most momentous changes and innovations occurred in the cotton textiles industry. E.J. Hobsbawm observed, "Whoever says industrial revolution says cotton." The **flying shuttle** by John Kay in 1733, a device which allowed a single weaver to operate a wider loom, greatly increased the output of each weaver and led to an enhanced demand for yarn. In 1767 James Hargreaves invented the **spinning jenny** which speeded up the production of yarn to an unprecedented level. In 1769, Richard Arkwright patented the water frame that produced a coarse, twisted yarn and could be powered by water. The existence of rivers and streams in England boosted the textile mills which were built on these waterbodies. After 1780s, with the application of steam power, **mills** grew up in urban areas. However, a formidable social crisis emerged in the textile mills in England. The workers fiercely resented the arrival of new machinery which to a considerable extent replaced human labour. The workers who were unemployed sharply resisted their loss of work and their anger was directed towards the machines which they in a fit of rage attacked and destroyed. This was the beginning of the 'Luddite' movement (machine breaking), named after the legendary labour leader, Ned Ludd.

Along with cotton, **iron** was also at the heart of the British industrialisation process. The old method of extracting coal from the pits was replaced by a new method. Up to 1709, furnaces could only use charcoal (made from wood) to produce iron. New methods of manufacturing iron, however, became imperative as wood was quickly getting depleted due to large-scale clearing of forests for farmland and timber. Coal was a good substitute and was also available in abundance, but it contained sulphur which made iron brittle. The situation improved when in 1709, a man called Abraham Darby succeeded in smelting iron using coke (made from coal). This technological innovation was a major breakthrough which accelerated the Industrial Revolution in England. After 1709, the small village of Coalbrookdale, where Darby made his discovery, saw the **first cast-iron bridge** built over the River Severn and the first cast-iron framed building built in Shrewsbury. Darby's blast furnace marked the beginning of a new development in the iron industry. The **iron age** began in England. In 1790 the first iron-built ship was launched in England.

Another revolutionary step was the **use of steam power** by James Watt, a Scottish scientist. Together with Matthew Boulton, who owned an engineering works in Birmingham, he began to manufacture more efficient steam engines. The demand for them came initially from mine owners but also extended to paper, flour and iron mills as well as distilleries, canals and waterworks. They proved particularly useful for pumping water out of the coal mines. Horse-drawn pumps could only draw water from depths up to 90 feet, making it almost impossible to extract coal that lay deeper. In 1712, Thomas Newcomen invented the first commercially successful steam engine or the atmospheric engine which had the power of 20 horses and pumped water from hundreds of feet below the ground. Watt's improvements in 1769 to the Newcomen steam engine were fundamental to the changes brought by the Industrial Revolution not only to England but to the entire world. According to Toynbee, "the two men who did the most to bring about (the revolution) were Adam Smith and James Watt…. They destroyed the old world and built a new one."[39] Plenty of coal was now accessible to the industrialists to boost their efforts. Coal-mining was further facilitated in 1815 with the invention of Humphry Davy's **safety lamp**, designed to be safely lit and used by miners, preventing the flame's heat from igniting concentrations of methane gas.

The whole system of communication was revolutionised at the same time. It facilitated the railways as well as the waterways. The first steamer, that is, ship propelled by steam power was constructed in 1802. Gradually new roads were built to connect industrial centres. A network of canals and waterways was constructed for the same purpose.

All the scientific innovations mentioned above were undoubtedly the culmination of the remarkable scientific revolution that swept across Europe through the 17th and the 18th centuries, motivating an intellectual movement which we call the Enlightenment or the Age of Reason. It was sparked by philosophers like Kant and Fichte, Bacon and Spinoza, Locke and Voltaire, scientists like Descartes and Newton, Halley and Herschel, Boyle and Cavendish. Enlightenment served as the foundation of the Industrial Revolution that heralded the beginning of the modern world.

The discussion above, of course, does not mean that Britain did not have any obstacles in her path to industrialisation. They might have been easy to overcome because, as Hobsbawm observed, "the fundamental social and economic conditions for it already existed, because the 18th century type of industrialisation was comparatively cheap and simple, and because the country was sufficiently wealthy and flourishing to be untroubled by inefficiencies which might have crippled less fortunate economies."[40] To give an example, *Britain knew exactly how much to produce and for whom.* So, they produced exquisite jewellery and fabric for the aristocrats and heaps of coarse cloth for the masses. The protracted wars were a serious impediment. Her participation in the **Seven Years' War** impoverished her to such an extent that she imposed a series of taxes on her American colonies in order to replenish her empty coffers, and such a measure became a serious bone of contention between them, eventually leading to the outbreak of the **American War of Independence**, which again proved to be disastrous for Britain. However, Britain turned her wars into an advantage by accelerating her production of ships and guns. Britain further capitalised on the weaknesses of her major competitors who were devastated by war. Her increasing population was turned into an asset rather than a burden, by being channelised into new avenues of production and consumption of goods.

Characteristics of the Industrial Revolution in Britain

The British Industrial Revolution, therefore, had certain characteristic features which we may now sum up. These could at the same time be looked upon as the impact of industrialisation on the English society, economy and polity. A very important aspect, for example, was the **breakup of the age-old, feudal agrarian relationship**. Earlier, peasants often failed to sustain themselves on the plots of land they owned. So, they worked on the lands of their landlords as tenant-farmers. The common lands in the villages were used for grazing cattle. This traditional pattern of the countryside changed with the multiplication of factories. The common lands were enclosed. *Large-scale migration of workers from villages to the towns began.* The landlords began to use their lands for commercial purposes. A new class of landless wage-earners was created. Pretensions of the Crown were reduced to the minimum. Government was subordinated to the will of the men of property as the British parliament was an aristocratic oligarchy. With the advent of capitalism, an advanced system of banking and credit geared to business needs emerged in Britain. It was far more intricate and efficient compared to what existed in the rest of the continent.

The Industrial Revolution in Britain was associated with enormous technological changes, as discussed above. The Industrial Revolution introduced machines in textile manufacturing, iron-mining, printing and engineering industries. Hargreave's spinning jenny, Arkwright's water-frame, Crompton's mule and Cartwright's power loom revolutionised the industry of cotton manufacturing. Invention of the steam engine, use of coal, and the use of coke in iron production had far-reaching effects. Two other features of British industrialisation were the enclosure movement and the principles of laissez-faire or least interference from the government. A weak guild system ensured freedom to the manufacturers.

FIG. 4.1: Smoke Pollution, Widnes

Historians Interpreting the First Industrial Revolution

It is no wonder that a path-breaking event such as the Industrial Revolution would be a subject matter of debate, discussion and analysis among scholars. Since the publication of Arnold Toynbee's *Lectures on the Industrial Revolution in England* in 1884, there has been a surge of interest in studying the origins, pattern and effects of the Industrial Revolution. Historians, economists and other social scientists have long debated different aspects of the Industrial Revolution. Some prominent viewpoints on the starting point and the origins of the Revolution we have already discussed. As far as the effects of the first Industrial Revolution are concerned, the vast literature of interpretations that we have today could broadly be classified into two types: *first*, those who judged it on the basis of its effects on human life. And *second*, those who scrutinised it from the point of view of the massive technological transformations that were taking place. A few significant interpretations of both the groups are as follows.

In the first category we may start with Toynbee himself. Toynbee considered the time of the Industrial Revolution as "a period as disastrous and terrible as any through which a nation ever passed."[41] Other early scholars, such as the husband-and-wife Fabian socialists Beatrice and Sidney Webb (writing in 1897), as well as J.L. and Barbara Hammond (writing in 1911), also followed in the footsteps of Toynbee and regarded the Industrial Revolution as a period of intense agony and hardship. Such a view was also endorsed by H. de Gibbins who in his *Industry in England* (1907) wrote, "it must be continually remembered that the condition of the mass of the people in the first of this (nineteenth century) was one of deepest depression...."[42]

This **thoroughly dismal picture** became slightly brighter with the writings of E. J. Hamilton as well as Colin Clark in 1952 when they talked about the **rise in income of workers** (though often disturbed by frequent unemployment) and also maintenance of real income. This trend had begun with J.H. Clapham who in his pioneering work *Economic History of Modern Britain* wrote in 1926:

> For every class of urban or industrial worker about which information is available, except—a grave exception—such dying trades as common handloom cotton weaving, wages had risen markedly during the intervening sixty years (since 1790). For fortunate classes, such as

London bricklayers or compositors, they had risen well over 40 per cent, and for urban and industrial workers in the mass, perhaps about 40 per cent.[43]

R.M. Hartwell, in his book *The Industrial Revolution and British Economic Growth* has coherently analysed the viewpoints of several scholars on the impact of the Industrial Revolution. He quotes extensively from the writings of Miss Foley (1893), Ivy Pinchbeck (1930) and Mrs D. George (1931), all of whom focussed on the conditions of women in industry. Pinchbeck and George were of the opinion that their standards of living were improving, while Miss. Foley observed how the factories took the girls out of the precincts of the four walls of their homes and taught them to be self-reliant and strong.[44] In 1830, **Macaulay**, the British historian and Whig politician, wrote convincingly in favour of the Industrial Revolution,

> We must confess ourselves unable to find any satisfactory record of any great nation, past or present, in which the working classes have been in a more comfortable situation than in England during the last thirty years…The serving man, the artisan and the husbandman, have a more copious and palatable supply of food, better clothing, and better furniture…Yet the country poorer than in 1790?[45]

Similar observations were made by Samuel Smiles, the Scottish author, and J. Ward, in the 1860s, thirty years after Macaulay. N. Scatcherd, writing in the same year as Macaulay, analysed the impact of the revolution on traditional family ties. The children who migrated to the cities or towns no longer remained under paternal control. *The old patriarchal notions of family, therefore, were slowly withering away.* This understanding was built upon by present-day writers like Louise A. Tilly and Joan W. Scott.[46]

The benefits of the Industrial Revolution were firmly established by the 20th century and, therefore, a host of 20th-century historians—such as T.S. Ashton, Phyllis Deane and G.D.H. Cole, Peter Mathias, David Landes, Patrick O'Brien, Carlo Cipolla and others—emphasised the scientific and material progress the Revolution brought about. However, many poets and literary figures, like **Wordsworth**, writing in the first half of the 19th century reacted sharply to it. As a romantic poet, Wordsworth rebelled against the **harsh realities of factory life**. So did **Shelly, Coleridge, Dickens**, as well as socialist theorists, **J.F. Bray, W. Thomson, and Friederich Engels**. Some thinkers like Whitaker considered factories to be the hot-beds of immorality and vice.[47] However, Hartwell categorically refutes this, citing the Factory Commission Report of 1833, according to which there was no evidence to show that proneness to vice was more prevalent among factory workers and the poor.[48]

Hobsbawm seemed to be in a dilemma. On the one hand he wrote, "The Industrial Revolution marks the most fundamental transformation of human life in the history of the world recorded in written documents … We have been profoundly marked by the experience of our economic and social pioneering and remain marked by it to this day."[49] But on the other hand, as a Marxist historian, Hobsbawm believed that the Industrial Revolution had indeed unleashed a **dark period of exploitation and misery for the common man**—a view he saw as widely shared among the intelligentsia. Hartwell strongly refuted this, and instead aligned himself with the optimism of Macaulay, Clapham, Ashton and others, who believed that the living standards of the average English worker had improved significantly. According to Hartwell, an increasing number of present-day historians subscribed to the Macaulay–Clapham view—not only because of the growing body of research supporting it, but because they were convinced that the Industrial Revolution had fundamentally transformed the world and human life for the better. Nevertheless, Hartwell pondered that

> in an age of many and massive inhumanities, the sustained capacity
> for indignation at the spectacle of children in factories and women in
> mines has been lost: facts and fictions that roused the humane passions
> of the Hammonds tend to leave the modern reader, well disciplined by
> familiarity with concentration camps, comparatively unmoved.[50]

Coming to the second category of historians, those who judged the Industrial Revolution on the basis of **economic and technological growth**—in other words material growth—reference might be made to an important debate which has come up in recent times. **Peter Temin** elaborated two prevalent views of the British Industrial Revolution in his scholarly essay published in *The Journal of Economic History* in 1997. One of them, he wrote, was the traditional one represented by T.S. Ashton and David Landes which emphasised the broad changes the Industrial Revolution brought about in the British society and economy. Ashton said, "It was not only gadgets, however, but innovations of various kinds—in agriculture, transport, manufacture, trade, and finance—that surged up with a suddenness for which it is difficult to find a parallel at any other time or place."[51] The other view, held by N.F.R. Crafts and C. Knick

Harley challenged the older view and saw the revolution as having brought about significant technical changes only in a few limited industries such as cotton and iron, and no overall transformation. The latter argument was taken to an extreme by Rondo Cameron who argued that the change was so small relative to the whole economy that it no longer deserved the title of Industrial Revolution. By using a Ricardian model of international trade to formulate a testable hypothesis about the nature of the Industrial Revolution, Peter Temin discarded the new 'Crafts-Harley' view, and confirmed and upheld the traditional view—the one held by Ashton and Landes—that **the technical change was widespread**. According to him, apart from cotton and iron, other sectors also contributed significantly towards increasing British productivity. Crafts and Harley, in their turn, examined technical change, growth and economic structure with the help of computational general equilibrium (CGE) modelling and rejected Temin's contention. Both views recognised that the structure of British economy underwent a rapid transformation during the classical period of the Industrial Revolution (1770 to 1830). However, the 'new view'— contrary to that of Ashton and Landes, who were supported by scholars such as Maxine Berg and Pat Hudson—argued that modern economic growth extended over a longer period of time, was concentrated in far fewer industries and was at the same time characterised by low agricultural productivity. The population, however, was rising rapidly and far exceeded the agricultural output, as Malthus had predicted. According to Crafts and Harley, "the export of manufactures financed food imports that provided partial relief to the straitened population."[52]

By way of conclusion, it could be argued that there is merit in both the viewpoints and further probe might bring forth a fresh approach. Even so, it seems to me that, although **cotton** and **iron** might have been the biggest industries, it would not be fair to restrict the Industrial Revolution to these two alone. Its range was wider. However, it is not my intention to undermine in any way the contribution of these two sectors that made England the '**workshop of the world**.' Nonetheless, the role of other sectors cannot be overlooked. **Coal**, for example, was an integral part of its success. So also was **agriculture** which sustained its growing population and helped to improve its standard of living. The woollen industry was the most dominant till the 18th century. According to Crouzet, "the wool trade and woollen manufacture early made England a part of the international economy and stimulated the rise of capitalism."[53] Technologies in all fields, big or small, together combined to bring about the great metamorphosis.

Notes

1. Theodore S. Hamerow, *The Birth of a New Europe: State and Society in the Nineteenth Century* (Chapel Hill and London: University of North Carolina Press, 1983), 3.

2. *The Fontana Dictionary of Modern Thought*, 3rd ed. (London: Fontana Press, 1999).

3. Paul Mantoux, *The Industrial Revolution in the Eighteenth Century: An Outline of the Beginnings of the Modern Factory System in England* (London: Jonathan Cape Ltd., 1928), 21.

4. BBC History, 'Why the Industrial Revolution Happened in Britain', 2013. Available at https://www.bbc.com/mediacentre/proginfo/2013/03/why-the-industrial-revolution (accessed May 2025).

5. Phyllis Deane, *The First Industrial Revolution* (Delhi: Foundation Books, 1994), 2.

6. Ibid.

7. T. S. Ashton, *Economic History of England: The Eighteenth Century* (London, 1955), 125; quoted in Phyllis Deane, 'The British Industrial Revolution,' in Mikuláš Teich and Roy Porter, eds, *The Industrial Revolution in National Context* (Cambridge: Cambridge University Press, 1996), 14.

8. Hoffmann quoted in W. O. Henderson, *The Industrial Revolution on the Continent*, 2nd ed. (London: Frank Cass & Co. Ltd., 1967), 3–4.

9. Ibid., 4.

10. Patrick K. O'Brien and Roland Quinault, eds, *The Industrial Revolution and British Society* (Cambridge: Cambridge University Press, 1993), 5.

11. Quoted in Ibid., 2.

12. Ibid.

13. Ibid., 5.

14. Ibid.

15. Ibid.

16. Ibid.

17. Ibid.

18. Mikuláš Teich and Roy Porter, eds., *The Industrial Revolution in National Context* (Cambridge: Cambridge University Press, 1996), 25.

19. Ibid., 26.

20. BBC History, 'Empire and Sea Power,' British History. Available at https://www.bbc.co.uk/history/british/empire_seapower/ (accessed May 2025).

21. Deane, *The First Industrial Revolution*, 22–23.

22. Tony Wrigley, 'English County Populations in the Later 18th Century,' Cambridge Group for the History of Population and Social Structure. University of Cambridge.

23. Ibid., 22.

24. G. T. Griffith, *Population Problems of the Age of Malthus* (Cambridge, 1926).

25. H. J. Habakkuk, 'English Population in the 18th Century,' *The Economic History Review*, New Series, 6(2) (1953): 128.

26. Ibid., 130–31.

27. Robert L. Heilbroner, *The Worldly Philosophers*, rev. ed. (New York: Touchstone, 1996), 95.

28. Thomas McKeown and R. G. Brown, 'Medical Evidence Related to English Population Changes in the 18th Century,' *Population Studies* 9(2) (November 1955): 119–41.

29. Ibid., 141.

30. R. M. Hartwell, ed., *The Causes of the Industrial Revolution in England* (London: Methuen & Co., 1970), 74.

31. E. J. Hobsbawm, *Industry and Empire* (London: Pelican Books, 1968), 42.

32. Roy Porter and Mikuláš Teich, eds, *Revolution in History* (Cambridge: Cambridge University Press, 1986), 21.

33. Deane, *The First Industrial Revolution*, 228.

34. O'Brien and Quinault, *The Industrial Revolution and British Society*, 130.

35. Deane, *The First Industrial Revolution*, 179.

36. William A. McColloch, 'Shackled Revolution? The Bubble Act and Finance Regulation in 18th Century England,' Working Paper No. 2013-06, Department of Economics, University of Utah. Also see Williamson, Jeffery G. 'Why Was British Growth So Slow during the Industrial Revolution?' *Journal of Economic History* 44 (3) (1984): 687–712; Black, Robert A. and Claire G. Gilmore. 'Crowding Out During Britain's Industrial Revolution.' *Journal of Economic History* 50 (1) (1990): 109–131; Temin, Peter and Hans-Joachim Voth. 'Credit Rationing and Crowding Out during the Industrial Revolution: Evidence from Hoare's Bank, 1702–1862.' *Explorations in Economic History* 42 (3) (2005): 325–348.

37. Ibid.

38. Adam Smith, *Wealth of Nations*, Book 1, Chap. 11, https://www.marxists.org/reference/archive/smith-adam/works/wealth-of-nations/book01/ch11a.htm (accessed June 2025).

39. Quoted in Hartwell, *The Causes of the Industrial Revolution*, 32.

40. Hobsbawm, *Industry and Empire*, 39–40.

41. Arnold Toynbee, *Lectures on the Industrial Revolution in England: Popular Addresses, Notes and Other Fragments* (Cambridge: Cambridge University Press, 2011 [1884]).

42. Quoted in R. M. Hartwell, *The Industrial Revolution and Economic Growth* (London: Methuen & Co., 1971), 84.

43. Ibid., 87.

44. Ibid., 88, 96–97.

45. Ibid., 92.

46. Louise A. Tilly and Joan W. Scott, *Women, Work and Family* (New York: Routledge, 1978), 116.

47. Hartwell, *The Industrial Revolution and Economic Growth*, 97.

48. Ibid.

49. Hobsbawm, *Industry and Empire*, 13.

50. Hartwell, *The Industrial Revolution and Economic Growth*, 104.

51. Quoted in Peter Temin, 'Two Views of the Industrial Revolution,' *The Journal of Economic History* 57(1) (March 1997): 64.

52. C. Knick Harley and N. F. R. Crafts, 'Simulating the Two Views of the British Industrial Revolution,' *The Journal of Economic History* 60(3) (September 2000): 820.

53. F. Crouzet, 'England and France in the 18th Century: A Comparative Analysis of Two Economic Growths,' in Hartwell, *The Causes of the Industrial Revolution in England*, 139.

Industrial Revolution on the Continent

There were three major waves of industrialisation in Europe in the period between 1750 and 1914, according to Clive Trebilcock. The **first wave** attained its climax in the decades between 1780s and 1820s. The **second** between 1840 and 1870 and the **third** blossomed in the two decades just preceding the First World War. Specific countries were associated with each of these phases or waves. He identified the first one with Britain, 'the world's first industrial economy'. In the second wave, in Trebilcock's view, countries like France and the German states (not yet unified) were included. The third wave related to countries like Italy, Sweden, the Austrian section of the Hapsburg Empire and Russia. The Industrial Revolution in Britain was primarily accelerated through a series of 'simple and cheap' innovations which sparked off the entire process.[1] We have already discussed at length the conditions favouring industrial development in Britain. Scholars have put forth a variety of causes, such as proximity to the sea facilitating easy transportation; ownership of colonies; abundant availability of coal; good ports; congenial climatic conditions; The list could go on, but as I mentioned earlier, many of these conditions prevailed in other countries as well. For instance, Holland and Spain both had large colonial empires, but lagged far behind as far as the advent of the Industrial Revolution was concerned. If climatic conditions were so important, then England should have had an industrial revolution much earlier. Germany too, like England, was rich in coal reserves, but had an industrial revolution much later—in Trebilcock's second wave. What then was so unique about **England** that she emerged as the **first industrial nation of the world**?

Hobsbawm argued that as a result of the economic crisis of the 17th century, the old pattern of expansion in the Mediterranean or the Baltic had perished and new centres of expansion along the borders of the North Sea and North Atlantic had emerged. The structure of relationship had changed widening the flows of commerce. This

> powerful, growing and accelerating currents of overseas trade which swept the infant industries of Europe with it—and in fact, sometimes actually created them—were hardly conceivable without this change. It rested on three things: in Europe, the rise of a market for products for everyday use; and overseas the creation of economic systems for producing such goods (such as, slave-operated plantations) and the conquest of colonies designed to serve the economic advantage of their European owners.[2]

New colonies with new relationships boosted economic growth and gave England a lead over others. According to historian Kenneth Pomerantz, the fundamental factor that made England different from the rest of the world was her access to the vast resources of the American empire. Though, of course, much of this advantage was soon lost with the victory of the American colonies against their coloniser England.

Another advantage which Britain had and which was mostly absent in other countries was a favourable political atmosphere and a supportive state. In England, the parliament was vocal and effective and played a very important role throughout the centuries. It not only strongly supported industrialisation efforts, but also passed acts which facilitated the process, like financing turnpike projects. In France, on the contrary, a rigid state mercantilism seriously hampered commercial activities. It reached its peak with Colbertism (the mercantilist theories of Jean Baptiste Colbert in the 17th century, especially his advocacy of high protective tariffs). In Italy and Germany, lack of unification forfeited entrepreneurs of any substantial help from the state. In Britain, some members of parliament were merchants themselves; naturally they, in their own self-interest, promoted commercial and industrial ventures. In France, on the contrary, involvement of the nobility in business and commerce was looked down upon. The ideal prevalent there was *vivre noblement*, that is, scornful attitude towards work. Further, enclosure was fiercely resisted in Britain as in other continental countries, but the British parliament supported it with legislation. In France, on the other hand, enclosures were severely obstructed due to lack of capital and incessant acrimony between the large landlords and merchants, and the small holding peasantry and landless labourers. And there was no parliament to solve this problem. As Rozental argued,

> In their intensity and spread, the enclosures in France cannot be compared with those of England. The incentives for commercial agriculture were far stronger in the latter country with its high degree of industrialisation, more rapid population growth, more elastic demand for cash crops, and above all, greater abundance of land in proportion to landowning population.[3]

In Russia, with her deep-rooted feudalism, the status of the landlord depended on the size of his land and the number of serfs. Serfdom being deeply entrenched, no official enclosure movement could begin in Russia before 1906 when Stolypin provided for the enclosure of the lands of individual peasant households in European Russia. In Germany, which was divided into 39 states since the days of the Congress of Vienna, different rules prevailed in different states and any comprehensive uniform land policy was not possible. Further, Britain had the advantage of the absence of a system of internal tolls and tariffs, which existed on the continent. This facilitated free movement of goods in Britain ensuring smooth flow of trade and commerce. In contrast, internal customs duties raised barriers in respect of movement of goods between different parts of France. In Germany, trade was hindered regularly till the *zollverein* (customs union) came into existence on 1 January 1834.

Finally, by far the most important phenomenon in Britain was the series of scientific inventions that accelerated the process of industrialisation and gave Britain the remarkable lead over others and established her as the first industrial nation of the world. Just as France had produced a number of brilliant philosophers who helped enormously in bringing about a revolution in France—a phenomenon that happened only in France and nowhere else in Europe—so England in the 18th century had produced a galaxy of extraordinary scientists whose amazing contributions transformed her into the strongest industrial nation in the world.

There is extensive contemporary literature that attempts to answer the oft-repeated question—'Why was England first?'. According to N.F.R. Crafts, the answers seemed to fall into three types. *First*, there were scholars who tried to explain why by giving only one reason. Kemp, for example, argued that the continuance of the traditional agrarian structure slowed down the process of industrialisation in France. Hagen explained

England's lead in terms of a natural or temperamental difference between the populace. He wrote, "…the Industrial Revolution occurred first in England and Wales…because British people were inwardly different from those of the continent." *Second*, a group of historians like Hartwell have regarded the Industrial Revolution as an outcome of "a long period of slow economic growth." A *third* viewpoint saw it as the culmination of a number of factors combined. Milward and Saul held that it was difficult to explain British economy in terms of one single factor not present in continental economies. Kranzberg, wrote, "…it was a multiplicity of factors—technological, social, economic, political and cultural—which came together in the mid-18th century to provide the stimulus for industrial advance."[4] W.W. Rostow ascribed it to the great innovational zeal present in England in the 18th century.[5]

The Industrial Revolution had certain typical characteristic features. Trebilcock enumerated a few. For one, industrialisation was undoubtedly a capital-intensive process. It was also a long-drawn, evolutionary process. Trebilcock disagreed with Rostow's theory that the industrial take-off entailed a period of about thirty years, and believed that it took at least five to eight decades (ten in case of Britain).[6] It was, therefore, *both a revolution as well as an evolution*. There was nothing sudden or dramatic about it as Charles Beard had called it in his 'melodramatic' remark, "a thunderbolt from a clear blue sky". It was basically a gradual and accumulative process.

Alexander Gerschenkron identified a significant trait among the late developers like Russia, Italy, Sweden, who industrialised after the 1880s. He called it the '**great spurt**' arising primarily out of their anxiety of lagging behind and, therefore, the haste amongst them to catch up. They also had the advantage of availing of the technology of countries which had already experienced industrialisation. They lost no time and quickly gathered momentum. The growth in their case was exceedingly rapid. *Russia, for example, by 1900 became the fourth country in the world in iron production and the fifth in steel.* Trebilcock expressed his reservation and said that Gerschenkron's theory was based mostly on his study of the case of Russia. Another prominent country that developed after the 1880s—Italy—did not reveal any sudden or rapid growth and was characterised by only an average growth of 5.4 per cent per annum, which was slower than Germany. Even Russian development was not sudden in the sense that even before the emancipation of serfs in 1861, Russian enterprise was visible in some fields like cotton textiles, sugar refining and distilling.[7] The 'great spurt' theory, therefore, suffers from the handicap of generalisation without evidence.

A significant aspect of the industrialisation was the existence of an **economic dualism**. Traditional agriculture as well as handicrafts existed side by side with new technological changes until 1914. Sewell showed how artisan corporate culture survived, in modified form, in the revolutions of 1830 and 1848 and also thereafter. The skilled population in France was less willing to change traditional ways in agriculture as well as in hand-produced luxury items and to produce consumer goods on a mass scale. As late as 1882, one-third of German textile workers were employed within the domestic system of manufacturing. In Russia till 1914, village manufacturing continued side by side with the modern factories. *Kustar* industries (the Russian word 'kustar' meant Russian cottage industry that made craft goods for sale) chiefly furniture, textile, toys, shoes etc. represented ethnic Russian culture and remained popular deep down into the middle of the 20th century. However, according to Wendy Salmond, the kustar industries suffered as Russia industrialised in the second half of the 19th century. Although their goods could not compete in price with factory-made products, yet many private individuals—primarily members of Moscow's elite merchant class—intervened and tried to save the industry. In 1876, for example, Elizaveta and Savva Mamontov established a kustar workshop on their estate Abramtsevo, with the purpose of helping peasant men in the villages to remain with their families rather than seeking factory work in the cities.[8] This aspect of dualism, at any rate, has not been accepted by most of the scholars, according to whom traditional artisanal production was almost crushed, except in a few cases, by the advent of the Industrial Revolution, and whatever was left was almost dwindling.

Notwithstanding this dual existence of tradition with modern technology, newly invented machines predominated the era of Industrial Revolution. David Landes highlights this factor while elaborating the **leading role of the cotton textiles industry** in precipitating the Industrial Revolution:

> On the one hand, (the Industrial Revolution) required machines which not only replaced hand labour but compelled the concentration of production in factories—in other words, machines whose appetite for energy was too large for domestic sources of power and whose mechanical superiority was sufficient to break down the resistance of older forms of hand production. On the other hand it required a big

industry producing a commodity of wide and elastic demand, such that (1) the mechanisation of any of its processes of manufacture would create serious strains in the others, and (2) the impact of improvements in this industry would be left throughout the economy.[9]

The preponderance of machines and factory was a central characteristic feature of the Industrial Revolution.

The Industrial Revolution had an international as well as **regional component**. The revolution cut across nations and exchanged or borrowed technology, ideas and intellectual capital from each other. In fact, English scientists and technicians were invited to many countries to share their knowledge, skills and experience. Goods were imported and exported on a wide scale. This regional element was extremely predominant. Each place had its own typical product which was famous by the name of its place of origin. For example, cotton of Lancashire, silk of Lyons, iron works of Essen. Professor Pollard observed that industrialisation was less a national circumstance than a regional event.

Institutions—educational academies, technical institutes, government ministries, private corporations, investment banks, financial organisations—played an important part in different stages of the Industrial Revolution. Gerschenkron observed that different countries, depending upon their levels of backwardness, were associated with different types of institutions. Chronic backwardness, for instance, required effective State intervention; medium backwardness needed the help of investment banks; suppressed backwardness or in other words, developed economies, could be safely managed by large-scale modern corporations.

The Industrial Revolution in France

WHY WAS THE REVOLUTION DELAYED IN FRANCE?

As historian Tom Kemp pointed out, industrial growth in France in the 19th century was marked by symptoms of retardation. In other words, the French economy had become somewhat stagnant. Even when France became a leading industrial country in the 19th century, this 'retard' continued. Many historians are more or less agreed on this point. If industrialisation meant a thorough technological transformation of the means of production or a radical shift from the agrarian to the manufacturing sector, "it must be emphasised that France entered the 19th century with a lag behind Britain of which contemporaries were well aware."[10] In fact, according to Clapham, "…France never went through an Industrial Revolution…The transformation accomplished in a century was in many ways less complete than that which Germany experienced in the forty years after 1871."[11] The question then is: why this lag? Scholars have tried to explain the phenomenon in several ways.

The 17th century crisis, which is an important subject of discussion among historians, created a long period of stagnation and decline in France. A series of demographic, religious, economic and political problems brought about a general breakdown in Europe in the spheres of economy, society and politics—a precarious situation which came to be called **the 17th-century crisis**. Various events such as the English Civil War, the Fronde in France, the revolts against the Spanish Crown in Portugal, Naples and Catalonia were all symptoms of the same 'general crisis'. Hobsbawm, Maurice Dobb and other Marxist historians saw it as primarily being economic and social in origin.[12] For Marxist scholars, it was a crisis of production—a conflict between the producing bourgeoisie and the retrograde feudal society. According to this view, the forces of capitalism triumphed early in England not only because they were more developed there, but because they were strongly backed by the Parliament. England was, therefore, the only country that broke the shackles of feudalism and marched forth towards a prosperous capitalistic future. The English Puritan Revolution was, therefore, a successful bourgeois revolution. Hugh R. Trevor-Roper, however, did not agree with this view. He saw this crisis broadly as a conflict between the 'court' and the 'country', that is, between the sovereign princely states who represented the court and the landed gentry representing the country; or in his words,

> it was a crisis not of the constitution, nor of the system of production, but of the State, or rather, of the relation of the State to society.…For by the seventeenth century the Renaissance Courts had grown so great, had consumed so much in "waste", and had sent their multiplying suckers so deep into the body of society, that they could flourish only for a limited time…[13]

He, in fact, looked upon the crisis as a 'general revolution', because, although the revolutions differed from place to place, they had numerous common elements, especially the element of discord between the State and society.[14] As we have discussed in Chapter 1, the **Wars of the Fronde** were a series of revolts that occurred in France due to conflicts in government between the nobility and the monarchy. Its failure paved the way for the absolutism of Louis XIV's reign. The 17th century was indeed a period of regression and even decline in France. As Francois Crouzet pointed out, there were frequent economic and demographic crises which in turn, crippled industrial enterprises, producing thereby unprecedented unemployment and deep-seated popular discontent.[15] Such a picture was in sharp contrast to that of England. Despite the frequent ups and downs, like the period of the Civil War, England, on the whole, prospered as far as her growth of capitalism was concerned. In Trevor-Roper's view, the reason for England's prosperity was clear. The princely courts had outgrown their utility everywhere in Europe, and had to be overhauled. While in countries like France (through the Wars of Fronde for example) and Holland it was achieved partially, in England it was complete. Not that England was free of problems—"the storm of the mid-century, which blew throughout Europe, struck the most brittle, most overgrown, most rigid Court of all and brought it violently down."[16]

Trevor-Roper's view has not been accepted by all historians. Jean Egret in his second work in 1970, J.H. Shennan in 1968, William Doyle in 1970 had expressed clearly sympathetic views in favour of the Parlements, portraying them as useful restraining agents against the arbitrary tendencies of the government.[17] At any rate, what is most pertinent in the present discussion is the fact that the crisis of the 17th century undoubtedly had far greater adverse repercussions on France than on England, as a result of which the Industrial Revolution could bring about a remarkable breakthrough in the latter while the former lagged behind. Jean-Baptiste Colbert, the minister of finance under Louis XIV had desperately endeavoured to revive the falling French economy—the aftermath of Fronde. Historians are divided in their opinion on Colbert's contributions. Historians like W.O. Henderson and Tom Kemp were of the opinion that this policy of mercantilism pursued by Colbert and the French government aided the industrialisation process. This was strongly contended by other scholars. Even Kemp agreed later that '**Colbertism**' was more a bureaucratic response to an economic stagnation and lacked a 'firm economic base.'[18] According to Crouzet, industrial growth under Colbert was not very pronounced. Many of his undertakings could not be sustained and "the general picture remains most unfavourable."[19] While Abbot Usher and Charles Cole argued that although partial, Colbert did contribute to the long-term economic development of the nation, Pierre Goubert was of the opinion that Colbert's measures, like those of his predecessors, were mostly transient, both in their content and impact, and that lasting economic achievements occurred only in the 18th century and were not the feats of **'Louis XIV's famous adviser'**.[20] France had always been a nation of mercantilism which reached such a climax in the era of Colbert that his policies collectively came to be called 'Colbertism'. Colbert engaged in a virtual orgy of grants of monopoly, subsidies of luxury and cartelizing privileges and created a network of spies and informers to ferret out any kind of violation of the regulations. The result of this network of restriction was that the industrial and economic growth of France was badly crippled.

The factor which historians have emphasised is the **aftermath of the Revolution and Napoleonic wars**. The upheaval that the country went through and the concomitant social and economic effects that they entailed were colossal enough to throw the nation off gear and put its economy out of track. Much of its resources were drained in unproductive expenditure. The nation was hardly in a position to devote itself to serious entrepreneurial pursuits. According to Tom Kemp, the post-revolutionary land-settlement, howsoever praiseworthy from a social point of view, was not economically viable as it kept a major portion of the rural population tied to the ground, curtailing thereby the supply of labour necessary for an industrial take-off. Moreover, as a large number of nobles emigrated (émigrés nobles), the main clientele for the products for which France was well-known—luxury items like silk, perfumes, laces, fine pottery, crockery—was gone, and the home market languished. Britain, on the other hand, had a flourishing home market to cater to.

The social and economic structures were old, conventional and anachronistic. It is true that the Constituent Assembly swept away all vestiges of feudalism by the Report of 4 August 1789, but Henderson observed that although seigneurial rights like special privileges of hunting, fishing, levying of tolls at markets, fairs, rivers or monopoly over mills, ovens and wine-presses were abolished, 'real rights' like quit-rents, annual tax on cultivated land, etc., continued.[21] And it were the **quit-rents** by which the peasants were vexed the most. The peasantry fiercely resisted the efforts of the physiocrats to introduce sweeping agricultural reforms. The enclosure movement encouraged in England by the parliament was strongly prevented in France from being introduced. The governments in charge were preoccupied in bringing the political situation under control, neglecting the economy as well as economic ventures, although general over-hauling of taxes and some financial reforms were undertaken.

During the Napoleonic regime, French colonial trade was both adversely and favourably affected. It was adversely affected because its colonial trade was almost destroyed since Britain had blocked her ports. A large part of her manufactures was dependent on colonial supply. The French refineries, for example, were nourished by the supply of raw materials from San Domingo. Her overseas trade as well as communication with her colonies were terribly hard hit as a result of the neglect of her crucially important ports like Bordeaux, Nantes and Marseilles. The exchange with the colonies—import of raw materials from there and sending finished products to their markets—broke down. Consequently, a large number of French workshops and factories were severely affected. However, in another way manufacture was encouraged by **Napoleon's Continental System**. Napoleon took several measures to encourage indigenous production. Cotton production of Ghent and Mulhouse (incorporated in France), and also of Paris as well as Roubaix got a boost. A reward was announced by Napoleon for the invention of a machine to produce wool from flax. The production of new dyes was initiated in Koechlin. In 1812, a small steam engine was set up by Dollfus-Mieg and Cie at Mullhouse to drive a spinning machine.

France's late entry in the industrial field has often been linked to her lack of coal, which had accelerated the Industrial Revolution in Britain. France imported coal at a huge cost, which automatically put brakes on her manufacture. Henderson, however, argued that this was significantly compensated by an abundance of iron. He wrote, "Until 1871 France had in Lorraine the largest iron-ore deposits in western Europe. The success of the Hayange ironworks showed what could be achieved in this region. But, on the whole, the French neglected to exploit the vast iron-ore resources of Lorraine."[22] As a result, in 1914, France was not the leading producer of pig-iron or steel.[23] This was also due to the fact that France lost Lorraine to Prussia after her severe defeat to Prussia in 1871.

The other factors that impeded the industrial growth in France were the slow development of railways, chequered expansion of ports and relatively slower increase of population when compared to Britain, Germany or the United States. It was only under the **Second Empire** that an **extensive network of railways** was built, and the *crédit mobilier* was established to thrust the flow of capital into the industrial sector. The conservative outlook of the financiers hampered the investment of funds in industrial enterprises. The progress of farmers and entrepreneurs, construction of railways and technological innovations—all these were hindered by want of capital. The financial needs of the railways helped the emergence of a capital market. The building of railways had started from the time of the July monarchy, that is, the regime of Louis Philippe, but picked up its momentum under the Second Empire. The lack of connectivity prior to the construction of railways had created a kind of monopoly of the local traders and had, therefore, prevented the development of a proper national market. With the coming of railways, better distribution of agricultural surpluses and other excess products was made possible. Easy means of communication facilitated the setting up of heavy industries as the transportation of raw materials and finished products became less cumbersome; although heavy industries always remained a less pronounced feature of French economy. Similarly, according to Henderson, the population of France grew only by 10 million over the span of 100 years from 1700 to 1799, while that of Britain rose from 10.5 million to 37 million.[24] Whereas on the one hand, the **slow rate of population increase** implied a reduced labour force, it also meant less pressure on the resources of France.

One of the most crucial factors that inspired the industrialisation of Britain and gave her a lead over all were the series of technical inventions her scientists brought about in the field of agriculture as well as industry. Improved methods of cultivation enhanced the output which not only fed a growing population, but created a reserve of capital which could be invested in industries. Here France, like all other countries, lagged behind. It is true that there were some **significant technical innovations in France** such as the **silk loom of Jacquard**, **Berthollet and Leblanc's innovations in the chemical industry**, **Gribeauval** in shipbuilding, the contributions of **Buffon** and **Réaumur** in the fields of natural history, entomology. But they were far less compared to what Britain witnessed throughout the 18th century. In fact, France, like many other countries, invited British technicians in order to learn from their experiences.

The factors elaborated above are the general comparative points which historians have enumerated in order to highlight the disadvantages from which France suffered vis-à-vis Britain in economic growth. These were also the causes of her so-called inevitable 'retard'. Crouzet, while agreeing with such an analysis, argued all the same that in the period between the end of the **War of the Spanish Succession in 1714** and the **French Revolution in 1789**, the situation changed drastically and the wide gap between the two countries narrowed considerably. Surprisingly enough, observed Crouzet, their rates of growth during this period were not dissimilar. The volume of French foreign trade reached almost the same level as that of Britain on the eve of the French Revolution. In the international markets Britain had to face a steep competition from French goods. French colonies expanded, her woollen industry prospered though not like Britain, her coal production multiplied and France was not lagging too far behind by the end of the 18th century. The agricultural growth of the two countries, argued Crouzet, was also roughly parallel. The fundamental difference between them was in the field of technology. France developed her industries within the traditional structure; Britain, on the other hand, transcended the age-old structures through a series of new technical innovations which indeed heralded a revolution. According to Crouzet, although France was not disastrously lagging behind, and the Industrial Revolution there might have taken off within a gap of a few years of British Industrial Revolution, her chances were ruined by the outbreak of the French Revolution and the protracted Revolutionary Wars which continued for 23 years—the 'national catastrophe', in the words of Crouzet.[25]

The theory of 'lag' or 'retard' has not, however, been accepted by recent historians. They have extended Crouzet's argument—that the wide gap between England and France had narrowed down in the 18th century—and remarked that even in the 19th and 20th centuries the overall rate of increase in real output per capita was hardly less than Britain. According to them, Clapham and his successors were mostly concerned with the outward manifestations of economic transformation like drastic innovation, growth of factories, rise of cities and towns, and overlooked the silent and sustained yet impressive upward changes in real output per capita.[26] *French industrial development, therefore, was not lagging behind, but was only of a different nature.*

PATTERN OF FRENCH INDUSTRIALISATION

The French industrialisation was marked by certain characteristic features which made it distinct from other countries in Europe. An important feature was, as we have already discussed, the symptoms of **retardation or stagnation**. There is no doubt that France entered the field of industrial growth with a lag. Many of the reasons of this lag we have enumerated above. One of the major reasons was the 17th-century crisis. It was sparked off by France's participation in various wars—starting with the Thirty Years' War, and then the Wars of Fronde. These wars sapped her energy and left her devastated economically and spiritually. France remained primarily an agricultural country until well into the 20th century. The land-settlement after the French Revolution distributed land among the poor and the landless, as a result of which they were more tied up with their land in the countryside and lost interest in migrating to the cities for work. The supply of labour for factories was adversely affected thereby. Industrialisation set in hesitantly and tentatively. In fact, French industry had begun to be crippled in the late 15th century, when the King issued gold charters and endeavoured to control the urban as well as rural guilds by setting standards of quality. Lyons was exempted from such restrictions and that was the major reason why it flourished in the 16th century. Under the pretext of controlling the standards, competition was throttled, production and imports were limited and prices kept high. Industrial Revolution in France was further delayed by the outbreak of the revolution in 1789 and later the Napoleonic Wars.

Another feature of the French Industrial Revolution was the **emphasis on quality**. This put a severe restriction on mass production—an extremely necessary condition for industrial development. **French aversion to mass production** was nothing new. The same trend was noticeable even earlier. One example was the loom invented in the early 17th century. Initially it was used to produce mainly luxury items, for example, silk stockings. Later, when the loom began to be used for the production of goods of mass consumption—like woollen and linen items—the hand-knitters resented vehemently the fresh competition it presented. So much so that eventually in 1680 Colbert had to outlaw the use of the loom on any article except silk. Colbert believed that product quality alone could ensure France's success in the international markets. If the private merchants and manufacturers were given unrestricted freedom, the quality might suffer due to their unbounded greed for profit. Hence, Colbert felt, the need for regulation. Colbert's policy of control was pursued even after his death in 1683. For example, the same fate befell the art of button-making—a trade mostly controlled by the cord and button-makers' guild who made cord buttons by hand. In the 1690s the tailors and dealers innovated the art of manufacturing buttons of the garment from the same cloth. Fierce resistance from the hand button-makers brought in state intervention, which immediately prohibited the production and sale of the new variety.[27] Innovation was strangled, and 'quality' was preserved at the cost of the spirit of industrialisation. Conservation of traditional skill and style of ethnic craftsmanship characterised French methods of production. Conventional industries also were encouraged thereby to resent the entry of any new entrepreneur. In the 1680s the indigenous woollen, silk and linen industries were outraged by the immense popularity of the printed calicoes which came from India and had become a craze among the ladies. The protest of the home industries eventually forced the government to ban the import of calicoes. However, the move did not succeed due to the vehement remonstrance from the women patrons and rampant smuggling went on. The domestic calico printers, however, were pushed out of their business so they had to emigrate to England and Holland and pursue their enterprise there.[28] Under such circumstances, heavy investments in modern plants were discouraged, meticulous production of 'quality' goods was the order of the day, and as Kemp observed, "new techniques were adopted on a piece-meal basis without necessarily bringing about great changes in the traditional structure."[29] The **absence of wide, expansive markets for cheap mass-produced goods** was a typical trait of the French economy in the 18th and 19th centuries. Piece-meal production had an added advantage. The goods produced were light and delicate items, and could be exported in bulk at a relatively lower cost. They had a huge demand in international markets. France was said to be the fashion trendsetter of the European continent. No wonder this was a matter of great vanity among the French people. This common French sentiment was expressed by the Parlement of Paris in the following words:

> Our merchandise has always won out in foreign markets…(It) is sought after all over Europe for its taste, its beauty, its finesse, its quality, the correctness of its design, the perfection of its execution, the quality of its raw materials…Our arts, brought to the highest degree of perfection, enrich your capital, of which the entire world has become the tributary.[30]

Mercantilism was an inseparable element of the French pattern of industrialisation. In fact, crippling regulation of French production had begun in the late 15th century when the king had issued a number of guild charters, conferring the power to control and to set the standards of quality of items produced, on the **guilds** and their masters. In 1581 King Henry III ordered all artisans to join the guilds. In the name of preservation of 'quality', **freedom** and **versatility** of manufacturers was **severely curtailed**. The same trend in similar austerity was carried out by Colbert, as we have seen. The industries producing luxury goods were heavily subsidised as their clientele consisted primarily of the members of the royal family and the aristocracy. The result was the increased taxes on the new mass production industries preventing them from investment in innovations. However, Colbert did encourage **private initiatives** by providing sops (or concessions) like outright gifts, tax exemptions including those on salt, wine etc. Protection against foreign competition was also assured. The guilds were finally abolished in France in 1791. The **regulatory policies of the French government** were in sharp contrast to the **laissez faire principles of the British government** allowing enough room for blossoming of new ideas and experiments. French tendencies of control continued way down the close of the 18th century. Lack of competition made the French entrepreneurs **complacent**. The zeal to improve the standards of production through new scientific inventions was not strong enough. Only during two periods—between 1786 and 1792 and again between 1860 and 1880s—liberal economic policy prevailed in France. The Anglo-French Commercial Treaty of 1786 ended briefly the economic war between France and England and set up a system to reduce tariffs on goods from either country. Unpopular with French merchants, it did not survive the outbreak of the war with Britain in 1793. Another treaty between these two countries was signed in 1860 which reduced French duties on British manufactured goods to levels not above 30 per cent and reduced British duties on French liquor. This explains, observed Henderson, why inventions like steam engines, coke blast furnaces etc. were so slow to be adopted by France, compared to other countries. "Without the spur of foreign competition they were frequently content to use traditional techniques."[31] In the absence of decisive innovations', France followed a different route to industrialisation—an 'unobtrusive one'. On the other hand, according to R. Davis, it was these decisive innovations which were responsible for the first Industrial Revolution in England. If these had occurred in France rather than in England, France would have had the first Industrial Revolution.[32]

French industrialisation before 1914, therefore, was marked *neither by a dramatic take-off as it happened in Britain and Germany, nor any 'great spurt' as it characterised Russia towards the end of the 18th century*. It was rather slow, emphasising upon delicate, luxury items like fine crockery, glassware, woven silk, leather goods, fine furniture, jewellery, tapestries, produced on a piecemeal basis. French manufacturers concentrated on finished products. **Absence of standardised mass-production** and an **effective mercantile policy** characterised French industrial system. The government vigorously directed trade, commerce and all kinds of industrial enterprises. The enclosure movement came late and was initiated by means of local acts by the parliament during the 18th and 19th centuries. This encouraged the small-scale forms of capitalism closely linked with commercialisation of agricultural products and petty production. Since France had relatively few resources of coal and iron, collieries and ironworks began to appear only in the middle of the 19th century to cater to the growing railway industry. Since the French mostly specialised in the production of luxury items, their demand in the markets was lower than that of British or German goods, as a limited clientele alone could afford and had the taste for such exquisite objects. This meant that France had far fewer factories, which in turn implied a lower rate of urbanisation and growth of towns and cities, as it was generally around the factories that the townships grew up. Of course, there were important French textile factories in cities like Rouen, Elbeuf, Lille, Roubaix, Mulhouse, Reims and Saint-Quentin, but they were certainly fewer than their British counterparts.

The other possible reasons for the **absence of heavy industries** and the prevalence of an **overall sluggish progress of industrial activities** were primarily the acquisition of land by the middle class and post-revolutionary land-settlement favourable to the peasantry. In a number of ways, it limited the scope for massive industrialisation. In fact, the continuance of the agrarian structure side by side with the industrial sector was the distinctive pattern of the Industrial Revolution in France. This feature, argued Sewell, could further be explained by the fact that the decline of artisans, which was a common element in the industrialised countries of Europe, did not happen in France. Some of the handicraft industries like metal-construction were in fact absorbed into the machine-construction factories which needed their skill and expertise, and these artisans were a distinctive group of highly paid proud craftsmen, quite distinct from the unskilled or semi-skilled workers. Even the handloom weavers in France were not so drastically wiped out as in Britain. Domestic weaving continued in full force till the introduction of power looms, which also came slowly and gradually. The fall of the handloom artisans, therefore, happened over a long span of time. The growth of factories being slow and of limited variety in France, several kinds of artisans thrived there, including stone-masons, carpenters, confectioners, butchers, potters. In fact, with the expansion of cities and markets, many French artisans changed their style of production from made-to-order items to "lower-quality, standardised, ready-made" items which had a larger demand. This system was known as 'confection'. Indeed, as per the estimates of Markovitch, in the first half of the 19th century, the numerical predominance of artisans over factory workers was clear enough and continued down the middle of the century.[33] In short, as Sewell points out, "In numerical terms, at least, this was an era of rise, rather than decline, for urban artisans."[34] This was undoubtedly, a unique pattern of French industrialisation. Further, the big agrarians who dominated the indigenous grain market always agitated against free trade and upheld the need for tariff protection in order to reduce competition and to retain thereby their own predominance in the home market. Their resistance to the treaty of 1860 led to the introduction of the protective measure of the Meline tariff in 1892. It marked a return to the earlier protectionist policies, effectively ending the period of free trade associated with the **1860 Cobden-Chevalier Treaty**. The basic feudal structure of the society with all its archaism, therefore, remained undisturbed by the industrialisation of the country.

All in all, by the middle of the 19th century, France was one of the leading industrial countries on the continent. A number of factors facilitated it. One of them was the construction of **railways**. It was under Louis Philippe that the first railways started in France in **1832**. Though it was not long after the first line had opened in Britain, the overall French progress in the expansion of railways was slower than those in other countries. According to Kemp, "it would be an exaggeration to claim that railway development sparked off a revolution in industry before 1848. Its pace was too leisurely and its spatial effects too limited to do that. However, a start had been made."[35] Another important point should also be taken into consideration that the construction of railways boosted the progress of several other facets of industrial development—for example, iron-mining, coal, financial establishments—thus promoting overall industrial advancement. It also paved the path for the emergence of a new and elite form of private or merchant banking, known as *haute banque*, for which the **support of bank finance and organisation of credit** was essential. The process that led to the creation of haute banque ended during the first of the 19th century. This term referred to approximately 20 respected banking houses in the capital which belonged to very rich banking families—Daillier, Delessert, Fould, Perier, Rothschild, and so on. Crédit Mobilier (literally, 'movable credit'), was a French banking company established in 1852 under the Second Empire and played a major role in the financing of numerous railroads and other infrastructure projects and thereby proved crucial for the nation's economic growth. Investment began in infrastructural projects like public roads, harbours, ports etc.

As in England, the textile industry was a pillar of industrial growth in France. Since the 16th century, the silk industry flourished in Lyon. Expanding demand and congenial climatic conditions stimulated the coming of an Industrial Revolution. France, like other continental countries, had the advantage of receiving the assistance of British technology. The development of France, especially Paris, reached its pinnacle under the **Haussmann era** which put the nation on the track of modernised transformation through various projects in which the Industrial Revolution played an essential role. It was through a collaboration of private capitalism and state initiative in the form of decision-making, management and financial investment that the renovation of Paris was accelerated with the aim of benefitting society in general and the poor in particular.

The Industrial Revolution in Germany

The period from 1870 to 1914 is known as the **Second Industrial Revolution**. Economist Joel Mokyr has explained why it is called so. *First*, the spate of inventions had slowed down in 1825, and had again gathered momentum in the last quarter of the century, although the indications had started showing from 1850s onwards. *Second*, there were distinct differences between the innovations of the first Industrial Revolution and the second. *The technologies of the Second Revolution had much stronger scientific foundations compared to those of the first, and therefore the inventions of the latter period were more profound and scientific.* The **First Industrial Revolution**, in the words of Mokyr, "had little or no scientific base. It created a chemical industry with no chemistry, an iron industry without metallurgy, power machinery without thermodynamics."[36] In fact, according to David Mowery and Nathan Rosenberg, the period 1859 to 1873 has been characterised as one of the most fruitful and dense in innovations in history.[37] It approximately started with the introducti[on] of **Bessemer steel** and culminated in the early **factory electrificatio[n] mass production** and the **production line**. One of the major countries involved was Germany and others in Europe were Britain, France and the Low Countries. We have referred above to Trebilcock's 'three waves of industrialisation'. The Second Industrial Revolution overlapped Trebilcock's second and third waves. While the countries in the first wave were Britain and Belgium, those in the second were France, German states (not unified into the German Empire until 1871) and the United States of America.

It is beyond doubt that Germany was a remarkably advanced nation from the point of view of its contribution to the fields of literature, music and philosophy since the days of the Reformation. Historians have also shown how trade and commerce flourished in medieval Germany. As Marie-Louise Kaplan has observed, even in the 17th century, trade and commerce in German Hanse flourished.[38] Until the advent of the 17th century, according to Friedrich Lutge, German economy was still prosperous and healthy. He insisted upon the prosperity of numerous North German small trade enterprises as an example.[39] In the 18th century, therefore, Germany was far from an under-developed country in Europe. Even so, industrialisation came late in Germany.

There were many reasons why the Industrial Revolution was **delayed** so much in Germany. First of all, Germany in the 18th century was not a unified country, but a conglomeration of nearly 300 principalities, which Napoleon had reduced to 100 principalities in a confederation—the **Confederation of the Rhine**—and became its Protector by abolishing the Holy Roman Empire in 1806. In 1815, at the Congress of Vienna, the Confederation of the Rhine was further reduced to the **German Confederation** comprising 39 states governed by independent German princes—an archaic system which hindered the emergence of modern industries. It was not until the **abolition of serfdom** in Germany that a steady supply of a free labour force became available for working in industries. Of course, the state did take initiative in setting up some industries. In some cases, *public and private enterprises went on side by side.* In the coal industry, for example, privately owned mines existed alongside the nationalised mines. In fact, it was the government which exercised much greater control over mining than over other industries. The methods of mining, fixation of prices, regulating wages, etc. were controlled under state supervision. As far as **Prussia**—where lay the **largest coal fields of the Ruhr, the Saar and Upper Silesia**—was concerned, the mining laws of 1851 removed excess control of the government and gave the coalmine owners the same control over their enterprises as the other industrialists had.

The effects of war—the Thirty Years' War and the political divisions created by the **Treaty of Westphalia**, the Continental System and the Napoleonic wars—had disastrous effects on German industrialisation. The Continental System **cut off Germany's trade with England** and seriously hampered the export trade of wool, timber, cereals. The situation was aggravated by the high tariffs of the neighbouring countries. Several enterprises were ruined in the process. Moreover, in order to cater to the **necessities of war**, many **new industries** sprang up like ironworks, manufacturers of arms and ammunitions, soldiers' uniforms, bandages etc. When the war was over, these factories had to be re-oriented to meet peace-time requirements. Due to the lack of unification, **no uniform system of tariffs and customs** prevailed for the purpose of preventing effectively the flow of foreign goods in German markets. This was dangerous to the efforts of reviving and rehabilitating the decadent industries producing war goods. While the home industries were confronted with the challenge of foreign imports, there came the harvest failures of 1847 which threw German economy completely out of gear.

Geographical factors also were serious obstacles in the path of industrialisation. One important factor was the **quality of soil**. Certain parts of the country were infertile, sandy and marshy and unfit for profitable cultivation. The location of the areas rich in minerals—the Ruhr, the Saar, Silesia, Saxony—were on the periphery and could hardly be properly utilised unless the communication system was improved. It was, therefore, not until the **railways** were constructed that these minerals— coal and steel particularly—could be optimally used for the purpose of industrial growth. Moreover, the ports of Germany were less strategically situated than those of England and France.

CONDITIONS FAVOURING GERMAN INDUSTRIALISATION

Although there were certain adverse conditions which dragged Germany behind on her path of industrialisation, there were some significant favourable factors as well. One of them was the **tariff of 1818**, initiated and nourished by the Prussian government and described by Clapham as "immeasurably the wisest and most scientific tariff then existing among the great powers."[40] In place of a medley of taxes and tolls that existed in the state, **a single tariff** was decided to be levied at the frontier. This example was soon followed by others, the first among them being Schwarzburg-Sondershausen, a small state which entered into a customs union with Prussia in 1819. Quickly enough, several other states followed suit. A **customs union or Zollverein** emerged which made the flow of trade and commerce smooth and simple. Gone were the days of cumbersome taxes and seizure of goods. This measure is generally looked upon as an important landmark as far as economic development was concerned.

The construction of railroads was another boon in the coming of the Industrial Revolution in Germany. It promoted economic unity by connecting different places and fostered all-round growth and development. The **first railroad in Germany** was the one connecting **Nuremberg** with **Fürth in Bavaria**. Opened in 1835 it pioneered the speedy construction of a national network of communication accelerating the process not only of industrialisation, but also of national unification. The **Dresden–Leipzig railway in Saxony in 1839** was extremely important from the point of view of connectivity. Henderson observed, "Railways were built more quickly in Germany than anywhere else on the continent except Belgium. In 1850 Germany already had 5,856 km of railways in operation while France had only 2,996 km."[41]

German industrialisation received a boost from banks and joint-stock companies. **Cartels** and **syndicates** were formed in order to fight jointly matters of common interest, to maintain research laboratories, to control prices and wages etc. The early cartels were in the field of heavy industries in the 1870s, but soon they spread to other industries like glass, chemicals, cement etc. Equally important was the role of **banks**. The early banks were set up in Cologne, Berlin, Darmstadt, Dresden. They not only lent money to the industries, but also took up blocks of shares themselves and put them in the markets for sale. That is how the banks encouraged investments and fostered industrial growth. At the same time, the banks supported Germany's foreign investments as well as vital foreign projects like the **Berlin–Baghdad Railroad** in the **Ottoman Turkish Empire**, the **Anatolian Railway Company** set up by the joint-cooperation of the Deutsche Bank and the Dresden Bank in 1889, while shares were acquired in the Oriental Railway Company by the Deutsche Bank and the Vienna Bank.

The rapid progress of German industries was to a large extent due to the various scientific inventions of the time. Henderson mentions a number of inventions like **Werner Von Siemen's electric dynamo, Otto's gas engine, Daimier's petrol engine,** the **Haber-Bosch process** for the fixation of nitrogen in the air by electrolysis. In different ways they helped the industries to march ahead.[42]

The development of ports and canals were the other facilitating factors. The **Kiel Canal** of 1895 connecting the North Sea and the Baltic Sea is one of the most important ones. The Rhine-Herne Canal, the Berlin-Stettin Canal, the Dortmund-Ems Canal, the Ems-Weser Canal followed suit. They enormously facilitated the export and import of goods.

Coal and iron industries developed rapidly as Germany was rich in these minerals. In fact, according to John Maynard Keynes "the German Empire was built more truly on coal and iron than on blood and iron."[43] Heavy industries was the most significant characteristic feature of the Industrial Revolution in Germany. Her output of coal went up to 190 million tons from 60 million tons in 1887. And her iron-ore output grew from 6.7 million tons in 1887 to more than 28 million tons in 1913.

Another factor—the availability of a substantial **labour force**—contributed largely to the take-off of the German Industrial Revolution. There were primarily two reasons behind this, the more important of them being the emancipation of serfs. The second one was the growth of population. As far as the emancipation of serfs is concerned, the conditions of the German peasants varied from place to place. As Kemp points out, in the north-west, serfdom had long been abolished. In the west and south, it lingered on for a long time and so also in the east.[44] Under such circumstances, came the attack of Napoleon and the consequent defeat of Prussia in the **Battle of Jena** in **1806**. This came both as a rude shock as well as an eye-opener to the German people. The result was the introduction of a series of agrarian reforms, which aimed to modernise the German society in general, and the Prussian society in particular. The **Stein-Hardenberg reforms of 1807** declared that serfdom was to be abolished by 1810. The emancipation released many serfs who found it increasingly difficult to make ends meet. They found work in the new factories coming up in the urban areas. The acute harvest failure in the 1840s had ruinous consequences on the peasant community in general, and those who could afford the cost of travel emigrated to the west of the Atlantic—the United States—in search of a better future. It was the poor and the landless who were available for swelling the number of workers in the factories. However, it should not be overlooked that despite the emigration of peasants, there was a demographic revolution in Germany in the 19th century. Kemp noted that the population rose about by 59 per cent between 1816 and 1865. In 1820 it had been 25 million, which rose to 40 per cent by 1871 and almost 65 million by 1910.[45] Improved medical knowledge, better hygienic habits, better sanitation might explain the growth in population during this time. As in England, so in Germany and other countries, significant rise in population was invariably followed by rapid industrialisation.

PATTERN OF INDUSTRIAL REVOLUTION IN GERMANY

We have seen that an effective economic unity prevailed in Germany by the time the country was unified in 1871. The economic unity was based upon a customs union (*zollverein*), a network of banking and railroad connectivity. This unity was also responsible for Germany's rapid industrial development. This rapidity was one of the most important characteristic features of the German Industrial Revolution. It is true that for reasons explained above, industrialisation took off quite late in Germany. But when it finally did, Germany closed the gap vis-à-vis the early starters with enormous speed and even went ahead in many respects. Indeed, it was Germany that fulfilled Rostow's theory of economic growth perfectly. As a result of the speedy expansion, the entire structure of her economy transformed.

A unique feature of her development was the boost it received from foreign powers in the shape of capital investment as well as technical training. As Kemp observed, "the resources of Germany, the potentialities of a market with a large and growing population, the existence of an abundant labour supply, had by the 'forties become attractive to foreign business."[46] The interest of **foreign countries** to **invest** in Germany was further stimulated by the fast construction of railroads, which facilitated the smooth transportation of raw materials from the mines and the fields to the factories and from factories to the markets. Germany's iron and coal mining and metallurgical industries were modelled especially on British technology. For the heavy and rapid industrial growth in Germany, large amounts of capital were needed, a substantial part of which came from foreign investments. The element of foreign assistance, therefore, formed an inseparable part of Germany's economic development.

With the passage of time, however, the foreign component of the German Industrial Revolution declined, as more and more Germans came forward to participate in the industrialisation process. They quickly learnt the new technology and skills from their foreign counterparts, assimilated them and even added their own innovations to them. The bank credits provided formidable support. A strongly business-minded middle class emerged. The situation improved further in the 1860s under **Bismarck's premiership**. **Freedom of enterprise** or economic liberalism was encouraged and the privileges of the guilds and corporations were put an end to. The road to rapid industrialisation thus became easier. Besides the initial help provided by foreign capital, the existing banks supplied capital to the nascent industries. In the 1850s, however, emerged a number of **joint-stock banks** which helped German industries flourish. Here lay a fundamental distinction between the German and the British industrialisation process. In Britain joint-stock companies played no such crucial role as they played in Germany. Based primarily upon heavy industry, Germany quickly overcame her late start, and in the export market, soon became a strong contender of Britain, the pioneer country.

The emphasis of German industries was, unlike in France, on heavy industries; in other words, either the goods produced or the processes involved were heavy, like production of railway coaches, construction of roads, buildings and bridges, chemical plants, etc. Goods were manufactured in bulk and the factories were bigger with bulky, heavy machineries. While France specialised in manufacturing delicate, piece-meal, intricate items, Germany took pride in the production of heavy objects in bulk like machinery, arms and ammunition, etc.

A significant element of German economic growth is to be noted here. The modernisation of German economy took place within a tightly rigid, conservative political and social construct. *Germany moved on a path of economic liberalism while being an archaic, interventionist state and an extremely conventional society dominated by the Junker aristocracy*—a queer combination indeed. Here Germany successfully fit Trebilcock's theory of **'technological dualism'**—the existence side by side of highly developed modern techniques and older, antiquated methods. He wrote,

FIG. 5.1: Krupp Factory, Essen; The Weapon's Forge of the German Reich, World War I

Even in Germany, where the rise of cartels in the 1870s and 1880s helped to carry large-scale industrial organisation further than anywhere else on the continent, traditional methods of production were by no means extinguished: as late as 1882 one-third of all German textile workers were still employed within the domestic system of manufacturing.[47]

And the difference between the old and the new went on widening. The modern sector was moving ahead with enormous speed while the traditional producers remained where they were. The gap naturally kept increasing.

German industries soon developed an exclusive pattern of organising themselves into **cartels or syndicates**. In this way sharp competition was transformed into close competition. *Companies producing the same kind of goods were organised into a single cartel.* Companies which were bitterly competitive before they entered into an alliance now concentrated on working together as a cartel and devoted themselves to their collective growth and welfare. The cartels began in heavy industries and spread throughout other industries. Cartels could be horizontal as well as vertical. The former included companies which produced the same kind of raw materials or finished products. The latter was an amalgamation of companies which were at different stages of production—some producing raw materials, others manufacturing finished goods. The formation of cartels was a new characteristic element of industrialisation which was carried down through the centuries. The earliest cartel was the **Neckar Salt Union of 1828**. During the economic depression that began in 1873, a number of cartels sprang up as the firms in crisis found a way of survival in this kind of association. Henderson disagreed with the view of some economists that cartels were generally born out of economic depression, and argued instead that several reasons explained the birth of cartels, and they emerged under prosperity as well. By 1900, there were 275 cartels in operation in Germany and by 1908 the number had shot up to 500.

Economic liberalisation which meant free exchange of goods among nations was another particular trait of the German Industrial Revolution in the 1860s. It favoured middle-class businessmen by wiping out the privileges of the guilds and corporations. It meant keener competition in the market. Indigenous markets were thrown open to foreign goods. In course of time, however, entrepreneurs from various fields began to feel the pinch and started demanding protection, as a result of which the German Reich in the 1870s discarded economic liberalism of the 1860s and adopted **protective tariffs**, which then came to assume the new character of German industrialisation.

Another distinctive feature of the German economy in the mid-19th century was the survival of the peasantry and the prominence of **a prosperous agrarian structure**. A technologically advanced heavy industry producing enormous quantities of steel, chemicals, electricity, strongly developed mining and engineering sectors, along with a flourishing agriculture using modern techniques and a rapidly growing export market where Germany competed on equal terms with Britain, obliterated her initial handicap as a latecomer and placed Germany on the same platform as the early birds.

However, Germany was indeed the pioneer in one field—that of **state socialism**. It provided German industrialisation with its own unique distinction. Like workers in all other countries, German factory workers were also in pitiable condition. The socialist parties capitalised on their miseries and won popularity among the working class by sympathising with them. In order to wean them from the socialist party, Bismarck started an experiment in state socialism by passing **Imperial Laws of Insurance in 1883, 1884 and 1889**, respectively against sickness, accident and old age. Whether they achieved any appreciable measure of success or not, it was undoubtedly a unique pattern of Germany as far as her industrial policies were concerned. These measures were also a manifestation of state interventionism which played a decisive role in the process of German industrialisation.

The Industrial Revolution in Russia

Russia, in the mid-20th century, was hardly different from any other country in Europe. In the 19th century, however, Russia was a long way behind the leading industrial nations. It were the policies of **Sergei Witte, the Russian Minister for Finance** from 1892 to 1903, that accelerated the Industrial Revolution in Russia. It was during Witte's regime that Russia began to catch up with the West. By raising Russian tariffs for imports, by encouraging the entrepreneurs to open up new ventures, and, most importantly, by convincing other nations to invest in Russian industry, Witte laid the foundations of an industrial base on which an edifice was rapidly erected.

It should not be assumed, however, that there was no manufacturing in Russia before the end of the 19th century. According to Mikhail I. Tugan-Baranovskii, the prominent Ukrainian economist,[48] Russian capitalist traditions had their roots in the *kustar* or cottage industry which became an important source of income for peasants in some parts of Russia by the 16th century, and developed extensively during the 19th century. **Kustar** mainly comprised the small enterprises of peasants who paid *obrok* or quit-rent to their landlords and thereby freed themselves to work on crafts in their own homes. Some craftsmen or artisans were also engaged in kustar to cater to the demands of a wealthy clientele. Kustar, had economic, social as well as cultural significance. It was economically extremely important to the local rural people as their means of livelihood; it was an instrument to keep the social structure intact by providing work to the youth and thereby preventing them from migrating to the cities with all their perceived notions of moral corruption and character debasement. Culturally, kustar was a symbol of ethnic Russian art that was coveted all over the world (the colourfully painted Russian dolls one inside the other, for example, was, and still is, the international icon of typical Russian cottage industry). Elaborating on this, Alexander Gerschenkron argues that state support, or the efforts of Sergei Witte, eventually became the basis for industrial development in Russia.[49]

It would be, however, wrong to assume that factories did not exist in Russia before the end of the 19th century. **Peter the Great** (1682–1725), also known as the 'father of Russian manufacturing industry', had started factories—**possessional factories**, as they were called—upon government contracts, primarily for the production of arms in order to fulfil the country's military and naval needs. It is said that nearly 233 industrial centres were established during Peter the Great's reign. These included mines, iron foundries, saltpetre plants, glass factories, etc. Henderson refers to some enterprises which existed in Russia even before Peter the Great ascended the throne. He wrote,

> The Stroganov family had manufactured salt on a large scale while Morozov operated potash plants, iron foundries, distilleries, brick-kilns and linen works. Among the foreigners Vinius (a Dutchman) and Koet (a Swede) deserve mention. The former had established ironworks near Tula (1632) while the latter had set up glassworks near Moscow (1634).[50]

Further, there were factories set up by nobles as well with the purpose of fulfilling their own daily requirements. These were called the **manorial factories**. Both these types of factories—the foreign owned as well as manorial—were based upon serf labour. Kemp felt that they were not very successful enterprises, first because their purpose was very limited, and second because most of Russia's general populace lacked money to buy the products. As a result, they never attracted private investments, and, therefore, never expanded beyond a point.[51] Professor James Mavor, however, observed that Czar Peter "showed his people in what the material wealth of Russia consisted, and he showed them how it might be exploited."[52] Henderson agreed with this view.[53] However, there did exist, although very few in number, a **fourth category of factories** which were indeed unique and remarkable in the sense that they were **founded and owned by some extraordinary individual serfs**. Mention may be made here of the textile factory of the small town of Ivanovo, northwest of Moscow. It was established by a serf with his master's permission and became a flourishing enterprise with power looms and an impressive labour force of 2600 by 1852.

OBSTACLES IN THE PATH OF INDUSTRIAL REVOLUTION IN RUSSIA

There were several reasons—geographical, infrastructural, economic, political and social—that were responsible for Russia's late entry in the field of industrialisation. Geographically, Russia was situated far from the centres of advanced industrial activity in Europe—England, France, Germany. The waves of industrialisation did not reach the Russian frontier. Within Russia also, the sites rich in mineral resources were located far apart and were not easily accessible as the **transport system** for such a vast country, much of it hostile terrain, was **poor and inadequate**. Scattered natural resources over sprawling areas without efficient means of communication made availability of raw materials, which were so very essential for the factories, extremely difficult. There was only one railroad in the 1840s and that served the iron mines of the Urals alone. The prominent railway connecting Moscow and St. Petersburg came as late as 1851. Waterways existed, but the boats were exceedingly slow due to **lack of steam power**. Moreover, over long periods in a year the rivers were frozen and were, therefore, beyond use. Similarly, the lands were covered with **snow** for the long winter months in Russia, making cultivation difficult. Even so, the country was agricultural. But cultivable land with fertile soil was very limited, as a result of which the harvests were never enough to be used as surplus capital for industrial growth.

Until the 1870s, the few Russian factories which existed had to compete with domestic products or the kustar industries, which enjoyed enormous popular demand as well as state encouragement. While in Britain and Germany, the factories wiped out a number of cottage industries, in Russia the case was completely different. It was only from the 1870s onwards when strong currents of industrialisation shook the vital economic bases of the Russian lands that the kustar industries suffered, as their goods could no longer compete in price with factory-made products.

The social structure of Russia was not favourable to industrial development. The Russian society, essentially **feudal** in character, did not have a middle class of any considerable size. Russian society was mostly divided into two broad classes—the landlords and the peasantry. Within the body of the peasantry, lay the huge number of serfs. In Russia, the different social layers varied depending upon the size of land belonging to them. The topmost level belonged to the big landlords or the **aristocrats**. They owned sprawling lands with a large number of **serfs** working on

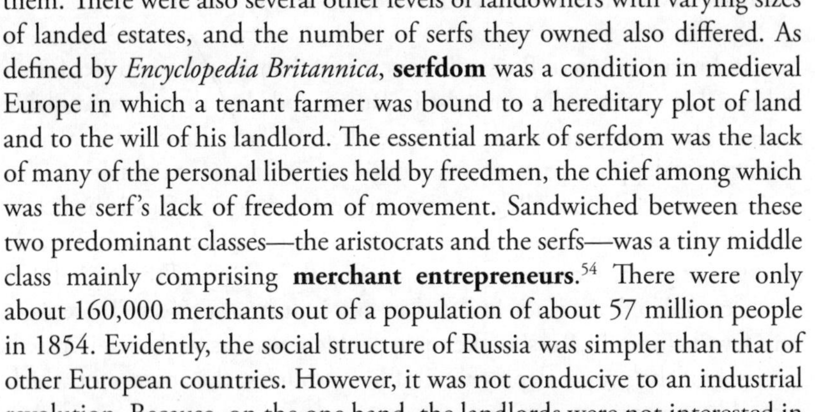

them. There were also several other levels of landowners with varying sizes of landed estates, and the number of serfs they owned also differed. As defined by *Encyclopedia Britannica*, **serfdom** was a condition in medieval Europe in which a tenant farmer was bound to a hereditary plot of land and to the will of his landlord. The essential mark of serfdom was the lack of many of the personal liberties held by freedmen, the chief among which was the serf's lack of freedom of movement. Sandwiched between these two predominant classes—the aristocrats and the serfs—was a tiny middle class mainly comprising **merchant entrepreneurs**.[54] There were only about 160,000 merchants out of a population of about 57 million people in 1854. Evidently, the social structure of Russia was simpler than that of other European countries. However, it was not conducive to an industrial revolution. Because, on the one hand, the landlords were not interested in entrepreneurial ventures as these were considered to be inferior pursuits for people of their stature. On the other, the serfs were tied to the lands of their masters and were not available for any other work. The irony of the situation, therefore, was that, despite the huge population, a steady supply of workforce for the industries was not forthcoming. The small middle class lacked the requisite man-power and capital as well as the autonomy, vision and resolution to bring about an industrial revolution.

The political situation was not ready either for an overwhelming economic transformation. Neither the church nor the state was favourable to any modern influence of the West. Any significant change, leave alone revolution, was perceived as a potential threat to their own power and authority, if not to their very existence. The vision of the rulers of the 17th and 18th centuries—Peter the Great and Catherine the Great, for example—was lacking among the rulers of the 19th century. They desperately **clung to the old order** and resolutely turned their faces away from the waves of change that were knocking at the doors of Russia. Economy in Russia was thus inextricably intertwined with an orthodox, reactionary political system. Even the reforms of **Alexander II, the Czar Liberator** as he was called, were not adequate and had many lacunae.

Moreover, Russia lagged far behind her western counterparts as far as adoption of technology and technical expertise were concerned. Bereft of modern scientific knowledge and technical skill, Russia failed to achieve any considerable breakthrough in the sphere of industrialisation till the last quarter of the 19th century.

FACTORS FAVOURING INDUSTRIALISATION IN RUSSIA

Late industrialisation in Russia did not imply that the pre-requisites for an industrial revolution did not exist in Russia and that they were available only in the countries which started earlier. In fact, Russia was a huge country overlapping parts of two continents and was extremely rich in natural resources, especially coal, iron-ore, oil and timber. Russia had close trade relations with other European countries and exported considerable amounts of grain. However, the revenue that flowed in and the capital that was accumulated were not invested in any industrial project. There were very few factories in Russia. The main problem was, as we have discussed, the issue of the proper deployment of her resources, the absence of which turned into a major constraint.

Russia had a large population to serve as **a potent labour force** for her industries. A major part of this population consisted of serfs, who could be effectively engaged in industrial enterprises. This is exactly what was done in the 'possessional factories' of Peter the Great and the 'manorial factories' of the nobles. But the serfs in the 19th century were closely tied to the lands of their landlords and could not be channelised into an effective mobile source of industrial workers. There were two serious obstacles in its way. First, there was hardly any industrial development in Russia where the serfs could be fruitfully absorbed. And second, even if there was any such development, the serfs themselves were not willing to leave their villages and neighbourhood and migrate to a new, unknown place. The serfs had to hand over most of what they cultivated to their landlords and the state, leaving bare subsistence for themselves and their families. In some areas where the land was not so fertile, the serfs paid quit-rent or obrok. The serfs then had to fend for themselves by working for wages in agriculture or factories or by setting up their own kustar industries, which were mostly run on a 'putting out' basis.

In short, therefore, Russia was a country of tremendous potential, which was yet to be exploited by overcoming the serious hurdles that eclipsed the benefits. In the second half of the 19th century, some important events took place which wholly transformed the existing situation, thereby paving the path for the advent of an Industrial Revolution. The first of these was the **Crimean War (1854–1856)** which severely exposed the weaknesses of the Russian army and its methods and techniques of warfare vis-à-vis the west European countries like England and France. Alexander II, the then Russian Czar, saw the military defeat of Russia as glaring evidence of the urgent need for a thorough overhaul of the entire system existing in Russia. He realised how stagnation and decay had crept deep into the roots of the vast empire. *The New York Times* reported,

> This conviction gave an enormous impulse to reform. It did not overthrow Czarism, for it reached the mind of the Czar as strongly as it did that of the nobles or the bourgeois class. All set to work with enthusiasm to correct those evils which had so plainly made Russia inferior to Western Europe when the fiery test of war was tried.[55]

It was clear that the Russian factories were unable to produce sufficient weapons, munitions and machinery, and that Russia was woefully lagging behind the other European countries, especially England, France, Germany in technology. At the same time, the Czar saw the pathetic state of the Russian serf-army as against the superior free troops from Britain and France. This revealed to him the need for emancipation. Consequently, the abolition of serfdom took place in Russia in 1861.

The **emancipation of serfs** was intended to release the serfs from the age-old grip of the conservative landowners and to utilise them as a mobile labour force that could be relocated to areas where industrial workers were needed. Not only would the freed serfs stimulate the industrial sector, but they would also contribute to the emergence of an **agrarian capitalism**. Given greater freedom, the peasants would develop more efficient and productive ways of farming. Historians, however, were sceptical of the usefulness of the serfs in bringing about the Industrial Revolution in Russia. Professor Baykov, for example, was of the view that 32 million or 42.3 per cent of the population were free of serf status and could effectively contribute to industrial development if other factors like availability of natural resources through better transport etc. were feasible. However, since natural resources were widely scattered and efficient transport was nearly non-existent, industrialisation was not possible. The scattered location of the natural resources, therefore, was a hurdle more irksome than the existence of serfdom.[56] Kemp observed that Baykov had overlooked the fact that although 32 million were free, they were **not a 'homogenous mass'** which could be mobilised as a viable labour force, because a considerable number of them were either not interested in factory work, or were simply unwilling to migrate to distant areas to take up jobs. The problem, according to Kemp, was not the existence of serfdom alone; but it was the entire system extant in Russia of which serfdom was an inextricable part, that was responsible for her backwardness. So, although the serfs became free, the rest of the archaic and putrefied system continued, with the result that the abolition alone could not lead immediately to any significant overhaul.[57] Indeed, the freed serfs, even after their emancipation, were tied to the prevalent old system because their freedom was saddled with certain conditions like redemption payments for the land which was allotted to them. This seemed to most of the ex-serfs extremely oppressive and vexatious. The responsibility for collection of redemption payments was vested in the village commune or *mir*. The result was that the serfs found it extremely difficult to make their ends meet after paying redemption and therefore continued, in many cases, to work on the lands of their old masters in return for wages. *The emancipation, for all practical purposes, remained a myth*. In fact, Gerschenkron referred to the political aspect of the decision. Stephen J. Lee, too, insisted on the political motives of Alexander II, one of whose intentions was to forestall a violent movement of the serfs to free themselves. He said to his nobles in 1856, "the existing conditions of owning souls [common parlance for serfs] cannot remain unchanged. It is better to begin to destroy serfdom from above than to wait until that time when it begins to destroy itself from below." The intended economic and social stability necessary for an industrial and commercial growth ended in failure. Trebilcock, too, did not accept the conventional theory that the emancipation gave a boost to industrial growth in Russia. He rather believed that it was the Crimean War which rang the fire-bell. He observed in 'The Industrialisation of Modern Europe, 1750–1914' (1998):

> The true stimulus for economic modernization was not the emancipation of the serfs but defeat in the Crimean war of 1854–1856. Backward Russia was trounced by the two most advanced industrial powers in the world at that time, Britain and France…If conservative, old regime Russia wished to remain a great power, she needed to attain a measure of advanced, new-regime industry.

The **Trans-Siberian Railway**, started in **1891**, played a crucial role in stimulating the Industrial Revolution in Russia. In Russia the 1880s saw the emergence of a brilliant statesman in the form of Sergei Witte, a mathematician with a proven track record of achievement. In 1889, he was placed as in-charge of the railway system and it was he who oversaw the completion of the massive project of the Trans-Siberian Railroad connecting western Russia with Siberia. It facilitated the transport of raw materials for Russia's heavy industries such as oil, steel and metallurgy.

Further, it promoted Siberian agriculture and helped significantly in exporting cheap grains towards the west, to central Russia and in the USA and Europe. The territories connected to it, either directly or through river transport, became major centres of export in Europe.

State help, particularly the sweeping economic reforms of Sergei Witte helped Russia enormously in catching up with the West. It was Witte who encouraged other countries to invest in Russia and thereby brought **substantial foreign capital**. By 1892, Witte was minister for transport, communication and finance. In 1897, he **moved** the **Russian rouble** to the **gold standard** and **improved foreign exchange**. Large amounts of capital flowed into Russia from France and Britain and funded not only new plants and factories, but also major infrastructural projects like railways, roads, telegraph lines, electrical plants, and chemical engineering. There were 269 foreign firms operating in Russia helping her to exploit her oil and mineral deposits. *By 1900 Russia was the world's fifth largest producer of steel, fourth in pig-iron and second in petroleum.* According to Soviet records, Russia's total production doubled during Witte's term of office, and the momentum he created enhanced it by 50 per cent more during the next decade.[58] Gordon Craig looked upon this Soviet estimate to be all the more credible for Czarist Russia, because, generally, the Soviet writers were scornfully critical even of the achievements of the Czarist regime.[59] Undoubtedly, a gigantic economic transformation took place which drastically changed the entire face of the Empire. "Russian industrial economy had progressed more in one decade than it had in the previous century."[60] This extraordinary rapidity in development was, argued Gerschenkron, the 'great spurt'.[61] And the state played a unique role in this amazing success story.

> The state participated directly in the nation's economy to an extent unequalled in any western country. In 1899 the state bought almost two-thirds of all Russia's metallurgical production. By the early 20th century, it controlled some 70 per cent of the railways and owned vast tracts of land, numerous mines, and oil fields, and extensive forests. The national budgets from 1903 to 1913 indicated that the government received more than 25 per cent of its income from various holdings. Russia's economic progress in the eleven years of Witte's tenure as minister of finance was, by every standard, remarkable. Railway trackage virtually doubled, coal output in southern Russia jumped from 183 million poods in 1890 to 671 million in 1900.[62]

In her industrialisation process, Russia had another advantage. Since she was a latecomer in the sphere of industrial growth, she had the **benefit of the experiences accumulated by her predecessors**. The technology of the early starters was available to her. She could benefit from the skill and innovations that the other industrialied countries, especially the pioneering country Britain possessed. Henderson had enlisted the assistance Russia received: It was **British capital, machinery and skilled labour** which helped Russia develop her **cotton** industry. John Ludwig Knoop, a cotton merchant and entrepreneur from the city-state of Bremen, used English credit and equipment to build cotton mills in Russia. The Thorntons, the British family of woollen merchants set up a large woollen mill in St. Petersburg on the banks of the river Neva. A Welshman, John Hughes, set up an ironworks in 1872 at the Donetz basin. During the 1880s, the Donetz basin developed into the principal iron and steel producing country; by 1913 it was making 74 per cent of all Russian pig iron. Coal mines were opened up in the Donetz basin by Belgian and French investors. Brothers from the USA, Ludwig and Robert Nobel, invested in the rich oil-fields of Baku on the Caspian Sea in 1877. The system of oil extraction in Russia at that time was very primitive. The oil was scooped out of the wells by hand and transported in wooden barrels on the carts pulled by donkeys.[63] Comparatively, in the USA, on the other hand, tank wagons had been in use for 10 years. The Nobel brothers wanted to start the process through pumps, pipes and railways. Pipes had to be brought from Glasgow. Since all these threatened the poor donkey drivers who would lose their means of livelihood, the authorities refused permission. Later permission was granted and work started in 1877. The donkey drivers and barrel-makers were given jobs in the oilfields. Ludwig Nobel himself constructed the world's first modern tanker. The Russian oil industry was completely revolutionised.

PATTERN OF RUSSIAN INDUSTRIALISATION

It is a fact that the pattern of Russian industrialisation was distinctly unique in several respects. One of the most important aspects was that like Germany, the Russian Industrial Revolution was based on heavy industry and goods were produced in bulk such as the cotton mills producing bulk cloth, iron-works, metallurgy, coal mining, oil drilling. Notwithstanding the fact that she was a late entrant, Russia developed her industries at a tremendous speed or 'great spurt'. Trebilcock, however, argued that the Russian Industrial Revolution did not happen all of a sudden. A very encouraging boost had been provided even before in 1857 by the passing of the 'railway *ukaz*' by Alexander II, the Czar Liberator who declared that "our fatherland, equipped with abundant gifts but divided by huge spaces, especially needs suitable communications."[64] This was in sharp contrast with the views of Czar Nicholas I's finance minister Count Igor Frantsevich Kankrin, who opposed the railways because he believed that they would lead to "frequent and useless travel, thus fostering the restless spirit of our age."[65] Railroads began to be constructed under Alexander II's reign. Mainly French funds supported the **Grand Societe de Fer Russes** that built several arterial lines which served both economic and military needs.[66] Since 1861 the industrial output growth rate had been maintained at approximately 6 per cent annual advance. And even before 1861 there existed industrial enterprises in Russia such as cotton textiles, sugar refining, distilling, etc. Moreover, Gerschenkron's theory was not applicable to other late developing countries. It thus becomes clear that Russia, no matter whether she had an industrial background or not, developed stupendously fast from the 1890s onwards and this itself gave Russian industrialisation a unique characteristic that distinguished it from that of other nations.

Russia's geographical terrain also defined her industrial pattern. Her huge spaces kept the modern factories and the village markets apart. It was difficult for the factories to send their products to remote corners of the country. The communication system was not developed enough for the purpose. Therefore, the peasant craft manufacturing or the kustar industries continued in full swing. In fact, industrialisation was a process of transition from limited handicraft products to bulk mechanised products. But this naturally took time. And, therefore, traditional modes continued in Russia well into the 20th century. Even in 1914, the industrial economy was characterised by this '**technological dualism**', that is, the co-existence of traditional methods alongside advanced modern technology. Not only handicrafts, the agrarian sector, too, dominated Russian economy as it did in Germany. As with the *junkers* in Germany, the big agriculturists and landlords in Russia began to sulk under the impact of the new socio-economic phenomena of loss of labour arising out of their migration to the urban areas in search of factory jobs, and also the impending introduction of free trade. This was a trend observable in all industrialised nations, but it varied in degree of intensity from country to country. In England, for example, the share of agriculture in national output was marginal, but in countries like France, Germany and Italy in 1910 it was significant—35 per cent, 25 per cent and 42 per cent, respectively while in Russia it was as high as 60 per cent.[67] This **predominance of agriculture in her economy** made her pattern of industrialisation quite distinct.

The **co-existence of backwardness and modernity**, therefore, was an essential feature of Russian economy in the 19th century. On the one hand, there was impressive industrial expansion with modern techniques, and on the other, a backward and feudal countryside with primitive methods of cultivation and a major component of impoverished peasantry. It was a paradoxical situation that Russia was a leading grain exporter in the last quarter of the 19th-century and accumulated significant capital from her grains when per capita food consumption among the people was low. Throughout the 19th century, the **Russian wheat crop** remained an important export commodity. By 1910, Russian wheat constituted 36.4 per cent of the total world export of wheat, although the general agricultural productivity was lower in Russia compared to other developed countries. Some of the surplus came from the larger estates which used wage labour and in the 20th century, benefited from the **reforms of Stolypin**. Some of the surplus also came from distressed peasants who were forced to sell portions of their produce above subsistence to meet the redemption payments. The peasants could not increase their produce as they exhausted the soil through their backward techniques. The opinions of the scholars are divided on the issue of peasants' misery. Kemp believed that the grains exported were not surplus in the true sense of the term, but beneath the apparent prosperity were **hidden signs of a deep subsistence crisis** among a significant part of the population. Geroid T. Robinson, the agrarian historian wrote, "The arrears (of redemption payments) present the best of all indices of the peasants' economic situation, …and the fact of their continued accumulation would seem to indicate a widespread and increasing distress in the village."[68] On the contrary, James Y. Simms Jr. argued that redemption arrears rather showed the losses incurred by the state, and that there was a significant rise in tax receipts in 1887, and this was not due to ruthless methods of tax collection, but due to excellent harvests which was an index of peasant well-being. There was also evidence that the peasants were paying indirect taxes on consumer goods, which proved, argued Simms Jr., that "they must have been the major consumer of the goods taxed, that is, sugar, matches, and so forth. Therefore, since they could purchase non-agricultural goods, one can hardly depict the rural sector as ravaged by a ruthless tax system."[69] However, there is no dispute on the issue of the co-existence in Russia of modern development and survival of aspects of antiquity and feudalism.

The investment of foreign capital was an indispensable part of Russian industrial growth. It was **British capital** which came first, as we have discussed above. From 1894 onwards, **France** became the principal creditor of Russia. The two countries came close to each other since the conclusion of the Triple Alliance of Germany, Austria-Hungary and Italy in 1882. It left Russia vulnerable, while France had been already diplomatically isolated after her disastrous defeat at the hands of Prussia in the Franco-Prussian War in 1871. From 1888, cheap loans were provided to Russia by the Paris Bourse (Paris Stock Exchange) with the purpose of aiding technologically deficient Russia to build her army as well as her railways so that they could bring troops to the German front. Relations between them were finally cemented by the signing of the **Franco-Russian Alliance in 1894**. Apart from France and Britain, capital poured in from **Germany, Belgium and Sweden** as well. A symbiotic relationship prevailed between Russia and her creditors. The former wanted foreign aid for her economic development, while the latter desired a favourable balance of trade. The primary aim of Russia's foreign policy was to scrupulously preserve foreign confidence in the rouble.

As we have already seen, the state played a significant role in the Russian scheme of development. Industrial revolution in this country occurred and continued under **severe state intervention**. There is a crucial difference between intervention and encouragement. In England, the role of the state could be perceived as encouragement, while in Russia it was nothing short of unmitigated intervention or control. There were tangible reasons behind this. Russia was predominantly an agricultural country whereas England was a 'nation of shop-keepers'. Trade and commerce was the backbone of British economy. It is true that the British government wanted to keep the landowners (a long-established class who were heavily represented in the Parliament) on their side, but at the same time, was deeply interested in industrial growth. The merchants and industrialists (not represented in Parliament) wanted to keep the wages low, which could only be done if the food prices were also kept low. The British

Government finally decided in 1846 in favour of **repealing the corn laws introduced in 1815**. In Russia, industrialism was a threat to the existence of the entire social and political structure and even to the Czardom. But at the same time the Crimean War had brutally exposed the weaknesses of the Russian government. Industrialisation was the only way to overcome these difficulties. The industrialisation in Russia, therefore, had to be done very cautiously under rigid governmental supervision.

There would be two water-tight compartments. On the one side there would be **the heavy industrial sector**, and on the other, the **village commune** which would keep its control over the peasants and hold them at bay from migrating to the factories and towns. Till 1890, despite reasonable industrial progress, Russia, in general, was considered by her state authorities as primarily an agricultural country. It was Witte who turned the focus to industrialism as the nation's key goal. We have seen how his efforts dramatically pushed forth an economically backward country to a platform which she shared proudly with other industrially advanced nations of the world. In the final reckoning, Russia despite all her industrial developments, continued to be predominantly anchored in a rural, pastoral culture. As Kemp remarked, "Surrounded by a sea of peasants an industrial proletariat of modern type had come into existence, highly concentrated around large, often foreign-owned, plants."[70] Even at the turn of the 20th century, 85 per cent of her population lived in villages. It was only the hopelessly destitute who, until 1914, moved to urban areas to work in factories and who went on to form **the revolutionary proletariat**. "But the enduring feature was village life. In the world's fifth biggest industrial economy, the vast majority of Russians would never have seen a factory."[71]

The Impact of Industrialisation

EMERGENCE OF CLASSES

A very important consequence of the Industrial Revolution was the changes in the traditional social structure. **Pre-industrial society**, as Pamela Pilbeam analysed, was a **society of orders or estates**. The first order was the clergy, the second the nobility and the third included the rest of the society. The Industrial Revolution gave rise to **a distinct new class—the**

working class or the proletariat. It was composed primarily of the new industrial workers. *A society of orders was slowly transformed into a society of classes.* The question is: What was the difference between these two? The distinctions among orders were based on the roles they played in society. The first order or the clergy, for instance, was involved in protecting the morals of the society and also in performing certain social responsibilities like births, deaths and marriages. The second order protected the state and society against foreign enemies as they were in high posts in the army. The third order took care of all the physical needs of the society by producing food, clothing and other essentials. The contributions of the nobles as magistrates, army officers etc. were considered valuable and commendable. With the passage of time, this particular social pattern was overhauled and a new structure emerged. The advent of industrialisation changed the entire basis of social distinctions. *Supreme social value was now attached to economic activities and the production of material goods. The society, therefore, was divided into groups on the basis of their economic contribution to the society.* Marx called these new social divisions **classes**. "Financial status and perceived status, the basis of a modern notion of class," wrote Pamela Pilbeam, "emerged within the vertical sub-sections of the society of orders."[72] Privileges acquired earlier through social status now gave way to power accessed through money.

A few critical factors determined the new pattern. The most important among them by far was the **impact of the French Revolution and Napoleonic Wars**. We have seen earlier that the Constituent Assembly, by its Report of 4 August 1789, had wiped out all vestiges of feudalism and the *Declaration of the Rights of Man and of the Citizen* of 27th August the same year had elaborated a list of rights and prerogatives of common man. The Napoleonic conquests ensured that the social changes in France extended to other countries subjugated by Napoleon. A very significant consequence of the French Revolution was the desecration of the Church and the suppression of the nobility. The Church was split up into 'constitutional' and 'refractory', and a large segment of the nobility migrated to other countries and came to be called the émigrés nobles. The Revolution ended in the triumph of the bourgeoisie. The predominance of the middle class was further heightened by their role in the Industrial Revolution. The accumulation of capital confirmed their newly exalted status in society. On the other hand, there emerged a whole body of workers who were the backbone of the factories. They were paid wages for the services they provided. In 19th-century Europe, these were the two most predominant social entities or classes—**capital and labour**.

The relationship between these two classes was acrimonious all through. Their fundamental interests clashed. The capitalists were interested in keeping the level of wages low, while the working class wanted higher wages to make ends meet. *The creation of the working class or the proletariat was one of the most vital legacies of the Industrial Revolution.* How did its formation take place? Scholars are divided on this: **Karl Marx** traced its origins to the rise of industrial capitalism which required the labour of a stream of workers who automatically became recognised as a class by themselves. As against this 'class in itself-for itself' model of Marx, **Ira Katznelson**, however, identified four distinct stages in the process of **class formation**. These were structure, way of life, disposition and collective action. The first two related to the Marxian model, that is, the beginning of enterprises, the employment of workers for wages, which constituted Katznelson's first level; the second level related to the living conditions, plight and miseries of the workers. This, according to Marx, contained the seeds of the emergence of a new socio-economic system that recognised the value of labour in the system of production. Disposition, the third level of Katznelson meant what the workers thought about their circumstances and their own lives and how they interacted with each other. Katznelson clarified that Marx was not in any way referring to class consciousness, but rather a kind of social and cultural exchange. "To say that people share dispositions," he wrote, "can mean that they have come to share understandings of the social system or that they have come to share values of justice and goodness."[73] The fourth level referred to collective action by workers to improve their own conditions and those of the society at large. Disposition, therefore, changed to behaviour. But while Katznelson made a clear distinction between disposition and collective action, and believed that interaction did not necessarily lead to movement, **E.P. Thompson**, on the contrary, considered the two almost inseparable, one necessarily leading to the other. In the words of Thompson,

> Class is a social and cultural formation (often finding institutional expression) which cannot be defined abstractly, or in isolation, but only in terms of relationship with other classes; and, ultimately, the definition can only be made in the medium of time—that is, action and reaction, change and conflict. When we speak of a class we are thinking of a very loosely defined body of people who share the same congeries of interests,

social experiences, traditions, and value-system, who have a disposition to behave as a class, to define themselves in their actions and in their consciousness in relation to other groups of people in class ways.[74]

Although Ira Katznelson deliberately eschewed a discussion on the issue of class consciousness, it did slowly creep in. It did not spring up all of a sudden, but developed over a span of time. Observed closely, it would be clear that **class consciousness** was indeed a by-product of the first three stages of Katznelson's scheme of class formation. The fourth level was a direct outcome of class consciousness, which was a strong feeling of solidarity and oneness among the workers. Their work conditions and ways of life were the foremost factors that led to the growth of class consciousness among them. 'De-skilling' and the prospect of proletarianisation created acute **fear among artisans** who, by dint of their proficiency and expertise considered themselves as distinct from ordinary unskilled workers. The advent of industries and machines posed a real threat to their traditional profession and the exclusive goods they produced. On the other hand, rigours of factory life, low wages and abominable living conditions cemented the bonds among workers and united them into a single organised class. According to E.P. Thomson, the factor of time or working hours as well as work-discipline were the other sources of deep-seated anguish. The workers who mostly migrated from the countryside were not habituated with the concept of time management of the urban factories and found it particularly onerous. Moreover, *time was regularly manipulated by the factory owners through tampering with the factory clocks to the benefit of the masters and to the disadvantage of the workers.*[75] Thompson quoted extensively from several verses of the Monitor's Order (Law Book of the Crowley Iron Works—a civil and penal code to regulate Crowley's refractory work force) to establish his point. Verse 31 declared:

> And whereas I have been informed that the sundry clerks have been so unjust as to reckon by clocks going the fastest and the bell ringing before the hour for going from business, and clocks too slow and the bell ringing after the hour for their coming to business,…it is therefore ordered that no person upon the account doth reckon by any other, bell, watch or dyall but the Monitor's, which clock is never to be altered but by the clock-keeper.[76]

These and other similar experiences of constant regulation, control and repression were responsible for the development of a unique class consciousness among the workers. It was argued by **C.A. Bayly** that most social historians until the 1970s felt that class consciousness was growing everywhere among the industrial proletariat.[77] The formation of **trade unionism** and **French style syndicalism** were the signs of the palpable forces of the time. Lenin, and later, British labour historians argued that an '**aristocracy of labour**' had been created, which was used to a middle-class lifestyle and thereby demanded what was perceived to be excessive wages, so much so that the major powers of Europe began to look for **cheaper sources of labour** elsewhere, especially overseas, and started carving out their own spheres of interest in different parts of the world. Thus began the reinforced version of what is called '**imperialism**' in the last quarter of the 19th century. In recent years, however, as Bayly observed, labour historians contended that the abysmal urban living conditions and the forms of industries with their particular work requisites determined the intensity of labour agitation, and not the impulse of class consciousness. Bayly wrote, "Just as nationalism was a consequence, more than a cause, of European wars, so working class consciousness was a consequence of turmoil and revolution, rather than its cause."[78] Such an understanding, he added, "liberates them (historians) from the assumption that 19th century working-class histories inevitably saw the growth of a united class consciousness which eventually exploded in revolution."[79]

Industrialisation and the growth of a substantial working class were not only inseparably linked, but also were strong political, economic and social symbols of the late 19th and early 20th century, and they engaged the attention of politicians, economists, socialist thinkers, litterateurs and artists alike. Whether a well-crystallised sense of class consciousness had come into being is a matter of debate, but "the idea of the working class as a world-wide phenomenon had become entrenched. In part, this was because governments now feared networks of syndicalists and anarchists, who had staged some extra-ordinary coups in the assassination of Russian czars and French presidents."[80] With the spread of Marxism, socialism as a tenet had assumed an international character. We shall study this in the following chapter.

EFFECTS OF URBANISATION: HISTORIANS' PERSPECTIVES

Industrialisation and population growth inevitably led to migration and urbanisation in 19th-century Europe. Urbanisation, despite its positive aspects like better job opportunities and income prospects, is always perceived as a negative trend in the sense that city life is associated with several concomitant problems—pollution, poverty, criminality, exploitation of children, lack of hygiene and sanitation, proliferation of slums, deforestation. In the new cities and urban centres, **new social classes** emerged. The social structure was transformed, leading to a divide within different classes in the society. While the working classes slogged long gruelling hours in dismal factories under unsafe conditions, only to go back completely exhausted to their crowded houses lacking sanitation and hygiene, and could barely make ends meet even after each family member put in labour, the factory owners accumulated immense profits and grew richer and more powerful. Society thus became broadly divided into two classes—**the rich** and **the poor**, or for that matter, **labour** and **capital**. This class divide motivated social thinkers to put forth several theories which would ameliorate the abysmal lives of the working classes and in course of time obliterate the sharp class distinctions that permeated European society of the 19th century.

Industrialisation and the growth of city life led to many **changes in the family structure** as well. In the pre-industrial society men were the primary 'bread-winners', although women and children too contributed to the combined family economy through the housework they put in. This picture changed with the Industrial Revolution. The wives and daughters went out for work and consequently attained a reasonable degree of independence from patriarchal control. *The traditional patriarchal predominance was substantially eroded.* The conventional role of women staying within the precincts of the four walls of the home and looking after children was radically transformed. Unmarried daughters took up jobs either in factories or as domestic help, trying to save their income for their own marriages and thus gained considerable autonomy. Many even lost touch with their families.

Paul M. Hohenberg and **Lynn Hollen Lees** referred to specific changes brought about by the Industrial Revolution. These were the **scale and density of urban growth**. The houses needed to be built in close proximity in order to save space. This further bred unhygienic conditions and had a serious impact on the health of the residents. Big spaces, on the other hand, were reserved for the bourgeois public. From the social point view, it helped develop new personal relationships. Being torn from their roots, individuals became more anonymous[81] and started building new relationships in their new environment. **New autonomous sub-cultures** were thereby created. Different people from different places, ethnicity, language and church merged together to form mosaics of disparate, heterogeneous groups. "However hard and unfamiliar the urban environment might be, it offered the chance to construct new lives with new webs of relationships, and multitudes grasped at that chance."[82]

According to **Bayly**, many old, traditional cities declined as a result of revolution as well as imperial expansion between 1776 and 1815. On the other hand, 'new' cities emerged as industrialisation and commercialisation expanded.[83] And these new cities developed distinctive social and cultural lives of their own, and were far more modern than the older cities. Hohenberg and Lees, however, did not agree with this close co-relation between industrialisation and development of new cities as pointed out by Bayly. Rather, in their view, "only twenty five new towns were created during this period, and they accounted for less than 10 per cent of the increase in urban population."[84] In Sweden, for example, 80 per cent of the growth took place in the existing cities irrespective of the fact that coal was not a main criterion in her industrialisation.

Historians, poets, novelists have persistently portrayed the horrifying state of moral depravity of the industrial towns. Charles Dickens' Coketown was a place of "unnatural red and black, like the painted face of a savage." Frederick Engels depicted industrial centres as the worst dreaded places of moral degradation, poverty, misery, violence and crime. Class warfare, alone could deliver the workers from such a deplorable state of affairs, Engels believed. Thomas Jefferson, the American president, wrote that "in the cities men are piled over one another and eat each other." Mental instability and psychological disorder were normal corollaries of such circumstances.

As far as the standard of living is concerned, apart from the examples of Coketown, the miserable conditions of the industrial towns were depicted by several writers, social and political thinkers. In 1838, a British member of Parliament described a cotton mill:

> [It was] a sight that froze my blood. The place was full of women, young, all of them, some large with child, and obliged to stand twelve hours a day. Their hours are from five in the morning to seven in the evening, two hours of that being for rest, so that they stand twelve hours a day. The heat was excessive in some of rooms, the stink pestiferous, and in all an atmosphere of cotton flue. I nearly fainted. The young women were

all pale, sallow, thin, yet generally fairly grown, all with bare feet—a strange sight to English eyes.[85]

In fact two broad groups of historians could be identified. A group of historians including the first great historian of the Industrial Revolution, **Arnold Toynbee**, and several well-known historians following him such as **J.L. Hammonds, E.J. Hobsbawm, E.P. Thompson**, as well as socialist thinkers such as **Auguste Blanqui, Frederich Engels** and others, were of the opinion that the standard of living and conditions of life were appalling in the days of the Industrial Revolution. However, another group of historians, like **M. Dorothy George**, **John Harold Clapham** and **Peter Lane** argued that the standard of life, in general, improved. In 1884 Toynbee wrote: "We now approach a darker period as disastrous and as terrible as any through which a nation ever passed; disastrous and terrible side by side with a great increase of wealth was seen an enormous increase of pauperism."[86]

As far as France is concerned, historian **Jacques Droz** has quoted extensively from several writings, especially from those of Auguste Blanqui. Dr. Guepin, for example, observed in 1845 that, "living meant not dying." In the Red Cross suburb of Lyons, **Auguste Blanqui** noted that the working girls earned "three hundred francs a year working fourteen hours a day at looms where they were hung from a strap in order to be able to use both their hands and their feet, and whose continuous and simultaneous movement was indispensable for the weaving of braid." Several travellers wrote that "the faces of the working women in England were bloated by gin, and their hair thick with grease;" while Blanqui came across "children in Rouen who were premature invalids, stunted to such a degree as to cause strange misconceptions as to their age," and in Lille "skeletal, hunch-backed, deformed and for the most part half-naked."[87] **Jacques Droz** offered certain data which showed a steady fall in wages, thereby meaning continuous fall in standard of living. In England, he noted,

> the domestic weavers earned only seven or eight shillings a week about 1840 instead of thirty shillings of 1820; they continued to eat oatmeal, but their consumption of wheat-flour and butter fell by half; as for meat and beer, they disappeared from their tables. In Germany, the index of real wages which stood at 86 units between 1820 and 1829, fell to 82 units between 1830 and 1839, and 74 units between 1840 and 1849, with even steeper falls in the crisis years (65 units in 1846 and 57 units in 1847).[88]

This kind of writing depicting a dismal picture of the lives of the common people came to be called **'pessimistic' history**. Engels and all other socialist and Marxist thinkers—E.J. Hobsbawm, E.P. Thompson for example—belonged to this category. These scholars were of the opinion that things were much better in pre-industrial Europe. Keeping England in mind, for example, Engels and Hammonds argued that the legislation of the Tudor and Stuart kings ensured a fair wage for the workers and this was destroyed during the Industrial Revolution as a result of which the sufferings of the workers at the hands of the employers increased immeasurably. According to them, things stabilised for the workers and started improving from 1820 onwards. According to **L.D. Schwarz**, real wages fell in London between 1750 and 1770 and between 1780 and 1800.

What happened then between 1770 and 1820? A group of **'optimist' historians** like **Peter Lindert** and **Jeffrey Williamson** noted a real-wage stability between 1755 and 1797; the wages fell after that till 1819, with a short period of rise between 1810 and 1815. **N.F.R. Crafts** reiterated that the industrialisation pattern in Europe in general, and in England in particular, was uneven and, therefore, consumption patterns also varied widely from place to place.

In fact, 'optimistic' history-writing began in 1925 when **M. Dorothy George** wrote *London Life in the Eighteenth Century*. Using mortality statistics as the basis of her work, she showed that standards of living on the whole improved in the 18th century. In 1926, Clapham wrote the leading 'optimistic' history and showed, on the basis of statistics of death rates, prices and wages, that the living conditions of English labourers certainly improved during the first Industrial Revolution. **Peter Lane**, too, disagreed with the 'pessimists' and noted that the Industrial Revolution undoubtedly created "an independent, self-confident and ambitious" wage-earning class—quite distinctive from their pre-industrial counterparts—who formed their own unions and strove to improve their conditions and status.[89] Moreover, argued Lane, conditions in pre-industrial England were often vitiated by rampant occurrences of harvest failures, famines and epidemics.[90] The indices prepared in the early 1980s by Lindert and Williamson strongly argued that standards of living sharply improved in Britain by as much as 50 per cent or more between 1780 and 1830 in particular, and about 100 per cent in the period between 1780 and 1850 in general. On the basis of north Staffordshire male wages, **E.H. Hunt** and **W. Botham** also concluded that real wages rose in much of north and mid-lands before 1820. The 'optimist' school, therefore, concluded that in general the Industrial Revolution brought about a rise in the standard of living of the people in Europe. As far as England was concerned, Lane put forth certain factors which helped to bring about a better lifestyle. One was a great increase in total production. Second, total exports were less compared to total production. For instance, he wrote that in 1830 exports constituted only 15 per cent of the national income. The rest were consumed by the people of the nation. A substantial volume of products—food, clothes, furniture, utensils, shoes, etc.—were available for the people to buy. The result was a fall in prices. In Lane's view, the fall was steepest in the period from 1820 to 1830.[91] All these factors contributed to a perceptible rise in the standard of living.

Anthropometrics in Britain innovated a unique method of assessing the living standards of British workers based on an **analysis of their height data**, on the assumption that height reflected the total and essential nutrients the body received. Following this method, **Stephen Nicolas** and **Richard H. Steckel** interpreted the living standards of English workers during 1770–1815 on the basis of the height data of 11,303 men tried in English courts and transported to the penal colony of New South Wales, Australia, between 1817 and 1840. These English convicts represented the working class at home. Their study revealed that the height of both rural and urban workers fell significantly after 1780. And there also urban Englishmen were a little shorter than the rural ones. This showed that urban workers received even less nourishment than their rural counterparts, perhaps due to the rise in food prices, unhygienic living conditions or harsh work conditions in the factories. In a recent study on heights of males from different parts of Europe, John Komlos, too, revealed that the heights, especially of men from western and northern Europe declined after 1760 and continued to decline till 1800. It recovered after that but again began to decline from 1830 till 1860.[92]

At any rate, although the real wages might have gone up, as the 'optimist' historians pointed out, and even the standard of living had marginally improved, or at least it had not fallen, the overall picture of the lives of workers was not satisfactory. The English workers were perhaps slightly better off than their continental counterparts. Even then, as John Merriman wrote, "human reality lay behind grim statistics."[93] The average life of a worker remained surrounded by '**dark satanic mills**', insanitary circumstances, exposure to diseases, insufficient or just about sufficient wages to meet his daily needs despite the fact that almost all family members put in their labour for basic sustenance, and low life expectancy. Wages might have been rising, but other indicators of life were quite abysmal. As we know, hard facts of life cannot always be measured by statistics alone.

Women in the Industrial Revolution

From times immemorial, women have always actively participated in keeping the structure of the family economy intact. The unmarried young girls as well as the married women who were wives as well as mothers contributed enormously to the income of the family in various ways. This role of women in the pre-industrial as well as industrial economy has been designated by Louise A. Tilly and Joan W. Scott as **women's work in the family economy**. Single unmarried girls contributed through housework like helping the mother in the kitchen or the garden, and also working as laundresses, seamstresses or spinners in proto-industrial units in order to augment the family income. In agricultural areas, they tended to the domestic animals, took care of the dairies and also engaged in cooking and stitching. Another category of female occupation was domestic service, which absorbed a substantial percentage of British as well as continental women. They worked 18 hours a day on average, but were generally well-fed. They worked to accumulate resources for their own marriages. Some of them sent money home, some did not. Many a times the girl's parents made arrangements with the employers to receive her wages directly from the latter. The married women were, in fact, the pivot of the family economy. They looked after the entire household and took care of all members and the farm and the poultry. They grew vegetables in the kitchen garden, tended the poultry and the cows, goats and sheep. The surplus farm or poultry products were taken by them to the local markets for sale. The money earned added to the family economy. A French rural proverb went thus: "No wife, no cow, hence no milk, no cheese, neither hens, nor chicks, nor eggs…"[94] Sometimes they did some extra work like shopping for others, tailoring, cooking part-time for other households or working in the fields in order to earn a little extra money. Lace-making, glove-making, hat-making, knitting, sewing—all came under the category of domestic manufacture. All of these tasks were of course in addition to bearing and nurturing children. In urban areas, women helped the male members in the family business. They functioned as shopkeepers, accountants, weavers, spinners. In both rural and urban areas women often served as nurses, especially wet-nurses.

Things went haywire with the death of the head of the family. The responsibility of running the household and rearing the children fell entirely on the widow. If she had grown-up children to support her, the situation would be better. But the task of young widows with small, orphaned children was the toughest. The money they earned through unskilled or even skilled jobs like lace-making, spinning, embroidering, etc., was extremely meagre. Such unfortunate families were forced to take recourse to charity. The children were mostly sent by their helpless mothers to charitable institutions and orphanages, where conditions were often quite appalling and heart-rending.

With the advent of industrialisation and consequent expansion of factory mode of production, there came a drastic change in the economy of the society in general, and the family in particular. Small home industries declined. To keep the family incomes intact, the women—both unmarried and married, mothers as well as daughters—started taking up jobs in factories in return for wages. *Family economy, therefore, gave way to family wage economy.* The lives of women in this new economy changed radically. The coming of industrialisation brought the opportunity of work in factories for the rural people. All the members of a family were engaged in industrial work and many of them migrated to cities and towns in search for work. The young girls, who generally worked in regional proto-industrial units like lace-making, spinning, weaving, etc., were mostly forced to take up jobs in industrial factories in urban locations primarily because as a result of fierce competition their traditional, old livelihoods were decaying. But, on the other hand, their financial contributions were of tremendous importance for the survival of their families. And once they moved out, they became used to city life, and seldom returned to the villages. The dilemma of married women was still more complicated. Need for money compelled them to work in industries, but they had to withdraw for childbirth and to look after infants. Financial urgencies, however, drove them to return to work as early as possible. Even after that, however, they found it extremely difficult to preserve a balance between the two worlds. The textile mills were the most congenial for the womenfolk and in France in 1856 half of the workforce in textile factories were constituted of women. At almost the same time, more than a third of all married women were employed in the textile mills of Lancashire in England. However, this did not mean that women were not engaged in other factories. Next to the **textile mills**, the **mines** drew the maximum number of female workforce.

Employment in industries brought about significant changes not only in the lives of women, but in the society at large. A very perceptible feature was a distinct change that crept into traditional family relationships. The daughters, as they migrated to the cities, became distinctly free of parental control and took life decisions themselves. This was **a clear erosion of patriarchal domination**, and one of the most important causes behind this was the **financial independence** that the young women experienced as they stepped out of the house. Abbe Cetty called this process a **"decline of paternal authority" in a working-class home**. The contribution of the daughters to the family fund gave them a certain voice in family decisions. In the family wage economy, all the family members contributed to a collective fund which supported family expenses. Till the children were small and the wife was pregnant or lactating, the man bore the burden of the family alone. But, "as the children grew, this situation improved; between 8 and 15 years of age, they stopped being a burden and became a resource; now all hands were occupied, and as small as their wages might be, they added a supplement to the budget that could not be disdained."[95] The significant input by the females of the house—single or married—in the wage economy silently transformed their status in the family as well.

The enhanced importance in the family, however, came at a very heavy expense. The **deplorable work conditions** in the factories and the drudgery at home made the lives of working-class women gruelling. Some of these challenges have been discussed above. The working hours were long and tiring. The children came home too tired to even eat properly. Again, they had to get up very early in the morning to be able to reach work on time. Sometimes after coming back from factories, they helped their mothers in housework or in some domestic enterprises like candle-making or sewing. In general, the daughters had enough sympathy and affection for their exhausted mothers. An Englishwoman wrote, "I have had many temptations in life, but my mother's face ('her poor and tired face') always seemed to stand between me and temptation."[96] Lottie Mary Cooper, born in 1890, wrote about her mother while visiting her in the cashmere rug weaving factory where her mother worked:

I can see our mother now, at her loom, there wasn't a stool to sit on, only a bar held by ropes. You couldn't sit on it properly, only lean against it while your feet worked the treadles. It was very hard work operating the treadles which worked the heddles … You could always tell someone who'd been working on the weaving all their lives for they walked in a special way, all that treadling.[97]

Often the works of the young girls were risky and dangerous. An English factory inspector reported that the children working at punching machines risked losing their fingers. An 8-year-old girl who opened the ventilation doors in the mines to let coal-wagons pass said, "I have to trap without a light, and I am scared. I go at four and sometimes half-past three… Sometimes I sing when I've light but not in the dark. I dare not sing then."[98]

FIG. 5.2: A Little Spinner in the Mollohan Mills, Newberry, South Carolina (1908)

Source: Library of Congress, Prints and Photographs division, Washington D.C. (Reproduction Number: LC-DIG-nclc-01451)

In spite of all their efforts and pains, women's jobs remained low paid in comparison to men's. That was because the women frequently left their

FIG. 5.3: Women Workers in New Gun Factory, Woolwich Arsenal, London, World War I

jobs to deliver and then nurture children. Young girls also got married and some of them quit working after marriage. The uncertain nature of their work kept their wages disproportionately low. Women were often forced to quit jobs due to domestic pressures and family responsibilities. This adversely affected the entrepreneurs as it resulted in an **instability in the labour market**; the absence of more and more married women created a scarcity of workforce and, therefore, an increasing demand for labour. Consequently, wages rose. This, obviously clashed with the interests of the manufacturers. Moreover, women's work was generally believed to be unskilled. Since they quit jobs off and on, they were not trusted with any specialised work. An overt discrimination between male and female workforce existed all along. Even the **lace industry** which was believed to be the largest employer of women, reserved its skilled jobs for men. **Sanya O. Rose** in her study 'Limited livelihoods' argued that until the end of the 19th century the lace industry was dominated by men. It was during this period that special machines were introduced which could be called 'women's machines'. They were so called because they could be easily manoeuvred by women. Earlier, the machines were too heavy and big to be handled by women. They could only work on smaller machines which were much less in use. However, according to Sanya O. Rose, that was not the sole reason. Even when hand machines were replaced with a wheel, boys were employed to turn the wheel under the supervision of men.[99] The general preference was for males. Women's work on the whole remained unskilled and low-paid. **Maxine Berg**, however, did not agree that there was ever any male predominance in the lace industry. Neither were the men interested in it. According to her, like lace there were certain other industries—the cotton textiles industry, woollen industry, silk manufacturing, hand-spinning, stocking, knitting, and so on—which were specifically 'women's industries'.[100] In the cotton factory, for example, women constituted a little more than half of the labour force in 1818. Many of these industries, for instance spinning and knitting, declined in the 18th century. They were replaced by some new industries—flax spinning in Scotland, silk throwing in Essex and jenny-spinning in Lancashire.[101] These new industries did not re-employ the women who worked in the old ones. Only those particular industries which required some special and fine aptitude—calico printing, spinning, painting on the biscuit etc.— employed women because it was felt that women had a knack for delicate work. Maxine Berg wrote, "Contemporary manufacturers believed that women and girls had a greater 'natural' aptitude for the manual dexterity and fine motor skills required by the new techniques …."[102] At any rate, these were exceptional cases. Introduction of new machineries or new technologies threw maximum women out of work. "Spinning jenny displaced nine in ten warp spinners and thirteen in fourteen weft spinners in the West of England."[103] Silk-throwing machinery, Jacquard loom, the flying shuttle, framework knitting machinery similarly ruined the opportunities of plenty of women.[104] The dismissed women then had to look to the fast growing domestic service or, as a last resort, to prostitution for their livelihood.

In fact, as far as women's work in the Industrial Revolution is concerned, limits and restrictions on the types of professions they could undertake were many. Apart from the technical snags, there were other **social restrictions** on the nature of women's work as well. Not all women's work was looked upon as respectable, especially for bourgeois women. Independent women entrepreneurs were not encouraged much as this would imply their interaction with several professional males like bankers, clerks, suppliers etc. This, it was assumed, transgressed the limits of gentility or respectability. As long as female enterprises remained restricted within the confines of the family, aided and assisted by family members, they were acceptable. But independent movements in the external world were definitely frowned upon. Women, in general, were looked upon as dependents. This was particularly applicable in case of middle-class women who were supposed to cling to their 'domesticity', otherwise their decent social status would be seriously at stake. The working-class women enjoyed greater freedom in this respect as they moved out of the precincts of the four walls of their homes to take up larger responsibilities in the industrial world and even migrated to distant towns and cities to sustain their families. However, in one respect, a point of similarity lay between the two. The women of both these classes played significant economic roles in their families by bringing in dowry (which varied from family to family depending upon their capacities), their own skill and talents and sometimes contacts. Women's role in the 19th century in private enterprises was undeniable. **Leonore Davidoff** and **Catherine Hall** have given many such instances. For, example, the son of an Essex farmer was educated and wanted to start a boys' school. He could eventually do so with 800 pounds that his wife had brought at marriage. An Ipswich baker, immensely hard-pressed with financial burdens, could pay off his flour supplier with the amount of 4 pounds lent by two of his sisters-in-law.[105] Several manufacturing units were dependent on the skills and talents of women. The food catering businesses like hotels and restaurants were often dependent on the recipes as well as culinary skills of their female family members. Even tailoring, embroidering and garment making enterprises were run on the basis of the talent of the wives, daughters, nieces of the entrepreneurs.

An important aspect of the time of Industrial Revolution was the **adoption of contraception in the lives of the workers**. The reason was their interest in keeping their families small. This contradicted their earlier notion of large families, which they believed meant more working hands bringing in more income. Life in industrial towns conflicted with this notion because the wife's wages were of crucial importance in a working-class household. The income of the head of the family was woefully inadequate to make ends meet. The need for money clashed with frequent pregnancies and childbirth, which bogged the women down at home.

Although they tried to go back to work as early as possible, the nature of factory labour and the long hours hampered infant care and child-rearing, as a result of which child sickness and infant mortality rose considerably. The health of the lactating mothers, too, was seriously affected due to excessive work both in and outside home. **Elinor Accampo**, in her study of the lives of ribbon-weavers and metal-workers of Saint Chamond, has shown how they hesitated to have a large number of children. They also chose not to have children immediately after marriage.[106] Understandably, this kind of mindset developed in working-class families in response to the pressures of the work culture that threatened their survival. The workers, therefore, decided to have fewer children in order to ensure their survival. This marked an essential difference from the middle class, who also preferred to have small families, but for different reasons. The middle class adopted fertility control in order to provide the maximum benefits to their children. They, unlike the working class, were driven to curtail the size of the family not for any financial constraint, but for the exclusive reason of maintaining a higher standard of living and for providing the best facilities to their children.

Another feature that industrialisation brought to modern society was a **significant rise in prostitution**. A large number of women who had moved out to urban areas in search of work in the newly emergent factories often found things much more arduous than they had imagined. Sometimes the number of workers far exceeded the quantum of work available. Further, there were lean seasons when the pressure of production in the industries was low, resulting in unemployment for many. During this time the unemployed female factory hands had no alternative but to find work as domestic help, or take to prostitution in order to survive. Occasionally, even married women took recourse to prostitution in return for money which they desperately needed to sustain their families under dire circumstances. Some women, however, were willing sexual workers without any moral compunction. The categories of prostitutes, therefore, ranged from high-class courtesans to impoverished working class or au-pair girls. Prostitution, however, went on surreptitiously behind common knowledge, with the government systematically discouraging them and the police regularly compelling the registered ones to undergo medical check-ups in order to prevent the spread of venereal diseases. Nevertheless, **John Merriman** wrote,

The number of prostitutes in London were so difficult to determine that estimates for the 1840s vary from 7,000 to 80,000. In St. Petersburg, there were over 4,000 registered prostitutes in 1870. In France, many prostitutes were former servants who, after an inopportune pregnancy, now walked the streets or beckoned from doorways....[107]

In the final reckoning, women's work, howsoever repetitive, exploitative or underpaid, contributed not only to their homes by raising the level of family economy, but also to the society and economy at large by making the Industrial Revolution successful. Undoubtedly there were certain sectors (discussed above) which employed women predominantly, and these sectors did achieve 'significant productivity gains'. Women's work, therefore, cannot in any way go unnoticed or unrecognised. In fact, they were the pivot around which the family, society and nations revolved.

Notes

1. Clive Trebilcock, 'The Industrialisation of Modern Europe, 1750–1914,' in *The Oxford Illustrated History of Modern Europe*, ed. T.C.W. Blanning (Oxford: Oxford University Press, 1998), 40–68.

2. E.J. Hobsbawm and Chris Wrigley, *Industry and Empire* (London: Penguin Adult, 1999), 52.

3. Alek A. Rozental, 'The Enclosure Movement in France,' *The American Journal of Economics and Sociology* 16(1): 55.

4. N.F.R. Crafts, 'The Industrial Revolution in England and France: Some Thoughts on the Question, "Why was England First?"' *Economic History Review* 30(3) (August 1977): 429–30.

5. W.W. Rostow, *The Stages of Economic Growth: A Non-communist Manifesto* (Cambridge: Cambridge University Press, 1991).

6. Trebilcock, 'The Industrialisation of Modern Europe, 1750–1914,' 46.

7. Ibid., 48.

8. Wendy Salmond, *Arts and Crafts in Late Imperial Russia: Reviving the Kustaar Art Industries, 1870–1917* (Cambridge: Cambridge University Press, 1996).

9. David S. Landes, *The Unbound Prometheus: Technological Change and Industrial Development in Western Europe from 1750 to the Present* (Cambridge: Cambridge University Press, 1969), 81.

10. Tom Kemp, *Industrialization in Nineteenth-Century Europe*, 2nd ed. (London and New York: Longman, 1985), 49.

11. William H. Sewell, 'Work and Revolution in France,' in *The Industrial Revolution*, ed. Steven M. Beaudoin (Boston and New York: Houghton Mifflin, 2003), 18.

12. E.J. Hobsbawm, 'The Crisis of the 17th Century—II,' *Past and Present* 6(1) (1954): 44–65.

13. H.R. Trevor-Roper, *The General Crisis of the Seventeenth Century: Reformation and Social Change* (Indianapolis: Liberty Fund, 1967), 80; see also *Past and Present* (16) (November 1959): 31–64.

14. Ibid., 43.

15. Francois Crouzet, 'England and France in the Eighteenth Century,' in *The Causes of the Industrial Revolution in England*, ed. R.M. Hartwell, 141–42.

16. Trevor-Roper, *The General Crisis of the Seventeenth Century*, 80–81.

17. William Doyle, *Origins of the French Revolution* (New York: Oxford University Press, 1980), 37–38.

18. Kemp, *Industrialization in Nineteenth-Century Europe*, 52.

19. Crouzet, 'England and France,' 142.

20. James Adams William, *Constructing the French Economy: Government and the Rise of Market* (Washington: The Brookings Institution, 1989), 46–47.

21. W.O. Henderson, *The Industrialization of Europe: 1780–1914* (New York: Harcourt, Brace & World, 1969), 98.

22. Ibid.

23. Ibid.

24. Ibid., 95.

25. Crouzet, 'England and France,' 173.

26. Sewell, 'Work and Revolution in France', 21.

27. 'Mercantilism and Colbertism in France,' The Centre for Economic Liberty, 21 April 2013. Available at https://centerforeconomicliberty.blogspot.com/2013/04/mercantilism-and-colbertism-in-france.html (accessed May 2025).

28. Ibid.

29. Kemp, *Industrialization in Nineteenth-Century Europe*, 59.

30. Sewell, 'Work and Revolution in France', 21.

31. Henderson, *The Industrialization of Europe*, 95.

32. Crafts, 'Industrial Revolution in England and France,' in *The Economics of the Industrial Revolution*, ed. Joel Mokyr (New Zealand: Allen and Unwin, 1985), 122.

33. Sewell, 'Work and Revolution in France', 22.

34. Ibid., 25.

35. Kemp, *Industrialization in Nineteenth-Century Europe*, 62.

36. Joel Mokyr, 'The Second Industrial Revolution, 1870–1914: Mutual Feedbacks of Science and Technology.' Available at https://faculty.wcas.northwestern.edu/jmokyr/castronovo.pdf (accessed May 2025).

37. David Mowery and Nathan Rosenberg, 'The Influence of Market Demand upon Innovation: A Critical Review of Some Recent Empirical Studies,' *Research Policy* 8(2) (April 1979).

38. Marie-Louise Pelus Kaplan, 'Merchants and Immigrants in Hanseatic Cities,' in *Cities and Cultural Exchange in Europe*, vol. 2 of *Cultural Exchange in Early Modern Europe*, eds, Donatella Calabi and Stephen Christensen (Cambridge: Cambridge University Press, 2007), 132–33.

39. Frederich Lutge, cited in Immanuel Wallerstein, *The Modern World System II: Mercantilism and Consolidation of the European World Economy 1600–1750* (Berkeley and Los Angeles: University of California Press, 1980), 22.

40. John Harold Clapham, *The Economic Development of France and Germany* (Cambridge: Cambridge University Press, 1966), 97; also quoted in Henderson, *The Industrialization of Europe*, 15.

41. Henderson, *The Industrialization of Europe*, 19.

42. Ibid., 65.

43. Ibid., 66.

44. Kemp, *Industrialization in Nineteenth-Century Europe*, 82.

45. Ibid., 85.

46. Ibid., 97.

47. Trebilcock, 'The Industrialisation of Modern Europe, 1750–1914,' 49.

48. Mikhail I. Tugan-Baranovskii, *The Russian Factory in the 19th Century* (Homewood: Georgetown, 1970).

49. Alexander Gerschenkron, 'The Rate of Industrial Growth in Russia since 1885,' *Journal of Economic History* 7(S1) (1947): 144–174.

50. Henderson, *The Industrialization of Europe*, 206.

51. Kemp, *Industrialization in Nineteenth-Century Europe*, 116–17.

52. Quoted in Henderson, *The Industrialization of Europe*, 206–7.

53. Ibid.

54. John Merriman, *A History of Modern Europe: From the French Revolution to the Present*, vol. 2 (London: W.W. Norton & Company, 1996), 688.

55. *The New York Times*, 5 October 1877.

56. Kemp, *Industrialization in Nineteenth-Century Europe*, 120.

57. Ibid.

58. Gordon A. Craig. *Europe Since 1815* (New York: Holt, Rinehart and Winston, 1966), 426.

59. Ibid.

60. 'Alpha History on Russian Industrialisation,' *Alpha History*. Available at https://alphahistory.com/russianrevolution/russian-industrialisation (accessed May 2025).

61. Trebilcock, 'The Industrialisation of Modern Europe, 1750–1914,' 46.

62. Alexander Ascher, quoted in 'Alpha History on Russian Industrialisation.'

63. Brita Asbrink, 'The Nobel Brothers Revolutionise Russian Oil Management,' *Branobel History*, https://www.branobelhistory.com.

64. Trebilcock, 'The Industrialisation of Modern Europe, 1750–1914,' 48.

65. T.G. Otte and Keith Neilson, eds., *Railways and International Politics: Paths of Empire, 1848–1945* (London: Routledge, 2012).

66. Ibid.

67. Trebilcock, 'The Industrialisation of Modern Europe, 1750–1914,' 51.

68. Geroid T. Robinson, quoted in James Y. Simms Jr., 'Crisis in Russian Agriculture at the End of the 19th Century: A Different View,' *Slavic Review* 36(3) (September 1977): 381.

69. Simms Jr., 'Crisis in Russian Agriculture,' 385.

70. Kemp, *Industrialization in Nineteenth-Century Europe*, 147.

71. Trebilcock, 'The Industrialisation of Modern Europe, 1750–1914,' 68.

72. Pamela Pilbeam, 'From Orders to Classes: European Society in the 19th Century,' in *The Oxford Illustrated History of Modern Europe*, ed. T.C.W. Blanning (Oxford: Oxford University Press, 1996), 100.

73. Ira Katznelson, 'Working-Class Formation,' in *The Industrial Revolution*, ed. Steven M. Beaudoin (Boston: Houghton Mifflin, 2003), 145.

74. E.P. Thompson, 'Time, Work-Discipline, and Industrial Capitalism,' in *The Industrial Revolution*, ed. Steven M. Beaudoin (Boston: Houghton Mifflin, 2003), 164.

75. Ibid.

76. Ibid.

77. C.A. Bayly, *The Birth of the Modern World, 1780–1914* (Malden, MA: Blackwell Publishing, 2004), 191.

78. Ibid.

79. Ibid., 192.

80. Ibid., 193.

81. Paul M. Hohenberg and Lynn Hollen Lees, *The Making of Urban Europe, 1000–1950*, in *The Industrial Revolution*, ed. Steven M. Beaudoin (Boston: Houghton Mifflin, 2003), 132–133.

82. Ibid.

83. Bayly, *The Birth of the Modern World*, 186.

84. Hohenberg and Lees, *The Making of Urban Europe*, 131.

85. Louise A. Tilly and Joan W. Scott, *Women, Work, and Family* (New York: Routledge, 1987), 64; also quoted in Merriman, *A History of Modern Europe*.

86. Arnold Toynbee, *Lectures on the Industrial Revolution in England* (London: Rivingtons, 1884).

87. Jacques Droz, *Europe Between Revolutions, 1815–1848* (Glasgow: Fontana Collins, 1981), 64.

88. Ibid., 65–66.

89. Peter Lane, *The Industrial Revolution: The Birth of the Modern Age* (UK: Barnes & Noble, 1978), 247.

90. Ibid., 248.

91. Ibid., 249.

92. John Komlos, 'Shrinking in a Growing Economy? The Mystery of Physical Stature during the Industrial Revolution,' *Journal of Economic History* 58(3) (1998).

93. Merriman, *A History of Modern Europe*, 703.

94. Quoted in Tilly and Scott, *Women, Work, and Family*, 45.

95. Ibid., 105–6, from Louis Reybaud, *Le Coton* (Paris, 1863), 115.

96. Ibid., 143.

97. Sonya O. Rose, 'Limited Livelihoods', in Beaudoin, *The Industrial Revolution*, 221.

98. Merriman, *A History of Modern Europe*, 698.

99. Rose, 'Limited Livelihoods', 218.

100. Maxine Berg, 'What Difference Did Women's Work Make to the Industrial Revolution?' *History Workshop Journal* 35(1) (1993): 27–29.

101. Ibid., 29.

102. Ibid., 35.

103. Ibid., 40.

104. Ibid.

105. Leonore Davidoff and Catherine Hall, 'Family Fortunes', in Beaudoin, *The Industrial Revolution*, 211–12.

106. Elinor Accampo, 'Industrialisation, Family Life, and Class Relations,' in Beaudoin, *The Industrial Revolution*, 200–201.

107. Merriman, *A History of Modern Europe*, 697.

CHAPTER 6

Socialism, Marxism and Utopia
International Working-Class Movements

In the wake of the Industrial Revolution, as we have seen in the last chapter, the society in Europe became divided into two broad classes—labour and capital. In material terms, the position of the two classes was diametrically opposite. The industrial class was becoming richer and richer while the working class was becoming poorer and poorer. Such disparity seriously disturbed a section of the population. Scholars and intellectuals began to propose varying solutions with a view to minimise this gaping divergence in society. These doctrines, starting in Europe from the late 18th century (that was the time when Industrial Revolution first happened in England), varied from time to time and from country to country. These egalitarian theories propounded by different scholars (also called the socialists) which emphasises public rather than private ownership and control over property and resources, are collectively called socialism. *Socialism refers to both an ideology and an economic system.* Under this particular 'ism', various theories of socialism as well as international working-class movements, which were founded upon socialist tenets, will be discussed.

Socialism and its Many Varieties

Socialism can be defined as a system or an organisation with deep and wide-ranging political, social and economic implications. It advocates that the means of production, distribution and exchange should be owned or regulated by the society or community as a whole. The word 'socialism' encompasses a variety of ideas—for example, communism, fabian socialism, syndicalism, anarchism—that have certain distinctive common elements that might bind them together in a common cluster, but, at the same time, exhibit unique characteristic concepts that clearly distinguish them from each other. Dictionaries often distinguish between socialism and communism by defining socialism as **midway between capitalism and communism**, advocating collective ownership of the means of production and distribution of goods.[1] The **communists** insisted upon radical egalitarianism and rejection of basic precepts of industrialisation, that is, accumulation of wealth and ownership of industries by a small group of capitalists. Their **emphasis on proletarian interests** distinguished them from other social thinkers who neither rejected the progress of technology, nor the industrial revolution, but rather desired large-scale reforms that aimed at mitigating the evil effects of industrialism in accordance with the spirit of enlightenment. *Socialism, in general, did not intend to restructure the entire social composition, but aspired to bring in reforms from within the order* to make it a better place to live in. The common element that bound communism and socialism together was their **indictment of liberalism**. Communism wanted everything that socialism stood for, and went farther ahead. In this sense, it can be said that all communists were socialists, but all socialists were not communists. That brings us to two broad divisions— **early or utopian socialism**, and **scientific socialism or the dialectic materialism of Marx**. There is also a third category that includes all other varieties of socialism.

The origins of socialism can be traced to the onset of the Industrial Revolution. Industrialisation led to accumulation of capital. Prior to the Industrial Revolution, in the days of what the socialists called 'bourgeois liberalism', protection of private property was one of the sacred duties of the King. Even in the heydays of absolutism, the monarchs of Europe were bound by the principle of **sanctity of private property**. Thinkers like **John Locke** (1632–1704), considered to be one of the earliest exponents of liberalism, assigned immense importance to private property. So had Aristotle, who believed that property earned by one's own labour was one's exclusive right. With the income one earned, one was entitled to have servants. The modern concept of capital and labour had not emerged then. Locke, too, was perfectly comfortable with the system of servants or serfs, as he himself was an absentee landlord and, as **George Lichtheim**, the well-known historian of socialism[2] pointed out, a stockholder in the slave trading Royal African Company. *Life, labour, property and liberty* were all interconnected, claimed Lichtheim. Society, whether agrarian or urban, was a feudal society based on the division of labour where everyone had an assigned role. It was a society based on the independence of the small peasant and the urban artisan.

This way of life changed drastically with the coming of the Industrial Revolution as the conventional system of production and distribution were radically altered with mechanisation. In England where the First Industrial Revolution happened, an agricultural revolution preceded the industrial. Under its impact, the small farmer and the artisan were almost wiped out. The peasants who became redundant due to the advent of machines migrated to the cities and towns in search of livelihoods. It swelled the number of labourers and immediately resulted in a fall in wages and living conditions. In Chapter 5, we have discussed in detail the abominable conditions of the working class. The political and social conditions of those days were generally favourable to the owners of factories and capitalists. The state paid little attention to the grievances and sufferings of the factory labourers. Instead of submitting to social and economic injustice, the workers began to organise themselves to improve their lot. This was the origin of the **trade union movement** which grew stronger as workers grew more aware of their rights, the extent of their exploitation, and found ways of articulating their demands. The state gradually gave up the laissez faire policy of the 18th century and state intervention provided for curtailment of the rights of the capitalist and expansion of the rights of the workers. But the movement of the state in this matter was slow. Intellectuals and social thinkers were unhappy and began to think of the **problem of labour-capital relationship** from a new perspective. Their ideas led to the development of a body of doctrines generally known as socialism.

It is indeed astonishing that although the First Industrial Revolution began in England, the **major early socialist theories**, with the exception of that of Robert Owen, **originated in France**. As Lichtheim argued in Hegelian style, "A simplified account of the birth of socialism might begin with the statement that the industrial revolution furnished the thesis and the French Revolution the anti-thesis, while socialism brought about a synthesis of these two parallel but unconnected phenomena."[3] The contention that the Industrial Revolution furnished the thesis seems clear. It was the Industrial Revolution which ended feudalism and gave birth to the eternal conflict between labour and capital. The French Revolution aimed at wiping out all inequalities, while the Industrial Revolution created new social classes but also deepened the existing divisions in society based upon inequality. But did the French Revolution really produce the antithesis? On the face of it, it is perplexing because it was the French Revolution that **transferred power** from the **aristocracy to the bourgeoisie**. And it was the bourgeoisie who comprised the **mercantile and capitalist class**. By concentrating economic as well as political power in the hands of the bourgeoisie—the mercantile entrepreneurs—*did not the French Revolution too foment the same class conflict as the Industrial Revolution?*

Like the Industrial Revolution, the French Revolution was a direct assault on the feudal order. However, on a deeper probe, the distinctions between the two revolutions become clear. Although the French Revolution symbolised the rise of the bourgeoisie, it was a **landed and professional bourgeoisie** all the same. The industrial, factory-owning bourgeoisie had not yet emerged in France. The bourgeois revolution in France confirmed the distribution of the émigrés as well as Church lands among the poor and landless peasants by parcelling out small plots of land. In the French Revolution, the bourgeoisie and the sans-culotte fought together against the feudal aristocracy. An industrial capitalist breakthrough had not yet appeared in France, which still clung to the fundamental precepts of *liberté*, *égalité*, and *fraternité* in its own way. *A distinct working class or proletariat, therefore, had not yet emerged in France.* The Industrial Revolution, on the other hand, symbolised conflict between the bourgeoisie and the proletariat; in other words, inequality was the key word. In that sense, the French Revolution was the anti-thesis of the Industrial Revolution. Between these two opposing forces, socialism acted as a third force—a midway path or a synthesis.

Utopian Socialists

The Latin word *utopia* means an imaginary place or society supposed to be ideally perfect in its social, political or moral aspects. Since it is not practically viable to translate such an idea or dream into reality, it is taken as a visionary concept. **Sir Thomas More** envisioned an imaginary island in 1516 and called it 'Utopia' representing a society flawless from every point of view—political, legal and moral.

An Early Socialist in England

The utopian socialists were those who, in tune with utopian ideology, aimed at creating a perfect, blissful society where people would live happily and harmoniously. Among the socialists who were identified as utopian, three were most prominent—Robert Owen of England and Claude Henri de Saint-Simon and Charles Fourier of France. **Robert Owen** was born in Newtown, Montgomeryshire, in the family of a saddlemaker and ironmonger. He left home at the age of nine and took up work in the shop of a draper, James McGuffog, who was also his neighbour in Newton. Prior to that, he had been briefly educated in a school where he excelled in "games, dancing and lessons". After a year of his apprenticeship in Newtown, he left for London and from there finally settled in a cotton factory in Manchester as its manager. His experiences there as the manager of 500 men and women transformed his views. He wrote:

> My reason taught me that I could not have made one of my own qualities,—that they were forced upon me by nature;—that my language, religion and habits were forced upon me by society … Thus was I forced, through seeing the error of their foundation, to abandon all belief in every religion which had been taught to Man. But my religious feelings were immediately replaced by the spirit of universal charity.[4]

Owen applied his notions of **universal charity** to the New Lanark Mills where he became the manager and eventually married Caroline, the daughter of David Dale who was the owner of the New Lanark Mills. His primary goal was to create a community with a good environment and good human beings. In his view, the noble qualities of a person depended on his environment and education. He abolished harsh treatment from the factory and the school because he believed that it was cruelty that debased human qualities. Owen wanted to improve the conditions of labour by reducing the hours of work. The working hours of children were reduced to 10. He also stopped the employment of children below 10. He opened schools for the children of the factory workers because he believed education helped the development of the potential and good qualities of an individual. Young children were supposed to attend school full-time, while older children were to attend school part-time after their factory work. The education at New Lanark aimed to produce loving, compassionate human beings. He believed that only children who were treated tenderly could love and respect their fellow beings. Owen's instructions to the teachers were as follows:

> They were on no account ever to beat any one of the children or to threaten them in any word or action or to use abusive terms; but were always to speak to them with a pleasant voice or in a kind manner. They should tell the infants and children (for they had all from 1 to 6 years under their charge) that they must on all occasions do all they could to make their playfellows happy—and that the older ones, from 4 to 6 years of age, should take especial care of younger ones, and should assist to teach them to make each other happy.[5]

Shops were opened for workers from where quality goods were available at reasonable prices. New Lanark, which was the base for his unique experiment, was internationally famous.

Owen's associates and acquaintances considered him to be crazy for his social ideas and concern for the poor, especially in view of the fact that he himself belonged to the capitalist class. Owen left for the United States as he became totally disillusioned with the attitude of the British middle class. He tried to establish an ideal society in the US, and spent almost two-thirds of his fortune on it. Unfortunately, it failed for several reasons. However, as Jacques Droz observed, Owen died a contented man that he was far ahead of his times and truly endeavoured to serve humanity.

Early Socialists in France

The three utopian socialists mentioned above were born and lived almost at the same time. The most utopian among the utopian socialists was **Charles Fourier**. He refused to accept the realities of the world around him. He rejected industrialism altogether. A humble shop-assistant of very limited education, Fourier was born in Besancon in France in 1772. He was moved by the drudgery of the life of the working class and wished to create a world **based not upon coercion but upon cooperation**. Adopting from the ancient Greek phalanx (the impenetrable fighting unit), he termed the world he conceived *phalanstère*. It meant a self-contained community in which 1,620 members lived together in perfect unity and harmony. Now the question is why this strange figure of 1,620? The answer is that, according to Fourier, there were 810 different psychological types. If this number is multiplied by two (male and female), we get 1,620. Of this, he believed, seven-eighths of the members ought to be cultivators and manufacturers; the rest would be capitalists, scholars and artists. He wrote,

> an experimental phalanx, being obliged to start out with agricultural labour, will not be in full operation until the month of May (in a climate of 50 degrees, say in the region around London or Paris); ... there will be barely five months of full practice in a region of 50 degrees: the work will have to be accomplished in that short space.[6]

His ideal, therefore, was an agricultural society. The world of commerce he detested for its immorality. In his book *The Social Destiny of Man*, he argued that "truth and commerce are as incompatible as Jesus and Satan." He was unhappy about the position of women which, in his opinion, was a kind of slavery. No social progress was possible without the equal treatment of women. Charles Fourier wanted to conduct a single experiment to show the world how successful and fantastic his concept was. He believed, "If an experiment is made in minimal harmony, with two or three hundred members, or on a limited scale with four hundred members, it would be possible, although difficult, to use a monastery or palace for the central edifice."[7] He only needed financial support from a benevolent philanthropist to translate his dream into practice. He made a public announcement that he would be at home everyday at noon to wait for any generous patron to turn up to facilitate his project. Regrettably, however, he waited for 12 long years but no kind-hearted donor ever came forward. Even so, it should not be assumed that Fourier's life was a failure. Posterity remembers him as a great thinker, and his *phalanstère* inspired later phalanxes like the short-lived Book Farm in Massachusetts (1841–1846), and also the North American Phalanx at Red Bank, New Jersey. He further inspired the founding of the community called La Reunion near present day Dallas, Texas. Fourier's ideas continued to influence the 1848 Revolution and the Paris Commune as well as the theories of Proudhon, Marx and Engels.

Claude Henri de Saint-Simon was the son of a minor noble in France. Born in Paris in 1760, he served in the French army and fought the American War of Independence in the battle of Yorktown and was imprisoned. He was also imprisoned in France during the Reign of Terror and barely escaped execution. After his release, he speculated in émigrés property and earned substantial wealth. He owned a salon that attracted many intellectuals and influential people. But soon his money was exhausted and his later years were marked by penury. However, his experiences during the Terror made him intensely bitter towards revolutionary brutality. He saw the excesses of feudalism in the pre-revolutionary period and the excesses of liberalism and radicalism during the Revolution in France. He, therefore, felt the necessity of reorganising society on the basis of industrialisation. He proposed that control of society be vested in the hands of the industrialists, and the administration of the Church in the hands of the scientists. A series of periodicals, *L'Industrie* (1816–1818), *La Politique* (1819), *L'Organisateur* (1819–1820) and *Du Systeme Industriel* (1821–1822) contain most of his socialist theories. His call for a 'science of society' encouraged the study of sociology and economics as fields of scientific study. In his prominent work, *Nouveau Christianisme* (1825) which he could not complete, he developed **a new interpretation of Christianity** as a religion founded upon the basic elements of both Catholicism and Protestantism in the interests of all sections of society. This was his "new Christianity" that would preach the teachings of Jesus to evolve a new society devoted to serve the poor and the needy.

The ideas of Saint-Simon raised a few important issues. *First*, why did he want society, or rather the political, economic and social systems to be organised and controlled by the '*industriels*'? The 'industriels' or the industrialists were, however, the bourgeoisie for Marx, Engels and other socialists, who viewed them as the exploiters of the hapless proletariat and who were, therefore, to be curbed. Marx asserted that the leadership of the bourgeoisie must be replaced by that of the proletariat. Saint-Simon, on the contrary, wished to entrust governance in the hands of the capitalists, whom he considered to be the competent and wise men of society. He wanted power to be shifted from the *oisifs* (idlers) who, in his opinion, were capable of doing nothing except monopolising capital, to the industrial capitalists who, he believed, were people with great organisational skill, proficiency and managerial qualities. There lay the difference between the early socialists like Saint-Simon and the later socialists. In the days of Saint-Simon, when industrialisation had emerged only in Britain, the political, economic and social power was in the hands of the nobles and the clergy who monopolised all the privileges. A revolution had to be fought for the transfer of power to the bourgeoisie. The triumph of the bourgeoisie was complete after the Revolution. Saint-Simon, being the son of the French Revolution during which he was close to the Jacobins, advocated this victory. To him, it was the victory of the Third Estate, that included the workers as well. The later socialists, especially those after the

Age of Revolution, spoke of the evils of bourgeois rule, primarily capitalist bourgeois rule, and advocated reforms and changes accordingly. Liberty and equality were not the main objects of Saint-Simonian ideology, they were the inevitable consequences of a well-governed, good society. *Second,* Saint Simon dreamed of a Church that would be run by logical, scientific minded people, and not a clergy that was subjected to scathing criticism from even erudite people like Voltaire.

Louis Blanc, prominent among the admirers of Saint-Simon, emphasised upon the role of the state in industrial world. He endorsed the principle of the Saint-Simonians of "having rehabilitated the authoritarian principle." Like **Villeneuve-Bargemont** who viewed the governments as "the common centre of light, effort and power, whose rays could reach the farthest ends of the kingdom", Louis Blanc believed that the state could very effectively, through various means, ameliorate the conditions of the poor and the needy. He was, therefore, the major spokesman for both socialism as well as Jacobin democracy. His valuable work *Organisation du Travail* preached the basic tenets of socialism to the working class by emphasising that the government's guarantee of employment as 'right to work' was the fundamental right of a citizen. However, his concept of factory was a worker-run industrial co-operative organised on a national level by a unicameral democratic parliament.

Pierre-Joseph Proudhon, also known as the '**father of anarchism**' was born in Besancon, France to Claude-Francois Proudhon, a brewer and a cooper—a simple and honest man who lived his life in poverty. Proudhon continued his study in the college of Besancon where his mother got him enrolled with the help of Claude Francois' former employer and later in the Academy of Besancon with great financial difficulty. Although he was a certified compositor in the printing trade as well, he took enormous interest in political and philosophical books and essays and chose to write. His ideas and concepts evoked passionate thoughts of great later thinkers like Marx and Mikhail Bakunin. In fact, Proudhon was the first to call himself an anarchist. He was an anarchist in the sense that he envisioned *a society in which individuals formed the sovereign power*. It was an anarchical state in which sovereignty rested in the people. This was Proudhon's concept of a "society without authority." In his work of 1851, *The General Idea of the Revolution*, he wrote a sub-chapter entitled 'What is a Government' where he explained,

> To be Governed is to be watched, inspected, spied upon, directed, law-driven, numbered, regulated, enrolled, indoctrinated, preached at, controlled, checked, estimated, valued, censured, commanded, by creatures who have neither the right nor wisdom nor the virtue to do so. To be Governed is to be at every operation, at every transaction noted, registered, counted, taxed, stamped, measured, numbered, assessed, licensed, authorised, admonished, prevented, forbidden, reformed, corrected, punished. It is under pretext of public utility, and in the name of the general interest, to be placed under contribution, drilled, fleeced, exploited, monopolised, extorted from, squeezed, hoaxed, robbed; then at the slightest resistance, the first word of complaint, to be repressed, fined, vilified, harassed, hunted down, abused, clubbed, disarmed, bound, choked, imprisoned, judged, condemned, shot, deported, sacrificed, sold, betrayed; and to crown all, mocked, ridiculed, derided, outraged, dishonoured. That is government; that is its justice; that is its morality.[8]

Not only was Proudhon against concentration of power in the hands of the government, but was also against the capitalist and the Church for the same reason. "This trinity of absolutism is as baneful in practice as it is in philosophy", he wrote. He identified himself in the form of an exchange with a fictitious interlocutor in the following words:

> "Well you are a democrat?"—"No."—"What! You would have a monarchy."—"No."—"A constitutionalist?"—"God forbid!"—"You are then an aristocrat?"–"Not at all."—"You want a mixed government?"–"Still less."—"What are you then?"—"I am an anarchist."[9]

In fact, Proudhon observed, **ownership of all sources of wealth**—mines, canals, railways, factories, agricultural units—should be handed over to **democratically organised workers' associations**. Together they would form a vast federation of companies and societies jointly combined on the basis of equality and co-operation. He called this economic system '**mutualism**'. He further elaborated his idea of ownership of property in his first work, *Qu'est-ce Que la Propriété* (What is Property?) in 1840. According to Proudhon, **property is theft**. Because, in his view, property can be accumulated only by depriving others of their basic dues. The workers, according to him, are never paid the real worth of their labour. They are paid a fixed wage which, Proudhon thought, was much below the value of the labour they had put in. The balance of the cost of production (including wage) and the actual price was pocketed wholly by the owner of the means of production instead of distributing it among the workers. This, in Proudhon's opinion, was nothing but theft.

Proudhon's mutualistic philosophy was largely influenced by **Hegel's dialectical method**—the co-relationship between thesis, anti-thesis and synthesis. There existed a thesis, that is, the existing society in which extreme inequality prevailed—for example, that between the capitalist and the worker. The anti-thesis of this was a world of equality which was Proudhon's ideal. Proudhon worked out a synthesis between these two opposites and the result was his vision of workers' associations combined on the basis of co-operation and equality.

Early Socialists in Germany

Another country which produced a plethora of socialist thinkers was **Germany**. The early English and French socialists had a profound influence on the German intellectual circle. Another source of inspiration were the Hegelians, especially the **neo-Hegelians**. The earliest German socialist, also called the '**father of German socialism**', was **Ludwig Gall** who was born in Trier, also the birthplace of Marx. In 1835 in a pamphlet Gall had divided the society into two broad classes—the labourers who produced all wealth, and the capitalist owners who reaped all the benefits. The advantages of the rich increased at the same rate as the conditions of the worker decreased. Gall wrote, "The privileged rich and the working classes are fundamentally opposed to each other by contrary interests; the situation of the former improves in the exact proportion in which the situation of the latter worsens, and becomes more precarious and wretched."[10] His dream was to establish a phalanstéré in the United states. Gall travelled far from home and went to America at the age of 28 with the purpose of encouraging the settling of German immigrants in Pennsylvania. He carried 11 indentured servants with him. He went to Pennsylvania in 1819 in search of a site for a phalanstéré. His efforts, however, failed and he returned to Germany almost a broke and lived in his home in Trier. At this time, he leaned deeply towards socialist thought and became an ardent follower of Charles Fourier. At any rate, Gall's writings made men who mattered in Germany look askance. According to Boris Nicolaievsky and Otto Maenchen-Helfen, "The police were aware of Gall's very suspicious way of thinking" and perceived that he "required a specially sharp watch to be kept on him".[11] Although his socialism falls under the category of utopia, his primary contribution was his influence on German intellectual and elitist thinking, and evoked different theories of socialism in Germany.

Among the early German social thinkers, **Lorenz Von Stein**[12] occupies a prominent place. Although not a socialist or a communist in the proper sense of the term, he was an erudite scholar of public administration, an economist and sociologist, whose ideas on industry and labour, (Stein called them the "social movement") left invaluable impression on the theories of socialism. Stein assigned considerable significance to the relationship between the worker and capitalist in society and the concomitant problems associated with it. Movements were required to solve these issues and Stein called them the "Social movements". Such movements were necessary to forestall a social revolution which was, Stein believed, likely to be much more catastrophic than the previous political revolutions led by the bourgeoisie.

The primary source of influence on Stein came from France, particularly from **Francois Babeuf** who for the first time brought about the concept of **national labour**. The concept was implemented by Louis Blanc in the provisional government after the Revolutions of 1848. National workshops were organised and right to work guaranteed. This "organisation of labour", which was **Louis Blanc**'s famous slogan was further expanded and clearly defined in Stein's notion of the "organisation of national labour by state authority." According to Bela Foeldes, Marx was familiar with Stein's concepts. Foeldes concluded that the concepts of the 'proletariat' and of 'class' were originally Stein's contribution.[13] The unattainable polarisation between labour and capital was further elaborated by Stein in his *Socialism and Communism*, but he advocated neither a revolution (proletarian revolution) like Marx, nor a utopia, but wanted reform through a widespread social movement. However, Stein believed that if the state did not carry out the movement, the proletariat would.

No discussion on early German socialists is complete without a reference to **Ludwig Feuerbach**, who also exerted a distinct influence on Marx and Engels. Feuerbach belonged to the category of neo-Hegelians or young Hegelians who further expanded the thought of Hegel and interpreted it in their own way. In fact, *Hegel and Feuerbach were the true philosophical forerunners of Marx*. It is necessary to understand first what Hegel's theory was in order to discuss Feuerbach and Marx. In the view of Hegel nothing in the universe is static. Everything is dynamic and changing constantly.

Everything is, therefore, dialectic. Every concept, every institution went through a course, reached a peak and met its opposite. Then takes place a fusion between the original and the opposite, and thus disappears the former. It is transformed by the fusion and creates the new base. This new base now forms the thesis. This, according to Hegel, is the constant interplay of thesis, anti-thesis and synthesis. This denotes that everything is changing constantly. Inherent change is the fact of life. This is one very predominant aspect of Hegelian philosophy. Another equally important feature of Hegel's thought is his proximity to the ideals of bourgeois philosophy that emerged in the wake of the rise of the modern age. In the preceding feudal era, which lasted from about the 7th century to the 15th century, the overwhelming power of the Church was the supreme. The doctrines, jurisprudence and preachings of the Church constituted the essence of the philosophy of the feudal age. It was also known as **scholastic philosophy**.

In the decline of the feudal age and rise of the modern, the emergence of natural science and of commercial capitalism played an indisputable role. The bourgeois mode of production led to a bitter struggle for power in the upper circles of the feudal society. The new scientific approach dealt a heavy blow at the retrograde practices as well as beliefs of the Church. The Reformation movement carried out a scathing attack against the Church. Philosophers and materialists like Diderot, Helvetius, Voltaire played a key role in shattering the ecclesiastical supremacy. The rise of a flourishing mercantile class or the bourgeoisie created a new crop of ideas that produced the bourgeois philosophy which first appeared in those countries of Europe where the prominence of bourgeoisie was most pronounced—England, France and finally Germany. The scholastic philosophy was replaced by the new bourgeois philosophy. The main features of **bourgeois philosophy** were its emphasis on the **triumph of reason over religious orthodoxy** and clerical predominance as well as state absolutism.

Hegel was the positive consummator of bourgeois philosophy. Three elements are particularly significant in the study of Hegel's philosophy. *First*, he was **an idealist**. Idea or thought of human mind, he believed, was the mover of the world. All worldly or material things were created and run by ideas. *Second*, Hegel believed that there was no sharp disagreement between religion and philosophy. Rather, philosophy was an expanded, analytical and metaphysical exposition of religion. *Third*, Hegel's firm conviction in dialectics, which I have already discussed, is by far the most important aspect of his philosophy. These three features form the main pillars of Hegelian philosophy. Hegel was not a political revolutionary as such, but his insistence on ideas which, in his view, created material reality and his perception of the intermingling of religion and philosophy, could be interpreted to provoke revolutionary thoughts. Philosophy, in Hegel's perception, only elucidated the truth and good, and benevolent aspects of religion. So if one analysed deeply the good ideas bequeathed by religion, the tyranny of the state would be intolerable. Hegel never stated them in explicit terms, and his philosophy was so obscure and abstract that the Prussian state could never fathom that it was in any way directed against them.

Against this backdrop, it is pertinent to discuss the thoughts of **Feuerbach**. While Hegel's ideas of religion and philosophy were subtle and abstract, they were pronounced and explicit in the writings and preachings of his student Feuerbach. Feuerbach was vociferous in his attack on both Christianity as well as philosophy. His book *Das Wesen des Christentums* (The Essence of Christianity) has invaluable impact on the history of social and religious thought and revealed the mindset of the post-Hegelian generation. Both religion and philosophy, argued Feuerbach, are nothing but the creation of man's own thought and imagination. Christianity believed that God created man. This belief was also the root of Hegel's cosmic reason. However, Feuerbach went farther ahead. According to him, God did not create man. Rather, it was just the opposite. *It was man who created God and endowed him with lofty qualities.* In that process, man, after transferring all the noble and sublime characteristics to God, became bereft of all inherent goodness and therefore turned into a selfish individual himself. He could be liberated only by changing his own concept of religion and reintegrating the qualities in himself. This thought is similar to what an ancient Greek philosopher maintained, "If oxen made a God, he would be an ox; if a negro made a God, he would have a flat nose and thick lips."[14] In other words, God is an image of man's own character. Philosophy, wrote Feuerbach, is a far more refined, analytical and reflective version of religion. It elaborates the finer tunings of human thoughts. This is also what Hegel believed. In other words, religion and philosophy are the reflections of human mind and its fertile thought-process. But, Feuerbach argued, nothing can be a figment of imagination in the material world. Something which cannot be seen or felt is not acceptable. Sense experience is the fundamental basis of true knowledge. Feuerbach's materialism was, therefore, **natural-science materialism** and was fixed and irreversible. It is also called **contemplative materialism**. This is in direct contradiction with Hegel who believed in dialectics. This led Marx and Engels to move on to dialectic materialism, which was a modification of the theories of their predecessors Hegel and Feuerbach. Marx wrote, "Feuerbach, not satisfied with abstract thinking, wants contemplation; but he does not conceive sensuousness as practical, human-sensuous activity."[15] Feuerbach attacked Christianity which was then the state religion. Naturally he attracted the ire of the Prussian state authorities and had to retreat to a village school as a private teacher.

Among the German Socialists, the Rhenish Jew intellectual **Moses Hess** has left an indelible impact. Referred to as the '**father of German Communism**', he was the chief protagonist of a movement called 'true socialism'. Like Hegel and Feuerbach, he, too, exerted considerable influence on both Marx and Engels, in the sense that he not only **converted Engels to communism**, but sufficiently inspired Marx as well. In fact, their relationship was rather a kind of love-hate relationship; on the one hand, Hess and Marx allied together in their criticism of Bruno Bauer, Feuerbach and Max Stirner, while on the other, Marx and Engels carried on a virulent polemic against Hess. In the *Communist Manifesto*, Marx even criticised the 'true socialists' for being allies of the feudal reaction.[16]

Hess was man of a pure nature, saintly in his behaviour and was passionate about all kinds of injustice in society. Following the philosophy of Feuerbach, he developed the **theory of alienation of a workman's labour** to the capitalist. This enriched the latter but impoverished the former. This was due to the fact that a worker's only asset was his labour which he drained out in favour of the capitalist who used it to amass his own wealth. This was the same way in which Feuerbach's man alienated all his good qualities to create the image of God. In this way Hess developed a unique kind of communism called 'true socialism'. Balance then, Hess believed, could be restored in society on the basis of altruism and brotherhood.

Hess' concept of true socialism had certain distinct characteristic features. In fact, **the true socialists—Hess, Luning, Kreige, Heinzen—** all had their own distinctive thoughts. However, they all shared a few common elements. Even so, it is almost impossible to draw up any general formula for 'true socialism'. The major views of Hess can be summarised as follows: *First,* the true socialists were deeply influenced by the French socialist thinkers and were opposed to the bourgeoisie class who had emerged as a powerful body in the society in the wake of the Napoleonic wars. By cutting off Germany's trade with Britain by his Continental System, Napoleon had paved the path for the rise of an industrial class in Germany committed to producing a variety of goods, including those that came from Britain and her colonies. They began to exert substantial influence by virtue of their immense financial aid to the government in times of need and by attracting the nobility to their lucrative investment schemes. The growth of a proletariat was the inevitable consequence of the industrial expansion. The true socialists in Germany, following the examples set by the French socialists, took up the cause of the proletariat whom they considered the symbol of humanity.

Second, apart from Hegel and Feuerbach, the works and ideas of Spinoza and Fichte had profound impact on the ideas of Hess. According to **Spinoza**, God is a singular self-subsistent substance of which matter and thought are attributes. A substance and its attributes are, therefore, separable from each other. Karl Jaspers wrote that Spinoza's God was *natura naturans*, that is, "a dynamic nature in action, growing and changing, not a passive or static thing."[17] In other words, God was all-pervasive and human beings, along with everything else in the universe, were His parts. Whatever was happening was God's will.[18] This he called religion. But Hess' sense of humanism and concern for the underdog clashed with the abstract, metaphysical aspects of the universe as conceptualised by Spinoza and Hegel. As Sydney Hook observed, Hess' 'underdog' was not confined unlike Marx and Engels, to the proletariat, but anybody who was in distress—even if he belonged to the nobility or bourgeoisie, the classes who exploited the proletariat. The true socialists were, therefore, humanists above all. Hess clearly distinguished between religion and morality. "The essence of religion is worship; the essence of morality conscientiousness."[19] To fulfil the dictates of his morality, Hess turned to Fichte who called his philosophical system the **Wissenschaftslehr** or **science of knowledge**. **Fichte** suggested the self as 'the I,' which constantly changes itself according to circumstances, and imposes upon itself the **task of action** or *tathandlung*. This he borrowed from the Kantian notion of autonomy in the form of self-inflicted discipline. Hess viewed communism as an altruistic ideal which transcended the narrow confines of one's own near and dear ones and diffused love and compassion among society as a whole. However, 'true socialists', like Hess, argued that the contradiction of communism lay in the fact that while it identified itself with humanitarianism of the society at large, it considered itself as a proletarian movement; but the proletariat, after all, was only a part of the society, not the whole society. Communism, therefore, represented only a fraction of the society.

Reference should be made to **Wilhelm Weitling** (1808–1871) who was regarded as the **epitome of German utopian communism**. He considered communistic society as the ideal society and the workers to be the true instrument through which a communist revolution would be possible. In order to bring about a profound transformation in the existing situation he joined an association of the communists among German workers. His dreams symbolised a true '**revolution from below**', because Weitling was a workman himself. A tailor by profession, the son of a domestic maid, he lacked any formal education except some elementary education in the public school of Magdeburg. Weitling invented a new and useful improvement in sewing machine for making button holes. He went to Switzerland in 1841 where he founded several workers' groups who united on their common link of poverty and through them he aimed at attaining justice for the society at large. He was deeply motivated by the ideas of Fourier, Owen and Cabet. His work *Die Garantien der Harmonie und Freiheit* (Guarantees of harmony and freedom), published in 1842 was appreciated by Bruno Bauer, Feurbach, Bakunin as well as Marx. In his *Das Evangelium eines armen Sunders* (Gospel of Poor Sinners) he linked communism to early Christianity for which he had earned the epithet of **Christian Communist**. Weitling, therefore, joined the **League of the Just** that made the slogan "All men are Brothers" its axiom. It was based upon the Christian principles of love, equality and justice. It was also primarily a workers' league organised in 1836 by workmen like Karl Schapper who was a printer, Heinrich Bauer, a shoemaker and Joseph Moll, a close friend of Weitling and a watchmaker by profession. It was an international organisation which later in 1847 merged with members of the Communist Corresponding Committee headed by Karl Marx and Friedrich Engels. Being an ardent lover of equality, liberty, fraternity and justice, Weitling staunchly supported the Revolutions of 1848. After the revolutions failed, he went back to America and became one of the **Forty-Eighters** (Europeans who supported the Revolutions of 1848 in Europe). Although, Weitling's movement came to nothing, and historians like George Lichtheim called him "a half-mad apostle of Christian communism",[20] Weitling made significant contribution both to revolutionary and communist movements. He looked upon Jesus as not only the apostle of love and liberty, but the first revolutionary whose battle against "the Pharisees and the rich gave the Gospels their real significance".[21]

Scientific Socialism

Socialism in the second half of the 19th century revolved round the theories and principles of Karl Marx, the most prominent socialist thinker and theoretician of all times to come. Marx was inspired by several socialists and economists who preceded him. As Lichtheim has pointed out, "Marx was able to bring German idealist philosophy, French socialist politics, and British classical economics together because they had all grown from a common root—the combined impact of liberalism and democracy."[22] He was particularly influenced by French socialist Proudhon, German socialists like Feuerbach and German philosophers like Hegel, British economists like Ricardo. Proudhon, Feuerbach and Hegel have been discussed earlier. The *similarity between Proudhon and Marx* lay in the fact that both believed *in transferring the means of production in the hands of the*

Fig. 6.1: Karl Marx

workers. Proudhon proposed handing over to the democratically organised workers' associations all sources of wealth. In his opinion, the exact value of a commodity should be equivalent to the value of labour that has gone into it. If the price was more than the stipulated value, then it amounted to profit, which Proudhon called theft. Therefore, according to Proudhon property is theft. Marx agreed with Proudhon on this and called this the **labour theory of value**. However, Marx differed from Proudhon markedly on the issue of **tolerance**. When Marx met Proudhon and requested him to join him and Engels, Proudhon clearly stated that he was ready to join only on the condition of running a tolerant and inclusive movement. He said, "Let us carry on a good and loyal polemic, let us give the world the example of an informed and farsighted tolerance, but let us not—simply because we are at the head of a movement—make ourselves into the leaders of a new intolerance, …"[23] Of course Marx, opposed to ideas of dissent as he was, refused to agree.

Hegel was the **greatest influence** on Marx. Marx's theory was founded on Hegel's principles of dialectics or inherent change. At the same time, it was founded upon the basic facts of the material world. Therefore, Marx's idea of socialism is known as dialectic materialism. According to

Fig. 6.2: Friedrich Engels

Marx, *every society is based upon an economic structure*. Prior to the advent of industrialisation, society's economic foundation constituted of pastoral activities. After the Industrial Revolution, the foundation was industrial pursuit. As Marx wrote, "The hand-mill gives you society with the feudal lord, the steam-mill, society with the industrial capitalist."[24] As the material world changed, society also changed correspondingly. Agricultural society changed into industrial society. Along with it, social relationships underwent constant transformation. For example, in the place of feudal lord and peasants there emerged the industrial capitalist and a large proletariat. The worst sufferers were the artisans or skilled craftsmen. They had to compete with the machine-made goods and consequently, large sections of them were wiped out. Bitter class conflicts followed. Moreover, the relationship of the capitalist as well as proletariat was also inimical. The reason was that the capitalist accumulated wealth or profit, while the worker received his wages which were not proportionate to the labour that went into them. The workers had nothing to offer but their labour. The artisans and small traders or small businessmen, (in other words the petty bourgeoisie) also were elbowed out of their business by the big capitalists. They, therefore, joined hands with the proletariat and created a bigger and bigger base. The **base** in Marxian philosophy related primarily to the aids and tools of production, like machines, land, factories etc. It also involved the varied relationships that emerged out of the methods of production. That is, the employer-employee relations, division of society and social relations into labour and capital etc. The **superstructure** which has apparently nothing to do with the base, and represented art, intellect, law, science, philosophy as well as the cultural aspects of the society, however, got indirectly but closely affected by the base. The inimical labour-capital relationship often led to social revolution, and this conflict within the base was bound to impact on the balance within the superstructure. Therefore, in the preface to *A Contribution to the Critique of Political Economy* Marx wrote, "The mode of production of material life conditions the general process of social, political and intellectual life." In other words, the **thesis** was the capitalist world established by the Industrial Revolution. An **anti-thesis** was created by the proletariat who fiercely resented the appropriation of wealth by the capitalist. The thesis and the anti-thesis would clash with each other and a **synthesis** would emerge, that is, the proletarian rule. The great proletarian revolution would eventually end in the destruction of the capitalists and establish its own rule. The ownership, distribution and exchange of all means of production would be in the hands of the proletariat. The state would disappear, and the wage-system would be abolished as well. Communism would follow, the main principle of which was 'from each according to his ability, to each according to his needs.' In other words, the resources accumulated on the basis of everybody's contribution, would be distributed according to needs alone, irrespective of all other considerations. Inevitably, the superstructure would undergo massive transformation as a result of the new synthesis (the establishment of proletarian rule). This synthesis would now become the new thesis. Marx and Engels looked upon the Revolutions of 1848 as the prelude to the proletarian revolution. Although it was started by the bourgeoisie, it was propelled by the proletariat. The working class pushed forth their demands forcefully—the right to work, a minimum wage, shorter hours of work, progressive taxation etc. Engels wrote about the Revolutions of 1848 in France, "The year 1848 is turning out well. By this glorious revolution, the French proletariat has again placed itself at the head of the European movement. All honours to the workers of Paris."[25] *So, while Hegel thought of thesis, anti-thesis and synthesis in terms of ideas, Marx translated them in material terms.*

Even so, Marx developed his concept of state and society on the basis of the dialectics of Hegel. Hegel's theory of state was quite contrary to that of Hobbes, Locke or Rousseau, who believed that there existed a contract between the state and the people, and the state existed to protect the rights and liberties of the people. Hegel, on the other hand, was of the opinion that the people subordinated their interests to the will of the state. Marx, following the Hegelian model, argued that *the state generally endeavoured to preserve the interests of the ruling order*, and that class conflict was rampant, especially between the owners of capital and the representatives of labour. *The Communist Manifesto* has interpreted the history of society as the history of class conflict. Economic issues which determined the political institutions. In fact, the bourgeois revolution was also a result of economic conflict—a conflict between the landed and the mercantile classes. *Material reality formed the foundation of the theories of Marx and Engels.* Marx had visualised the obliteration of the bourgeois state. But at the same time, both Engels and Marx aimed at the application of their philosophy to historical reality. That is why their philosophy is known as **historical materialism**. However, Marx, according to Lichtheim, "did not try to forecast the transition from the existing social order to another."[26]

There was the lack of an adequate and exact political theory which left the room for enough interpretation and speculation among his followers.

Although based upon Hegel, Marx differed from him on certain important aspects. While Hegel's dialectics were based upon an ideological foothold, because Hegel's notion of the 'spirit of the age' was merely imaginary, Marx's attitude towards the world was **empirical**. Hegel's philosophy was essentially conservative, whereas Marx's thoughts were distinctly radical. Marx was an avowed atheist. He believed that his concepts would bring about *a social revolution which was more radical than a political revolution*. Even after a political revolution like the French Revolution, argued Marx, complete equality did not prevail and the distinctions between capital and labour continued. It was only after a social revolution, as Marx envisaged, that means of production were socialised so that all social inequality was wiped out. As American philosopher **George H. Sabine** has pointed out, "materialism for Marx had an ethical meaning: the root of social inequality is economic; by comparison all political reform is superficial, leaving the source of inequality untouched…"[27] Marx believed that the way a society used its material resources for producing goods to fulfil its needs determined its social structure by creating a hierarchy of classes on the basis of the role each individual played in that system of production. This also decided its political and cultural system.

This is, in a nutshell, Marx's theory of economic determinism—a phenomenon linked inextricably to his dialectical materialism. The mode of production and the definite relations into which men enter as a result of it create the economic base of society on which are created social, political and cultural institutions which constitute the superstructure. The base and superstructure are to a large extent determined by the technology, skill and knowledge that are applied. Accumulation of capital and consequent appropriation and exploitation depend on the scale of science and technology used. Marx's theory, therefore, is also called 'scientific'. Scientific discoveries have supreme social importance as they govern technology. Of course, accumulation of capital cannot always be related to economic factors. Marx himself had cited the expropriation of monasteries as a source of capital in explaining rise of capitalism in England. But this involved political and religious reasons rather than economic.

Both Marx and Engels elaborated their philosophy most exhaustibly in *The Communist Manifesto* and *Das Kapital*. Both held that dialectic was a working hypothesis and the conclusion might not be substantive.

Both agreed that economic factor was the most important determining element that explained almost all social conflicts. But while Marx believed that the base and the superstructure were clearly distinct, and that the base causes the superstructure and not vice versa, Engels contended that under specific conditions the superstructure influenced the base. For example, laws restricting long hours of work did affect the base of labour–capital relationship. "In effect, Engels has undermined any meaning that Marx attached to historical 'inevitability'."[28] Critiquing what he read as an internal inconsistency between Marx's 'scientific' view of history and Engels' own interpretations of it, British philosopher and historian **G.S.L. Tucker** argued that Engels diluted the idea of a strict inevitable path of history, which Marx emphasised as **scientific socialism**—thus undermining its credibility as a predictive, scientific doctrine.

British economist **David Ricardo** was a scholar who wielded considerable influence on Marx. Professor Schumpeter used to say, "Marx had a master then? Yes. Real understanding of his economics begins with recognising that, as a theorist, he was a pupil of Ricardo."[29] The two men, however, widely differed from each other—in ideas as well as in personalities. Even so, as G.S.L. Tucker observed, "The reason for linking the two names appears simply to be that Ricardo, unwittingly and with different ends in mind, developed a theory which was later used to provide the essential foundations of Marxian economics."[30] The essential points which Marx adopted from Ricardo were as follows:

First, Ricardo, like Marx, believed that the workers were a lot who were always pushed to the subsistence level, but while Marx argued that this misery of the workers was due to the greed of their employers, that is the capitalists whose inherent tendency was to accumulate profit by depriving the workers of their due which is the actual value of the labour that has gone into the production, Ricardo observed that the workers themselves were responsible for their own distress. Even when the wages rose as a result of demand for labour (because the capitalists wanted to expand and invest their profit in further enterprises), the workers went on to perpetuate as they were hopelessly addicted to "the delights of domestic society". Consequently, their number proliferated, bringing down the wages. Therefore, according to Ricardo, "over the long run they are condemned by their own weakness to a life at the margin of subsistence."[31]

Second, both Marx and Ricardo believed that the sole aim of the capitalists was to earn profit. Their "entire purpose on earth is to accumulate—that is, to save their profits and to re-invest them by hiring more men to work for them."[32] But here also lay a difference between the two. In Marx's view, the capitalists were the exploiters who sucked the proletariat dry and amassed enormous wealth. So, a proletarian revolution would follow and the capitalist as a class would be purged from society. Ricardo, on the contrary, sympathised with the capitalists, because they, in his view, were "put in a double squeeze."[33] But how? Ricardo explained that as the number of proletariat increased due to their love for said "delights of domestic society", the demand for grain went up and the landlords were greatly benefitted. But the capitalists suffered as they now had to pay higher wages in view of the rising price of bread. So, while the landlords profited, the capitalists were pushed to the margin. The capitalist was being "squeezed" from both sides—by the landlords from the top and the workers from below.

Marx observed that Ricardo, like Adam Smith, did not think that competition which occurred during progressive accumulation led to higher wages. Because, in Ricardo's view, the tendency of the workers to perpetuate always kept their number higher than the demand. This was also the opinion of Say, the French physiocrat.

Lichtheim further elaborated that the history of one generation had a tremendous impact on the formation of the history of the next, because, in his words, "The tradition of all the dead generations weighs like a nightmare on the brains of the living."[34] In that sense, socialism was indebted to the bourgeois revolution which gave birth to a social reality (irrespective of the intention of its creators) that socialism could not deny. Marx was also no exception. He fused the intellectual contents of the previous generations—socialism and sociology of France and theoretical economics of England—with German philosophy, especially that of Kant and Hegel. So, as Lichtheim has claimed, Marx's materialism was 'historical materialism' which was distinct from the 'dialectical materialism' of Engels.[35] However, for all practical purposes, dialectical materialism is inextricably linked with both Marx and Engels, and was developed largely in Russia and the Soviet Union.

Critics of Marx

The several critics of Marx, especially the **social democrats** dismissed summarily his concept of a proletarian revolution. The anarchists did not accept Marx's theory of a brief spell of the bourgeois state before the final take-over by the proletariat. **V.K. Dmitriev**[36] and **Ladislaus Von Bortkiewicz**[37] have refuted Marx's **labour theory of value** and also his law of '**the tendency of the rate of profit to fall**'. Both, they believed, were inherently self-contradictory. On the one hand, Marx argued that since the workers were not paid wages in proportion to the volume of labour that went into the production of a particular commodity, the difference between the labour and market price constituted the profit pocketed by the capitalist. This labour theory of value contradicted Marx's law of the tendency of the rate of profit to fall. Explaining this law in Chapter 14 of the third volume of *Capital*, Marx borrowed from Ricardo, who propounded that profits had a natural tendency to fall because more production meant more demand for more labour and, therefore, higher wages. This, however, Ricardo contended, could be checked at repeated intervals with improvements in science of machinery as well as agriculture, and this helped to dispense with a substantial portion of labour and "therefore to lower the price of the prime necessaries of the labourer." Marx elaborated this by contending that constant capital, that is, plants, machinery, raw materials, etc., was in the long run more expensive than variable capital, that is, labour. So profits fell. **N. Okishio**, a Japanese economist, on the other hand established his theorem in 1961 that if a capitalist introduced a cost-cutting technique, while the wage of the workers in general remained the same, the profit on the whole was bound to increase.[38] This created a sensation among the economists because it contradicted Marx's theory of the tendency of the rate of profit to fall. Therefore, according to Okishio and others like Paul Sweezy, David Laibman, etc., Marx's theory was internally inconsistent.

There are, however, critics of these economists who consider that Marx's theory was quite consistent if the theory is considered to be 'temporal' or non-simultaneous and 'single-system'. They are called the proponents of the **Temporal Single-System Interpretation** (TSSI). This school of economists include Guglielmo Carchedi, John Ernst, Alan Freeman, Andrew Kliman, Nick Potts, Alajandro Ramos Martinez. This interpretation emerged in the 1980s and endeavoured to show that Marx's rate of profit can fall even in circumstances in which Okishio has tried to prove that the rate of profit would rise. The value of a commodity and its price constitute a single system, that is they are inseparably linked but are not simultaneous. That is, they are determined independently. This is what is meant by 'temporal single system'. Seen from this point of view, no inconsistency can be found. In such a framework, **Alan Freeman**, for example, established that the rate of profit rose continuously regardless of whether or not there was a technical change, unless capitalist consumption exceeded profit as it occurrs in a slump. He considered Okishio's method to be theoretically deficient and utterly unrealistic.[39]

Contention also arises regarding the relationship between the base and the superstructure. According to Marx, the modes of production and subsequent capital-labour relations, or in other words, economic factors formed the base of society. These economic factors influenced society's cultural, political, ideological aspects which composed the superstructure. The critics of Marx argued that it is indeed perplexing to decide *whether the base influenced the superstructure, or it was the other way round.* This leads to the famous chicken or the egg argument. However, the fact remains that to Marx the economic forces were the most vital. He truly believed that the means of production was the controlling factor in society, and, therefore, the only way for man to be free from servitude was to **seize the means of production**. This, according to **Peter Singer**, was the goal of history and the superstructure constituted the tools of history.[40] **P.R. Sarkar** criticised Marx by saying that Marx's folly was that he considered only one factor, that is the economic forces to be deciding the historical evolution. This approach, Sarkar argued, was rather simplistic and narrow. Several other forces like progress of science and technology, spiritualism, intellect, etc, for example, were responsible for the processes of history and society. In fact, the revolution should not be led only by the proletariat but should be a combined effort of dignified intellectuals as well as workers and labourers against the rapacity of the capitalists.[41] Marx, therefore, was guilty of the charges of **oversimplification** and **mono-causality** (or explaining complex events and processes through a single dominant cause). Engels strongly refuted the charges by saying,

> According to the materialist conception of history, the ultimately determining element in history is the production and reproduction of real life. More than this neither Marx nor I ever asserted. Hence if somebody twists this into saying that the economic element is the only determining one he transforms that proposition into a meaningless, abstract, senseless phrase.[42]

Lichtheim points out two very important aspects of Marxist thought. *First,* he objected to the Marxian notion of class conflict as analysed in the *Manifesto.* Marx stated that society of all times was regulated by **class**

conflict. In the *Manifesto* Marx and Engels wrote, "the history of all existing society is the history of class struggles." Later, however, they realised that class conflict in economic terms was a by-product of bourgeois revolution. *Second*, Lichtheim argued, Marx, a liberal in his early life, transformed into a socialist after his encounter with the French socialists, and propounded a theory of the **final purging of the state**. Unfortunately, however, Marx was never very candid in his idea as to what political structure would there be in the absence of the state. This lack of an adequate political theory was inherent in Marxist communism and "[t]his did not begin to trouble his followers for another generation, but the lack of an adequate political theory then made itself felt."[43]

Marx was indeed quite **myopic in his perception of human relations**. **Marvin Perry** also observed that Marx never understood that material possessions were not the only reason for which man strove. There were several other causes of human conflict, such as struggle for power and status.[44] Perry opined that Marx did not appreciate that even under capitalist governments the condition of workers could improve. Western workers saw substantial improvement in their working and living conditions. So did middle class professionals, small entrepreneurs, and so on. This "belies Marx's prediction that capitalist society would be polarised into a small group of very rich capitalists and a great mass of destitute workers." Moreover, Marx's philosophy transcended the barriers of nation. Marx believed that workers had no nation in the sense that everywhere in the world their miseries were the same. Therefore, they represented a universal class. In reality, however, according to Marvin Perry, things did not happen that way. Intense sentiments of nationalism united workers and capitalists alike of a nation in the First World War against their enemies. The class polarisation of Marx did not work then. "The French workers did not make common cause with the German workers against the ruling capitalists in their respective countries."[45]

Furthermore, Marx was wrong in thinking that price should be determined primarily by the value of labour that has gone into making the product. As the British economist **Alfred Marshall** has pointed out, it is *not only labour but also capital and entrepreneurial skill as well as market demand* which play an important part in deciding the price of a product.

The greatest criticism against Marxist theory was the **element of coercion** it involved. Free enterprise is an essential component of individual freedom. The encroachment of communism on free enterprise throttled freedom. Economists like Milton Friedman, John Maynard Keynes believed that a capitalist free market economy alone could ensure individual liberty.

Not only in economic terms, Marxism *did not tolerate any kind of political disagreement* either. Within the International, for example, no free discussion of different viewpoints and varying individual notions were allowed by Marx who wanted to keep the control of the organisation confined in the hands of a few. This was his main point of conflict with the anarchist Mikhail Bakunin who was practically banished by Marx from the International in 1872. Authoritarianism was ingrained in the movement he organised. **Robert L. Heilbroner** wrote, "This was the most quarrelsome and intolerant of men, and from the beginning he was unable to believe that anyone who did not follow his line of reasoning could possibly be right…He called his opponents 'louts', 'rascals', even 'bedbugs'."[46] Marx clashed with innumerable people, even socialist thinkers like Proudhon who as we have seen refused to join him on this very issue of intolerance, even though there were striking resemblances between the two. Like Marx, Proudhon too struck a synthesis between philosophy, economics and politics. Moreover, Proudhon's theory of 'property is theft' was based upon the principle that the price of a product should be proportionate to the amount of labour that has gone into it. This same principle was the basis of Marx's labour theory of value. Moses Hess bitterly resented **Marx's intolerant, authoritarian stance**. Force and intimidation were, therefore, regrettably also a part of communism and resembled in many aspects the totalitarian regimes of the communist governments of the 20th century. Suppression of individual rights reached their heights under the Stalinist regime. The record of Stalin's mass killings is no less impressive than that of Hitler's. Glimpses of communist intolerance are very well reflected in novels, such as George Orwell's *Animal Farm* as well as Arthur Koestler's *Darkness at Noon*.

The main principle of Marxist economic thought was, as has been mentioned above, "**from each according to his ability to each according to his needs**." This kind of income-sharing had its own inevitable problems, which have been pointed out by critics. *First*, the entire concept went against the fundamental laws of nature. It was *opposed to intrinsic human character*. Since times immemorial, man has developed the trait of accumulation. Forced parting with it or forced sharing is against human nature. In that sense, communism was tantamount to swimming against the current. Obviously, it would result in vehement resentment. *Second,* it was bound to *reduce incentives.* No human being would like the idea of incessant toiling for the benefit of others. So, production would tend to diminish. Also, it would encourage lethargy. If automatically a man's needs were taken care of at somebody else's cost, he would naturally tend to become slothful. Eventually, a nation's economy would suffer. John Stuart Mill wrote in 1848,

> It is the common error of socialists to overlook the natural indolence of mankind; their tendency to be passive, to be the slaves of habit, to persist indefinitely in a course once chosen. Let them once attain any state of existence which they consider tolerable, and the danger to be apprehended is that they will thenceforth stagnate; will not exert themselves to improve, and by letting their faculties rust, will lose even the energy required to preserve them from deterioration. Competition may not be the best conceivable stimulus, but it is at present a necessary one, and no one can foresee the time when it will not be indispensable to progress.[47]

Without extreme force and pressure from above, such an unnatural system as communism could never be sustained. Marxism was, therefore, synonymous with tyranny. And history has shown time and again that extreme tyranny was bound to perish. So, it is perhaps no wonder that most communist regimes in different parts of the world crumbled in the long run. The algorithm of its destruction was written in the system itself.

Nevertheless, Marx had an immense impact upon his times and posterity. His theory—inconsistent in many respects, incomplete in numerous details—was powerful enough to forge armies of followers through the ages. He not only created a movement, or led a revolution, but initiated an entire philosophy. Marx therefore, ranks with the greatest philosophers of all times. Engels wrote in 1883 at the funeral of Marx that "Just as Darwin discovered the law of evolution in organic nature, so Marx discovered the law of evolution in human history."[48]

The German Socialist Movement

The most prominent socialist movement in Germany started with the foundation of the **Social Democratic Party**. It was born out of the merger of the General German Workers' Association led by Ferdinand

Lassalle and the Social Democratic Workers' Party, headed by August Bebel and Wilhelm Liebknecht. **Ferdinand Lassalle**, founder of the General German Workers' Party in 1863 was a student of philosophy in the University of Bresalau and later that of Berlin and a devotee of Georg Hegel. From the very beginning, he was a committed republican and started his political career in the wake of the Revolutions of 1848. He gave fiery speeches supporting the republican movement and was thrown into prison for six months. He was barred from entering Berlin and began to reside in Rhineland when he defended the case of a countess who was fighting a legal case for equitable division of property against her husband from whom she was separated. The case was settled finally in 1854 consequent upon which Countess Sophie Von Hatzfeldt won a substantial fortune and paid Lassalle an annual income of 5000 thalers for the rest of his life. In 1857, his book on the life of philosopher Heraclitus was published and won him considerable renown. He became famous for the published speech he delivered in Berlin in 1862. It came to be called the Workers' Programme and sold almost 3000 copies, after which he was convicted of three months' imprisonment. He became a member of the **Communist League**—an international Marxist political party established

FIG. 6.3: Ferdinand Lassalle

in 1847 in London through the merger of the League of the Just headed by Karl Schapper and the Communist Correspondence Committee of Brussels. In 1863 he founded the General German Workers' Association in Leipzig. Lassalle **advocated universal suffrage** which would enable the workers to outnumber the bourgeois politicians and ultimately capture sufficient political power by which they would be able to win over the entire fruit of their labour. Lassalle, therefore, believed that seizure of political power alone could liberate the workers. **August Bebel**, one of his close followers, wrote in his autobiography in 1911 that Lassalle's political ideas did not appeal to the workers much. Lassalle insisted upon the formation of productive associations of workers subsidised by the state, of which workers did not have a very clear idea. Nor were they very concerned about universal suffrage. They valued freedom of speech and assembly, freedom to settle down, liberty to wander and exemption from passports, among other things. He was deeply criticised by Marx as well. His thoughts became popular later. He was killed in a duel over a girl in August 1864.

FIG. 6.4: August Bebel

Lassalle's General German Workers' Association (ADAV) merged with the Social Democratic Workers' Party of Germany founded by August Bebel and Wilhelm Liebknecht in 1869. After the two parties merged at a conference in Gotha in 1875, the Socialist Workers' Party of Germany (SAPD) was formed. It was banned by Bismarck in 1878 for its anti-monarchist sentiments. But it was legalised again in 1890 after the fall of Bismarck from power. Then it changed its name to **Social Democratic Party (Sozialdemokratishe Partei Deutschlands, SPD)** in **1890**.

One of the most prominent members of the Social Democratic Party or SPD was **Eduard Bernstein** born in Berlin in 1850 of Jewish parents. He joined SPD in 1872. The success of SPD in the elections of 1877 in which it won 12 seats worried Bismarck who passed an anti-socialist law. Bernstein thereupon moved to Switzerland where he became the editor of the underground socialist journal *Der Sozialdemokrat*. He was expelled from Switzerland and emigrated to London and started working with the Fabian socialists.

In the meanwhile, the socialists split into two distinct groups—the revisionists and the purists. The **revisionists** were those who believed in participating in the government through contesting the elections and then by occupying important posts in the state to carry out reforms for the working class. The trend in this direction had already been set by Lassalle. The **purists**, on the contrary, led by Marx himself, were of the firm conviction that any kind of cooperation with any political party or the state would only delay the proletarian revolution that could be carried out by the proletariat alone without any outside aid, and not cooperation but overthrow of the bourgeois state was the ultimate end of the working-class movement. **Eduard Bernstein** was, like Lassalle, a revisionist in the sense that he too believed that through trade union activity and parliamentary politics, socialism could be achieved in a capitalist state. He contradicted Marxist thoughts and strategies in his influential book *Evolutionary Socialism* published in 1899. Slowly the SPD became divided into two distinct groups—the **right wing** and the **left wing**. The right wing consisted of the revisionists like **Bernstein**, while the left wing included the Marxists like **Bebel, Karl Kautsky, Karl Liebknecht** and **Rosa Luxemburg**. The latter were out and out purists and were convinced that a proletarian revolution was inevitable and the only goal of the socialists, and that collaboration would lead to corruption and denigration of the working class. Bernstein returned to Germany in 1901 and was elected to the Reichstag twice—once from 1902 to 1906 and again from 1912 to 1918. Later on, however, he tilted towards the left wing over the issue of the First World War and refused to join it as he believed like the other left-wing members that it was a capitalist war.

In **1917**, the left-wing members of the SPD formed the **Independent Socialist Party**. The members were Eduard Bernstein, Karl Kautsky, Julius Leber, Rudolf Breitscheild and Rudol Hilferding. In the meanwhile, some members of the SPD including Rosa Luxemburg had been imprisoned for short spells. Earlier, on the release of Rosa Luxemburg in February 1916, a secret political organisation was formed called ***Spartakusbund*** or **Spartacus League**. The members included Karl Liebknecht, Rosa Luxemburg, Leo Jogiches, Clara Zetkin, Ernest Meyer, Paul Levi, Julian Marchlewski, Hermann Duncker and Hugo Eberlein. Its views were published in its newspaper *Spartacus Letters*. It aimed at "using all instruments of political power to achieve socialism, to expropriate the capitalist class, through and in accordance with the will of the revolutionary majority of the proletariat." In November 1918 in the wake of Germany's crushing defeat in the First World War, widespread revolution broke out all over Germany. The members of the Spartacus League formed the **German Communist Party** or **KPD** led by **Rosa Luxemburg** and **Karl Liebknecht**. It was formed at a founding congress held in Berlin between 30 December 1918 and 1 January 1919.

FIG. 6.5: Karl Liebknecht

FIG. 6.6: Rosa Luxemburg

Immediately after the formation of the party, its goal of seizing political power through capturing the governmental authority clashed severely with the interests of the Social Democratic Party, which formed the **Weimar Republic** that came into power in Germany after the **fall of the Wilhelmine monarchy** as a consequence of World War I. A number of anti-communist parliamentary groups were organised by the Social Democratic Party called '**Freikorps**' or **free corps**. They were mostly demobilised armed forces of the war, but also included native volunteers, enemy deserters, vagabonds and other disgruntled elements. They were an extreme militant and belligerent group and were responsible for the capture and assassination of Karl Liebknecht and Rosa Luxemburg in 1919.

Socialist Movements in Other Countries

By the second half of the 19th century, socialism made its headway in a number of European countries. The first socialist venture in **Belgium**, for example, was started with the socialist congress of 1877. Its leader was

Edward Anseele. He organised a cooperative bakery **Vooruit** in 1880. In this way, he endeavoured to present a counter against capitalism. In April 1885, a meeting of 112 workers took place at Grand Place in Brussels. At this meeting, the **Belgian Labour Party** was created. The socialist party of Anseele was also a significant part of it. Its achievements included an eight-hour workday, an old-age pension, inheritance taxes, a graduated income tax, and the repeal of a law that prohibited picketing.

The **Italian Labour Party** was a socialist party in **Italy** founded by **Giuseppe Croce and Costantino Lazzari** in 1882. A year before in 1881, the **Revolutionary Socialist Party** was founded in Romagna by Andrea Costa, originally an anarchist but who converted into a social democrat after his marriage with Anna Kuliscioff. In 1892, it merged in Genoa with the Italian Labour Party to form the Italian Workers' Party and changed its name to **Italian Socialist Party** in 1893 led by **Filippo Turati**. It had its newspaper *Avanti* of which later Benito Mussolini was the editor. The Italian Socialist Party was soon split into two groups—the **reformists led by Lazzari** and the **maximalists led by Mussolini**. The reformists believed in cooperating with Prime Minister Giovanni Giolitti. The other prominent leaders were Leonida Bissolati, Giacomo Matteotti, Ivanoe Bonomi and Meuccio Ruini. They were expelled from the Italian Socialist Party and they formed the Italian Reformist Socialist Party in 1912. The maximalists supported revolutionary reforms. Over the issue of Italy's joining the World War I, Mussolini also later broke away from the Socialist Party and founded in 1921 the **National Fascist Party** (Partito Nazionale Fascista).

Spanish Socialist Workers' Party (Partido Socialsta Obero Espanol), better known by its initials, PSOE was founded on 2 May 1879 in the Casa Labra Pub in Madrid by the Spanish workers' leader **Pablo Iglesias**. There were only 40 people initially, but the party gained in popularity through its participation in strikes. It also collaborated with the main Republican Party and took part in elections and finally in 1910, Pablo Iglesias was elected as the first socialist leader in the Parliament of Spain (known as the 'Cortes Generales').

The two main leaders of the Socialist Party were **Francisco Largo Caballero** and **Indalecio Prieto**. When Miguel Primo de Rivera established a military dictatorship in Spain in September 1923, and aimed at eliminating corruption and regenerating Spain, Largo Caballero joined hands with **Primo de Rivera** as he believed that it was the only way for the Socialist Party to attain power. Prieto, however, disagreed and formed his left-wing alliance against the new regime. At this time the **Union General de Trabajadores** (UGT) was the most prominent trade union organisation in Madrid established by a group of printers. The UGT was recognised by Primo de Rivera's regime as the regime's trade union. This was also accepted by Caballero, while Prieto opposed it vehemently. In 1925, Caballero became the sole leader of the PSOE. He wanted to gain political power for the party and the working class by whatever means possible. By 1930, PSOE had 20,000 members. However, Indalecio Prieto joined the Republican coalition known as the **Pact of San Sebastian** along with Francisco Caballero and both joined the coalition government of Niceto Alcala Zamora in 1931. Prieto was appointed the Minister of Public Works. Caballero became the Minister of Agriculture. In October, Manuel Azana replaced Zamora as the Prime Minister of the Second Republic. The PSOE was his main pillar of support.

Meanwhile, some other extremist left parties like that of the anarchists and syndicalists emerged in Spain. In September 1933, the Government of Azana fell and the Republican-Socialist coalition came to an end. In the elections of November 1933, the conservatives were voted to power in Spain. On the eve of the elections of 1936, thanks to the efforts of **Manuel Azana**, a **coalition of the left parties** was formed. This included the Socialist Party, the Communist Party and the Republican Union Party and came to be known as the Popular Front. The right-wing groups in Spain formed the National Front. In the elections of Spain in February 1936, the Popular Front won 263 seats out of 473 and formed the new government. Soon, however, some army officers in Spain like Emilo Mola, Francisco Franco, Gonzalo Queipo de Llano, etc., started conspiring against the Popular Front. Thus began the **Spanish Civil War** in **1936**.

In **Paris**, a **radical socialist revolutionary government** was set up in the wake of the establishment of the Third Republic and the six months' siege by the German forces of Paris that followed the crushing defeat of Napoleon III at the hands of the Prussian army in the Franco-Prussian War at the **Battle of Sedan** in **1871**. It ruled Paris from 18 March to 28 May 1871 and was known as the **Paris Commune**. It was organised by the workers and the lower middle-class people who were very badly affected by the breakdown of the factories and other enterprises because of war. The people belonging to the upper classes left Paris in large numbers. But here was an influx of people, especially belonging to the lower classes, from the areas occupied by the Germans. This created a crunch on the existing resources, further enraging the people. Again, some people desired their own government in Paris with their own elected council (as was the case with many small provinces or departments as they were called) and not a national government. The Commune was defended by the National Guard comprising men conscripted to part-time service as reservists. Their indignation was directed in full measure against the Third Republican government led by **Adolphe Thiers** that signed a **humiliating armistice with Prussia**. According to the terms of the armistice, the French National Army, not the National Guard, was disarmed. The fierce radicals of the Commune who engaged in violent clashes against the army and the Third Republic resembled the Jacobins of the French Revolution and advocated wide distribution of private property. Marx called it **the first successful workers' revolution**. In his pamphlet entitled 'Civil War in France' he extolled the Communards as the revolutionaries who fulfilled the transitional phase of the proletarian revolution as prescribed by the Marxists. The Commune received strong support from socialists like Auguste Blanqui and Proudhon.

We have already seen the distinction between the revisionists and the purists within the body of German socialists. A similar division could be identified within the French socialists as well. There were **Jules Guesde**, the purist and leader of the Marxist French Workers' Party that later merged with Blanquist Central Revolutionary Committee to form the **Parti Socialiste de France**. **Jean Jaures**, the leader of the Parti Socialiste Francaise and **Alexander Millerand**, were the revisionists. Support for the revisionists, however, evaporated as it was increasingly felt that participation in and cooperation with the government did not yield satisfactory and expected results. For example, conditions and prospects of the workers had not improved substantially; nor did the rise in prices always match the rise in wages. As a result, faith and confidence in revisionism gradually waned and prominent leaders like Alexander Millerand, who was a minister in a non-socialist government, lost a lot of support despite his significant contributions to the amelioration of the conditions of labour as a minister of commerce under the Republican cabinet of **Pierre Waldeck-Rousseau**. Millerand's contribution as the labour minister included the introduction of substantial reforms like reduction of work days from 11 to 10, an eight-hour workday for postal employees, and prescription of maximum hours and minimum wages for all work. He is specially known for his project of old age pensions which became law in 1905. He formed a small party called the Independent Socialist Party in 1907.

Between 1890 and 1914, a group of socialists emerged in **France** known as the **Syndicalists** led by **Georges Sorel**. **Syndicalism, anarcho-syndicalism, or revolutionary syndicalism** is an economic system and a form of socialism in which syndicates or groups of workers (trade unions) own the means of production. It aimed at abolition of the wage system because in the view of its proponents, wage was the main element that eventually led to slavery. Syndicalism, therefore, advocated direct action by workers and was a revolutionary concept. It was private ownership of property that denied a vast majority of the population the opportunity to enjoy material independence and concentrated economic, social and political privileges emanating from ownership of property in the hands of a few. To recall, that is why Proudhon had equated property to theft. From France, syndicalism spread to England, Spain, Italy and the Latin-American countries, and was a predominant form of socialism till the end of World War II. Its two major exponents in France were Georges Sorel and **Fernand Pelloutier**. The two main labour organisations which propagated syndicalism mostly through strikes were the **Confederation Generale du Travail** and the **Federation des Bourses du Travail**. Immensely inspired by the thoughts of Pierre Proudhon and Auguste Blanqui, syndicalism, like Marxism, was opposed to capitalism and **advocated class war**. Sorel's ideas first appeared in a series of articles in *Le Mouvement Socialiste* in early 1906 and were translated in various languages. They were compiled together in the form of a book in 1908 entitled *Reflexions sur la Violence*. Sorel propounded that workers should be made to believe in the effectiveness of **strikes by the proletariat** that would eventually lead to the end of bourgeois rule. A great admirer of his ideas was Benito **Mussolini**, who based his corporatist state on the syndicalist thoughts of Georges Sorel.

In England, several reforms had already taken place in the 19th century. The political reforms like widening of the franchise had immense effect on the common people and was an important reason why the country successfully avoided a revolutionary upsurge. In **England**, a new kind of socialism was prominent in the late 19th and 20th centuries. It was known as **Fabian socialism**. Fabian Society was an organisation founded in England in 1884 to *spread socialist principles gradually by peaceful means*. They wanted to avoid violent revolution. The movement was so called because they were founded on the principles of the **Roman General**

Fabius Cunctator who won the battles over the powerful Carthaginian army of Hannibal, the military commander of Carthage in the **Second Punic War** through his unique, patient and elusive tactics. He is also known as the **father of guerrilla warfare**, a novel and distinctive method that became popular and is applied even in modern times. He developed the remarkable strategy of delaying frontal attack, thereby successfully tiring out the enemy. He therefore, earned the epithet 'Cunctator' which was a Latin word meaning 'delayer'. Likewise, the Fabian socialists aimed at reforming society slowly and gradually in a peaceful manner. Later they founded the **Labour Party** in **1906**. Prominent members of the Fabian Society were poets Edward Carpenter and John Davidson, George Bernard Shaw, Sidney and Beatrice Webb, Annie Besant, H.G. Wells, Jawaharlal Nehru, etc. Their activities included creating a universal health care system, guaranteeing a minimum wage, fixing hours of work, educating the people by organising seminars, conferences, summer schools, public speeches, discussion groups, by publishing research articles, papers, pamphlets, news bulletins in order to attract the attention of the people towards their ideal and objective of delivering social justice and popular welfare in a placid, humanitarian but forceful way. In England, a revolutionary working-class movement was also organised by the **Chartists** in the late 1830s and 1840s, which is said to be the first mass movement driven by the working classes (see Chapter 7). Whereas in Russia, an efflorescence of socialist ideas led to the Russian Revolution.

Notes

1. 'Definition of Socialism,' *Urban Dictionary*. Available at https://www.urbandictionary.com (accessed May 2025).

2. George Lichtheim, *A Short History of Socialism* (London: Widenfeld & Nicolson, 1970), 14.

3. Ibid., 41.

4. Frank Podmore, *Robert Owen: A Biography* (New York: Haskell House Publishers Ltd., 1971), 20.

5. Ian Donnachie, 'Education in Robert Owen's New Society: The New Lanark Institute and Schools,' *The Encyclopedia of Informal Education* (2000).

6. Charles Fourier, *Selections from the Works of Fourier*, trans. Julia Franklin (1851), Marxist Internet Archive. Available at https://www.marxists.org (accessed May 2025).

7. Charles Fourier, *The Utopian Vision of Charles Fourier: Selected Texts on Work, Love and Passionate Attraction* (Boston: Beacon Press, 1971).

8. Pierre-Joseph Proudhon, *The General Idea of the Revolution in the Nineteenth Century*, trans. John Beverly Robinson (London: Freedom Press, 1923), 293–94.

9. Pierre-Joseph Proudhon, *Property is Theft: A Pierre-Joseph Proudhon Anthology*, ed. Iain McKay (Edinburgh, Oakland, and Baltimore: AK Press, 2011), 133.

10. Jacques Droz, *Europe Between Revolutions, 1815–1848* (Glasgow: Fontana Collins, 1981), 80–81.

11. Boris Nicolaievsky and Otto Maenchen-Helfen, *Karl Marx: Man and Fighter*, trans. G. David and Eric Mosbacher (London: Methuen & Co., 1936).

12. Keathe Mengelberg, 'Lorenz Von Stein and His Contribution to Historical Sociology,' *Journal of the History of Ideas* 22(2) (April–June 1961): 267–274.

13. August Thalheimer, *Introduction to Dialectical Materialism*, 1927, Marxist Internet Archive. Available at https://www.marxists.org (accessed May 2025).

14. Sydney Hook, 'Marx and Feuerbach,' *New International* 3(2) (April 1936): 47–57. Also, Sydney Hook, 'Karl Marx and Moses Hess,' *New International* 1(5) (December 1934): 140–144.

15. Hook, 'Marx and Feuerbach'.

16. Hook, 'Karl Marx and Moses Hess,' 140–144.

17. Jaspers, *Spinoza*, in *The Great Philosophers*, vol. II,14.

18. Ibid.

19. Hook, 'Karl Marx and Moses Hess,'140–144.

20. Lichtheim, *A Short History of Socialism*, 74.

21. Robert L. Heilbroner, *The Worldly Philosophers* (New York: Touchstone, 1999), 153.

22. Lichtheim, *A Short History of Socialism*,145.

23. Friedrich Engels, *Marx Engels Collected Works*, vol. 6 (1976), 558. Also quoted in Rob Sewell, 'The 1848 Revolutions: The Hoped-for Prelude to the Proletarian Revolution,' *In Defence of Marxism*, Marxist Internet Archive.

24. Lichtheim, *A Short History of Socialism*, 97–98.

25. George H. Sabine and Thomas L. Thorson, *A History of Political Theory*, 4th ed. (New Delhi: Oxford & IBH Publishing Company, 1973), 690.

26. Lichtheim, *A Short History of Socialism*, 74

27. Sabine and Thorson, *A History of Political Theory*, 690.

28. Tucker, Ibid.

29. Heilbroner, *The Worldly Philosophers*, 95. Joseph A. Schumpeter, *Capitalism, Socialism and Democracy*, 2nd ed. (Virginia: Wilder Publications Inc., 2011). Also quoted in G.S.L. Tucker, 'Ricardo and Marx,' *Economica*, n.s., 28, no. 111 (August 1961): 252

30. Tucker, 'Ricardo and Marx,' 252.

31. Ibid.

32. Tucker, 'Ricardo and Marx,'.

33. Ibid., 85.

34. Lichtheim, *A Short History of Socialism*, 82.

35. Ibid.

36. V.K. Dimitriev, *Economic Essays on Value, Competition and Utility* (Cambridge: Cambridge University Press, 1974).

37. Ladislaus von Bortkiewicz, 'Value and Price in the Marxian System,' *International Economic Papers*, no. 2 (1952).

38. N. Okishio. 'Technical Changes and Rate of Profit,' *Kobe University Economic Review*, no. 7 (1961): 85–89.

39. Alan Freeman, 'A General Refutation of Okishio's Theorem and a Proof of the Falling Rate of Profit,' *MPRA (Munich Personal RePEc Archive)*, 1998.

40. Peter Singer, *Marx: A Very Short Introduction* (Oxford: Oxford University Press, 1980), 50.

41. Lichtheim, *A Short History of Socialism*, 98.

42. Ibid.

43. Ibid.

44. Marvin Perry, *An Intellectual History of Modern Europe* (Boston: Houghton Mifflin Company, 1992), 265.

45. Ibid., 265.

46. Heilbroner, *The Worldly Philosophers*, 152.

47. John Stuart Mill, *Principles of Political Economy* (London: John W. Parker, 1848), Book 4, Chap. 7.

48. *Marx Engels Collected Works* (Moscow: Progress Publishers, vol. 24), 467. Also quoted in Ian Angus, 'Marx and Engels… and Darwin?' *International Socialist Review*, no. 71 (May 2010).

CHAPTER 7

Parliamentary and Institutional Reforms in Britain
Chartists and Suffragettes

Constitutionalism, springing from the ideas of **John Locke**, is the doctrine that espouses the belief that the powers and authority of a government ought to be contained by a body of laws called the Constitution, which aims to protect the interests of the people by preventing a government from becoming arbitrary. It is understood that the Constitution emerges through a democratic procedure and popular consent. Under this particular 'ism', I seek to elaborate the growth of democracy in *Britain, the only country that had a parliament since the 13th century.*

From the Magna Carta to the Establishment of the Parliament

The Parliament evolved in England in the 11th century in the form of a council created by **King Henry I**. It consisted of prominent nobles and church dignitaries. It was not exactly what we call a parliament today, but rather a talking session between the King and the nobles. The King asked for their advice, but actually did what he wanted. This eventually developed into the **House of Lords**. The most important development in the formation of the Parliament was the **acceptance of the *Magna Carta*** (Latin for the Great Charter) by **King John** on **15 June 1215**. It was a charter for the protection of the barons from illegal imprisonment, the preservation of Church rights, protection from overtaxation, and so on. During the reign of **Henry III**, there was **a civil war in England in 1264–1267** led by **Simon de Montford**, the sixth Earl of Leicester, against the King, ostensibly over the issue of overtaxation, though there had been general dissatisfaction over his methods of governance, which intensified in the wake of a widespread famine. The rebels demanded more power for the baronial council and reassertion of the *Magna Carta*. After his victory over the King, Montford established a Parliament summoning the barons, knights, burgesses and other key town administration authorities to discuss matters. Montford came to be referred to as the **founder of the Commons**. The House of Lords already existed since the 11th century, and now the formation of the Commons in the 13th century created **the first two-chamber, or bicameral, English Parliament**.

The bicameral Parliament was not a popularly elected body and its power during the Tudor rule remained insignificant. The Parliament started asserting itself under the absolute rule of the **Stuart kings** and the conflict between the monarchy and the Parliament intensified. In fact, the right of the Parliament to criticise the Crown and its ministers developed more strongly towards the end of the 14th century. The **Good Parliament of 1376**, for example, severely criticised the government of **Edward III**, and also saw the **first procedure of impeachment** by which an offender could be brought to trial before the House of Lords. The main cause of conflict of the Parliament and the Crown from the beginning was the extraction of money by the kings from the nobility and the wealthy merchants without the sanction of the Parliament. It reached its peak at the time of Charles I when he was engaged in war with Scotland and needed money. The Parliament refused and the **Civil War** started in **August 1642**. It ended in the defeat of **Charles I** who was publicly executed in 1649. The Parliament established a Republic. **Oliver Cromwell**, a soldier and a Member of Parliament, was made the 'Lord Protector'. He led the New Model Army which was formed in 1645 by the parliamentarians to fight the Civil War. As a rule, the army's leaders were prohibited from having a seat in either the House of Lords or House of Commons. Cromwell ruled for eleven years. After his death in 1658, **Charles II**, the son of the executed King Charles I was invited to be the king. This was called the **Restoration** of the Stuart monarchy, which took place in **1660**. The period from the execution of Charles I to the Restoration is known as the **Interregnum** declared by the Rump Parliament in May 1649. In 1653, after forcible dissolution of the Rump Parliament, Oliver Cromwell was declared Lord Protector of a united 'Commonwealth of England, Scotland and Ireland'.

Both Charles II and after him his son and successor **James II** believed in the absolute power of the King and endeavoured to assert their supreme authority over the Parliament. Charles II had become a Roman Catholic on his deathbed and James II was a devout Roman Catholic. His **overt Roman Catholicism** created considerable discontent in the country. In 1688, **William of Orange**, *stadtholder* (a provincial executive officer or governor who holds a position on behalf of the monarch or the state) of Netherlands, and the husband of Mary, the daughter of James II, was invited by some prominent politicians of England to redress the nation's grievances. As William advanced towards London, James II fled to France. The crown was offered to William and Mary jointly. This bloodless revolution is known in history as the **Glorious Revolution**. The Revolution was *a clear triumph of the Parliament over the monarchy*, and established the Parliament as the ruling power of England. The doctrine of divine right of kings was completely destroyed. The Parliament enacted a **Bill of Rights** in **1689** which provided that suspension of laws, levying of taxes and raising an army could be done only with the consent of Parliament which would meet more frequently. It also provided for trial by jury, right to petition and freedom from excessive bails, fines and punishment of persons accused of crime.

This kind of relationship persisted and the power and activities of the King were clearly defined. The King was the 'King in Parliament' which meant that the King was the repository of wide legislative powers; and he was also the 'King in Council' indicating the supreme executive and judicial authorities. It was amply clarified that the monarch enjoyed the following powers: the right to grant pardon or clemency; to coin money; to command army in battles; to appoint to public office; to confer nobility; and the last but of supreme importance, to summon Parliament and to dismiss Commons and to arrest without a magistrate's warrant. The King was assisted in his work by a **Privy Council**. The Privy Council was in essence the British sovereign's private council. It wielded a lot of political and judicial powers. It sprang from the *Curia Regis*, or a court composed of people who helped the sovereign in social, political and judicial matters, though of course these functions were not as clear and distinct initially as they were to become later. Its composition and functions varied from time to time and from country to country. With the passage of time, however, the *curiae* became so overloaded with work that much of their judicial activities were delegated to special courts of law, such as the Court of King's Bench in England, much like the Parlements in France.

The Privy Council system worked well as long the King was competent enough to choose the right men for the right task. Later, however, these councils became pothouses of jealousy and bickering. Its power atrophied as gradually most political responsibilities of the monarch were transferred to the Prime Minister, who in his turn formed his own Cabinet which was a core group of ministers aiding the King in his executive powers. However, the modern parliamentary system of the entire cabinet resigning in the event of **no-confidence** of the government had not emerged then. That system developed later during the time of **Robert Walpole**, who remained the Prime Minister of King George I from 1721–1742. In 1782 the government of Lord North resigned because the Commons did not support his policies. The **Reform Bill in 1832**, discussed in detail in a later section, elaborated two basic principles of the cabinet government:

> (*i*) the cabinet should be formed of members belonging to the political party which was in majority in the House of Commons;
>
> (*ii*) the cabinet was to be collectively responsible to the Commons for the activities of the government.

The British Parliament Consolidates its Power

Several stages contributed to the strengthening of the power of the Parliament. One was the development of the system of **petition**. It had its origin in the encouragement of **Edward I** (1272–1307). Petitions of various kinds—requests for favour, justice, redress—were presented by individuals or organisations like town authorities or merchant guilds both to the Crown as well as to the Parliament. This gave the Parliament the status of a court of justice. At the time of the revolt of the American colonies against the mother country, that is Britain, the revolutionaries were divided into two groups—the extremists and the moderates. While the former wanted to present a petition only before the King, the latter pleaded to present it both before the King and the Parliament. Another very significant power that fortified the position of the Parliament was **the authority to grant taxation**. The kings were compelled to bestow on the Parliament the authority to levy taxes. The outbreak of prolonged wars like the Hundred Years' War or the War of Roses enhanced the importance of the Parliament's function of consenting to the levy of taxes. Furthermore, the maturing of the British democratic system began with the passing of a number of Acts or legislative measures. The spirit of reform was invigorated and *the reform movement became an inseparable and distinctive feature of British parliamentary growth.*

The most significant reform was that of the **criminal code by Robert Peel** as Secretary of State for the Home Department. He humanised the prison system and modernised the police administration. Between 1825 and 1830, he effected the fundamental consolidation and comprehensive reorganisation of the criminal code. In 1829, he carried through the Metropolitan Police Act which set up the first disciplined police force for the Greater London area.

Another important democratic reform brought forth by the Parliament was the **Catholic Emancipation Act** of **April 1829**. After Reformation, the Roman Catholics faced serious restrictions regarding purchase of land, holding civil and military posts, or seats in the Parliament. The Irish Catholics were not allowed to vote in parliamentary elections. A Catholic Association was formed by **Daniel O'Connell**, the prominent Irish lawyer and orator, to mobilise the movement for Catholic emancipation. Robert Peel, who was the Home Secretary at this time, offered to resign on this issue. He and his Conservative Party were dogmatically opposed to the measure as maintaining the supremacy of the Church was one of their main concerns. **Prime Minister Wellington** looked upon the issue of Catholic emancipation as a political rather than a religious issue and was tilted in its favour since 1825. He requested Peel to hold on to his resignation because the situation had become complicated in the meantime over the issue of **O'Connell**'s victory in the **County Clare Elections**, which he had contested irrespective of his ineligibility to stand in elections (a Roman Catholic in Ireland could neither vote nor stand in parliamentary elections). Wellington now had two options. Either he could get the Catholic Emancipation Bill passed and give O'Connell his seat, or he could declare the elections null and void. In the latter case loomed the overwhelming danger of eruption of major violence in Ireland, which was under the British Empire at the time. He decided to choose the former and realised the pressing need for Peel's support in convincing the King. He said to Peel, "I tell you frankly that I do not see the smallest chance of getting the better of these difficulties if you should not continue in office."[1] Peel saw the necessity for the emancipation, placed the interests of the nation before his personal principles and agreed to put the Bill before the

Commons. He convinced the King, and on 29 February 1829 proposed the Bill to the House of Commons in the face of savage criticism from his party members and the press for betraying the cause of Protestantism. Finally, the Catholic Emancipation Bill became an Act in April.

The Reform Bill of 1832 and Franchise

The years 1832 to 1884 were indeed momentous in England's parliamentary history as far as elections and voting were concerned. Till 1832, **voting rights** in England were most **unevenly distributed** as they were mostly concentrated in the old traditional rural areas. It is here where the landed classes lived. The upcoming industrial cities which were rapidly growing in the wake of the Industrial Revolution were completely unrepresented. Even large industrial cities like Birmingham and Manchester did not have any parliamentary seat. Regrettably, many of these rural constituencies had ceased to have enough population and had been reduced to what the reformers called "**rotten boroughs**" (uninhabited or depopulated rural districts). But they still retained their original representation. On the eve of the passing of the Reform Act of 1832, more than 140 parliamentary seats of a total of 658 were in rotten boroughs, 50 of which had fewer than 50 voters. In addition, there were **pocket boroughs** which were controlled by one person or family. The relatively small populations in these boroughs were either bribed or browbeaten to return their representatives to the Parliament. The sparsely populated Cornwall county returned 44 members, while the city of London with more than 100,000 people, returned only four members.[2] Similarly, Old Sarum with only seven members dominated two seats.[3] The situation needed an urgent change.

John Wilkes and **Major John Cartwright** had made demands for parliamentary reforms in the 1760s and also in the first decade of the 19th century, respectively. John Cartwright, an English naval officer, advocated **taxpayer franchise reform** to generate parliamentary support for a redefined programme of reform without which, he believed, corruption could not be checked and Britain's ability to resist foreign invasion would be seriously mitigated.[4] In 1776 he published his pamphlet 'Take Your Choice!' advocating annual parliaments, the secret ballot and manhood suffrage. He came to be known as the 'father of reform'. These demands were later on picked up by the Chartists and became part of their 'six points'". Wilkes, the journalist and British MP from Middlesex between 1774 and 1790, had introduced the first bill for parliamentary reform in the British Parliament in 1776. But no reform of the Parliament had followed. Since the formation of the modern party system in England in late 18th century, in the form of the two political parties—the Tory and the Whig—it was the Tory party which was ruling (with a brief interregnum of the regime of Baron Grenville in 1806–1807) till 1830 when **Earl Grey** from the **Whig party** became the Prime Minister. The **Tories** were the pillars of conservatism in England (that is why they were renamed the **Conservative Party**) and opposed reform in general, and parliamentary reform in particular. They were the supporters of the monarchy vis-à-vis the Parliament in the Civil War. Therefore, it is not surprising that no worthwhile reform of Parliament took place as long as they were in power. Things, however, began to change with the coming of the Whigs at the helm of affairs

Even before Earl Grey became the Prime Minister, **Lord John Russell**, the prominent Whig leader had introduced in 1820 a scheme for **disenfranchising the rotten boroughs**, especially the worst cases. The measure for disfranchising Grampound was accepted by both the Houses in 1821. Although composed mostly of aristocrats, with only three commoners, the Ministry of Grey was favourable to reforms. Asa Briggs observed, "While their opponents in 1830 believed that a considerable measure of parliamentary reform would lead to national catastrophe, the Whigs maintained that only a considerable measure could prevent a catastrophe."[5] He convinced the King accordingly. The people who supported the Whigs were the bankers, financiers, industrialists, dissenters like William Smith, John Wilkes, utilitarians like Bentham, popular Radicals like William Cobbett and Henry Hunt. Bentham commented,

> The Tories are the people's avowed enemies … On no occasion under the ever-increasing weight of the yoke of oppression and misrule, from any hand other than that of the parliamentary Whigs can the people receive any of the slightest chance (talk not of relief) for the retardation of increase.[6]

The **popular radicals** in 19th-century England were mainly working class and middle-class people who agitated for parliamentary reforms like the right to vote, freedom of press and free trade.

A committee of four was formed for the framing of the **Reform Bill**. The **four members** were **Lord Durham, J.W. Ponsonby, Sir James**

Graham and **John Russell**. Russell outlined the Reform Bill of 1832 and was known to be its primary architect. It evoked fierce opposition from the Tories. The Tory speaker Sir Robert Inglis called it "a revolution that will overturn all the natural influence of rank and property".[7] In fact, the Tories were apprehensive of a number of discrepancies that might follow the reform. *First,* they feared the overwhelming representation of the general public that would eventually curb severely the pre-eminence of several existing institutions, like the House of Lords, the Church, even the monarchy. In the words of Crocker, who had expressed his apprehensions to Sir Walter Scott, "All will be levelled to the plane of petty shop-keepers and small farmers."[8] They considered it **a serious intrusion of property rights** in general. They were deeply concerned that the reform would pave the path for several other reforms in future that would completely disrupt the existing social, political and economic fabric. The Whigs, however, maintained emphatically that nothing was going to encroach upon the rights of property. It was only an effort **to ensure a fair representation of the rising industrial and manufacturing populace**. It was unfair that large industrial centres like Manchester and Birmingham were unrepresented. In the words of a local Wolverhampton businessman:

> Fifty years ago we were not in that need of Representatives, which we are at present, as we then manufactured nearly exclusively for home consumption, and the commercial and manufacturing districts were then identified with each other; where one flourished, both flourished. But the affairs are now changed—we now manufacture for the whole world, and if we have not members to promote and extend our commerce, the era of our commercial greatness is at an end.[9]

The debates on Russell's first proposal of the Reform Bill began in March 1831. The small boroughs with less than 2000 inhabitants were completely disfranchised. The representation of boroughs with less than 4000 people were reduced by 50 per cent. As a result, 168 vacancies were created out of which 42 were to be given to new boroughs and about 55 to counties. The rest were not to be filled up at all, with the consequence that the House of Commons would now be smaller in size than before; a 40 shilling freeholder vote (those who had the parliamentary franchise to vote, by virtue of possessing freehold property, or directly holding lands of the king, for an annual rent of at least 40 shillings) was retained in the counties; in the boroughs whoever occupied a building worth 10 pounds annual—whether a tenant or a landlord—was eligible for a vote.

The **cost of elections** was designed to be kept low, and that is why the poll was decided to be limited to two days. The large constituencies were to be divided into separate polling districts. It is significant to note that the Reform Bill **excluded women** from the electorate by defining voters as 'male persons'. The Bill passed the Commons by one vote, but got stuck in the House of Lords. Under pressure from the Whigs, the House was dissolved and fresh elections were ordered by **King William IV** on the question of reform. Reform was the main agenda in the **elections of 1831**, although the kind of reform aspired for varied from place to place.

REFORM ISSUES OTHER THAN FRANCHISE

Franchise was not the only burning issue. **Birmingham**, for example, under its leader Thomas Attwood focussed upon **currency reform**. Manchester yearned **for repeal of corn laws**. In general, there was a public outcry in favour of reform. The homes of staunch conservative leaders like the Duke of Newcastle and Wellington were attacked. There were violent demonstrations at Nottingham and Derby, Worcester and Bath. On 29 October 1831, there was serious rioting in Bristol. Arson and vandalism were at their worst.[10] The whole town was mercilessly ransacked. Russell prepared a new Reform Bill with minor modifications from the first. *This time the Bill passed the Commons with a large margin, but on 8th October it again failed to pass the House of Lords.* In May, a frustrated Earl Grey requested the King to grant him the authority for the creation of some liberal peers who would get the Bill cleared in the House of Lords. The King refused and Grey resigned. The King invited Wellington to form the government. Although Wellington tried to form a team of ministers, in the end he found the task too difficult, and the King had to depend on Grey again and gave in to Grey's demand for creating **additional peers**. The threat of creation of new peers was, however, enough signal for the House of Lords, and the Bill was passed on 4 June 1832.

CRITICS FOR AND AGAINST THE REFORM BILL

Ever since the Bill was passed, it became a subject of controversy. Voices were heard both for and against the Reform Bill. In the words of

Phillips and Wetherell, "Opponents viewed the Bill's probable impact as an unqualified disaster, while proponents saw it as nothing less than political salvation."[11] Members of the aristocracy naturally denounced it vehemently. The **Duke of Wellington** regretted that "in a short time… nothing will remain of England but the name and the soil."[12] **Lord Wharncliffe** thought that England was "gravitating towards a revolution" because the influence of "respectable persons of the middle class" was "overwhelmed by the numerical strength of the low voters, who want to go to all lengths."[13] **Karl Marx**, on the other hand, was very disappointed that the working class gained nothing out of it. He condemned the Reform Act as nothing but "a series of the most extra-ordinary tricks, frauds, and juggles…calculated not for increasing middle-class influence, but for the exclusion of Tory and the promotion of Whig patronage."[14] **Benjamin Disraeli** too agreed with Marx that the Act was designed by the Whigs "to root up the power of their opponents; and to destroy the happy balance of the parties in the state."[15]

On the other hand, there were several opinions in favour of the Bill as well. An article in *Westminster Review*, for example, considered the Act as **equivalent to going to Bastille** which inspired in England a great political change.[16] **Francis Place**, the son of an overseer and himself a leather-breeches maker and the founder of the National Political Union in 1831, saw it as a great start that would eventually open up the way to several other reforms in future. In the view of **John Cannon**, 1832 marked not just "the beginning of the transformation from one political system to another but also the foundation achievement of modern conservatism."[17] **Richard W. Davis** believed that the Whigs wanted to give the middle class a voice in the political system and it was the responsibility of the elite to abide by public opinion. And this indeed brought about a significant change in the political attitude of the English people.

In recent years, a group of **revisionist historians** have endeavoured to strike a balance between these two extreme views. **Norman Gash** and later **Frank O'Gorman** have shown that the new reform was more a continuity than change. According to Gash, the influence of the political patrons continued unabashed. The old political climate prevailed, which encouraged corruption and electoral violence.[18] Similarly, O'Gorman argued that the old electoral system, despite all its shortcomings and inadequacies, corruption and lack of transparency, undoubtedly played a vital role in the field of politics in England. The new Reform Bill was only a continuation.[19] According to the early Whig historians like **J.R.M. Butler** and **G.M. Trevelyan**, the reform was a *well-thought out 'concession' of liberal-minded aristocrats to the people with their yearning for reforms*. According to later historians like **D.C. Moore**, the Reform Act was less a 'concession' rather than a 'conservative cure'.[20] He, therefore, called it an act of deference on the part of the reformers. Its main purpose was to consolidate the political powers of the landed promoters by separating urban and rural constituencies. **Cannon** went on to call it a "compromise rather than a surrender."[21] **W.N. Molesworth**, however, felt that the Whigs were being pushed into reform out of apprehension of the wrath of the "great social and popular forces". Nevertheless, he believed at the same time that the Reform Bill should "be regarded by every Englishman with feelings of unmixed pride and satisfaction."[22] **E.A. Wasson**, however, firmly believed that whatever be the other motivations, the primary purpose of the Whigs was to bring about a change in the state of affairs. In his essay 'The Spirit of Reform, 1832–67', Wasson observed that the most significant underlying factor of the Great Reform Bill was the spirit of aristocratic decline. The enfranchisement of a section of the middle class constituted a landmark in the political outlook of the country. In the view of Wasson, in the curtailment of the political monopoly and privileges of the aristocracy lay the true Whig spirit of reform. Indeed, "Humpty Dumpty fell off the wall in 1832." This made the Reform Bill more than either a 'concession' or a 'cure'.[23] It was a genuine concern for improvement.

The Poor Law Amendment Act of 1834

After their success with the Reform Act of 1832, the *Whigs began to call themselves Liberals and were predominant in the House of Commons. The Tories, henceforth, were referred to as the Conservatives.* The next important reform that the Whigs brought about was the **Poor Law Amendment Act of 1834**. By this law "outdoor relief" was to be reserved for the sick and the aged alone. All able-bodied poor were subsequently required to earn their needs by serving in workhouses. The conditions of the workhouses were to be made so stringent that only people in dire need would try to avail of their benefits.

Some people welcomed it because it would reduce the cost of the government to maintain the poor. The poor would henceforward have shelter against vicissitudes of weather and would be clothed and fed in the workhouses. Poor children in the workhouses would receive some schooling. Moreover, **the poor would be fruitfully engaged** and would learn to work hard to earn their living. The beggars would be taken off the streets. The Poor Law Amendment Act was passed on the basis of a Report issued by **a Royal Commission** appointed by the government of Earl Grey to investigate the workings of the existing Poor Law and to make suggestions for improvement. Led by **Thomas Frankland Lewis** and with **Edwin Chadwick** as the Secretary, the Commission outlined the fundamental provisions on which the law was based. However, the law was inspired by a number of other factors. One major driving force was the publication of *An Essay on the Principle of Population* by **Thomas Robert Malthus** in 1798. In the eyes of Malthus, poverty was neither accidental nor an act of God. It was the creation of man's own folly. It was the *geometric growth of population that exceeded the earth's capacity of food supply*. Poor relief, therefore, should be abolished as it would only encourage the poor to propagate endlessly to the utter detriment of the earth and humanity as a whole. Economist and politician **David Ricardo**'s '**Iron Law of Wages**' which laid down that *real wages should be equal to the amount necessary to sustain the life of a worker*, underlined the argument that poor aid adversely affected the wages of other workers. **Jeremy Bentham**'s theory of utilitarianism that upheld the doctrine of greatest happiness for the greatest number of people underpinned the new Poor Law. Greatest happiness of the society could be ensured by curbing poor relief and by making the poor work hard for a living.

However, rancour against the new law was quite sharp and intense. **Thomas Carlyle** criticised it vehemently saying that the framers of the law did not take into consideration the **agony of involuntary unemployment**, especially in industrial England north of the Trent. In 1839 Carlyle wrote,

> The New Poor Law is an announcement…that whosoever will not work ought not to live. Can the poor man that is willing to work always find work and live by his work? A man willing but unable to find work is… the saddest thing under the sun.[24]

Richard Oastler, a Tory radical and an ardent social reformer (also known as the 'Factory King') who was instrumental in getting the **Factory Act of 1847** passed, which restricted the working hours of women and children to ten hours per day, regarded the workhouses as nothing less than 'prisons' where a poor man lost all his liberty and was subjected to utmost drudgery in exchange of some clothes and meagre food. **Charles**

Dickens' *Oliver Twist* is a vivid portrayal of the miserable conditions of an English workhouse. There the dress provided was a kind of uniform and food mostly consisted of brown bread and watery soup devoid of any nourishment. Dickens, a sharp critic of the new Poor Law, observed that the poor people of his times had two choices: "being starved by a gradual process in the house or by a quick one out of it."[25] **John Walter**, the editor of *The Times*, highlighted the evils of the new Poor Law by exposing in his newspaper the abysmal miseries of the **Andover Workhouse** where the manager kept the inmates starving by stealing the supplies allocated. As it is, the diet decreed by the Poor Law Commission was nowhere followed properly and the poor were underfed and severely malnourished everywhere. But matters had reached an extreme at Andover and the scandal caught the attention of several politicians and journalists, and eventually led the Parliament to set up a Select Committee to enquire into it in 1846. Those in the workhouses were mostly cut off from their families and were psychologically devastated. Undoubtedly, the conditions of the poor under the new law were materially dehumanising and emotionally shattering. It needed urgent redressal. The Select Committee found the Andover Workhouse manager Colin McDougal to be a drunken bully, and he was sacked. The Select Committee condemned both the Poor Law Commission as well as the Andover House guardians for negligence of duty, as a result of which matters had reached such a pathetic state of affairs. At any rate,

> The most that the anti-poor Law movement could realistically hope to achieve was what had been achieved by 1844, delay, a demonstration of the inadequacy of the law, and some modification of its rigours. Anything more substantial would have to wait until a positive alternative to the New Poor Law was put forward, and that was not to happen for more than half a century.[26]

Repeal of the Corn Laws

The era of empowerment of the bourgeoisie reached its height with the repeal of the vexatious corn laws in 1846, where Prime Minister Robert Peel was instrumental. The **Anti-Corn Law League** was founded in Manchester in 1839 and protests by the industrial classes backed by the radicals against the landlords were organised. *The corn laws were designed to* *favour the domestic producers by imposing tariffs on imported grain.* They kept the prices of bread high and favoured the landed class, while the industrial and merchant classes faced stiff restrictions in other countries, suffered from over-production and the balance of trade was seriously damaged. The capitalists strongly condemned the corn laws and demanded their repeal. In 1843, with the support of the Anti-Corn Law League, Scotsman James Wilson founded London's weekly magazine *The Economist,* which was vocal against the corn laws. The outbreak of the severe Irish famine in 1845 helped strengthen the movement and Prime Minister Robert Peel supported the repeal of all corn laws, which was achieved in 1846.

The benefits of the major reforms of this 'Age of Improvement' were mostly restricted to a limited section of the society—the middle class. These had not trickled down to the lower echelons—the working class, the artisans, the ordinary peasants. Economically as well as politically, they were at the lowest ebb. The Industrial Revolution had created a large working class. Their **material conditions were abysmal**. Their working hours were very long, and the wages were low. The housing system and sanitation conditions were miserable. With the advent of the Industrial Revolution, a large number of skilled artisans lost their traditional livelihood as they failed to compete with machines. Inevitably, they were pushed to accept what they dreaded the most—**proletarianisation**. Politically, they were deprived of the right to vote or the right to be elected. After the passing of the Reform Act of 1832, workers and artisans started agitating for an extension of franchise, but were rebuffed when Lord Russell declared that the reforms of the Act of 1832 were "final". The workers from different parts of the country, therefore, began to **coalesce themselves into the Chartist Movement**, which started in the late 1830s.

The Chartist Movement

In England, a revolutionary working-class movement was organised by the Chartists in the late 1830s and 1840s. It is said to be **the first mass movement driven by the working classes**. It was a direct result of the failure of the Reform Act of 1832 to provide voting rights to those outside the propertied classes, and the passing of the New Poor Act of 1834. The aim of the Chartists was to gain political rights and prominence for the working classes. The organisers of this movement were **William Lovett,**

Francis Place and **Henry Hetherington** who established the **London Working Men's Association** in London in **1836** in order to give a base to the movement. Many enlightened men from prosperous families led the movement. Feargus O'Connor was an estate owner, George Binns was a businessman, Peter McDougall was a surgeon while Thomas Cooper was a journalist. They were called the Chartists because Lovett drew up a charter called the **People's Charter** that comprised **six main demands**. These were:

(*i*) All men to have the vote (universal manhood suffrage)

(*ii*) Voting should take place by secret ballot

(*iii*) Parliamentary elections every year, not once every five years

(*iv*) Constituencies should be of equal size

(*v*) Members of Parliament should be paid

(*vi*) The property qualification for becoming a Member of Parliament should be abolished.

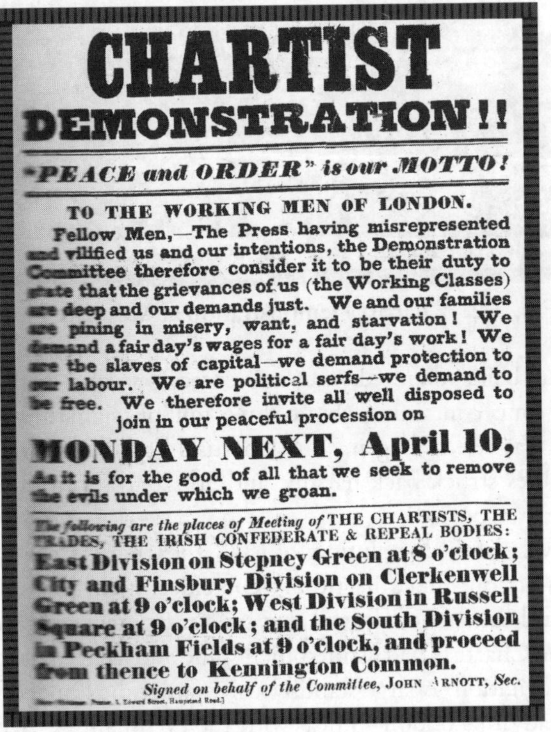

FIG. 7.1: A Pamphlet on a Chartist Demonstration

The Chartists presented petitions before the Parliament three times: in **1839**, in **1842** and the last one in **1848**. In June 1839, the Chartists presented a petition before the House of Commons with over 1.25 million signatures. It was rejected by the Parliament. This provoked widespread unrest. The Chartists reacted quite fiercely. On 4 November 1839, a large number of Chartists led by **John Frost** rebelled against the authorities in Newport. The uprising was severely quelled and nearly 22 demonstrators were killed while many, including John Frost, were transported for life.

FIG. 7.2: Chartist Demonstration at Westgate Hotel

Without being daunted, they presented a second petition in May 1842, this time containing about three million signatures; regrettably, however, it was rejected again. The Chartists began agitating in Preston. The authorities struck back harshly, and 56 Chartists from the Potteries region were transported.

In the wake of the Revolutions of 1848, the Chartists were again stirred to vigorous action. Since its timing coincided with the Revolutions of 1848, the authorities were fearful that serious repercussions would follow, although the Chartists had assured them time and again that they believed in peaceful agitation. A large standby army under the Duke of Wellington was kept ready in London to deal with the eventualities. A meeting was organised on Kennington Common in South London led by **Feargus**

O'Connor, the editor of *The Northern Star*, a weekly newspaper that promoted the Chartist cause. This time the petition contained six million signatures which were carried in three cabs with the leaders, including Feargus O'Connor, Thomas Clark and others, walking alongside the cabs from Kennington Common to the House of Commons. The Parliament claimed that a large number of signatures was fictitious and the petition was rejected.

After this the Chartist movement slowly fizzled out. Many of its leaders died prematurely. Feargus O'Connor died in 1855. George Binns died at the age of 31. John Frost was exiled for a long time. Another leader Robert Peddie was never heard of again. There were many reasons behind this withering away of the movement. *First*, the suppression of its leaders by the authorities was an important dampening agent. The movement failed to win the support of the men in power. Although influential political figures like **Thomas Attwood**, **Benjamin Disraeli** and **Lord John Russell** sympathised with the Chartists, it was not enough to get their petition approved by the Parliament. In July 1839, the House of Commons rejected by 235 votes to 46 the motion brought by Attwood that the Chartist petition should be taken up by the committee for consideration. *Second*, there was no unity among the leaders. There was animosity between O'Connor on the one hand and Lovett, Bronterre O'Brien and Henry Vincent. Lovett even decided to leave the National Charter Association in disgust. Cooper and O'Connor broke out against each other over the Land Scheme. *Third*, as Mark Hovell and Thomas Frederick Tout have pointed out in their book *The Chartist Movement*, the return of prosperity mitigated the effectiveness of the campaign. Asa Briggs too believed that though its main emphasis was on political rights, it was essentially the economic questions that kept the embers of Chartism simmering. He wrote, "Only in years of economic crisis when 'the knife and fork question' dominated politics had they any real opportunity of winning sufficient working-class support to intimidate if not to convince the government. When economic conditions improved after 1842 they inevitably lost ground."[27]

As we have seen, Chartism was born primarily on account of the political shortcomings of the Reform Act of 1832 and hard times arising out of economic and social distress that reached its height in many parts of western and central Europe, especially in Ireland, Flanders, Netherlands and Germany in the 1840s. However, in the rest of Britain, with the exception of Ireland, there was relative prosperity. In England and Scotland, the harvests were improving; railway construction was started with zeal; cotton industry was booming. As a result, employment opportunities increased. All these coincided with the effective administration of Sir Robert Peel. It brought about factory legislations like the **Mines Act of 1842** with the objective of protecting children and women miners, and the **Factory Act of 1842** making the underground employment of women and boys under 10 illegal. The harshness of the new Poor Law was attempted to be attenuated; unemployment was reducing; wages were rising. These reforms diluted the effectiveness of the Chartist movement. Between 1843 to 1846, the price of bread fell remarkably. With some improvement in living conditions and economic relief, the significance and urgency of the six-point political programme demanded by the Chartist movement waned considerably. *Finally*, the swelling influence of the Anti-Corn Law League as well as the persistent growth of trade unionism spelt the ruination of the Chartist movement. It was to some extent revived again in the wake of the economic crisis of 1847–1848, but by then the original leadership was mostly gone and much of the steam of the movement had already evaporated. Moreover, in 1848 the abolition of the corn laws brought down the price of bread—the prime concern of the workers. All these made Chartism ineffective.

Even the **Chartist land plan** chalked out by O'Connor in 1845 was not successful. The plan of O'Connor was to raise funds to buy a large estate, which would be divided up into little farms and sold among subscribers on the basis of lottery. In return tenants would pay a rent at the rate of 5 per cent per annum. With this money the company would go on buying more lands until every subscriber was happily settled. He established the National Land Company in 1847. The plan failed due to bad planning and by 1850, the National Land Company was virtually bankrupt and the plan failed miserably.

Even so, the spirit of Chartism continued. The working-class movement received ample impetus and became an integral part of English public life. The movement was particularly popular among the handloom weavers who were suffering badly in the wake of the Industrial Revolution. Five out of the six Chartist demands were later passed into law. The print media was used by the Chartists effectively. They owned many newspapers, many of which sold thousands of copies per week. O'Connor's newspaper *Northern Star* for example, was the best seller in 1839, with a circulation of 50,000 copies. *Its greatest achievement was to give the workmen a voice in the law-making procedure in the country.*

The Emergence of Trade Unions

What followed in fact was an era of political and social cleavage. The main theme of the next thirty years was, in the words of Asa Briggs, '**divergence**'. It was divergence among political parties, leaders as well as classes. There was cleavage between the Conservatives and the Liberals; the working class and the middle class, or in other words, between labour and capital; the professionals and the businessmen; the unskilled worker and masterful artisan; the factory operative and handloom weaver and so on and so forth.

Working-class movements began to be organised even before the Chartist movement started. Attempts were made to sink the divergences among workers and to weld them into unions with the view of concerted action. The **Grand National Consolidated Trades Union** (G.N.C.T.U.) of 1834 was one such early attempt to form a national workers' confederation. A few months earlier the followers of Robert Owen had formed a Grand National Moral Union of the Productive Classes of the United Kingdom in 1833. However, as early as 1830, the most influential labour organisation was the **Builders' Union**. A federation of existing builders' associations was founded in Manchester and was named **An Operative Builders' Union**. Its highest authority was a Grand Lodge or Builders' Parliament which met twice every year. In 1936, William Lovett, Francis Place and Henry Hetherington established the **London Working Men's Association** (L.W.M.A.). It was one of the basic organs of Chartism. In 1845 the **National Association of United Trades for the Employment of Labour** was founded. It was a sister concern of the **National Association for the Protection of Labour** established in 1830 by John Doherty, a radical Irish factory reformer. The early efforts of the union aimed to address economic and physical welfare like security, intemperance, bad housing, sanitation, better wages, shorter hours of work etc. As we have seen above, the Chartists first drew up a charter demanding political rights and parliamentary reforms like universal suffrage, annual parliaments, secret ballot, etc. Francis Place and L.W.M.A. were instrumental in drawing up the Charter.

Despite many working-class agitations, the issue of workers' political rights was not taken up in the Parliament for a long time to come. Members of Parliament were still not comfortable with reforms, especially political reforms. Nevertheless, a series of **Factory Acts** were passed by the Parliament in order to regulate the conditions of industrial employment. Although the early Acts aimed at regulating the hours of work and health conditions of child labour employed in factories, particularly in cotton mills, they were not effectively enforced until the Act of 1833 established a professional Factory Inspectorate. The **Coal Mines Act** was passed in **1842**. The regulation of working hours was then extended to women by an Act of 1844. An Act in 1847, also known as the **Ten Hour Act** (amended in 1850 and 1853 to seal the defects of the 1847 Act), was passed in response to a long-standing demand of the workers for a 10-hour day. The **Bank Charter Act of 1844** and the **Companies Act of 1844** were designed to put banking and finances in order. But these were all economic and industrial reforms. Even the prominent trade union leaders like **William Allen** (the leader of the engineers), **George Odger** (leader of the London Trades Council), **Robert Applegarth** (Secretary of the Amalgamated Society of Carpenters and Joiners), concentrated more on the physical and economic problems of the workers, rather than on their political rights. However, George Potter founded a smaller organisation in 1866, borrowing the Chartist name London Working Men's Association and the Chartist programme in order to boost support and demonstration for reform. He also started in 1861 a trade union weekly newspaper *Bee-Hive* that primarily advocated strike action, so much so that Applegarth accused Potter of being a "manufacturer of strikes". *Bee-Hive*, however, lacked adequate circulation and eventually landed Potter into bankruptcy.

The Reform Act of 1867

The political divergences on several issues among the leading statesmen obstructed the path of reform. The acute differences of opinion between **John Russell**, the Prime Minister and **Lord Palmerston**, the Foreign Secretary over the policies of the latter in Austria and the Near East in 1848–1849, and the disapproval of the Queen herself of Palmerston's action led to his removal from office at the end of 1851. However, Palmerston took his revenge on Russell in 1852. Russell's government lost in the House of

Commons that year by only nine votes through the vigorous and persistent opposition of Palmerston. Till this time, governments were formed on an individual and not on a party basis. Palmerston himself being a Liberal, took the initiative to get his Liberal Prime Minister ousted. Russell was succeeded by a Peelite (follower of Robert Peel), Prime Minister **Aberdeen**. Palmerston was given the Home Office. Again, here it is to be noted that Palmerston, a Liberal, was invited to a Peelite cabinet. This is how the British Parliament functioned in the mid-19th century.

Palmerston was a staunch opponent of any further reform. This was one of the primary reasons why, inspite of the favourable attitude of a number of Members of Parliament like Russell, Gladstone, Cobden, Graham and Disraeli towards reform, nothing substantial happened as far as reformist change was concerned. Palmerston succeeded Aberdeen in 1855, was out of power in 1858, was soon back again in 1859 and continued till 1865. During this entire period Palmerston successfully blocked the passing of any progressive reform proposal. By the end of his office, that is 1865, the mood of the country was changing rapidly. The working class was becoming increasingly restive. Their demand for political rights, especially extension of franchise, grew more emphatic and forceful. The brewing disquiet could no longer be overlooked. They sullenly resented Palmerston's intransigent approach towards reform. He was now looked upon as an apostle of conservatism. Asa Briggs alludes to a striking incident of 1864. In Bradford, where Palmerston went to address a workingmen's meeting, it was decided that he would be received in conspicuous silence.[28] Already in 1860, a landmark reform had taken place. **William Gladstone**, as the Chancellor of Exchequer had put an end to protection by concluding the famous **Cobden-Chevalier Treaty** with France. It ended French duties on most British manufactured goods and reduced British duties on French wines and brandy. Gladstone now seriously took up the cause of parliamentary reform and even made a speech in the House of Commons to that effect. He was then severely criticised by Prime Minister Palmerston, but Gladstone remained unscathed.

Three significant events paved the path for the passing of the **Reform Act of 1867** that *conferred voting rights to the working class*. The *first* was the visit of **Garibaldi**, the hero of Italian unification, to England in April 1864. Garibaldi was regarded in Europe as the embodiment of the triumph of republicanism and democratic rights. He received a tumultuous welcome from a massive crowd that came to listen to him. It kindled the fire of desire for reform among the masses of the English people. A **Reform League** was formed to intensify the agitation for extension of franchise and other radical reforms. *Second*, the **conclusion of the American Civil War in 1865** marked the victory of the democratic republic and symbolised the freedom of man from the chains of oppression and servitude. *Third*, the **death of Palmerston** in October 1865 removed the last obstacle from the path of reform.

Palmerston was succeeded by **Lord Russell** who was now in his 74th year. Russell was always in favour of 'improvement', and in fact is said to have carried a draft reform Bill in his pocket since 1854.[29] There were, however, a number of staunch critics of reform like **Robert Lowe**, a true Palmerstonian, who warned the House of Commons of the dangers of the 'rule by trade unions'. Real leadership in the Parliament would be completely destroyed, he noted. Nevertheless, Gladstone introduced a mild Bill on 12 March 1866. In the counties, any tenant paying an annual rent of 14 pounds or more would be eligible to vote. In the boroughs, the property qualification for franchise rights was lowered from 10 pounds to 7 pounds. This was fiercely criticised by the radicals. Even among the Liberals, there were dissenters such as Lord Grosvenor, whom Richard Cobden and John Bright (a prominent Liberal who founded the Anti-Corn Law League) referred to as '**Adullamites**'—a short-lived anti-reform faction within the Liberal Party. Gladstone and Russell then passed another Bill (again a cautious one) in May. This was also turned down by 315 votes against 304. Russell resigned.

Lord Russell was succeeded by the conservative leader **Earl of Derby**, with **Benjamin Disraeli** of the Conservative Party as his Chancellor of Exchequer. It was finally the **Derby-Disraeli government** that pushed through the Reform Bill in 1867. Disraeli, who is generally viewed as its prime architect, wanted the entire credit for the achievement of its passage for his own party and to belittle the Liberals at the same time. The passing of the Bill amidst turmoil would help Disraeli emerge as a great statesman of his times. In Disraeli's assessment, the British working class was predominantly conservative. This was also the analysis of 19th-century political analyst, commentator and editor of *The Economist*, **Walter Bagehot**. Much later, Norman Gash[30] in 1953 and M. Ostrogorski[31] in 1964 reiterated the conservative character of the workers in Victorian England. Regrettably, this is what Gladstone, although a shrewd statesman otherwise, failed to grasp.[32] Furthermore, the economic crisis that followed the crash in the stock market in May 1866, coupled with harvest failure due to heavy rain, and the outbreak of cholera in England and the continent as well as across the Atlantic, created panic among the common people. Popular disaffection could no longer be contained. Political exigencies along with economic and social crises raged across the whole country. A huge public **demonstration in Hyde Park** in **May 1867** signalled an impending popular outburst. Majority of the Members in the Parliament realised that the issue of reform could no longer be postponed. In August 1867, the long-debated Reform Bill was eventually passed.

Here it is interesting to note that **Gertrude Himmelfarb** in her essay on the Reform of 1867 did not assign either the American Civil War or the death of Palmerston or the economic crisis of 1866 any special significance for expediting the passage of the Bill in 1867. According to her, even after the success of the North (that is the democratic republican spirit) in the American Civil War, Gladstone complained of public apathy as far as the Reform Bill was concerned. Neither did Palmerston's death bring about any change in general principles. As far as the economic crisis is concerned, the repercussions of the crash and harvest failure with the resultant unemployment and high food prices might have influenced the workers' movement, but how far it impacted parliamentary behaviour is very difficult to assess. Even during the demonstration at Hyde Park, the main focus of protest was not on the right to vote but the right to assembly as they had earlier been denied access to the park.[33] The Reform Bill as it was passed was more the outcome of politics of the party leaders than the efforts of the reformers inside or outside the House.[34]

The 1867 Reform Act enfranchised 1,500,000 men. All urban male householders and tenants paying 10 pounds a year as rent got the right to vote. The electorate was doubled. Seats were redistributed on the basis of population growth. As many as 52 seats were transferred from the small towns (with less than 10,000 people) like Chichester, Harwich and Windsor to the growing industrial towns like Birmingham, Liverpool, Manchester and Leeds. The small towns lost one of their M.Ps. The University of London was given a seat. Women were completely excluded.

It is interesting to note that all of Disraeli's pre-Reform calculations went wrong. He pushed the Reform Bill with the hope of winning popularity for his party among the newly enfranchised population. He, therefore, went farther than Gladstone in his concessions and enfranchised many more men than Gladstone had desired. Disraeli wanted to secure his party's position in the next election when, he assumed, the new voters would vote for his party in huge numbers out of gratitude. However, his dream of wooing the voters was dashed to the ground. In the elections of 1868, the Liberals led by Gladstone won with a substantial margin of over 100 seats. Gladstone remained Prime Minister from 1868 till 1874. But the question is why did this happen? One answer may be that the vote share increased more in the urban boroughs than in the counties, while the latter was the main pillar of conservative support. Second, prior to 1867, in many boroughs conservative candidates generally won unopposed. After the reform, Liberals wanted to explore their fate by competing with the Conservatives in such constituencies and fortune favoured them. Change in electoral circumstances along with well-calculated strategies accounted for Liberal success in 1868. Gary Cox has shown that political competition really intensified at the constituency level as more seats were opened to contestation.[35] In 1868 it favoured the Liberals, though, however, in the long run, it benefited the Conservatives as is evident from the electoral results of 1874.

Voices for and Against

It is true that the Reform Bill became an Act under various considerations, but the stream of apprehensions and misgivings did not end. The most virulent attack came from **Lowe**, who had believed all along that control of the House of Commons should remain in the hands of 'wealth' and 'intellect' rather than 'numbers'. **Thomas Carlyle** expressed his helpless frustration in his diatribe *Shooting Niagara: And After?* and was convinced that the 'Great Unwashed', as the working classes were often called, were about to take the "Niagara leap of democracy", after which the nation was to be ruled by a "swarmery of men buzzing, humming…tumbling in infinite noise and darkness"; the poet Coventry Patmore wrote in despair, "the orgies of the multitude…now begin."[36] According to British historian, jurist and statesman **James Bryce**, "The real danger to England is not from the working class…but from the isolation of classes…and the alarming increase in the political, and still more in the social, power of wealth."[37] The *Quarterly Review* wrote, "In the social pyramid, the possession of the suffrage will unquestionably give to the poorer millions the power of plundering the wealthier thousands."[38] The proponent of the Bill, the Earl of Derby himself was full of apprehensions and referred to the action as a "leap in the dark" in his speech at its third reading.

On the other hand, significant support for the Bill came from eminent members like **John Stuart Mill**. He used the 'class theory' which was the Conservative theory of the Constitution. Applying that theory in the case of the Reform, Mill countered the Conservatives, "There is a class which has not yet had the benefit of the theory….We claim, then, a large and liberal representation of the working classes, on the Conservative theory of the Constitution."[39] Notwithstanding, Mill, irrespective of all his sympathies for socialism, harboured certain misgivings also of a "governing majority of manual labourers",[40] who he feared would tend to protect the home producer against foreign trade. This would obviously hamper policies of free trade. **John Bright**, British radical and liberal statesman who sat in the House of Commons from 1843 to 1889, portrayed himself as a promoter of public welfare and criticised those who called the workers as the embodiments of "poverty and passion."[41] He pleaded the House to pass the Bill. Equating the US decision of elimination of slavery to the question of extension of franchise in England, Gladstone held both as greatly momentous and epoch-making landmarks in the history of their respective countries. He referred to the workers as "our fellow subjects, our fellow-Christians, our own flesh and blood", who could not be so discriminated against.[42]

At any rate, the Reform of 1867 was a momentous decision—no less momentous than the Great Reform Act of 1832. The latter was the first stepping stone, the first opening account, upon which the former was a further elaboration. Posterity has shown, notwithstanding the misgivings of the time, that it **was a 'leap' into the formation of a true democracy**. And after that, there was no looking back. *England was the first country to confer voting rights to its women in 1918*. It is true that much was left to be achieved even after 1867. Several acts followed—in 1884, 1918, 1928. Britain set the trend of a liberated Parliament, which others followed.

The Reform of 1867 gave votes to the industrial workers and artisans in urban areas, but the farm workers of rural areas were left out. So in **1884**, Gladstone, who had succeeded Disraeli and become the Prime Minister for the second time in April 1880, introduced the **Third Reform Bill**. It primarily aimed at bringing the farm labourers within the fold of the electorate. The Conservative Party led by Salisbury opposed it as it was his belief that the poorer farmers in the countryside would never vote for the

Conservatives, who in their eyes represented the 'rich' and the 'privileged'. Therefore, Salisbury argued, it was not in the interest of the Conservatives to expand the electorate with people who were inimical to them. Moreover, they would remain obliged only to the party that enfranchised them, that is the Liberals. Extending votes to the counties would only mean strengthening the Liberals further. So, the Bill, although cleared by the Commons, was rejected by the Conservative-dominated House of Lords. Gladstone, however, was not deterred by this setback. He reintroduced the Bill. This time the Lords agreed to pass it, on an agreement with Gladstone that the Reform Act would be followed by a **Redistribution Bill**. Gladstone agreed, and the Reform Bill of 1884 became a law. The people of the counties were enfranchised on the same terms as those in the boroughs—all adult male householders and 10 pound lodgers were given the right to vote, taking the number of enfranchised men to 5,500,000. Gladstone, true to his word, introduced the Redistribution Bill, as a result of which 79 towns with less than 15,000 inhabitants lost their right to elect an M.P., and 36 towns with population between 15,000 and 50,000 lost one M.P. Towns with populations between 50,000 and 165,000 were given two seats.

The nation was still far from achieving universal adult franchise although majority of adult males had the vote. Women were completely excluded from the scope of franchise, even if they owned sufficient property. Migratory labourers and the very poor who were unable to produce any residence or property qualification were also excluded. Thus, all women and about 40 per cent males were still outside the purview of voting rights. It was not until 1928 that adult suffrage in the true sense of the term was accomplished in Britain.

The Movement for Women's Suffrage

An intensified women's movement for suffrage henceforth started. The discussion, however, had started as far back as 1865 when a group of women had initiated a discussion group known as **Kensington Society**. It was so named because they held their meetings at 44 Phillimore Gardens in Kensington. A draft petition was drawn up by two members, **Barbara Bodichon** and **Helen Taylor**, to be submitted before the Parliament. Henry Fawcett and John Stuart Mill supported the cause of women's suffrage. In 1867 Mill introduced an amendment to the 1867 Reform Act that would give women votes on the same terms as those of men. The amendment was rejected by 194 votes to 73. The members of Kensington Society were naturally crestfallen, but decided to carry on their struggle. With this end in view, they formed the **London Society for Women's Suffrage**. Similar societies sprang up in different parts of the country. Eventually on 14 October 1897, a number of them merged together to form the **National Union of Women's Suffrage Societies** (NUWSS). The first president of the organisation was **Lydia Becker**. After her death, **Millicent Fawcett** became the new president.

From its foundation, the NUWSS played an important role in the **Independent Labour Party** (ILP), which was established in January 1893 at Bradford with **Keir Hardy**, a Gladstonian Liberal and a Member of the House of Commons from the Scottish Labour Party, as the leader. The Independent Labour Party was the first working-class socialist party in Britain. The main objective of the party would be to secure the collective ownership of the means of production, distribution and exchange. Hardy advocated women's rights from the beginning, and after resigning from the House of Commons devoted his energy primarily to promoting the cause of women's suffrage, among other issues. By the end of the 19th century, there were two prominent cross sections among the women who campaigned to win vote—the **suffragists** and the **suffragettes**. The Suffragists were those who used peaceful, moderate and law-abiding methods to attain their objectives. NUWSS was their main organisation. Women who used militant tactics and were members of the **Women's Social and Political Union** (WSPU) were called suffragettes, a name given to them by the *Daily Mail* in 1906. The WSPU was established by **Emmeline Pankhurst** in Manchester in 1903. But even before that she had been a local ILP leader. In 1904 ILP accepted WSPU's demand of immediate granting of votes to women on the same terms as men, but the Labour Party rejected it. The Labour Party had been created in 1900 by the 29 candidates who won seats in the election of that year with the sponsorship of the Labour Representation Committee (founded in 1900 with the object of supporting working-class candidates in elections). After 1900, the ILP became an affiliate of the Labour Party which also represented the big trade unions, many of whose officials were of a conservative cast of mind when it came to women's suffrage. The WSPU as a consequence severed its links with the ILP and, led by Emmeline Pankhurst's daughter **Christabelle Pankhurst**, assumed a militant character, bent upon attacking forcefully the political setup to extract demand of votes for women. The Liberal Government retaliated with matching ruthlessness taking the shape of jail sentences and the notorious Cat and Mouse Act.*

FIG. 7.3: Black Friday Attack on Suffragettes, London

The women's suffrage campaign in Britain stopped more or less completely in August 1914 with the outbreak of the Great War. Emmeline Pankhurst, Christabelle and their followers in WSPU stopped campaigning for vote and threw themselves wholeheartedly into anti-German propaganda and recruiting women war workers for the home front. Women from all social classes helped the war effort by doing heavy jobs such as heaving coal, portering, labouring in the fields and working in munitions factories. As large numbers of men were serving at the front,

---

*The Cat and Mouse Act, 1913, was the name popularly given to special legislation framed during the suffragette agitation of 1906-1914 to meet the problem caused by women who went on 'hunger strike' while undergoing terms of imprisonment. The Act authorised the Home Secretary to liberate a prisoner on licence which could be revoked, without further trial, on a repetition of the offence.

many of their jobs were done by women, like serving as conductors on buses and trams, as labourers on farms and as secretaries and assistants in offices. By the end of the War, women had demonstrated that they were not weak, frail or unintelligent creatures; that they had helped to win the war and at the same time, overturned society's views about the relative roles of men and women.

FIG. 7.4: Annie Kenney and Christabelle Pankhurst

During the World War, the Labour Party shot into prominence. The first war-time coalition government was formed in May 1915, mainly comprising the Liberals and the Conservatives. The need of rapprochement with the Labour Party during the War induced the Home Secretary Walter Long to suggest in August 1916 the calling of an all-party Conference to consider all questions of electoral reform. The Speaker agreed to convene and preside over the Conference. At this conference held in January 1917 all parties were unanimous on every point barring the issue of women's suffrage. Sir John Simon proposed a motion to enfranchise women and kept a hard fight with the government. Meanwhile, on 5 December

Fig. 7.5: Woman Van Driver

1916, Prime Minister **Herbert Henry Asquith**, known to be a diehard 'anti' resigned and **Lloyd George**, who had sympathies with the issue of women's suffrage, became the Prime Minister. He wanted the Conference to continue. The Report of the Speaker's Conference, dated 27th January was issued a few days later. The recommendations of the Conference were embodied in **Representation of the People Bill of 1917**; women's suffrage and proportional representation were left to the M.P.s' votes according to their conscience, without any central party directive (what was known as a 'free vote'). Eventually, a coalition government passed the **Representation of the People Act 1918** that **enfranchised women over 30** if they were local government electors or wives of local government electors. Ten years later, in **1928**, the Conservative government led by Stanley Baldwin passed the **Representation of the People (Equal Franchise) Act** giving the vote to all British women **over the age of 21**.

FIG. 7.6: Women Casting Votes

Source: Available at https://www.flickr.com/photos/nationaalarchief/3333357159/ in/photolist-65yjXa (accessed July 2025)

Often the women's vote in England is linked to their contributions during the War. According to some historians like Gifford Lewis it was a token of gratitude for their contribution during the war. He held that the highly skilled and dangerous work done by women during the war was probably the greatest factor in the granting of the vote to women. Some others like Martin Pugh and Arthur Marwick thought that it was not only public gratitude but **their mature political response** during the War that earned women a credible public identity. It highlighted their strength, capabilities as well as courage. According to Pugh, the non-militants or the Suffragists were the real heroines. They were quiet revolutionaries who helped to attain voting rights by *broadening the base of the movement by fusing it with a working-class component*. It was this mass appeal which convinced the government on the issue of women's franchise.[43] However, many have argued, on the contrary, that War efforts were only a partial cause. The French women, for example, contributed a lot during the War but achieved their votes much later, after World War II. One argument, therefore, is that French women had not fought as vigorously as the

British women prior to the War for their political rights. The suffrage movements of British women undoubtedly had prepared the backdrop for the attainment of votes. A devastated England, after the War, wanted peace above everything and did not want a re-enactment of the violent demonstrations organised by the suffragettes. Had it been only their War efforts, then the young women who had worked so hard in the munitions factories or served as conductors in public transport would have been enfranchised. But they were not. Only mature, responsible women above 30 got it. Evidently, there were factors other than contributions in the War that played a crucial role.

Further Stages of the Evolution of the Parliamentary System

The British Parliamentary system of government evolved through three distinct stages: (*i*) extension of suffrage; (*ii*) development of the cabinet system of government; (*iii*) supremacy of the House of Commons. Apart from universal suffrage, the maturing of the cabinet system was also an important part of a developed parliamentary system of administration. From the earliest times, as we have seen, Britain had Privy Council to assist the King. It consisted of a limited number of members specially selected by the King himself. It enjoyed the full confidence of the monarch. The system changed a little after the supremacy of the Parliament was established over the monarchy in the Glorious Revolution in 1688. King James II abdicated in favour of his daughter Mary and son-in-law Prince William of Orange dynasty of Holland. While they ascended the throne of England, they accepted the demand that the members of their Council should be approved by the legislature, especially the House of Commons. Therefore, the practice developed of choosing the members from the party or coalition of parties who formed the majority in the Parliament. Notwithstanding, the power remained concentrated primarily in the hands of the King till the time of George I, the prince from the German state of Hanover, who was the King of England from 1714 till his death in 1727. Language being a serious constraint, George I delegated the functions of the government in the hands of his ministers, particularly Sir Robert Walpole, who for all practical purposes became the first Prime Minister. That is how the post of Prime Minister was created. Walpole held this post from April 1721 to

February 1742. He served two kings George I and George II. Disputes broke out in the Parliament over many issues, particularly in the 1730s over the question of war against Spain on trade matters (Walpole was against war while the majority of members in the House of Commons opposed him), though finally Walpole agreed to commence the **War of Jenkins' Ear** in 1739. In 1742 in the by-election in Chippenham, Walpole and his supporters lost the motion of no confidence and resigned. Till the end, however, Walpole enjoyed the full support and confidence of the King, who wept when the former resigned, but could not help it as Walpole was outvoted in the House of Commons. This shows the evolution of the pre-eminence of the Parliament by this time. It was not the confidence of the King but that of the House of Commons that the Cabinet was required to enjoy.

Another important stage in the growth of the parliamentary system in England was the establishment of the supremacy of the House of Commons over the House of Lords. In other words, the House of Commons emerged as the most powerful organ of the Parliament. This symbolised the evolution of true democracy since the House of Commons represented the voice of the nation. Its supremacy meant the predominance of the people in important issues. But how was this supremacy established? After all, the Members of the House of Lords belonged to the nobility and princely class and enjoyed much higher status and influence in society than the members of the lower chamber. It was, therefore, not an easy task to uphold the importance of the **House of Commons**. It came through stages. In the first stage, the cabinet was made exclusively responsible to the House of Commons. A second stage came in the early 19th century when financial matters became a subject of final decision by the lower House. Even so, the upper chamber retained the power of veto over general legislation. So, any law passed by the House of Commons could be obstructed in the House of Lords. The Lords, therefore, had tremendous power of harassment in their hands. However, the King of England had the supreme power of creating unlimited number of peers. But since he acted only on the advice of the Prime Minister, the latter could create a number of new peers loyal to him. This would obviously drive a wedge in the House of Lords, a situation the Lords wanted sincerely to avoid.

Nevertheless, conflict between the two Houses was rampant. The Upper Chamber being composed mostly of Tories, the clashes were sharper on occasions when the Lower Chamber was majorly Liberal. A classic example of such conflict is what happened in 1909 when the Lords blocked the budget proposal of the then Chancellor of Exchequer David Lloyd George and Prime Minister Asquith. It was a pro-poor budget that Lloyd George intended earnestly to bring about. Being brought up in poverty, Lloyd George always wanted to do something to improve the conditions of the poor. He was a Liberal M.P. and when the Liberals won the elections in 1905 with a substantial majority, he said that the new government should come up with something new "to cope with the social condition of the people, to remove the national degradation of slums and widespread poverty and destitution in a land glittering with wealth."[44] He was appointed the Chancellor of Exchequer by Asquith in 1908. Lloyd George then had the opportunity to help the distressed and he prepared a budget "to wage implacable warfare against poverty and squalidness." He drew up a budget that came to be called the 'People's Budget'. It introduced enormous and unprecedented taxes on the wealthy and large-scale welfare programmes for the needy. It also included a tax on the "unearned increment" of land value by industrial or other developments nearby. The Lords, who were mostly Conservatives and rich, opposed it fiercely although it was the convention that the Upper House would not block it. But it was decisively voted down on 30 November by 350 votes to 75. Inevitably, fresh elections were held in January when, curiously enough, the Liberals got through with a slender margin. However, the 1909 budget now was passed by both the Houses.

Asquith and Lloyd George now seriously contemplated curtailing the powers of the House of Lords which had broken the convention by rejecting the Bill of 1909. The result was the drawing up of the **Parliament Bill of 1911**. It was *indeed a milestone in the relationship between the House of Commons and the House of Lords*. This Act, passed on 10 August 1911 in the British Parliament deprived the House of Lords of its absolute power of veto on legislation. This Act was passed with the support of the Liberal majority in the House of Commons. The Act provided that any Bill passed by the House of Commons in three separate sessions without being altered would automatically become a law even without the consent of the Lords if only two years had elapsed since the Bill has been introduced. In case of money Bills, they would become law automatically after one month of their passing by the House of Commons irrespective of the disapproval of the House of Lords. In case of other legislation, the Lords only had a suspensive veto. If they were passed by the Commons in three successive sessions, they would become law even if they were opposed by the Lords. Needless to say, the Upper House did not agree easily to such a curtailment of their age-old power by passing the law. However, Asquith and Lloyd George had the support of the King, who threatened the predominantly Conservative Upper House of sweeping the House by creating a Liberal majority. The King in Britain had the prerogative to elevate an unlimited number of men to nobility rank. In this way the supremacy of the voice of the people's representatives over that of the aristocracy was clearly established. It was certainly a great leap forward in the gradual democratisation of the British Parliament. The Lower House or the voice of the people emerged triumphant and henceforth, asserted the strength of its position over the formerly ascendant class, the repository of phenomenal power—the nobility who represented the Upper House of the British Parliament.

Notes

1. Marjie Bloy, 'Peel and Catholic Emancipation,' *The Victorian Web*, 2002. Available at https://victorianweb.org/history/pms/peel/peel5.html (accessed May 2025).

2. *Encyclopaedia Britannica*, 'Reform Bill.' Available at https://www.britannica.com/event/Reform-Bill (accessed May 2025).

3. Glenn Everett, 'The Reform Acts,' *The Victorian Web*, 2001. Available at https://victorianweb.org/history/hist2.html (accessed May 2025).

4. Rachel Eckersley, 'Of Radical Design: John Cartwright and the Redesign of the Reform Campaign, 1800–1811,' *History* 89(4) (October 2004): 560–580.

5. Asa Briggs, *The Age of Improvement: 1783–1867* (London: Longman, 1959), 239.

6. Ibid., 238.

7. Ibid., 241.

8. Quoted from 'Crocker Papers, II, 113,' in James Ramsay Montagu Butler, *The Passing of the Great Reform Bill* (London: Frank Cass and Co., 1964), 249; also quoted in Briggs, *The Age of Improvement*, 251.

9. Ibid., 246.

10. Ibid., 253.

11. John A. Phillips and Charles Wetherell, 'The Great Reform Bill of 1832 and the Rise of Partisanship,' *Journal of Modern History* 63(4) (December 1991): 621.

12. Ibid., 622.

13. Ibid.

14. Ibid., 623.

15. Ibid.

16. Ibid.

17. John Cannon, *Parliamentary Reform 1640–1832* (Cambridge: Cambridge University Press, 1973), 246.

18. Norman Gash, *Politics in the Age of Peel: A Study in the Technique of Parliamentary Representation, 1830–1850* (London: Longman, 1953), quoted in Phillips and Wetherell, 'The Great Reform Bill,' 624.

19. Frank O'Gorman, 'Electoral Deference in Unreformed England, 1760–1832,' *Journal of Modern History* 56 (1984): 393.

20. D. C. Moore, *The Politics of Deference: A Study of the Mid-Nineteenth Century English Political System* (Hassocks: Harvester Press, 1976), 151.

21. Cannon, *Parliamentary Reform*, 165.

22. W.N. Molesworth, *The History of the Reform Bill of 1832* (London: Chapman and Hall, 1865), 1–3.

23. Ellis A. Wasson, 'The Spirit of Reform, 1832 and 1867,' *Albion: A Quarterly Journal Concerned with British Studies* 12(2) (Summer 1980): 164–74.

24. Thomas Carlyle, quoted in Marjie Bloy, 'The Poor Law Amendment Act.' Available at https://www.historyhome.co.uk/peel/poorlaw/poorlaw.htm (accessed May 2025).

25. Charles Dickens, *Oliver Twist* (London: Richard and Bentley, 1838), 20.

26. Nicholas C. Edsall, *The Anti-Poor Law Movement, 1834–44* (Manchester: Manchester University Press, 1971), 262.

27. Briggs, *The Age of Improvement*, 306.

28. Ibid., 489.

29. Ibid., 498.

30. Gash, *Politics in the Age of Peel.*

31. M. Ostrogorski, *Democracy and the Organisation of Political Parties*, ed. S.M. Lipset (New York: Routledge, 1964).

32. Gertrude Himmelfarb, 'The Politics of Democracy: The English Reform Act of 1867,' *Journal of British Studies* 6(1) (November 1966): 114.

33. Ibid., 104.

34. Ibid., 106–107.

35. Gary Cox, *The Efficient Secret: The Cabinet and the Development of Political Parties in Victorian England* (Cambridge: Cambridge University Press, 1987).

36. Quoted in Janice Carlisle, 'On the Second Reform Act, 1867,' in *BRANCH: Britain, Representation and Nineteenth Century History*, ed. Dino Franco Felluga. Available at https://branchcollective.org/?ps_articles=janice-carlisle-on-the-second-reform-act-1867 (accessed May 2025).

37. Briggs, *The Age of Improvement*, 516.

38. Ibid., 319.

39. Quoted in Carlisle, 'On the Second Reform Act, 1867.'

40. John Stuart Mill, *Considerations on Representative Government* (London: Parker, Son and Bourn, 1861).

41. Quoted in Carlisle, 'On the Second Reform Act, 1867.'

42. Quoted in Richard Shanon, *Gladstone: God and Politics* (London: Continuum, 2007), 193.

43. Martin Pugh, *March of Women: A Revisionist Analysis of the Campaign for Women's Suffrage 1866–1914* (Oxford: Oxford University Press, 2000).

44. Richard Cavendish, 'The House of Lords Rejects the 1909 People's Budget,' *History Today* 59(11) (November 2009).

CHAPTER 8

Culture and Society
1789–1850s

Popular Consumption of Culture: Neo Classical Art, Romanticism and Realism in Art and Literature

The history of art and culture in Europe witnessed the evolution of several distinctive styles and forms, starting from the ancient times down to the present day. In the 18th and 19th centuries, each of the different art forms was a well-defined movement with its own distinct characteristics and expression. They encompassed painting, literature, architecture, sculpture, music, and so on. In the late 18th and early 19th century, the predominant cultural form was **Romanticism**, which developed **in reaction to Classicism**. The latter started in the late 15th century in Rome and continued till the beginning of the 18th century, only to be revived in the late 18th century as **Neo-classicism**.

The great artists who represented the classical style were Michelangelo (1475–1564), Raphael (1483–1520), Correggio (1489–1534), Mantegna (1431–1506), Anton Raffael Mengs (1728–1779) and Johan Joachim Winckelman (1717–1768). Both Classicism and Neo-classicism were based on the art of Greece and Rome in antiquity. Their special features were sobriety, clarity, order and harmony. The classical period also coincides with the **Baroque** style whose early manifestations were seen in the latter decades of the 16th century. The term 'baroque' originated from the Italian word *barocco* meaning obstacle. Baroque style, therefore, came to denote anything contorted, misshaped and warped, especially an idea or vision. Though, however, Heinrich Wolfflin (1864–1945) in his scholarly work *Renaissance und Barock* (1888) contested this view and called the baroque art a "stylistic designation".[1] Its main characteristics were a portrayal of the efforts of the Roman Catholic Church to counter the impact of the Reformation, and also the consolidation of the absolute monarchy and aristocratic nobility. The hallmark of this art form was richness in colour, design, drama and emotion in ornamental and decorative style. The themes depicted the grandeur and heroism of the Church and the royal traditions. In this sense, the typical baroque form and classicism intermingled with each other on several occasions.

Rococo or '**Late Baroque**' was a distinct art form which manifested in painting, architecture and sculpture, and like Baroque, depicted the royal and aristocratic lifestyle and romantic moods, but mostly in natural settings, and in pastel colours, soft lines, and ornate design. It began approximately in 1700 and continued till mid-18th century, almost till the 1770s. The main artists and literary figures of this art form were Jean-Antoine Watteau (1684–1721), Jean-Honore Fragonard (1732–1806), Francois Boucher (1703–1770), Giovanni Battista Tiepolo (1696–1770), Thomas Gainsborough (1727–1788), Elizabeth Vigee Le Brun (1755–1842), Jean-Baptiste-Simeon Chardin (1699–1779), Thomas Chippendale (1718–1779), and others. It was in vogue mainly in the period from early 18th to mid-18th century. It first appeared in France but soon spread to central Europe.

ROMANTICISM

Romanticism succeeded the Rococo style and was prevalent in the late 18th century to mid-19th century. It was a kind of reaction against the spirit of Enlightenment and rationalism which were driven by reason and empiricism, the main force behind which was experience. Romanticism, on the other hand, emphasised upon emotion, imagination and visionary romantic sensitivities. Romanticism was the theme of many works of literature, painting, music, architecture and other art forms. Romanticism has nothing to do with love or romance. Rather it is a movement of rebellion against the spirit of reason and progress of the preceding era. It **abhorred the emphasis on mechanisation** as envisaged and executed by the Industrial Revolution. Their art and literature is a protest against the evils and excesses of industrialisation and its impact upon human life and society.

The Romantics emphasised upon spiritual bliss hidden in nature and quested for that divine and spiritual rapture beneath the chaos and harshness of everyday material life. So, the Romantic movement advocated a simple and natural life. They painted sublime seas and vast natural landscapes in contrast to and as a pleasant relief from the oppressive, crowded, smoke-filled, dismal cityscapes. As against the dark side of urban industrial life, the Romantics celebrated the awe and grandeur of the countryside. Poet William Wordsworth (1770–1850) wrote volumes of poems on daffodils, oak trees, butterflies and rivers. So did the American painter Thomas Cole (1801–1848), who painted the Niagara Falls and other captivating natural scenes. Another great portrayal of nature was the *Wanderer Above the Sea of Fog* painted by the German Romantic landscape painter Casper David Friedrich (1774–1840). French Romantic painter Eugene Delacroix's (1798–1863) *Death of Sardansapalus* was based on the oriental play by Lord Byron. Delacroix's passion for liberty against tyranny was given free rein in his famous painting *July 28: Liberty Leading the People* on the 1830 Revolution. A sublime scene of early morning was

FIG. 8.1: *View on Lake Winnipiseogee* (1828) by Thomas Cole; Oil on Canvas

painted by the German painter Philipp Otto Runge (1777–1810). The French Romantic painter Theodore Gericault (1791–1824) was fascinated by battle scenes and moved by shipwrecks. He painted *Portrait of an Officer of the Chasseurs Commanding a Charge*, based on a military officer of the Napoleonic era. Gericault's work *The Raft of the Medusa* is based on a survivor of a shipwreck off the African coast of Senegal. *The Desperate Man* by the French painter Gustave Courbet (1819–1877), and *The Third of May 1808* by the Spanish painter Francisco Goya (1746–1828) commemorating the Spanish resistance to Napoleon were the other great masterpieces of the Romantic period.

The Romantics loved Gothic and medieval art, the best example being the rebuilding of the Westminster Palace, the Parliament of England. Although built in 1835 when the Neo-classical style was prevalent, the Westminster Palace was rebuilt by its Romantic architect Augustus Pugin (1812–1852) who was staunchly devoted to Gothic architecture, which preserved the conservative style. The Romanticists were well aware of the dark and horrifying dimensions of life. Novelist Mary Shelly (1797–1851), married to poet Percy Bysshe Shelly (1792–1822), wrote *Frankenstein* in which she depicted how ordinary men were at the mercy of dark and terrible forces.

The Romantics, unlike the representatives of Classicism and Enlightenment, were **believers in unconventional practices**. William Blake (1757–1827), the English poet and artist, for example, believed in free love. The famous love story *The Sorrows of Young Werther*, written in 1774 by the German author Johann Wolfgang von Goethe (1749–1832), depicts the unconventional love between Werther and Charlotte, their union being impossible as Charlotte was already married. In his *Emile, ou de l'Education* (*Emile or On Education*), Rousseau (1712–1778) praised the natural goodness and innocence of children as against adult behaviour. It was a sort of parental guide for raising children. However, in a certain section of the book, Rousseau had questioned traditional tenets of religion and opposed Christian orthodoxy, which led to the book being banned in Paris and Geneva and burned down in the very year of its publication. However, the English poet William Blake condemned Britain's war against the French revolutionaries, as that was, in Blake's view, an assault upon liberty and freedom. His poem 'The French Revolution' was never allowed to be published in England. Romantic literature was extremely rich with the contributions of many other great Romantic philosophers and writers like Frederich Von Schiller (1759–1805), Friedrich Wilhelm Joseph Schelling (1775–1854), Johann Gottlieb Fichte (1762–1814), Georg Wilhelm Friedrich Hegel (1770–1831); occult and supernatural writers like Edgar Allan Poe (1809–1849), Nathaniel Hawthorne (1804–1864); poets, novelists and fiction writers like Ludwig Tieck (1773–1853), Heinrich Von Klieist (1777–1811), Friedrich Holderlin (1770–1843) and others. The great English Romantic poets apart from Blake, Shelly and Wordsworth mentioned earlier, were Samuel Taylor Coleridge (1772–1834), John Keats (1795–1821) Lord Byron (1788–1824), novelists Jane Austen (1775–1817), Charles Dickens (1812–1870), Thomas Hardy (1840–1928); Scottish poets were James Macpherson (1736–1796) and Sir Walter Scott (1771–1832).

In the field of music, the greatest composers of the earlier part of the era were the German composer Wolfgang Amadeus Mozart (1756–1791), Russian composer Rachmaninoff (1873–1943), Polish composer Chopin (1810–1849), German composers Beethoven (1770–1827), Schumann (1810–1846), Mendelssohn (1809–1847), Johannes Brahms (1833–1897), Austrian composer Schubert (1797–1828), Italian composer Bellini (1801–1835), French composer Berlioz (1803–1869), the Italian violinist Nicolo Paganini (1782–1840), Hungarian composer Franz Liszt (1811–1866). During the Romantic period, a magnificent dance form known waltz became fashionable in Vienna. Mainly composed for ballroom dances and large coffee houses, the waltz spread from Vienna and caught the imagination of the whole of Europe. The most famous composer of this music was Johann Strauss the Younger (1825–1899), also known as the Waltz–King. His most well-known waltz was the *An Der Schonen Blauen Donau* (*The Blue Danube*). The others included Morgenblatter (*Morning Papers*), *Kunstlerlaben* (*Artists' Life*) and *Wein, Weib und Gesang* (*Wine, Women and Song*). By far, the Romantic era produced the maximum number of magnificent musicians of the world.

The Romantic period was undoubtedly **the golden age of European art and culture**. Artistic and literary splendour reached its zenith during this era. However, some scholars like Marvin Perry observed that the Romantics in their 'excessive zeal' of glorifying the past and ancient traditions whipped up the unbridled passions of radical nationalism that snowballed into totalitarian fascism of the 20th century. He wrote,

> …the romantics undermined respect for the rational tradition of the Enlightenment and thus set up a precondition for the rise and triumph

of fascist movements. Although their intention was cultural and not political, by idealizing the past and glorifying ancient folkways, legends, native soil, and native language, the romantics introduced a highly charged non-rational component into political life.[2]

NEO-CLASSICISM

Another art form belonging to the same timeline as Romanticism was Neo-classicism, which we have mentioned, was a revival of old Classicism. It was a strong reaction against the rich, overtly ostentatious and ornamental Baroque and Rococo styles. Neo-classicism stood for simple, geometric, symmetrical patterns. It was an art form developed in tune with the Enlightenment and the revolutionary age, starting with the American Revolution and the French Revolution. It emerged in the 1760s and attained its peak in the 1850s. Breaking from the passionate Baroque and sensuous Rococo styles, it looked back to the classical age with symmetry, accurate proportionate lines and sombre pattern. Its cornerstones were patriotism, honour, justice, victory of the revolution and constitution, and human rights. It drew its inspiration from the ancient art that came to the limelight with the unearthing of the remains of the city of Pompeii in 1748 and Herculaneum of ancient Italy in the 1750s. The excavation of these cities, which were buried by the eruptions of Mount Vesuvius in 79 AD, brought into light ruins of buildings, numerous beautiful artefacts, magnificent paintings and statues which provide glimpses of the wonderful art and architecture of the time. This motivated the neo-classical artists and architects. Pompeii was a symbol of the ancient Roman civilisation, while Herculaneum was of Greek origin and became a Roman municipium in 89 BC. The Graeco-Roman style of art and architecture of these ancient cities heavily influenced neo-classical art. Jean-Antoine Houdon (1741–1828), the neo-classical French sculptor, made several bronze statues of anonymous men and women (his *Anatomical Man* and *La Frileuse* meaning the shivering woman) as well as marble busts of great men like Mirabeau, Thomas Jefferson, Benjamin Franklin, Marquis de Condorcet and full marble statues of Washington and Voltaire. Of course, he depicted them not in Roman or Greek attire, but in the garments of their times. He made statues of saints like Bruno and John the Baptist in 1766–1767. Houdon belonged to the era of revolution, and the Enlightenment was his main theme.

One of the great neo-classical architects was the French architect Etienne-Louis Boullee (1728–1799), whose speciality lay in symmetrical geometric shapes, with emphasis on ancient Roman columns and arches the Doric order—elaborate use of cylinders, cones, spheres and pyramids. Newton's cenotaph, the National Assembly Hall of France, the Opera Building and the National Library are some of his spectacular creations. He brought simple geometrical lines and shapes to life through the impressive, original effects of light and shadow. Another striking example of neo-classical architecture was the *Arc de Triomphe*, one of the most famous monuments in Paris, built to commemorate the soldiers who had died for France in the French Revolutionary Wars and the Napoleonic wars. The beauty of its straight columns and proportionate structure is indeed amazing. It was built in 1806 by the neo-classical French architect Jean-Francois-Therese-Chalgrin (1739–1811). He was a pupil of the prophet of neo-classicism, French architect and designer Giovanni Niccolo Servandoni, as well as Boullee. Among Servandoni's more prominent works are the Church of Saint Sulpice, completed in 1870. Servandoni was a student of the Italian painter and decorator Giovanni Paolo Panini (1691–1765), who was famous as a Vedutisti (view painter). His most well-known works are the interior of the Pantheon—a circular structure in tune with typical neo-classical style, Veduta (paintings of picture galleries with views of Rome).

The most famous painter of the neo-classical order was Jacques-Louis David (1748–1825). His well-known work was *The Oath of the Horatii*, which depicts patriotism and self-sacrifice. Three brothers of the family of Horatii take the oath to finish the war between the two warring cities Rome and Alba Longa. The other well-known paintings of Jacques-Louis David include *The Death of Marat*, *The Death of Socrates*, *The Coronation of Napoleon*, *Napoleon Crossing the Alps* and *The Intervention of Sabine women* all mostly based on revolutionary, patriotic and historical themes, sacrifice and martyrdom. Another neo-classical scholar of David's tradition was his student the French painter Jean-Auguste-Dominique Ingres (1780–1867), who, although of the neo-classical school, adopted some characteristic features of his own that made him a source of inspiration for exponents of modern art like Picasso and Matisse. The prominent paintings of Ingres include *The Ambassadors of Agamemnon in the tent of Achilles*, *The Vow of Louis XVIII*, *Portrait of Monsieur Bertin* and *The Turkish Bath*.

Antonio Canova was a famous Italian sculptor of the neo-classical school, known for his marble sculptures. Though he followed the simplicity, precision, order and restrained beauty of neo-classicism, he was clearly influenced by the Baroque and classical forms as well. Canova's famous works include *Psyche Revived by Cupid's Kiss, Orpheus, Theseus and Minotaur, Perseus Triumphant* and *The Three Graces*, all based upon mythological characters. He also sculpted a marble bust of Napoleon, a statue of Napoleon's mother Maria-Letizia Ramolino, and a marble statue of George Washington for the North Carolina State House. When Washington's statue was destroyed by fire in 1831, a plaster cast of the original was sent by the King of Italy in 1910, which is now on display at the North Carolina Museum of History.

Neo-classical literature, too, followed its tradition of practical rather than utopian, visionary style of the Romantic age. Rationality was the hallmark of the literature of this time, and much influenced by the Graeco-Roman writing style. One of the greatest writers of the time was the German scholar and art historian Johann Joachim Winckelmann (1717–1768). His great admirer was the early neo-classical German Bohemian painter Anton Raphel Mengs who made his portrait. Winckelmann was highly impressed by Alexander Pope's *Homer*. His *Gestichichte der Kunst des Alterthums* (History of Art in Antiquity,) published in 1764 became a classic in European literature and attracted people's interest towards classical art.

REALISM

Realism as an art movement started in the mid-19th century in France and expanded to other countries of Europe. It depicted the world as it was, and not what it should be or what people wanted it to be. The Realists honestly portrayed everyday life in society with all its aspects, contrasts and perspectives, good and evil, and used art as an instrument to combat the wrongs of our surroundings. Portrayal of real and existing things and objects which people could touch, feel and view were their subject matter. Emile Zola wrote about the great Realist painter Edouard Manet,

> It is a question, here, of searching for an 'absolute' of beauty. The artist is neither painting history nor his soul…And it is because of this that he should neither be judged as a moralist nor as a literary man. He should be judged simply as a painter.[3]

The Realists painted urban as well as rural life as they existed, uninfluenced by any imaginary vision. So Realism is also called naturalism. The prominent artists of this genre are Gustave Courbet (1819–1877) Edouard Manet (1832–1883), Honore Daumier (1808–1879), Jean Francois Millet (1814–1875), Ilya Repin (1844–1930), Thomas Eakins (1844–1914), Jules Breton (1827–1906) and others. *Rue Transnonain* by Honore, *The Stone Breakers* by Courbert, *Olympia* by Manet, *Song of the Lark* by Breton are eternal paintings depicting human emotions, pain and cruelty in their pristine form. Even poets like Charles Baudelaire and socialist Pierre–Joseph Proudhon were leading exponents of this school.

Realist thought influenced literature as well. *A Doll's House* by the Norwegian author Henrik Ibsen (1828–1906), *The Cherry Orchard* by the Russian author Anton Chekov (1860–1904), Fyodor Dostoyevsky (1821–1881) with his priceless works *Brothers Karamazov* and *Crime and Punishment*, *A Sportsman's Sketches* as well as *Fathers and Sons* by Ivan Turgenev (1818–1883), Alexander Pushkin (1799–1837), Gustave Flaubert's (1821–1880) *Madame Bovary*, Leo Tolstoy's (1828–1910) *War and Peace, The Portrait of a Lady* by Henry James (1843–1916) were outstanding masterpieces of Realist literature depicting the harsh everyday lives of ordinary people. Realist literature were characterised by simple plots and complex characters focussing on the daily life of the lower and middle class people. The Russian authors mostly depicted the harsh realities of feudal Russian society, the oppression of the serfs at the hands of the intransigent, self-centred nobility. The consequences of Napoleonic invasion of Russia was portrayed masterfully by Leo Tolstoy in his *War and Peace*. The cravings and desires of a reckless bourgeois lady was shown in Flaubert's masterpiece, *Madame Bovary*. The psychological torment of a young Russian student Raskolnikov in Dostoyevsky's *Crime and Punishment* is another example of a realistic novel.

For a more expansive understanding on art and culture, please refer to Chapter 1 of this volume, the section on 'Art and Culture in the French Revolution', particularly the subsection titled 'Trends in Art and Architecture'.

The City in Industrial Europe

Industrialisation and population growth strongly encouraged migration and urbanisation in 19th-century Europe. Rise in population created extraordinary pressure on the countryside and consequently food became inadequate. This induced people to move to the cities and towns in search of livelihood. In 1800, for example, about one-fifth of the British population lived in towns and cities. During the following century, a largely rural society became predominantly urban, with three-fourth of the population working and living in cities. This pattern repeated itself in continental Europe with the result that new, modernised urban centres sprang into existence. A close connection has been made, therefore, between these two developments. On the one hand, Marx and Engels refer to the creation of a substantial working class or proletariat who became the most significant redeeming feature of the newly grown cities. Sociologist Emile Durkheim probed the effects of urban lifestyle on traditional social ties. On the other hand, a large number of social thinkers considered the influences of the industrial world on urbanisation as minimal. Franklin Mendel observed in 1972 that proto-industrialisation (or the **putting out system**, the chief characteristic of which was to produce for distant, sometimes overseas markets by village artisans or peasants) supplied the maximum number of workers.[4] The entire industrialisation process was a rather slow one. Peter Cain and Anthony Hopkins called British industrialism "gentlemanly capitalism", at the core of which was financial services—banking and stock-exchange—and not factory production. It was more financial capitalism rather than industrial capitalism.[5] According to Martin Weiner, anti-industrial values in Britain were so strong that the entrepreneurial spirit got subdued.[6] Jan de Vries has referred to what he called the "industrious revolution" which constituted the origin of the Industrial Revolution. Taking the household as an economic unit, he showed how low wages were compensated by greater intensity of work by the family members through curtailing their time of leisure; and how in this way they produced not only for their own consumption but also for the market. Through diligent and incessant labour they became consumers and producers at the same time. This was the genesis of new aspirations, new supplies of labour "in which the special contribution of the Industrial Revolution inserted itself."[7] Clearly, all these scholars undermined the inevitable connection between industrialisation and the growth of cities. Paul M. Hohenberg and Lynn Hollen Lees wrote, "These two phenomena should be seen as related, but distinct, changes. Their interaction cannot be reduced to a two-way accretion of towns around factories and spread of factories in towns."[8] They argued that Italy which saw a late industrialisation, however, experienced a high rate of urban growth much before her Industrial Revolution, while in Switzerland and some parts of France, industries developed rapidly, but urbanisation was pretty slow.[9] Some reasons for such a phenomenon were the location of raw materials, hazards of transportation, advantages of the entrepreneurs, reactions of the elitist urban people. For instance, the cost of transporting coal was so high that factories requiring heavy coal consumption tended to grow around the coal mines, which were mostly situated in rural areas. The landed gentry and elite of the older towns were extremely resistant to the idea of the settlement of workers in urban areas close to them; they, therefore, did not at all welcome modern industry. According to Hohenberg and Lees, industrialisation and urbanisation merged together for the first time in the latter part of the 19th century in western and central Europe.[10] It was primarily due to the **centralisation of railway tracks** that industries began to be concentrated in large cities. C. A. Bayly argued that there was one important common element that cemented industrialisation and urbanisation together. "These two phenomena," he wrote, "were linked in the broader sense, however, in that they represented radically different ways of creating, consuming and living from those which had been common 150 years earlier."

And these new ways of living and consuming attracted common people who found it more feasible to seek employment in the newly created sector, as it also seemed more promising. People who settled in the towns called other friends and relatives and helped them to acquire jobs and find accommodations to live in. John Merriman observed that between 1816 and 1850, at least 5 million Europeans booked passage across the seas, particularly during the "hungry forties".[11] The rapid urbanisation had left an enormous impact on the life and society of Europe.

Notes

1. Wolfflin, Heinrich, *Principles of Art History: The Problem of the Development of Style in Later Art*, Dover Publications, USA, 1929, p. 64.

2. Marvin Perry, *An Intellectual History of Modern Europe* (Boston: Houghton Mifflin Company, 1993), p. 185.

3. Translated from the original, Émile Zola. *Édouard Manet: Biographical and Critical Study*. Originally published in *La Revue d'histoire du XIXe Siècle* (Dentu, Paris, 1867).

4. C.A. Bayly, *The Birth of the Modern World, 1780–1914* (Malden, MA: Blackwell Publishing, 2004), 171; see also Steven M. Beaudoin, ed., *The Industrial Revolution* (Boston and New York: Houghton Mifflin, 2003), 79.

5. Bayly, *The Birth of the Modern World*, 171.

6. Ibid.

7. Jan de Vries, 'The Industrial Revolution and the Industrious Revolution,' in Beaudoin, *The Industrial Revolution*, 87.

8. Paul M. Hohenberg and Lynn Hollen Lees, *The Making of Urban Europe, 1000–1950*, in Beaudoin, *The Industrial Revolution*, 128.

9. Ibid.

10. Ibid., 131.

11. John Merriman, *A History of Modern Europe: From the Renaissance to the Present* (New York: W.W. Norton & Company, 1996), 694.

Bibliography

Abray, Jane. *The American Historical Review*. Vol. 80, February 1975.

Accampo, Elinor. 'Industrialisation, Family Life, and Class Relations.' In *The Industrial Revolution*, edited by Steven M. Beaudoin, 200–201. Boston: Houghton Mifflin, 2003.

Acton, Edward. *Rethinking the Russian Revolution*. London: Bloomsbury Academic, 1990.

Aftalion, Florin. *The French Revolution: An Economic Interpretation*. Cambridge: Cambridge University Press, 1990.

Alexandre, Charles. 'Women's Participation in Riots over the Price of Sugar, February 1792.' In *Women in Revolutionary Paris, 1789–1795*, edited by Darline Gay Levy, Harriet Branson Applewhite, and Mary Durham Johnson, 115–118. Illinois: Illinois University Press, 1979.

Amariglio, Jack and Bruce Norton. 'Marxist Historians and the Question of Class in the French Revolution.' *History and Theory* 30(1) (February 1991).

Anderson, Eugene. *Nationalism and Cultural Crisis in Prussia: 1806–1815*. New York: Octagon Press, 1966.

Anderson, Patricia, *The Printed Image and the Transformation of Popular Culture, 1790-1860*. New York: Clarendon Press of Oxford University Press, 1992.

Andries, Lise. 'Radicalism and the Book in Paris during the French Revolution.' CNRS Paris, 2006. Available at https://www.princeton.edu/csb/conferences/march_2006/…/andries.doc (accessed September 2013).

Angus, Ian. 'Marx and Engels… and Darwin?' *International Socialist Review*, no. 71 (May 2010).

Asbrink, Brita. 'The Nobel Brothers Revolutionise Russian Oil Management.' *Branobel History*, 2011. Available at https://www.branobelhistory.com/distribution/the-nobel-brothers-revolutionise-russian-oil-management/ (accessed June 2025).

Ascher, Abraham. *The Revolution of 1905: Russia in Disarray*. Stanford: Stanford University Press, 1988.

Ascher, Alexander. Quoted in 'Alpha History on Russian Industrialisation.' *Alpha History*. Available at https://alphahistory.com/russianrevolution/russian-industrialisation (accessed May 2025).

Asher, Harvey. 'The Kornilov Affair: A Reinterpretation.' *Russian Review* 29(2) (1970): 296.

Ashton, T. S. *Economic History of England: The Eighteenth Century*. London, 1955.

Baker, Keith Michael. 'Ideological Origins of the French Revolution.' In *The French Revolution*, edited by Roland Schechter, 71–73. Wiley-Blackwell, 2000.

_____. 'Sieyès and the Creation of the French Revolutionary Discourse.' 1989. Available at http://hdl.handle.net/1803/7172 (accessed June 2025).

_____. *Inventing the French Revolution: Essays on French Political Culture in the Eighteenth Century.* Cambridge: Cambridge University Press, 1990

Batra, Ravi. 'Sarkar, Toynbee and Marx.' *Progressive Socialism*, September 2011. Available at https://www.proutglobe.org (accessed May 2025).

Bayly, C.A. *The Birth of the Modern World, 1780–1914*. Malden, MA: Blackwell Publishing, 2004.

BBC History, 'Empire and Sea Power,' British History. Available at https://www.bbc.co.uk/history/british/empire_seapower/ (accessed May 2025).

_____. 'Why the Industrial Revolution Happened in Britain', 2013. Available at https://www.bbc.com/mediacentre/proginfo/2013/03/why-the-industrial-revolution (accessed May 2025).

Beaudoin, Steven M., ed. *The Industrial Revolution*. Boston and New York: Houghton Mifflin Company, 2003.

Berg, Maxine. 'What Difference Did Women's Work Make to the Industrial Revolution?' *History Workshop Journal* 35(1) (1993): 22–44.

Berger, Helge, and Mark Spoerer. 'Economic Crises and the European Revolutions of 1848.' *Journal of History* 61(2) (June 2001).

Beryl, William. *The Russian Revolution, 1917–1921*. Oxford: Basil Blackwell, 1987.

Billig, M. 'The Extreme Right: Continuities in Anti-Semitic Conspiracy Theory in Post-War Europe'. In Peter Davies, *The Debate on the French Revolution*. Manchester: Manchester University Press.

Blanchard, Ian. 'Eighteenth Century Russian Economic Growth: State Enterprise or Peasant Endeavour?' *Jahrbücher für Geschichte Osteuropas* 45(4) (1997).

Blanning, T.C.W., ed. *The Oxford Illustrated History of Modern Europe*. Oxford: Oxford University Press, 1998.

_____., ed. *The Rise and Fall of the French Revolution*, Chicago University Press, Chicago, 1996.

Bloy, Marjie. 'Peel and Catholic Emancipation,' *The Victorian Web*, 2002. Available at https://victorianweb.org/history/pms/peel/peel5.html (accessed May 2025).

_____. 'The Poor Law Amendment Act.' Available at https://www.historyhome.co.uk/peel/poorlaw/poorlaw.htm (accessed May 2025).

Blum, Jerome. *Lord and Peasant in Russia*. Princeton: Princeton University Press, 1961.

Boime, Albert. *Social History of Modern Art: Art in the Age of Revolution 1750–1800*, Vol. 1. Chicago: University of Chicago Press, 1987.

Bortkiewicz, Ladislaus von. 'Value and Price in the Marxian System.' *International Economic Papers*, no. 2 (1952).

Breunig, Charles. *The Age of Revolution and Reaction*. New York and London: W. W. Norton and Company, 1977.

Briggs, Asa. *The Age of Improvement, 1783–1967*. London: Longmans, Green and Co. Ltd., 1959.

Britt, Albert Sidney. *The Wars of Napoleon*. New York: Avery Publishing Group, 1985.

Buchanon, G. *My Mission to Russia*. New York: Arno Reprint, 1977.

Bullock, Alan, Oliver Stallybrass, and Stephen Trombley, eds. *The Fontana Dictionary of Modern Thought*, 2nd ed. London: Fontana Press, 1988.

Butler, James Ramsay Montagu. *The Passing of the Great Reform Bill*. London: Frank Cass and Co., 1964.

Byron, Lord. 'Ode to Napoleon'. 1814.

Campbell, Peter, ed. *The Origins of the French Revolution*. UK: Palgrave Macmillan, 2006.

Cannon, John. *Parliamentary Reform 1640–1832*. Cambridge: Cambridge University Press, 1973.

Carlisle, Janice. 'On the Second Reform Act, 1867.' In *BRANCH: Britain, Representation and Nineteenth Century History*, edited by Dino Franco Felluga. Available at https://branchcollective.org/?ps_articles=janice-carlisle-on-the-second-reform-act-1867 (accessed May 2025).

Cavanaugh, Gerald J. 'The Present State of French Revolutionary Historiography: Alfred Cobban and Beyond.' *French Historical Studies* 7(4) (Autumn 1972): 588–595.

Cavendish, Richard. 'The House of Lords Rejects the 1909 People's Budget.' *History Today* 59(11) (November 2009).

Chartier, Roger. 'Cultural Origins of the French Revolution.' In *The French Revolution*, edited by Roland Schechter, 75–105. Wiley-Blackwell, 2000.

Chase, William, and John A. Getty. Quoted in Ronald Kowalski, *The Russian Revolution, 1917–1921*. London and New York: Routledge, 1997.

Chubarov, Alexander. *The Fragile Empire: A History of Imperial Russia*. New York, 1999.

Cipolla, Carlo M., ed. *Fontana Economic History of Europe: The Industrial Revolution*. William Collins Sons & Co. Ltd., 1973.

Cliff, Tony. *Russia: A Marxist Analysis*. Marxist Internet Archive.

Clapham, John Harold. *The Economic Development of France and Germany*. Cambridge: Cambridge University Press, 1966.

Cliff, Tony. *Class Struggle and Women's Liberation*. London, 1984. Marxists' Internet Archive. Available at https://www.marxists.org/archive/cliff/works/1984/women/00-intro.htm (accessed April 2025).

Cobb, Richard. *The French and Their Revolution: Selected Writings*. New York: The New Press, 1998.

Cobban, Alfred. *A History of Modern France 1799–1871*, Vol. 2. London: Penguin Books Ltd., 1961.

———. *The Social Interpretation of the French Revolution*, 2nd ed. New York: Oxford University Press.

Collingwood, R.G. *The Idea of History*. Posthumously published (1946; rev. ed., 1993).

Cox, Gary. *The Efficient Secret: The Cabinet and the Development of Political Parties in Victorian England*. Cambridge: Cambridge University Press, 1987.

Crafts, N.F.R. 'The Industrial Revolution in England and France: Some Thoughts on the Question, "Why was England First?"' *Economic History Review* 30(3) (August 1977): 429–430. Reprinted in *The Economics of the Industrial Revolution*, edited by Joel Mokyr, 122. New Zealand: Allen and Unwin, 1985.

Craig, Gordon. *Europe since 1815*. New York: Holt, Rinehart and Winston, 1966.

Crook, Malcolm. *Elections in the French Revolution: An Apprenticeship in Democracy, 1789–99*. Cambridge: Cambridge University Press, 1996.

Crouzet, F. 'England and France in the 18th Century: A Comparative Analysis of Two Economic Growths.' In *The Causes of the Industrial Revolution in England*, edited by R. M. Hartwell, 133–154. London: Methuen & Co., 1970.

Darnton, Robert. *The Forbidden Bestsellers of Pre-Revolutionary France*. New York: W. W. Norton, 1996.

Darrow, Margaret H. 'Economic Terror in the City: The General Maximum in Montauban.' *French Historical Studies* 17(2) (Autumn 1991): 498–502.

Davidoff, Leonore, and Catherine Hall. 'Family Fortunes'. In *The Industrial Revolution*, edited by Steven M. Beaudoin, 211–12. Boston: Houghton Mifflin, 2003.

Davies, Natalie Zemon. *Society and Culture in Early Modern Europe*. Stanford: Stanford University Press, 1975.

Davies, Peter. *The Debate on the French Revolution*. Manchester: Manchester University Press.

de Soto, Jesús Huerta. *Money, Bank Credit and Economic Cycles*. 2nd ed. Translated by Melinda A. Stroup. Auburn: Ludwig von Mises Institute. Available at https://mises.org/books/desoto.pdf (accessed May 2025).

de Vries, Jan. 'The Industrial Revolution and the Industrious Revolution.' In *The Industrial Revolution*, edited by Steven M. Beaudoin, 87. Boston: Houghton Mifflin, 2003.

Deane, Phyllis. *The First Industrial Revolution*. Delhi: Foundation Books, 1994.

Devlin, Roger F. *From Salon to the Guillotine*. Translated by Nancy Derr Polin. Rockford: Chronicles Press, 2007.

Dickens, Charles. *Oliver Twist*. London: Richard and Bentley, 1838.

Dimitriev, V.K. *Economic Essays on Value, Competition and Utility.* Cambridge: Cambridge University Press, 1974.

Domar, Evsey D., and Mark J. Machina. 'On the Profitability of Russian Serfdom.' *The Journal of Economic History* 44(4) (December 1984): 925–955.

Donnachie, Ian. 'Education in Robert Owen's New Society: The New Lanark Institute and Schools.' *The Encyclopedia of Informal Education*, 2000. Available at https://infed.org/mobi/education-in-robert-owens-new-society-the-new-lanark-institute-and-schools/ (accessed June 2025).

Doyle, William. *Origins of the French Revolution.* New York: Oxford University Press, 1980.

Droz, Jacques. *Europe Between Revolutions, 1815–1848.* Glasgow: Fontana Collins, 1981.

Eckersley, Rachel. 'Of Radical Design: John Cartwright and the Redesign of the Reform Campaign, 1800–1811.' *History* 89(4) (October 2004): 560–580.

Edsall, Nicholas C. *The Anti-Poor Law Movement, 1834–44.* Manchester: Manchester University Press, 1971.

Elias, Norbert. *The Civilising Process: The History of Manners*, Vol. 1. Oxford: Blackwell Publishers Ltd., 1978.

Ellis, Geoffrey. 'The Marxist Interpretation of the French Revolution.' *The English Historical Review* 93(367) (April 1978): 360–378.

Ellison, Herbert J. 'Economic Modernisation in Imperial Russia.' *The Journal of Economic History* 25(4) (December 1965): 523–533.

Encyclopaedia Britannica, 'Reform Bill.' Available at https://www.britannica.com/event/Reform-Bill (accessed May 2025).

Engels, Friedrich. *Marx Engels Collected Works*, Vol. 24. Moscow: Progress Publishers.

______. *Marx Engels Collected Works*, Vol. 6. 1976.

Engelstein, Laura. *Moscow, 1905: Working-Class Organization and Political Conflict.* Stanford: Stanford University Press, 1982.

Everett, Glenn. 'The Reform Acts,' *The Victorian Web*, 2001. Available at https://victorianweb.org/history/hist2.html (accessed May 2025).

Figes, Orlando. *A People's Tragedy: The Russian Revolution, 1891–1924.* New York: Viking Penguin, 1998.

Fitzpatrick, Sheila. *The Russian Revolution.* New York: Oxford University Press, 2017.

'Flight of Kerensky.' Australian and New Zealand Cable Association. *National Library of New Zealand.*

Fourier, Charles. *Selections from the Works of Fourier.* Translated by Julia Franklin. Marxist Internet Archive, 1851. Available at https://www.marxists.org (accessed May 2025).

_____. *The Utopian Vision of Charles Fourier: Selected Texts on Work, Love and Passionate Attraction.* Boston: Beacon Press, 1971.

Freeman, Alan. 'A General Refutation of Okishio's Theorem and a Proof of the Falling Rate of Profit.' MPRA (Munich Personal RePEc Archive), 1998.

Furet, François. 'Napoleon Bonaparte.' In *Recent Debates and New Controversies*, edited by Gary Kates. New York: Routledge, 1998.

_____. *The French Revolution, 1770–1814.* New Jersey: John Wiley and Sons, 1987.

_____. *Interpreting the French Revolution.* Cambridge: Cambridge University Press, 1981.

Gash, Norman. *Politics in the Age of Peel: A Study in the Technique of Parliamentary Representation, 1830–1850.* London: Longmans, 1953.

Gerschenkron, Alexander. 'The Rate of Industrial Growth in Russia since 1885.' *Journal of Economic History* 7(S1) (1947): 144–174.

Geyl, Peter. *Napoleon: For and Against.* New Haven and London: Yale University Press, 1964.

Ginsborg, Paul. 'Peasants and Revolutionaries in Venice and Veneto, 1848.' *Historical Journal* 3 (1974): 503.

Goodman, Dena. *The Republic of Letters: A Cultural History of the French Enlightenment.* Ithaca: Cornell University Press, 1994.

Griffith, G. T. *Population Problems of the Age of Malthus.* Cambridge, 1926.

Gulick, Edward Vose. *Europe's Classical Balance of Power.* Connecticut: Green Wood Press, 1955.

Habakkuk, H. J. English Population in the 18th Century.' *The Economic History Review*, New Series, 6(2) (1953): 128–152.

Hamerow, T. S. 'History and the German Revolution.' *American Historical Review* 60(1) (October 1954): 27–44.

Hampson, Norman. *A Social History of the French Revolution.* London: Routledge, 1963.

Harley, C. Knick, and N. F. R. Crafts. 'Simulating the Two Views of the British Industrial Revolution.' *The Journal of Economic History* 60(3) (September 2000): 819–841.

Hartwell, R. M. *The Industrial Revolution and Economic Growth*. London: Methuen & Co., 1971.

———. ed. *The Causes of the Industrial Revolution in England*. London: Methuen & Co., 1970.

Hazen, C. D. *The Long Nineteenth Century: A History of Europe from 1789 to 1918*. e-artnow, 2019.

Heilbroner, Robert L. *The Worldly Philosophers*, revised ed. New York: Touchstone, 1996.

Henderson, W. O. *The Industrial Revolution on the Continent*, 2nd ed. London: Frank Cass & Co. Ltd., 1967.

———. *The Industrialization of Europe: 1780–1914*. New York: Harcourt, Brace & World, 1969.

Himmelfarb, Gertrude. 'The Politics of Democracy: The English Reform Act of 1867.' *Journal of British Studies* 6(1) (November 1966): 104–114.

Hobsbawm, E. J. *The Age of Revolution*. Delhi: Rupa & Co., 1992.

———. *Industry and Empire*. London: Penguin Adult, 1999.

———. 'The Crisis of the 17th Century—II.' *Past and Present* 6(1) (1954): 44–65.

Hoch, Steven L. 'Did Russia's Emancipated Serfs Really Pay Too Much for Too Little Land? Statistical Anomalies and Long-Failed Distributions.' *Slavic Review* 63(2) (Summer 2004): 274.

Hohenberg, Paul M. and Lynn Hollen Lees. *The Making of Urban Europe, 1000–1950*. In *The Industrial Revolution*, edited by Steven M. Beaudoin, 128–133. Boston: Houghton Mifflin, 2003.

Hook, Sydney. 'Karl Marx and Moses Hess.' *New International* 1(5) (December 1934): 140–144.

———. 'Marx and Feuerbach.' *New International* 3(2) (April 1936): 47–57.

Hovell, Mark and Thomas Frederick Tout. *The Chartist Movement*. Manchester: Manchester University Press, 1966.

Hufton, Olwen. 'Women in Revolution 1789–1796.' In *French Society and Revolution*, edited by Douglas Johnson. Cambridge: Cambridge University Press, 1976.

Hunt, Lynn. 'Band of Brothers.' In *The French Revolution: The Essential Readings*, edited by Roland Schechter, 236–262. Oxford: Wiley-Blackwell, 2000.

———. 'The Many Bodies of Marie Antoinette.' In *The French Revolution: Recent Debates and New Controversies*, edited by Gary Kates, 279–297. New York: Routledge, 1998.

Jaspers, Karl. *Spinoza*. In *The Great Philosophers*, Vol. II, edited by Hannah Arendt. New York: Harvest Books, 1974.

Jones, P. M. *The Peasantry in the French Revolution*. Cambridge: Cambridge University Press, 1988.

Jones, Peter. *The 1848 Revolutions*. Longman Group, U.K., 1981.

Juneja, Monica. 'Imaging the Revolution: Gender and Iconography in French Political Prints.' *Studies in History* 12(1) (January–June 1996): 12–38.

Kale, Steven. *French Salons: High Society and Political Sociability from the Old Regime to the Revolution of 1848*. Baltimore: Johns Hopkins University Press, 2006.

Kaplan, Marie-Louise Pelus. 'Merchants and Immigrants in Hanseatic Cities.' In *Cities and Cultural Exchange in Europe*, vol. 2 of *Cultural Exchange in Early Modern Europe*, edited by Donatella Calabi and Stephen Christensen, 132–33. Cambridge: Cambridge University Press, 2007.

Katznelson, Ira. 'Working-Class Formation.' In *The Industrial Revolution*, edited by Steven M. Beaudoin, 145. Boston: Houghton Mifflin, 2003.

Kavanagh, Julia. *Women in France during the Enlightenment Century*. New York: G.P. Putnam's Sons, 1893.

Kelly, Joan. *Women, History and Theory: The Essays of Joan Kelly*. Chicago: University of Chicago Press, 1984.

Kemp, Tom. *The Historical Patterns of Industrialisation*. London: Longman, 1978.

————. *Industrialization in Nineteenth-Century Europe*, 2nd ed. London and New York: Longman, 1985.

Kennedy, Emmet. *A Cultural History of the French Revolution*. New Haven, Connecticut: Yale University Press, 1989.

Kerensky, A. F. *The Catastrophe*. Millwood: Kraus Reprint, 1977.

Klíma, Arnošt. 'The Bourgeois Revolution of 1848–9 in Central Europe.' In *Revolution in History*, edited by Roy Porter and Mikulas Teich. Cambridge: Cambridge University Press, 1986, 74–100.

Komlos, John. 'Shrinking in a Growing Economy? The Mystery of Physical Stature during the Industrial Revolution.' *Journal of Economic History* 58(3) (1998).

Kowalski, Ronald. *The Russian Revolution, 1917–1921*. London and New York: Routledge, 1997.

Kowlaklovski, L. *Main Currents of Marxism: Its Origin, Growth and Dissolution*. Oxford: Oxford University Press, 1978.

Kries, Steven. 'The French Revolution: The Radical Stage, 1792–1794.' *Lectures on European Intellectual History*, Lecture 13. Available at https://www.historyguide.org/intellect/intellect.html (accessed June 2025).

Ladurie, Emmanuel Le Roy. *The French Peasantry, 1450–1660*. Translated by Alan Sheridan. Berkeley and Los Angeles: University of California Press, 1987.

Landes, David S. *The Unbound Prometheus: Technological Change and Industrial Development in Western Europe from 1750 to the Present*. Cambridge: Cambridge University Press, 1969.

Landes, Joan B. *Women and the Public Sphere in the Age of the French Revolution*. Ithaca: Cornell University Press, 1988.

Lane, Peter. *The Industrial Revolution: The Birth of the Modern Age*. UK: Barnes & Noble, 1978.

Langhorne, Richard. 'Reflections on the Significance of the Congress of Vienna.' *Review of International Studies* 12(4) (October 1986): 319–324.

Lee, Alexander. 'Beethoven and Napoleon.' *History Today* 68(3), March 2018.

Lee, Stephen J. *Aspects of European History, 1789–1980*. London and New York: Routledge, 1982.

Lefebvre, Georges. *The Coming of the French Revolution*. Translated by R. R. Palmer. Princeton: Princeton University Press, 2005.

____. *The French Revolution: From Its Origins to 1793*. Translated by Elizabeth Moss Evanson. Vol. 1. New York: Columbia University Press, 1962.

Lenin, V. I. *April Theses*. In *Collected Works*, Vol. 24. Moscow: Progress Publishers, 1964. Also in Marxist Internet Archive.

____. Speech at the Third All-Russia Congress of Soviets, January 10–18 (23–31), 1918. *Lenin Internet Archive*, November 2000.

Les Révolutions de Paris. No. 106, July 16–23, 1791.

Levy, Darline Gay, Harriet Branson Applewhite, and Mary Durham Johnson, eds. *Women in Revolutionary Paris, 1789-1795*. Illinois: University of Illinois Press, 1979.

Lichtheim, George. *A Short History of Socialism*. London: Widenfeld & Nicolson, 1970.

Lipson, E. *Europe in the 19th and 20th Centuries*. London: Adam and Charles Black, 1960.

Llewellyn, J., et al. 'Provisional Government.' *Alpha History*, 2014. Available at https://alphahistory.com/russianrevolution/provisional-government/ (accessed August 2018).

______., et al. 'The Kornilov Affair.' *Alpha History*, 2014. Available at https://alphahistory.com/russianrevolution/kornilov-affair/ (accessed August 2018)

Lougee, Carolyn. 'Women, Salons and Social Stratification in Seventeenth Century France.' *Journal of Social History* 12(2) (December 1, 1978): 327–331.

Lowe, Norman. *Mastering Twentieth Century Russian History*. New York: Palgrave, 2002.

Lucas, Colin. *The French Revolution and the Creation of Modern Political Culture*, Vol. II. Oxford: Pergamon Press, 1988.

Lutge, Frederich. Cited in *The Modern World System II: Mercantilism and Consolidation of the European World Economy 1600–1750* by Immanuel Wallerstein. Berkeley and Los Angeles: University of California Press, 1980.

Lynch, Michael. *Reaction and Revolution: Russia, 1894–1924*, 4th ed. London: Hodder Education, 2015.

Mantoux, Paul. *The Industrial Revolution in the Eighteenth Century: An Outline of the Beginnings of the Modern Factory System in England*. London: Jonathan Cape Ltd., 1928.

Markham, Felix. *Napoleon and the Awakening of Europe*. England: Penguin Books, 1975.

Markoff, John. 'Peasant Grievances and Peasant Insurrection: France in 1789.' *The Journal of Modern History* 62(3) (September 1990): 150–179.

Marxist Internet Archive. 'Student Movements in Pre-Revolutionary Russia.' *Encyclopedia of Marxism*.

Mathias, P. *The First Industrial Nation: An Economic History of Britain, 1700-1914*. London: Methuen & Co., 1969.

Matteson, Keiko. 'The Revival of Tradition in France's Forests.' *Solutions Journal* 3(6) (February 2013).

McColloch, William A. 'Shackled Revolution? The Bubble Act and Finance Regulation in 18th Century England.' Working Paper No. 2013–06. Department of Economics, University of Utah, 2013.

McKean, Robert B. and Ian D. Thatcher. *Late Imperial Russia: Problems and Prospects*. Manchester: Manchester University Press, 2005.

McKeown, Thomas, and R. G. Brown. 'Medical Evidence Related to English Population Changes in the 18th Century.' *Population Studies* 9(2) (November 1955): 119–41.

McLellan, David. *Marx: A Biography.* UK: Palgrave Macmillan, 2006.

____. *Marxism after Marx.* UK: Palgrave Macmillan, 2007.

McPhee, Peter, *Living the French Revolution 1789-1799,* Palgrave Macmillan, UK, 2006

Memoirs of Madame de Rémusat: 1802–1808. Document 4. New York: D. Appleton and Company, 1880.

Mengelberg, Keathe. 'Lorenz Von Stein and His Contribution to Historical Sociology.' *Journal of the History of Ideas* 22(2) (April–June 1961): 267–74.

'Mercantilism and Colbertism in France.' The Centre for Economic Liberty, 21 April 2013. Available at https://centerforeconomicliberty. blogspot.com/2013/04/mercantilism-and-colbertism-in-france. html (accessed May 2025).

Merriman, John. *A History of Modern Europe: From the French Revolution to the Present*, Vol. 2. New York: W. W. Norton & Company, 1996.

Mignet, F. *Histoire de la Révolution Française.* London, 1913.

Mill, John Stuart. *Considerations on Representative Government.* London: Parker, Son and Bourn, 1861.

____. *Principles of Political Economy.* London: John W. Parker, 1848.

Mokyr, Joel. 'The Second Industrial Revolution, 1870–1914: Mutual Feedbacks of Science and Technology'. Available at https://faculty. wcas.northwestern.edu/jmokyr/castronovo.pdf (accessed May 2025).

Molesworth, W. N. *The History of the Reform Bill of 1832.* London: Chapman and Hall, 1865.

Montesquieu. *Persian Letters.* Translated by C.J. Betts. Harmondsworth: Penguin, 1973.

Moore, D. C. *The Politics of Deference: A Study of the Mid-Nineteenth Century English Political System.* Hassocks: Harvester Press, 1976.

Mousnier, Roland. 'Recherches sur les soulèvements populaires en France avant la Fronde.' *Revue d'Histoire Moderne et Contemporaine* (1958).

Mowery, David, and Nathan Rosenberg. 'The Influence of Market Demand upon Innovation: A Critical Review of Some Recent Empirical Studies.' *Research Policy* 8(2) (April 1979).

Namier, Sir Lewis. *1848: The Revolution of the Intellectuals*, The Raleigh Lecture on History. London: British Academy, 1944.

Nicolaievsky, Boris, and Otto Maenchen-Helfen. *Karl Marx: Man and Fighter*. Translated by G. David and Eric Mosbacher. London: Methuen & Co., 1936.

Nicolson, Harold. *The Congress of Vienna: A Study in Allied Unity, 1812–1822*. London: Methuen & Co. Ltd., 1970.

Nove, Alec. *An Economic History of the USSR*. Great Britain: Penguin Books, 1984.

O'Brien, Patrick K. and Roland Quinault, eds. *The Industrial Revolution and British Society*. Cambridge: Cambridge University Press, 1993.

O'Gorman, Frank. 'Electoral Deference in Unreformed England, 1760–1832.' *Journal of Modern History* 56 (1984): 391–409.

Okishio, N. 'Technical Changes and Rate of Profit.' *Kobe University Economic Review*, no. 7 (1961): 85–89.

Ostrogorski, M. *Democracy and the Organisation of Political Parties*, edited by S. M. Lipset. New York: Macmillan, 1964.

Otte, T.G., and Keith Neilson, eds. *Railways and International Politics: Paths of Empire, 1848–1945*. London: Routledge, 2012.

Ozouf, Mona. 'Revolutionary Festival: A Transfer of Sacrality.' In *The French Revolution*, edited by Roland Schechter, 306–308. Wiley-Blackwell, 2000.

______. *Festivals and the French Revolution*, trans. Alan Sheridan. Cambridge, MA: Harvard University Press, 1988.

Parsons, T.G. 'The Popular Movement during the French Revolution: A Note on Recent Work.' *Labour History*, no. 7 (November 1964): 11–13.

Pekacz, Jolanta T. 'Les Amies des Philosophes: The Making of Enlightenment Salons in Nineteenth Century France.' *Conservative Tradition in Pre-Revolutionary France*, no. 36. Toronto: Carinal Press, University of Toronto Press. Available at https://h-france.net/rude/vol1/peckacz5 (accessed April 2025).

Perry, Marvin. *An Intellectual History of Modern Europe*. Boston: Houghton Mifflin Company, 1992.

Phillips, John A., and Charles Wetherell. 'The Great Reform Bill of 1832 and the Rise of Partisanship.' *Journal of Modern History* 63(4) (December 1991): 621–658.

Pierson, George W. *The Moving American*. Bombay: Allied Publishers, 1972.

Pilbeam, Pamela. 'From Orders to Classes: European Society in the Nineteenth Century.' In *The Oxford History of Modern Europe*, edited by T. C. W. Blanning, 101–125. Oxford: Oxford University Press, 2000.

Pilbeam, Pamela M. *The Middle Classes in Europe 1789–1914: France, Germany, Italy and Russia*. Chicago: Lyceum Books, 1990.

Pinkney, David H. 'A New Look at the French Revolution of 1830.' *Review of Politics* 23: 217–219, 1961.

Pipes, Richard. *The Russian Revolution, 1899–1919*. London: Collins Harvill, 1990.

Podmore, Frank. *Robert Owen: A Biography*. New York: Haskell House Publishers Ltd., 1971.

Pokrovsky, M. N. *Brief History of Russia*, Vol. 1. London, 1933.

Porter, Roy and Mikuláš Teich, eds. *Revolution in History*. Cambridge: Cambridge University Press, 1986.

Proudhon, Pierre-Joseph. *Property is Theft: A Pierre-Joseph Proudhon Anthology*, edited by Iain McKay. Edinburgh, Oakland, and Baltimore: AK Press, 2011.

_____. *The General Idea of the Revolution in the Nineteenth Century*. Translated by John Beverly Robinson. London: Freedom Press, 1923.

Pugh, Martin. *March of Women: A Revisionist Analysis of the Campaign for Women's Suffrage 1866–1914*. Oxford: Oxford University Press, 2000.

Reed, John. *Ten Days That Shook the World*. 1922. Marxist Internet Archive.

Reybaud, Louis. *Le Coton*. Paris, 1863.

Robinson, Geroid T. Quoted in Simms Jr., James Y. 'Crisis in Russian Agriculture at the End of the 19th Century: A Different View.' *Slavic Review* 36(3) (September 1977): 381.

Robinson, James Harvey. 'Aulard's Political Theory of the French Revolution.' *Political Science Quarterly* 26 (March 1911): 139.

Rose, Holland J. *The Revolutionary and Napoleonic Era, 1789–1815*. Cambridge: Cambridge University Press, 1935.

Rose, Sonya O. 'Limited Livelihoods'. In *The Industrial Revolution*, edited by Steven M. Beaudoin, 218–221. Boston: Houghton Mifflin, 2003.

Rostow, W.W. *The Stages of Economic Growth: A Non-communist Manifesto*. Cambridge: Cambridge University Press, 1991.

Rozental, Alek A. 'The Enclosure Movement in France.' *The American Journal of Economics and Sociology* 16(1): 55.

Rudé, George F. E. *The French Revolution*. London: Weidenfeld and Nicolson, 1988.

——. *Revolutionary Europe, 1783–1815*. Great Britain: Fontana, 1975.

——. *The Crowd in the French Revolution*. Oxford: Oxford University Press, 1967.

Sabine, George H. and Thomas L. Thorson. *A History of Political Theory*, 4th ed. New Delhi: Oxford & IBH Publishing Company, 1973.

Salmond, Wendy. *Arts and Crafts in Late Imperial Russia: Reviving the Kustaar Art Industries, 1870–1917*. Cambridge: Cambridge University Press, 1996.

Schumpeter, Joseph A. *Capitalism, Socialism and Democracy*, 2nd ed. Virginia: Wilder Publications Inc., 2011.

Scott, Joan Wallach. 'French Feminists and the Rights of Man.' In *The French Revolution: The Essential Readings*, edited by Roland Schechter. Wiley-Blackwell, 2000.

Seaman, L. C. B. *From Vienna to Versailles*. London: Methuen & Co. Ltd., 1955.

Service, Robert. *Lenin: A Biography*. UK: Pan Macmillan, 2000.

Seton-Watson, Hugh. *The Decline of Imperial Russia*. London: Methuen & Co., 1966.

Sewell, William H., Jr. 'Work and Revolution in France'. In *The Industrial Revolution*, edited by Steven M. Beaudoin, 18. Boston and New York: Houghton Mifflin, 2003.

Shanon, Richard. *Gladstone: God and Politics*. London: Continuum, 2007.

Simms Jr., James Y. 'Crisis in Russian Agriculture at the End of the 19th Century: A Different View.' *Slavic Review* 36(3) (September 1977): 381–385.

Singer, Peter. *Marx: A Very Short Introduction*. Oxford: Oxford University Press, 1980.

Smith, Adam. *An Inquiry into the Nature and Causes of the Wealth of Nations*. Book 1, Chapter XI. Available at https://www.marxists.org/ reference/archive/smith-adam/works/wealth-of-nations/book01/ ch11a.htm (accessed June 2025).

Smith, S. A. 'Moscow Workers and Revolutions of 1905 and 1917.' *Soviet Studies* 36(2) (April 1984): 288.

Soboul, Albert. *A Short History of the French Revolution, 1789–1799*. Berkeley: University of California Press, 1977.

——. *Les Sans-culottes Parisiens en l'an II*. Paris, 1962.

Soboul, Albert. *Précis d'Histoire de la Révolution Française*, 2nd ed. Paris, 1963.

———. *The Sans-culottes: The Popular Movement and Revolutionary Government, 1793–1794*. Princeton: Princeton University Press, 1980.

———. *Understanding the French Revolution*. New Delhi: People's Publishing House, 1989.

Sperber, Jonathan. *The European Revolutions, 1848–1851*. Cambridge: Cambridge University Press, 1994.

Stearns, Peter. *1848: The Revolutionary Tide in Europe*. New York: W.W. Norton & Company, 1974.

Sweet, Paul R. *Frederich von Gentz: Defender of the Old Order*. Madison: University of Wisconsin Press, 1941.

Taine, Hippolyte. 'Napoleon's Views of Religion.' *The North American Review* 152(414): 567. May 1891.

Tallentyre, S.G. *Women of the Salons*. New York: G.P. Putnam's Sons, 1926.

Taylor, A. J. P. *Revolutions and Revolutionaries*. Oxford: Hamilton, 1980.

Taylor, Brian D. Quoted in J. Llewellyn et al., 'The Kornilov Affair'. *Alpha History*, 2014.

Teich, Mikuláš and Roy Porter, eds. *The Industrial Revolution in National Context*. Cambridge: Cambridge University Press, 1996.

Temin, Peter. 'Two Views of the Industrial Revolution.' *The Journal of Economic History* 57(1) (March 1997): 63–82.

Thalheimer, August. *Introduction to Dialectical Materialism*, 1927. Marxist Internet Archive. Available at https://www.marxists.org (accessed May 2025).

The Fontana Dictionary of Modern Thought. 3rd ed. London: Fontana Press, 1999.

The New York Times. 5 October 1877.

Thompson, E.P. 'Time, Work-Discipline, and Industrial Capitalism.' In *The Industrial Revolution*, edited by Steven M. Beaudoin, 164. Boston: Houghton Mifflin, 2003.

Thompson, Dorothy. *Chartists: Popular Politics in the Industrial Revolution*. Knopf Publishing Group, University of Michigan, 1984.

Thompson, E.P. *The Making of the English Working Class*. London: Pelican Books, 1968.

Thomson, David. *Europe Since Napoleon*. London: Penguin Books, 1966.

Tilly, Louise A. and Joan W. Scott. *Women, Work, and Family*. New York: Routledge, 1987.

Tocqueville, Alexis de. *Democracy in America*. Vol. 1, Part 1, Chap. 3. Chicago: University of Chicago.

Toynbee, Arnold. *Lectures on the Industrial Revolution in England: Popular Addresses, Notes and Other Fragments*. Cambridge: Cambridge University Press, 2011[1884].

Trebilcock, Clive. 'The Industrialisation of Modern Europe, 1750–1914.' In *The Oxford Illustrated History of Modern Europe*, edited by T.C.W. Blanning, 40–68. Oxford: Oxford University Press, 1998.

Trevor-Roper, H. R. *The Crisis of the Seventeenth Century: Religion, the Reformation, and Social Change*. Indianapolis: Liberty Fund, 2001.

____. 'The General Crisis of the Seventeenth Century.' *Past and Present*, no. 16 (November 1959): 31–64.

Tucker, G.S.L. 'Ricardo and Marx.' *Economica*, n.s., 28(111) (August 1961): 252.

Tugan-Baranovskii, Mikhail I. *The Russian Factory in the 19th Century*. Homewood: Georgetown, 1970.

Turner, Frederick Jackson. *The Frontier in American History*. Bombay: Allied Publishers, 1947.

Ulam, Adam. *The Bolsheviks: The Intellectual and Political History of the Triumph of Communism in Russia*. Cambridge, MA: Harvard University Press, 1965.

Urban Dictionary. 'Definition of Socialism.' Available at https://www.urbandictionary.com (accessed May 2025).

Vanhaute, Eric, Richard Paping, and Cormac Ó Gráda. 'The European Subsistence Crisis of 1845–1850: A Comparative Perspective.' Paper presented at IEHC, Helsinki, 2006. Available at https://www.researchgate.net/publication/24140493 (accessed May 2025).

Vega, Judith. 'Feminist Republicans and Etta Palm d'Aelders on Justice, Virtue and Men.' *History of European Ideas* 10(3): 391.

Vincent, David. *Literacy and Popular Culture: England 1750–1914*. Cambridge: Cambridge University Press, 1989.

Volkogonov, Dimitri. Quoted in Lucy Ryan. 'Historiography of the Russian Revolution.'

'Wars of Vendee.' *Encyclopedia Britannica*.

Warner, Marina. *Monuments and Maidens: The Allegory of the Female Form*. California: University of California Press, 2000.

Wasson, Ellis A. 'The Spirit of Reform, 1832 and 1867.' *Albion: A Quarterly Journal Concerned with British Studies* 12(2) (Summer 1980): 164–174.

William, James Adams. *Constructing the French Economy: Government and the Rise of Market*. Washington: The Brookings Institution, 1989.

Winks, Robin, and Joan Neuberger. *Europe and the Making of Modernity, 1815–1914*. New York: Oxford University Press, 2005.

Wood, Alan. *Bolshevism: The Road to Revolution*. London: Aakar Books/ Wellred Publications, 2009.

———. *The Origins of the Russian Revolution, 1861–1917*. 2nd ed. London: Routledge, 1993.

Wrigley, Tony. 'English County Populations in the Later 18th Century.' Cambridge Group for the History of Population and Social Structure. Department of Geography, University of Cambridge.

Zamoyski, Adam. *Rites of Peace: The Fall of Napoleon and the Congress of Vienna*. London: Harper Press, 2007.

Zenkovsky, Serge A. 'The Emancipation of the Serfs in Retrospect.' *Russian Review* 20(4) (October 1961): 289–291.

Zohrab, Irene. 'The Socialist Revolutionary Party, Kerensky and the Kornilov Affair: From the Unpublished Papers of Harold W. Williams.' *New Zealand Slavonic Journal* (1991): 153–154.